Theory of
Valuation

Rowman & Littlefield Studies in Financial Economics
Jonathan E. Ingersoll, Jr., General Editor

Theory of Financial Decision Making
 Jonathan E. Ingersoll, Jr.

Financial Markets and Incomplete Information:
Frontiers of Modern Financial Theory
 Edited by Sudipto Bhattacharya and George M. Constantinides

Theory of Valuation

Frontiers of Modern Financial Theory

edited by

Sudipto Bhattacharya

and

George M. Constantinides

Rowman & Littlefield Publishers, Inc.

ROWMAN & LITTLEFIELD PUBLISHERS, INC.

Published in the United States of America
by Rowman & Littlefield Publishers, Inc.
8705 Bollman Place, Savage, Maryland 20763

Library of Congress Cataloging-in-Publication Data

Theory of valuation: frontiers of modern financial theory/edited by
    Sudipto Bhattacharya and George M. Constantinides
        (Rowman & Littlefield studies in financial economics)
        Includes index.
        ISBN 0-8476-7486-X
        ISBN 0-8476-7487-8 (pbk.)
        1. Finance.   2. Economics.   3. Valuation theory.
    I. Bhattacharya, Sudipto.   II. Constantinides, George M.
    III. Series.
    HG174. T53.   1988   87-32123
    332—dc 19   CIP

Printed in the United States of America

to

Usha Bhattacharya and K.K. Anaskevic

Maria, Michalis, Stylianos, Olvia and Mikis

Contents

Acknowledgments

Major credit for the potential success of the two volumes is due to the contributors of original essays published in these volumes and to the authors and journal publishers who have given us permission to reprint earlier published articles. Several professional colleagues, particularly the series editor, Jonathan Ingersoll, have given us invaluable advice throughout this project. The staff of Rowman & Littlefield has provided the expert advice and has shown the patience that has made this project possible. Myrtle Sims and Stella Padmore have provided expert secretarial assistance. The first editor acknowledges financial and secretarial support from the Berkeley program in finance, the School of Business at University of Michigan, and Bell Communications Research. The second editor acknowledges the financial support of his home institution, the Graduate School of Business, University of Chicago, and of the Marvin Bower fellowship program at the Harvard Business School.

Preface

The contemporary theory of financial economics is the beneficiary of major developments over the last 35 years in valuation theory and information economics. Developments in valuation theory over this period include the general equilibrium theory of Arrow and Debreu; the portfolio selection theory of Markowitz and the equilibrium valuation theory of Sharpe and Lintner; the no-arbitrage valuation theory of Modigliani and Miller and its application in corporate finance; the intertemporal no-arbitrage valuation theory of Black and Scholes; the intertemporal valuation theory of Merton; and the asymptotic no-arbitrage theory of Ross. Developments in information economics pertaining to the theory of finance include the role of prices in aggregating and communicating information; the signaling of asymmetrically known attributes through quantity-dependent, nonlinear prices; the revelation of information through contingent contracting; and the analysis of strategic coordination across multiple-informed agents.

We have collected some important papers published from 1973 to 1986 and original essays contributed by eminent researchers with the goal of presenting a summary statement of recent research progress in theoretical financial economics to both specialist and nonspecialist financial economists. The second goal, and perhaps the most ambitious one, is to forecast, through the distillation of the opinions of these researchers, trends in the theory of financial economics. The third goal is to provide ready material for one Ph.D.-level course in financial economics or for a sequence of two courses covering valuation theory and information economics. Segments of these volumes may also be used for elective M.B.A., M.S., and advanced undergraduate courses.

In order to present a coherent picture within the confines of two volumes we focus exclusively on theoretical issues. Thus major strides in empirical research are, at best, noted in passing. A complementary book covering the empirical side is clearly warranted.

In selecting the eighteen articles reprinted in these volumes, we have applied the criteria of originality, coherence, comprehensiveness, and pedagogical clarity. This means that occasionally the earliest important, or landmark, article in an area has not been chosen. Furthermore, the task of spanning the entire field of theoretical finance with eighteen articles has proved awesome. In narrowing down the selection to the eighteen articles, we have been forced to make some arbitrary choices, and we offer our sincere apologies to authors whose worthy articles are not reprinted in these volumes.

An innovation of these volumes is the inclusion of original essays in addition to the reprinted articles. These essays provide comprehensive reviews of important topics in finance, update and extend the contribution of the reprinted articles, and offer directions for future research. Furthermore each of us has provided a detailed overview, one addressing the first volume on valuation theory and the other addressing the second volume on the application of information economics in finance.

We hope that the contributions collected in these volumes communicate the excitement of the field of financial economics to beginners and specialists alike and stimulate further research.

1 | Theory of Valuation: Overview and Recent Developments

George M. Constantinides

**Graduate School of Business
University of Chicago**

I. INTRODUCTION

The reprinted articles and contributed essays gathered in this volume present valuation theories put forth and tested in finance. An important class of valuation theories, pioneered by Modigliani and Miller (1958) and by Black and Scholes (1973), are based on the equilibrium condition that there exist no arbitrage opportunities. These essentially preference-free theories generate results of great generality without necessitating the specification of the equilibrium in its full detail.

A second important class of valuation theories makes assumptions on preferences and derives more specific pricing restrictions than do the preference-free theories. This essay provides an overview of these latter preference-dependent valuation theories. The unifying theme is that the various preference-dependent valuation theories are specializations (or sometimes generalizations) of the fundamental valuation equation, which equates the price of a claim to the expectation of the product of the future payoff and the marginal rate of substitution of the representative investor. Our goal is to stress the similarities rather than the differences of these theories and thereby provide the reader with a conceptual framework for some of the theories in this book.

Within the space limitations of one essay, I address a subset of the interesting issues, in particular, the filtering of information in an intertemporal economy of homogeneously informed agents, and the role of conditioning information on the empirically testable implications of these theories. In this essentially theoretical essay I have attempted to bridge the theoretical and empirical research in finance by referencing representative empirical papers.

Papers referenced with an asterisk (*) are included in this and the companion volume. I would like to thank Sudipto Bhattacharya, Wayne Ferson, Chi-fu Huang, and Ken Singleton for constructive criticism on an earlier draft.

The essay steers away from several important topics, such as economies with heterogeneously informed agents, existence and other technical aspects of an equilibrium, the application of valuation theory to corporate finance, corporate and personal taxes, and transaction costs. Some of these issues are dealt with elsewhere in these volumes. In particular, Sudipto Bhattacharya's overview and the articles and essays in the second volume address the economics of information and its application in finance.

To convey the economics to a broad readership, including the beginning student of finance and economics, I sometimes sacrifice mathematical rigor. In specific applications I rely upon the simplifying assumption that prices and per capita consumption are multivariate normal. This implies that prices may be negative and that utility may be undefined if it is unbounded from below. These technical problems are often resolved in a continuous-time framework in which prices and consumption are modeled as an Itô process. Thus whenever I invoke the simplifying property that prices and per capita consumption are multivariate normal, it is to be understood that in a more rigorous treatment I would be modeling prices and consumption as an Itô process.

II. THE BASIC MODEL

Consider an exchange economy that extends over $T + 1$ periods, $t = 0, 1, 2, \ldots, T, T < \infty$. The assumptions on the discreteness of the trading interval and on the finiteness of the time horizon are intended to keep the discussion simple. I make references, when appropriate, to the continuous-trading economies, such as in Merton (1973a), and to the infinite-horizon recursive economies, such as in Lucas (1978).

There is one nonstorable consumption good only. The numeraire at date t is the consumption good at date t.

Information at date t is the vector $\phi^t \in R^L$, a Markov process. The cumulative probability distribution of ϕ^{t+1} is $F^t(\phi^{t+1} | \phi^t)$. Consumers know the functions $F^t(\cdot | \cdot)$ at all times and know the vector ϕ^t at date t. Thus consumers have homogeneous information.

There are n firms, indexed $i = 1, 2, \ldots, n$. The ith firm pays net dividend $D_i^t(\phi^t)$ at date t, where the functions $D_i^t(\cdot)$ are known at all times. In this exchange economy the net dividend functions $D_i^t(\phi^t)$ are primitives. If storage of the consumption good is permitted, it may be modeled with a firm that provides the storage service.

That the functions $D_i^t(\phi^t)$ are primitive does not imply that firms are passive in their investment and financing decisions. Production economies, such as those in Brock (1982), Cox, Ingersoll, and Ross (1985a), and Prescott and Mehra (1980), endogenously determine the firms' investment and financing policy functions, which in turn map into net dividend functions, $D_i^t(\phi^t)$. Thus production economies impose additional restrictions on the observables of the economy, and these restrictions involve the net dividend functions. If an empirical test rejects the restrictions imposed by an exchange economy, it also rejects some of the restrictions imposed by the corresponding production economy.

I simplify the presentation with the assumption that the market is complete, or at least "effectively" complete. Although the assumption that the market is complete requires the existence of a large number of traded securities, Arrow (1964) and Kreps (1982) prove that the requirements on the number of traded securities may be considerably reduced. In economies where the information revelation is modeled by a finite-dimensional Brownian motion or diffusion process, Duffie and Huang (1985*) prove that the market can be effectively completed by a finite number of long-lived securities equal in number to the dimension of the information process plus one. See also the insightful discussion by Scheinkman (1988*).

When the market is complete, *equilibrium* prices and aggregate consumption remain unchanged when we replace the heterogeneous consumers with one consumer (the "representative" consumer) with chosen preferences and with endowment equal to the sum of the heterogeneous consumers' endowments. An equilibrium in a heterogeneous-consumer economy is observationally equivalent to the equilibrium in some homogeneous-consumer economy. Hereafter I refer to the representative consumer as simply the "consumer." This result is foreshadowed by Prescott and Mehra (1980). Existence of a representative consumer is shown by Constantinides (1982, Lemma 1). In the same paper Lemma 2 states that, if the heterogeneous consumers have time-additive, von Neumann–Morgenstern utility functions, the representative consumer's utility function inherits these properties. Note that the conditions for the existence of a representative consumer are less stringent than the conditions for the aggregation of preferences, yet they are sufficient for our purposes. See also the related papers by Bhattacharya (1981), Breeden and Litzenberger (1978), Constantinides (1980), Dybvig and Ingersoll (1982), Dybvig and Ross (1982), and Rubinstein (1974).

I assume that the consumer receives no labor or other exogenous income. In equilibrium the consumer must hold all the stock of each firm and consume the aggregate dividend $c^t = \sum D_i^t(\phi^t)$ at date t. The consumer has von Neumann–Morgenstern preferences and expected utility at t given by

$$E\left[\sum_{\tau=t}^{T} u^\tau(c^\tau)|\phi^t\right] \equiv E\left[\sum_{\tau=t}^{T} u^\tau\left(\sum_{i=1}^{n} D_i^\tau(\phi^\tau)\right)\middle|\phi^t\right],$$

where the direct utility function $u^\tau(\cdot)$ is monotone increasing and strictly concave.

In equilibrium, the ex dividend (shadow) price, P_i^t, of the ith firm at date t is such that the consumer holds all the stock and is indifferent (at the margin) to buying or selling a fraction α of the stock; that is, the objective function

$$\max_{\alpha} E\left[u^t(c^t - \alpha P_i^t) + \sum_{\tau=t+1}^{T} u^\tau(c^\tau + \alpha D_i^\tau)|\phi^t\right]$$

is maximized at $\alpha = 0$. Since the objective function is strictly concave in α, the first-order necessary condition of optimality is also sufficient. With simple manipulation this condition yields the fundamental valuation equation

$$(1) \qquad P_i^t = E\left[\sum_{\tau=t+1}^{T} \frac{u_c^\tau(c^\tau)}{u_c^t(c^t)} \cdot D_i^\tau \Big| \phi^t\right],$$

where the subscript c denotes a derivative. Since the right side is a known function of ϕ^t, the equilibrium stock price is a known function of the information ϕ^t and is sometimes denoted by $P_i^t(\phi^t)$.

Since some of the net dividends may be negative, there is nothing in equation (1) to guarantee that a firm's price is nonnegative. I impose the restriction that the net dividends are nonnegative for all ϕ^t. This restriction is actually too strong. In production economies the nonnegativity of prices is guaranteed by the stockholders' limited liability.

The fundamental valuation equation is derived by Rubinstein (1976*), Lucas (1978), Breeden and Litzenberger (1978), and undoubtedly by others. It serves as the starting point of the valuation theories discussed in this essay. For future reference I rewrite it in terms of a firm's rate of return from date $t - 1$ to date t, defined as $R_i^t \equiv (P_i^t + D_i^t)/P_i^{t-1}$. Since

$$P_i^{t-1} = E\left[\sum_{\tau=t}^{T} \frac{u_c^\tau(c^\tau)}{u_c^{t-1}(c^{t-1})} \cdot D_i^\tau \Big| \phi^{t-1}\right]$$

$$= E\left[\frac{u_c^t(c^t)}{u_c^{t-1}(c^{t-1})} \cdot \left\{D_i^t + \sum_{\tau=t+1}^{T} \frac{u_c^\tau(c^\tau)}{u^t(c_c^t)} \cdot D_i^\tau\right\}\Big| \phi^{t-1}\right]$$

$$= E\left[\frac{u_c^t(c^t)}{u_c^{t-1}(c^{t-1})} \cdot \left\{D_i^t + E\left[\sum_{\tau=t+1}^{T} \frac{u_c^\tau(c^\tau)}{u_c^t(c^t)} \cdot D_i^\tau \Big| \phi^t\right]\right\}\Big| \phi^{t-1}\right]$$

(by the law of iterated expectations)

$$= E\left[\frac{u_c^t(c^t)}{u_c^{t-1}(c^{t-1})} \cdot (D_i^t + P_i^t)\Big| \phi^{t-1}\right] \quad \text{[by equation (1)],}$$

I divide both sides by P_i^{t-1} and use the definition of the rate of return to obtain

$$(2) \qquad E\left[\frac{u_c^t(c^t)}{u_c^{t-1}(c^{t-1})} \cdot R_i^t \Big| \phi^{t-1}\right] = 1.$$

The riskless rate of interest from date $t - 1$ to date t, denoted by R_0^t, may be shown to satisfy the valuation equation (2). The excess rate of return on the ith firm, defined as $r_i^t \equiv R_i^t - R_0^t$, satisfies

$$E\left[\frac{u_c^t(c^t)}{u_c^{t-1}(c^{t-1})} \cdot r_i^t \Big| \phi^{t-1}\right] = 0,$$

which simplifies to

$$(3) \qquad E[u_c^t(c^t) \cdot r_i^t \Big| \phi^{t-1}] = 0.$$

Equations (2) and (3) are restatements of the valuation equation (1).

The rate of return in equations (2) and (3) is defined between adjacent consumption periods, but it need not be. For example, the compound rate of return of the ith firm from date $t - 2$ to date t is easily shown to satisfy the following generalized version of equation (2):

$$E\left[\frac{u_c^t(c^t)}{u_c^{t-2}(c^{t-2})}\cdot\frac{(P_i^t + D_i^t)(P_i^{t-1} + D_i^{t-1})}{P_i^{t-1}P_i^{t-2}}\middle|\phi^{t-2}\right] = 1.$$

The same reasoning that led to equation (1) shows that the price $V(\mathbf{X}^t)$ at date t of any claim or contract (which may or may not be the stock of a firm) with cash flows $\mathbf{X}^t = (X^t\ X^{t+1}\ \cdots\ X^T)$ is

(4)
$$V(\mathbf{X}^t) = E\left[\sum_{\tau=t}^{T}\frac{u_c^\tau(c^\tau)}{u_c^t(c^t)}\cdot X^\tau\middle|\phi^t\right].$$

The fundamental valuation equation, as stated in equations (1)–(4), is conditional on the information ϕ^{t-1}. By the law of iterated expectations I may take the expectation of the valuation equation with respect to any information subset of ϕ^{t-1}. In particular, I take the expectation of equation (3) with respect to the subset ϕ^0 to obtain the unconditional valuation equation

(5)
$$E[u_c^t(c^t)\cdot r_i^t|\phi^0] = 0.$$

Examples that display the role of conditioning information are in Grossman and Shiller (1982), Hansen and Richard (1985), and Hansen and Singleton (1982, 1983).

In the following sections I specialize the conditional valuation equation (3) or the unconditional valuation equation (5) and derive versions of the consumption-based asset pricing model (CCAPM), the capital asset pricing model (CAPM), the intertemporal capital asset pricing model (ICAPM), the arbitrage pricing model (APT), and the intertemporal arbitrage pricing model. Typically, I relate the conditional (or unconditional) expected excess return to the conditional (or unconditional) covariance of the asset's return with consumption, the market portfolio return, state variables, or economywide factors.

III. CONSUMPTION-BASED ASSET PRICING MODELS

Consumption-based asset pricing models are developed in Rubinstein (1976*), Breeden and Litzenberger (1978), and Breeden (1979*). These models make assumptions on the form of the utility function and/or the joint probability distribution of consumption and excess asset returns with the objective of simplifying the fundamental valuation equation and relating expected excess returns to the covariance of excess returns with consumption. Subsequent related work includes Bhattacharya (1981), Grossman and Shiller (1982), and Kraus and Litzenberger (1983). See also Ross (1988*).

One way to simplify the valuation equation (3) is to set $u^t(c^t) = A^t\cdot c^t - B^t\cdot(c^t)^2/2$, where $A^t \equiv A^t(\phi^{t-1})$, $B^t \equiv B^t(\phi^{t-1})$. Then we obtain

$$E[(A^t - B^t\cdot c^t)\cdot r_i^t|\phi^{t-1}] = 0,$$

which simplifies to

$$(6) \qquad E[r_i^t|\phi^{t-1}] = \left(\frac{B^t}{A^t - B^t\bar{c}^t}\right) \cdot \mathrm{cov}(r_i^t, c^t|\phi^{t-1})$$

where $\bar{c}^t \equiv E[c^t|\phi^{t-1}]$. The expected excess return is proportional to the asset's covariance with consumption or, equivalently, to the asset's consumption beta, defined as $\mathrm{cov}(r_i^t, c^t|\phi^{t-1})/\mathrm{var}(c^t|\phi^{t-1})$. In the definition of the consumption beta, the consumption may be replaced by the change in consumption, $c^t - c^{t-1}$, or by the consumption growth rate, c^t/c^{t-1}, without affecting the basic result. If A^t and B^t are independent of ϕ^{t-1}, I substitute the quadratic utility in the unconditional valuation equation and obtain the unconditional version of equation (6), where ϕ^{t-1} is replaced by ϕ^0. Note that in the definition of the consumption beta I may not replace consumption by the change in consumption or by the consumption growth rate because c^{t-1} is not in the information set ϕ^0.

An alternative way to simplify the valuation equation is to invoke Stein's (1973) lemma. Suppose that (x, y) are bivariate normally distributed, $g(y)$ is everywhere differentiable, and $E|g'(y)| < \infty$; then $\mathrm{cov}(x, g(y)) = E[g'(y)]\,\mathrm{cov}(x, y)$. (See also Rubinstein (1976*), the appendix.) Thus, if c^t and r_i^t are bivariate normally distributed, conditional on ϕ^{t-1}, and the marginal utility satisfies the differentiability and boundedness condition, the valuation equation simplifies to

$$(7) \qquad E[r_i^t|\phi^{t-1}] = -\frac{E[u_{cc}^t(c^t)|\phi^{t-1}]}{E[u_c^t(c^t)|\phi^{t-1}]} \cdot \mathrm{cov}(r_i^t, c^t|\phi^{t-1}).$$

If c^t and r_i^t are bivariate normally distributed, conditional on ϕ^0, the unconditional version of equation (7) holds, where ϕ^{t-1} is replaced by ϕ^0. Furthermore, I may replace consumption by the consumption growth rate if the relative risk aversion is constant.

In Breeden's (1979*) continuous-time model, the assets' rates of return and consumption are driven by a joint diffusion process. Breeden proves that the assets' expected excess returns are proportional to their consumption betas. An intuitive interpretation of the result is that an asset's rate of return and the consumption rate are locally bivariate normal. The assumption of a diffusion process (or, more generally, of an Itô process) bypasses the undesirable property that multivariate normal variables are unbounded from below.

Examples of CCAPM tests are in Breeden, Gibbons, and Litzenberger (1986), Dunn and Singleton (1986), Ferson (1983), Grossman, Melino, and Shiller (1985), Grossman and Shiller (1981), Hall (1981, 1985), Hansen and Singleton (1983), Litzenberger and Ronn (1986), and Mehra and Prescott (1985).

IV. THE CAPITAL ASSET PRICING MODEL

The CAPM, originated by Sharpe (1964) and Lintner (1965), has played an important role in finance and has been a focal point in the empirical finance literature. The CAPM is a single-period specialization of the fundamental valuation equation. At the end of the period, $t = 1$, firms pay a liquidating dividend, and consumption equals aggregate wealth; hence $c^1 = \sum D_i^1 \equiv W^1$. The fundamental valuation equation becomes

$$(8) \qquad E[u_w^1(W^1) \cdot r_i^1 | \phi^0] = 0,$$

thereby relating the assets' excess return to the marginal utility of aggregate wealth.

If the end-of-period dividends are multivariate normal, then the end-of-period returns and the end-of-period wealth are multivariate normal, and the fundamental valuation equation, with the aid of Stein's lemma, simplifies to

$$(9) \qquad E[r_i^1 | \phi^0] = -\frac{E[u_{ww}^1(W^1) | \phi^0]}{E[u_w^1(W^1) | \phi^0]} \cdot \operatorname{cov}(r_i^1, W^1 | \phi^0).$$

Thus a firm's expected excess return is proportional to the covariance of the excess return with the end-of-period wealth or, equivalently, to the covariance of the excess return with the market portfolio return, defined as $W^1/\sum P_i^0$.

The contribution of the CAPM is that it relates the expected excess returns to the market portfolio return. The model's reliance on the market portfolio return is criticized by Fama (1976), Roll (1977), Ross, and others, who point out that the model is testable only if the market portfolio return is observable. The only empirically testable implication of the CAPM is that the market portfolio is mean-variance efficient.

Multivariate normality is sufficient but not necessary for the derivation of the CAPM. Chamberlain (1983b) and Owen and Rabinovitch (1983) characterize the elliptical distributions, which imply that expected utility of wealth is completely specified by its mean and variance, hence they imply the CAPM. Ross (1978*) provides a complete characterization of the class of distributions that imply the CAPM. Another sufficient condition is that utility be quadratic.

Empirical tests of the CAPM include Black, Jensen, and Scholes (1972), Fama and MacBeth (1973), Ferson, Kandel, and Stambaugh (1987), Gibbons (1982), Gibbons and Ferson (1985), Gibbons, Ross, and Shanken (1985), Shanken (1985a), and Stambaugh (1982).

V. THE INTERTEMPORAL CAPITAL ASSET PRICING MODEL

Whereas I may think of the state at date t as being the information at date t, there is a parsimonious way to define the state. Suppose there exists an m-vector $\mathbf{s}^t(\phi^t)$ and a function $\hat{c}^t(\cdot, \cdot)$ such that

$$(10) \qquad \hat{c}^t(\phi^{t-1}, \mathbf{s}^t) \equiv c^t(\phi^t) \text{ for all } \phi^t.$$

Although $\mathbf{s}^t = \phi^t$ satisfies the definition, the definition is useful if there exists a vector $\mathbf{s}^t$ that is of small dimension even when ϕ^t is of large dimension. The definition in equation (10) asserts that $(\phi^{t-1}, \mathbf{s}^t)$ is a sufficient statistic of ϕ^t in determining consumption at date t. There is no presumption that $(\phi^{t-1}, \mathbf{s}^t)$ is a sufficient statistic of ϕ^t in determining the asset prices $P_i^t(\phi^t)$. Therefore (ϕ^{t-1}, s^t) is not generally a sufficient statistic of ϕ^t to describe the investment opportunity set available to consumers at date t—that is, the probability distribution of returns, R_i^{t+1}, conditional on ϕ^t. The identification of state variables and sufficient statistics for an agent's dynamic choice problem in the case of diffusion information are discussed by Huang (1986). Without loss of generality I assume that the elements of s^t are uncorrelated with each other.

The ICAPM relates an asset's expected excess return to the covariance of the asset's excess return with each component of the state. I write the valuation equation (3) as

(11) $$E[u_c^t(\hat{c}^t(s^t, \phi^{t-1})) \cdot r_i^t | \phi^{t-1}] = 0.$$

Under the assumption that the assets' excess returns and the elements of s^t are multivariate normal, conditional on the information ϕ^{t-1} and that marginal utility satisfies the differentiability and boundedness conditions, I obtain the conditional ICAPM:

(12) $$E[r_i^t | \phi^{t-1}] = \sum_{j=1}^{m} \frac{-E[u_{cc}^t \cdot \hat{c}_j^t | \phi^{t-1}]}{E[u_c^t | \phi^{t-1}]} \cdot \text{cov}(s_j^t, r_i^t | \phi^{t-1}),$$

where $\hat{c}_j^t$ denotes the derivative of $\hat{c}^t$ with respect to the jth element of s^t. In Merton's (1973a) original derivation of the ICAPM, the state variables and prices are assumed to follow a joint diffusion process. The diffusion process implies that the assets' excess returns and the elements of s^t are locally multivariate normal—hence the result. See also the diffusion models of Breeden (1979*), Chamberlain (1985), and Cox, Ingersoll, and Ross (1985a) and the discrete-time models of Long (1974) and Stapleton and Subrahmanyam (1978).

The ICAPM attains economic significance once the state variables are identified. In a single-period framework the end-of-period consumption equals the end-of-period wealth; hence wealth is identified as the sole state variable. In an intertemporal context, Fama (1970) identifies three sources of state variables. The first source is state-dependent direct utility; that is, $u^t = u^t(c^t; s^t)$. The second and closely related source of state dependence is the relative prices of consumption goods in a multigood economy. Then the direct utility of consumption of the different goods implies an indirect utility of consumption of a basket of goods, where the indirect utility also depends on the state variables, which stand for the relative prices of these goods. Note that neither one of these sources of state variables exists in the economy presented in this essay.

The third source of state dependence is the changing investment opportunity set. Candidate state variables are the distribution of wealth among consumers in a heterogeneous-consumer economy. As I argued earlier, if the market is complete, or at least effectively complete, the equilibrium is observationally equivalent to an equilibrium in a homogeneous-consumer economy; hence the distribution of wealth among consumers is described by redundant state variables. Other candidate state variables describe the evolution of dividends and of the aggregate endowment.

Beyond the definition in equation (10), the theory does not provide an operational procedure for identifying the state variables. Chen, Roll, and Ross (1986) propose macroeconomic variables as proxies for state variables. They test whether these variables relate to contemporaneous stock returns and whether they explain part of the contemporaneous expected excess return of the assets.

The conditional ICAPM reduces to the conditional CAPM under the assumption that utility is logarithmic; that is, $u'(c^t) = \rho^t \cdot \ln c^t$, and ρ^t is independent of ϕ^t. I substitute the logarithmic utility in the valuation equation (1) and sum across firms to obtain the wealth at time t:

(13)
$$W^t = \sum_{i=1}^{n} (P_i^t + D_i^t) = \sum_{i=1}^{n} E\left[\sum_{\tau=t}^{T} \frac{\rho^\tau \cdot c^t \cdot D_i^\tau}{\rho^t \cdot c^\tau} \middle| \phi^t \right]$$

$$= c^t \cdot \sum_{\tau=t}^{T} \frac{\rho^\tau}{\rho^t}, \quad \text{since } c^\tau = \sum_{i=1}^{n} D_i^\tau.$$

I compare equation (13) with the definition of the state in equation (10) and conclude that the state may be represented by the wealth alone. Hence, the ICAPM in equation (12) states that an asset's expected excess return is proportional to $\text{cov}(r_i^t, W^t | \phi^{t-1})$. Since the market return is $W^t / \sum P_i^{t-1}$, and $\sum P_i^{t-1}$ is an element of the information set ϕ^{t-1}, an asset's expected excess return is proportional to the covariance of the asset's excess return with the market return, conditional on ϕ^{t-1}.

In the conditional ICAPM of equation (12), the moments are conditional on the information ϕ^{t-1}. I may derive the ICAPM in unconditional form by augmenting the state as the vector $(s^t(\phi^t) \quad q^{t-1}(\phi^{t-1}))$ such that

(14)
$$\hat{c}^t(\phi^0, s^t(\phi^t), q^{t-1}(\phi^{t-1})) \equiv c^t(\phi^t) \quad \text{for all } \phi^t$$

by analogy with equation (10). I substitute (14) in the unconditional valuation equation (5) and proceed as before to relate the unconditional excess return of an asset with the unconditional covariance of the return with each element of $s^t(\phi^t)$ and $q^{t-1}(\phi^{t-1})$. The unconditional ICAPM involves covariances of the asset's excess return with the elements of both s^t and q^{t-1}, unlike the conditional ICAPM, which involves covariances with only the elements of s^t. Empirical studies by Fama (1981, 1984a, b, c), Fama and French (1986), Fama and Schwert (1977), Keim and Stambaugh (1986), Merton (1980), Nelson (1972), and others find evidence that variables derived from the information set ϕ^{t-1} have forecasting power on the assets' returns over the period $(t-1, t)$. These variables are candidates for the augmenting vector $q^{t-1}(\phi^{t-1})$.

With logarithmic utility the unconditional ICAPM may be reduced to the unconditional CAPM. I substitute c^t from equation (13) in equation (3), multiply by $\sum_{i=1}^{n} P_i^{t-1}$, and use the definition of the market's rate of return, $R_m^t \equiv W^t / \sum_{i=1}^{n} P_i^{t-1}$, to obtain $E[r_i^t / R_m^t | \phi^{t-1}] = 0$. Taking the expectation with respect to ϕ^0, I obtain $E[r_i^t / R_m^t | \phi^0]$, which leads to the unconditional CAPM, if r_i^t and R_m^t are unconditionally (locally) bivariate normal.

An important application of the intertemporal valuation theory is in the study of the term structure of interest rates. Campbell (1986), Cox, Ingersoll, and Ross (1981, 1985b*), and Donaldson, Johnsen, and Mehra (1985) present term structure theories. Singleton (1988*) surveys the theories and empirical evidence and, in particular, discusses the role of money. Constantinides and Ingersoll (1984*) present a term structure theory that incorporates personal and corporate taxes.

Brennan (1970) presents a static valuation theory that incorporates personal taxes on dividends and capital gains. Constantinides (1983, 1984) presents a dynamic valuation theory in the presence of personal taxes, in which investors follow an optimal policy on the realization of their capital gains and losses.

VI. THE ARBITRAGE PRICING THEORY

The arbitrage pricing theory (APT), put forth by Ross (1976, 1977), addresses the criticism on the observability of the market portfolio return leveled against the CAPM. I first discuss the APT and its variations in a single-period context and then explore the implications of the theory in an intertemporal context.

The APT asserts that the excess returns of a given subset, $i = 1, 2, \ldots, n'$, of the n firms and/or the zero-net-supply assets have a factor structure

$$(15) \qquad r_i = \bar{r}_i + \sum_{k=1}^{K} \beta_{ik}\delta_k + \varepsilon_i, \qquad i = 1, 2, \ldots, n',$$

where the noise terms ε_i have bounded variance and are uncorrelated with each other and with the K factors δ_k. Time subscripts and the conditioning information ϕ^0 are suppressed in this single-period framework. Without loss of generality, the factors and noise terms have zero mean so that $\bar{r}_i$ is the expected excess return of the ith asset. Although there always exists a factor structure with $K = n'$, the spirit of the APT is that the number of factors is small (though unspecified) compared to the number of assets.

I substitute equation (15) in the fundamental valuation equation (3) and, upon simplification, obtain

$$(16) \qquad \bar{r}_i = \sum_{k=1}^{K} \left\{ \frac{E[-u_c(c)\cdot\delta_k]}{E[u_c(c)]} \right\} \beta_{ik} + \frac{E[-u_c(c)\cdot\varepsilon_i]}{E[u_c(c)]}.$$

As a motivation for the APT, Ross (1977) points out that if the assets' returns are spanned by the factors (i.e., if $\varepsilon_i \equiv 0$ for $i = 1, 2, \ldots, n'$), then the second term on the right side of equation (16) is zero and each asset's expected excess return is linear in its factor loadings $\beta_{ik}, k = 1, \ldots, K$. This result also follows directly from no-arbitrage arguments without the need to invoke the fundamental valuation equation.

The spirit of the APT is that the residuals, $E[-u_c(c)\cdot\varepsilon_i]/E(u_c(c))]$, are small even when the noise terms ε_i are nonzero; hence each asset's expected excess return is approximately linear in its factor loadings. Ross (1976) introduces the concept of asymptotic no-arbitrage and argues that the sum of the squared residuals is bounded as the number of assets in the subset n' tends to infinity.

Huberman (1982*) defines asymptotic no-arbitrage and provides a simple proof of the result that the sum of the squared residuals is bounded. Chamberlain (1983a) and Connor (1984) provide conditions that lead to the asymptotic APT. Chamberlain and Rothschild (1983) and Ingersoll (1984) derive the APT when asset returns only have an approximate factor structure. Chamberlain (1983a), Chen and Ingersoll (1983), Connor (1984), Grinblatt and Titman (1987), and Ross (1978*) relate the exact APT to the CAPM. Some of this work is reviewed in Connor's (1988*) essay.

I present a variant of the asymptotic APT wherein the number of assets in the economy remains finite, and seek conditions under which the residuals are small. Brock (1982) and Cragg and Malkiel (1982) initiate this approach, and Dybvig (1983) and Grinblatt and Titman (1983) derive bounds for the residuals.

I write consumption in the second period as

$$(17) \qquad c^1 = \sum_{i=1}^{n} D_i^1 = \sum_{i=1}^{n} \left(\frac{D_i^1}{P_i^0} \right) P_i^0 = \sum_{i=1}^{n} (r_i^1 + R_0^1) \cdot P_i^0.$$

I assume that aggregate consumption and the noise terms ε_i are bivariate normal. I also assume that the returns of all (n) positive-net-supply assets have the factor structure given by equation (15). I substitute c^1 from equation (17) and r_i^1 from equation (15) in the residual term, invoke Stein's lemma and, upon simplification, obtain

$$(18) \qquad \frac{E[-u_c(c^1) \cdot \varepsilon_i]}{E[u_c(c^1)]} = \left\{ -\left(\sum_{i=1}^{n} P_i^0 \right) \frac{E[u_{cc}(c^1)]}{E[u_c(c^1)]} \right\} \left(\frac{P_i^0}{\sum_{i=1}^{n} P_i^0} \right) \cdot \mathrm{var}(\varepsilon_i).$$

The term in braces is some measure of the relative risk aversion coefficient. The second term is the weight of the ith asset in the market portfolio in the first period. This term illustrates the intuition of the asymptotic APT: as the number of assets grows such that the weight of the ith asset in the market portfolio tends to zero, the residual also tends to zero. Reasonable estimates of these parameters for the U.S. stock market indicate that the residual is small in a finite-asset economy.

Under the maintained hypotheses that the economy is single period and that *all* positive-net-supply assets have a factor structure with factors extracted from the observable subset of assets, the APT is testable. The second maintained hypothesis may be weakened by stating that only the subset of observable assets has a factor structure with noise terms uncorrelated with the return of all positive-net-supply unobservable assets. The second maintained hypothesis makes an assertion on the unobservable assets and is the counterpart of the maintained hypothesis in the testing of the CAPM that a weighted portfolio of the observable assets is a proxy for the market. The testability of the APT is discussed by Dybvig and Ross (1985) and Shanken (1982, 1985b). Examples of APT tests are in Brown and Weinstein (1983), Chen (1983), Cho (1984), Connor and Korajczyk (1986), Conway and Reinganum (1986), Dhrymes, Friend, and Gultekin (1984), Huberman and Kandel (1985), Jobson (1982), Lehman and Modest (1985), and Roll and Ross (1980).

VII. THE INTERTEMPORAL ARBITRAGE PRICING THEORY

In this section I explore the implications of embedding Ross's single-period APT in an intertemporal economy. Related work includes Connor and Korajczyk (1986), Ohlson and Garman (1980), Reisman (1986), and Stambaugh (1983).

As in the discussion of the ICAPM, suppose that there exists an m-vector of state variables $s^t(\phi^t)$ defined by equation (10). In the intertemporal context, the assertion that the returns of the n firms have a factor structure is expressed as follows:

$$(19) \qquad r_i^t = \bar{r}_i^t + \sum_{k=1}^{K} \beta_{ik}^t \delta_k^t + \varepsilon_i^t, i = 1, 2, \ldots, n,$$

where the noise terms ε_i^t have bounded variance and are uncorrelated with each other and with the K factors δ_k^t, conditional on ϕ^{t-1}. The parameters $\bar{r}_i^t$ and β_{ik}^t are understood to be known functions of ϕ^{t-1}. Without loss of generality, the factors and noise terms have zero mean, conditional on ϕ^{t-1}.

I substitute (19) in the valuation equation (11) and obtain

$$(20) \qquad E\left[u_c^t(\hat{c}^t(s^t, \phi^{t-1})) \cdot \left(\bar{r}_i^t + \sum_{k=1}^{K} \beta_{ik}^t \delta_k^t + \varepsilon_i^t \right) \Big| \phi^{t-1} \right] = 0.$$

I keep the notation tractable by considering the special case that the state s^t consists of two components, the one of which is the wealth at date t, $W^t \equiv \sum_{i=1}^{n}(P_i^t + D_i^t)$, and the other of which is denoted by the scalar s^t. Although it is not necessarily the case that wealth may proxy for one of the state variables, I develop this special case because I wish to illustrate the relation between the ICAPM and the intertemporal APT.

Under the assumption that $W^t, s^t, \{\delta_k^t\}$, and $\{\varepsilon_i^t\}$ are multivariate normal, conditional on ϕ^{t-1}, I invoke Stein's lemma and simplify the valuation equation to

$$E[r_i^t | \phi^{t-1}] = \sum_{k=1}^{K} \beta_{ik}^t \cdot \frac{1}{E[u_c^t | \phi^{t-1}]} \{ - \text{cov}(\delta_k^t, W^t | \phi^{t-1}) \cdot E[\hat{c}_W^t \cdot u_{cc}^t | \phi^{t-1}]$$

$$- \text{cov}(\delta_k^t, s^t | \phi^{t-1}) \cdot E[\hat{c}_s^t \cdot u_{cc}^t | \phi^{t-1}]\}$$

$$(21) \qquad\qquad - \text{cov}(\varepsilon_i^t, W^t | \phi^{t-1}) \cdot \frac{E[\hat{c}_W^t \cdot u_{cc}^t | \phi^{t-1}]}{E[u_c^t | \phi^{t-1}]}$$

$$- \text{cov}(\varepsilon_i^t, s^t | \phi^{t-1}) \cdot \frac{E[\hat{c}_s^t \cdot u_{cc}^t | \phi^{t-1}]}{E[u_c^t | \phi^{t-1}]}.$$

This equation states that the conditional expected excess return of the ith asset is linear in the asset's conditional factor loadings, β_{ik}^t, as in the asymptotic single-period APT. However, the expected excess return also depends on two residual terms that are proportional to the covariances $\text{cov}(\varepsilon_i^t, W^t | \phi^{t-1})$ and $\text{cov}(\varepsilon_i^t, s^t | \phi^{t-1})$.

The first residual term may be simplified by invoking the same arguments that allow me to write the residual in the single-period approximate APT as in equation (18):

(22)
$$\text{cov}\,(\varepsilon_i^t, W^t | \phi^{t-1}) \cdot \frac{E[\hat{c}_W^t \cdot u_{cc}^t | \phi^{t-1}]}{E[u_c^t | \phi^{t-1}]}$$

$$= \left\{ \left(\sum_{i=1}^n P_i^{t-1} \right) \frac{E[\hat{c}_W^t \cdot u_{cc}^t | \phi^{t-1}]}{E[u_c^t | \phi^{t-1}]} \right\} \cdot \left(\frac{P_i^{t-1}}{\sum_{i=1}^n P_i^{t-1}} \right) \cdot \text{var}\,(\varepsilon_i | \phi^{t-1}).$$

The intuition of the asymptotic single-period APT carries over to this residual term of the intertemporal APT: as the number of assets in the economy grows such that the weight of the ith asset in the market portfolio tends to zero, this residual also tends to zero.

The second residual term that is proportional to $\text{cov}\,(\varepsilon_i^t, s^t | \phi^{t-1})$ is specific to the intertemporal APT. Note that in the single-period APT end-of-period consumption equals end-of-period wealth, and we set $s^t \equiv 0$, thereby eliminating this residual term. But in the intertemporal APT no assumption has yet been made to lead to the conclusion that the terms $\text{cov}\,(\varepsilon_i^t, s^t | \phi^{t-1})$ and/or $E[\hat{c}_s^t \cdot u_{cc}^t | \phi^{t-1}]$ are small, even in the asymptotic case when the weight of the asset in the market portfolio tends to zero. Thus the intertemporal APT is subject to the same limitation as the ICAPM in that the theory does not provide an operational procedure for identifying the state variables.

Under the plausible maintained hypotheses that (1) the observable subset of assets has a factor structure, (2) the noise terms of the observable assets are uncorrelated with the returns of the unobservable assets, and (3) the factors span the state variables that influence the rates of return of the observable assets, then the intertemporal APT becomes testable. Specifically, the noise terms of the observable assets are uncorrelated with the state variables, and the second residual term in equation (21) vanishes. Note that under the same maintained hypothesis the state variables are identified and the ICAPM also becomes testable. See also the discussion in Chen, Roll, and Ross (1986).

An alternative way to make the intertemporal APT testable is to introduce the maintained hypothesis that utility is logarithmic. Then equation (13) implies that $s^t \equiv 0$, the second residual term vanishes, and the intertemporal APT is reduced to the APT.

Finally, I derive the intertemporal APT in unconditional form. I assume that the returns of the n firms have the factor structure given by equation (19), where the noise terms have bounded variance and are uncorrelated with each other and with the K factors, conditional on ϕ^0 (or on any other subset of ϕ^{t-1}). I also augment the state as $(s^t(\phi^t) \quad q^{t-1}(\phi^{t-1}))$ satisfying equation (14). I start with the unconditional valuation equation (5) and proceed as before to obtain the unconditional counterpart of equation (21). It differs from equation (21) in two respects. First, ϕ^{t-1} is replaced everywhere by ϕ^0. Second, there is one more term on the right side, namely

$$- \text{cov}\,(\varepsilon_i^t, q^{t-1} | \phi^0) \cdot \frac{E[\hat{c}_q^t \cdot u_{cc}^t | \phi^0]}{E[u_c^t | \phi^0]},$$

in the special case that q^{t-1} is scalar. As in the conditional equation, I argue that no assumption has yet been made that leads to the conclusion that the two terms proportional to the covariances $\text{cov}(\varepsilon_i^t, s^t|\phi^0)$ and $\text{cov}(\varepsilon_i^t, q^{t-1}|\phi^0)$ are small. These terms vanish if utility is assumed to be logarithmic, or if the factors span the state variables $(\mathbf{s}^t(\phi^t)\mathbf{q}^{t-1}(\phi^{t-1}))$.

VIII. INCOMPLETE MARKET

When the market is incomplete, interesting questions arise on portfolio separation, spanning, and Pareto efficiency. These issues are addressed by Ingersoll (1988*), Ross (1978*, 1988*), Rubinstein (1976*), Scheinkman (1988*), and Stiglitz (1988*), and in references therein.

The fundamental valuation equation and its derivative restrictions such as the consumption CAPM and the CAPM are often rejected in empirical tests. Grossman and Shiller (1981) find that the representative consumer must have an implausibly high degree of risk aversion if the valuation equation is to fit the data. Hansen and Singleton (1983) and Mehra and Prescott (1985) find that the difference in mean returns on risky assets cannot be explained by differences in consumption risk. Mehra and Prescott (1985) suggest that the problem may lie with the complete market/representative consumer economic paradigm. Bewley (1982), Mankiw (1986), Scheinkman (1988*), and Scheinkman and Weiss (1986) present incomplete market models and address some of these issues.

I focus on a subset of the issues that arise in an incomplete market. Specifically, I explore the robustness of the valuation theories presented in the earlier sections to a particular kind of market incompleteness. I do so in the context of a modified version of the two-date, incomplete-market economy presented by Mankiw (1986). In the next section I review the pricing restrictions imposed by a necessary condition of equilibrium—the absence of arbitrage.

At the first date consumers are identical in terms of their endowments, beliefs, and tastes. At the second date each consumer receives a dividend c plus an endowment. A fraction λ of the consumers receive endowment $-x/\lambda$, and a fraction $1-\lambda$ receive endowment $x/(1-\lambda)$. The aggregate endowment is zero; hence per capita consumption is c. At the first date c and x are random variables with known joint distribution. Each consumer does not know which of the two types of endowment he or she will receive; furthermore the type of endowment is independent of c and x.

In a Pareto optimal allocation each consumer consumes c. This allocation is attainable in a competitive economy in which each consumer's endowment is observable by everybody ex post and in which an insurance market exists that pools the endowments. Market incompleteness is introduced in this model by banning the insurance of endowments.

The counterpart of the fundamental valuation equation (3) is

(23) $$E[y \cdot r_i] = 0,$$

where

(24)
$$y \equiv (1 - \lambda)u_c\left(c + \frac{x}{1 - \lambda}\right) + \lambda u_c\left(c - \frac{x}{\lambda}\right).$$

The fundamental valuation equation (23) may be tested directly, where now marginal utility is replaced by the weighted sum of marginal utilities.

In the special case that utility is quadratic, marginal utility is linear in its argument and the weighted sum of marginal utilities becomes $y = u_c(c)$. The consumption CAPM in terms of the per capita consumption remains unaltered, despite the fact that the market is incomplete and the allocation is not Pareto optimal. This result is presented in Grossman and Shiller (1982). In another special case, Breeden (1979) assumes that the consumption and endowment are a diffusion process. This implies that utility is (locally) quadratic and, as in the previous special case, the consumption CAPM remains unaltered, even though the market is incomplete and the allocation is not Pareto optimal. Bewley (1982), Mankiw (1986), and Scheinkman (1988*) present models in which the third derivative of the utility function is positive and show that market incompleteness increases the consumption risk premium.

In the discussion below I steer away from the assumption of quadratic (or locally quadratic) utility and highlight the effect of market incompleteness on valuation theories. I assume that c, x, and r_i are multivariate normal, invoke Stein's lemma, and obtain the following:

(25)
$$E[r_i] = \text{cov}(r_i, c) \cdot E\left[(1 - \lambda)u_{cc}\left(c + \frac{x}{1 - \lambda}\right) + \lambda u_{cc}\left(c - \frac{x}{\lambda}\right)\right] \Big/ E[y]$$
$$+ \text{cov}(r_i, x) \cdot E\left[u_{cc}\left(c + \frac{x}{1 - \lambda}\right) - u_{cc}\left(c - \frac{x}{\lambda}\right)\right] \Big/ E[y].$$

If x is constant, the second term on the right side vanishes. The consumption CAPM and the CAPM hold despite the fact that the allocation is not Pareto optimal.

If the size of the endowment shock, x, is a random variable, the consumption CAPM in terms of per capita consumption and the CAPM generally do not hold. Equation (25) states that an asset's expected excess return is linear in both the per capita consumption risk, $\text{cov}(r_i, c)$, and the endowment shock risk, $\text{cov}(r_i, x)$. The coefficient of $\text{cov}(r_i, x)$ may be of either sign. If $x \geq 0$ $(x \leq 0)$ the coefficient is nonpositive (nonnegative). In special cases, such as quadratic utility, the coefficient of $\text{cov}(r_i, x)$ is zero. In general, however, the consumption CAPM and CAPM are not robust to market incompleteness. In contrast, the single-period, equilibrium APT remains valid with y replacing u_c in equation (16). However, the magnitudes of the factor risk premia and of the residual term change.

One source of market incompleteness is transaction costs. Constantinides (1986*) studies a two-asset intertemporal consumption-investment model with proportional transaction costs. The demand for assets is shown to be sensitive to these costs. However, transaction costs have only a second-order effect on the liquidity premia implied by equilibrium asset returns because investors accommodate large transaction costs by drastically reducing the frequency and volume of trade. Hence, in intertemporal models in which the only motivation to trade is consumption or rebalancing of the portfolio, transaction costs have a second-order effect on the theory of valuation. By contrast, transaction costs may play an important role in models in which there is some other reason to trade, such as private information.

IX. PRICING IMPLICATIONS OF THE NO-ARBITRAGE RESTRICTION

The justly famous Modigliani-Miller (1958) theorem represents a brilliant application of the no-arbitrage restriction and marks the beginning of modern finance. The key concept introduced by Modigliani and Miller is that of a risk class or spanning. The power of the theorem is that it is preference free, except to the extent that arbitrageurs prefer more to less. The theoretical developments of the no-arbitrage restriction proceed on three fronts.

First, the theory of the firm is extended by Modigliani and Miller and others to incorporate taxes and institutional restrictions. This literature is represented in the second volume with Miller's (1977*) influential paper and the essays by Kim (1988*) and Scholes and Wolfson (1988*).

Second, in his important paper Ross (1976) proposes an arbitrage pricing theory under the assumption that asset returns are generated by a K-factor model. In an asymptotic sense, as the number of assets tends to infinity, or in an approximate sense in a finite-asset economy, the K factors determine K risk classes. This literature is represented in this volume with Huberman's (1982*) paper and Connor's (1988*) essay.

The third theoretical development of the no-arbitrage restriction is pioneered by Black and Scholes (1973) in their celebrated option pricing model. The use of arbitrage in the Modigliani-Miller theory is a static, one-shot exploitation by the arbitrageur of a potential relative price discrepancy. Although the stock and the option do not belong to the same risk class in a static sense, when the stock price follows a geometric Brownian motion a dynamically adjusted portfolio of the stock and a bond does belong to the same risk class as the option and makes possible the pricing of the option relative to the stock and the bond. The Black and Scholes paper has had a profound influence on the theory of valuation.

In the first part of his paper, Merton (1973b*) employs the Modigliani-Miller concept of a risk class and through static no-arbitrage arguments develops distribution-free and preference-free restrictions on the price of an option relative to a bond and the underlying security. In the second part Merton employs the Black-Scholes concept of a risk class and through dynamic no-arbitrage arguments extends the Black-Scholes theory. As a historical note, footnote 43 of Merton's paper contains the germ of term structure theories.

Cox and Ross (1976) develop the concept of "as if risk neutral economy" and apply it in the valuation of options under different stochastic processes. The concept that state probabilities, suitably normalized, may be viewed as prices in an "as if risk neutral" economy is due to Arrow (1964) and is formalized in a dynamic hedging context in the influential paper of Harrison and Kreps (1979). The theory is reviewed by Cox and Huang (1988*) and in the remainder of this section.

Define by B^t, $B^t = B^t(\phi^t)$, the price at date t of a discount bond which pays one unit of the consumption good at date T. Normalize the firms' dividends and prices with B^t as the numeraire at date t. The normalized dividend of firm i at date t is $\hat{D}_i^t \equiv D_i^t/B^t$ and the price is $\hat{P}_i^t = P_i^t/B^t$. In terms of the representative-consumer economy of Section II, define $\xi^t \equiv \lambda u_c^t(c^t)B^t$, where λ is an arbitrary constant. Eliminate $u_c^t(c^t)$ from the valuation equation (1) and obtain

$$(26) \qquad \hat{P}_i^t = E\left[\sum_{\tau=t+1}^{T} \xi^\tau \hat{D}_i^\tau \mid \phi^t \right] \bigg/ \xi^t.$$

I now relax the assumptions that the market is complete and that consumers have homogeneous, time-additive and von Neumann–Morgenstern utility functions. Under the assumption of no-arbitrage opportunities and some other weak technical assumptions, it may be shown that a random variable ξ^t exists such that the generalized valuation equation (26) applies. This is an important result because the absence of arbitrage opportunities is a necessary condition of any equilibrium.

The generalized valuation equation states that ξ^t is a martingale. To prove this, consider firm i which pays dividend $\hat{D}_i^\tau - 1$ at date τ, $t + 1 \leqslant \tau \leqslant T$, and zero dividend at other dates. Note that the dividend may be reinvested at date τ in a discount bond which has unit price (with B^t as the numeraire) and one unit of the consumption good at date T. The price of firm i at date t is $P_i^t = B^t/B^t = 1$. Equation (26) becomes

$$(27) \qquad 1 = E[\xi^\tau \mid \phi^t]/\xi^t$$

and states that ξ^t is a martingale.

By analogy with equation (10) I may define the state at date t as an m-vector $s^t = s^t(\phi^t)$ if there exists a function $\hat{\xi}^t(\cdot, \cdot)$ such that

$$(28) \qquad \hat{\xi}^t(\phi^{t-1}, s^t) = \xi^t(\phi^t).$$

One may proceed as in Section V to derive an intertemporal capital asset pricing model. Related results are presented by Chamberlain (1985) and Reisman (1986).

X. FUTURE DIRECTIONS

An important theme of this essay is the role of conditioning information in valuation theory. The intertemporal asset pricing model requires the identification of the state variables in order to become an economic theory with empirically testable implications. Likewise the equilibrium version of the intertemporal arbitrage pricing theory requires the identification of the state variables, or at least requires the maintained hypothesis that the factors span the space of the state variables. Furthermore, the state vector needs to be augmented in both theories if the testable economic implications are to be stated in terms of unconditional moments.

The interface of valuation theory and the empirical identification of instruments of the state variables is an exciting direction for future research. There is substantial empirical research underway to identify the time-series and cross-sectional properties of asset returns. This includes the identification of factors, asset portfolios, and macroeconomic variables as instruments of the state variables. A challenge to the theory is to explain why a particular set of state variables is important in the determination of prices.

A second exciting direction for future research lies in the development of an equilibrium valuation theory when the market is incomplete. As I illustrated in Sections VIII and IX, this theory has richer implications than the valuation theory based on the complete market/representative consumer economic paradigm and already provides an explanation to some empirical puzzles. However, the full development and the empirical testing of the incomplete market theory remain a task for the future.

REFERENCES

Arrow, K. 1964. "The Role of Securities in the Optimal Allocation of Risk-Bearing." *Review of Economic Studies* 31: 91–96. This paper is the English translation of Arrow, K. 1953. "Le Rôle des Valeurs Boursiéres pour la Répartition la Meilleure des Risques," *Econométrie* (C.N.R.S. Paris): 41–47; discussion 47–48.

Bewley, T. F. 1982. "Thoughts on Tests of the Intertemporal Asset Pricing Model." Northwestern University (mimeo).

Bhattacharya, S. 1981. "Notes on Multiperiod Valuation and the Pricing of Options." *Journal of Finance* 36: 163–80.

Black, F.; Jensen, M.; and Scholes, M. S. 1972. "The Capital Asset Pricing Model: Some Empirical Tests." In M. Jensen (ed.), *Studies in the Theory of Capital Markets.* New York: Praeger, pp. 79–121.

Black, F., and Scholes, M. S. 1973. "The Pricing of Options and Corporate Liabilities." *Journal of Political Economy* 81: 637–54.

Breeden, D. T. 1979. "An Intertemporal Asset Pricing Model with Stochastic Consumption and Investment Opportunities." *Journal of Financial Economics* 7: 265–96.

Breeden, D. T.; Gibbons, M. R.; and Litzenberger, R. H. 1986. "Empirical Tests of the Consumption-Oriented CAPM." Duke University and Stanford University, unpublished manuscript.

Breeden, D. T., and Litzenberger, R. H. 1978. "Prices of State-Contingent Claims Implicit in Option Prices." *Journal of Business* 51: 621–51.

Brennan, M. J. 1970. "Taxes, Market Valuation and Corporate Financial Policy." *National Tax Journal* 23: 417–27.

Brock, W. 1982. "Asset Prices in a Production Economy." In J. McCall (ed.), *The Economics of Information and Uncertainty.* Chicago: University of Chicago Press.

Brown, S., and Weinstein, M. 1983. "A New Approach to Testing Asset Pricing Models: The Bilinear Model." *Journal of Finance* 38: 711–43.

Campbell, J. Y. 1986. "Bond and Stock Returns in a Simple Exchange Model." *Quarterly Journal of Economics* 101: 785–803.

Chamberlain, G. 1983a. "Funds, Factors, and Diversification in Arbitrage Pricing Models." *Econometrica* 51: 1305–23.

———. 1983b. "A Characterization of the Distributions that Imply Mean-Variance Utility Functions." *Journal of Economic Theory* 29: 185–201.

———. 1985. "Asset Pricing in Multiperiod Security Markets." Working paper No. 8510, University of Wisconsin, August.

Chamberlain, G., and Rothschild, M. 1983. "Arbitrage, Factor Structure, and Mean-Variance Analysis on Large Asset Markets." *Econometrica* 51: 1281–1304.

Chen, N. 1983. "Some Empirical Tests of the Theory of Arbitrage Pricing." *Journal of Finance* 39: 1393–1414.

Chen, N., and Ingersoll, J. E., Jr. 1983. "Exact Pricing in Linear Factor Models with Finitely Many Assets: A Note." *Journal of Finance* 38: 985–88.

Chen, N.; Roll, R.; and Ross, S. A. 1986. "Economic Forces and the Stock Market: Testing the APT and Alternative Asset Pricing Theories." *Journal of Business* 56: 383–403.

Cho, D. C. 1984. "On Testing the Arbitrage Pricing Theory: Inter-Battery Factor Analysis." *Journal of Finance* 39: 1485–1502.

Connor, G. 1984. "A Unified Beta Pricing Theory." *Journal of Economic Theory* 34: 13–31.

———. 1988. "Notes on the Arbitrage Pricing Theory." Discussion, Chapter 9, this volume.

Connor, G., and Korajczyk, R. A. 1986. "Risk and Return in an Equilibrium APT: Theory and Tests." University of California, Berkeley and Northwestern University, unpublished manuscript.

Constantinides, G. M. 1980. "Admissible Uncertainty in the Intertemporal Asset Pricing Model." *Journal of Financial Economics* 8: 71–86.

———. 1982. "Intertemporal Asset Pricing with Heterogeneous Consumers and without Demand Aggregation." *Journal of Business* 55: 253–67.

———. 1983. "Capital Market Equilibrium with Personal Tax." *Econometrica* 51: 611–36.

———. 1984. "Optimal Stock Trading with Personal Taxes: Implications for Prices and the Abnormal January Returns." *Journal of Financial Economics* 13: 65–90.

———. 1986. "Capital Market Equilibrium with Transaction Costs." *Journal of Political Economy* 94: 842–62.

Constantinides, G. M., and Ingersoll, J. E. 1984. "Optimal Bond Trading with Personal Taxes." *Journal of Financial Economics* 13: 299–335.

Conway, D. A., and Reinganum, M. R. 1986. "Capital Market Factor Structure: Identification through Cross Validation." Working paper No. 183, Center for Research in Security Prices, University of Chicago.

Cox, J. C., and Huang, C. 1988. "Option Pricing Theory and Its Applications." Discussion, Chapter 8, this volume.

Cox, J. C.; Ingersoll, J. E.; and Ross, S. A. 1981. "A Reexamination of Traditional Hypotheses about the Term Structure of Interest Rates." *Journal of Finance* 36: 769–99.

———. 1985a. "An Intertemporal General Equilibrium Model of Asset Prices." *Econometrica* 53: 363–84.

———. 1985b. "A Theory of the Term Structure of Interest Rates." *Econometrica* 53: 385–407.

Cox, J. C., and Ross, S. A. 1976. "The Valuation of Options for Alternative Stochastic Processes." *Journal of Financial Economics* 3: 145–66.

Cragg, J. G., and Malkiel, B. G. 1982. *Expectations and the Structure of Share Prices.* Chicago: University of Chicago Press.

Dhrymes, J.; Friend, I.; and Gultekin, N. 1984. "A Critical Reexamination of the Empirical Evidence on the Arbitrage Pricing Theory." *Journal of Finance* 39: 323–46.

Donaldson, J. B.; Johnsen, T.; and Mehra, R. 1985. "On the Term Structure of Interest Rates" (mimeo).

Duffie, D., and Huang, C. 1985. "Implementing Arrow-Debreu Equilibria by Continuous Trading of Few Long-Lived Securities." *Econometrica* 53: 1337–56.

Dunn, K. B., and Singleton, K. J. 1986. "Modeling the Term Structure of Interest Rates under Nonseparable Utility and Durability of Goods." *Journal of Financial Economics* 17: 27–55.

Dybvig, P. H. 1983. "An Explicit Bound on Individual Assets' Deviations from APT Pricing in a Finite Economy." *Journal of Financial Economics* 12: 483–96.

Dybvig, P. H., and Ingersoll, J. 1982. "Mean-Variance Theory in Complete Markets." *Journal of Business* 55: 233–51.

Dybvig, P. H., and Ross, S. A. 1982. "Portfolio Efficient Sets." *Econometrica* 50: 1525–46.

———. 1985. "Yes, the APT Is Testable." *Journal of Finance* 40: 1173–88.

Fama, E. F. 1970. "Multiperiod Consumption-Investment Decisions." *American Economic Review* 60: 163–74.

———. 1976. *Foundations of Finance.* New York: Basic Books.

———. 1981. "Stock Returns, Real Activity, Inflation and Money." *American Economic Review* 71: 545–65.

———. 1984a. "Information in the Term Structure." *Journal of Financial Economics* 13: 509–28.

———. 1984b. "Term Premiums in Bond Returns." *Journal of Financial Economics* 13: 529–46.

———. 1984c. "Forward and Spot Exchange Rates." *Journal of Monetary Economics* 14: 319–38.

Fama, E. F., and French, K. R. 1986. "Permanent and Temporary Components of Stock Prices." Working paper No. 128, University of Chicago, January.

Fama, E. F., and MacBeth, J. 1973. "Risk, Return and Equilibrium: Empirical Tests." *Journal of Political Economy* 81: 607–36.

Fama, E. F., and Schwert, G. W. 1977. "Asset Returns and Inflation." *Journal of Financial Economics* 5: 115–46.

Ferson, W. E. 1983. "Expectations of Real Interest Rates and Aggregate Consumption: Empirical Tests." *Journal of Financial and Quantitative Analysis* 18: 477–97.

Ferson, W. E.; Kandel, S.; and Stambaugh, R. 1987. "Tests of Asset Pricing with Time-Varying Expected Risk Premiums and Market Betas." Working paper No. 159, Center for Research in Security Prices, University of Chicago, November.

Gibbons, M. R. 1982. "Multivariate Tests of Financial Models: A New Approach." *Journal of Financial Economics* 10: 3–27.

Gibbons, M. R., and Ferson, W. 1985. "Testing Asset Pricing Models with Changing Expectations and an Unobservable Market Portfolio." *Journal of Financial Economics* 14: 217–36.

Gibbons, M. R.; Ross, S. A.; and Shanken, J. 1985. "Testing Portfolio Efficiency in the Presence of a Riskless Asset." Graduate School of Business, University of California, Berkeley.

Grinblatt, M., and Titman, S. 1983. "Factor Pricing in a Finite Economy." *Journal of Financial Economics* 12: 497–507.

———. 1987. "The Relation between Mean-Variance Efficiency and Arbitrage Pricing." *Journal of Business* 60: 97–112.

Grossman, S. J., and Shiller, R. J. 1981. "The Determinants of the Variability of Stock Market Prices." *American Economic Review, Papers and Proceedings* 71: 222–27.

――――. 1982. "Consumption Correlatedness and Risk Measurement in Economies with Non-Traded Assets and Heterogeneous Information." *Journal of Financial Economics* 10: 195–210.

Grossman, S. J., Melino, A., and Shiller, R. J. 1985. "Estimating the Continuous Time Consumption Based Asset Pricing Model." National Bureau of Economic Research, manuscript.

Hall, R. 1981. "Intertemporal Substitution in Consumption." Stanford University, manuscript.

――――. 1985. "Real Interest Rates and Consumption." Working paper No. 1694, National Bureau of Economic Research, August.

Hansen, L. P., and Richard, S. E. 1985. "The Role of Conditioning Information in Deducing Testable Restrictions Implied by Dynamic Asset Pricing Models." University of Chicago and Carnegie-Mellon University, manuscript.

Hansen, L. P., and Singleton, K. J. 1982. "Generalized Instrumental Variables Estimation of Nonlinear Rational Expectations Models." *Econometrica* 50: 1269–86.

――――. 1983. "Stochastic Consumption, Risk Aversion, and the Temporal Behavior of Asset Returns." *Journal of Political Economy* 91: 249–65.

Harrison, M., and Kreps, D. 1979. "Martingales and Arbitrage in Multiperiod Securities Markets." *Journal of Economic Theory* 20: 381 408.

Huang, C. Forthcoming. "An Intertemporal General Equilibrium Asset Pricing Model: The Case of Diffusion Information." *Econometrica.*

Huberman, G. 1982. "A Simple Approach to Arbitrage Pricing Theory." *Journal of Economic Theory* 28: 183–91.

Huberman, G., and Kandel, S. 1985. "A Size Based Stock Returns Model." Working paper No. 148, Graduate School of Business, University of Chicago.

Ingersoll, J. E., Jr. 1984. "Some Results in the Theory of Arbitrage Pricing." *Journal of Finance* 39: 1021–39.

――――. 1987. *Theory of Financial Decision Making.* Totowa, N.J.: Rowman & Littlefield.

――――. 1988. "Spanning in Financial Markets." Discussion, Chapter 4, this volume.

Jobson, J. D. 1982. "A Multivariate Linear Regression Test for the Arbitrage Pricing Theory." *Journal of Finance* 37: 1037–42.

Keim, D. B., and Stambaugh, R. F., 1986. "Predicting Returns in the Bond and Stock Markets." *Journal of Financial Economics* 17: 357–390.

Kim, E. H. 1988. "Optimal Capital Structure in Miller's Equilibrium." Discussion, Chapter 2, volume 2.

Kraus, A., and Litzenberger, R. 1983. "On the Distributional Conditions for a Consumption-Oriented Three Moment CAPM." *Journal of Finance* 38: 1381–91.

Kreps, D. 1982. "Multiperiod Securities and the Efficient Allocation of Risk: A Comment on the Black-Scholes Option Pricing Model." In J. McCall (ed.), *The Economics of Uncertainty and Information.* Chicago: University of Chicago Press.

Lehman, B. N., and Modest, D. M. 1985. "The Empirical Foundations of the Arbitrage Pricing Theory I: The Empirical Tests." Research paper No. 821, Stanford University.

Lintner, J. 1965. "The Valuation of Risk Assets and the Selection of Risky Investments in Stock Portfolios and Capital Budgets." *Review of Economics and Statistics* 47: 13–37.

Litzenberger, R., and Ronn, E. 1986. "A Utility-Based Model of Common Stock Returns." *Journal of Finance* 41: 67–92.

Long, J. B. 1974. "Stock Prices, Inflation, and the Term Structure of Interest Rates."

Journal of Financial Economics 2: 131–70.

Lucas, R. 1978. "Asset Prices in an Exchange Economy." *Econometrica* 46: 1429–45.

Mankiw, N. G. 1986. "The Equity Premium and the Concentration of Aggregate Shocks." Working paper No. 1788, National Bureau of Economic Research.

Mehra, R., and Prescott, E. C. 1985. "The Equity Premium: A Puzzle." *Journal of Monetary Economics* 15: 145–61.

Merton, R. C. 1973a. "An Intertemporal Capital Asset Pricing Model." *Econometrica* 41: 867–87.

―――. 1973b. "Theory of Rational Option Pricing." *Bell Journal of Economics and Management Science* 4: 141–83.

―――. 1980. "On Estimating the Expected Return on the Market: An Exploratory Investigation." *Journal of Financial Economics* 8: 323–62.

Miller, M. H. 1977. "Debt and Taxes." *Journal of Finance* 32: 261–75.

Modigliani, F., and Miller, M. H. 1958. "The Cost of Capital, Corporation Finance and the Theory of Investment." *American Economic Review* 48: 261–97.

Nelson, R. 1972. *The Term Structure of Interest Rates.* New York: Basic Books.

Ohlson, J. A., and Garman, M. B. 1980. "A Dynamic Equilibrium for the Ross Arbitrage Model." *Journal of Finance* 35: 675–84.

Owen, J., and Rabinovitch, R. 1983. "On the Class of Elliptical Distributions and Their Applications to the Theory of Portfolio Choice." *Journal of Finance* 38: 745–52.

Prescott, E., and Mehra, R. 1980. "Recursive Competitive Equilibrium: The Case of Homogeneous Households." *Econometrica* 48: 1365–79.

Reisman, H. 1985. "Intertemporal Arbitrage Pricing Theory." University of Minnesota, mimeographed.

Roll, R. 1977. "A Critique of the Asset Pricing Theory's Tests—Part I: On Past and Potential Testability of the Theory." *Journal of Financial Economics* 4: 129–76.

Roll, R., and Ross, S. A. 1980. "An Empirical Investigation of the Arbitrage Pricing Theory." *Journal of Finance* 35: 1073–1103.

Ross, S. A. 1976. "The Arbitrage Theory of Capital Asset Pricing." *Journal of Economic Theory* 13: 341–60.

―――. 1977. "Risk, Return and Arbitrage." In I. Friend and J. Bicksler (eds.), *Risk and Return in Finance.* Cambridge, Mass.: Ballinger.

―――. 1978. "Mutual Fund Separation in Financial Theory—The Separating Distributions." *Journal of Economic Theory* 17: 254–86.

―――. 1988. "Intertemporal Asset Pricing." Discussion, Chapter 3, this volume.

Rubinstein, M. 1974. "An Aggregation Theorem for Security Markets." *Journal of Financial Economics* 1: 225–44.

―――. 1976. "The Valuation of Uncertain Income Streams and the Pricing of Options." *Bell Journal of Economics and Management Science* 7: 407–25.

Scheinkman, J. A. 1988. "Market Incompleteness and the Equilibrium Valuation of Assets." Discussion, Chapter 2, this volume.

Scheinkman, J. A., and Weiss, L. 1986. "Borrowing Constraints and Aggregate Economic Activity." *Econometrica* 54: 23–45.

Scholes, M. S., and Wolfson, M. A. 1988. "Issues in the Theory of Optimal Capital Structure." Discussion, Chapter 2, volume 2.

Shanken, J. 1982. "The Arbitrage Pricing Theory: Is It Testable?" *Journal of Finance* 37: 1129–40.

―――. 1985a. "Multivariate Tests of the Zero-Beta CAPM." *Journal of Financial Economics* 14: 327–48.

―――. 1985b. "Multi-Beta CAPM or Equilibrium APT? A Reply." *Journal of Finance* 40: 1189–96.

Sharpe, W. 1964. "Capital Asset Prices: A Theory of Market Equilibrium under Conditions of Risk." *Journal of Finance* 19: 425–42.

Singleton, K. J. 1988. "Modelling the Term Structure of Interest Rates in General Equilibrium." Discussion, Chapter 5, this volume.

Stambaugh, R. 1982. "On the Exclusion of Assets from Tests of the Two-Parameter Model: A Sensitivity Analysis." *Journal of Financial Economics* 10: 237–68.

———. 1983. "Arbitrage Pricing with Information." *Journal of Financial Economics* 12: 357–69.

Stapleton, R., and Subrahmanyam, M. 1978. "A Multiperiod Equilibrium Asset Pricing Model." *Econometrica* 46: 1077–96.

Stein, C. 1973. "Estimation of the Mean of a Multivariate Normal Distribution." *Proceedings of the Prague Symposium on Asymptotic Statistics.*

Stiglitz, Z. 1988. "Mutual Funds, Capital Structure, and Economic Efficiency." Discussion, Chapter 10, this volume.

The valuation of uncertain income streams and the pricing of options

Mark Rubinstein

■ Since the theoretical breakthrough leading to a simple single-period valuation formula for uncertain income consistent with rational risk averse investor behavior and equilibrium in financial markets (Sharpe, 1964), there have been various attempts to extend this model to a multiperiod context. Fama (1970) proved that even though a risk averter maximized the expected utility from the stream of consumption over his lifetime, his choices in each period would be indistinguishable from that of a properly specified rational risk averse investor with a single-period horizon. Moreover, if his investment (and consumption) opportunities followed a (possibly nonstationary) random walk, then the induced single-period utility would be a nonstochastic function. These observations implied that the simple single-period model could apply to successive periods in a multiperiod setting. Subsequently, Merton (1973b) and later Long (1974) generalized the single-period formula to intertemporally stochastically dependent opportunity sets. While their resulting formulae were more complex, they still possessed the merit of empirical promise.

However, of greater interest than the anchoring of a single-period valuation formula in a multiperiod setting, is development of a simple multiperiod formula, that is, a method of determining the present value of a series of cash flows received over many future dates. The early certainty-equivalent and risk-adjusted discount rate approaches (Robichek and Myers, 1965) were flawed by failing to specify determinants of the adjustment parameters. In effect, they remained little more than definitions of these parameters. More recently, implicitly making use of Fama's result that the simple single-period model could be applied successively, Bogue and Roll (1974) have indeed derived a method for discounting an uncertain income stream consistent with rational risk averse investor behavior. In the spirit of dynamic pro-

Research for this paper was supported in part by a grant from the Dean Witter Foundation. The author would like to acknowledge comments on the original version of this paper from John Cox, Robert Geske, Robert Merton, and Stephen Ross.

gramming, they apply the single-period mean-variance model to the last period determining the date $T - 1$ present value of income received at date T. Knowing the determinants of this uncertain present value and the additional uncertain income received at date $T - 1$, the single-period model is again applied determining the date $T - 2$ present value, etc. By this means, the date zero present value of the income stream is determined. Unfortunately, the resulting formula, even for convenient special cases, is far from simple. The comfortable elegance of the formula for discounting a certain income stream does not seem to carry over to uncertainty.

This is all the more discouraging considering the obvious importance of valuing uncertain income streams for research in financial markets. The primary purpose of this paper is to develop the needed valuation formula that satisfies the tests of uncertain income received over time, consistency with rational risk averse investor behavior and equilibrium in financial markets, as well as simplicity and statement in terms of empirically observable inputs. Section 2 presents a general approach for valuation of uncertain income streams, but the formula contains inputs which are not easily observable. Section 3 remedies this defect for the special case of constant proportional risk aversion (CPRA). With a simple valuation formula in hand, in Section 4 it is applied to the multiperiod problem of the valuation of an option in terms of its associated stock. To my surprise, the resulting option pricing formula is *identical* to the Black-Scholes (1973) formula even though only costless *discrete-time* trading opportunities are available so that investors cannot create a perfect hedge, investors are risk averse, and must simultaneously choose among a large number of securities.

■ Assume there exist states of nature so that given the revelation of the state[1] at any date, the cash flow (i.e., dividend) received by the owner of any security is known with certainty. Let $t = 0,1,2, \ldots$ denote dates, $s(t)$ (random variable) denote the state at date t, $X[s(t)]$ the dividend received from a security in state $s(t)$, and $P[s(t)]$ the price of the security in state $s(t)$.

The requirement that securities with identical returns should have the same value is probably the most basic condition for equilibrium in financial markets. In particular, assume

(1) *Single-price law of markets:* If two securities, or more generally two portfolios of securities,[1] yield the same dividends for every future state, then their current prices are the same.

Since there then can be no more linearly independent securities than states, there must exist a set of random variables $\{Z[s(t)]\}$, *the same for all securities*, such that for any security

$$P_0 = \sum_{t=1}^{\infty} \sum_{s(t)} Z[s(t)]X[s(t)].$$

---

[1] Extension of the single-price law of markets to portfolios of securities (i.e. convex combinations of dividends) is inconsistent with transactions costs which vary with the scale of investment in any security. However, it insures that any pricing formula for arbitrary securities will possess the "portfolio property" that it applies to arbitrary portfolios as well.

Of course, the random variables will not be unique unless the number of linearly independent securities equals the number of states. A normalized riskless security for any date t has a certain dividend $X[s(t)] = 1$ at date t and a certain dividend of zero at any other date. Therefore, denoting R_{Ft}^{-1} as the current price of a date t normalized riskless security, then $R_{Ft}^{-1} = \Sigma_{s(t)} Z[s(t)]$. If, additionally, we assume

(2) *Nonsatiation: Ceteris paribus,* the larger its dividends for any state, the greater current price of a security.

then $Z[s(t)] > 0$ for all states.[2]

These two assumptions motivate the following theorem:

Theorem 1: Given assumptions 1 and 2, there exists a positive random variable $Y[s(t)]$, the same for all securities, such that for any security[3]

$$P_0 = \sum_{t=1}^{\infty} \frac{E(X_t) + \text{Cov}(X_t, Y_t)/E(Y_t)}{R_{Ft}}. \tag{1}$$

Proof: Let $\pi[s(t)]$ be a probability,[4] assessed at date $t = 0$, that state $s(t)$ will occur. Define random variable $Z'[s(t)] \equiv Z[s(t)]/\pi[s(t)]$; then $P_0 = \Sigma_t E(X_t Z'_t)$. Second, define random variable $Y[s(t)] \equiv E(Y_t)R_{Ft}Z'[s(t)]$; then $P_0 = \Sigma_t E(X_t Y_t)/[R_{Ft}E(Y_t)]$. The result follows from the definition of covariance. Q.E.D.

The valuation formula implies that the current price of a security (or portfolio of securities) equals the sum of the discounted certainty equivalents of its dividends discounted at the riskless rate. The risk adjustment factor applied to the mean dividend at each date is its "coefficient of covariation" with a random variable common to all securities. Not only will this random variable $\tilde{Y}_t$ not be unique if the number of states exceeds the number of different securities, but even if the number of states and different securities are equal, Y_t will be unique only up to a positive multiplicative constant.[5]

However, until more is said about $\tilde{Y}_t$ other than its sign, the theory has little empirical content. While we shall shortly provide a simple characterization of $\tilde{Y}_t$, first we develop the natural uncertainty analogue to the Williams-Gordon (1938, pp. 87–89) perpetual dividend growth model. Let one plus the rate of growth of $\tilde{X}_t$ be denoted by $\tilde{g}_t$ and one plus the rate of growth of $\tilde{Y}_t$ be denoted by $\tilde{y}_t$ so that $\tilde{X}_t = X_0(\tilde{g}_1\tilde{g}_2 \ldots \tilde{g}_t)$ and $\tilde{Y}_t = Y_0(\tilde{y}_1\tilde{y}_2 \ldots \tilde{y}_t)$. Letting $R_{Ft} = r_{F1}r_{F2} \ldots r_{Ft}$, equation (1) becomes

$$P_0 = X_0 \left\{ \sum_{t=1}^{\infty} \frac{E[g_1g_2 \ldots g_t y_1 y_2 \ldots y_t]/E[y_1 y_2 \ldots y_t]}{r_{F1}r_{F2} \ldots r_{Ft}} \right\}.$$

Analogous to the stationary riskless rate and stationary dividend

---

[2] If it were also assumed that a security existed insuring a non-negative rate of return to which all investors had access (i.e., cash), then $0 < Z[s(t)] < 1$ and indeed $\Sigma_{s(t)} Z[s(t)] \leq 1$ for all dates. Moreover, $R_1 \leq R_2 \leq R_3. \ldots$

[3] $E(\cdot)$ denotes expectation, $\text{Cov}(\cdot)$ covariance, $\text{Var}(\cdot)$ variance, and $\text{Std}(\cdot)$ standard deviation.

[4] These probabilities need not be held homogeneously by all investors, or indeed by any investor. They may be viewed as a purely mathematical construct. However, every state must be interpreted as possible so that $\pi[s(t)] > 0$.

[5] Beja (1971) has developed similar results to equation (1).

growth rate assumptions adopted by Williams and Gordon under certainty, we assume that $r_{Ft} \equiv r_F$ is stationary, that $\tilde{g}_t \equiv \tilde{g}$ follows a stationary random walk with a stationary correlation with $\tilde{y}_t$, and that $\tilde{y}_t \equiv \tilde{y}$ follows a stationary random walk.[6]

Theorem 2: Given assumptions 1 and 2, if the riskless rate is stationary and the rate of growth of a security's dividend stream follows a stationary random walk with stationary correlation with the rate of growth of $\tilde{Y}_t$, which also follows a stationary random walk, then

$$P_0 = X_0 \left[\frac{\mu_g + \sigma_{gy}/\mu_y}{r_F - (\mu_g + \sigma_{gy}/\mu_y)} \right].$$

Proof: From the premise, $\tilde{g}_t$ is serially uncorrelated, $\tilde{y}_t$ is serially uncorrelated, and lagged values of $\tilde{g}_t$ and $\tilde{y}_t$ are uncorrelated. Therefore, $E[g_1 g_2 \ldots g_t y_1 y_2 \ldots y_t] = E(g_1 y_1)E(g_2 y_2) \ldots E(g_t y_t)$; moreover $E[y_1 y_2 \ldots y_t] = E(y_1)E(y_2) \ldots E(y_t)$. Applying the stationary assumptions,

$$P_0 = X_0 \sum_{t=1}^{\infty} \left(\frac{\mu_{gy}/\mu_y}{r_F} \right)^t.$$

The result then follows from the formula for the sum of an infinite geometric series and the definition of covariance. Q.E.D.

Observe that, excepting the stationarity of the stochastic process of the dividend stream, the formula is quite general relying primarily on the single-price law of markets. If a security has no "nondiversifiable risk" so that $\sigma_{gy} = 0$, then the formula simplifies to $P_0 = X_0 \mu_g/(r_F - \mu_g)$. However, again since $\tilde{y}$ is not well-specified, the formula appears empty of empirical content. But this is not quite the case. Let the expression in brackets be denoted ϕ so that $P_0 = X_0 \phi$. At date $t = 1$, $\tilde{P}_1 = \tilde{X}_1 \phi$. Moreover, since $\tilde{X}_1 = X_0 \tilde{g}_1$, then the rate of return of the security $(\tilde{X}_1 + \tilde{P}_1)/P_0 = \tilde{g}[(1 + \phi)/\phi]$ follows a stationary random walk. In short, we have derived important properties of the stochastic process of the rate of return of a security from the stochastic process of its dividend stream.[7]

Corollary: Under the conditions of Theorem 2, the rate of return of a security follows a stationary random walk.[8]

Define $\tilde{X}_1/(\tilde{X}_1 + \tilde{P}_1 - P_0)$ as the date $t = 1$ "payout ratio" from market-determined earnings. Since this equals $[1 + \phi - (\phi/g)]^{-1}$, the payout ratio also follows a stationary random walk, varying *inversely* with the growth rate of dividends. That is, although the absolute level of dividends increases, it must be accompanied by a lower payout to

---

[6] By definition, $\mu_g \equiv E(g)$, $\mu_y \equiv E(y)$, $\sigma_{gy} \equiv \text{Cov}(g, y)$, $\mu_{gy} \equiv E(gy)$.

[7] From much of the literature on "efficient markets," it may have been expected that security rates of return should follow a random walk irrespective of the stochastic process of dividends. For example, see Granger and Morgenstern (1970, p. 26). Clearly, this is not true for default-free pure-discount bonds. Moreover, I have argued elsewhere (1974b) that in an important case, the rate of return of the market portfolio will be serially independent if and only if the rate of growth of aggregate consumption (i.e., the social dividend) is serially independent. This result is generalized in Section 3.

[8] Samuelson (1973) has derived a more general proposition, which unlike the simple case here, does not require stationary discount rates over time. However, like the present case, it does require that discount rates be nonstochastic functions of time; that is, future interest rates are assumed to be known in advance. I have shown elsewhere (1974a) that this may lead to unrealistic implications.

assure continuation of the stationary dividend process. This harmonizes with Lintner's (1956) empirical observation that in order to maintain a target payout ratio (i.e., $[1 + \phi - (\phi/\mu_g)]^{-1}$), firms will under (over) shoot it in times of unusually high (low) earnings.

Corollary: Under the conditions of Theorem 2, the payout ratio varies inversely with the growth rate of dividends.

Returning now to general dividend processes, we shall identify the positive random variable $\tilde{Y}_t$ by enriching the economic environment. Specifically, we shall assume

(3) *Perfect, competitive and Pareto-efficient financial markets:* There are no scale economies in the purchase of any security, every participant acts as if he cannot influence the price of any security, all investors can purchase the same security at the same date for the same price, and there exist a sufficient diversity of securities such that no investor desires the costless creation of a new security.[9]

(4) *Rational time-additive tastes:* Every investor acts as if he maximizes his expected utility over his lifetime dollar value of consumption which is concave and additive in consumption at each date.

(5) *Weak aggregation:*[10] There exists an average investor such that

    (i) *homogeneity:* every homogeneous economic characteristic also characterizes the average investor

    (ii) *commensurability:* if an economic characteristic is denominated in units of wealth, then this characteristic for the average investor is an unweighted arithmetic average over the corresponding characteristic of every investor

    (iii) *consensus:* prices are determined as if every investor were average.

Under these assumptions, we can meaningfully define an average investor who

$$\max_{\{C[s(t)]\}} \ \Sigma_t \Sigma_{s(t)} \pi[s(t)] U_t\{C[s(t)]\}$$

subject to $W_0 = \Sigma_t \Sigma_{s(t)} Z[s(t)] C[s(t)]$,

where U_t denotes his date t utility over consumption $C[s(t)]$ and $W_0 \equiv \Sigma_t \Sigma_{s(t)} Z[s(t)] \bar{C}[s(t)]$ is his initial wealth defined in terms of endowed claims to consumption $\bar{C}[s(t)]$. With these assumptions, we can identify $\tilde{Y}_t$.

Theorem 3: Given assumptions 1–5, $\tilde{Y}_t = U'_t(\tilde{C}_t)$ for all dates and states.

Since this is a classic and easily obtainable result from the first-order

---

    [9] This last condition would be satisfied if the financial market were complete, or if, as in the familiar mean-variance model, a riskless security exists and all investors divide their wealth after consumption between it and the market portfolio. The condition is required for Pareto-efficient exchange arrangements.

    [10] If all investors were identical this assumption is trivially satisfied. I have developed elsewhere (1974a, 1974b) more general sets of conditions. Perhaps the most appealing is the case where investors are heterogeneous with respect to the scale and composition of endowed resources, lifetime, time-preference, beliefs, and whether proportional risk aversion is increasing, constant, or decreasing. Additive generalized logarithmic utility is the only homogeneity requirement.

conditions to the programming problem, no proof will be given. The economic content of this theorem is that (1) the randomness of $\tilde{Y}_t$ is solely determined by per capita consumption $\tilde{C}_t$ and (2) $\tilde{Y}_t$ is a decreasing function of $\tilde{C}_t$ (since U_t is concave). From equation (1), this implies that securities tend to be more valuable if they tend to have high dividends in dates and states with relatively low per capita consumption.

Time-additive tastes prevent $\tilde{Y}_t$ from depending as well on past per capita consumption, and in general, weak aggregation is required to prevent $\tilde{Y}_t$ from depending on the distribution of consumption across investors. Since we are aiming at simple formulas, these two assumptions are useful. However, in one well-known case we can obtain even greater simplicity without requiring weak aggregation, but at the price of an alternative assumption: the joint distribution of $\tilde{X}_t$ and $\tilde{C}_t$ is bivariate normal for each date t and all investors have homogeneous beliefs. The Appendix shows that, subject to a mild regulatory condition, if x and y are bivariate normal and $g(y)$ is any at least once differentiable function of y, then $\text{Cov}(x, g(y)) = E[g'(y)]\text{Cov}(x, y)$. Applying this to equation (1), individual i would choose his lifetime consumption $C_0{}^i, \tilde{C}_1{}^i, \ldots, \tilde{C}_t{}^i, \ldots$ such that for every security

$$P_0 = \sum_{t=1}^{\infty} \frac{E(X_t) - \theta_t{}^i \text{Cov}(X_t, C_t{}^i)}{R_{Ft}},$$

where $\theta_t{}^i \equiv -E[U_t{}^{i\prime\prime}(C_t{}^i)]/E[U_t{}^{i\prime}(C_t{}^i)]$. Since financial markets are Pareto-efficient, prices are set as if there were complete markets. For every date t, we can therefore "manufacture" a risky security which pays off only at that date, so that $P_0 R_{Ft} = E(X_t) - \theta_t{}^i \text{Cov}(X_t, C_t{}^i)$. Summing this over all investors i and dividing by the number of investors I in the economy, produces a similar result to that found in single-period models, $P_0 R_{Ft} = E(X_t) - \theta_t \text{Cov}(X_t, C_t)$, where $\tilde{C}_t \equiv \Sigma_i \tilde{C}_t{}^i/I$ and $\theta_t \equiv [\Sigma_i (\theta_t{}^i)^{-1}/I]^{-1}$. Applying this for each date,

$$P_0 = \sum_{t=1}^{\infty} \frac{E(X_t) - \theta_t \text{Cov}(X_t, C_t)}{R_{Ft}}.$$

Again, since $\theta_t > 0$, securities are penalized which, *ceteris paribus*, have high dividends in dates and states with relatively high per capita consumption.

■ While our description of the economic environment has identified $\tilde{Y}_t$, the resulting valuation formula is not easily empirically useful. With weak aggregation, we need to determine the average utility function and even with the apparently simplified result from homogeneous joint normality, we require measurement of the stochastic process of per capita consumption. Moreover, to obtain the simple relationships of the familiar single-period model, we need to characterize $U'_t(\tilde{C}_t)$ as a function of the market rates of return $\tilde{r}_{Mt} \equiv \tilde{W}_t/(\tilde{W}_{t-1} - \tilde{C}_{t-1})$, where $\tilde{W}_t$ is per capita wealth at date t. $\tilde{C}_t$ has the natural interpretation of a social dividend on the market portfolio. In other words, we need to inquire under what circumstances does there exist a nonrandom function g_t such that $g_t(\tilde{r}_{M1}, \tilde{r}_{M2}, \ldots, \tilde{r}_{Mt}) = U'_t(\tilde{C}_t)$?

In particular, $g_t(\cdot)$ cannot be separately dependent on per capita wealth $\tilde{W}_\tau$ for any date $0 < \tau \leq t$. For then, $g_t(\cdot)$ would be a random function. It is known from portfolio theory that optimal portfolio composition is independent of wealth if and only if utility is constant proportional risk averse (CPRA); that is, if and only if

$$U_t(\tilde{C}_t) = \rho_1\rho_2 \ldots \rho_t \frac{1}{1-b} \tilde{C}_t^{1-b},$$

where $b > 0$ and $\rho_t > 0$.[11] ρ_t is a measure of time-preference and since $b = -\tilde{C}_t U''_t(\tilde{C}_t)/U'_t(\tilde{C}_t)$, b is the measure of CPRA. Since only in this case can $U'_t(\tilde{C}_t)$ be expressed in terms of $\tilde{r}_{M1}, \tilde{r}_{M2}, \ldots, \tilde{r}_{Mt}$ and otherwise independent of $\tilde{W}_\tau$ for $0 < \tau \leq t$, CPRA acquires empirical significance.

Theorem 4: Given assumptions 1–5, and if average utility is CPRA and if either $b = 1$ or the rate of growth of per capita consumption follows a (possibly nonstationary) random walk, then

$$\tilde{Y}_t = \tilde{R}_{Mt}^{-b}$$

for all dates and states, where $\tilde{R}_{Mt} \equiv \tilde{r}_{M1}\tilde{r}_{M2} \ldots \tilde{r}_{Mt}$.

Proof: Hakansson (1971) and Rubinstein (1974b) have shown that for an investor with CPRA his average propensity to consume wealth at any date is independent of his wealth. Indeed, this independence holds only under CPRA. In particular, in this case, there exists a random variable $\tilde{k}_t$ independent of wealth at any date such that $\tilde{C}_t = \tilde{k}_t\tilde{W}_t$. Moreover, if $b = 1$ (logarithmic utility) then while k_t depends on the date (through date dependent time-preference $\rho_1\rho_2 \ldots \rho_t$ and the time remaining until his death), it is nonstochastic. When $b \neq 1$, then k_t will also be nonstochastic if the rate of growth of per capita consumption follows a (possibly nonstationary) random walk.[12] The assumptions of the theorem therefore imply k_t is a nonstochastic function of time. Since $\tilde{W}_t = (\tilde{W}_{t-1} - \tilde{C}_{t-1})\tilde{r}_{Mt}$, then $\tilde{C}_t = (\tilde{W}_{t-1} - \tilde{C}_{t-1})k_t\tilde{r}_{Mt}$. Similarly, $\tilde{C}_t = (\tilde{W}_{t-2} - \tilde{C}_{t-2})(1 - k_{t-1})k_t\tilde{r}_{Mt-1}\tilde{r}_{Mt}$. Continuing to work backwards

$$\tilde{C}_t = [W_0(1 - k_0)(1 - k_1) \ldots (1 - k_{t-1})k_t]\tilde{R}_{Mt}.$$

Substituting this into equation (1), noting [·] is nonstochastic and $U'_t(\tilde{C}_t) = \rho_1\rho_2 \ldots \rho_t\tilde{C}_t^{-b}$, yields the conclusion of the theorem. Q.E.D.

In brief, given the conditions of the theorem, for any security (or portfolio)

$$P_0 = \sum_{t=1}^{\infty} \frac{E(X_t) - \lambda_t\kappa(X_t, - R_{Mt}^{-b})\text{Std } X_t}{R_{Ft}}, \tag{2}$$

---

[11] In the limiting case of $b = 1$, $U_t(\tilde{C}_t) = \rho_1\rho_2 \ldots \rho_t\ln \tilde{C}_t$.

[12] Specifically, it follows from Rubinstein (1974b), that

$$\tilde{k}_t^{-1} = 1 + \rho_{t+1}{}^B\tilde{E}_t(r_{Ct+1}{}^{1-b}) + \rho_{t+1}{}^B\rho_{t+2}{}^B\tilde{E}_t(r_{Ct+1}{}^{1-b}r_{Ct+2}{}^{1-b}) + \ldots,$$

where $B \equiv b^{-1}$, $\tilde{r}_{Ct} \equiv \tilde{C}_t/\tilde{C}_{t-1}$, and expectations are assessed with respect to information available at date t. When the rate of growth of per capita consumption follows a random walk, then k_t is nonstochastic, since

$$k_t^{-1} = 1 + \rho_{t+1}{}^B E_t(r_{Ct+1}{}^{1-b}) + \rho_{t+1}{}^B\rho_{t+2}{}^B E_t(r_{Ct+1}{}^{1-b})E_t(r_{Ct+2}{}^{1-b}) + \ldots.$$

Moreover, it is easy to see when $b = 1$ that k_t is nonrandom even if the rate of growth of per capita consumption does not follow a random walk.

where $\lambda_t \equiv \text{Std}(R_{Mt}^{-b})/E(R_{Mt}^{-b})$ and $\kappa(\cdot)$ is a correlation coefficient.

Although no stochastic restrictions have been placed on the rates of return of securities, the premise that the rate of growth of per capita consumption follows a random walk is sufficiently strong to imply important stochastic properties for "basic" portfolios.

Corollary: Under the conditions of Theorem 4, if $b \neq 1$

(1) *market portfolio:* the rate of return of the market portfolio follows a (possibly nonstationary) random walk;

(2) *default-free bonds:* the term structure of interest rates is un-biased in the sense that at each date the next period expected rates of return of default-free pure discount bonds of all maturities are the same.

Moreover, if $b = 1$, then conclusion (1) holds if and only if the rate of growth of per capita consumption follows a (possibly nonstationary) random walk; and conclusion (2) holds if and only if the inverse one plus rate of growth of per capita consumption is serially uncorrelated.

Proof: To prove assertion (1), recall that $\tilde{C}_t = k_t \tilde{W}_t$, $\tilde{r}_{Mt} \equiv \tilde{W}_t/(\tilde{W}_{t-1} - \tilde{C}_{t-1})$ and one plus the rate of growth of per capita consumption $\tilde{r}_{Ct} \equiv \tilde{C}_t/\tilde{C}_{t-1}$ for all t. Therefore $\tilde{r}_{Mt} = \tilde{r}_{Ct}[k_{t-1}/k_t(1 - k_{t-1})]$ so that $\kappa(r_{Mt}, r_{Ct}) = 1$. When $b = 1$, we do not require the premise that $\tilde{r}_{Ct}$ follow a random walk to keep k_t and k_{t-1} nonstochastic. To prove assertion (2), let $_{t-1}R_{Ft+1}^{-1}$ denote the price at date $t - 1$ of one dollar for sure at *date* $t + 1$. From the first-order conditions of the programming problem of Section 2, it follows that

$$r_{Ft}^{-1} = \rho_t E_{t-1}(r_{Ct}^{-b}), \quad r_{Ft+1}^{-1} = \rho_{t+1} \tilde{E}_t(r_{Ct+1}^{-b})$$

and

$$_{t-1}R_{Ft+1}^{-1} = \rho_t \rho_{t+1} E_{t-1}(r_{Ct}^{-b} r_{Ct+1}^{-b})$$

if utility is CPRA, where $\tilde{\ }$ indicates random variables from the perspective of information available at date $t - 1$. Additionally, if $_{t-1}\tilde{r}_{Ft}$ denotes the one plus rate of return on the two-period bond from date $t - 1$ to date t, then in conformity with the single-price law of markets

$$_{t-1}R_{Ft+1} = {}_{t-1}\tilde{r}_{Ft}\tilde{r}_{Ft+1}.$$

From this it follows that

$$E_{t-1}(_{t-1}r_{Ft}) = [E_{t-1}(r_{Ct+1}^{-b})][\rho_t E_{t-1}(r_{Ct}^{-b} r_{Ct+1}^{-b})]^{-1}.$$

When $b \neq 1$ and by premise $\tilde{r}_{Ct}$ and $\tilde{r}_{Ct+1}$ follow a random walk, then this simplifies to $E_{t-1}(_{t-1}r_{Ft}) = [\rho_t E_{t-1}(r_{Ct}^{-b})]^{-1}$ so that $r_{Ft} = E_{t-1}(_{t-1}r_{Ft})$. When $b = 1$, this same conclusion is reached if and only if $\tilde{r}_{Ct}^{-1}$ and $\tilde{r}_{Ct+1}^{-1}$ are serially uncorrelated. This proof is easily extended to default-free bonds of all maturities. Q.E.D.

Whether or not (1) the market portfolio follows a random walk or (2) the term structure is unbiased depends critically on the stochastic process of per capita consumption over time. The underlying real *intertemporal* stochastic process of per capita consumption is mir-rored in the equilibrium financial process governing the prices of "basic" portfolios. Moreover, when $\tilde{r}_{Ct}$ follows a random walk or $b = 1$, then the real *contemporaneous* stochastic process of per capita consumption is also mirrored in the market portfolio. From the above proof, $\tilde{r}_{Mt} = \tilde{r}_{Ct}[k_{t-1}/k_t(1 - k_{t-1})]$ so that $\tilde{r}_{Ct}$ is normal (lognormal) if and only if $\tilde{r}_{Mt}$ is normal (lognormal).

When the rate of growth of per capita consumption follows a stationary random walk and average time-preference is stationary, then equation (2) can be further simplified.

Corollary: Under the conditions of Theorem 4, if the rate of growth of per capita consumption follows a stationary random walk and average time-preference is stationary over an infinite life-time, then

$$P_0 = \sum_{t=1}^{\infty} \frac{E(X_t) - \lambda_t \kappa(X_t, - r_M^{-bt})\text{Std } X_t}{r_F^t},$$

where

$$\lambda_t = \sqrt{(1 + \lambda^2)^t - 1} \text{ and } \lambda \equiv \text{Std}(r_M^{-b})/E(r_M^{-b}).$$

Proof: From the proof of the previous corollary, $\tilde{r}_{Mt} = \tilde{r}_{Ct}[k_{t-1}/k_t(1 - k_{t-1})]$. From the expression for k_t in note 12, under the premise of the above corollary since $\tilde{r}_{Ct} \equiv \tilde{r}_C$ and $\rho_t \equiv \rho$, then $k_t \equiv k$ is stationary. Therefore, $\tilde{r}_{Mt} \equiv \tilde{r}_M$ is likewise stationary. In general, if any random variable $\tilde{r}_t$ follows a stationary random walk (or is merely stationary and serially uncorrelated), then

$$\text{Var}(x_1 x_2 \ldots x_t) = (\sigma_x^2 + \mu_x^2)^t - (\mu_x^2)^t.$$

And, of course, $E(x_1 x_2 \ldots x_t) = \mu_x^t$. From these properties, it follows that $\lambda_t = \sqrt{(1 + \lambda^2)^t - 1}$. Similarly, from the proof of the previous corollary, since $\tilde{r}_{Ft}^{-1} = \rho_t \bar{E}_{t-1}(r_{Ct}^{-b})$, then $\tilde{r}_{Ft} = r_{Ft} \equiv r_F$ is a stationary constant. Q.E.D.

Under these stationarity conditions, the "market price of risk" λ_t increases with the time to the receipt of the cash flow so that risk averse investors tend to penalize more distant risks more than near risks. Compounding this effect is the tendency of Std X_t to increase with t. For example, if the growth rate $\tilde{g}_t$ of $\tilde{X}_t$ follows a stationary random walk, then Std $X_t = X_0[(\sigma_g^2 + \mu_g^2)^t - (\mu_g^2)^t]^{\frac{1}{2}}$, which clearly increases with t. However, since r_F^t increases with t (assuming $r_F > 1$), the net effect on present value of the influence of time to receipt of income on risk is indefinite.

Although Theorem 4 identifies $\tilde{Y}_t$ as $\tilde{R}_{Mt}^{-b}$, unless b, the level of CPRA, were known in advance, empirical application of the valuation formula (2) would prove difficult. Even the implied single-period formula

$$P_{t-1} = \frac{\overline{E(X_t)} - \hat{\lambda}_t \text{Cov}(\overline{X_t, - r_{Mt}^{-b})} \text{Std } \overline{X_t}}{r_{Ft}} \tag{3}$$

where $\bar{\tilde{X}}_t \equiv \tilde{X}_t + \tilde{P}_t$ and $\hat{\lambda}_t \equiv \text{Std}(r_{Mt}^{-b})/E(r_{Mt}^{-b})$ is difficult to apply. Standard linear regression techniques cannot be used to estimate b, since the formula is nonlinear in b. Nonetheless, there are three interesting methods to overcome this difficulty. As Blume and Friend (1975) and Cohen *et al.* (1975) have recently attempted, it may be possible to measure b from empirical surveys of consumer wealth allocation. Second, and possibly more promising, is to infer b by trial and error from the behavior of the rate of return of the market portfolio. Since equation (3) holds for the market portfolio, dividing by P_{t-1} and rearranging, $r_{Ft} = E(r_{Mt}^{1-b})/E(r_{Mt}^{-b})$. Partially differentiating the right-hand side by b, the Schwartz inequality can be used to show that $\partial[E(r_{Mt}{}^{1-b})/E(r_{Mt}{}^{-b})]/\partial b > 0$. Therefore, a trial-and-error procedure will quickly converge to a good estimate of b which approximately satisfies the above equality. Third, is to infer b from the rate of return of the market portfolio when it is assumed to conform to a given stochastic process.

Corollary: Under the conditions of Theorem 4, if the single-period one plus rate of return of the market portfolio is lognormal, then

$$b = \frac{E(\ln r_{Mt}) - \ln r_{Ft}}{\text{Var}(\ln r_{Mt})} + \tfrac{1}{2}.$$

Proof: Since equation (3) holds for the market portfolio, dividing by P_{t-1} and rearranging, $r_{Ft} = E(r_{Mt}{}^{1-b})/E(r_{Mt}{}^{-b})$. From the Appendix, if $\tilde{r}_{Mt}$ is lognormal, then $\tilde{r}_{Mt}{}^{1-b}$ and $\tilde{r}_{Mt}{}^{-b}$ are lognormal. Therefore, $E(r_{Mt}{}^{1-b}) = \exp[(1 - b)E(\ln r_{Mt}) + \tfrac{1}{2}(1 - b)^2\text{Var}(\ln r_{Mt})]$ and $E(r_{Mt}{}^{-b}) = \exp[-bE(\ln r_{Mt}) + \tfrac{1}{2}b^2\text{Var}(\ln r_{Mt})]$. The result follows by dividing these two expressions, setting the quotient equal to r_{Ft} and taking logarithms. Q.E.D.

Equation (2) with b estimated from the corollary, requires only that $\tilde{r}_{Mt}$ be lognormal and (unless $b = 1$) follow a (possibly nonstationary) random walk; no distributional restrictions have been placed on the rates of return of other securities. This is fortunate since the rates of return of many securities such as options and default-free bonds near maturity, as well as the rates of return of capital budgeting projects, are neither lognormal nor follow a random walk. However, for securities with one plus rates of return $\tilde{r}_t$ jointly lognormal with $\tilde{r}_{Mt}$, a similar argument to the corollary can be used to show

$$\ln[E(r_t)] = \ln r_{Ft} + b\,\text{Cov}(\ln r_t, \ln r_{Mt}).$$

Although this formula has been derived in discrete time, it is consistent with Merton's (1973b) continuous-time model as interpreted over discrete intervals by Jensen (1972, p. 386). CPRA has substituted for continuous trading opportunities to achieve the same end.[13]

■ The similarity between the valuation results derived in discrete and continuous time suggests that other security pricing relationships may also be immune from this distinction. In particular, it is known that the Black-Scholes (1973) option pricing equation for dividend-protected options,

$$Q = SN(z^* + \sigma\sqrt{t}) - Kr_F{}^{-t}N(z^*), \tag{4}$$

where

$$z^* \equiv \frac{\ln(S/K) + (\ln r_F - \tfrac{1}{2}\sigma^2)t}{\sigma\sqrt{t}},$$

holds either with continuous trading opportunities or risk neutrality.[14]

---

[13] See Kraus and Litzenberger (1975) for similar remarks.

[14] Merton (1973a) mentions that Samuelson and Merton (1969) have uncovered yet a third set of assumptions for equation (4): (a) the average investor has CRPA, (b) only three securities exist—a default-free bond, the option, and its associated stock, and (c) the net supply of both the options and the bonds is zero.

Clearing up the notation:

Q = current price of option (i.e., call)
S = current price of associated stock
K = striking price
t = time to expiration
r_F = one plus the interest rate
σ^2 = the variance of the logarithm of one plus the rate of return of the associated stock
$N(\cdot)$ = the standard normal cumulative density function.

Although proofs are available elsewhere, to ease understanding of the subsequent discrete-time analysis under risk aversion, it will be useful to sketch a proof here. Following Sprenkle (1961), we first derive a simplified expression for the expected future value of the option at expiration and then discount this value back to the present. Let $\tilde{Q}_t$ and $\tilde{S}_t$ be the respective values of the option and its associated stock at expiration. Since[15] $\tilde{Q}_t = 0$ if $\tilde{S}_t < K$ and $\tilde{Q}_t = \tilde{S}_t - K$ if $\tilde{S}_t \geq K$, then $E(Q_t) = E[S_t - K|\tilde{S}_t \geq K]$. Defining $\tilde{R} \equiv \tilde{S}_t/S$, $E(Q_t) = SE[R - (K/S)|\tilde{R} \geq (K/S)]$. Defining $\tilde{r} \equiv \ln \tilde{R}$, $E(Q_t) = SE[e^r - (K/S)|\tilde{r} \geq \ln (K/S)]$. Since $\tilde{S}_t$ is lognormal, $\tilde{R}$ is lognormal and $\tilde{r}$ is normal, therefore

$$E(Q_t) = S \int_{\ln(K/S)}^{\infty} \left(e^r - \frac{K}{S}\right) f(r) dr,$$

where $f(\cdot)$ is the normal density function. Breaking this apart into the difference between two integrals, using equations (1) and (2) of the Appendix to evaluate them, and noting the transformation of the mean of a lognormal variable, we obtain

$$E(Q_t) = S\mu_R N(z^* + \sigma_r) - KN(z^*),$$

where

$$z^* \equiv \frac{\ln(S/K) + \mu_r}{\sigma_r}.$$

Since $\mu_R = \exp[\mu_r + \frac{1}{2}\sigma_r^2]$, then $\mu_r = \ln \mu_R - \frac{1}{2}\sigma_r^2$. Finally discounting $E(Q_t)$ back to the present by the expected compound rate of return μ_Q of the option through expiration, we obtain

$$Q = [S\mu_R N(z^* + \sigma_r) - KN(z^*)]/\mu_Q$$

where

$$z^* \equiv \frac{\ln(S/K) + \ln \mu_R - \frac{1}{2}\sigma_r^2}{\sigma_r}.$$

The usefulness of this result is hampered primarily by measurement of μ_Q and secondarily by measurement of μ_R. However, assuming risk neutrality, the expected rates of return of the stock and option are equal and moreover equal to the riskless rate so that $R_F = \mu_Q = \mu_R$. If, additionally, the riskless rate is constant over time so that $r_F = (\mu_R)^{1/t} = (\mu_Q)^{1/t}$, and the rate of return of the associated stock follows a stationary random walk so that $\sigma_r^2 = t\sigma^2$, then the Black-Scholes equation follows exactly.

---

[15] Merton (1973a) has shown that rational nonsatiated investors will not exercise a call option prior to expiration if it is properly dividend protected and if the striking price is fixed. He also proves this will *not* generally be true for puts.

Recently, Black and Scholes have stimulated academic interest in options by showing that the valuation formula derived under risk neutrality holds under seemingly much more general conditions. They argue that if the associated stock price follows a continuous stochastic process in time[16] and if investors can costlessly continuously revise their portfolios, then investors can create a perfectly hedged (i.e., riskless) portfolio by selling a call against a long position in the associated stock. Cox and Ross (1975) have argued that since, in equilibrium, this portfolio must earn the riskless rate, then given the current price of the stock, the interest rate, and agreement about the relevant statistics characterizing the rate of return of the stock, the current price of the call will be independent of the characteristics of other securities and the preferences of investors. Therefore, the same current price of the option will be derived irrespective of investor preferences. To simplify matters, we are then free to assume risk neutrality without loss of generality. But, by the previous analysis, the Black-Scholes equation again holds.

On the surface, the existence of continuous trading opportunities to insure the riskless hedge seems critical to the Black-Scholes analysis. How else (except in the trivial risk neutrality case) could the pricing formula be independent of investor preference datum and opportunities for diversification? Although Merton (1975, p. 2) claims that the continuous trading formula appears in the limit as the trading interval shrinks to zero, it remains unclear what kind of an approximation is involved even for small finite trading intervals.

The following theorem proves that the Black-Scholes pricing formula is robust within lognormality conditions, even with only discrete trading opportunities and risk aversion.

Theorem 5: Given assumptions 1 and 2, if S_t and Y_t are jointly lognormal, investors agree on σ, and the associated stock pays no dividends through expiration of the option, then

$$Q = SN(z^* + \sigma) - KR_F^{-1}N(z^*), \tag{5}$$

where

$$z^* \equiv \frac{\ln(S/K) + \ln R_F}{\sigma} - \tfrac{1}{2}\sigma$$

and R_F is the riskless discount rate through the expiration of the option and σ is the standard deviation of the logarithm of the compound one plus rate of return of the associated stock through the expiration of the option (i.e., Std(ln R)).

Proof: Recalling the proof to Theorem 1, we can define a random variable $\tilde{Z}'_t$ such that $\tilde{Z}'_t \equiv \tilde{Y}_t R_{Ft}^{-1}/E(Y_t)$. Since the stock is assumed to pay no dividends, $S = E(S_t Z'_t)$. Moreover $Q = E[(S_t - K)Z'_t|\tilde{S}_t \geq K]$ and $R_F^{-1} = E(Z'_t)$. By defining $\tilde{R} \equiv \tilde{S}_t/S$, these relationships become

$$E(RZ'_t) = 1, \quad R_{Ft}^{-1} = E(Z'_t)$$

and

$$Q = SE[(R - (K/S))Z'_t|\tilde{R} \geq (K/S)].$$

---

[16] See Cox and Ross (1975) and Merton (1975) for analyses of option pricing when its associated stock price follows a jump process.

Defining $\tilde{r} \equiv \ln \tilde{R}$ and $\tilde{y} \equiv \ln \tilde{Z}'_t$, $Q = SE[(e^r - (K/S))e^y | \tilde{r} \geq \ln(K/S)]$. Since $\tilde{S}_t$ and $\tilde{Z}'_t$ are jointly lognormal, then $\tilde{r}$ and $\tilde{y}$ are jointly normal, therefore

$$Q = S \int_{-\infty}^{\infty} \int_{\ln(K/S)}^{\infty} \left(e^r - \frac{K}{S} \right) e^y f(r, y) dr \, dy,$$

where $f(\cdot)$ is the bivariate normal density function. Breaking this apart into the difference between two integrals, using equations (3) and (4) of the Appendix to evaluate them, and noting the transformations of the mean of a lognormal variable and the mean of the product of two lognormal variables, we obtain

$$Q = SE(RZ'_t)N(z^* + \sigma_r) - KE(Z'_t)N(z^*),$$

where

$$z^* \equiv \frac{\ln(S/K) + \mu_r + \kappa \sigma_r \sigma_y}{\sigma_r}.$$

Since $E(RZ'_t) = 1$ and $E(Z'_t) = R_F$ [1], this simplifies to

$$Q = SN(z^* + \sigma_r) - KR_F^{-1}N(z^*).$$

Since $E(RZ'_t) = \exp[\mu_r + \frac{1}{2} \sigma_r^2 + \mu_y + \frac{1}{2} \sigma_y^2 + \kappa \sigma_r \sigma_y] = 1$ and $E(Z'_t) = \exp[\mu_y + \frac{1}{2} \sigma_y^2] = R_F^{-1}$, then $\mu_r + \frac{1}{2} \sigma_r^2 - \ln R_F + \kappa \sigma_r \sigma_y = 0$. Substituting this into the expression for z^* proves the theorem. Q.E.D.

Appending the Black-Scholes stationarity conditions converts equation (5) into equation (4). However, the derivation presented here shows that under the strengthened lognormality assumption, these stationarity conditions are in no way necessary to retain the important features of equation (4).[17] Under what conditions will $\tilde{Y}_t$ be jointly lognormal with $\tilde{S}_t$? Theorem 4 supplies an interesting sufficient condition. $\tilde{Y}_t = \tilde{R}_{Mt}^{-b}$ will be jointly lognormal with $\tilde{S}_t$ if $\tilde{R}_{Mt}$ and $\tilde{S}_t$ are jointly lognormal.[18]

To extend equation (5) to dividend paying stock, assume through the life of the option, the dividend yield of the associated stock is a known nonstochastic function of time. Let $\delta_t \equiv \tilde{X}_t / \tilde{S}_t$ denote the dividend yield of the stock at any date t through the life of the option. Then the one plus the compound rate of return of the stock to the expiration date, $\tilde{R} = (\tilde{S}_t/S)(1 + \delta_1)(1 + \delta_2) \ldots (1 + \delta_t)$. Defining $\Delta \equiv (1 + \delta_1)(1 + \delta_2) \ldots (1 + \delta_t)$, then $\tilde{R} = \tilde{S}_t/(S\Delta^{-1})$. In the proof of Theorem 5, replacing S with $S\Delta^{-1}$,

---

[17] Merton (1973a) has relaxed the stationarity conditions on the interest rate and allows the standard deviation of the logarithm of one plus the rate of return of the associated stock (σ) to be a known nonstochastic function of time; here σ can be stochastic as well, extending the model to more realistic stochastic processes. See Rosenberg (1972).

[18] The Samuelson-Merton (1969) assumptions (see note 14) are clearly a special case. Their assumptions (b) and (c) imply that $Y_t = \tilde{R}^{-b}$, since the associated stock is the market portfolio. The risk neutrality justification is a degenerate special case where $\tilde{Y}_t$ is nonstochastic. It should also be noted that the premise of Theorem 5 is stronger than necessary. We actually require a random variable $\tilde{Y}_t$ shared *only* by the option, its associated stock, and the default-free bond, which is jointly lognormal with $\tilde{S}_t$. In effect, as in the Black-Scholes analysis, equation (5) will apply even if S and R_{Ft} are not in equilibrium with the other securities in the market. Finally, agreement on $\text{Var}(\ln S_t)$ is not required if heterogeneous investor beliefs can be meaningfully aggregated; see Rubinstein (1976).

Corollary: Under the conditions of Theorem 5, except that the associated stock, through the expiration of the option, has a dividend yield which is a known nonstochastic function of time, and the option cannot be exercised prior to its expiration date, then

$$Q = S\Delta^{-1}N(z^* + \sigma) - KR_F^{-1}N(z^*)$$

where

$$z^* \equiv \frac{\ln(S\Delta^{-1}/K) + \ln R_F}{\sigma} - \frac{1}{2}\sigma$$

and R_F is the riskless discount rate through the expiration of the option and σ is the standard deviation of the logarithm of the compound one plus rate of return of the associated stock through the expiration of the option (i.e., Std(ln R)).

When will the dividend yield be nonstochastic? Theorem 2 provides a sufficient condition in its premise. An "American" option, one that can be exercised prior to its expiration date, will be worth more than Q as given by the above formula.[19]

■ This paper has developed a simple and practical formula for the valuation of uncertain income streams, consistent with rational risk averse investor behavior and equilibrium in financial markets. Since the formula places virtually no stochastic restrictions on the income stream, it can be used to value securities or other assets such as capital budgeting projects with serially correlated cash flows or rates of return, securities with or without limited liability, and derivative securities such as options in terms of their underlying securities. The formula was used to derive simple sufficient restrictions on real economic variables for the rate of return of the market portfolio to follow a random walk and the term structure to be unbiased. When applied to the pricing of options, it was shown, given appropriate stochastic restrictions, to imply the Black-Scholes option pricing formula, even though a perfect hedge cannot be constructed.

Appendix

■ Random variables x and y are said to be bivariate *normal* if their joint density function is

$$f(x, y) = \frac{1}{2\pi\sqrt{\sigma_x^2\sigma_y^2(1 - \kappa^2)}}$$

$$\times \exp\left\{\frac{-1}{2(1 - \kappa^2)}\left[\frac{(x - \mu_x)^2}{\sigma_x^2} - 2\kappa\frac{(x - \mu_x)(y - \mu_y)}{\sigma_x\sigma_y} + \frac{(y - \mu_y)^2}{\sigma_y^2}\right]\right\},$$

---

[19] See Samuelson and Merton (1969). The corollary generalizes Merton (1973a, p. 171) by allowing the dividend yield to depend on time. In a succeeding working paper, Geske (1976) has further generalized the option pricing model for underlying stock with a stochastic but lognormal dividend yield. Since a perfect hedge cannot be constructed in this case, even if investors can make continuous revisions, his generalization requires the preference-specific approach developed in this paper.

where $\mu_x \equiv E(x)$, $\mu_y \equiv E(y)$, $\sigma_x^2 \equiv \text{Var } x$, $\sigma_y^2 \equiv \text{Var } y$, $\kappa \equiv \kappa(x, y)$. Defining the *marginal* density function of x, $f(x) \equiv \int_{-\infty}^{\infty} f(x, y)dy$ (and similarly for y), it is not difficult to prove that $f(x)$ (and $f(y)$) is a normal density function; that is,

$$f(x) = \frac{1}{\sigma_x\sqrt{2\pi}} \exp\left[\frac{-1}{2\sigma_x^2}(x - \mu_x)^2\right].$$

Defining the *conditional* density function of y given x, $f(y|x) \equiv f(x, y)/f(x)$, it follows that

$$f(y|x) = \frac{1}{\sqrt{2\pi(1 - \kappa^2)\sigma_y^2}}$$

$$\times \exp\left\{\frac{-1}{2(1 - \kappa^2)\sigma_y^2}\left[(y - \mu_y) - \kappa\frac{\sigma_y}{\sigma_x}(x - \mu_x)\right]^2\right\}.$$

Observe that this conditional density is itself a normal density with mean and variance, respectively,

$$E(y|x) = \mu_y + \kappa(\sigma_y/\sigma_x)(x - \mu_x)$$

and

$$\text{Var}(y|x) = (1 - \kappa^2)\sigma_y^2.$$

One very useful but little known[20] property of the bivariate normal distribution is that if x and y are bivariate normal and $g(y)$ is any at least once differentiable function of y, then, subject to mild regularity conditions,

$$\text{Cov}(x, g(y)) = E[g'(y)]\text{Cov}(x, y).$$

To see this, since

$$\text{Cov}(x, g(y)) = \iint xg(y)f(x, y)dx\, dy - \mu_x E[g(y)],$$

then using the conditional density

$$\text{Cov}(x, g(y)) = \int g(y)E(x|y)f(y)dy - \mu_x E[g(y)]$$

or, more particularly, for bivariate normal variables

$$\text{Cov}(x, g(y)) = \kappa\left(\frac{\sigma_x}{\mu_y}\right)\int g(y)(y - \mu_y)f(y)dy$$

$$= \text{Cov}(x, y)\int g(y)\left[\frac{y - \mu_y}{\sigma_y^2}\right]f(y)dy.$$

Defining $h'(y) \equiv \left[\frac{y - \mu_y}{\sigma_y^2}\right]f(y)$ and integrating by parts, we obtain

$$\text{Cov}(x, g(y)) = \text{Cov}\left(x, y\left[g(\infty)h(\infty) - g(-\infty)h(-\infty) - \int g'(y)h(y)dy\right]\right).$$

Since $f(y) = \frac{1}{\sigma_y\sqrt{2\pi}} e^{-(y-\mu_y)^2/2\sigma_y^2}$, then $h(y) = -f(y)$. In addition, since then $f(-\infty) = f(\infty) = 0$ and if $g(y)$ is bounded above and below or, more generally, if

$$\lim_{y \to -\infty} g(y)f(y) = \lim_{y \to \infty} g(y)f(y) = 0,$$

---

[20] To my knowledge, this property of bivariate normal variables was first noted in Rubinstein (1971). Stein (1973) has independently made its discovery.

then

$$\text{Cov}(x, g(y)) = \text{Cov}(x, y)\left[\int g'(y)f(y)dy\right] = E[g'(y)]\text{Cov}(x, y).$$

In the process of deriving an analytic solution for the discrete-time valuation of options, we need to evaluate several definite integrals over the marginal and conditional normal density functions:

$$\int_a^\infty f(x)dx = N\left(\frac{-a + \mu_x}{\sigma_x}\right), \tag{A1}$$

where $N(z^*)$ is the standard cumulative normal distribution from $-\infty$ to z^*; that is, $N(z^*) \equiv \int_{-\infty}^{z^*} \frac{1}{\sqrt{2\pi}} e^{-z^2/2}\, dz$. This is proved by first converting $f(x)$ into the standard normal density function $f(z) \equiv \frac{1}{\sqrt{2\pi}} e^{-z^2/2}$ and then observing that since z is symmetric around zero, the limits of integration can be interchanged. That is,

$$\int_a^\infty f(x)dx = \int_{\frac{a-\mu_x}{\sigma_x}}^\infty f(z)dz = \int_{-\infty}^{\frac{-a+\mu_x}{\sigma_x}} f(z)dz = N\left(\frac{-a + \mu_x}{\sigma_x}\right).$$

Second, we show that

$$\int_a^\infty e^x f(x)dx = (e^{\mu_x + \frac{1}{2}\sigma_x^2}) N\left(\frac{-a + \mu_x}{\sigma_x} + \sigma_x\right). \tag{A2}$$

To see this,

$$\int_a^\infty e^x f(x)dx = \int_a^\infty \frac{1}{\sigma_x\sqrt{2\pi}} \exp\left[\frac{-1}{2\sigma_x^2}(x - \mu_x)^2 + x\right]dx.$$

Since the exponent of e is equal to $\mu_x + \frac{1}{2}\sigma_x^2 - \frac{1}{2\sigma_x^2}(x - \mu_x - \sigma_x^2)^2$,

$$\int_a^\infty e^x f(x)dx = (e^{\mu_x + \frac{1}{2}\sigma_x^2}) \int_a^\infty \frac{1}{\sigma_x\sqrt{2\pi}} \exp\left\{\frac{-1}{2\sigma_x^2}[x - (\mu_x + \sigma_x^2)]^2\right\}dx.$$

Again, the result follows by converting this density into the standard normal density and interchanging the limits.

As an interim result, we will need to prove that

$$\int_{-\infty}^\infty e^y f(y|x)dy = \exp\left[\mu_y + \kappa \frac{\sigma_y}{\sigma_x}(x - \mu_x) + \frac{1}{2}(1 - \kappa^2)\sigma_y^2\right].$$

This is equivalent to finding the expected value of e^y where y is normally distributed with mean $\mu_y + \kappa(\sigma_y/\sigma_x)(x - \mu_x)$ and variance $(1 - \kappa^2)\sigma_y^2$. This is analogous to integral (2) where $a = -\infty$. In this case, $N(\cdot) = N(\infty) = 1$, so that the exponent of e may be replaced by $\mu_y + \kappa(\sigma_y/\sigma_x)(x - \mu_x) + \frac{1}{2}(1 - \kappa^2)\sigma_y^2$.

Now we are prepared to prove

$$\int_{-\infty}^\infty \int_a^\infty e^y f(x,y)dx\, dy = (e^{\mu_y + \frac{1}{2}\sigma_y^2}) N\left(\frac{-a + \mu_x}{\sigma_x} + \kappa\sigma_y\right). \tag{A3}$$

From our interim result

$$\int_{-\infty}^\infty \int_a^\infty e^y f(x,y)dx\, dy = \int_a^\infty f(x)\left[\int_{-\infty}^\infty e^y f(y|x)dy\right]dx$$

$$= \int_a^\infty e^{\mu_y + \kappa \frac{\sigma_y}{\sigma_x}(x-\mu_x) + \frac{1}{2}(1-\kappa^2)\sigma_y^2} f(x)dx.$$

Combining terms in the exponents of e, this, in turn, equals

$$\int_a^\infty \frac{1}{\sigma_x\sqrt{2\pi}} \exp\left[\mu_y + \kappa\frac{\sigma_y}{\sigma_x}(x - \mu_x)\right.$$
$$\left. + \frac{1}{2}(1 - \kappa^2)\sigma_y^2 - \frac{1}{2\sigma_x^2}(x - \mu_x)^2\right]dx.$$

Since the exponent of e is equal to $\mu_y + \frac{1}{2}\sigma_y^2 - \frac{1}{2\sigma_x^2}\left[(x - \mu_x)\right.$
$\left. - \kappa\sigma_x\sigma_y\right]^2$,

$$\int_{-\infty}^\infty \int_a^\infty e^y f(x,y)dx\, dy = (e^{\mu_y + \frac{1}{2}\sigma_y^2})$$

$$\times \int_a^\infty \frac{1}{\sigma_x\sqrt{2\pi}} \exp\left\{\frac{-1}{2\sigma_x^2}[x - (\mu_x + \kappa\sigma_x\sigma_y)]^2\right\}dx.$$

Again, the result follows by converting this density into the standard normal density and interchanging the limits.
Finally,

$$\int_{-\infty}^\infty \int_a^\infty e^x e^y f(x,y)dx\, dy = (e^{\mu_x + \mu_y + \frac{1}{2}(\sigma_x^2 + 2\kappa\sigma_x\sigma_y + \sigma_y^2)})$$

$$\times N\left(\frac{-a + \mu_x}{\sigma_x} + \kappa\sigma_y + \sigma_x\right). \text{(A4)}$$

Again from our interim result,

$$\int_{-\infty}^\infty \int_a^\infty e^x e^y f(x,y)dx\, dy = \int_a^\infty e^x f(x)\left[\int_{-\infty}^\infty e^y f(y|x)dy\right]dx$$

$$= \int_a^\infty e^{\mu_y + \kappa\frac{\sigma_y}{\sigma_x}(x - \mu_x) + \frac{1}{2}(1 - \kappa^2)\sigma_y^2} e^x f(x)dx.$$

Combining terms in the exponents of e, this, in turn, equals

$$\int_a^\infty \frac{1}{\sigma_x\sqrt{2\pi)}} \exp\left[\mu_y + \kappa\frac{\sigma_y}{\sigma_x}(x - \mu_x) + \frac{1}{2}(1 - \kappa^2)\sigma_y^2\right.$$
$$\left. + x - \frac{1}{2\sigma_x^2}(x - \mu_x)^2\right]dx.$$

Since the exponent of e is equal to

$$\mu_x + \mu_y + \frac{1}{2}(\sigma_x^2 + 2\kappa\sigma_x\sigma_y + \sigma_y^2)$$

$$- \frac{1}{2\sigma_x^2}\left[(x - \mu_x) - (\kappa\sigma_x\sigma_y + \sigma_x^2)\right]^2,$$

substituting this into the integral, converting this density into the standard normal density, and interchanging the limits yields (A4).

If x and y are bivariate normal, then random variables $X \equiv e^x$ and $Y \equiv e^y$ are said to be bivariate *lognormal*. Since sums of jointly normal variables are normal, products of jointly lognormal variables are lognormal. Moreover, if a and b are constants, since $y = a + bx$ is normally distributed if x is normally distributed, then $Y = aX^b$ is lognormally distributed if X is lognormally distributed. Since $x = \ln X$ and $y = \ln Y$ are normally distributed and since $d(\ln X) = dX/X$ and $d(\ln Y) = dY/Y$, then from the bivariate normal density function, the bivariate lognormal density function of X and Y is $F(X, Y) = \frac{1}{XY}$ $f(x, y)$, where $f(x, y)$ is again the bivariate normal density function. Consequently, the *marginal* lognormal density function of X, usually called simply the lognormal density, is $F(X) = \frac{1}{X} f(x)$.

Using the lognormal density and integrating

$$\mu_X \equiv \int_0^\infty XF(X)dX \text{ and } \sigma_X^2 \equiv \int_0^\infty (X - \mu_X)^2 F(X)dX,$$

it can be shown that the mean and variance of the lognormal variables, μ_X and σ_X^2, are related to the mean and variance of their corresponding normal variables, μ_x and σ_x^2 by[21]

$$\mu_X = e^{\mu_x + \frac{1}{2}\sigma_x^2} \text{ and } \sigma_X^2 = (e^{\mu_x + \frac{1}{2}\sigma_x^2})^2(e^{\sigma_x^2} - 1).$$

With these relationships, since the product XY is itself lognormal,

$$E(XY) - \exp[\mu_x + \mu_y + \tfrac{1}{2}\sigma_x^2 + \sigma_{xy} + \tfrac{1}{2}\sigma_y^2].$$

References

BEJA, A. "The Structure of the Cost of Capital under Uncertainty." *Review of Economic Studies* (July 1971).

BLACK, F. AND SCHOLES, M. "The Pricing of Options and Corporate Liabilities." *Journal of Political Economy* (May-June 1973).

BLUME, M. AND FRIEND, I. "The Asset Structure of Individual Portfolios and Some Implications for Utility Functions." *Journal of Finance* (May 1975).

BOGUE, M. AND ROLL, R. "Capital Budgeting of Risky Projects with 'Imperfect' Markets for Physical Capital." *Journal of Finance* (May 1974).

COHEN, R., LEWELLEN, W., LEASE, R., AND SCHLARBAUM, G. "Individual Investor Risk Aversion and Investment Portfolio Composition." *Journal of Finance* (May 1975).

COX, J. AND ROSS, S. "The Pricing of Options for Jump Processes." University of Pennsylvania, Wharton Working Paper #2–75, 1975.

FAMA, E. "Multiperiod Consumption-Investment Decisions." *The American Economic Review*, Vol. 60, No. 1 (March 1970).

GESKE, R. "The Pricing of Options with Stochastic Dividend Yield." Unpublished manuscript, March 1976.

GRANGER, C. AND MORGENSTERN, O. *Predictability of Stock Market Prices.* Lexington, Mass.: Heath Lexington Books, 1970.

HAKANSSON, N. "Optimal Entrepreneurial Decisions in a Completely Stochastic Environment." *Management Science* (March 1971).

JENSEN, M. "Capital Markets: Theory and Evidence." *The Bell Journal of Economics and Management Science*, Vol. 3, No. 2 (Autumn 1972).

KRAUS, A. AND LITZENBERGER, R. "Market Equilibrium in a Multiperiod State Preference Model with Logarithmic Utility." *Journal of Finance*, in press.

LINTNER, J. "Distribution of Income of Corporations Among Dividends, Retained Earnings, and Taxes." *The American Economic Review*, Vol. 46, No. 2 (May 1956).

LONG, J. "Stock Prices, Inflation and the Term Structure of Interest Rates." *Journal of Financial Economics* (July 1974).

MERTON, R. "Theory of Rational Option Pricing." *The Bell Journal of Economics and Management Science*, Vol. 4, No. 1 (Spring 1973a).

———. "An Intertemporal Capital Asset Pricing Model." *Econometrica* (September 1973b).

———. "Option Pricing when Underlying Stock Returns are Discontinuous." MIT Working Paper #787–75, April 1975.

MILLER, M. AND MODIGLIANI, F. "Dividend Policy, Growth and the Valuation of Shares." *Journal of Business* (October 1961).

ROBICHEK, A. AND MYERS, S. *Optimal Financing Decisions.* Englewood Cliffs, N.J.: Prentice-Hall, 1965.

ROSENBERG, B. "The Behavior of Random Variables with Nonstationary Variance and

---

[21] The general formula for the nth order central moment of a lognormal variable is

$$E[(X - \mu_X)^n] = (\mu_X)^n \left[\sum_{r=0}^{n} \frac{n}{r!(n - r)!} (-1)^{n-r} e^{\frac{1}{2}r(r-1)\sigma_x^2} \right]$$

the Distribution of Security Prices." University of California, Berkeley, Research Program in Finance, Working Paper #11, December 1972.

RUBINSTEIN, M. "A Comparative Statics Analysis of Risk Premiums," Essay 2 in *Four Essays in the Theory of Competitive Security Markets.* Ph.D. dissertation, UCLA; appeared in *Journal of Business,* October 1973.

————. "An Aggregation Theorem for Security Markets." *Journal of Financial Economics* (September 1974a).

————. "A Discrete-Time Synthesis of Financial Theory." University of California, Berkeley, Research Program in Finance, Working Papers #20 and #21, May, June 1974b.

————. "Securities Market Efficiency in an Arrow-Debreu Economy." *The American Economic Review,* Vol. 65, No. 5 (December 1975).

————. "The Strong Case for the Generalized Logarithmic Utility Model as the Premier Model of Financial Markets." *Journal of Finance* (May 1976).

Samuelson, P. "Proof That Properly Discounted Present Values of Assets Vibrate Randomly." *The Bell Journal of Economics and Management Science,* Vol. 4, No. 2 (Autumn 1973).

———— AND MERTON, R. "A Complete Model of Warrant Pricing that Maximizes Utility." *Industrial Management Review* (Winter 1969).

SHARPE, W. "Capital Asset Prices: A Theory of Market Equilibrium under Conditions of Risk." *Journal of Finance* (September 1964).

SPRENKLE, C. "Warrant Prices as Indicators of Expectations and Preferences." *Yale Economic Essays* (1961).

STEIN, C. "Estimation of the Mean of a Multivariate Normal Distribution." *Proceedings of the Prague Symposium on Asymptotic Statistics,* September 1973.

WILLIAMS, J. *The Theory of Investment Value.* Amsterdam: North-Holland Publishing Company, 1938.

discussion | **Market Incompleteness and the Equilibrium Valuation of Assets**

José A. Scheinkman

Department of Economics
University of Chicago

Equilibrium asset pricing formulas of the type developed in the preceding article by Mark Rubinstein and in related papers by LeRoy (1973), Lucas (1978), Brock (1982), and Prescott and Mehra (1985) have played an important role in furthering our understanding of the behavior of securities prices and in providing testable restrictions on intertemporal asset prices. In the first part of this chapter we discuss possible weakenings of the single-investor assumption used by Rubinstein. In the second part we show how market incompleteness affects the asset pricing formula. In particular, we demonstrate, with the aid of a simple example, how ignoring the presence of uninsurable individual risk may lead us to conclude for exaggerated degree of risk aversion on the part of the agents.

I. THE REPRESENTATIVE CONSUMER

Though Rubinstein postulates the presence of an average investor, one can derive the asset pricing formula by assuming the following: (i) there is no private information, all agents have a common subjective probability, and each has preferences given by an additively separable, concave, state-independent expected utility function; that is,

$$(1) \qquad U^i(c) = E \sum_{t=1}^{\infty} u_t^i(c(s^t)),$$

where E denotes the expected value operator, and $s^t = (s_1, \ldots, s_t)$ denotes a "history" of the states of the world that occurred up to and including time t; and (ii) there is a complete set of contingent claims markets. Hypothesis (i) is self-explanatory, but (ii) needs to be made explicit, especially in situations where the number of contingent commodities is infinite. By the presence of a complete set of contingent markets, one means the existence of a (continuous) linear functional p defined over a space that includes all possible individual

I would like to thank M. Boldrin, G. Constantinides, L. Hansen, N. Kocherlakota, B. LeBaron, and R. Lucas for comments.

contingent consumptions and initial endowments and that agents may purchase any contingent consumption that has (under p) a value not exceeding that of their initial endowment.

Under these two conditions one may use the Pareto optimality of a competitive equilibrium (Debreu 1954) to show that, for a finite number of agents, associated with any equilibrium there exists a utility function of the same type as (1) that is maximized at the equilibrium (Constantinides 1982). Further, if $u_t^i(c(s^t)) = \delta^t u^i(c(s^t))$ (i.e., all agents have a common discount factor), then so will the stand-in consumer. For an economy with an infinite number of consumers, one must further assume that the value (under p) of the aggregate endowment is finite. It is important to notice that establishing the existence of the stand-in consumer is much simpler than the problem of "aggregating" the demand functions of several heterogeneous agents into the demand of a single agent as in Rubinstein (1974). For in the case we are interested in, the demand of the stand-in consumer must agree with the aggregate demand only at the *equilibrium price*.

Since complete markets involve a large number of claims, it is quite interesting to try to reduce requirement (ii). Arrow (1953) had already noticed that we can price "by arbitrage" all contingent claims if we are willing to assume that at each t history s^t there exist complete spot markets and contingent markets for at least one commodity for every $t + 1$ history s^{t+1} that may follow s^t and, further, that consumers have perfect foresight about the spot and contingent prices that would prevail in all future date-event pairs.[1]

A further result along these lines was established by David Kreps (1982). Consider an economy with a finite set of dates $t = 1, \ldots, T$, where at each date t a "state" is drawn from a finite set S with l elements. There is a simple consumption good, and there are N "long-lived" securities, each a contingent claim to consumption at the terminal date T. At each date $t \leqslant T$, prices $p_n(s^t)$ for each of the N securities are determined (as a function of the history obtained), and again it is assumed that consumers know which prices will prevail in the future contingent on the history that occurs. Let $p(s^t) = (p_1(s^t) \ldots p_N(s^t))$. For given s^t consider the l vectors $p(s^t, s_{t+1}) \in \mathscr{R}^N$ of prices at all possible[2] histories that may follow s^t. If these vectors are linearly independent, then the equilibrium is Pareto optimal. The idea is to be able to generate at s^t a contingent consumption claim that yields one unit of consumption at $t + 1$ if s_{t+1} occurs, and zero otherwise, for each $s_{t+1} \in S$ (and hence an arbitrary claim by forming appropriate contingent plans). This can be achieved by choosing an adequate portfolio at t—that is, one that solves

$$(2) \qquad \lambda P = e^i,$$

where $e_j^i = 0$ if $j \neq i$, $e_i^i = 1$, and P is the $N \times l$ matrix formed by the l column vectors $p(s^t, s_{t+1})$. If P has rank l, then (2) has a solution for each e^i. Notice that this requires $N \geqslant l$. This result is unsatisfactory since it involves an assumption on endogenous variables, the equilibrium prices. Kreps (1982) solves this problem by considering a fixed economy (i.e., states of the world, number of agents and utility functions) except for the payoff of the N long-lived securities—that is, a vector in $\mathscr{R}^q$, where $q = Nl^T$, describing the payoff of each security at each T-history. It is then shown that if $N \geqslant l$, except for a subset of $\mathscr{R}^q$ whose closure has Lebesgue measure zero, the economy will admit an equilibrium with $\text{rank}(P) = l$—that is, that "most" economies with $N \geqslant l$ have an efficient equilibrium. The basic idea is to notice that the set of complete market equilibria of each economy is independent of the chosen vector $d \in \mathscr{R}^q$ of payoffs of each long-lived security at each T-history. By selecting a particular complete market equilibrium, we may thus price the long-lived securities as a linear function of the final payoffs and see that if $N \geqslant l$ the linear independency condition will hold for "most" d's. Duffie and Huang (1985) generalize these results for continuous time.

The results of Arrow and Kreps considerably reduce the number of securities needed to yield Pareto optimality.[3] Unfortunately, for an infinite-time horizon—which is necessary to generate the kind of stationarity used in empirical testing—two difficulties remain. First, one needs to impose some restrictions on allowable trades to rule out the strategy of consuming at each t arbitrary amounts, financing the consumption by the sale of goods for delivery at time $t + 1$ and repeating this operation ad infinitum (Ponzi schemes). Without such a restriction no equilibrium would exist. This is usually accomplished by placing some lower bound on net debt at each t. Second, though one can use the same reasoning as in the finite-horizon case to price claims, one must also show that the implied prices assign an unambiguous value to all admissible contingent consumptions and finite value to the aggregate endowment in order to conclude the efficiency of equilibria.

To understand this point, we believe it is best to examine the following example, known as the overlapping generations model (Samuelson 1973). Consider an economy extending over $t = 1, 2, \ldots$, where in each period a single consumption good exists. A consumption bundle is thus a sequence $\{c_t\}_{t=1}^{\infty}, c_t \geqslant 0$. There are also M individuals of each type $i = 1, 2, \ldots,$[4] and an individual of type i has utility function given by $U^i(c) = \log c_i + \log c_{i+1}$, and endowment $\{w_t^i\}_{t=1}^{\infty}$ where $w_t^i = 0$ if $t \neq i,\ i+1$; $w_i^i = 1$, $w_{i+1}^i = \frac{1}{2}$. At each t suppose there are markets for exchanging the consumption good at $t + 1$ for the consumption good at t at a price p_t. In order to rule out Ponzi schemes, we forbid any individual of type i to make net sales for future delivery at any period $t > i + 1$—which is natural here since the individual's endowment after period $i + 1$ is always zero. Then if $p_t = 2$, it is easy to verify that each individual would consume exactly his or her initial endowment. This allocation is not efficient because it is dominated by an allocation where an individual of type i consumes $c_i = \frac{3}{4}$, $c_{i+1} = \frac{3}{4}$ (except for $i = 1$, which consumes $c_1 = 1$, $c_2 = \frac{3}{4}$). Notice that, as in Arrow (1953), we may use arbitrage to price any finite contingent claim—if a claim yields y_t units of the consumption good at t, then it is worth $2^{t-1} y_t$ units of the consumption good at time 1. However, a claim to the aggregate endowment has infinite value.

Usually one avoids such problems by assuming a priori bounds on contingent prices. An alternative approach for utility functions as (1) consists of obtaining certain bounds from "transversality conditions at infinity" (see, e.g., Weitzman 1973 and Benveniste and Scheinkman 1982) and showing directly that a functional of the same type as (1) is maximized at a competitive equilibrium (see, e.g., Scheinkman 1977 and Brock 1982).

In any case, once the representative consumer is obtained, one then has that Theorem 3 of Rubinstein's paper holds and, in particular, if $p(s^t)$ denotes the price of any asset at time t if history s^t occurs, then

$$(3) \qquad p(s^t) = E_t \left\{ \frac{U'_{t+1}(c(s^{t+1}))}{U'_t(c(s^t))} [p(s^{t+1}) + \chi(s^{t+1})] \right\},$$

where $c(s^t)$ denotes the aggregate consumption at t if history s_t occurs, $\chi(s^{t+1})$ is the dividend if history s^{t+1} occurs, and E_t is the expected value conditional on the information available at t (i.e., the realized history s^t). If all consumers use the same discount factor δ, then (3) reduces to

$$(3') \qquad p(s^t) = \delta E_t \left\{ \frac{U'(c(s^{t+1}))}{U'(c(s^t))} [p(s^{t+1}) + \chi(s^{t+1})] \right\}.$$

Equations such as (3') are tested and preference parameters estimated by postulating a constant relative risk-aversion utility function and by either (i) choosing an asset (really a combination of assets) and regressing its prices on measures of aggregate consumption or (ii) choosing a pair of assets and writing (3') for each and looking at differences in the rates of return.

II. INCOMPLETE MARKETS

A series of studies using aggregate data to test formulas like (3') and to estimate preference parameters has appeared (cf., Grossman and Shiller 1981, Hall 1981, or Hansen and Singleton 1982, 1983). The results are at best mixed. The model is sometimes definitely rejected, and the estimates of risk-aversion parameters are implausibly high and with large standard errors. Prescott and Mehra (1985) constructed a model economy with a single asset claim to GNP. There is a representative consumer that maximizes a discounted sum of utilities. The growth rate of the asset's dividends is a stochastic process chosen such that the rate of growth, variance, and intertemporal covariance of dividends are grossly comparable to those of the American aggregate consumption series. They then compute the risk premium that such a claim should have over a risk-free asset with "reasonable" risk-aversion coefficients (less than 10) and find that it is much smaller than the actual risk premium that the S & P 500 composite stock index commands over short-term government debt. They went on to suggest part of that discrepancy might be due to uninsured individual risk, that is, the lack of (essentially) complete contingent markets.

We present here a simple example to illustrate this point. First notice that (3') must hold if we replace the mean consumption $c(s^t)$ with an individual's consumption $c^i(s^t)$. Writing (3') for two distinct assets and taking the difference, we obtain

(4) $$0 = E_t\{U'(c^i(s^{t+1}))[r^1(s^{t+1}) - r^2(s^{t+1})]\},$$

where $r^i(s^{t+1})$ is the rate of return of the ith asset if history s^{t+1} occurs. In particular, if $c(s^{t+1})$ is known with certainty (or U' is a constant), then the mean returns must be the same.

Now consider a two-period economy in which there is one state of the world in the first period, four possible and equally probable states of the world in period 2, and a single consumption good. There are two types of individuals with common utility function $U(c^1, c^2) = u(c^1) + Eu(c^2)$. In period 1 all individuals have one unit of the consumption good, whereas in period 2 their initial endowments are

State	Endowment of Type 1	Endowment of Type 2
1	x	y
2	y	x
3	x	y
4	y	x

where $y > x$.

There is also a single machine whose output per capita is $z > 0$ in states 1 and 2 and 0 in states 3 and 4. All individuals own initially equal shares of the machine.

There are only two assets traded. One is "risk free" with a rate of return r. The other is a claim to the per capita output of the machine; in other words, for a price p one acquires the right to z units of the consumption good if states 1 or 2 occur. Clearly, if a competitive equilibrium exists, there also exists one where the consumption of each type, denoted c_i, $i = 1, 2$, is

State	c_1	c_2
1	$x + z$	$y + z$
2	$y + z$	$x + z$
3	x	y
4	y	x

Using (4) we have

(5) $$\frac{u'(x+z) + u'(y+z)}{u'(x) + u'(y)} = \frac{r}{z/p - r}.$$

If we could only observe aggregate data (i.e., states 1 and 2 look identical, as do states 3 and 4), then we would believe that the common utility function v should satisfy

(6) $$\frac{v'((x+y)/2 + z)}{v'((x+y)/2)} = \frac{r}{z/p - r}.$$

If we know that the common utility function is of the type $u(c) = c^{1-\alpha}/(1-\alpha)$, $\alpha > 0$, then we would estimate α to satisfy

(7)
$$\frac{(((x+y)/2)+z)^{-\hat{\alpha}}}{((x+y)/2)^{-\hat{\alpha}}} = \frac{r}{z/p - r},$$

whereas the true $\tilde{\alpha}$ would satisfy

(8)
$$\frac{(x+z)^{-\tilde{\alpha}} + (y+z)^{-\tilde{\alpha}}}{x^{-\tilde{\alpha}} + y^{-\tilde{\alpha}}} = \frac{r}{z/p - r}.$$

It is easy to show that $\hat{\alpha} > \tilde{\alpha}$—that is, that one overestimates the degree of relative risk aversion using aggregate data. To see this, note first that

(9)
$$\frac{x^{-\alpha} + y^{-\alpha}}{((x+y)/2)^{-\alpha}} > \frac{(x+z)^{-\alpha} + (y+z)^{-\alpha}}{(((x+y)/2)+z)^{-\alpha}}$$

for all $\alpha > 0$, $z > 0$.[5] Hence when $\tilde{\alpha}$ solves (8), we have

(10)
$$\frac{(((x+y)/2)+z)^{-\tilde{\alpha}}}{((x+y)/2)^{-\tilde{\alpha}}} > \frac{r}{z/p - r}.$$

Further, the left side decreases with $\tilde{\alpha}$. Hence $\hat{\alpha} > \tilde{\alpha}$.

Two remarks are in order. First, Bewley (1982), who developed the Prescott-Mehra idea of how uninsurable risks could cause their "excess" returns to risk to appear, gives examples where ignoring the lack of insurance and estimating the risk premium from aggregate consumption (and known utility functions, etc.) leads to errors in *either direction*.[6] Second, though the example has only two periods, it could easily be extended to an infinite-horizon economy.

Scheinkman and Weiss (1986) study a dynamic model where borrowing constraints prevent individuals from sharing their human capital risk. Their simulations show that if each individual has logarithmic utility (i.e., a unitary coefficient of relative risk aversion), an estimate of relative risk aversion based on aggregate consumption is about 3. Mankiw (1986) presents another example that illustrates the role of incomplete markets on the overestimation of risk aversion.

NOTES

[1] Arrow dealt only with the case $t = 1, 2$. His reasoning, however, is perfectly general.

[2] For simplicity we assume that given s^t all states in S have a positive probability of occurrence.

[3] Note, however, that Kreps (1982) shows only that for most d there exists *an* equilibrium that is an optimum and not that all equilibria associated with such d are Pareto efficient.

[4] Usually individual types are interpreted as generations, but this frequently leads to a confusion as to the reason of the inefficiency of the equilibrium.

[5] Simply differentiate $((x+z)^{-\alpha} + (y+z)^{-\alpha})/(((x+y)/2)+z)^{-\alpha}$ w.r.t. z and observe that the derivative is always negative if $y > x$.

[6] The property that u' is convex was used in our example.

REFERENCES

Arrow, K. 1953. "Le Rôle des Valeurs Boursiére pour la Répartition la Meilleure des Risques." *Econométrie* (C.N.R.S. Paris): 41–47, 47–48. Translated in *Review of Economic Studies* 31 (1964): 91–96.

Benveniste, L. M., and Scheinkman, J. A. 1982. "Duality Theory for Dynamic Optimization Models of Economics: The Continuous Time Case." *Journal of Economic Theory* 27: 1–19.

Bewley. T. F. 1982. "Thoughts on Tests of the Intertemporal Asset Pricing Model." Northwestern University (mimeo), July.

Brock, W. A. 1982. "Asset Prices in a Production Economy." In J. J. McCall, ed., *The Economics of Information and Uncertainty*. Chicago: University of Chicago Press.

Constantinides, G. M. 1982. "Intertemporal Asset Pricing with Heterogeneous Consumers and without Demand Aggregation." *Journal of Business* 55: 253–67.

Debreu, G. 1954. "Valuation Equilibrium and Pareto Optimum." *Proceedings of the National Academy of Sciences of the U.S.A.* 40: 588–92.

Duffie, D., and Huang, C. 1985. "Implementing Arrow-Debreu Equilibria by Continuous Trading of Few Long-Lived Securities." *Econometrica* 53: 1337–56.

Grossman, S., and Shiller, R. 1981. "The Determinants of the Variability of Stock Market Prices." *American Economic Review* 71: 222–27.

Hall, R. E. 1981. "Intertemporal Substitution in Consumption." Working paper No. 720, National Bureau of Economic Research.

Hansen, L., and Singleton, K. 1982. "Generalized Instrumental Variables Estimation of Nonlinear Rational Expectations Models." *Econometrica* 50: 1269–86.

————. 1983. "Stochastic Consumption, Risk Aversion, and the Temporal Behavior of Asset Returns." *Journal of Political Economy* 91: 249–65.

Kreps, D. 1982. "Multiperiod Securities and the Efficient Allocation of Risk: A Comment on the Black-Scholes Option Pricing Model." In J. J. McCall, ed., *The Economics of Information and Uncertainty*. Chicago: University of Chicago Press.

LeRoy, Stephen. 1973. "Risk Aversion and the Martingale Property of Stock Prices." *International Economic Review* 14: 436–46.

Lucas, R. E., Jr. 1978. "Asset Prices in an Exchange Economy." *Econometrica* 46: 1429–45.

Mankiw, N. G. 1986. "The Equity Premium and the Concentration of Aggregate Shocks." National Bureau of Economic Research.

Prescott, E., and Mehra, R. 1985. "The Equity Premium: A Puzzle." *Journal of Monetary Economics* 15(2): 145–62.

Rubinstein, Mark. 1974. "An Aggregation Theorem for Security Markets." *Journal of Financial Economics* 1: 225–44.

Samuelson, P. A. 1973. "Optimality of Profit, Including Prices under Social Ideal Planning." *Proceedings of the National Academy of Sciences of the U.S.A.* 70: 2109–11.

Scheinkman, J. A. 1977. "Notes on Asset Pricing." University of Chicago, manuscript.

Scheinkman, J. A., and Weiss, L. 1986. "Borrowing Constraints and Aggregate Economic Activity." *Econometrica* 54: 23–45.

Weitzman, M. 1973. "Duality Theory for Infinite Horizon Convex Models." *Management Science* 19: 783–89.

Journal of Financial Economics 7 (1979) 265–296. © North-Holland Publishing Company

AN INTERTEMPORAL ASSET PRICING MODEL WITH STOCHASTIC CONSUMPTION AND INVESTMENT OPPORTUNITIES

Douglas T. BREEDEN*

Stanford University, Stanford, CA 94305, USA

Received October 1978, revised version received July 1979

This paper derives a single-beta asset pricing model in a multi-good, continuous-time model with uncertain consumption goods prices and uncertain investment opportunities. When no riskless asset exists, a zero-beta pricing model is derived. Asset betas are measured relative to changes in the aggregate real consumption rate, rather than relative to the market. In a single-good model, an individual's asset portfolio results in an optimal consumption rate that has the maximum possible correlation with changes in aggregate consumption. If the capital markets are unconstrained Pareto-optimal, then changes in all individuals' optimal consumption rates are shown to be perfectly correlated.

1. Introduction

The capital asset pricing model (CAPM) of Sharpe (1964) and Lintner (1965) is an important theory of the structure of equilibrium expected returns on securities in the capital markets. Empirical tests of the model have had mixed results, in that security returns do appear to be positively related to their respective measured market 'betas', but not in the precise manner implied by the CAPM.[1] By relaxing the assumptions involved in the derivation of the CAPM, the model has been extended to more general economies, usually at the expense of simplicity in the structure of equilibrium expected returns. This paper further develops the intertemporal extension of the CAPM that was initiated by Merton (1973) in a continuous-time model.

Merton's intertemporal CAPM with stochastic investment opportunities states that the expected excess return on any asset is given by a 'multi-beta' version of the CAPM with the number of betas being equal to one plus the number of state variables needed to describe the relevant characteristics of

---

*I am grateful for the helpful comments of Sudipto Bhattacharya, George Constantanides, Eugene Fama, Nils Hakansson, Jon Ingersoll, John Long (the referee), Merton Miller, Stephen Ross, Myron Scholes, and especially Robert Litzenberger. Of course, they are not responsible for any remaining errors.

[1]See Jensen (1972) for a survey of many of these results.

the investment opportunity set. Since all of those state variables are not easily identified, this intertemporal extension, while quite important from a theoretical standpoint, is not very tractable for empirical testing, nor is it very useful for financial decision-making. This paper utilizes the *same* continuous-time economic framework as that used by Merton, likewise permitting stochastic investment opportunities. However, it is shown that Merton's multi-beta pricing equation can be collapsed into a single-beta equation, where the instantaneous expected excess return on any security is proportional to its 'beta' (or covariance) with respect to aggregate consumption alone. In this paper, it is also demonstrated that this result extends to a multi-good world, with an asset's beta measured relative to aggregate real consumption. The fact that this model involves a single beta relative to a specific variable, rather than many betas measured relative to unspecified variables, may make it easier to test and to implement, given certain stationarity assumptions on the joint distributions of rates of return and aggregate consumption.

Section 2 presents the continuous-time economic model with stochastic investment opportunities. General versions of the 'mutual fund' theorem of Merton (1973) and Long (1974) and of their multi-beta CAPM are briefly derived. The single-beta, single-good intertemporal CAPM as described above is derived and discussed in section 3. This derivation also generalizes a similar single-beta CAPM derived in a multi-period state preference model by Breeden and Litzenberger (1978). They derived the same pricing equation, but only for assets with cash flows that are jointly lognormally distributed with aggregate consumption. Neither consumption nor asset prices need be lognormally distributed here, but they are assumed to follow diffusion processes. A simple example is presented in section 4 to illustrate the point that the relation of an asset's return with aggregate consumption precisely measures its relevant risk, whereas the return's relation to aggregate wealth is not an adequate measure of an asset's risk.

Section 5 demonstrates that there are intertemporal analogs to the single-period results that state that all individuals' wealths will be perfectly correlated and that each individual's portfolio beta is proportional to his Pratt (1964) – Arrow (1965) measure of relative risk tolerance. In particular, it is proven that changes in all individuals' optimal consumption rates are perfectly correlated at each instant, and each individual's optimal instantaneous standard deviation of changes in consumption is proportional to his relative risk tolerance, if the capital markets permit an unconstrained Pareto-optimal allocation of consumption. For general capital markets, it is shown that each individual's optimal portfolio is such that changes in the individual's optimal consumption rate have the maximum possible correlation with changes in the aggregate consumption rate.

Section 6 presents a derivation of a 'zero-beta' intertemporal CAPM for an economy with no riskless asset. The expected return on the zero-beta portfolio is obtained from a portfolio with returns that are uncorrelated with changes in aggregate consumption. This pricing model is an intertemporal analog to the single-period zero-beta model of Lintner (1969), Black (1972), and Vasicek (1971).

A multi-good extension of the intertemporal CAPM is presented in section 7. Long (1974) has extended Merton's multi-beta model to the multi-good case in a discrete-time economy, but this extension resulted in a pricing equation with even more terms. The focus of this section of the paper is on the derivation of a single-beta CAPM in the multi-good world. It is shown that equilibrium expected excess real returns on assets are proportional to the assets' betas with respect to aggregate *real* consumption, where aggregate real consumption is computed for an instantaneously additive price index with aggregate expenditure fractions on the various goods as weights. This result also extends the single-risk-measure asset pricing equation of Grauer and Litzenberger (1979) from a multi-good economy with strong 'homothetic' restrictions on consumption preferences to an economy with general and diverse consumption preferences. The continuous-time framework permits their covariance of an asset's return with the marginal utility of aggregate consumption to be written as a function of the asset's consumption-beta.

2. The economic model

The continuous-time model of this paper is very similar to the models utilized by Merton (1971, 1973), Lucas (1978), and Cox, Ingersoll and Ross (CIR) (1977). Therefore, in the interest of brevity, common facets of this model will only be sketched, with the unfamiliar reader being referred to those earlier developments of the model. Readers familiar with these continuous-time models may skip this section without losing the thrust of the paper.

Initially, it is assumed that there is a single good that may be consumed by individuals or invested via firms; a multi-good extension is presented in section 7. Individuals are assumed to behave as price takers in perfectly competitive, but possibly incomplete capital markets that are frictionless. They may trade continuously and may short-sell any assets with full use of the proceeds. Trading takes place only at equilibrium prices. Also, it is assumed that all investors have identical probability beliefs for states of the world. Individuals hold wealth in the form of risky asset shares or in an instantaneously riskless asset; the case where no riskless asset exists is presented in section 6. W^k is individual k's wealth and w^k is his $A \times 1$ vector of fractions of wealth invested in the various risky assets. (Throughout this paper, vectors will appear as bold italic and multi-column matrices will appear as bold roman.) Letting 1 be a vector of ones, $w_0^k = 1 - 1'w^k$ is individual k's fraction of wealth invested in the riskless asset. Each individual k has a stochastic number of labor units, y^k, that yield a continuous wage income rate of ly^k.[2]

It is assumed that there exists an $N \times 1$ vector of state variables, θ that (with time) describes the state of the world. For example, asset prices, dividend yields, and income rates may be written as $P(\theta, t)$, $\delta(\theta, t)$, and $l(\theta, t)y^k(\theta, t)$, respectively. Assuming that the state vector θ follows a continuous-time vector Markov process of the Ito type, the following stochastic differential equations may be written as

$$d\theta = \mu_\theta(\theta, t)\,dt + \sigma_\theta(\theta, t)\,dz_\theta, \tag{1}$$

$$\frac{dP_a}{P_a} = [\mu_a(\theta, t) - \delta_a(\theta, t)]\,dt + \sigma_a(\theta, t)\,dz_a \quad \text{for each asset } a, \tag{2}$$

$$dy^k = \mu_{yk}(\theta, t)\,dt + \sigma_{yk}(\theta, t)\,dz_{yk} \qquad \begin{array}{l}\text{for each} \\ \text{individual } k,\end{array} \tag{3}$$

where the drift and diffusion coefficients in (2) and (3) may be obtained from those in (1) by Ito's Lemma.[3] Throughout, $\mu_j(\theta, t)$ represents the expected rate of change in variable j at time t, when the state vector is θ at that time. Similarly, $\sigma_j(\theta, t)$ represents the standard deviation of that rate of change, which depends upon time and the state vector; σ_θ is the diagonal matrix of the instantaneous standard deviations of the state variables. The z_θ variables are correlated Weiner processes, having zero means, unit variances per unit of time, and variance–covariance matrix and correlation matrix $V_{\theta\theta}$, which may depend upon θ and t.

Although there are a number of technical conditions that functions of Ito processes must meet for the application of Ito's Lemma [and for the representations of (2) and (3) to be rigorous], the economic restrictions on the movement of asset prices and incomes are not severe. Asset prices, dividends and incomes must follow continuous sample paths, but their levels, their mean rates of change and their variances and covariances may be stochastic, depending upon the evolution of the state vector over time. Thus,

---

[2]The labor–leisure choice is not examined in this paper. The formal model of sections 2–6 treats an individual's labor units supplied as stochastic and possibly correlated with all other economic variables, but there is no disutility for labor supplied. The multi-good model of section 7 could be adapted to handle the labor–leisure choice.

[3]For discussions of stochastic differential equations and of Ito's Lemma, see Merton (1978), Arnold (1974, sec. 5.3–5.5), Gihman and Skorohod (1972, part II, ch. 2, sec. 6), Kushner (1967, sec. 1.4), or McKean (1969, ch. 2). For discussions of the optimal control of these stochastic processes, see Arnold (1974, sec. 13.1–13.2) or Kushner (1967, ch. 6). For less technical discussions of these processes and theorems and for applications of them in economic models, see Merton (1971, 1973), Garman (1976), and Cox, Ingersoll and Ross (1977).

in Merton's (1973) terminology, the 'investment opportunity set' may be stochastic here. The state variables need not be restricted in number, nor do they need to be specified for the purposes of this paper. Restrictions on their number would restrict the dimensionality of the price system, as noted by Rosenberg and Ohlson (1976).

For the derivations that follow, it is not necessary to explicitly examine firms' production decisions and the supply of asset shares, provided that the assumptions made are consistent with optimal behavior of firms in a general equilibrium model. To be consistent with general equilibrium, prices must be recognized to be endogenously determined through the equilibrium of supply and demand. The model presented is consistent with endogenously determined prices if, as assumed, all random shocks to the economy are captured as elements of the state vector, θ. These random shocks may affect both the supplies and demands for shares. However, assuming that both supply and demand functions are functions of the state variables (shocks) that follow Ito processes, the equilibrium prices that arise will also follow Ito processes that are representable as in (2). This statement follows from Ito's Lemma, subject to the qualification that the supply and demand functions be sufficiently smooth for Ito's Lemma to apply.[4] Thus, the economic model of (1)–(3) is consistent with endogenously-determined prices.

As an example of a supply side that can be imbedded in this model without changing any of the analysis, consider the following economy. The output of the economy is produced by F different productive units (firms) under conditions of uncertainty about current investment productivity and about future investment technology. Firms buy stocks of the good and rent labor units of the good for use in their production processes. The current stock of the good that firm f owns is x_f, and the current amount of labor employed by it is y_f. The $F \times 1$ vectors of capital investment and labor employment by the various firms are denoted x and y, respectively, and the current wage rate is l. Changes in the amount of the good that a firm has are caused by its production, less its wage payments and dividends, d_f, and plus any new capital infusions, η_f, from sales of stock (negative η_f represents stock repurchases). It is assumed that such changes in the stock of the good that productive units have may be described by a system of stochastic differential equations of the Ito type,

$$dx = [\mu_x(x, y, e, t) - ly - d + \eta] \, dt + \sigma_x(x, y, e, t) \, dz_x, \tag{4}$$

and

$$de = \mu_e(e, t) \, dt + \sigma_e(e, t) \, dz_e, \tag{5}$$

---

[4]See footnote 3.

where e is an $E \times 1$ vector of indices that describe the productivity of current technology, and z_x and z_e are vectors of correlated Wiener processes. The vector of expected production rates is μ_x, and σ_x is the diagonal matrix of instantaneous standard deviations of the various production rates. Both expected and random components of a firm's production may depend upon the capital and labor employed and upon the current level of technology. As indicated by (5), technological change is assumed to be random, with the productivity indices following a vector Markov process. Although it is not done here, it is also possible (with more notation) to model expenditures on research and development that would affect the rates of technological change in the various production processes.

In the example, each firm may issue a number of different securities, such as debt and equity, that contractually partition its cash flows over time among investors in the firm. Each firm is assumed to maximize the value of its securities, net of input costs. For slightly greater generality, it is also assumed that individuals may issue or purchase a number of contractually defined securities ('side bets') that have zero net supplies. Options and forward contracts are permissible in this class of financial assets.

In a rational expectations equilibrium, asset prices in this economy are functions of the consumption preferences of individuals and time, which are non-stochastic, and the following stochastic variables: (1) the current productivities of the production processes, (2) the current supplies of capital and labor, and (3) the current distribution of income and wealth among individuals. Since all of these stochastic variables follow Ito processes in this model, and since they jointly comprise a Markov system, the initial representation of prices, dividends and income rates as functions of a Markov vector of state variables and time, as given by eqs. (1)–(3), is consistent with the existence of a production sector as sketched and with the endogenous determination of asset prices. Changes in the state vector, θ, for this economy are the results of stochastic production and stochastic technological change, which are the underlying exogenous variables of this example. Any other economies with supply side structures that are consistent with (1)–(3), given the preference and the other assumptions, are also governed by the theorems and pricing relations of this paper.

It is possible, with certain preference and/or probabilistic assumptions, that fluctuations in some of the elements of the state vector θ do not affect any individual's expected utility of lifetime consumption, given the individual's wealth. For example, certain elements of the state vector may affect the distribution of payoffs between two assets in such a way that the total payoff to the two is unaffected. If all individuals hold identical fractions of the two assets, then their expected utilities are unaffected by fluctuations in those state variables, assuming that the state variables have no other effects. To distinguish between state variables that do affect at least one individual's expected utility, given the person's wealth, it is convenient to define another state vector, s, that contains those state variables that do affect at least one individual's expected utility, given his wealth. This $S \times 1$ vector of variables is a subset of the comprehensive state vector, θ, and is assumed to follow a vector Markov process. Summarizing, each individual's expected utility of (remaining) lifetime consumption may be written as a function of his wealth, the vector of relevant state variables, and time, $J^k = J^k(W^k, s, t)$, where

$$ds = \mu_s(s, t) \, dt + \sigma_s \, dz_s. \tag{1'}$$

As all of the subsequent analysis and theorems are in terms of only these state variables, s, they are referred to throughout the paper as the 'state vector' or as the 'vector of state variables'.

Each individual k is assumed to maximize the expected value at each instant in time of a time-additive and state-independent von Neumann–Morgenstern utility function for lifetime consumption,

$$E_t \left\{ \int_t^{t^k} U^k(c^k(\tau), \tau) \, d\tau + B^k[W^k(t^k), t^k, s(t^k)] \right\}, \tag{6}$$

where t^k is individual k's time of death, and U^k and B^k are his strictly quasiconcave utility and bequest functions of consumption, c^k, and terminal wealth, $W^k(t^k)$, respectively.[5] E_t is the expectation operator at time t, conditional upon the state of the world at that time.

At each instant, individual k chooses an optimal rate of consumption, c^k, and an optimal portfolio of risky assets, $w^k W^k$. Given these choices, Merton (1971) has shown that the individual's wealth will follow the stochastic differential equation,

$$dW^k = \lceil w^{k'}(\mu_a - r) + r \rceil W^k \, dt + (ly^k - c^k) \, dt + W^k w^{k'} \sigma_a(dz_a), \tag{7}$$

where r is the instantaneously risk-free interest rate, $r = r \cdot 1$, μ_a is the $A \times 1$ vector of expected total (capital gains and dividends) rates of return on assets, and σ_a is the $A \times A$ diagonal matrix of assets' instantaneous standard deviations. Thus, μ_a, σ_a, and dz_a are all as presented in (2).

Let $J^k(W^k, s, t)$ be the maximum expected utility of lifetime consumption in (6) that is obtainable with wealth W^k and opportunities s at time t. Under certain conditions, if there exists a well-behaved function $J^k(W^k, s, t)$ and controls $c^k(W^k, s, t)$ and $w^k(W^k, s, t)$ that solve the following problem subject

---

[5]Under certain conditions, individuals' lifetimes may be uncertain. See Merton (1973) or Richard (1975). See the Richard paper for an analysis of optimal life insurance rules in a continuous-time model.

to the constraint of (7), then the consumption and portfolio decisions are optimal (with superscript k suppressed),[6]

$$0 = \max_{\{c, w\}} \left\{ U(c, t) + (J_W J'_s J_t) \begin{pmatrix} [w'(\mu_a - r) + r]W + ly - c \\ \mu_s \\ 1 \end{pmatrix} \right.$$
$$\left. + \frac{1}{2} \begin{pmatrix} V_{WW} & V_{Ws} \\ V_{sW} & V_{ss} \end{pmatrix} \square \begin{pmatrix} J_{WW} & J_{Ws} \\ J_{sW} & J_{ss} \end{pmatrix} \right\},$$

(8)

where subscripts of the J function represent partial derivatives with respect to wealth (J_W) and the various state variables (J_s). The matrix of V's is a partitioning of the variance–covariance matrix of the individual's wealth and the state variables. The box multiply sign implies that corresponding elements of the two matrices are multiplied, then summed. Note that the individual's variance rate for wealth is $V_{WW}^k = (W^k)^2 w^{k'} V_{aa} w^k$, and his vector of covariances of wealth with the state variables is $V_{Ws}^k = W^k w^{k'} V_{as}$, where V_{aa} is the $A \times A$ variance–covariance matrix of asset returns, and V_{as} is the $A \times S$ matrix of covariances of asset returns with state variables.

First-order conditions for an interior maximum in (8) may be stated as

$$U_c^k(c^k, t) = J_W^k(W^k, s, t),$$

(9)

and

$$w^k W^k = (-J_W^k/J_{WW}^k) V_{aa}^{-1} (\mu_a - r) - V_{aa}^{-1} V_{as} (J_{sW}^k/J_{WW}^k).$$

(10)

These conditions give the individual's optimal risky asset portfolio, (10), and state that the marginal utility of another unit of consumption must equal the indirect marginal utility of wealth for an optimal policy.

The following portfolio allocation theorem is obtained directly from individuals' portfolio demands as given by (10). Its proof is in appendix 1.

Theorem 1. S+2 Funds. All individuals in this economy, regardless of preferences, may obtain their optimal portfolio positions by investing in at most S+2 funds. These funds may be chosen to be: (1) the instantaneously riskless asset, (2) the S portfolios having the highest correlations, respectively, with the S state variables summarizing investment and income opportunities, and (3) the market portfolio.

Of course, any $S+2$ funds that span the same vector space would also suffice.

[6]See footnote 3 for references for this result and the conditions under which it is valid.

To see that Merton's (1973) 'multi-beta' asset pricing model obtains in this economy when betas are measured with respect to aggregate wealth and the returns of assets that hedge against changes in the various state variables, aggregate individuals' portfolio demands in (10) and substitute in equilibrium expected excess returns for the market portfolio, $(\mu_M - r)$, and for assets perfectly correlated with the state variables, $(\mu_s - r)$, assuming that such assets exist. Doing this, Merton's model is obtained,[7]

$$\mu_a - r = \beta_{a,Ms} \left(\frac{\mu_M - r}{\mu_s^* - r} \right), \tag{11}$$

where $\beta_{a,Ms}$ is the $A \times (S+1)$ matrix of 'multiple-regression' betas for all assets on the market and on the assets perfectly correlated with the state variables. This type of multi-beta equation was also derived in a discrete-time model by Long (1974). As both Merton and Long noted, the Sharpe–Lintner CAPM will not generally hold in these intertemporal economic models – expected excess returns are not proportional to market betas in these models with stochastic investment opportunities.

As shown by Garman (1976) and by Cox, Ingersoll and Ross (1977), each asset's price in this economy is a solution to a second-order partial differential equation in its price. This 'fundamental valuation equation' may be obtained for any asset by using Ito's Lemma to find its expected

---

[7]When assets with returns that are perfectly correlated with the state variables do not exist, a multi-beta CAPM as in (11) holds with one modification: expected excess returns for the S portfolios in (11) are those of the S portfolios with the maximum correlations with the S state variables, respectively, which have portfolio weights that are proportional to the columns of $V_{aa}^{-1}V_{as}$. Similarly, the S non-market betas required for each asset for (11) may be measured relative to the returns on these S most highly correlated portfolios. Briefly, the proof is as follows. From Appendix 1, (A.1),

$$w^M = k_1 V_{aa}^{-1}(\mu_a - r) + w_{s'} k_2,$$

where $w_{s'}$ is the $A \times S$ matrix of S portfolios with the maximum correlation of returns with the various state variables, respectively. Pre-multiplying this equation by V_{aa} gives

$$\mu_a - r = V_{aM}(1/k_1) + V_{as'}(-k_2/k_1) = V_{a,Ms'} \left(\frac{1/k_1}{-k_2/k_1} \right),$$

$$\left(\frac{\mu_M - r}{\mu_{s'} - r} \right) = V_{Ms',Ms'} \left(\frac{1/k_1}{-k_2/k_1} \right),$$

where $V_{Ms',Ms'}$ is the $(S+1) \times (S+1)$ variance–covariance matrix for the market and the most correlated portfolios' returns. Substituting this result into the previous equation gives

$$\mu_a - r = V_{a,Ms'} V_{Ms'Ms'}^{-1} \left(\frac{\mu_M - r}{\mu_{s'} - r} \right) = \beta_{a,Ms'} \left(\frac{\mu_M - r}{\mu_{s'} - r} \right),$$

which is the result stated.

instantaneous return from the function $P(\theta, t)$ and then by equating this drift rate to the equilibrium drift rates implied by the multi-beta model of (11). An interpretation of the general mathematical solution to the valuation equation is given in the CIR paper, but useful closed-form solutions are known only for a few assets, and then only under highly restrictive preference and state assumptions. In particular, CIR assume logarithmic utility functions and a single state variable to derive their closed-form solution for the term structure of interest rates. In this paper, no restrictions on state variables are imposed, and only the relatively weak preference assumption of (6) is made. Consequently, the goal here is to simplify the expression relating asset risks and returns, rather than to solve for an explicit pricing function, $P(\theta, t)$. The next section demonstrates that the multi-beta intertemporal CAPM of (11) can be collapsed into a single-beta intertemporal CAPM, with no additional assumptions.

3. A 'single-beta' intertemporal asset pricing model

Up to this point, the consumption–investment analysis is virtually the same as in Merton's (1973) continuous-time development, but with slightly more discussion of the supply side. An individual's portfolio holdings are found in terms of his indirect utility function for wealth, $J^k(W^k, s, t)$, and equilibrium expected asset returns are correspondingly found in terms of aggregate wealth and the returns on assets that are perfectly correlated with changes in the various state variables, if they exist. This paper focuses upon the individual's direct utility function for consumption, $U^k(c^k, t)$, in the analysis of equilibrium expected returns on assets. The two approaches are intimately linked by the optimality condition that the marginal utility of consumption equals the marginal utility of wealth.

To restate the optimal portfolio demands in terms of the individual k's optimal consumption function, $c^k(W^k, s, t)$, note from (9) that: $J_W^k = U_c^k$, which implies that $J_{Ws}^k = U_{cc}^k c_s^k$ and $J_{WW}^k = U_{cc}^k c_W^k$, where subscripts of U, J and c denote partial derivatives. Define T^k to be individual k's absolute risk tolerance: $T^k = -U_c^k/U_{cc}^k$. Then the optimal portfolio may be written as

$$w^k W^k = (T^k/c_W^k)\mathbf{V}_{aa}^{-1}(\mu_a - r) - \mathbf{V}_{aa}^{-1}\mathbf{V}_{as}(c_s^k/c_W^k), \tag{12}$$

where $\mu_a - r$ is the vector of instantaneous expected excess returns on assets, $\mathbf{V}_{aa}$ is their variance–covariance matrix, and $\mathbf{V}_{as}$ is the $A \times S$ matrix of covariances of asset returns with changes in the state variables.

Pre-multiplying (12) by $c_W^k \mathbf{V}_{aa}$ and rearranging terms gives

$$T^k(\mu_a - r) = V_{aW_k}c_W^k + \mathbf{V}_{as}c_s^k, \tag{13}$$

where V_{aW_k} is the vector of covariances of asset returns with k's wealth change. Since k's optimal consumption is a function, $c^k(W^k, s, t)$, of his wealth, the state variables and time, Ito's Lemma implies that the local covariances of asset returns with changes in k's consumption rate are given by

$$V_{ac_k} = V_{aW_k} c_W^k + V_{as} c_s^k, \tag{14}$$

which is the right-hand side of (13). Intuitively, (14) can also be seen by noting that the random change in k's consumption rate is locally linear in the random changes in k's wealth and the state variables, with the weights in the linear relation being the partial derivatives of k's consumption with respect to wealth and the state variables. Thus, the local covariance of asset j's return with k's change in consumption is

$$\operatorname{cov}(\tilde{r}_j, \mathrm{d}\tilde{c}^k) = \operatorname{cov}\left(\tilde{r}_j, c_W^k(\mathrm{d}\tilde{W}^k) + \sum_i c_{s_i}^k(\mathrm{d}\tilde{s}_i)\right)$$
$$= c_W^k \operatorname{cov}(\tilde{r}_j, \mathrm{d}\tilde{W}^k) + \sum_i c_{s_i}^k \operatorname{cov}(\tilde{r}_j, \mathrm{d}\tilde{s}_i), \tag{15}$$

which is what is stated by (14).

By substituting (14) into (13), it is seen that each individual will choose an optimal portfolio in such a way that the local covariance of each asset's return with changes in his optimal consumption is proportional to the asset's expected excess return,

$$V_{ac_k} = T^k(\mu_a - r). \tag{16}$$

This relation holds for each individual k and can be aggregated by summing over all individuals in (16). Using the aggregate relation, defining the aggregate consumption rate to be C, and defining a measure of aggregate risk tolerance to be $T^M = \sum_k T^k$, it follows that the expected excess returns on assets in equilibrium will be proportional to their covariances with changes in aggregate consumption,

$$\mu_a - r = (T^M)^{-1} V_{aC}. \tag{17}$$

By dividing both the random consumption change and aggregate risk tolerance by current aggregate consumption, (17) may be expressed in terms of aggregate relative risk tolerance and return covariances with changes in the logarithm of consumption (percentage rates of change of consumption),

$$\mu_a - r = (T^M/C)^{-1} V_{a, \ln C}. \tag{17'}$$

For any portfolio M with weights w^M, pre-multiplying (17′) by those weights gives

$$(\mu_M - r)/\sigma_{M,\ln C} = (T^M/C)^{-1}, \tag{18}$$

and

$$\mu_a - r = (V_{a,\ln C}/\sigma_{m,\ln C})(\mu_M - r)$$
$$= (\beta_{aC}/\beta_{MC})(\mu_M - r), \tag{19}$$

where β_{aC} and β_{MC} are the 'consumption-betas' of asset returns and of portfolio M's return. The consumption-beta for any asset j's return is defined to be

$$\beta_{jC} = \mathrm{cov}(\tilde{r}_j, \mathrm{d}\ln \tilde{C})/\mathrm{var}(\mathrm{d}\ln \tilde{C}). \tag{20}$$

If there exists a security whose return is perfectly correlated with changes in aggregate consumption over the next instant, then the risk–return relation of (19) can be written in terms of assets' betas measured relative to that security's return, β_C, and the expected excess return on this security, $\mu_C^* - r$,[8]

$$\mu_a - r = \beta_C(\mu_C^* - r). \tag{21}$$

Portfolio M may be any measure of the market portfolio or any other portfolio. Eq. (19) states that the ratio of expected excess returns on any two assets or portfolios in equilibrium will be equal to the ratio of their betas measured relative to aggregate consumption. Thus, the relevant risk of a security's return may be summarized by a single beta with respect to consumption – a considerable simplification over the Merton multi-beta derivation, at no loss of generality in assumptions.

The intertemporal asset pricing relation of (19) or (21) holds at each instant in time, but does not necessarily hold for returns and betas that are measured over finite periods of time. Breeden and Litzenberger (1978) have shown that assumptions of identical constant relative risk aversion utility functions for individuals and lognormally distributed consumption are sufficient to derive (19) for returns and consumption-betas measured over finite time periods.

There are two ways to understand the economic intuition of this result:

---

[8]In general, even if there does not exist a portfolio whose return is perfectly correlated with aggregate consumption, the consumption-betas in (19), (20), and (21) may be equivalently derived as the betas measured relative to the returns on the asset portfolio that has the most highly correlated returns with changes in aggregate consumption. The proof is a univariate version of footnote 7, working from (17) and the fact that the most correlated portfolio has weights proportional to $V_{aa}^{-1} V_{aC}$.

the first focuses upon the marginal rates of substitution between consumption today and consumption in the future, whereas the second interpretation focuses upon the level of wealth and the productivity of investments at future dates and states. Both explanations are briefly presented here. Although capital market completeness was not necessary for the ICAPM of (19), the first explanation is cast in the simplified framework of complete markets.[9]

Any asset may be described for valuation purposes by its total payoff, price and dividend, in the various possible states of the world in the next instant (a period in discrete time). The value in equilibrium of a \$1 payoff in a particular state of the world at a future date is equal to the state's probability multiplied by the ratio of the marginal utility of consumption at the future state to the marginal utility of consumption in the current period. That is,

$$\lambda_{t_1 s_1} = \pi_{t_1 s_1} (U_c^k(c_{t_1 s_1}^k, t_1)/U_c^k(c_t^k, t)) \quad \text{for all } k, \tag{22}$$

where $\lambda_{t_1 s_1}$ is k's shadow price at time t of \$1 received at time t_1 if state s_1 occurs, $\pi_{t_1 s_1}$ is the probability of that state, $c_{t_1 s_1}^k$ is k's optimal consumption if that state occurs, and c_t^k is k's current consumption. The value of any asset having a dividend, $d_{t+1,s}$, and price, $P_{t+1,s}$, at time $t+1$ in different states of the world is

$$P_t = \sum_s (d_{t+1,s} + P_{t+1,s})\lambda_{t+1,s}, \tag{23}$$

which must be the same for all individuals behaving optimally. Thus, the price per unit of probability for these elementary state-contingent claims varies among states only as planned consumption varies among states. The relation is inverse between planned consumption and the price/probability ratio for the state, due to the diminishing marginal utility of consumption. Therefore, holding the expected payoff on an asset constant, the value of the asset will be negatively related to its covariance with the individual's consumption. As seen from (22), for each date in this economy, if the capital markets are Pareto-optimal, the larger $\lambda_{t_1 s_1}/\pi_{t_1 s_1}$ is, the smaller each individual's consumption is in state s_1.[10] Since each individual's planned consumption in various states is positively and monotonically related to aggregate planned consumption, it can also be said that, holding the

---

[9]Theorem 3 of section 6 characterizes the relation of individuals' optimal consumption rates to the aggregate consumption rate for the general case of incomplete capital markets. Following that theorem, additional discussion of the pricing results of (19) and (21) is presented.

[10]For a detailed analysis of optimal consumption allocations in a multi-period state preference framework, see Breeden and Litzenberger (1978).

expected payoff on an asset constant, the value of the asset will be negatively related to its covariance with aggregate consumption. This implies relatively large (small) equilibrium expected returns on assets with relatively large (small) covariances with aggregate consumption, as is indicated by (19).

The key to this analysis is the relation between low levels of aggregate consumption and highly-valued state payoffs via the relation between value and marginal rates of substitution of consumption. The reason that payoff covariances with more distant levels of aggregate consumption (or their present value, aggregate wealth) do not appear explicitly in the pricing equation is that they are already reflected in the levels of equilibrium asset prices that will occur in alternative states at the next instant. That is, the asset's value in the next period appropriately reflects the covariances of its more distant payoffs with more distant levels of aggregate consumption.

The alternative, equivalent explanation is presented somewhat less rigorously, but may be more intuitive in light of the development of the finance literature. Holding expected payoffs constant between two assets, one asset's payoff probability distribution is preferred to the other's, if it tends to pay more highly in states where another dollar to invest gives large benefits (high marginal utility) and tends to pay relatively less in states where another dollar invested gives small benefits (low marginal utility). Whether an additional dollar invested is more or less beneficial depends upon: (1) the wealth of the economy in that state, via the diminishing marginal utility of wealth (future consumption), and (2) the physical productivity of investments in the state, that is, the marginal rate of transformation of goods today into goods in the future. The diminishing marginal utility of wealth was the driving force for the single-period CAPM and its portfolio diversification theorem. In the intertemporal model, as Merton (1973) has shown, changing investment opportunities create what he terms 'hedging demands' for assets, with their concomitant implications for equilibrium expected returns on assets.

An asset's covariance with aggregate consumption is all that is necessary for asset pricing, because aggregate consumption is perfectly negatively correlated with the marginal utility of an additional dollar of wealth invested through the optimality condition: $U_c(c,t)=J_W(W,s,t)$. Holding investment opportunities constant, if wealth is relatively high in a state, then the value per dollar of payoffs in that state is low. Optimal consumption is relatively high in that state. Holding wealth constant, if investment opportunities are relatively good in a state, then the present value of a dollar payoff in that state is high, as it can be invested quite profitably. In this case, optimal consumption is relatively low for individuals. *Always*, when the value of an additional dollar payoff in a state is high, consumption is low in that state, and when the value of additional investment is low, optimal consumption is high. This is *not* always true for wealth, when investment opportunities are uncertain. It is quite possible that there are states of the world where wealth is high and, yet, the marginal utility of a dollar is high due to the excellent investment opportunities in the state. Similarly, it is quite possible that there are states where wealth is low and, yet, the marginal utility of a dollar is low due to poor investment opportunities. Given preferences, wealth is not a sufficient statistic for the marginal utility of a dollar – consumption is.[11] For optimum consumption and portfolio choices, an individual's marginal utility of wealth or consumption is a monotonically decreasing function of consumption. For this reason, holding the expected payoff on an asset constant, its present value is a decreasing function of its covariance with aggregate consumption. Consequently, the higher that an asset's beta with respect to consumption is, the higher its equilibrium expected rate of return.

Note that this analysis is consistent with the derivations of the market-oriented CAPM by Sharpe (1964) and Lintner (1965) in a single-period context, and by Merton (1973) and Long (1974) in an intertemporal model. In the single-period model, all wealth is consumed at the end of the period, so investment opportunities are irrelevant. In Merton's model, investment opportunities are required to be constant for the derivation of the single-beta CAPM; thus, wealth is a sufficient statistic for marginal utility in that model. Merton and Long's multi-beta pricing models are derived with stochastic investment opportunities, as in this paper; the foregoing analysis demonstrates that wealth is not a sufficient statistic for marginal utility in their models.

4. An example

A simple example more graphically illustrates the main point. Consider a 3-date economy with many identical individuals and a single good called wheat. The current stock of wheat is the entire wealth of the economy. At each date, the amount of wheat to be consumed and the (residual) amount to be invested must be determined; wheat invested produces more wheat that will be available for future consumption. Assume that the optimal consumption/investment decision has already been made for date 1 and that the amount of wheat available for consumption and investment at date 2 will either be 200 bushels/person or 231 bushels/person, depending upon the state of the world. Furthermore, assume that the physical productivity of wheat invested at date 2 for consumption at date 3 may either be 0% or 20%, depending upon the state of the world. This 're-investment rate' will be

---

[11]The fact that consumption is a sufficient statistic for an individual's marginal utility is due to the assumption that individuals have time-additive and state-independent preferences for consumption.

known for certain at date 2, but is unknown at date 1. Constant returns to scale are assumed.

At date 2, each individual chooses consumption, c_2, and investment, $W_2 - c_2$, which results in consumption at date 3 of $c_3 = (W_2 - c_2)(1 + r_2)$, where r_2 is the physical productivity of investment at date 2. Each individual's utility function is $u(c_2, c_3) = c_2^{0.5} + c_3^{0.5}$. It may be verified that the optimal consumption at date 2 is $c_2 = W_2/(2 + r)$. At date 2 there are four possible states of the world, representing the different possible combinations of wealth and productivity, W_2 and r, respectively. Consumption and the marginal utility of another bushel of wheat at date 2 for either consumption or investment will depend upon the state of the world as shown in table 1.

It is seen from table 1 that marginal utility tends to be negatively related to wealth, but not perfectly. In particular, note that wealth in state 4 is greater than that in state 1, but marginal utility in state 4 is higher than that in state 1. This is true because the difference in physical productivity between the two states has offset the decline in marginal utility caused by the wealth differential. Since marginal utilities at time 2 are essential in the determination of prices of assets at time 1 from their state-contingent payoffs, covariances with wealth are inadequate risk measures, even in a mean-variance model.

Table 1

Consumption, wealth, and marginal utility: An example.

State	Wealth	Physical productivity	Optimal consumption	Marginal utility
1	220	0%	110	0.0476
2	220	20%	100	0.0500
3	231	0%	115.5	0.0465
4	231	20%	105	0.0488

From table 1, it is seen that consumption is perfectly negatively related to marginal utility, as it must be with state-independent preferences. As a consequence, in the locally mean-variance, continuous-time model, covariance with consumption is the relevant risk measure for the pricing of assets.

5. Properties of individuals' optimal consumption functions

In the single-period portfolio theory of Markowitz (1952), Sharpe (1964), Lintner (1965) and Mossin (1966), two important results were obtained: (1) all individuals hold the same risky asset portfolio or, alternatively stated, all individuals' rates of return on wealth are perfectly positively correlated, and (2) each individual's optimal portfolio beta or portfolio standard deviation is proportional to his Pratt (1964) – Arrow (1965) measure of relative risk tolerance. Clearly, from the portfolio theory of section 2, neither of these results holds in the intertemporal choice model with stochastic investment opportunities. This section presents two analogous results that do obtain in the intertemporal model, if the capital markets permit an unconstrained Pareto-optimal allocation: (1) at any instant, the changes in all individuals' optimal consumption rates are perfectly positively correlated, and (2) at each instant, every individual's instantaneous standard deviation of changes in his consumption rate is proportional to his Pratt–Arrow measure of relative risk tolerance.[12]

The first result, which was discussed in section 3, is stated more precisely by the following theorem:

Theorem 2. Optimal Consumption Paths. Given the continuous time econ omic model and the assumption that the capital markets permit an unconstrained Pareto-optimal allocation of consumption, at every instant in time, the change in each individual's optimal consumption rate is perfectly positively correlated with the change in every other individual's optimal consumption rate and with the change in the aggregate consumption rate for the economy.

Proof. The assumption of Pareto-optimal capital markets implies that the state-contingent allocation of consumption is the same as when there exists, at each instant in time, the market portfolio, a riskless asset, and a set of portfolios whose returns are perfectly correlated with the various state variables that affect individuals' optimal consumption rates, $c^k(W^k, s, t)$.[13] As shown in section 2, individuals would need only to trade in those assets to achieve their optimal portfolios. Letting μ and V represent the $(S+1) \times 1$ drift vector and the $(S+1) \times (S+1)$ incremental covariance matrix for the market portfolio and those S portfolios' rates of return, respectively, it is shown in appendix 2 that the instantaneous covariance between individual k's changes in consumption and individual j's is

$$\text{cov}(c^k, c^j) = T^k T^j (\mu - r)' \, V^{-1} (\mu - r). \tag{24}$$

From (24) letting $\gamma = (\mu - r)' V^{-1} (\mu - r)$, the correlation between k's and j's

---

[12]The relative risk tolerance referred to is calculated from the individual's (direct) utility function for consumption; it is not necessarily equal to the individual's risk tolerance measured by his (indirect) utility function for wealth. The 'direct' measure does not depend upon the state of the world, given the individual's consumption, whereas the 'indirect' measure in general does depend upon the state vector, given wealth.

[13]For a proof, see Breeden (1977, ch. 5).

changes in consumption is (where 'std' represents an instantaneous standard deviation)

$$\text{corr}(c^k, c^j) = \frac{\text{cov}(c^k, c^j)}{\text{std}(c^k)\,\text{std}(c^j)} = \frac{T^k T^j \gamma}{\sqrt{(T^k)^2 \gamma}\sqrt{(T^j)^2 \gamma}} = 1. \tag{25}$$

Similarly, by aggregating in (24) each individual's correlation of consumption with the aggregate is seen to be unity.   Q.E.D.

Theorem 2 could have been anticipated by noting that Breeden and Litzenberger (1978) proved that an individual's optimal consumption at any date in the multiperiod economy may be expressed as a function of only aggregate consumption at that date. They utilized an assumption of partial homogeneity in beliefs and they assumed that individuals' preferences for consumption were time-additive and state-independent, as is assumed in section 2, eq. (6). With homogeneous beliefs as assumed here, the functional relationship between each individual's consumption rate and the aggregate consumption rate is strictly monotonic and increasing. Given their results, Ito's Lemma provides Theorem 2 in the continuous-time economy, since by Ito's Lemma any random variable that follows an Ito process is (locally) perfectly positively correlated with any positive, strictly monotonic function of it.

To see that risk tolerance (or, inversely, risk aversion) is reflected proportionally in each individual's standard deviation of changes in his optimal consumption path, note that from (24): $\text{std}(c^k) = T^k \sqrt{\gamma}$ and that $\text{std}(c^k)/\text{std}(C) = T^k/T^M$. Similarly, in terms of standard deviations of growth *rates*, $\text{std}(\ln c^k)/\text{std}(\ln C) = T^{*k}/T^{*M}$, where $T^{*k} = T^k/c^k$ is k's relative risk tolerance and $T^{*M} = T^M/C$ is an aggregate measure of relative risk tolerance. The implication is intuitive: those who are very risk averse will choose consumption paths with low variability, compared to those chosen by individuals who are less risk averse. Of course, in the limiting case of an individual with infinite risk aversion, the individual would choose complete insurance against any fluctuation in his consumption path. His wealth would be variable in such a way as to offset any impact of changing investment opportunities on his optimal consumption. In general, those who are more or less risk averse than average can be identified by empirically observing the standard deviations of individuals' consumption rates. They cannot be identified merely from their asset portfolios, as was implied by single-period portfolio theory.

In general capital markets, it may or may not be possible to achieve an unconstrained Pareto-optimal allocation of consumption with portfolios of available securities. For example, this situation may occur if there does not exist a portfolio of assets with a return that perfectly 'hedges' (in Merton's terminology) against changes in one of the state variables. When an unconstrained Pareto-optimal allocation is not possible, one assumption of Theorem 2 is violated and changes in individuals' optimal consumption rates are not necessarily perfectly correlated with each other or with changes in the aggregate consumption rate. In a general capital market, the following theorem holds:

Theorem 3. Consumption Allocations in General Capital Markets. Given a continuous-time economic model with general capital markets, at every instant in time, the optimal portfolio for each individual results in changes in the individual's optimal consumption rate that have the maximum possible correlation with changes in the aggregate consumption rate.

Proof. Individual k's optimal portfolio given in (12) maximizes the covariance of k's changes in consumption with changes in aggregate consumption for a given variance of k's changes in consumption. That is: $w^k W^k$ solves

$$\max_{w} c_W^k w' V_{aC} + \iota_s' V_{sC}$$

$$+ \lambda \left[(c_W^k w' c_s^{k'}) \begin{pmatrix} V_{aa} & V_{as} \\ V_{sa} & V_{ss} \end{pmatrix} \begin{pmatrix} c_W^k w \\ c_s^k \end{pmatrix} - \text{var}(dc^k) \right].$$

By maximizing k's covariance of consumption changes with changes in aggregate consumption, for given variances of k's consumption changes and aggregate consumption changes, the correlation coefficient between the individual's consumption and aggregate consumption is maximized. Q.E.D.

This result provides an explanation for the fact that the derivation of the intertemporal CAPM does not require Pareto-optimal capital markets, i.e., the fact that perfect hedges against changes in all of the state variables are not necessary for the derivation. Since each individual's optimal portfolio maximizes the correlation of his consumption with aggregate consumption, fluctuations in each individual's consumption and marginal utility that are uncorrelated with aggregate consumption are also uncorrelated with the returns on all assets. Thus, an asset's risk premium, which is determined by the covariance of its return with individuals' marginal utilities of consumption, is unaffected by the fluctuations in individuals' consumption rates that are unrelated to aggregate consumption, because those fluctuations are also unrelated to all asset returns. The reason that asset betas with respect to only aggregate consumption are in the intertemporal CAPM is that the assets available have betas equal to zero when measured relative to the components of individuals' consumption risks that are uncorrelated with aggregate consumption.

6. Asset pricing with no riskless asset

This section derives for an economy with no riskless asset a 'zero-beta' intertemporal CAPM that corresponds to the zero-beta CAPM derived by Lintner (1969), Black (1972) and Vasicek (1971) in a single-period model. The differences between the models are: (1) an asset's beta is measured relative to aggregate consumption, rather than relative to aggregate wealth, and (2) the zero-beta portfolio, whose expected return replaces that of the riskless return in (19), is a portfolio with returns uncorrelated with aggregate consumption, rather than a portfolio with returns uncorrelated with the market portfolio's return.

The only formal modification to the individual's optimization problem [eqs. (6)–(8), section 2] is that the expected rate of return on invested wealth, which was $w'\mu_a + (1 - 1'w)r$, is now simply a weighted average of risky asset returns, $w'\mu_a$. The wealth constraint is now that the risky asset portfolio weights sum to unity, which may be enforced by the use of a Lagrange multiplier in (8). The first-order condition that the marginal utility of consumption equals the marginal utility of wealth is unchanged; however, the optimal risky asset portfolio of (10) now becomes

$$w^k W^k = (-J^k_w/J^k_{WW}) \mathbf{V}_{aa}^{-1} \mu_a$$

$$+ (\lambda^k/W^k J^k_{WW}) \mathbf{V}_{aa}^{-1} \mathbf{1} - \mathbf{V}_{aa}^{-1} \mathbf{V}_{as} (J^k_{sW}/J^k_{WW}), \tag{10'}$$

where λ^k is individual k's Lagrange multiplier for his budget constraint.

By an extension of the proof in appendix 1 for the $(S+2)$-fund theorem of section 2, it is seen that an $(S+2)$-fund theorem holds in this economy with no riskless asset. The funds may be chosen to be (1) the S portfolios having the highest correlations, respectively, with the S state variables summarizing investment opportunities, (2) the market portfolio, and (3) the zero consumption-beta portfolio of the risky assets that has minimum variance.

Substituting partial derivatives of individual k's direct utility function for consumption and k's optimal consumption function for the partials of the indirect utility function in (10'), and proceeding as in eqs. (12)–(16) in section 3, gives

$$V_{ac_k} = T^k \mu_a + (\lambda^k \mathbf{1}/W^k U^k_{cc}). \tag{16'}$$

Aggregating (16') over all individuals gives

$$V_{aC} = T^M \mu_a + v\mathbf{1}, \tag{17''}$$

where

$$v = \sum_k \lambda^k / W^k U_{cc}^k.$$

For any portfolio z with returns that are uncorrelated with aggregate consumption, from (17'') above,

$$v = -T^M \mu_z. \tag{17'''}$$

Substituting this into (17'') gives

$$(\mu_M - \mu_z)/\sigma_{MC} = (T^M)^{-1}, \tag{18'}$$

and

$$\mu_a - \mu_z \mathbf{1} = (\beta_{aC}/\beta_{MC})(\mu_M - \mu_z). \tag{19'}$$

Thus, if there is no riskless asset in the single-good continuous-time model, then the equilibrium expected return on an asset is equal to the expected return on a portfolio with returns uncorrelated with aggregate consumption plus a risk premium proportional to the asset's consumption-beta. Both the mutual fund theorem of section 2 and the intertemporal CAPM of section 3 hold with no riskless asset when 'the riskless asset' in those results is replaced by 'the zero consumption-beta portfolio that has minimum variance'.[14]

The next section examines asset pricing in the multi-good continuous-time model, when a nominally riskless asset is assumed to exist.

7. Asset pricing with many consumption-goods

The derivations of the consumption, portfolio and pricing results thus far have been in the context of a rather general *single-good* economy. This section discusses some modifications of the results that would occur in a multi-good economy. The major focus will be on conditions that permit the derivation of a 'single-beta' intertemporal capital asset pricing model with stochastic investment *and* consumption opportunities (similar to that of section 3, which had only stochastic investment opportunities).

[14]The choice of a zero-beta, minimum-variance portfolio is intuitive, but not unique. For example, in the mutual fund theorem of section 2, the unconstrained minimum variance portfolio can also replace the riskless asset under the assumptions of this section. Also, the zero-beta intertemporal CAPM can be written in terms of the expected return on any zero consumption-beta portfolio.

Let there be Q goods in the economy and let $q^k(t)$ be individual k's $Q \times 1$ vector of the rates at which quantities are consumed of the various goods at time t. Each individual is assumed to maximize the expected utility of a time-additive utility function as in (6), but with $U^k(c^k, t)$ being replaced by $u^k(q^k, t)$. The vector of consumption-goods prices is P_c, and individual k's rate of nominal expenditures is $c^k = P_c'q^k$. Individual k's indirect utility function for consumption expenditures is now defined as

$$U^k(c^k, P_c', t) = \max_{\{P_c'q^k = c^k\}} u^k(q^k, t). \tag{26}$$

The analysis of section 2 is virtually unchanged in the multi-good model; first-order conditions (9) and (10) still hold when the state vector s is assumed to include as a subset P_c and its probability distribution. The $(S+2)$-fund theorem obtains with instantaneous-maturity commodity futures contracts being perfect hedges for changes in consumption-goods prices. Similarly, the multi-beta asset-pricing model given by (11) holds in this model, with expected excess returns on those futures contracts (if they exist) being a subset of $(\mu_s^* - r)$.[15]

Although, in the multi-good case, the form of the demand equations for assets is unchanged from section 2's eq. (10), section 3's translation of those demands in terms of the individual's optimal consumption function is somewhat different in the multi-good case. The difference arises from the fact that the utility of a given level of consumption expenditure now depends upon relative prices, P_c. Mathematically, in section 2, $U_c^k(c^k, t) = J_W^k(W^k, s, t)$ implied that $U_{cc}^k c_s^k = J_{Ws}^k$, but in the multi-good case we have: $U_c^k(c^k, P_c(s), t) = J_W^k(W^k, s, t)$ implies that $U_{cc}^k c_P^k + U_{cP}^k = J_{WP}^k$ by the implicit function theorem. Thus, individual k's asset demand functions, written in terms of his optimal consumption function, are [from (10) and above, assuming the first Q state variables are the logarithms of consumption-goods prices]

$$w^k W^k = (T^k/c_W^k)\mathbf{V}_{aa}^{-1}(\boldsymbol{\mu}_a - r) - \mathbf{V}_{aa}^{-1}\mathbf{V}_{as}(c_s^k/c_W^k)$$

$$- \mathbf{V}_{aa}^{-1}\mathbf{V}_{as}\begin{pmatrix} U_{\ln P, c}^k/U_{cc}^k c_W^k \\ 0 \end{pmatrix}. \tag{27}$$

The last term in (27) represents long or short components of asset demands for the portfolios that are most highly correlated with the prices of consumption-goods; this term arises from the dependence of the individual's

---

[15]Since futures contracts require no investment and, therefore, rates of return are undefined, the expected excess return on a contract in this context should be viewed as the expected rate of return to a portfolio of the futures contract and an instantaneously riskless bond that has face value equal to the price of the futures contract.

indirect marginal utility for nominal expenditure on consumption-goods prices.

Let $\boldsymbol{\alpha}^k$ be the $Q \times 1$ vector of individual k's budget shares, i.e., $\alpha_j^k = P_j q_j^k / c^k$, and let $\boldsymbol{m}^k$ be individual k's vector of incremental ('marginal') budget shares, i.e., $m_j^k = P_j(\partial q_j^k / \partial c^k)$. The vector $\boldsymbol{m}^k$ is the set of fractions of an additional dollar of total expenditure that would be spent on the various consumption-goods. The new term in (27) due to the multi-good model may be expressed in terms of the average and marginal vectors of budget shares as shown in appendix 3, giving asset demands

$$w^k W^k = (T^k/c_W^k)\mathbf{V}_{aa}^{-1}(\boldsymbol{\mu}_a - \boldsymbol{r}) - \mathbf{V}_{aa}^{-1}\mathbf{V}_{as}(c_s^k/c_W^k)$$

$$+ \mathbf{V}_{aa}^{-1}\mathbf{V}_{as}\begin{pmatrix} c^k\boldsymbol{\alpha}^k/c_W^k - (T^k/c_W^k)\boldsymbol{m}^k \\ 0 \end{pmatrix}. \tag{28}$$

Multiplying (28) by $(\mathbf{V}_{aa}c_W^k)$ and rearranging terms gives

$$T^k\left[\boldsymbol{\mu}_a - \boldsymbol{r} - \mathbf{V}_{as}\begin{pmatrix} \boldsymbol{m}^k \\ 0 \end{pmatrix}\right] = \mathbf{V}_{aW_k}c_W^k + \mathbf{V}_{as}c_s^k - \mathbf{V}_{as}\begin{pmatrix} \boldsymbol{\alpha}^k c^k \\ 0 \end{pmatrix}$$

$$= \mathbf{V}_{ac_k} - \mathbf{V}_{as}\begin{pmatrix} \boldsymbol{\alpha}^k c^k \\ 0 \end{pmatrix}, \tag{29}$$

where the second line recognizes that $c^k = c^k(W^k, s, t)$ and Ito's Lemma implies that $\mathbf{V}_{aW_k}c_W^k + \mathbf{V}_{as}c_s^k = \mathbf{V}_{ac_k}$.

Aggregating the optimality condition in (29) for all individuals gives a similar relation in terms of aggregate consumption and aggregate vectors of average budget shares and marginal budget shares,

$$\boldsymbol{\mu}_a - \boldsymbol{r} - \mathbf{V}_{as}\begin{pmatrix} \boldsymbol{m} \\ 0 \end{pmatrix} = (T^M/C)^{-1}\left[\mathbf{V}_{a,\ln C} - \mathbf{V}_{as}\begin{pmatrix} \boldsymbol{\alpha} \\ 0 \end{pmatrix}\right], \tag{30}$$

where

$$\boldsymbol{\alpha} = \left(\sum_k \boldsymbol{\alpha}^k c^k\right)\bigg/ C \quad \text{and} \quad \boldsymbol{m} = \left(\sum_k \boldsymbol{m}^k T^k\right)\bigg/ T^M.$$

The calculation of the economy-wide vector of average budget shares, $\boldsymbol{\alpha}$, requires only data on the aggregate dollars spent on the various goods; no other preference information is required. These shares are the fractions of aggregate expenditure that are spent on the various consumption-goods. These budget shares are, in principal, the weights used in the computation of the price deflator for consumption expenditures in the National Income and Product Accounts.[16]

---

[16]See the *Survey of Current Business* of the U.S. Department of Commerce.

The vector of aggregate marginal budget shares, m, is the set of fractions of an additional dollar of aggregate expenditure (allocated optimally among individuals) that would be spent on the various consumption goods, holding prices constant. The reason that this statement can be made, without explicit reference to the risk tolerances of individuals, is that the optimal allocation among individuals of an individual dollar of aggregate nominal expenditure is according to individuals' risk tolerances relative to aggregate risk tolerance, (T^k/T^M). Thus, the aggregate marginal budget shares for goods may be written as

$$m_j = \sum_k (\partial c^k/\partial C) P_j (\partial q_j^k/\partial c^k) = P_j (\partial q_j/\partial C). \tag{31}$$

Note that the aggregate marginal budget share for each good can be computed as the product of (1) the aggregate average budget share for the good and (2) the aggregate expenditure elasticity of demand for the good, $(\partial \ln q_j)/(\partial \ln C)$.

It is useful for the subsequent analysis to define the local percentage changes in two price indices – one based upon average budget shares for the economy and one based upon the marginal budget shares for the economy,[17]

$$dI/I \equiv \sum_j \alpha_j (dP_j/P_j), \qquad dI_m/I_m \equiv \sum_j m_j (dP_j/P_j). \tag{32}$$

The two terms in eq. (30) that involve m and α can be rewritten in terms of these price indices, giving

$$\mu_a - r - \dot{V}_{aI_m} = (T^M/C)^{-1} [V_{a, \ln C} - V_{aI}], \tag{33}$$

where V_{aI_m} and V_{aI} are the vectors of the covariances of asset returns with the local percentage changes in the price indices.

Since it can be shown that a feasible (but not necessarily optimal) allocation exists such that everyone in the economy has a consumption

---

[17]A globally valid price index that is invariant to the level of nominal expenditure exists for an individual if and only if his indifference curves are 'homothetic'. This implies unitary demand elasticities for all goods. When they are not unitary, the individual's budget shares depend upon his level of nominal expenditure, making the weights in his price index vary with the level of expenditure. A survey of price index results is provided by Samuelson and Swamy (1974). Identical and homothetic consumption preferences for all individuals are typically assumed to justify the use of aggregate budget shares to compute a price index for the economy. The price indices used in this paper do not require that individuals be identical, nor that they have homothetic preferences. The continuity of the continuous-time framework and the weaker requirement that the price indices be locally (not globally) valid permits the greater generality of consumption preferences of this paper. For a paper that utilizes preference restrictions that give a globally valid price index, see Grauer and Litzenberger (1979).

allocation that is preferable to his current allocation if and only if the percentage change in aggregate nominal expenditure exceeds the percentage change in the average budget share price index, I, aggregate *real* consumption is defined as $C^* = C/I$.[18] Given this definition, note that the vector of covariances of real asset returns with aggregate real consumption is

$$V_{a^*C^*} = V_{a,\ln C} - \dot{V}_{aI} - \dot{V}_{IC^*}1, \tag{34}$$

where $\dot{V}_{IC^*}$ is the covariance of the aggregate average-weighted price index with aggregate real consumption. Defining an asset's 'real consumption-beta', β_j^*, as the local covariance of its real return with percentage changes in aggregate real consumption, divided by the variance rate of changes in aggregate real consumption, then (33) can be re-written in terms of assets' real consumption-betas,

$$\mu_a - r - \dot{V}_{aI_m} = (T^M/C\sigma_{C^*}^2)^{-1}[\beta_a^* - \beta_r^*1], \tag{35}$$

where β_r^* is the real consumption-beta of the nominally riskless asset.

The left-hand side of (35) can be interpreted as the differences of the expected real returns on assets from the expected real return on the nominally riskless asset, where these expected real returns are evaluated relative to the price index with aggregate marginal budget shares. To see this, first note that the instantaneous expected percentage rate of change of an asset's real price, P_a/I, is given by Ito's Lemma as the expected nominal return on the asset, minus the expected rate of inflation measured by the index, and minus the covariance of the asset's nominal return with inflation. The covariance term is explained by the fact that an asset with high nominal payoffs when prices are low and low nominal payoffs when prices are high buys more real goods on average than an asset with positive covariance of its nominal returns with inflation, assuming that expected nominal payoffs are the same for both assets. Since the covariance of the nominal return on the nominally riskless asset with inflation is zero, the LHS of (35) is the difference between the expected real returns on assets, μ_a^*, and the expected real return on the nominally riskless asset, μ_r^*. It can be easily verified that for any three assets i, j and k,

$$(\mu_i^* - \mu_j^*)/(\beta_i^* - \beta_j^*) = (\mu_k^* - \mu_j^*)/(\beta_k^* - \beta_j^*) \quad \text{for all } i, j, k. \tag{36}$$

Letting z represent a portfolio with real returns that are uncorrelated with

---

[18]For a proof of the result stated, see Breeden (1977, ch. 3).

changes in aggregate real consumption, it is seen that a multi-good, zero-beta intertemporal CAPM obtains

$$\mu_i^* - \mu_z^* = (\beta_i^*/\beta_k^*)(\mu_k^* - \mu_z^*). \tag{37}$$

The use of the price index based upon aggregate marginal shares for calculation of expected real returns, while using the price index with aggregate average shares as weights for calculation of real consumption-betas, requires some intuitive explanation. Before proceeding with an explanation, note that there is no difference between the indices if aggregate expenditure elasticities of demand for goods are all unity. This aggregate 'homothetic' case involves strong preference assumptions and is not assumed to hold. As in the single-good economy, asset prices are determined from their payoffs and from individuals' marginal utilities of a dollar of consumption expenditure in the various states of the world. The marginal utility of a dollar to an individual depends upon: (1) the quantities of goods consumed, via diminishing marginal utilities for the consumption of goods, and (2) the quantities of goods that a dollar can buy. By the definition of the marginal budget share vector, an additional dollar is spent on goods in the proportions given by the marginal vector; thus, the price index with marginal weights evaluates the quantities of goods that another dollar purchases. As Samuelson and Swamy (1974) observed, real consumption is a quantity index. As a quantity index, the larger real consumption is, the smaller the marginal utility of goods consumed is. The role of the price index with average budget shares as weights in risk measurement arises from its use in the computation of aggregate real consumption, which is inversely related to the marginal utilities of consumption-goods.

To this point, a real riskless asset is not assumed to exist, nor are futures contracts that can create a real riskless return assumed to exist. If a real riskless asset or portfolio is assumed to exist and have a real return of r^*, then the expected return on a zero real consumption-beta portfolio in the pricing eq. (37) can be replaced by r^*,

$$\mu_i^* - r^* = (\beta_i^*/\beta_k^*)(\mu_k^* - r^*). \tag{38}$$

This is an intertemporal asset pricing model developed in a multi-good world with stochastic consumption and investment opportunities.

The results obtained here may be compared to those obtained in the explicitly multi-commodity economies of Long (1974) and Grauer and Litzenberger (1979). Long makes no restrictions on preferences for goods, but assumes joint normality of consumption-goods prices. The effect of many goods in his model is to extend the number of betas that must be calculated to find the expected excess return on any asset from the expected excess returns on futures contracts and on portfolios that hedge against investment opportunity set changes. The derivation in this paper of instantaneous expected excess returns in terms of a single beta for each asset is a contribution to the literature.

Grauer and Litzenberger work with a multi-commodity, two-period state preference model and derive asset prices with particular attention to the prices of commodity futures contracts. They make no assumptions about the probability distribution of states of the world, but they assume that the capital markets are Pareto-optimal and that each individual has 'homothetic' preferences for consumption-goods, i.e., that all income elasticities of demand are unity for all goods, for each individual. They derive an asset's risk premium from its return covariance with a single variable, the social marginal utility of wealth. This variable is a function of aggregate wealth deflated by a price index that is assumed to be the same for all individuals. The derivation in this paper of a single-beta measure of risk in a multi-commodity world is similar to theirs, but knowledge of the social marginal utility function is not needed for the beta computation of this paper. The difference between their focus upon wealth and the present focus on consumption is a product of their two-period world, which does not require an analysis of changing investment opportunities. Finally, the preference assumptions needed for the existence of a price index in a discrete-time model are not needed for the local statements of the continuous-time model.

8. Conclusion

An intertemporal capital asset pricing model has been derived in an economic environment permitting both stochastic consumption-goods prices and stochastic portfolio opportunities. The paper is an extension and generalization of Merton's (1973) continuous-time model, deriving equivalent pricing equations that are simpler in form and are potentially empirically testable.

The use of aggregate consumption in empirical tests, rather than the market portfolio that has been used, has both virtues and difficulties. Difficulties with consumption numbers that are available include: (1) instantaneous consumption rates are not measured; rather, weekly, monthly, quarterly, or annual integrals of these rates are measured,[19] (2) only the part of the measured consumption of goods that gives current utility should be included, which excludes a large fraction of current purchases of durables, and (3) the actual data that are available contain considerable measurement error, whereas the prices and numbers of shares used in the market portfolio

---

[19]With power utility functions and lognormal consumption, this is not a problem, since the pricing model holds with betas and returns measured over any interval. See Breeden and Litzenberger (1978) for a proof of this result.

C

computations are measured with very little error. The principal virtue of aggregate consumption measures, in comparison with the market proxies used, is that the consumption measures available cover a greater fraction of the true consumption variable than the fraction that the market portfolio measures cover of the true market portfolio (mainly because of the lack of coverage of human capital, real estate, and consumer durables in market measures). Note also that proposed capital expenditure projects typically have cash flows that are more significantly related to aggregate consumption, than to the market portfolio. This may make the distinction of projects with different risk levels more precise and more intuitive, thereby facilitating the use of asset pricing theory in capital budgeting.

In the continuous-time model, areas that need additional theoretical development include the role of firms and their optimal investment and capital structure decisions, and the impact of transaction costs, information costs, and diverse beliefs upon optimal consumption–investment decisions and upon the structure of asset returns.

Appendix 1: Proof of Theorem 1

By aggregating the optimal portfolio demands of all individuals given by (10) the market portfolio must be

$$w^M M = \sum_k w^k W^k = T_W^M V_{aa}^{-1}(\mu_a - r) + V_{aa}^{-1} V_{as} H_s^M, \tag{A.1}$$

where

$$T_W^k = -J_W^k/J_{WW}^k \quad \text{and} \quad H_s^k = -J_{Ws}^k/J_{WW}^k,$$

and where

$$T_W^M = \sum_k T_W^k \quad \text{and} \quad H_s^M = \sum_k H_s^k.$$

Substituting (A.1) into (10) allows the individual's portfolio demands to be written as

$$w^k W^k = (T_W^k/T_W^M) M(w^M) + V_{aa}^{-1} V_{as}(H_s^k - H_s^M T_W^k/T_W^M). \tag{A.2}$$

This proves that all individuals may obtain their optimal portfolio positions by trading in $(S+2)$ 'mutual funds', with one of them being the market portfolio, one being the riskless asset, and S of them being given by $V_{aa}^{-1}V_{as}$.

Next, note that column j of $V_{aa}^{-1}V_{as}$, i.e., $V_{aa}^{-1}V_{as_j}$, is the solution to the following problem (up to a factor of proportionality):

$$\frac{1}{2\lambda} V_{aa}^{-1} V_{as_j} \quad \text{solves} \quad \max_{w_j} \{w_j' V_{as_j} + \lambda(\sigma^2 - w_j' V_{aa} w_j)\}. \tag{A.3}$$

In (A.3), by maximizing covariance of the portfolio with s_j for a given level of variance, we effectively find the portfolio of assets that maximizes the correlation coefficient of its returns with changes in state variable j. Given this, the theorem is proven from (A.2) and the fact that wealth not in risky assets is placed in the nominally riskless asset. Q.E.D.

Appendix 2

Since $c^k = c^k(W^k, s, t)$ and $c^j = c^j(W^j, s, t)$, Ito's Lemma implies that the covariance of c^k and c^j is

$$\text{cov}(c^k, c^j) = (c_W^k \; 0 \; c_s^{k'}) \begin{pmatrix} V_{W_k W_k} & V_{W_k W_j} & V_{W_k s} \\ V_{W_j W_k} & V_{W_j W_j} & V_{W_j s} \\ V_{s W_k} & V_{s W_j} & V_{ss} \end{pmatrix} \begin{pmatrix} 0 \\ c_W^j \\ c_s^j \end{pmatrix}, \tag{A.4}$$

$$= c_s^{k'} V_{sW_j} c_W^j + c_s^{k'} V_{ss} c_s^j + c_W^k V_{W_k s} c_s^j + c_W^k V_{W_k W_j} c_W^j,$$

where subscripted V's represent covariance matrices with appropriate dimensions and subscripted c's represent partial derivatives or gradients of those consumption functions.

First, the assumption is that

$$\mathbf{V}_{aa} = \begin{pmatrix} V_{MM} & V_{Ms} \\ V_{sM} & V_{ss} \end{pmatrix} \equiv \mathbf{V}, \tag{A.5}$$

and

$$\mu_a - r = \begin{pmatrix} \mu_M - r \\ \mu_s^* - r \end{pmatrix} \equiv \mu - r. \tag{A.6}$$

Define an $S \times (S+1)$ matrix $\mathbf{L}$ to be

$$\mathbf{L} = (\mathbf{0} \quad \mathbf{I}), \tag{A.7}$$

where $\mathbf{0}$ is an $S \times 1$ vector of zeros and $\mathbf{I}$ is an $S \times S$ identity matrix. Note that

$$\mathbf{L}(\mu - r) = \mu_s^* - r, \tag{A.8}$$

and

$$\mathbf{L}\mathbf{V} = \mathbf{V}_{s, Ms} \equiv (V_{sM} \quad V_{ss}). \tag{A.9}$$

From individuals' optimal asset demands, (12), it is seen that

$$c_W^k w^k W^k = \mathbf{V}^{-1}[T^k(\mu - r) - \mathbf{VL}'c_s^k],$$
(A.10)

which implies that

$$c_W^k V_{sW_k} = \mathbf{LV}[c_W^k w^k W^k]$$
$$= T^k \mathbf{L}(\mu - r) - \mathbf{LVL}'c_s^k.$$
(A.11)

Next, evaluate the last term of (A.4),

$$c_W^k V_{W_k W_j} c_W^j = c_W^k W^k w^{k'} \mathbf{V} w^j W^j c_W^j$$
$$= [T^k(\mu - r)' - c_s^{k'} \mathbf{LV}]\mathbf{V}^{-1}[T^j(\mu - r) - \mathbf{VL}'c_s^j]$$
$$= T^k T^j (\mu - r)' \mathbf{V}^{-1}(\mu - r) - T^k(\mu - r)' \mathbf{L}'c_s^j$$
$$- T^j c_s^{k'} \mathbf{L}(\mu - r) + c_s^{k'} \mathbf{LVL}'c_s^j.$$
(A.12)

Substituting the results of (A.11) and (A.12) into (A.4) gives the covariance of changes in individual k's optimal consumption rate with changes in j's optimal consumption rate,

$$\text{cov}(c^k, c^j) = c_s^{k'}[T^j \mathbf{L}(\mu - r) - \mathbf{LVL}'c_s^j] + c_s^{k'} \mathbf{LVL}'c_s^j$$
$$+ [T^k(\mu - r)' \mathbf{L}' - c_s^{k'} \mathbf{LVL}']c_s^j$$
$$+ T^k T^j \gamma - T^k(\mu - r)' \mathbf{L}'c_s^j$$
$$- T^j c_s^{k'} \mathbf{L}(\mu - r) + c_s^{k'} \mathbf{LVL}'c_s^j$$
$$= T^k T^j \gamma,$$
(A.13)

where $\gamma = (\mu - r)' V^{-1}(\mu - r)$. Eq. (A.13) is eq. (24) of the text, as was to be shown.

Appendix 3

The definition of the consumer's indirect utility function is

$$U(c, t, \mathbf{P}_c) = \max_{P_c q = c} u(q, t) = \max_q \{u(q, t) + \lambda(c - \mathbf{P}_c q)\}$$
(A.14)

and the first order conditions for a maximum imply that

$$u_q = \lambda \mathbf{P}_c, \qquad U_p = -\lambda q,$$
(A.15)

and the shadow price $\lambda = U_c$.

By differentiating the optimality conditions in (A.15),

$$-U_{\ln P_j, c}/U_{cc} = (U_c/U_{cc})P_j(\partial q_j/\partial c) + P_j q_j = -Tm_j + c\alpha_j. \qquad (A.16)$$

Substitute (A.16) into (21), and (22) is obtained.

References

Arnold, L., 1974, Stochastic differential equations: Theory and applications (Wiley, New York).

Arrow, K.J., 1964, The role of securities in the optimal allocation of risk-bearing, Review of Economic Studies, 91–96.

Arrow, K.J., 1965, The theory of risk aversion, in: Aspects of the theory of risk-bearing (Helsinki).

Black, F., 1972, Capital market equilibrium with restricted borrowing, Journal of Business 45, no. 3, July.

Breeden, D.T., 1977, Changing consumption and investment opportunities and the valuation of securities, Ph.D. dissertation (Stanford University, Stanford, CA).

Breeden, D.T. and R.II. Litzenberger, 1978, Prices of state-contingent claims implicit in option prices, Journal of Business, Oct.

Cox, J.C., J.E. Ingersoll and S.A. Ross, 1977, A theory of the term structure of interest rates, Econometrica, forthcoming.

Cox, J.C. and S.A. Ross, 1977, Some models of capital asset pricing with rational anticipations, Mimeo., Sept.

Debreu, G., 1959, The theory of value (Wiley, New York).

Fama, E.F., 1970, Multiperiod consumption–investment decisions, American Economic Review, March, 163–174.

Garman, M., 1976, A general theory of asset valuation under diffusion state processes, Working paper no. 50 (Graduate School of Business, University of California, Berkeley, CA).

Gihman, I.I. and A.V. Skorohod, 1972, Stochastic differential equations (Springer-Verlag, New York).

Grauer, F.L.A. and R.H. Litzenberger, 1979, The pricing of commodity futures contracts, nominal bonds and other risky assets under commodity price uncertainty, Journal of Finance, March, 69–84.

Hakansson, N.H., 1970, Optimal investment and consumption strategies under risk for a class of utility functions, Econometrica, 587–607.

Hakansson, N.H., 1977, Efficient paths toward efficient capital markets in large and small countries, in: H. Levy and M. Sarnat, eds., Financial decision making under uncertainty (Academic Press, New York).

Hakansson, N.H., 1978, Welfare aspects of options and supershares, Journal of Finance, June, 759–776.

Harrison, J.M. and D.M. Kreps, 1978, Martingales and the valuation of redundant assets, Research paper no. 444, May (Stanford University, Stanford, CA).

Jensen, M.C., 1972, Capital markets: Theory and evidence, Bell Journal of Economics and Management Science, Autumn, 357–398.

Kushner, H.J., 1967, Stochastic stability and control (Academic Press, New York).

Lintner, J., 1965, Valuation of risk assets and the selection of risky investments in stock portfolios and capital budgets, Review of Economics and Statistics, 13–37.

Lintner, John, 1969, Aggregation of investors' diverse judgements and preferences in purely competitive security markets, Journal of Financial and Quantitative Analysis, Dec.

Long, J.B., 1974, Stock prices, inflation, and the term structure of interest rates, Journal of Financial Economics, 131–170.

Lucas, R.E., 1978, Asset prices in an exchange economy, Econometrica 46, Nov., 1429–1445.

Markowitz, H., 1952, Portfolio selection, Journal of Finance, March.

McKean, H.P., 1969, Stochastic integrals (Academic Press, New York).

Merton, R.C., 1971, Optimum consumption and portfolio rules in a continuous-time model, Journal of Economic Theory, 373–413.

Merton, R.C., 1973, An intertemporal capital asset pricing model, Econometrica 41, 867–887.

Merton, R.C., 1978, On the mathematics and economic assumptions of continuous-time models, M.I.T. Working paper no. 981–78, March (Massachusetts Institute of Technology, Cambridge, MA).

Mossin, J., 1966, Equilibrium in a capital asset market, Econometrica, Oct.

Mossin, J., 1973, Theory of financial markets (Prentice–Hall, Englewood Cliffs, NJ).

Muth, J.F., 1961, Rational expectations and the theory of price movements, Econometrica.

Pratt, J., 1964, Risk aversion in the small and in the large, Econometrica 32.

Pye, G., 1972, Lifetime portfolio selection with age dependent risk aversion, in: G. Szego and K. Shell, Mathematical methods in investment and finance (North-Holland, Amsterdam) 49–64.

Richard, S.F., 1975, Optimal consumption, portfolio and life insurance rules for an uncertain lived individual in a continuous time model, Journal of Financial Economics 2, 187–203.

Roll, R., 1977, A critique of the asset pricing theory's tests; Part I: On past and potential testability of the theory, Journal of Financial Economics 4, March, 129–176.

Rosenberg, B. and J.A. Ohlson, 1976, The stationary distribution of returns and portfolio separation in capital markets: A fundamental contradiction, Journal of Financial and Quantitative Analysis, Sept.

Ross, S.A., 1976, The arbitrage theory of capital asset pricing, Journal of Economic Theory 3, Dec., 343–362.

Ross, S.A., 1978, The current status of the capital asset pricing model, Journal of Finance, June, 885–901.

Rubinstein, M., 1974, An aggregation theorem for securities markets, Journal of Financial Economics 1, 225–244.

Rubinstein, M., 1976, The valuation of uncertain income streams and the pricing of options, Bell Journal of Economics and Management Science 7, no. 2, 407–425.

Samuelson, P.A. and S. Swamy, 1974, Invariant economic index numbers and canonical duality: Survey and synthesis, American Economic Review 64, Sept., 566–593.

Sharpe, W.F., 1964, Capital asset prices: A theory of market equilibrium under conditions of risk, Journal of Finance, 429–442.

Stapleton, R.C. and M.G. Subrahmanyam, 1978, A multiperiod equilibrium asset pricing model, Econometrica 46, Sept., 1077–1096.

U.S. Department of Commerce, 1966, The national income and product accounts of the United States 1929–1965 (Washington, DC).

Vasicek, Oldrich, 1971, Capital market pricing model with no riskless asset, Unpublished manuscript, March (Wells Fargo Bank).

discussion | Intertemporal Asset Pricing

Stephen A. Ross

Yale School of Management

The reprinting of Doug Breeden's (1979) watershed piece offers an appropriate occasion to reflect on the current state of affairs in the theory of intertemporal asset pricing. We have learned a great deal about the intertemporal theory of asset pricing, but, to paraphrase an old adage, it is amazing how much of it we already knew. Breeden's piece is a wonderful example of the basic point I wish to make. In large measure the modern development of the theory can be understood as resulting from the interplay of two basic themes, each of which takes on different forms.

The first theme is the search for and the development of intertemporal models that extend the fundamental intuitions of the static, single-period asset pricing models to a dynamic setting. This comes under the heading of "what we already know." The second theme is the recognition and study of forces that can only arise in the intertemporal framework and that are irrelevant to the static models. These two themes, though central, do not describe the only forces at work in this area. Intertemporal asset pricing models can also be understood in terms of the more traditional breakdown into those that are supply or technology driven and those that emphasize demand. Perhaps more interestingly, a distinction can also be made between those that rely largely on the forces of arbitrage and those that more fully articulate an equilibrium.

The focus of this brief discussion will be on the above issues and on what we have accomplished to date, but I will save some time at the end to consider what we do not know and what remains to be done. Since the bulk of the work to date has been theoretical, it should not be surprising that this discussion reflects that emphasis. It also should come as no surprise that it is in the empirical area that the most work must be done.

I. THE EARLY MODELS

Leaving aside intertemporal and deterministic growth theory, the first work on intertemporal asset pricing models began by generalizing static portfolio

I wish to acknowledge the assistance of Jon Ingersoll, Rick Antle, Philip Dybvig, Sudipto Bhattacharya, and George Constantinides. Any errors are my own responsibility, as are the opinions expressed.

models to a dynamic setting. Hakansson (1971, 1974) and Mossin (1969), in particular, established the solutions to a canonical set of individual consumption-portfolio allocation problems and demonstrated the primary role played by the linear risk tolerance class of utility functions. It was through this work that we learned that the constant risk tolerance utility functions have constant optimal portfolio policies in an unchanging stochastic environment. Furthermore, the optimal policies can be determined myopically. In other words, the optimal dynamic path comes from stringing together a sequence of optimal static decisions. From Hakansson and later Merton's (1971, 1973) work, we also learned that these results would no longer hold with a changing investment opportunity set (with the exception of the log utility function), but, at first, this was not the central feature of the analysis.

The methodology of these studies was that of dynamic programming and backward recursion. In effect, this was the device that converted the intertemporal problems with time-dependent policies as their objects of study into more familiar static problems. At any moment of time an indirect utility function could be defined, and its local or myopic maximization would provide the necessary conditions for global optimality. To some extent this mode of reasoning has guided the intertemporal theory up to now.

The aggregation of these models into intertemporal equilibrium models occurred with Merton's (1973) publication of the intertemporal asset pricing model (ICAPM). Merton first recast and extended the earlier work on individual accumulation models, using Ito's version of the stochastic calculus (1971). Employing a dynamic programming approach to find the individual optimal policies in a competitive model, he then aggregated these policies to obtain necessary conditions on asset demands and pricing in equilibrium (Merton 1973).

The static models of asset pricing take preferences and technology as exogenous and derive current prices and asset holdings. Included in the specification of technology is an assumption about what the terminal payoffs to the assets will be. In the intertemporal model of Merton this is carried one step further. In a similar fashion to the static theory, Merton begins his analysis with a specification of the price paths followed by assets. After these paths are exogenously specified, the model is closed on the demand side by an investor whose goal is to maximize the expectation of an integral of discounted additively separable future utility flows. At any moment the utility function is assumed to be state independent and a function only of that moment's consumption flow.

The central conclusion of the model is an instantaneous equilibrium condition that neatly generalized the static condition of the CAPM, but this pat description of its conclusion is misleading as to its true contribution. Aside from its methodological extension to the diffusion approach to modeling such problems, this was the first such model that went beyond simple analogies with the static models to introduce and approach a new phenomenon that is intrinsically intertemporal in nature.

As the economy moves over time, the statically optimal decisions that individuals make are generally not intertemporally optimal. To be fully optimal such decisions must take account of the way in which the economy changes. In the Merton model a collection of state variables was a priori assumed to be sufficient to describe changes in the economy's production set. In such a world the indirect utility functions of individuals depend not only on their current wealth but also on the current state of the economy. The indirect utility captures the expected future utility along an optimal path. Since this will depend on the future path of technology, it follows that it must also depend on the current state of the economy. In an economy endowed with current supplies and where production conditions are expected to be strong, the indirect utility will be larger than one in which production is expected to be weak. As a consequence, risk-averse individuals making portfolio and consumption decisions will take into account the possibility of hedging against adverse shifts in the production possibility set. Since production is only a means to an end, what they are really concerned with is shifts in their consumption possibility sets, and it is this that they are hedging against.

As a result of these considerations, the necessary conditions of the ICAPM differ from those of the static CAPM to account for such hedging possibilities. No longer could we expect the static CAPM and the security market line to hold intertemporally and risk premia to depend only on the beta coefficients of asset returns with the market return. In an intertemporal world the static market beta risk premium for any asset must be augmented by including for every state variable a term that is proportional to the beta of the asset's return with that state variable. Merton also considered the possibility of using observable variables such as the risk-free interest rate as surrogates for the state variables. Interest-rate betas, for example, would then be used to augment the market beta.

II. THE CONSUMPTION BETA MODEL

Acquiring a new intuition about asset pricing, namely that intertemporal state changes mattered, was both exhilarating and puzzling. Although it was clear that the result was a unique feature of intertemporal models, it was also clear that it fitted uncomfortably with the intuitions of the static CAPM.

In the static CAPM, individuals took portfolio positions that evaluated assets in terms of their marginal contributions to future wealth. Since realized wealth was a consequence of all of the possible state changes, the question of why this intuition did not hold in an intertemporal setting remained.

It was this paradox that Breeden's (1979) paper resolved, and it was the contribution of his paper to restore the appropriate dynamic analog to the static result. (See, too, Rubinstein's 1976 paper, which also emphasized the role of consumption, although it did not address the reconciliation with the Merton model.) Breeden reasoned that what mattered in the intertemporal model was the individual's consumption policy and that consumption played the role of wealth in a static setting. Indeed, in the one-period model, terminal wealth was assumed to be fully consumed. Just as the individual evaluated an asset in terms of its marginal contribution to terminal wealth in a static model, in an intertemporal setting what mattered was its marginal relation with the consumption flow. This insight produced the consumption beta model, in which all of the state variables that were priced in the Merton ICAPM were collapsed into a single consumption beta in Breeden's analysis.

Two ways of seeing this same point are worth examining. The actual mathematics of the analysis of the ICAPM was based on the observation that along an optimal path an individual sets the marginal utility of consumption equal to the marginal utility of wealth. It is the latter that is the primitive notion of the theory, and it is at this step that the central assumption of the consumption beta models is most clearly seen. Given the current wealth and state of nature, an indirect utility function, when it exists, describes the current value to an individual of the future lifetime utility to be obtained from following optimal policies. It is always true that along an optimal path the individual evaluates assets in terms of the correlation (covariance in a diffusion model) of their returns with changes in the marginal utility of wealth. When utility is determined as the expected discounted value of a stream of utilities of the consumption flow, then at any instant the optimal policy will set the marginal utility of this consumption flow equal to the marginal utility of wealth. Breeden's analysis of the Merton model exploited the observation that if the local utility function was not dependent on the state of nature other than through the dependence of the optimal consumption choice on the state, then along an optimal path the marginal utility of wealth would depend only on consumption. The key to the result is the state independence of the utility function.

An alternative approach to the matter brings further insight. Suppose that the model is cast in a framework with complete markets. In such a setting, an individual optimizes by purchasing consumption in each future state of nature at each future time point by setting the marginal rate of substitution between consumption in different states equal to the relative prices. Since (with homogeneous beliefs) the prices of wealth in each state per unit of probability are equal across individuals, with von Neumann–Morgenstern (state-independent) utilities each individual will order consumption in the different states in the same fashion. In the diffusion model this implies that if perfect hedges for the state variables can be formed, then all individuals will have locally perfectly correlated consumption policies (see Bhattacharya 1981). Just as consumption is the intertemporal analogue of wealth in the static setting, this result is the analogue of the CAPM's finding that all individuals will hold the market portfolio.

Whether or not markets are complete, the Breeden model still prices assets in terms of their covariance with aggregate consumption. It is particularly important to understand what drives the Breeden model in making an assessment of it. The model uses additively separable preferences to establish an analogy between the static CAPM and the ICAPM. From Breeden we learned that wealth in the static model was really just a one-period version of the consumption flow. We had been confused because wealth and consumption are the same in a world that lives for only one period.

III. INTERTEMPORAL RATIONALITY

The above models followed the static tradition of specifying technology and preferences exogenously and deriving the necessary conditions for equilibrium. A consequence of this was that the uncomfortable relation with the static CAPM was not the only paradox in the ICAPM. After all, if these were models of the pricing of assets, then how was it possible to exogenously specify the price paths of the assets? Was it not the role of the model to determine the prices?

When looked at in this fashion, the ICAPM has an oddly dated appearance. In essence, it provides a specification of the necessary conditions on the demand side of the economy for investors to be in equilibrium given a particular price path. It says nothing about what the price path will be, and, in particular, it is divorced from the discussion of rational expectations that was the cornerstone of the early study of efficient markets and that had led to the revolution in macroeconomics. It is not so much that the ICAPM is irrational; rather it is silent on the whole matter of rationality and the price formation process.

An attempt to address these issues was made contemporaneously with the ICAPM in Ross (1975). In this model, preferences were assumed to be myopic, and the equilibrium diffusion price paths for assets were determined for particular neoclassical specifications of the technology. However, the paths were rational only in the limited sense that the actual distribution of the intertemporal price movement coincided in expectation with the ex ante distribution employed by investors.

The first full rational expectations intertemporal asset equilibrium model was constructed by Cox, Ingersoll, and Ross (CIR) (1985a) in a diffusion setting. In the CIR model a production technology was specified ex ante along with preferences. Prices were solved for by using the contingent-claims analysis of option pricing theory. The result was a complete model in which the rational equilibrium price paths emerged as functions of the underlying specification of the technology. The application of this model to the term structure of interest rates is discussed by Ken Singleton in this volume. A somewhat different approach to the construction of a rational expectations model that focused on the role of consumption, analogous to the Breeden model, was constructed by Lucas (1978).

It is instructive at this point to recall the early work on efficient markets. This work was largely empirical, but it was guided by some marvelous intuitions that still inspire theory to this day. The basic idea is summarized in the simple statement that "prices reflect all of the available information."

Such a statement is too loose for analytical purposes, and it really came to be less of a statement about the role of information in markets and more of a statement about the actual empirical aspects of price processes: for example, that prices followed random walks or that they were serially uncorrelated. When precision was sought, usually such theories were given a formal representation in the martingale statement that

$$E\{p_{t+1}|I_t\} = (1 + r_t)p_t,$$

where I_t denotes the information set available to "the market" at time t and incorporated in the price p_t, and r_t is the sure rate of interest prevailing over the unit period at time t.

This representation also makes it clear that *the* efficient market theory is really a class of theories defined by the information set, I_t, assumed to be used for pricing. Fama (1970) coined the terminology "strong-form efficiency" to denote the case where the information set contained, in effect, all that was known and pertinent to the assessment of value. A notch down was semistrong efficiency, which referred to the situation when the information set contained all of the "publicly available information," and at the far end of the spectrum was weak-form efficiency, which referred to the case when the information set contained only the past prices.

The emphasis on the central role of the information set established one path of development for the construction of intertemporal asset pricing models, and it was this path that was revived with the CIR model. But there is another theme present in the early work and in the CIR model.

IV. ARBITRAGE MODELS AND MARTINGALE ANALYSIS

In Ross (1976) it was first shown that the absence of arbitrage implied the existence of state contingent (Arrow-Debreu) prices and, therefore, of a linear operator that could be used to price all assets. This was extended to an intertemporal setting in Ross (1978). In Harrison and Kreps (1979) it was shown that the operator could be represented as an expectation taken with respect to a martingale measure.

The work of Harrison and Kreps unified two divergent strands in intertemporal pricing theory: arbitrage-free pricing and option pricing. The Cox and Ross (1976) risk-neutral pricing "trick" for solving option pricing problems could now be seen as a consequence of a general structure of pricing in arbitrage-free economies. The work on the implications of the absence of arbitrage has been extended in many different directions, particularly by Harrison and Pliska (1981, 1983), Hansen and Richard (1984), Dybvig, Ingersoll, and Ross (1986), and by Müller (1985).

From the absence of arbitrage alone, we can derive an important relation between the state variables that define the information set of the economy and the prices of assets. In precise analogy with the arbitrage-pricing theory (APT) (Ross 1976a, b), at any moment the absence of arbitrage requires the excess expected return on assets to be a linear function of their covariances with the state variables. This is precisely the result of the ICAPM, and, as CIR note, it is solely a consequence of the absence of arbitrage and is not dependent on the further assumptions of the model that characterize the equilibrium. Since the observation that pricing depends only on the state variables is a consequence of the absence of arbitrage, the role played by these additional assumptions in an intertemporal model is to establish the determinants of the risk premia associated with each state variable. (We are ignoring the ICAPM's addition of local production uncertainty in this discussion, but this could be accounted for by simply expanding the state space. Without such a device, the market portfolio enters as a priced index, just as it does in the static CAPM, and it has influence for pricing beyond the influence of the state variables. The importance of this for pricing, though, is more of an empirical issue than a theoretical one. The issue turns on the relative size of local production uncertainty—innovations in earnings—versus changes in asset values.)

This provides us with an interesting format within which to study the different intertemporal asset pricing models. All of them are consistent with the absence of arbitrage, and, therefore, in all of them pricing is determined by the covariances between the asset returns and the state variables. What the different models do is specify the state variables and the risk premia in different fashions. For example, the Breeden model and the ICAPM assume that the state variables are arbitrary and make strong assumptions about individual preferences, namely that they are intertemporally additive and state independent. This permits the state risk premia and covariances to be aggregated into a single covariance with an endogenous variable, aggregate consumption. The CIR model, on the other hand, points in the direction of a more careful and limiting specification of the information set. This is coupled, if desired, with whatever parametric restrictions on preferences are required to solve the model, as in the term structure work of Cox, Ingersoll, and Ross (1985a, b).

The most recent work on intertemporal asset pricing can best be understood as blending the integral representation of no-arbitrage conditions with complete markets. In a complete market setting, decisions can be thought of as specifications of complete contingent plans; thus, the intertemporal problem is ultimately reduced to a static problem. Cox and Leland (1982), Cox (1984), and Duffie and Huang (1985) use the observation that with a binomial or lognormal process the price per unit probability will be independent of the path followed by the economy. As a consequence, along an optimal path an individual with a state-independent utility function will choose the same wealth at any point in a tree generated by such a process, independent of the path to that point. This makes intertemporal choice isomorphic to static choice without the usual expansion of the state space to include all future paths. Using these techniques, Cox and Leland (1982) and Cox (1984) were able to solve optimal accumulation problems with boundaries on consumption that had not yielded to the usual dynamic programming techniques.

The arbitrage arguments come into play in the emphasis in this work on the dynamics of the pricing standard (i.e., the price per unit probability) whose existence is implied by the absence of arbitrage. In Dybvig (1985), Dybvig, Ingersoll, and Ross (1986), and Ross (1986), assets are priced by directly specifying the motion of the pricing standard or by deriving its motion from the price dynamics of other assets. This reduces intertemporal problems to static ones and allows us to dispense with dynamic programming by specifying pricing directly in terms of integrals with respect to the martingale measure.

I will not go any further into this work because it is treated in this volume in more detail in Jon Ingersoll's discussion of the Duffie and Huang paper and in Cox and Huang's of Merton's work. To briefly summarize, though, it represents the final completion of the analogy between the intertemporal asset pricing models and the static state-space market theories. When markets are complete, it exploits the isomorphism between pricing in the dynamic theory and the static theory. A weaker, but still quite useful, isomorphism exists for incomplete markets in which the absence of arbitrage implies the existence of prices for state contingent claims, whether marketed or not.

V. NEW DIRECTIONS, UNRESOLVED MATTERS, AND EMPIRICAL WORK

By now it has become traditional in discussions of intertemporal asset pricing to bemoan the lack of a suitable model that takes account of the role played by asymmetric information. I will pay the usual homage to this deficiency, since I have nothing very substantial to contribute to the issue. I also will not dwell on the attempts to build such a model except to say that there does not currently exist a satisfactory intertemporal asset pricing model with asymmetric information, where "satisfactory" should mean, at the least, empirically relevant. We will return to this matter briefly, but for now let us turn our attention to the empirical literature on testing intertemporal asset pricing theories. To some extent this overlaps with the body of literature that tests static theories, and it is worth noting where this does and does not occur.

Tests of the CAPM are best interpreted as static tests, since intertemporal models in which the CAPM is valid period by period appear as special and somewhat odd restrictive forms. If we are too zealous in applying this standard, though, it is difficult to find any pure tests of the ICAPM. An exception to this is the work by Schipper and Thompson (1979) in which an explicit attempt was made to test the ICAPM. By contrast, tests of intertemporal models in which a specific set of state variables explains pricing look much like static tests of the APT. The APT is, after all, a necessary snapshot of the CIR rational expectations models. Thus, a test that is sufficiently sensitive to conditioning can be interpreted as a true test of an intertemporal pricing model. The exploration of such tests is just beginning, and the work of Chen, Roll, and Ross (1986) and the subsequent work of Keim and Stambaugh (Forthcoming) are examples.

Perhaps because the data requirements are less severe, extensive testing has been conducted on the consumption beta model. To mention a few papers, Breeden, Gibbons, and Litzenberger (1986) have examined the theory using stock market data, Hansen and Singleton (1983) have conducted extensive tests using aggregate data, and Chen, Roll, and Ross (1986) have tested for the influence of consumption for pricing portfolios of stocks. To summarize the results of these tests, and to paraphrase Hansen and Singleton (as well as to take their words out of context), the marginal significance levels of the test statistics were essentially zero. Chen, Roll, and Ross (1986) found that consumption betas had no significance for pricing by themselves, and that in the presence of alternatives they basically added noise to the tests.

Why have these tests been unsuccessful at verifying the mere influence of aggregate consumption on asset pricing, let alone that it has a determinate effect? I believe that the poor results should have been expected. Despite its immense theoretical appeal, it is naive to think that consumption can compete with more fundamental state variables as an explanator of asset prices. The heart of the theory is the view that individuals adjust their marginal rates of substitution for consumption at different times and in different states to equal the relative prices in the different states. This is far more heroic than, for example, expecting consumers to adjust their marginal rates of substitution for different goods at the same point in time to the prevailing *and observable* relative prices of the goods. (We pause here to clear up a common misconception about the consumption beta model. It is wrong to think of consumption as *determining* asset prices in some causal sense; rather, in the best competitive tradition the model assumes that competitive consumers *adjust* their choices to the intertemporal prices they face. In equilibrium both consumption and the prices are determined endogenously.)

The consumption beta theory is really an intertemporal extension of a particular separable form of the neoclassical theory of consumer choice, and that explains both its appeal as a theory and its poor performance empirically. The lengthy effort that goes into even verifying the law of demand for a single consumer good pales beside the attempt to verify the intertemporal consumption beta model. The further assumption that consumers allocate their budget choices at a point in time according to an additively separable utility function has proven even less successful at explaining ordinary demand functions. Given this shaky basis of support, the hope that consumers make intertemporal decisions as assumed by the separable structure of the consumption beta theory seems to me to reach too far to expect it to be empirically valid. To put the point simply, what is being tested in the empirical work on the consumption beta theory is not so much a theory of asset pricing as it is a theory of individual choice.

By contrast, the success of financial asset pricing theories comes from their appeal to the stronger force of arbitrage rather than from a neoclassical demand and supply equilibrium. The most empirically successful theories in finance succeed by emphasizing the relative pricing of assets in terms of close substitutes. Furthermore, taking this perspective is less limiting than might at first appear. Although we will not be able to explain macroeconomic aggregates by this methodology, we can examine their influence on the economy through their impact on the capital markets.

Finally, we can only make mention of the volatility tests initiated by Shiller (1981). This work has spawned a large literature, some supportive of the original assertion of inefficiency and some opposed to it (see, e.g., Flavin 1983, Grossman and Shiller 1983, Kleidon 1985, Mankiw, Romer, and Shapiro 1985, Marsh and Merton 1984, and Müller 1985). Like the earlier and voluminous literature on regression tests, these papers are directed at the more general question of market efficiency, but, despite their proximity to our concerns, to discuss them adequately here is beyond our reach.

VI. SOME FINAL POINTS

I will end this discussion with the lament that began the preceding section. All of the tests we have mentioned are very much in the spirit of the pricing models themselves, which is to say that they use price data. There is no serious research as yet on volume data. This is in large part because we have no serious theories that purport to explain the volume of trade, and this brings us back to the deficiency with which this section began.

This is unfortunate, because it is difficult to imagine that the volume of trade in securities markets has very much at all to do with the modest amount of trading required to accomplish the continual and gradual portfolio rebalancing inherent in our current intertemporal models. It seems clear that the only way to explain the volume of trade is with a model that is at one and the same time appealingly rational and yet permits divergent and changing opinions in a fashion that is other than ad hoc. If I had to point to a single priority order of business for intertemporal pricing theory, it would be the construction of such a theory. Surely there can be nothing more embarrassing to an economist than the ability to explain the price in a market while being completely silent on the quantity. There are, of course, a number of other loose ends such as the impact of taxes—the Constantinides and Ingersoll (1984) work is discussed by Robert Litzenberger elsewhere in this volume—and human capital and other forms of nontraded assets, but in my mind the failure to explain the volume of trade looms as the major dark continent for explorers of this terrain.

REFERENCES

Bhattacharya, S. 1981. "Notes on Multi-Period Valuation and the Pricing of Options." *Journal of Finance* 36: 163–80.

Breeden, D. T. 1979. "An Intertemporal Asset Pricing Model with Stochastic Consumption and Investment Opportunities." *Journal of Financial Economics* 7: 265–96.

Breeden, D. T.; Gibbons, M. R.; and Litzenberger, R. H. 1986. "Empirical Tests of the Consumption-Oriented CAPM." Working paper No. 879, Stanford University Business School.

Chen, N.; Roll, R.; and Ross, S. A. 1986. "Macrovariables and Asset Pricing." *Journal of Business* 58.

Constantinides, G., and Ingersoll, J. E., Jr. 1984. "Optimal Bond Trading with Personal

Tax." *Journal of Financial Economics* 11: 299–335.

Cox, J. C. 1984. "Optimal Consumption and Portfolio Policies When Asset Returns Follow a Diffusion Process." MIT, unpublished working paper.

Cox, J. C.; Ingersoll, J. E., Jr.; and Ross, S. A. 1985a. "An Intertemporal General Equilibrium Model of Asset Prices." *Econometrica* 53: 363–84.

――― 1985b. "A Theory of the Term Structure of Interest Rates." *Econometrica* 53: 385–407.

Cox, J. C., and Leland, H. 1982. "On Dynamic Investment Strategies." *In Proceedings Seminar on the Analysis of Security Prices*, vol. 26, no. 2. Center for Research in Security Prices, Graduate School of Business, University of Chicago.

Cox, J. C., and Ross, S. A. 1976. "The Valuation of Options for Alternative Stochastic Processes." *Journal of Financial Economics* 3: 145–66.

Duffie, D., and Huang, C. F. 1985. "Implementing Arrow-Debreu Equilibria by Continuous Trading of Few Long-Lived Securities." *Econometrica* 53: 1337–56.

Dybvig, P. 1985. "The Payoff Distribution Approach." Yale School of Management, manuscript.

Dybvig, P.; Ingersoll, J. E., Jr.; and Ross, S. A. 1986. "Notes on Arbitrage and Martingales." Yale School of Management, manuscript.

Fama, E. F. 1970. "Efficient Capital Markets: A Review of Theory and Empirical Work." *Journal of Business* 43: 383–417.

Flavin, M. A. 1983. "Excess Volatility in the Financial Markets: A Reassessment of the Empirical Evidence." *Journal of Political Economy* 91: 929–56.

Grossman, S. J., and Shiller, R. J. 1983. "Consumption Correlatedness and Risk Measurement in Economies with Non-Traded Assets and Heterogeneous Information." *Journal of Financial Economics* 10: 195–210.

Hakansson, N. 1971. "On Optimal Myopic Portfolio Policies, with and without Serial Correlation of Yields." *Journal of Business* 44: 324–34.

――― 1974. "Convergence in Multiperiod Portfolio Choice." *Journal of Financial Economics* 1: 201–24.

Hansen, L., and Richard, S. 1984. "A General Approach for Deducing Testable Restrictions Implied by Asset Pricing Models." Unpublished manuscript.

Hansen, L., and Singleton, R. 1983. "Stochastic Consumption, Risk Aversion, and the Temporal Behavior of Asset Returns." *Journal of Political Economy* 91: 249–65.

Harrison, J. M., and Kreps, D. M. 1979. "Martingales and Arbitrage in Multiperiod Securities Markets." *Journal of Economic Theory* 20: 381–408.

Harrison, J. M., and Pliska, S. 1981. "Martingales and Stochastic Integrals in the Theory of Continuous Trading." *Stochastic Processes and Their Applications* 11: 215–60.

――― 1983. "A Stochastic Calculus Model of Continuous Trading: Complete Markets." *Stochastic Processes and Their Applications* 15: 313–16.

Keim, D. B., and Stambaugh, R. F. Forthcoming. "Predicting Returns in the Stock and Bond Markets." *Journal of Financial Economics*.

Kleidon, A. W. 1985. "Variance Bounds Test and Stock Price Valuation Models." Research paper No. 806, Stanford Graduate School of Business.

Lucas, R. E., Jr. 1978. "Asset Prices in an Exchange Economy." *Econometrica* 46: 1426–46.

Marsh, T. A., and Merton, R. C. 1984. "Dividend Variability and Variance Bounds for the Rationality of Stock Market Prices." Working paper No. 1584-84, Sloan School. *American Economic Review*, forthcoming.

Mankiw, N. G.; Romer, D.; and Shapiro, M. D. 1985. "An Unbiased Reexamination of Stock Market Volatility." *Journal of Finance* 40: 677–87.

Merton, R. C. 1971. "Optimum Consumption and Portfolio Rules in a Continuous Time Model." *Journal of Economic Theory* 3: 373–413.

————. 1973. "An Intertemporal Capital Asset Pricing Model." *Econometrica* 41: 867–87.

Mossin, J. 1969. "Optimal Multiperiod Portfolio Policies." *Journal of Business* 41: 215–29.

Müller, S. 1985. *Arbitrage Pricing of Contingent Claims.* New York: Springer-Verlag.

Ross, S. A. 1975. "Uncertainty and the Heterogeneous Capital Good Model." *Review of Economic Studies* 42: 133–46.

————. 1976a. "Return, Risk and Arbitrage." In I. Friend and J. Bicksler (eds.), *Risk and Return in Finance.* Cambridge, Mass.: Ballinger.

————. 1976b. "The Arbitrage Theory of Capital Asset Pricing." *Journal of Economic Theory* 13: 341–60.

————. 1978. "A Simple Approach to the Valuation of Risky Streams." *Journal of Business* 51: 453–75.

————. 1986. "Timing and Variability." Yale University, manuscript.

Rubinstein, M. E. 1976. "The Valuation of Uncertain Income Streams and the Pricing of Options." *Bell Journal of Economics* 7: 407–25.

Shiller, R. J. 1981. "Do Stock Prices Move Too Much to Be Justified by Subsequent Changes in Dividends?" *American Economic Review* 71: 421–36.

Schipper, K., and Thompson, R. 1981. "Common Stocks as Hedges Against Shifts in the Consumption or Investment Opportunity Set." *Journal of Business* 54: 305–28.

Econometrica, Vol. 53, No. 6 (November, 1985)

IMPLEMENTING ARROW-DEBREU EQUILIBRIA BY CONTINUOUS TRADING OF FEW LONG-LIVED SECURITIES

By Darrell Duffie and Chi-fu Huang[1]

A two-period (0 and T) Arrow-Debreu economy is set up with a general model of uncertainty. We suppose that an equilibrium exists for this economy. The Arrow-Debreu economy is placed in a Radner (dynamic) setting; agents may trade claims at any time during $[0, T]$. Under appropriate conditions it is possible to implement the original Arrow-Debreu equilibrium, which may have an infinite-dimensional commodity space, in a Radner equilibrium with only a finite number of securities. This is done by opening the "right" set of security markets, a set which effectively completes markets for the Radner economy.

1. INTRODUCTION

Figure 1 depicts a simple event tree information structure. Let's momentarily consider an exchange economy with endowments of and preferences for random time T consumption, depending on the state $\omega \in \Omega$ chosen by nature from the final five nodes of this event tree. A competitive equilibrium will exist under standard assumptions (Debreu [5, Chapter 7]), including markets for securities whose time T consumption payoff vectors span R^5. This entails at least five security markets, while intuition suggests that, with the ability to learn information and trade during $[0, T]$, only three securities which are always available for trading, or *long-lived securities* [13], might be enough to effectively complete markets. This is the maximum number of branches leaving any node in the tree. The reasoning is given by Kreps [13] and in alternative more general form later in this paper. An early precurser to this work is Arrow [1], which showed the spanning effectiveness of financial securities when trade can occur twice in a two-period model.

One major purpose of this paper is to verify this intuition for a very general class of information structures, including those which cannot be represented by event trees, such as the filtration generated by continuous-time "state-variable" stochastic processes. In some cases, where an Arrow-Debreu style equilibrium would call for an infinite number of securities, we show how a continuous trading Radner [20] *equilibrium of plans, prices and price expectations* can implement the same Arrow-Debreu consumption allocations with only a finite number of long-lived securities. It is misleading, of course, to use the number of security markets alone as a measure of the efficiency of the market structure; the number of transactions which must be performed to achieve a given allocation must also be considered. Largely for want of a reasonable model to study this tradeoff, we have not addressed the issue of the efficiency of market structure.

A comparison of Event Trees A of Figure 1 and B of Figure 2, which are intended to correspond to the same two-period Arrow-Debreu economy, obviates the role of the information structure in determining the number of long-lived

[1] We would like to thank David Kreps, John Cox, Michael Harrison, and David Luenberger for helpful comments. We are also grateful to Larry Jones, Donald Brown, and David Kreps for pointing out an error in the earlier version of this paper. That and any remaining errors are our own.

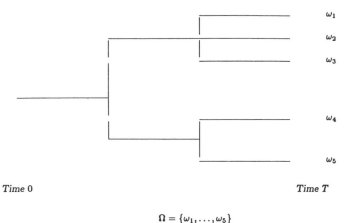

Time 0   Time T

$$\Omega = \{\omega_1, \ldots, \omega_5\}$$

FIGURE 1.

securities required to dynamically "span" the consumption space, or the *spanning number*. We later give this term a more precise meaning. Since all uncertainty is resolved at once in Event Tree *B*, the spanning number is five, instead of three for Event Tree *A*. Intuitively speaking, the maximum number of "dimensions of uncertainty" which could be resolved at any one time is the key determining property. This vague notion actually takes a precise form as the *martingale multiplicity* of the information structure, defined in the Appendix. A key result of this paper is that the spanning number is the martingale multiplicity plus one. The "plus one" is no mystery; in addition to spanning uncertainty, agents must have the ability to transfer purchasing power across time.

The notion that certain securities are redundant because their payoffs can be replicated by trading other securities over time, yielding arbitrage pricing relationships among securities, was dramatized in the Black–Scholes [2] option pricing

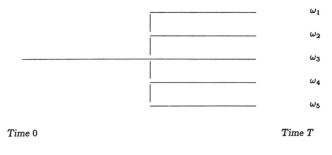

Time 0   Time T

$$\Omega = \{\omega_1, \ldots, \omega_5\}$$

FIGURE 2.

formula.[2] Provided the equilibrium price process for one security happens to be a geometric Brownian Motion, and for another is a (deterministic) exponential of time, then any contingent claim whose payoff depends (measurably) on the path taken by the underlying Brownian Motion, such as a call option on the risky security, is redundant and priced by arbitrage. This discovery curiously preceded its simpler logical antecedents, such as the corresponding results for event tree information structures. Only in the past few years have the implications of the spanning properties of price processes (e.g., [13]), the connection between martingale theory and equilibrium price processes (e.g., [8]), and the mathematical machinery for continuous security trading [9] been formalized.

In all of the above mentioned literature the takeoff point is a given set of security price processes, implicitly imbedded in a Radner equilibrium. Our second major goal is to begin more primitively with a given Arrow-Debreu equilibrium, one in which trading over time is not of concern since markets are complete at time zero. From that point we construct the consumption payoffs and price processes for a set of long-lived securities in such a way that agents may be allocated trading strategies allowing them to consume their original Arrow-Debreu allocations within a Radner style equilibrium. In short, we implement a given Arrow-Debreu equilibrium by continuous trading of a set of long-lived securities which is typically much smaller in number than the dimension of the consumption space. Merton [19; p. 666] recently predicted that results such as ours would appear.

The paper unfolds in the following order. First we describe the economy (Section 2) and an Arrow-Debreu equilibrium for it (Section 3). Section 4 provides a constructive proof of a Radner equilibrium which implements a given Arrow-Debreu equilibrium under stated conditions, based on a martingale representation technique. Section 5 characterizes the spanning number in terms of martingale multiplicity. Section 6 discusses the continuous trading machinery, some generalizations, and two examples of the model. Section 7 adds concluding remarks.

2. THE ECONOMY

Uncertainty in our economy is modeled as a complete probability space $(\Omega, \mathcal{F}, P)$. The set Ω constitutes all possible states of the world which could exist at a terminal date $T > 0$. The *tribe* $\mathcal{F}$ is the σ-algebra of measurable subsets of Ω, or events, of which agents can make probability assessments based on the probability measure P. Events are revealed over time according to a *filtration*, $F = \{\mathcal{F}_t, t \in [0, T]\}$, a right-continuous increasing family of sub-tribes of $\mathcal{F}$, where $\mathcal{F}_T = \mathcal{F}$ and $\mathcal{F}_0$ is almost trivial (the tribe generated by Ω and all of the P-null sets). We can interpret this by thinking of $\mathcal{F}_t$ as the set of all events which could occur at or before time t. The assumption that F is increasing, or $\mathcal{F}_t \subset \mathcal{F}_s$ for $s > t$, means simply that agents do not forget that an event has occurred once it

---

[2] Merton [18] is also seminal in this regard. Similar results were obtained by Cox and Ross [3] for other models of uncertainty.

is revealed. The above descriptions of $\mathcal{F}_0$ and $\mathcal{F}_T$ means that no information is known at time 0, and all uncertainty is resolved at time T.

Each agent in the economy is characterized by the following properties: (i) a known endowment of a perishable consumption good at time zero, (ii) a random, that is, state-dependent, endowment of the consumption good at time T, and (iii) preferences over consumption pairs (r, x), where r is time zero consumption and x is a random variable describing time T consumption, $x(\omega)$ in state $\omega \in \Omega$.

We will only consider consumption claims with finite variance. The consumption space is thus formalized as $V = R \times L^2(P)$, where $L^2(P)$ is the space of (equivalence classes) of square-integrable random-variables on $(\Omega, \mathcal{F}, P)$, with the usual product topology on V given by the Euclidean and L^2 norms.

The agents, finite in number, are indexed by $i = 1, \ldots, I$. The preferences of agent i are modeled as a complete transitive binary relation, or *preference order*, $\succcurlyeq_i$ on $V_i \subset V$, the ith agent's consumption set.

The whole economy can then be summarized in the usual way by the collection

$$\mathscr{E} = (V_i, \hat{v}_i, \succcurlyeq_i; i = 1, \ldots, I),$$

where $\hat{v}_i = (\hat{r}_i, \hat{x}_i) \in V_i$ is the ith agent's endowment. It is not important for this paper whether or not one assumes positive consumption or endowments.

3. ARROW–DEBREU EQUILIBRIUM

An Arrow–Debreu equilibrium for $\mathscr{E}$ is a nonzero linear (price) functional $\Psi: V \to R$ and a set of allocations $(v_i^* \in V_i; i = 1, \ldots, I)$ satisfying, for all i,

$$\Psi(v_i^*) \leq \Psi(\hat{v}_i),$$

(3.1) $\qquad v >_i v_i^* \quad \Rightarrow \quad \Psi(v) > \Psi(v_i^*) \quad \forall v \in V_i,$

$$\sum_{i=1}^{I} v_i^* = \sum_{i=i}^{I} \hat{v}_i.$$

We will assume that at least one agent i has strictly monotonic preferences. Specifically, if $v \in V_i$ and $v' \geq v$ (in the obvious product order on V), then $v' \in V_i$ and $v' >_i v$ provided $v \neq v'$. This ensures that in equilibrium Ψ is a strictly positive linear functional. Since V is a Hilbert lattice [21], this then implies that Ψ is a continuous linear functional on V, which can therefore be represented by some element (a, ξ) of V itself in the form:

$$\Psi(r, x) = ar + \int_\Omega x(\omega)\xi(\omega) \, dP(\omega) \quad \forall (r, x) \in V.$$

Without loss of generality we can normalize Ψ by a constant so that the positive random variable ξ has unit expectation, in order to construct the probability measure Q on $(\Omega, \mathcal{F})$ by the relation

$$Q(B) = \int_B 1_B(\omega)\xi(\omega) \, dP(\omega) \quad \forall B \in \mathcal{F}.$$

Equivalently, ξ is the Radon-Nikodym derivative dQ/dP. This leaves the simple representation

(3.2) $\quad \Psi(r, x) = ar + E^*(x) \quad \forall (r, x) \in V,$

where E^* denotes expectation under Q. Thus the equilibrium price of any random consumption claim $x \in L^2(P)$ is simply its expected consumption payoff under Q. For this reason we call Q an *equilibrium price measure*.

For tractability we will want any random variable which has finite variance under P to have finite variance under Q, and *vice versa*. A necessary and sufficient condition is that P and Q are *uniformly absolutely continuous*, denoted $Q \approx P$ (Halmos [7, p. 100]), or equivalently, that the Radon-Nikodym derivative dQ/dP is bounded above and below away from zero. Sufficient conditions for this can be given when preferences can be represented by von-Neumann-Morgenstern utility functions, in terms of bounds on marginal utility for time T consumption. We do not pursue this here since we are taking ξ as a primitive, rather than deriving it from preferences.[3]

A second regularity condition which comes into play is the separability[4] of $\mathcal{F}$ under P. This assumption should not be viewed as too restrictive. One can, for example, construct Brownian Motion on a separable probability space. Given $Q \approx P$ it is then easy to show the separability of $\mathcal{F}$ under Q by making use of the upper essential bound on dQ/dP.

Since uniform absolute continuity of two measures implies their equivalence (that is, they give probability zero to the same events), we can use the symbol a.s. for "almost surely" indiscriminately in this paper.

4. RADNER EQUILIBRIUM

A *long-lived security* is a consumption claim (to some element of $L^2(P)$) available for trade throughout $[0, T]$. A *price process* for a long-lived security is a semimartingale[5] on our given probability space adapted to the given information structure F. In general the number of units of a long-lived security which are held by an agent over time defines some stochastic process θ. We will say θ is an *admissible* trading process for a long-lived security with price process S if it meets the following regularity conditions:

(i) *predictability*, defined in the Appendix and denoted $\theta \in \mathcal{P}$;

(ii) *square-integrability*, or $\theta \in L^2_P[S] \equiv \{\phi \in \mathcal{P}: E(\int_0^T \phi_t^2 \, d[S]_t) < \infty\}$, where $[S]$ denotes the quadratic variation process for S (Jacod [11]); and

---

[3] Work subsequent to this paper shows extremely general continuity assumptions which yield these bounds [6].

[4] A tribe $\mathcal{F}$ is said to be separable under P if there exists a countable number of elements $B_1, B_2, \ldots$ in $\mathcal{F}$ such that, for any $B \in \mathcal{F}$ and $\varepsilon > 0$ there exists B_n in the sequence with $P\{B \Delta B_n\} < \varepsilon$, where Δ denotes symmetric difference.

[5] See Jacod [11], for example, for the definition of a semimartingale. This is not at all a severe restriction on price processes if one is to obtain a meaningful model of gains and losses from security trades.

(iii) the *gains process* $\int \theta \, dS$ is well defined as a stochastic integral. We will be dealing with price processes in this paper for which square-integrability (ii) is sufficient for this condition. Memin [16] gives a full set of sufficient conditions in the general case.

The stochastic integral $\int_0^t \theta(s) \, dS(s)$ is a model of the gains or losses realized up to and including time t by trading a security with price process S using the trading process θ. Interpreted as a Stieltjes integral this model is obvious, but the integral is generally well defined only as a stochastic integral. This model, formalized by Harrison and Pliska [9], is discussed further in Section 6, as are the other regularity conditions on θ.

Taking $S = (S_1, \ldots, S_N)$, $N \leq \infty$, as the set of all long-lived security price processes, any corresponding set of admissible trading processes $\theta = (\theta_1, \ldots, \theta_N)$ must also meet the accounting identity:

$$(4.1) \qquad \theta(t)^\top S(t) = \theta(0)^\top S(0) + \int_0^t \theta(s)^\top \, dS(s) \quad \forall t \in [0, T] \qquad \text{a.s.,}$$

meaning that the current value of a portfolio must be its initial value plus any gains or losses incurred from trading. The symbol $^\top$ denotes the obvious shorthand notation for summation from 1 to N. We'll adopt the notation $\Theta(S)$ for the space of trading strategies $\theta = (\theta_1, \ldots, \theta_N)$ meeting the regularity conditions (i)-(ii)-(iii) for each long-lived security and satisfying the "self-financing" restriction (4.1).

A *Radner equilibrium* for $\mathscr{E}$ is comprised of:

(1) a set of long-lived securities claiming $d = (d_1, \ldots, d_N)$, $d_n \in L^2(P)$, $1 \leq n \leq N \leq \infty$, with corresponding price processes $S = (S_1, \ldots, S_N)$;

(2) a set of trading strategies $\theta^i \in \Theta(S)$, one for each agent $i = 1, \ldots, I$; and

(3) a price $a \in R_+$ for time zero consumption;

all of these satisfying:

(4) budget constrained optimality: for each agent i,

$$\left(\hat{r}_i - \frac{\theta^i(0)^\top S(0)}{a}, \hat{x}_i + \theta^i(T)^\top d \right)$$

is $\succcurlyeq_i$-maximal in the budget set:

$$\left\{ \left(\hat{r}_i - \frac{\theta(0)^\top S(0)}{a}, \hat{x}_i + \theta(T)^\top d \right) \in V_i \colon \theta \in \Theta(S) \right\},$$

and

(5) market clearing:

$$\sum_{i=1}^I \theta^i(t) = 0 \quad \forall t \in [0, T].$$

The space of square-integrable martingales under Q, denoted $\mathscr{M}_Q^2$; its multiplicity, denoted $M(\mathscr{M}_Q^2)$; and a corresponding orthogonal 2-basis of martingales, $m = (m_1, \ldots, m_N)$, where $N = M(\mathscr{M}_Q^2) \leq \infty$; are all defined in the Appendix. The central concept is that any of the martingales associated with the given information structure can be represented as the sum of $M(\mathcal{M}_Q^2)$ stochastic integrals against the fixed 2-basis of martingales m, in the manner given by the following theorem. This result is a direct consequence of the definition of martingale multiplicity. The content of the result lies with specific examples in which martingale multiplicity is characterized. Details, beyond those in the Appendix, may be found in the fourth chapter of Jacod [11]. Kunita and Watanabe [14] as well as Davis and Varaiya [4] also include the essentials.

THEOREM 4.1: *For any $X \in \mathcal{M}_Q^2$ there exists $\theta = (\theta_1, \ldots, \theta_N)$, where $\theta_n \in L_Q^2[m_n]$ for all n, such that*

$$X_t = \int_0^t \theta(s)^\top \, dm(s) \quad \forall t \in [0, T] \quad \text{a.s.}$$

We should remark that when $Q \approx P$, the spaces $L_Q^2[m_n]$ and $L_P^2[m_n]$ are identical because of the bounds implied on dQ/dP. We also use the fact that a martingale under Q is a semimartingale under P given the equivalence of P and Q. Thus any element of $\mathcal{M}_Q^2$ is a valid price process. This can be checked in Jacod [11, Chapter 7], along with the existence of $\int \theta_n \, dm_n$ as a stochastic integral under P whenever $\theta_n \in L_P^2[m_n]$.

Now we have the main result.

THEOREM 4.2: *Suppose $(\Psi, v_i^*, i = 1, \ldots, I)$ is an Arrow-Debreu equilibrium for $\mathcal{E}$, where without loss of generality Ψ has the representation (a, Q) given by relation (3.2). Provided $Q \approx P$ and $\mathcal{F}$ is separable under P, there is a Radner equilibrium for $\mathcal{E}$ achieving the Arrow-Debreu equilibrium allocations.*

PROOF: The proof takes four steps:

(1) Specify a set of long-lived securities.

(2) Announce a price for time zero consumption and price processes for the long-lived securities.

(3) Allocate a trading strategy to each agent which generates that agent's Arrow-Debreu allocation and which, collectively, clears markets.

(4) Prove that no agent has any incentive to deviate from the allocated trading strategy.

STEP 1: Select the following elements of $L^2(P)$ as the claims of the available long-lived securities:

$$d_0 = 1_\Omega,$$

$$d_n = m_n(T), \quad 1 \leq n \leq N = M(\mathcal{M}_Q^2),$$

where 1_Ω is the random variable whose value is identically 1 (the indicator function on Ω), and $m = (m_1, \ldots, m_N)$ is an orthogonal 2-basis for $\mathcal{M}_Q^2$. Since $Q \approx P$, the final values of the martingales, $m_n(T)$, are elements of $L^2(P)$.

STEP 2: For $0 \le n \le N$ let $S_n(t)$, the price of d_n at time t, be announced as $E^*[d_n | \mathcal{F}_t]$. In other words, each long-lived security's current price is the conditional expectation under Q of its consumption value. For convenience we actually take RCLL[6] versions of these price processes. There is obviously some forethought here, for the result is $S_0 \equiv 1$ and $S_n = m_n$, $1 \le n \le N$, implying that the last N price processes are themselves an orthogonal 2-basis for $\mathcal{M}_Q^2$, suggesting their ability to "span" (in the sense of Theorem 4.1) all consumption claims not actually available for trading. The first security serves as a "store-of-value", since its price is constant. We also announce the positive scalar a given in the statement of the theorem as the price of time zero consumption.

STEP 3: For any agent i, for $1 \le i \le I-1$, let $e_i = x_i^* - \hat{x}_i$. Then the process

$$(4.2) \qquad X_i(t) = E^*(e_i | \mathcal{F}_t) - E^*(e_i), \quad t \in [0, T],$$

is an element of $\mathcal{M}_Q^2$, given $Q \approx P$, which can be reconstructed via Theorem 4.1 as

$$(4.3) \qquad X_i(t) = \sum_{n=1}^N \int_0^t \theta_n^i(s) \, dS_n(s), \quad \forall t \in [0, T] \quad \text{a.s.,}$$

for some $\theta_n^i \in L_P^2[S_n]$, $1 \le n \le N$.

In order to meet the accounting restriction (4.1), we set the following trading process for the "store-of-value" security:

$$(4.4) \qquad \theta_0^i(t) = E^*(e_i) + \sum_{n=1}^N \int_0^t \theta_n^i(s) \, dS_n(s) - \theta_n^i(t)S_n(t), \quad t \in [0, T].$$

Of course $\int \theta_0^i \, dS_0 \equiv 0$ since $S_0 \equiv 1$. A technical argument showing $\theta_0^i \in \mathcal{P}$ is given as Appendix Lemma A.1, which then implies $\theta_0^i \in L_P^2[S_0]$.

Substituting (4.4) into (4.3), noting that $m_n(0) = 0 \, \forall n$, we then have

$$(4.5) \qquad \theta^i(t)^\top S(t) = \theta^i(0)^\top S(0) + \int_0^t \theta^i(s)^\top dS(s) \quad \forall t \in [0, T], \quad \text{a.s.,}$$

confirming (4.1). This yields the final requirement for claiming the trading strategy is admissible, or $\theta^i = (\theta_0^i, \ldots, \theta_N^i) \in \Theta(S)$. Evaluating (4.5) at times T and 0, using the definitions of e_i and X_i yields:

$$\theta^i(T)^\top d + \hat{x}_i = \theta^i(T)^\top S(T) + \hat{x}_i = x_i^* \quad \text{a.s.}$$

and

$$\theta^i(0)^\top S(0) = E^*(x_i^* - \hat{x}_i) = \Psi(0, x_i^*) - \Psi(0, \hat{x}_i) = (\hat{r}_i - r_i^*)a,$$

the last line making use of the budget constraint on the Arrow–Debreu allocation for agent i. Thus by adopting the trading strategy θ^i, and faced with the time–zero consumption price of a, agent i can consume precisely $(r_i^*, x_i^*) = v_i^*$.

The above construction applies for agents 1 through $I-1$. For the last agent, agent I, let $\theta^I = -\sum_{i=1}^{I-1} \theta^i$. By the Kunita–Watanabe inequality [14], $\Theta(S)$ is a

[6] An *RCLL* process is one whose sample paths are right continuous with left limits almost surely.

linear space, so $\theta^I \in \Theta(S)$. Market clearing is obviously met by construction. To complete this step it remains to show that θ^I generates the consumption allocation $(r_i^*, x_i^*) = v_i^*$, but this is immediate from the linearity of stochastic integrals and market clearing in the Arrow-Debreu equilibrium.

STEP 4: We proceed by contradiction. Suppose some agent j can obtain a strictly preferred allocation $(r, x) >_j (r_j^*, x_j^*)$ by adopting a different trading strategy $\theta \in \Theta(S)$. Then the Arrow-Debreu price of (r, x) must be strictly higher than that of (r_j^*, x_j^*), or

$$ar + E^*(x) > ar_j^* + E^*(x_j^*).$$

Substituting the Radner budget constraint for r and x,

$$a\hat{r}_j - \theta(0)^\top S(0) + E^*\left[\hat{x}_j + \theta(0)^\top S(0) + \int_0^T \theta(t)^\top \, dS(t)\right] > ar_j^* + E^*(x_j^*),$$

or

(4.6) $$a\hat{r}_j + E^*(\hat{x}_j) > ar_j^* + E^*(x_j^*).$$

The last line uses the fact that $E^*[\int_0^T \theta(t)^\top \, dS(t)] = 0$ since $\int \theta^I \, dS$ is a Q-martingale for any $\theta \in \Theta(S)$, from the fact that $\int \phi \, dS_n \in \mathcal{M}_Q^2 \; \forall \phi \in L_Q^2[S_n]$ [11, Chapter 4]. But (4.6) contradicts the Arrow-Debreu budget-constrained optimality of (r_j^*, x_j^*). This establishes the theorem.   Q.E.D.

Of course, under the standard weak conditions ensuring that an Arrow-Debreu equilibrium allocation is Pareto optimal, the resulting Radner equilibrium allocation of this theorem is also Pareto optimal as it implements the Arrow-Debreu allocation.

5. THE SPANNING NUMBER OF RADNER EQUILIBRIA

The key idea of the last proof is that an appropriately selected and priced set of long-lived securities "spans" the entire final period consumption space in the sense that any $x \in L^2(P)$ can be represented in the form

(5.1) $$E^*[x \mid \mathscr{F}_t] = \theta(t)^\top S(t) = \theta(0)^\top S(0) + \int_0^t \theta(s)^\top \, dS(s) \quad \forall t \in [0, T] \quad \text{a.s.,}$$

where $S = (S_0, \ldots, S_N)$ is the set of $(N+1)$ security price processes constructed in the proof and $\theta \in \Theta(S)$ is an appropriate trading strategy. In particular, $E^*[x \mid \mathscr{F}_T] = x$ a.s. As examples in the following section will show, this number of securities, $N+1$, or the multiplicity of $\mathcal{M}_Q^2$ plus one, can be considerably smaller than the dimension of $L^2(P)$. But is this the "smallest number" which will serve this purpose, or the "spanning number" in some sense? To be more precise, we will prove the following result, still assuming $Q \approx P$ and the separability of $\mathscr{F}$.

PROPOSITION 5.1: *Suppose long-lived security prices for $\mathscr{E}$ are square-integrable martingales under Q, the equilibrium price measure for $\mathscr{E}$. Then the minimum number of long-lived securities which completes markets in the sense of (5.1) is $M(\mathscr{M}_Q^2)+1$.*

PROOF: That $M(\mathscr{M}_Q^2)+1$ is a sufficient number is given by construction in the proof of Theorem 4.2. The remainder of the proof is devoted to showing that at least this number is required.

If $M(\mathscr{M}_Q^2) = \infty$ we are done. Otherwise, suppose $S = (S_1, \ldots, S_K)$, $K < \infty$, is a set of square-integrable Q-martingale security price processes with the representation property (5.1). By the definition of multiplicity it follows that $K \geq M(\mathscr{M}_Q^2)$. It remains to show that $K = M(\mathscr{M}_Q^2)$ implies a contradiction, which we now pursue.

Let $x = k + 1^{\mathsf{T}} S(T) \in L^2(P)$, where k is any real constant and 1 is a K-dimensional vector of ones. If S has the representation property (5.1) there exists some $\theta \in \Theta(S)$ satisfying (5.1) for this particular x. Furthermore, since S is a vector of Q-martingales,

$$(5.2) \qquad E^*[x \mid \mathscr{F}_t] = k + 1^{\mathsf{T}} S(t) = k + 1^{\mathsf{T}} S(0) + \int_0^t 1^{\mathsf{T}} \, dS(s) \quad \forall t \in [0, T] \quad \text{a.s.}$$

Since $\theta(0)^{\mathsf{T}} S(0) = E^*(x) = k + 1^{\mathsf{T}} S(0)$, equating the right hand sides of (5.1) and (5.2) yields

$$\int_0^t \theta(s)^{\mathsf{T}} \, dS(s) = \int_0^t 1^{\mathsf{T}} \, dS(s) \quad \forall t \in [0, T] \quad \text{a.s.}$$

Appendix Lemma A.2 then implies

$$Q\{\exists t \in [0, T]: \theta(t) = 1\} > 0.$$

Since $Q \approx P$, the above event also has strictly positive P-probability, and equating the second members of (5.1) and (5.2) yields

$$P\{\exists t \in [0, T]: 1^{\mathsf{T}} S(t) = 1^{\mathsf{T}} S(t) + k\} > 0,$$

an obvious absurdity if $k \neq 0$. Q.E.D.

The reader will likely have raised two points by now. First, having shown that the "spanning number" is $M(\mathscr{M}_Q^2)+1$ when long-lived securities are square-integrable martingales under Q, what do we know about the spanning number in general? From the work of Harrison and Kreps [8], we see that a "viable" Radner equilibrium *must* be of the form of security price processes which are martingales under *some* probability measure. Their framework, somewhat less general than ours, was extended in Huang [10] to a setting much like our own. Readers may wish to confirm that the same result can be proved in the same manner for the present setting. We have chosen to announce prices as martingales under Q, rather than some other probability measure, as this follows from the natural selection of a numeraire claiming one unit of consumption in every state, the security claiming d_0 in Theorem 4.2. Other numeraires could be chosen; if a random numeraire is selected then in equilibrium security prices will be martingales under some other probability measure, say $\hat{P}$, and the spanning number will be $M(\mathcal{M}_{\hat{P}}^2) + 1$, if the appropriate regularity conditions are adhered to. Does this number differ from $M(\mathcal{M}_Q^2) + 1$; that is, can the martingale multiplicity for the same information structure change under substitution of probability measures? Within the class of equivalent probability measures, those giving zero probability to the same events, this seems unlikely. It is certainly not true for event trees. We put off a direct assault on this question to a subsequent paper. We will show later, however, that if the information is generated by a Standard Brownian Motion, then $M(\mathcal{M}_P^2) = M(\mathcal{M}_Q^2)$.

The second point which ought to have been raised is the number of securities required to implement an Arrow-Debreu equilibrium in a Radner style model, *dropping the requirement for complete markets.* For example, with only two agents, a single security which pays the difference between the endowment and the Arrow-Debreu allocation of one of the agents will obviously allow the two to trade to equilibrium at time zero. This is not a very robust regime of markets, of course. By fixing such agent-specific securities, any perturbation of agents' endowments or preferences which preserves Arrow–Debreu prices will generally preclude an efficient Radner equilibrium. Agents will generally be unable to reach their perturbed Arrow-Debreu allocations without a new set of long-lived securities. A set of long-lived securities which completes markets in the dynamic sense of relation (5.1) is constrastingly robust, although the selection still depends endogenously on Arrow-Debreu prices. It remains a formidable challenge to show how markets can be completed by selecting the claims of long-lived securities entirely on the basis of the exogenous information structure F. (As an aside, however, this is easily done for event trees. From this proof of the Proposition it is apparent that a selection of consumption payoffs for long-lived securities can be designed which (generically) completes markets for any Arrow–Debreu equilibrium prices.) There are no economic grounds, of course, precluding the selection of security markets from being an endogenous part of the equilibrium. One would in fact expect this to be the case, an interesting problem for future theoretical and empirical research.

Nothing precludes the fact that some of the martingale price processes in our model may take negative values, even if a positive constant (which is innocuous) is added. For a "spanning" set of positive price processes, one could split each of the original spanning martingales into its positive and negative parts, for a set of $2M(\mathcal{M}_Q^2) + 1$ price processes in all. The existence of the required stochastic integrals follows easily.

6. DISCUSSION

In this section we discuss some definitional issues, generalizations of the model, and some specific examples.

6.1. *The Gains Process and Admissible Trading Strategies*

Why is $L_P^2[S]$ an appropriate restriction on trading strategies for a security with price process S? Why is the stochastic integral $\int \theta \, dS$, for $\theta \in L_P^2[S]$, then the appropriate definition of gains from such a strategy? These are questions raised earlier by Harrison and Pliska [9].

Following Harrison and Pliska [9], we will say that a predictable trading strategy is *simple*, denoted $\theta \in \Lambda$, if there is a partition $\{0 = t_0, t_1, \ldots, t_{n-1}, t_n = T\}$ of $[0, T]$ and bounded random variables $\{h_0, \ldots, h_{n-1}\}$, where h_i is measurable with respect to $\mathcal{F}_{t_i}$, satisfying

$$\theta(t) = h_i, \quad t \in (t_i, t_{i+1}].$$

A simple trading strategy θ, roughly speaking, is one which is piecewise constant and for which $\theta(t)$ can be determined by information available up to, *but not including*, time t. The latter restriction is the basic content of *predictability*. This is not an unreasonable abstraction of "real" trading strategies. The gains process $\int \theta \, dS$, for $\theta \in \Lambda$, is furthermore defined path by path as a Stieltjes integral. That is, the gains at time t_i are

$$\int_0^{t_i} \theta(s) \, dS(s) = \sum_{j=0}^{i-1} \theta(t_j)[S(t_{j+1}) - S(t_j)],$$

simply the sum of profits and losses realized at discrete points in time.

We will give the space $\mathcal{M}_Q^2$ the norm

$$\|m\|_{\mathcal{M}_Q^2} = [E^*([m]_T)]^{1/2} \quad \forall m \in \mathcal{M}_Q^2,$$

and give $L_P^2[S]$ the semi-norm

$$\|\theta\|_{L_P^2[S]} = \left[E \left(\int_0^T \theta^2(t) \, d[S]_t \right) \right]^{1/2}.$$

PROPOSITION 6.1: *For every trading strategy $\theta \in L_P^2[S]$ there exists a sequence (θ_n) of simple trading strategies converging to θ in $L_P^2[S]$ (in the given semi-norm). For any such sequence, the corresponding gains processes $\int \theta_n \, dS$ converge to $\int \theta \, dS$ in $\mathcal{M}_Q^2$ in the given norm.*

PROOF: This is the way Ito originally extended the definition of stochastic integrals. His theorem uses the fact that Λ is dense in $L_Q^2[S]$ and shows that $\theta \mapsto \int \theta \, dS$, $\theta \in \Lambda$, extends uniquely to an isometry of $L_Q^2[S]$ in $\mathcal{M}_Q^2$. These facts can be checked, for instance, in Jacod [11, Chapter 4]. Since dQ/dP is assumed to be bounded above and below away from zero, the semi-norms $\|\cdot\|_{L_P[S]}$ and $\|\cdot\|_{L_Q^2[S]}$ are equivalent, and the result is proved. *Q.E.D.*

Interpreting this result: for any admissible strategy $\theta \in \Theta(S)$ there is a sequence of simple trading strategies converging (as agents are able to trade more and more frequently) to θ, with the corresponding gains processes converging to that generated by θ. The sequence of simple trading strategies can also be chosen to be self-financing (4.1) by using the same construction shown in the proof of Theorem 4.2 for the "store-of-value" strategy. A store-of-value security, one whose price is identically one for instance, is again called for. The minimal requirements for a "store-of-value" security price process have not been fully explored.

In what way have we limited agents by restricting them to $L_P^2[S]$ trading strategies? It is known, for instance, that by removing this constraint the so-called "suicide" and "doubling" strategies may become feasible, as discussed by Harrison and Pliska [9] and Kreps [12]. A suicide strategy makes nothing out of something almost surely, which no one would want to do anyway. A doubling strategy, however, generates a "free lunch," which shouldn't happen in equilibrium. More precisely, an equilibrium can't happen if doubling strategies are allowed. There are no doubling strategies in $L_P^2[S]$ since these strategies only generate martingales (under Q). There is also some comfort in knowing that, since $L_P^2[S]$ is a complete space, there is no sequence of simple or even general $L_P^2[S]$ strategies which converges to a doubling strategy in the sense of Proposition 6.1.

6.2. *Some Generalizations*

There is of course no difficulty in having heterogeneous probability assessments, provided all agents' subjective probability measures on $(\Omega, \mathscr{F})$ are uniformly absolutely continuous. This preserves the topologies on the consumption and strategy spaces across agents.

As a second generalization we could allow the consumption space to be $R \times L^q(P)$ for any $q \in [1, \infty)$, relaxing from $q = 2$. The allowable trading strategies should be generalized to $L_P^q[\underline{S}]$, as defined by Jacod [11, (4.59)], since there is then no guarantee of an orthogonal q-basis for $\mathscr{M}_Q^2$. It is a straightforward task to carry out all of the proofs in this paper under both of these generalizations. All interesting models of uncertainty we are aware of, however, are for $q = 2$.

It is also easy, but cumbersome, to extend our results to an economy with production and with a finite number of different consumption goods.

6.3. *Example: Economies on Event Trees*

If the information structure F is such that $\mathscr{F}_t$ contains only a finite number of events at each time t, then it can be represented in the form of an event tree, as in Figure 1.

For finite horizon problems, the terminal nodes of the tree can be treated as the elements of Ω. They are equal in number with the contingent claims forming a complete regime of Arrow–Debreu "simple securities." Yet, as the following proposition demonstrates, a complete markets Radner equilibrium can be established with far fewer securities, except in degenerate cases. Since integrability is not a consideration when Ω is finite, we characterize martingale multiplicity directly in terms of the "finite" filtration F, limiting consideration to probability measures under which each $\omega \in \Omega$ has strictly positive probability.

PROPOSITION 6.2: *The multiplicity of a finite filtration* F, *under any of a set of equivalent probability measures, is the maximum number of branches leaving any node of the corresponding event tree, minus one.*

The proof, given in the Appendix, presents an algorithm for constructing an orthogonal martingale basis. Just as in Section 4, a complete markets Radner equilibrium can be constructed from any given Arrow–Debreu equilibrium provided there are markets for long-lived securities paying the terminal values of such a Q-martingale basis in time T consumption, and one store-of-value security paying one unit of consumption at time T in each state $\omega \in \Omega$.

By drawing simple examples of event trees, however, it soon becomes apparent that many other choices for the spanning securities will work. This is consistent with Kreps [13]. His Proposition 2 effectively states that a necessary and sufficient condition for a complete markets Radner economy is that at any node of the event tree the following condition is met: The dimension of the span of the vectors of "branch-contingent" prices of the available long-lived securities must be the number of branches leaving that node. Kreps goes on to state that the number of long-lived securities required for implementing an Arrow–Debreu equilibrium in this manner must be at least K, the maximum number of branches leaving any node, consistent with our "spanning number" (the martingale multiplicity plus one), as demonstrated by the previous proposition. Kreps also obtains the genericity result: except for a "sparse" set of long-lived securities, a set of measure zero in a sense given in the Kreps article, *any* selection of K or more long-lived security price processes admits a complete markets Radner economy. (The economy needn't be in equilibrium of course.) This result seems exceedingly difficult to extend to a general continuous-time model.

One should beware of taking the "limit by compression" of finite filtrations and expecting the spanning number to be preserved. For example, we have seen statements in the finance literature to the following effect: "In the Black–Scholes option pricing model it is to be expected that continuous trading on *two* securities can replicate any claim since Brownian Motion is the limit of a normalized sequence of coin-toss random walks, each of which has only two outcomes at any toss." If this logic is correct it hides some unexplained reasoning. For example, two simultaneous independent coin-toss random walks generate a martingale space of multiplicity *three* (four branches at each node, minus one), whereas the corresponding Brownian Motion limits (Williams [22, Chapter 1]) generate a martingale space of multiplicity *two*. Somehow one dimension of "local uncertainty" is lost in the limiting procedure.

6.4. *A Brownian Motion Example*

This subsection illustrates an infinite dimensional consumption space whose economy (under regularity conditions) has a complete markets Radner equilibrium including only two securities!

Suppose uncertainty is characterized, and information is revealed, by a Standard Brownian Motion, W. To be precise, each $\omega \in \Omega$ corresponds to a particular sample path chosen for W from the continuous functions on $[0, T]$, denoted $C[0, T]$, according to the Wiener probability measure P on $\mathscr{F}$, the completed Borel tribe on $C[0, T]$. The probability space, then, is the completed Wiener triple $(\Omega, \mathscr{F}, P)$ and the filtration is the family $F = \{\mathscr{F}_t, t \in [0, T]\}$, where $\mathscr{F}_t$ is the completion of the Borel tribe on $C[0, t]$. For conciseness, we'll call (Ω, F, P) the completed filtered Wiener triple. More details on this construction are given in the first chapter of Williams [22].

To construct a complete markets Radner equilibrium from a given Arrow-Debreu equilibrium, as in Section 4, we need an orthogonal 2-basis for $\mathscr{M}_Q^2$, where Q is an equilibrium price measure for the Arrow-Debreu economy. In this case we can actually show that a particular Standard Brownian Motion on (Ω, F, Q) is just such a 2-basis!

It is a well known result (e.g. [14]) that the underlying Brownian Motion W is a 2-basis for $\mathscr{M}_P^2$. Assuming $Q \approx P$, the process

$$Z(t) = E\left[\frac{dQ}{dP}\bigg|\, \mathscr{F}_t\right], \quad t \in [0, T],$$

is a square-integrable martingale on (Ω, F, P), with $E[Z(T)] = 1$. Then, by Theorem 4.1, there exists some $\rho \in L_P^2[W]$ giving the representation:

$$Z(t) = 1 + \int_0^t \rho(s)\, dW(s) \quad \forall t \in [0, T] \quad \text{a.s.}$$

It follows from Ito's Lemma that, defining the process $\eta(t) - \rho(t)/Z(t)$, we have the alternative representation:

$$Z(t) = \exp\left\{\int_0^t \eta(s)\, dW(s) - \tfrac{1}{2}\int_0^t \eta^2(s)\, ds\right\} \quad \forall t \in [0, T] \quad \text{a.s.}$$

From this, the new process

(6.1) $$W^*(t) = W(t) - \int_0^t \eta(s)\, ds, \quad t \in [0, T],$$

defines a Standard Brownian Motion on (Ω, F, Q) by Girsanov's Fundamental Theorem (Lipster and Shiryayev [15, p. 232]). It remains to show that W^* is itself a 2-basis for $\mathscr{M}_Q^2$, but this is immediate from Theorem 5.18 of Liptser and Shiryayev [15], using the uniform absolute continuity of P and Q. This construction is summarized as follows.

PROPOSITION 6.3: *Suppose W is the Standard Brownian Motion underlying the filtered Wiener triple (Ω, F, P) and $Q \approx P$. Then W^* defined by (6.1) is a Standard Brownian Motion under Q which is a 2-basis for $\mathcal{M}_Q^2$. In particular, $M(\mathcal{M}_P^2) = M(\mathcal{M}_Q^2) = 1$.*

By a slightly more subtle argument, we could have reached the same conclusion under the weaker assumption that P and Q are merely equivalent, but $Q \approx P$ is needed for other reasons in Theorem 4.1.

In short, by marketing just two long-lived securities, one paying $W^*(T)$ in time T consumption, the other paying one unit of time T consumption with certainty, and announcing their price processes as $W^*(t)$ and 1 (for all t), a complete markets Radner equilibrium is achieved.

This example can be extended to filtrations generated by vector diffusion processes. Under well known conditions (e.g. [8]) a vector diffusion generates the same filtration as the underlying vector of independent Brownian Motions. An orthogonal 2-basis for $\mathcal{M}_P^2$ is then simply these Brownian Motions themselves [14]. By generalizing the result quoted from Lipster and Shiryayev [15, Theorem 5.18], one can then demonstrate a vector of equally many Brownian Motions under Q which form a martingale basis for $\mathcal{M}_Q^2$ in the sense of Theorem 4.1. Since the manipulations are rather involved, and because the results raise some provocative issues concerning the "inter-temporal capital asset pricing models" (e.g., [17]) which are also based on diffusion uncertainty, we put off this development to a subsequent paper. It is also known that the filtration generated by a Poisson process corresponds to a martingale multiplicity of one [11].

7. CONCLUDING REMARKS

We are working on several extensions and improvements suggested by the results of this paper.

The first major step will be to demonstrate the existence of continuous trading Radner equilibria "from scratch," that is, taking endowments and preferences as agent primitives and proving the existence of an equilibrium such as that demonstrated in Theorem 4.2. In particular, the existence of an Arrow–Debreu equilibrium and the condition $Q \approx P$ must be proven from exogenous assumptions, rather than assumed. A full-blown Radner economy is also being examined, one with consumption occurring over time rather than at the two points 0 and T.

The Brownian Motion example of Section 6.4, as suggested there, is being extended to the case in which uncertainty and information are characterized by a vector of diffusion "state-variable" processes. This will allow us to tie in with, and provide a critical evaluation of, the inter-temporal capital asset pricing models popular in the financial economics literature.

We left off in Section 5 by characterizing the spanning number in terms of (endogenous) Arrow–Debreu prices through the equilibrium price measure Q. Our next efforts will be directed at showing that, subject to regularity conditions, martingale multiplicity is invariant under substitution of equivalent probability measures. In that case the spanning number can be stated to be the exogenously given number, $M(\mathcal{M}_P^2) + 1$.

Stanford University
and
Massachusetts Institute of Technology

Manuscript received December 1983; final revision received January, 1985.

APPENDIX

MARTINGALE MULTIPLICITY

What follows is a heavily condensed treatment, taken mainly from the fourth chapter of Jacod [11].

A square-integrable martingale on the filtered probability space (Ω, F, P) is an F-adapted[7] process $X = \{X_t; t \in [0, T]\}$ with the properties: (i) $E[X(t)^2] < \infty$ for all $t \in [0, T]$, and (ii) $E[X(t)\mid \mathcal{F}_s] = X(s)$ a.s. for all $t \geq s$.

We will also assume without loss of generality for this paper that each martingale is an RCLL process. The first property (i) is *square-integrability*, the second (ii) is *martingale*, meaning roughly that the expected future value of X given current information is always the current value of X.

The space of square-integrable martingales on (Ω, F, P) which are null at zero (or $X(0) = 0$) is denoted $\mathcal{M}_P^2$. The spaces $\mathcal{M}_P^2$ and $L^2(P)$ are in one to one correspondence via the relationship, between some $X \in \mathcal{M}_P^2$ and $x \in L^2(P)$:

$$X(t) = E[x\mid \mathcal{F}_t], \quad t \in [0, T],$$

where all RCLL versions of the conditional expectation process are indistinguishable and therefore identified.

An F-adapted process is termed *predictable* if it is measurable with respect to the tribe $\mathcal{P}$ on $\Omega \times [0, T]$ generated by the left-continuous F-adapted processes. At an intuitive level, θ is a predictable process if the value of $\theta(t)$ can be determined from information available up to, *but not including*, time t, for each $t \in [0, T]$.

Two martingales X and Y are said to be *orthogonal* if the product XY is a martingale. From this point we'll assume that $\mathcal{F}$ is a separable tribe under P. In that case the path breaking work of Kunita and Watanabe [14] shows the existence of an orthogonal *2-basis* for $\mathcal{M}_P^2$, defined as a minimal set of mutually orthogonal elements of $\mathcal{M}_P^2$ with the representation property stated in Theorem 4.1. By "minimal," we mean that no fewer elements of $\mathcal{M}_P^2$ have this property. The number of elements of a 2-basis, whether countably infinite or some positive integer, is called the *multiplicity* of $\mathcal{M}_P^2$, denoted $M(\mathcal{M}_P^2)$.

The following lemma makes a technical argument used in the proof of Theorem 4.2.

LEMMA A.1: *Suppose the process X is defined by*

$$X(t) = \sum_{n=1}^{N} \left[\int_0^t \theta_n(s)\, dS_n(s) - \theta_n(t) S_n(t) \right], \quad t \in [0, T],$$

where $\int \theta_n\, dS_n$ is the stochastic integral of a predictable process θ_n with respect to a semi-martingale S_n, for $1 \leq n \leq N < \infty$. Then X is predictable.

PROOF: For any left-limits process Z, let $Z(t-)$ denote the left limit of Z at $t \in [0, T]$, and denote the "jump" of Z at t by $\Delta Z(t) = Z(t) - Z(t-)$, where we have used the convention that $Z(0-) = Z(0)$. Then we can write

$$X(t) = \sum_{n=1}^{N} \left[\int_0^{t-} \theta_n(s)\, dS_n(s) - \theta_n(t) S_n(t) + \theta_n(t)\, \Delta S_n(t) \right]$$

---

[7] A stochastic process $X = \{X_t; t \in [0, T]\}$ is adapted to a filtration $F = \{\mathcal{F}_t; t \in [0, T]\}$ if X_t is measurable with respect to $\mathcal{F}_t$ for all $t \in [0, T]$.

since

$$\Delta\left(\int_0^t \theta_n(s)\, dS_n(s)\right) = \theta_n(t)\,\Delta S_n(t)$$

by the definition of a stochastic integral. Then, using

$$\theta_n(t)S_n(t) = \theta_n(t)[S_n(t-) + \Delta S_n(t)],$$

we have

$$X(t) = \sum_{n=1}^{N}\left[\int_0^{t-}\theta_n(s)\, dS_n(s) - \theta_n(t)S_n(t-)\right], \quad t \in [0, T].$$

Since $\int_0^{t-}\theta_n\, dS_n$ and $S_n(t-)$ are left-continuous processes, and therefore predictable, and $\theta_n(t)$ is predictable, we know X is predictable because sums and products of measurable functions are measurable.
$\hspace{10cm}$ Q.E.D.

For any two elements X and Y of $\mathcal{M}_P^2$, let $\langle X, Y \rangle$ denote the unique predictable process with the property that $XY - \langle X, Y \rangle$ is a martingale and $\langle X, Y \rangle_0 = 0$.

LEMMA A.2: *Suppose* $(m_1, \ldots, m_N)$ *constitute a finite set of elements of* $\mathcal{M}_Q^2$ *with the representation property given in the statement of Theorem 4.1, where* $N = M(\mathcal{M}_Q^2)$. *If* θ_n *and* ϕ_n *are elements of* $L_Q^2[m_n]$, *for* $1 \leq n \leq N$, *satisfying (with the obvious shorthand)*

(a.1) $\hspace{1.5cm}\int_0^t \theta^\top\, dm = \int_0^t \phi^\top\, dm \quad \forall t \in [0, T]$ *a.s.*,

then

$$Q\{\exists t \in [0, T]: \theta(t) = \phi(t)\} > 0.$$

PROOF: Jacod [11] shows the existence of a predictable positive semi-definite $N \times N$ matrix valued process c and an increasing predictable process C with the property, for any α_n and β_n in $L_Q^2[m_n]$, $1 \leq n \leq N$,

(a.2) $\hspace{1cm}\left\langle \int \alpha^\top\, dm, \int \beta^\top\, dm \right\rangle_t = \int_0^t \alpha(s)^\top c(s)\beta(s)\, dC(s) \quad \forall t \in [0, T]$ *a.s.*

The process C also defines a Doléans measure (also denoted C) on $(\Omega \times [0, T], \mathcal{P})$ according to

$$C(B) = \int_\Omega \int_{[0,T]} 1_B(\omega, s)\, dC(\omega, s)\, dQ(\omega) \quad \forall B \in \mathcal{P}.$$

By (4.43) of Jacod [11], the matrix process c reaches full rank, and is thus positive definite, on some set $B^* \in \mathcal{P}$ of strictly positive C-measure. But, by (a.1) and (a.2),

(a.3) $\hspace{1cm}\int_0^t [\theta(\omega, s) - \phi(\omega, s)]^\top c(\omega, s)[\theta(\omega, s) - \phi(\omega, s)]\, dC(\omega, s) = 0 \quad \forall t \in [0, T]$ *a.s.*

Ignoring without loss of generality the Q-null set on which (a.3) does not hold, this implies that $\theta(\omega, t) = \phi(\omega, t)$ for all time points of increase of C on B^*, which have strictly positive Q-probability since the projection of B^* on Ω must have strictly positive Q-measure for B^* to have strictly positive C-measure.
$\hspace{10cm}$ Q.E.D.

PROOF OF PROPOSITION 6.2—MULTIPLICITY OF AN EVENT TREE: Let N denote the maximum number of branches leaving any node of the event tree, minus one. The proposition will be proved by constructing an orthogonal martingale basis on this filtration consisting of the N processes $m_1, \ldots, m_N$.

Any martingale on a finite filtration is characterized entirely by its right-continuous jumps at each node in the corresponding event tree. Denote the jump of m_j at a generic node with L departing branches by the vector $\delta_j = (\delta_{j1}, \ldots, \delta_{jL})$. That is, $\delta_j \in R^L$ represents the random variable which takes the real number δ_{jl} if branch l is the realized event at this node. Let $p = (p_1, \ldots, p_L) \in R^L$ denote the vector of conditional branching probabilities at this node.

The processes $m_1, \ldots, m_n$ are then mutually orthogonal martingales if they satisfy the following two conditions at each node:

(i) $p^T \delta_j = 0$, $j = 1, \ldots, N$ (zero mean jumps, the martingale property), and

(ii) $\delta_j^T [p] \delta_k = 0$, $\forall j \neq k$, where $[p]$ denotes the diagonal matrix whose lth diagonal element is p_l (mutually uncorrelated jumps, implying mutually orthogonal martingales).

We construct the processes $m_1, \ldots, m_N$ by designing their jumps at each node of the event tree, in any order, taking $m_j(0) = 0$ $\forall j$. At a given node (with L branches), it is simple to choose nonzero vectors $\delta_1, \ldots, \delta_{L-1}$ in R^L satisfying

(a.4) $\qquad \Delta_j[p]\delta_j = 0$, $\quad 1 \leq j \leq L-1$,

where Δ_j is the $j \times L$ matrix whose first row is a vector of ones and whose kth row is, for $k \geq 2$, δ_{k-1}^T. This cannot be done for $j \geq L$ since $\Delta_L[p]^{1/2}$ is a full rank $L \times L$ matrix (its rows are nonzero and mutually orthogonal). Instead, let $\delta_L, \ldots, \delta_N$ each be zero vectors. One can quickly verify that this construction meets the conditions (i)-(ii) for $m_1, \ldots, m_N$ to be mutually orthogonal martingales. They are nontrivial since there is at least one node with $N+1$ branches, by definition of N. They form a basis (in the sense of Theorem 4.1) for all martingales since at each node the subspace $\{\delta \in R^L : \delta^T p = 0\}$ has linearly independent spanning vectors $\delta_1, \ldots, \delta_{L-1}$. That is, the jump of any given martingale at this node is a linear combination of the jumps of the first $L-1$ martingales of the set $\{m_1, \ldots, m_N\}$. At least N martingales are needed for a martingale basis since at some node this subspace has dimension N, by definition of N. $\hfill$ Q.E.D.

EXAMPLE: A MARKOV CHAIN: As a simple example, consider a finite state-space Markov chain information structure. Transition probabilities are given by the matrix

$$\Pi = (\pi_{\alpha\beta}) \quad 1 \leq \alpha \leq n; 1 \leq \beta \leq n;$$

where $\pi_{\alpha\beta}$ denotes the one-step transition probability from state α to state β. Let π^α denote the αth row of Π and $\delta_j^\alpha \in R^n$ denote the vector of jumps of the process m_j at any node corresponding to state α, for $1 \leq j \leq n-1$. We will assume at least one row of Π has no zero elements. Then the multiplicity of the space of martingales on this Markov chain is $n-1$, and the processes $m_1, \ldots, m_{n-1}$ form an orthogonal martingale basis provided, for $\alpha = 1, \ldots, n$,

$$\pi^{\alpha T} \delta_j^\alpha = 0, \quad 1 \leq j \leq n-1,$$

and

$$\delta_j^{\alpha T} [\pi^\alpha] \delta_k^\alpha = 0, \quad j \neq k,$$

corresponding to conditions (i)-(ii) above, and $\delta_j^\alpha \neq 0$ for all α and all j.

If, for instance,

$$\Pi = \begin{pmatrix} 0.3 & 0.3 & 0.4 \\ 0.3 & 0.3 & 0.4 \\ 0.3 & 0.3 & 0.4 \end{pmatrix},$$

then the two martingales m_1 and m_2 are an orthogonal martingale basis, where, at any node, m_1 jumps $+2$ if state 1 follows, jumps $+2$ if state 2 follows, and jumps -3 if state 3 follows, or $\delta_1 = (2, 2, -3)$; and similarly m_2 is characterized by jumps $\delta_2 = (1, -1, 0)$. To be even more explicit, if state 2 occurs at time 1, state 3 at time 2, and the chain terminates at time 2.5, the sample path for m_1 is

$$m_1(t) = 0, \quad 0 \leq t < 1,$$

$$m_1(t) = 2, \quad 1 \leq t < 2,$$

$$m_1(t) = -1, \quad 2 \leq t \leq 2.5.$$

REFERENCES

[1] ARROW, K.: "Le rôle des valeurs boursières pour la repartition la meillure des risques," *Econometrie*, 40(1952), 41–48; translated in *Review of Economic Studies*, 31(1964), 91–96.

[2] BLACK, F., AND M. SCHOLES: "The Pricing of Options and Corporate Liabilities," *Journal of Political Economy*, 81(1973), 637–654.

[3] COX, J., AND S. ROSS: "The Valuation of Options for Alternative Stochastic Processes," *Journal of Financial Economics*, 3(1976), 145–166.

[4] DAVIS, M. H., AND P. VARAIYA: "The Multiplicity of an Increasing Family of σ-Fields," *The Annals of Probability*, 2(1974), 958–963.

[5] DEBREU, G.: *Theory of Value*. Cowles Foundation Monograph 17. New Haven: Yale University Press, 1959.

[6] DUFFIE, J. D.: "Advances in General Equilibrium Theory," Ph.D. Dissertation, Stanford University, 1984.

[7] HALMOS, P.: *Measure Theory*. Princeton: Van Nostrand, 1950.

[8] HARRISON, J., AND D. KREPS: "Martingales and Arbitrage in Multiperiod Securities Markets," *Journal of Economic Theory*, 20(1979), 381–408.

[9] HARRISON, J., AND S. PLISKA: "Martingales and Stochastic Integrals in the Theory of Continuous Trading," *Stochastic Processes and Their Applications*, 11(1981), 215–260.

[10] HUANG, C.: "Information Structure and Equilibrium Asset Prices," *Journal of Economic Theory*, 35(1985), 33–71.

[11] JACOD, J.; *Calcul Stochastique et Problémes de Martingales, Lecture Notes in Mathematics, No. 714*. Berlin: Springer-Verlag, 1979.

[12] KREPS, D.: "Three Essays on Capital Markets," Technical Report 298, Institute for Mathematical Studies in The Social Sciences, Stanford University, 1979.

[13] ———: "Multiperiod Securities and the Efficient Allocation of Risk: A Comment on the Black–Scholes Option Pricing Model," *The Economics of Uncertainty and Information*, ed. by J. McCall. Chicago: University of Chicago Press, 1982.

[14] KUNITA, H., AND S. WATANABE: "On Square-Integrable Martingales," *Nagoya Mathematics Journal*, 30(1967), 209–245.

[15] LIPTSER, R., AND A. SHIRYAYEV: *Statistics of Random Processes I: General Theory*. New York: Springer-Verlag, 1977.

[16] MEMIN, JEAN: "Espaces de semi Martingales et Changement de Probabilité," *Zeitschrift für Wahrscheinlichkeitstheorie*, 52(1980), 9–39.

[17] MERTON, R.: "An Intertemporal Capital Asset Pricing Model," *Econometrica*, 41(1973), 867–888.

[18] ———: "The Theory of Rational Option Pricing," *Bell Journal of Economics and Management Science*, 4(1973), 141–183.

[19] ———: "On the Microeconomic Theory of Investment Under Uncertainty," in *Handbook of Mathematical Economics, Vol. II*, ed. by K. Arrow and M. Intriligator. Amsterdam: North-Holland Publishing Company, 1982.

[20] RADNER, R.: "Existence of Equilibrium of Plans, Prices and Price Expectations in a Sequence of Markets," *Econometrica*, 40(1972), 289–303.

[21] SCHAEFER, H. H.: *Banach Lattices and Positive Operators*. New York: Springer-Verlag, 1974.

[22] WILLIAMS, D.: *Diffusions, Markov Processes, and Martingales, Vol. 1*. New York: Wiley, 1979.

discussion | Spanning in Financial Markets

Jonathan E. Ingersoll, Jr.

**School of Organization and Management
Yale University**

The property of spanning in markets is one of enormous interest to financial economists. Indeed, many, if not most, of the theories in finance depend crucially on some aspect of spanning. There seem to be three distinct foci of spanning research, which I shall call *welfare results, pricing results*, and *basis augmenting results*.

The focus of welfare results is on the change in utility for investors or consumers that is caused by a change in spanning opportunities. The Pareto efficiency of complete markets as demonstrated by Arrow (1964) and Debreu (1959) is the best-known result in this area.

The no-arbitrage pricing results in finance come directly from spanning. The Black-Scholes (1973) option pricing model and its derivative contingent-claims models are prime examples, as is the arbitrage pricing theory (APT). Some versions of the latter have aspects of welfare results as well.

The third strand of research is somewhat different. Rather than examining the results of spanning, our concern is on methods of creating new securities that increase the dimension of the basis. Arrow and Debreu pioneered in this area with the development of the concept of state-contingent claims—often called Arrow-Debreu securities. More recent research has been concerned primarily with the basis augmenting properties of options or other derivative securities based on existing assets.

Most of the spanning results in financial economics can be demonstrated in single-period models. Indeed, in order to understand our multiperiod models completely, we often limit them so that they can be reduced to a series of single-period models. In some cases, when enough of the time-state outcomes are spanned, the intertemporal nature of the problem disappears completely and there is no trading after the first period. The first three sections of this chapter discuss each of the areas previously mentioned in a discrete-time setting. The final section deals with intertemporal extensions.

I would like to thank the editors for their comments on earlier drafts. I have also benefited from discussions with my colleagues, in particular R. Antle, P. Dybvig, and S. Ross.

I. WELFARE RESULTS

The social welfare effects of spanning are not a primary area of interest within financial economics, so I will not spend much time on them. On the other hand, lack of familiarity has also led to some misinterpretation of these results.

Much of the social welfare literature can be summarized in these two theorems: (i) Any competitive equilibrium is Pareto efficient among all allocations spanned by the existing opportunities for trade. (ii) With convex preference orderings and convex consumption and production possibility sets and in the absence of any externalities, any Pareto-efficient allocation can be realized as a *compensated competitive equilibrium*.

In finance we usually concern ourselves only with the first result. In addition, we confine our attention to pure competitive equilibria without compensation (i.e., equilibria with no redistribution of endowments).[1]

The unconstrained Pareto efficiency of complete markets is a special case of the first theorem. In the context of the finance problem, if there is a complete market for assets (i.e., there are as many linearly independent assets as states[2]), then the resulting allocation of *wealth* (or consumption) is Pareto efficient.

More generally, if the financial markets are incomplete, then the resulting allocation of the *assets* is Pareto efficient. A central planner could not redistribute the existing assets to improve anyone's welfare without decreasing someone else's utility. Typically, however, the planner would be able to improve the final allocation of *wealth* by creating opportunities for trade beyond those spanned by the existing assets. From the proved Pareto superiority of a complete market, one might be led to the "obvious" conclusion that investors will always introduce a sufficient number of derivative assets to complete the market, provided the creation process is not too costly.

This conclusion is correct, but it is not an immediate consequence of the Pareto efficiency of complete markets. The introduction of new financial assets, something that the market could accomplish without a central planner, is not sufficient to ensure Pareto dominance of the completed market. Their introduction might change prices leading to income (or wealth) effects that hurt some investors more than the increased opportunities to trade can compensate. It is the central planner's ability to alter endowments (to create a *compensated* equilibrium) that ensures that these income effects can be offset. Nevertheless, as Satterthwaite (1981) has shown: "... if the observable component [of the state space] is not spanned, then entrepreneurs can make a riskless profit by introducing new securities."[3] Thus, in the context of a financial market where states are determined by observable outcomes, we should expect that the market will be complete or effectively so.[4]

If all investors have state-independent utility and homogeneous beliefs, then the Pareto-efficient allocation resulting from a complete market will create the same ordering of wealth across states for every investor. That is, for any two states with the same aggregate wealth, each investor will have the same end-of-period wealth, and if the states are ordered by aggregate wealth, then every investor's end-of-period wealth will be ordered as well.

A corollary to this result is that with complete markets the set of optimal (or efficient) portfolios is convex, so there must exist a representative investor who (optimally) holds the market portfolio.[5] This result, although of recent vintage, lies at the heart of many long-known theories in finance. I will discuss this issue further in the next section.

One aspect of Pareto efficiency that is often confused is its connection with "informational efficiency" as defined in the rational expectations literature. Although the word used is the same, the two concepts are quite different.[6] An informationally efficient market does not necessarily lead to a desirable allocation of risk, so it need not be Pareto efficient. Likewise, a Pareto-efficient market need not be informationally efficient. However, a market that has achieved a Pareto-efficient allocation with homogeneous beliefs among investors will be informationally efficient with respect to new heterogeneous (speculative) information that does not alter any current consumption or physical investment plans.[7]

II. PRICING RESULTS

The most direct, and certainly most important, pricing result that derives from spanning is the existence of a linear pricing rule or operator. This result is usually stated as follows: In the absence of arbitrage opportunities, there must exist positive state prices, p_s, that correctly value all assets. Formally, if V_i denotes the current value of asset i, and its (cum dividend) value in each state s next period is given by X_{si}, then $V_i = \sum_s p_s X_{si}$. Generally, these state prices are not unique; however, if the market is complete, then the set of state prices is unique.

Ross (1976a, 1978b) was the first to prove the equivalence of the absence of arbitrage and the existence of a linear pricing rule.[8] Now, the result is so well known (and so "apparently obvious") that it is easy to forget it is not an axiom but a theorem with far-reaching consequences and sometimes subtle interpretations. For example, all of the preference-free restrictions on option prices in Merton (1973b) and Cox and Ross (1976b) (including the theorem that an American call should not be exercised prior to maturity) follow immediately from the linear pricing result.[9]

This basic result can be presented in many different guises. Two alternative treatments are to price assets in terms of risk-neutral probabilities and to price assets using a pricing standard.[10]

If we define the *risk-neutral* (or *martingale*) *probabilities* to be $\pi_s^* \equiv p_s(1 + r)$, where r is the riskless interest rate, then the "expected" rate of return on each asset is equal to the interest rate: $(\sum_s \pi_s^* X_{si})/V_i = 1 + r$. Note that these "probabilities" must be positive because the state prices are, and they must sum to unity. They bear no direct relation to the true probabilities, however. This method is employed in option pricing or contingent-claims models and is usually referred to as the Cox-Ross or "risk-neutral" pricing method. A great number of pricing results have been developed with this methodology;

however, I will go no further into this area. It is covered at length in the discussion by Cox and Huang in this volume.

If we define the *pricing standard* $\tilde{\rho}$ as a random variable with realizations $\rho_s = (1 + r)p_s/\pi_s$, then the no-arbitrage pricing result can also be stated as $E[\tilde{X}_i\tilde{\rho}] = (1 + r)V_i$. This last result can be reexpressed using rates of return as

$$E\left[\frac{\tilde{X}_i}{V_i}\right] = (1 + r) - \text{Cov}\left(\frac{\tilde{X}_i}{V_i}, \tilde{\rho}\right).$$

This equation decomposes the expected gross return on any asset into two portions. The first is 1 plus the interest rate, or compensation for the use of funds. The second is the risk premium. It is equal to the negative of the covariance between the asset's return and the pricing standard. The portion of the return on an asset that is uncorrelated with $\tilde{\rho}$ bears no risk compensation in equilibrium.

In equilibrium $\tilde{\rho}$ must be proportional to the marginal utility of every investor.[11] Not surprisingly, since it is the marginal equilibrium condition for each investor, its basic form is the same as that of the CAPM (capital asset pricing model), the consumption beta model, a single-factor APT, and similar models. The distinction between the models is in their special interpretations of the pricing standard. For the CAPM, $\tilde{\rho}$ is proportional to the return on the market portfolio. For the consumption model it is proportional to aggregate consumption. For a single-factor APT it is proportional to the factor.

The similarity between these models and the general pricing equation is more than mere form. In each of these financial models, all investors' levels of utility are monotonically related. (That is, all investors rank the outcome states in the same order using their own welfare as criteria.) With the assumed state-independent (and separable for multiperiod models) utility functions, this guarantees that every investor's wealth (or consumption) is monotonically related to aggregate wealth (or consumption).

As discussed previously, this monotone relation among investors' wealths is also a property of complete markets, with the corollary that there exists a representative investor. The general result that the pricing standard, $\tilde{\rho}$, is proportional to the marginal utility of every investor yields in these cases the specific result that it is proportional to the "marginal utility of the market." Consequently, that portion of the return on any asset that is uncorrelated with aggregate wealth (or consumption) bears zero risk compensation in equilibrium.[12] Thus, there is a simple relation among all the common definitions of diversifiable risk. In each of these models of financial equilibrium, it is only correlation with the marginal utility of the "market" or, more precisely, the representative investor that requires compensation.

A similar result will generally obtain even if the structure of asset returns is not one for which a special model like the CAPM holds, provided investors are unfettered in the creation of new assets. As discussed previously, there will always be arbitrage opportunities for some entrepreneur to complete the market unless it is already effectively complete. And once the market is completed, there will be a representative investor whose marginal utility can serve as the pricing standard $\tilde{p}$.

There is another type of spanning in the CAPM—namely all portfolios of interest to investors (in equilibrium) are combinations of the riskless asset and the market portfolio. This spanning result is central to the model, but it is quite fragile. If the CAPM holds because the returns on the assets have a multivariate normal distribution or, more generally, are drawn from an elliptical distribution,[13] then the introduction of a single asset with a nonnormal return will cause the CAPM equilibrium to dissolve. This one non-Gaussian asset contributes to the market such different spanning properties that the previous equilibrium is not sustainable even as to form.[14] Once the market has been (effectively) completed by the addition of a sufficient number of derivative assets, however, the CAPM pricing result (but not the separation result) will again hold for the original assets. If we believe that the market is effectively complete and that the primitive assets, like stocks, have returns distributions that are approximately normal, this can justify the use of the CAPM for pricing them even though some assets, like options, clearly have highly nonnormal returns.

III. BASIS AUGMENTING RESULTS

The theoretical efficiency and pricing results that can be derived in a complete market setting are both simple and pleasing. Unfortunately, it requires an enormous amount of faith to believe that existing financial markets are close to being complete, at least when measured by the number of securities required. As Koopmans (1974) so aptly described it, the Arrow-Debreu model is "in the nature of a magnificent *tour de force*, enriching our insight, but with a somewhat strained relation to reality." The third strand of research that I will discuss addresses the issue of augmenting the span of the market by creating new securities and shows that the relation may not be so strained as one might have imagined.

To complete an existing market, we must add new securities, but in the process we certainly do not wish to create any new states. It follows that the new securities should be derivative securities (that is, securities whose value depends only on the value of other assets). Options are the most obvious example.

Pure Arrow-Debreu state securities can then be created by combining options in portfolios. Consider the sale of a call on a particular asset with striking price X and the purchase of a call on the same asset with striking price $X - \Delta$. This option spread will be worth Δ if the underlying asset ends up worth more than X, and will be worth 0 if the underlying asset ends up worth less than $X - \Delta$. Now combine this spread with a short position in a similar spread of options with striking prices X' and $X' + \Delta$ with $X' > X$. This portfolio of spreads will be worth Δ if the price of the underlying asset falls in the range (X, X'), and 0 if the price of the underlying asset falls outside the range

$(X - \Delta, X' + \Delta)$. If we choose Δ small enough so that the price of the underlying asset never falls in the ranges $(X - \Delta, X)$ and $(X', X' + \Delta)$, then this portfolio is always worth either 0 or Δ. A holding of $1/\Delta$ units of this portfolio will be a security that pays one dollar only on the occurrence of particular outcomes on this particular asset. If we choose X' and X sufficiently close together so that the underlying asset has only one possible price in the range (X, X'), then the portfolio pays one doller only upon the occurrence of a particular price on this asset.

This final portfolio is not an Arrow-Debreu security for any state unless the price of the underlying asset has this particular value in only one state. An Arrow-Debreu security for a particular state can be fashioned by writing call options on a portfolio of such portfolios of spreads for the different assets. Ross (1976b) demonstrated that this last step of the rather complicated procedure could be eliminated. He proved that if it is always possible to construct some portfolio that has a different value in each state, then the set of options on this portfolio can be used to provide a complete set of Arrow-Debreu securities. Arditti and John (1980) proved that in a finite state-space such a portfolio can always be constructed under the definition of states used here. In fact they prove that *almost any* (in a measure-theoretic sense) portfolio is such a "state-resolving" portfolio.

With a continuum of states, however, such a portfolio will not exist, and a more complex construction is required. Fortunately, there is no need to do this for many purposes. As discussed in the previous sections, when markets are complete, each investor forms a portfolio that gives the same end-of-period wealth in states with the same aggregate wealth. That is, in terms of the utility derived by each investor, all states with the same aggregate wealth are equivalent. The irony is that in a complete market investors (with state-independent utility and homogeneous expectations) will not need a complete set of Arrow-Debreu securities, provided they can trade pure claims to each metastate with a distinct level of aggregate wealth.[15]

If the market is complete with respect to at least these metastates, then the Pareto efficiency results of a truly complete market will obtain. The portfolio construction problem is then immediately solved. Since the market portfolio has a distinct value in each metastate with a different level of aggregate wealth, portfolios of spreads of options on the market can be used to provide an Arrow-Debreu security for each metastate. This observation is the key to the Hakansson (1978) supershares idea.[16]

IV. INTERTEMPORAL EXTENSIONS

Most of the spanning results discussed above have immediate extensions in an intertemporal context. One of the key features of a complete static market in an intertemporal setting is that all trading can take place at the start of the economy. Because investors can purchase pure claims against all contingencies, there is no need for any further trading at any later date. Essentially they can purchase insurance against the need to rebalance their portfolios. The resulting allocations are Pareto efficient, and the prices of Arrow-Debreu securities for each time-state event can be used as the linear pricing rule that values all assets. As with single-period models, the economy need not have a market that has pure securities for all of these time-state contingencies for the important complete market results to hold; it need only have pure securities for the important metastates.

The preceding Duffie-Huang article discusses conditions under which "continuous trading of few long-lived securities" can be used to implement an Arrow-Debreu equilibrium. As shown there and elsewhere, frequent trading of a few assets can substitute for many state-specific assets that investors might otherwise wish. If investors trade each period, then the number of (linearly independent) assets needed at any point in time to ensure that the market is intertemporally complete is just equal to the number of states that can obtain in the next period.

When an asset price follows a diffusion process, then its price path is continuous, and in an instant of time its price can only increase or decrease by a tiny amount. Essentially, over an instant there are only two states that are distinguished by this asset's price. These two states can be spanned by the asset itself and a riskless asset. This is the important feature behind the Black-Scholes option pricing model that permits the pricing of puts, calls, and more complex options without knowledge of the equilibrium. Because the option is a redundant asset, in the absence of arbitrage, its price must be completely determined by the prices of the primitive asset and the riskless asset.

In equilibrium models with many assets whose prices follow diffusion processes, complete spanning is not obvious. For a model with N risky assets, it might appear that there are as many as 2^N distinct states at the next instant. This is not true. It can be shown that, regardless of the covariance structure, N diffusion processes require only $N + 1$ states for their representation.[17] Since these $N + 1$ states are fully spanned by the N risky assets and the riskless asset, continuous trading can still make the market complete in the sense that we have been describing.

In a single-period model it is reasonable to assume that an investor's utility depends only on the wealth realized and, therefore, only on the values of the various assets. This is not so in an intertemporal model. Even if the investor is maximizing a utility function defined over terminal wealth, utility at intermediate points of time depends on certain features of the state of nature— for example, the investment opportunities available.

As Merton (1973a) has shown, investors will form portfolios in such a way as to hedge against unfavorable changes in the investment opportunity set. Thus, the market is intertemporally complete only if all the states describing such opportunity shifts are also spanned so that perfect hedges against these opportunity changes are available. If markets are complete in this more detailed sense, then the intertemporal market is Pareto efficient and all of the results discussed previously still obtain. The marginal utilities of all investors are perfectly correlated. With state-independent utility of consumption, all individual consumption flows are monotonic in aggregate consumption. Furthermore, since each investor's consumption flow is itself a diffusion process, individual consumption flows are perfectly correlated as well, so aggregate consumption can be used as the pricing standard to value assets in a mean-variance fashion as described by Breeden (1979).

In the absence of perfect hedges against changes in the opportunity set, the market is not Pareto efficient. Typically, investors would benefit from the introduction of assets to provide hedges, and entrepreneurs would certainly provide them as in the single-period model. Nevertheless, Breeden's (1979) consumption-based CAPM still obtains. The reason for this lies in the assumption of diffusion processes, which guarantees that investors are only making linear trade-offs. Their individual consumption flows are no longer perfectly correlated; however, the partial correlation between the return on each asset and aggregate consumption given each investor's consumption is zero.[18] This guarantees that the portion of the return on any asset that is uncorrelated with aggregate consumption is uncorrelated with each investor's consumption as well. Therefore, the individual pricing standard result, which always holds, can be aggregated to use per capita consumption.

V. CONCLUSION

In this review I have been able to discuss only a few of the most important applications of spanning. Other important issues, such as the Modigliani-Miller irrelevancy proposition, have not been treated. It should be clear, even from this short treatment, that spanning is at the core of many of our most powerful and useful ideas of finance.

Spanning is the mathematical handmaiden of linear systems, and, as in nearly all analytical sciences, linearity is the central mathematical assumption of our models. The role of linearity is not simply an assumption of tractability or convenience; it is at the heart of a competitive economy with price-taking agents. If one widget costs 50 cents, then two must cost one dollar, and this is true whether or not they are purchased in conjunction with shmoos. These price-taking assumptions may not be strictly true in any economic situation, but if they are good approximations for any market, those studied in finance must be at the top of our list.

NOTES

[1] The reader is referred to Stiglitz's discussion in this volume for a further elaboration of Pareto efficiency issues, including subtle ones arising with multiple commodities.

[2] In the first three sections of this chapter I will define a state to be an outcome that can be distinguished solely by the observed pattern of returns on marketed assets. That is, in two distinct states at least one asset has different values. This definition is commonly used in finance, and it avoids differentiation among states based on private information, since every investor can observe all prices.

[3] The intuition for Satterthwaite's result is as follows. In a complete market the first-order conditions guarantee that each state price must be proportional to the expected marginal utility of every investor in that state; i.e., $p_s = \lambda_k \pi_s u'_k(W^k_s)$. The quantity on the right side of this equation also defines an investor-specific subjective or effective state price when markets are not complete. Whenever two of these effective state prices are not in the same ratio for all investors, an entrepreneur could make a riskless profit by arranging a trade between two investors. Each investor would give up a little in the state relatively less valued and receive in the other state more than required at his or her current marginal rate of substitution. Because there is a divergence in the marginal rates of substitution (effective state price ratios), the entrepreneur could make an arbitrage profit. Under these conditions, there is always an incentive to create new markets at the margin. However, if the markets are used beyond the incipient level, the equilibrium might change, and this could well hurt the entrepreneur by more than the profit realized.

[4] Whenever the marginal rates of substitution (effective state prices as defined in note 3) are in the same ratio for all investors, then we may say that the market is *effectively complete*. An effectively complete market is Pareto efficient.

[5] The representative investor result here is slightly weaker than that in Rubinstein (1974). Under severe restrictions, Rubinstein shows how to construct a representative investor with "average" beliefs, "average" tastes, and "average" endowments. The averages are defined in such a way that if all the investors were average, then the same prices would prevail as in the actual economy. Here the averaging is only along the dimension of tastes and endowments. Beliefs are assumed to be homogeneous, so no "averaging" need be done along that dimension. In addition, the theorem only guarantees the existence of the average investor; it does not tell how to construct one from the individuals. See Dybvig and Ross (1982) for a proof of the convexity of the efficient set. See Dybvig and Ingersoll (1982) for a discussion of pricing issues using this representative investor.

[6] The word "efficient" is apparently too useful to economists to be put to just a single use. The ideas of Pareto efficiency and informational efficiency have already been mentioned. (See Stiglitz's and Admati's discussions in this volume for more details.) Productive efficiency is also discussed in economics. A productively efficient economy is one in which resources are being put to their best use. This idea is closely connected with a Pareto-efficient allocation of consumption. In addition, a portfolio is said to be efficient if it belongs to the set of portfolios that some investor in a given class (e.g., those with increasing concave utility functions) would optimally hold. This use is most common in the CAPM, where mean-variance efficient portfolios consist of those with the maximum expected return at each level of variance.

[7] See Ingersoll (1986, chapter 9) for a proof in the context of a standard financial model or Milgrom and Stokey (1982) for a general proof.

[8] Beja (1971) was probably the first to make use of this rule outside of a complete market setting, but he simply asserted its truth (p. 360).

[9] See Cox and Ross (1976a) for a proof. Garman (1976) also discusses these issues.

[10] The *pricing standard* is also called the *state price per unit probability* and the *state price density*.

[11] See Ingersoll (1986, chapter 5).

[12] In general, the representative investor result would only guarantee that the portion of the return that was *statistically independent* of aggregate wealth would have zero compensation in equilibrium. However, in the CAPM the monotone relation between wealth of every investor is a perfect correlation, so we have the stronger result that any portion of the return *uncorrelated* with aggregate wealth is not compensated. In the intertemporal consumption beta model, individual consumption flows are not necessarily perfectly correlated, but they are as highly correlated as is possible given the

investors' tastes and the market structure. The instantaneous linear structure of the diffusion model gives us again the stronger result. See Ingersoll (1986, chapters 13, 15) for a further discussion of these points.

[13] See Ross (1978a) for the development of the theory of two-fund separation. See Ingersoll (1986, chapter 4) for a discussion of its relation to the normal and elliptical distributions and the CAPM.

[14] This is true even if the introduced asset is in zero net supply, like an option or futures contract, and is therefore not in the market portfolio. See Dybvig and Ingersoll (1982) for a discussion of the breakdown of the CAPM when assets are added and of its limited applicability when markets are complete.

[15] The situation here is akin to that with separation or mutual fund theorems. For example, the entire efficient set can be shown to be spanned by only two mutual funds by restricting either investors' tastes (Cass and Stiglitz 1970) or the distribution of returns (Ross 1978a). Similarly, effectively complete spanning can be achieved by creating an Arrow-Debreu security either for every state that the returns distributions resolve or for every metastate that investors find "important."

[16] For further details, the reader is referred to Banz and Miller (1978), Hakansson (1978), and Ingersoll (1986, chapter 8). Breeden and Litzenberger (1978) treat this same issue in a multiperiod context using aggregate consumption in place of the market portfolio.

[17] See Ingersoll (1986, chapter 15) for a discussion of this representation with two risky assets. More assets can be handled similarly.

[18] See Ingersoll (1986, chapter 15) for a proof and more detailed discussion.

REFERENCES

Admati, A. 1988. "Information in Financial Markets: The Rational Expectations Approach." Discussion, Chapter 4, volume 2.

Arditti, F., and John, K. 1980. "Spanning the State Space with Options." *Journal of Financial and Quantitative Analysis* 15: 1–9.

Arrow, K. 1964. "The Role of Securities in the Optimal Allocation of Risk-Bearing." *Review of Economic Studies* 31: 91–96.

Banz, R., and Miller, M. H. 1978. "Prices for State-Contingent Claims: Some Estimates and Applications." *Journal of Business* 51: 653–72.

Beja, A. 1971. "The Structure of the Cost of Capital under Uncertainty." *Review of Economic Studies* 38: 359–68.

Black, F., and Scholes, M. J. 1973. "The Pricing of Options and Corporate Liabilities." *Journal of Political Economy* 81: 637–54.

Breeden, D. T. 1979. "An Intertemporal Asset Pricing Model and Stochastic Investment and Consumption Opportunity Sets." *Journal of Financial Economics* 7: 265–96. Reprinted this volume, Chapter 3.

Breeden, D. T., and Litzenberger, R. H. 1978. "Prices of State-Contingent Claims Implicit in Options Prices." *Journal of Business* 51: 621–51.

Cass, D., and Stiglitz, J. E. 1970. "The Structure of Investor Preferences and Asset Returns and Separability in Portfolio Allocation." *Journal of Economic Theory* 2: 122–60.

Cox, J. C., and Huang, C. 1988. "Option Pricing Theory and Its Applications." Discussion, Chapter 8, this volume.

Cox, J. C.; Ingersoll, J. E., Jr.; Ross, S. A. 1985. "An Intertemporal General Equilibrium Model of Asset Prices." *Econometrica* 53: 363–84.

Cox, J. C., and Ross, S. A. 1976a. "The Valuation of Options for Alternative Stochastic

Processes." *Journal of Financial Economics* 3: 145–66.

―――. 1976b. "A Survey of Some New Results in Financial Option Pricing Theory." *Journal of Finance* 31: 383–402.

Debreu, G. 1959. *Theory of Value.* New York: John Wiley.

Duffie, D., and Huang, C. F. 1986. "Implementing Arrow-Debreu Equilibria by Continuous Trading of Few Long-Lived Securities." *Econometrica* 53: 1337–56. Reprinted this volume, Chapter 4.

Dybvig, P. H., and Ingersoll, J. E., Jr. 1982. "Mean-Variance Theory in Complete Markets." *Journal of Business* 55: 233–51.

Dybvig, P. H., and Ross, S. A. 1982. "Portfolio Efficient Sets." *Econometrica* 50: 1525–46.

Garman, M. B. 1976. "An Algebra for Evaluating Hedge Portfolios." *Journal of Financial Economics* 3: 403–27.

Hakansson, N. H. 1978. "Welfare Aspects of Options and Supershares." *Journal of Finance* 33: 759–76.

Ingersoll, J. E., Jr. 1986. *Theory of Financial Decision Making.* Totowa, N.J.: Rowman & Littlefield.

Koopmans, T. 1974. "Is the Theory of Competitive Equilibrium with It?" *American Economic Review* 44: 325–29.

Merton, R. C. 1973a. "An Intertemporal Capital Asset Pricing Model." *Econometrica* 41: 867–87.

―――. 1973b. "The Theory of Rational Option Pricing." *Bell Journal of Economics and Management Science* 4: 141–81. Reprinted Chapter 8, this volume.

Milgrom, P., and Stokey, N. 1982. "Information, Trade, and Common Knowledge." *Journal of Economic Theory* 26: 17–27.

Ross, S. A. 1976a. "The Arbitrage Theory of Capital Asset Pricing." *Journal of Economic Theory* 13: 341–60.

―――. 1976b. "Options and Efficiency." *Quarterly Journal of Economics* 90: 75–89.

―――. 1978a. "Mutual Fund Separation in Financial Theory—The Separating Distributions." *Journal of Economic Theory* 17: 254–86.

―――. 1978b. "A Simple Approach to the Valuation of Risky Streams." *Journal of Business* 51: 453–75.

―――. 1988. "Intertemporal Asset Pricing." Discussion, Chapter 3, this volume.

Rubinstein, M. 1974. "An Aggregation Theorem for Securities Markets." *Journal of Financial Economics* 1: 225–44.

Satterthwaite, M. A. 1981. "On the Scope of the Stockholder Unanimity Theorems." *International Economic Review* 22: 119–33.

Stiglitz, J. E. 1988. "Mutual Funds, Capital Structure, and Economic Efficiency." Discussion, Chapter 10, this volume.

Econometrica, Vol. 53, No. 2 (March, 1985)

A THEORY OF THE TERM STRUCTURE OF INTEREST RATES[1]

By John C. Cox, Jonathan E. Ingersoll, Jr., and Stephen A. Ross

This paper uses an intertemporal general equilibrium asset pricing model to study the term structure of interest rates. In this model, anticipations, risk aversion, investment alternatives, and preferences about the timing of consumption all play a role in determining bond prices. Many of the factors traditionally mentioned as influencing the term structure are thus included in a way which is fully consistent with maximizing behavior and rational expectations. The model leads to specific formulas for bond prices which are well suited for empirical testing.

1. INTRODUCTION

THE TERM STRUCTURE of interest rates measures the relationship among the yields on default-free securities that differ only in their term to maturity. The determinants of this relationship have long been a topic of concern for economists. By offering a complete schedule of interest rates across time, the term structure embodies the market's anticipations of future events. An explanation of the term structure gives us a way to extract this information and to predict how changes in the underlying variables will affect the yield curve.

In a world of certainty, equilibrium forward rates must coincide with future spot rates, but when uncertainty about future rates is introduced the analysis becomes much more complex. By and large, previous theories of the term structure have taken the certainty model as their starting point and have proceeded by examining stochastic generalizations of the certainty equilibrium relationships. The literature in the area is voluminous, and a comprehensive survey would warrant a paper in itself. It is common, however, to identify much of the previous work in the area as belonging to one of four strands of thought.

First, there are various versions of the expectations hypothesis. These place predominant emphasis on the expected values of future spot rates or holding-period returns. In its simplest form, the expectations hypothesis postulates that bonds are priced so that the implied forward rates are equal to the expected spot rates. Generally, this approach is characterized by the following propositions: (a) the return on holding a long-term bond to maturity is equal to the expected return on repeated investment in a series of the short-term bonds, or (b) the expected rate of return over the next holding period is the same for bonds of all maturities.

The liquidity preference hypothesis, advanced by Hicks [16], concurs with the importance of expected future spot rates, but places more weight on the effects of the risk preferences of market participants. It asserts that risk aversion will cause forward rates to be systematically greater than expected spot rates, usually

[1] This paper is an extended version of the second half of an earlier working paper with the same title. We are grateful for the helpful comments and suggestions of many of our colleagues, both at our own institutions and others. This research was partially supported by the Dean Witter Foundation, the Center for Research in Security Prices, and the National Science Foundation.

by an amount increasing with maturity. This term premium is the increment required to induce investors to hold longer-term ("riskier") securities.

Third, there is the market segmentation hypothesis of Culbertson [7] and others, which offers a different explanation of term premiums. Here it is asserted that individuals have strong maturity preferences and that bonds of different maturities trade in separate and distinct markets. The demand and supply of bonds of a particular maturity are supposedly little affected by the prices of bonds of neighboring maturities. Of course, there is now no reason for the term premiums to be positive or to be increasing functions of maturity. Without attempting a detailed critique of this position, it is clear that there is a limit to how far one can go in maintaining that bonds of close maturities will not be close substitutes. The possibility of substitution is an important part of the theory which we develop.

In their preferred habitat theory, Modigliani and Sutch [25] use some arguments similar to those of the market segmentation theory. However, they recognize its limitations and combine it with aspects of the other theories. They intended their approach as a plausible rationale for term premiums which does not restrict them in sign or monotonicity, rather than as a necessary causal explanation.[2]

While the focus of such modern and eclectic analyses of the term structure on explaining and testing the term premiums is desirable, there are two difficulties with this approach. First, we need a better understanding of the determinants of the term premiums. The previous theories are basically only hypotheses which say little more than that forward rates should or need not equal expected spot rates. Second, all of the theories are couched in ex ante terms and they must be linked with ex post realizations to be testable.

The attempts to deal with these two elements constitute the fourth strand of work on the term structure. Roll [29, 30], for example, has built and tested a mean-variance model which treated bonds symmetrically with other assets and used a condition of market efficiency to relate ex ante and ex post concepts.[3] If rationality requires that ex post realizations not differ systematically from ex ante views, then statistical tests can be made on ex ante propositions by using ex post data.

We consider the problem of determining the term structure as being a problem in general equilibrium theory, and our approach contains elements of all of the previous theories. Anticipations of future events are important, as are risk preferences and the characteristics of other investment alternatives. Also, individuals can have specific preferences about the timing of their consumption, and thus have, in that sense, a preferred habitat. Our model thus permits detailed predictions about how changes in a wide range of underlying variables will affect the term structure.

---

[2] We thank Franco Modigliani for mentioning this point.

[3] Stiglitz [35] emphasizes the portfolio theory aspects involved with bonds of different maturities, as do Dieffenbach [9], Long [18], and Rubinstein [31], who incorporate the characteristics of other assets as well. Modigliani and Shiller [24] and Sargent [33] have stressed the importance of rational anticipations.

The plan of our paper is as follows. Section 2 summarizes the equilibrium model developed in Cox, Ingersoll, and Ross [6] and specializes it for studying the term structure. In Section 3, we derive and analyze a model which leads to a single factor description of the term structure. Section 4 shows how this model can be applied to other related securities such as options on bonds. In Section 5, we compare our general equilibrium approach with an alternative approach based purely on arbitrage. In Section 6, we consider some more general term structure models and show how the market prices of bonds can be used as instrumental variables in empirical tests of the theory. Section 7 presents some models which include the effects of random inflation. In Section 8, we give some brief concluding comments.

2. THE UNDERLYING EQUILIBRIUM MODEL

In this section, we briefly review and specialize the general equilibrium model of Cox, Ingersoll, and Ross [6]. The model is a complete intertemporal description of a continuous time competitive economy. We recall that in this economy there is a single good and all values are measured in terms of units of this good. Production opportunities consist of a set of n linear activities. The vector of expected rates of return on these activities is α, and the covariance matrix of the rates of return is GG'. The components of α and G are functions of a k-dimensional vector Y which represents the state of the technology and is itself changing randomly over time. The development of Y thus determines the production opportunities that will be available to the economy in the future. The vector of expected changes in Y is μ and the covariance matrix of the changes is SS'.

The economy is composed of identical individuals, each of whom seeks to maximize an objective function of the form

$$(1) \qquad E \int_t^{t'} U(C(s), Y(s), s) \, ds,$$

where $C(s)$ is the consumption flow at time s, U is a Von Neumann–Morgenstern utility function, and t' is the terminal date. In performing this maximization, each individual chooses his optimal consumption C^*, the optimal proportion a^* of wealth W to be invested in each of the production processes, and the optimal proportion b^* of wealth to be invested in each of the contingent claims. These contingent claims are endogenously created securities whose payoffs are functions of W and $\dot{Y}$. The remaining wealth to be invested in borrowing or lending at the interest rate r is then determined by the budget constraint. The indirect utility function J is determined by the solution to the maximization problem.

In equilibrium in this homogeneous society, the interest rate and the expected rates of return on the contingent claims must adjust until all wealth is invested in the physical production processes. This investment can be done either directly by individuals or indirectly by firms. Consequently, the equilibrium value of J is given by the solution to a planning problem with only the physical production processes available. For future reference, we note that the optimality conditions for the proportions invested will then have the form

$$(2) \qquad \Psi \equiv \alpha WJ_W + GG'a^* W^2 J_{WW} + GS' WJ_{WY} - \lambda^* 1 \leqslant 0$$

and $a^{*\prime} \Psi = 0$, where subscripts on J denote partial derivatives, J_{WY} is a $(k \times 1)$ vector whose ith element is J_{WY_i}, 1 is a $(k \times 1)$ unit vector, and λ^* is a Lagrangian multiplier. With J explicitly determined, the similar optimality conditions for the problem with contingent claims and borrowing and lending can be combined with the market clearing conditions to give the equilibrium interest rate and expected rates of return on contingent claims.

We now cite two principal results from [6] which we will need frequently in this paper. First, the equilibrium interest rate can be written explicitly as

$$(3) \qquad r(W, Y, t) = \frac{\lambda^*}{WJ_W} = a^{*\prime}\alpha + a^{*\prime}GG'a^* W \left(\frac{J_{WW}}{J_W} \right) + a^{*\prime}GS' \left(\frac{J_{WY}}{J_W} \right)$$

$$= a^{*\prime}\alpha - \left(\frac{-J_{WW}}{J_W} \right) \left(\frac{\text{var } W}{W} \right) - \sum_{i=1}^{k} \left(\frac{-J_{WY_i}}{J_W} \right) \left(\frac{\text{cov } W, Y_i}{W} \right),$$

where (cov W, Y_i) is the covariance of the changes in optimally invested wealth with the changes in the state variable Y_i, with (var W) and (cov Y_i, Y_j) defined in an analogous way; note that $a^{*\prime}\alpha$ is the expected rate of return on optimally invested wealth. Second, the equilibrium value of any contingent claim, F, must satisfy the following differential equation:

$$(4) \qquad \tfrac{1}{2}a^{*\prime}GG'a^* W^2 F_{WW} + a^{*\prime}GS' WF_{WY} + \tfrac{1}{2}\text{tr}\,(SS'F_{YY})$$

$$+ (a^{*\prime}\alpha W - C^*)F_W + \mu'F_Y + F_t + \delta - rF$$

$$= \phi_W F_W + \phi_Y F_Y,$$

where $\delta(W, Y, t)$ is the payout flow received by the security and

$$(5) \qquad \phi_W = (a^{*\prime}\alpha - r)W,$$

$$\phi_Y = \left(\frac{-J_{WW}}{J_W} \right) a^{*\prime}GS'W + \left(\frac{-J_{WY}}{J_W} \right)' SS'.$$

In (4) subscripts on F denote partial derivatives; F_Y and F_{WY} are $(k \times 1)$ vectors and F_{YY} is a $(k \times k)$ matrix. The left hand side of (4) gives the excess expected return on the security over and above the risk free return, while the right hand side gives the risk premium that the security must command in equilibrium. For future reference, we note that (4) can be written in the alternative form:

$$(6) \qquad \tfrac{1}{2}(\text{var } W)F_{WW} + \sum_{i=1}^{k} (\text{cov } W, Y_i)F_{WY_i} + \tfrac{1}{2} \sum_{i=1}^{k} \sum_{j=1}^{k} (\text{cov } Y_i, Y_j)F_{Y_iY_j}$$

$$+ [rW - C^*]F_W + \sum_{i=1}^{k} \left[\mu_i - \left(\frac{-J_{WW}}{J_W} \right)(\text{cov } W, Y_i) \right.$$

$$\left. - \sum_{j=1}^{k} \left(\frac{-J_{WY_j}}{J_W} \right)(\text{cov } Y_i, Y_j) \right] F_{Y_i} + F_t - rF + \delta = 0.$$

To apply these formulas to the problem of the term structure of interest rates, we specialize the preference structure first to the case of constant relative risk aversion utility functions and then further to the logarithmic utility function. In particular, we let $U(C(s), Y(s), s)$ be independent of the state variable Y and have the form

(7) $U(C(s), s) = e^{-\rho s}\left[\dfrac{C(s)^\gamma - 1}{\gamma}\right],$

where ρ is a constant discount factor.

It is easy to show that in this case the indirect utility function takes the form:[4]

(8) $J(W, Y, t) = f(Y, t)U(W, t) + g(Y, t).$

This special form brings about two important simplifications. First, the coefficient of relative risk aversion of the indirect utility function is constant, independent of both wealth and the state variables:

(9) $\dfrac{-WJ_{WW}}{J_W} = 1 - \gamma.$

Second, the elasticity of the marginal utility of wealth with respect to each of the state variables does not depend on wealth, and we have

(10) $\dfrac{-J_{WY}}{J_W} = \dfrac{-f_Y}{f}.$

Furthermore, it is straightforward to verify that the optimal portfolio proportions a^* will depend on Y but not on W. Consequently, the vector of factor risk premiums, ϕ_Y, reduces to $(1 - \gamma)a^{*'}GS' + (f_Y/f)SS'$, which depends only on Y. In addition, it can be seen from (3) that the equilibrium interest rate also depends only on Y.

The logarithmic utility function corresponds to the special case of $\gamma - 0$. For this case, it can be shown that $f(Y, t) = [1 - \exp[-\rho(t' - t)]]/\rho$. The state-dependence of the indirect utility function thus enters only through $g(Y, t)$. As a result, ϕ_Y reduces further to $a^{*'}GS$. In addition, the particular form of the indirect utility function allows us to solve (2) explicitly for a^* as

(11) $a^* = (GG')^{-1}\alpha + \left(\dfrac{1 - 1'(GG')^{-1}\alpha}{1'(GG')^{-1}1}\right)(GG')^{-1}1$

when all production processes are active, with an analogous solution holding when some processes are inactive.

In the remainder of the paper, we will be valuing securities whose contractual terms do not depend explicitly on wealth. Since with constant relative risk aversion neither the interest rate r nor the factor risk premiums ϕ_Y depend on wealth, for such securities the partial derivatives F_W, F_{WW}, and F_{WY} are all equal to zero and the corresponding terms drop out of the valuation equation (4).

---

[4] This type of separability has been shown in other contexts by Hakansson [15], Merton [22], and Samuelson [32].

By combining these specializations, we find that the valuation equation (4) then reduces to

$$(12) \qquad \tfrac{1}{2} \operatorname{tr} (SS'F_{YY}) + [\mu' - a^{*'}GS']F_Y + F_t + \delta - rF = 0.$$

Equation (12) will be the central valuation equation for this paper. We will use it together with various specifications about technological change to examine the implied term structure of interest rates.

3. A SINGLE FACTOR MODEL OF THE TERM STRUCTURE

In our first model of the term structure of interest rates, we assume that the state of technology can be represented by a single sufficient statistic or state variable. This is our most basic model, and we will examine it in some detail. This will serve to illustrate how a similarly detailed analysis can be conducted for the more complicated models that follow in Sections 5 and 6.

We make the following assumptions:

ASSUMPTION 1: *The change in production opportunities over time is described by a single state variable, $Y(\equiv Y_1)$.*

ASSUMPTION 2: *The means and variances of the rates of return on the production processes are proportional to Y.[5] In this way, neither the means nor the variances will dominate the portfolio decision for large values of Y. The state variable Y can be thought of as determining the rate of evolution of the capital stock in the following sense. If we compare a situation where $Y = \bar{Y}$, a constant, with a situation in which $Y = 2\bar{Y}$, then the first situation has the same distribution of rate of return on a fixed investment in any process over a two-year period that the second situation has over a one-year period. We assume that the elements of α and G are such that the elements of a^* given by (11) are positive, so that all processes are always active, and that $1'(GG')^{-1}\alpha$ is greater than one.[6]*

ASSUMPTION 3: *The development of the state variable Y is given by the stochastic differential equation*

$$(13) \qquad dY(t) = [\xi Y + \zeta]\, dt + \upsilon \sqrt{Y}\, dw(t),$$

where ξ and ζ are constants, with $\zeta \geq 0$, and υ is a $1 \times (n+k)$ vector, each of whose components is the constant υ_0.

---

[5] Although our assumptions in this section do not satisfy all of the technical growth restrictions placed on the utility function and the coefficients of the production function in [6], they do in combination lead to a well-posed problem having an optimal solution with many useful properties. The optimal consumption function is $C^*(W, Y, t) = [\rho/(1 - \exp(-\rho(t'-t)))]W$ and the indirect utility function has the form $J(W, Y, t) = a(t) \log W + b(t) Y + c(t)$, where $a(t)$, $b(t)$, and $c(t)$ are explicitly determinable functions of time.

[6] The condition $1'(GG')^{-1}\alpha > 1$, together with (13) and (14), insures that the interest rate will always be nonnegative. If $1'(GG')^{-1}\alpha < 1$, the interest rate will always be nonpositive.

This structure makes it convenient to introduce the notation $\alpha \equiv \hat{a}Y$, $GG' \equiv \Omega Y$, and $GS' \equiv \Sigma Y$, where the elements of $\hat{a}$, Ω, and Σ are constants.

With these assumptions about technological change and our earlier assumptions about preferences, we can use (3) to write the equilibrium interest rate as

$$(14) \qquad r(Y) = \left(\frac{1'\Omega^{-1}\hat{a} - 1}{1'\Omega^{-1}1} \right) Y.$$

The interest rate thus follows a diffusion process with

$$(15) \qquad \text{drift } r = \left(\frac{1'\Omega^{-1}\hat{a} - 1}{1'\Omega^{-1}1} \right) (\xi Y + \zeta) \equiv \kappa(\theta - r),$$

$$\text{var } r = \left(\frac{1'\Omega^{-1}\hat{a} - 1}{1'\Omega^{-1}1} \right)^2 vv'Y \equiv \sigma^2 r,$$

where κ, θ, and σ^2 are constants, with $\kappa\theta \geq 0$ and $\sigma^2 > 0$. It is convenient to define a new one-dimensional Wiener process, $z_1(t)$, such that:

$$(16) \qquad \sigma\sqrt{r}\, dz_1(t) \equiv v\sqrt{Y}\, dw(t);$$

this is permissible since each component of $w(t)$ is a Wiener process. The interest rate dynamics can then be expressed as:

$$(17) \qquad dr = \kappa(\theta - r)\, dt + \sigma\sqrt{r}\, dz_1.$$

For κ, $\theta > 0$, this corresponds to a continuous time first-order autoregressive process where the randomly moving interest rate is elastically pulled toward a central location or long-term value, θ. The parameter κ determines the speed of adjustment.[7]

An examination of the boundary classification criteria shows that r can reach zero if $\sigma^2 > 2\kappa\theta$. If $2\kappa\theta \geq \sigma^2$, the upward drift is sufficiently large to make the origin inaccessible.[8] In either case, the singularity of the diffusion coefficient at the origin implies that an initially nonnegative interest rate can never subsequently become negative.

The interest rate behavior implied by this structure thus has the following empirically relevant properties: (i) Negative interest rates are precluded. (ii) If the interest rate reaches zero, it can subsequently become positive. (iii) The absolute variance of the interest rate increases when the interest rate itself increases. (iv) There is a steady state distribution for the interest rate.

The probability density of the interest rate at time s, conditional on its value at the current time, t, is given by:

$$(18) \qquad f(r(s), s; r(t), t) = c\, e^{-u-v} \left(\frac{v}{u} \right)^{q/2} I_q(2(uv)^{1/2}),$$

---

[7] The discrete time equivalent of this model was tested by Wood [38], although, being concerned only with expectations, he left the error term unspecified.

[8] See Feller [12].

where

$$c \equiv \frac{2\kappa}{\sigma^2(1 - e^{-\kappa(s-t)})},$$

$$u \equiv cr(t) e^{-\kappa(s-t)},$$

$$v \equiv cr(s),$$

$$q \equiv \frac{2\kappa\theta}{\sigma^2} - 1,$$

and $I_q(\cdot)$ is the modified Bessel function of the first kind of order q. The distribution function is the noncentral chi-square, $\chi^2[2cr(s); 2q+2, 2u]$, with $2q+2$ degrees of freedom and parameter of noncentrality $2u$ proportional to the current spot rate.[9]

Straightforward calculations give the expected value and variance of $r(s)$ as:

$$E(r(s)|r(t)) = r(t) e^{-\kappa(s-t)} + \theta(1 - e^{-\kappa(s-t)}),$$

(19) $$\text{var}(r(s)|r(t)) = r(t)\left(\frac{\sigma^2}{\kappa}\right)(e^{-\kappa(s-t)} - e^{-2\kappa(s-t)}) + \theta\left(\frac{\sigma^2}{2\kappa}\right)(1 - e^{-\kappa(s-t)})^2.$$

The properties of the distribution of the future interest rates are those expected. As κ approaches infinity, the mean goes to θ and the variance to zero, while as κ approaches zero, the conditional mean goes to the current interest rate and the variance to $\sigma^2 r(t) \cdot (s - t)$.

If the interest rate does display mean reversion ($\kappa, \theta > 0$), then as s becomes large its distribution will approach a gamma distribution. The steady state density function is:

(20) $$f[r(\infty), \infty; r(t), t] = \frac{\omega^\nu}{\Gamma(\nu)} r^{\nu-1} e^{-\omega r},$$

where $\omega \equiv 2\kappa/\sigma^2$ and $\nu \equiv 2\kappa\theta/\sigma^2$. The steady state mean and variance are θ and $\sigma^2\theta/2\kappa$, respectively.

Consider now the problem of valuing a default-free discount bond promising to pay one unit at time T.[10] The prices of these bonds for all T will completely determine the term structure. Under our assumptions, the factor risk premium in (12) is

(21) $$\left[\hat{\alpha}'\Omega^{-1}\Sigma + \left(\frac{1 - 1'\Omega^{-1}\hat{\alpha}}{1'\Omega^{-1}1}\right)1'\Omega^{-1}\Sigma\right]Y \equiv \lambda Y.$$

---

[9] Processes similar to (17) have been extensively studied by Feller. The Laplace transform of (18) is given in Feller [12]. See Johnson and Kotz [17] for a description of the noncentral chi-square distribution. Oliver [27] contains properties of the modified Bessel function.

[10] A number of contractual provisions are sufficient to preclude default risk and make the value of a bond independent of the wealth of its seller. For example, the terms of the bond could specify that the seller must repurchase the bond at the price schedule given by (23) whenever his wealth falls to a designated level.

By using (15) and (21), we can write the fundamental equation for the price of a discount bond, P, most conveniently as

(22)· $\quad \frac{1}{2}\sigma^2 r P_{rr} + \kappa(\theta - r)P_r + P_t - \lambda r P_r - rP = 0,$

with the boundary condition $P(r, T, T) = 1$. The first three terms in (22) are, from Ito's formula, the expected price change for the bond. Thus, the expected rate of return on the bond is $r + (\lambda r P_r / P)$. The instantaneous return premium on a bond is proportional to its interest elasticity. The factor λr is the covariance of changes in the interest rate with percentage changes in optimally invested wealth (the "market portfolio"). Since $P_r < 0$, positive premiums will arise if this covariance is negative ($\lambda < 0$).

We may note from (22) that bond prices depend on only one random variable, the spot interest rate, which serves as an instrumental variable for the underlying technological uncertainty. While the proposition that current (and future) interest rates play an important, and to a first approximation, predominant role in determining the term structure would meet with general approval, we have seen that this will be precisely true only under special conditions.[11]

By taking the relevant expectation (see Cox, Ingersoll, and Ross [6]), we obtain the bond prices as:

$$P(r, t, T) = A(t, T) e^{-B(t,T)r},$$

where

$$A(t, T) \equiv \left[\frac{2\gamma e^{[(\kappa + \lambda + \gamma)(T-t)]/2}}{(\gamma + \kappa + \lambda)(e^{\gamma(T-t)} - 1) + 2\gamma} \right]^{2\kappa\theta/\sigma^2},$$

(23) $\quad B(t, T) \equiv \dfrac{2(e^{\gamma(T-t)} - 1)}{(\gamma + \kappa + \lambda)(e^{\gamma(T-t)} - 1) + 2\gamma},$

$$\gamma \equiv ((\kappa + \lambda)^2 + 2\sigma^2)^{1/2}.$$

The bond price is a decreasing convex function of the interest rate and an increasing (decreasing) function of time (maturity). The parameters of the interest rate process have the following effects. The bond price is a decreasing convex function of the mean interest rate level θ and an increasing concave (decreasing convex) function of the speed of adjustment parameter κ if the interest rate is greater (less) than θ. Both of these results are immediately obvious from their effects on expected future interest rates. Bond prices are an increasing concave function of the "market" risk parameter λ. Intuitively, this is mainly because higher values of λ indicate a greater covariance of the interest rate with wealth. Thus, with large λ it is more likely that bond prices will be higher when wealth is low and, hence, has greater marginal utility. The bond price is an increasing

---

[11] In our framework, the most important circumstances sufficient for bond prices to depend only on the spot interest rate are: (i) individuals have constant relative risk aversion, uncertainty in the technology can be described by a single variable, and the interest rate is a monotonic function of this variable, or (ii) changes in the technology are nonstochastic and the interest rate is a monotonic function of wealth.

concave function of the interest rate variance σ^2. Here several effects are involved. The most important is that a larger σ^2 value indicates more uncertainty about future real production opportunities, and thus more uncertainty about future consumption. In such a world, risk-averse investors would value the guaranteed claim in a bond more highly.

The dynamics of bond prices are given by the stochastic differential equation:

$$(24) \qquad dP = r[1 - \lambda B(t, T)]P\,dt - B(t, T)P\sigma\sqrt{r}\,dz_1.$$

For this single state variable model, the returns on bonds are perfectly negatively correlated with changes in the interest rate. The returns are less variable when the interest rate is low. Indeed, they become certain if a zero interest rate is reached, since interest rate changes are then certain. As we would intuitively expect, other things remaining equal, the variability of returns decreases as the bond approaches maturity. In fact, letting t approach T and denoting $T - t$ as Δt, we find that the expected rate of return is $r\Delta t + O(\Delta t^2)$ and the variance of the rate of return is $O(\Delta t^2)$ rather than $O(\Delta t)$, as would be the case for the returns on an investment in the production processes over a small interval. It is in this sense that the return on very short-term bonds becomes certain.

Bonds are commonly quoted in terms of yields rather than prices. For the discount bonds we are now considering, the yield-to-maturity, $R(r, t, T)$, is defined by $\exp\left[-(T - t)R(r, t, T)\right] \equiv P(r, t, T)$. Thus, we have:

$$(25) \qquad R(r, t, T) = [rB(t, T) - \log A(t, T)]/(T - t).$$

As maturity nears, the yield-to-maturity approaches the current interest rate independently of any of the parameters. As we consider longer and longer maturities, the yield approaches a limit which is independent of the current interest rate:

$$(26) \qquad R(r, t, \infty) = \frac{2\kappa\theta}{\gamma + \kappa + \lambda}.$$

When the spot rate is below this long-term yield, the term structure is uniformly rising. With an interest rate in excess of $\kappa\theta/(\kappa + \lambda)$, the term structure is falling. For intermediate values of the interest rate, the yield curve is humped.

Other comparative statics for the yield curve are easily obtained from those of the bond pricing function. An increase in the current interest rate increases yields for all maturities, but the effect is greater for shorter maturities. Similarly, an increase in the steady state mean θ increases all yields, but here the effect is greater for longer maturities. The yields to maturity decrease as σ^2 or λ increases, while the effect of a change in κ may be of either sign depending on the current interest rate.

There has always been considerable concern with unbiased predictions of future interest rates. In the present situation, we could work directly with equation (19), which gives expected values of future interest rates in terms of the current rate and the parameters κ and θ. However, in the rational expectations model we have constructed, all of the information that is currently known about the future movement of interest rates is impounded in current bond prices and the term structure. If the model is correct, then any single parameter can be determined from the term structure and the values of the other parameters.

This approach is particularly important when the model is extended to allow a time-dependent drift term, $\theta(t)$. We can then use information contained in the term structure to obtain $\theta(t)$ and expected future spot rates without having to place prior restrictions on its functional form.

Now, the future expected spot rate given by (19) is altered to:

$$(27) \qquad E(r(T)|r(t)) = r(t)\, e^{-\kappa(T-t)} + \kappa \int_t^T \theta(s)\, e^{-\kappa(T-s)}\, ds.$$

The bond pricing formula (30), in turn, is modified to:

$$(28) \qquad P(r, t, T) = \hat{A}(t, T)\, e^{-B(t,T)r},$$

where

$$(29) \qquad \hat{A}(t, T) = \exp\left(-\kappa \int_t^T \theta(s)\, B(s, T)\, ds\right),$$

which reduces to (23) when $\theta(s)$ is constant.

Assuming, for illustration, that the other process parameters are known, we can then use the term structure to determine unbiased forecasts of future interest rates. By (28), $\hat{A}(t, T)$ is an observable function of T, given the term structure and the known form of $B(t, T)$, and standard techniques can be invoked to invert (29) and obtain an expression for $\theta(t)$ in terms of $\hat{A}(t, T)$ and $B(t, T)$. Equation (27) can now be used to obtain predictions of the expected values of future spot rates implicit in the current term structure.

Note that these are not the same values that would be given by the traditional expectations assumption that the expected values of future spot rates are contained in the term structure in the form of implicit forward rates. In a continuous-time model, the forward rate $\hat{r}(T)$ is given by $-P_T/P$. Then, by differentiating (28):

$$(30) \qquad \hat{r}(T) = -P_T(r, t, T)/P(r, t, T)$$

$$= rB_T(t, T) + \kappa \int_t^T \theta(s)\, B_T(s, T)\, ds.$$

Comparing (27) and (30), we see they have the same general form. However, the traditional forward rate predictor applies the improper weights $B_T(s, T) \neq e^{-\kappa(T-s)}$, resulting in a biased prediction.

A number of alternative specifications of time dependence may also be included with only minor changes in the model. One particularly tractable example leads to an interest rate of $\bar{r}(t) + g(t)$, where $\bar{r}(t)$ is given by (17) and $g(t)$ is a function which provides a positive lower bound for the interest rate. The essential point in all such cases is that in the rational expectations model, the current term structure embodies the information required to evaluate the market's probability distribution of the future course of interest rates. Furthermore, the term structure can be inverted to find these expectations.

Other single variable specifications of technological change will in turn imply other stochastic properties for the interest rate. It is easy to verify that in our model if α and GG' are proportional to some function $h(Y, t)$, then the interest rate will also be proportional to $h(Y, t)$. By a suitable choice of $h(Y, t)$, $\mu(Y, t)$, and $S(Y, t)$, a wide range of a priori properties of interest rate movements can be included within the context of a completely consistent model.

4. VALUING ASSETS WITH GENERAL INTEREST RATE DEPENDENT PAYOFFS

Our valuation framework can easily be applied to other securities whose payoffs depend on interest rates, such as options on bonds and futures on bonds. This flexibility enables the model to make predictions about the pricing patterns that should prevail simultaneously across several financial markets. Consequently, applications to other securities may permit richer and more powerful empirical tests than could be done with the bond market alone.

As an example of valuing other kinds of interest rate securities, consider options on bonds. Denote the value at time t of a call option on a discount bond of maturity date s, with exercise price K and expiration date T as $C(r, t, T; s, K)$.[12] The option price will follow the basic valuation equation with terminal condition:

$$(31) \qquad C(r, t, T; s, K) = \max\left[P(r, T, s) - K, 0\right].$$

It is understood that $s \geq T \geq t$, and K is restricted to be less than $A(T, s)$, the maximum possible bond price at time T, since otherwise the option would never be exercised and would be worthless. By again taking the relevant expectations, we arrive at the following formula for the option price:

$$(32) \qquad C(r, t, T; s, K)$$

$$= P(r, t, s)\chi^2\left(2r^*[\phi + \psi + B(T, s)]; \frac{4\kappa\theta}{\sigma^2}, \frac{2\phi^2 r\, e^{\gamma(T-t)}}{\phi + \psi + B(T, s)}\right)$$

$$- KP(r, t, T)\chi^2\left(2r^*[\phi + \psi]; \frac{4\kappa\theta}{\sigma^2}, \frac{2\phi^2 r\, e^{\gamma(T-t)}}{\phi + \psi}\right),$$

where

$$\gamma \equiv ((\kappa + \lambda)^2 + 2\sigma^2)^{1/2},$$

$$\phi \equiv \frac{2\gamma}{\sigma^2(e^{\gamma(T-t)} - 1)},$$

$$\psi \equiv (\kappa + \lambda + \gamma)/\sigma^2,$$

$$r^* \equiv \left[\log\left(\frac{A(T, s)}{K}\right)\right] / B(T, s),$$

[12] Since the underlying security, a discount bond, makes no payments during the life of the option, the analysis of Merton [23] implies that premature exercise is never optimal, and, hence, American and European calls have the same value.

and $\chi^2(\cdot)$ is the previously introduced noncentral chi-square distribution function. r^* is the critical interest rate below which exercise will occur; i.e., $K = P(r^*, T, s)$.

The call option is an increasing function of maturity (when the expiration date on which the underlying bond matures remains fixed). Call options on stocks are increasing functions of the interest rate, partly because such an increase reduces the present value of the exercise price. However, here an increase in the interest rate will also depress the price of the underlying bond. Numerical analysis indicates that the latter effect is stronger and that the option value is a decreasing convex function of the interest rate. The remaining comparative statics are indeterminate.

5. A COMPARISON WITH BOND PRICING BY ARBITRAGE METHODS

In this section, we briefly compare our methodology to some alternative ways to model bond pricing in continuous time. It is useful to do this now rather than later because the model of Section 3 provides an ideal standard for comparison.

Our approach begins with a detailed description of the underlying economy. This allows us to specify the following ingredients of bond pricing: (a) the variables on which the bond price depends, (b) the stochastic properties of the underlying variables which are endogenously determined, and (c) the exact form of the factor risk premiums. In [21], Merton shows that if one begins instead by imposing assumptions directly about (a) and (b), then Ito's formula can be used to state the excess expected return on a bond in the same form as the left-hand side of (4). If the functional form of the right-hand side of (4) were known, then one could obtain a bond pricing equation. For example, if one arbitrarily assumed that bond prices depend only on the spot interest rate r, that the interest rate follows the process given by (17), and that the excess expected return on a bond with maturity date T is $Y(r, t, T)$, then one would obtain

$$(33) \quad \tfrac{1}{2}\sigma^2 r P_{rr} + \kappa(\theta - r)P_r + P_t - rP = Y(r, t, T).$$

If there is some underlying equilibrium which will support the assumptions (a) and (b), then there must be some function Y for which bond prices are given by (33). However, as Merton notes, this derivation in itself provides no way to determine Y or to relate it to the underlying real variables.

An arbitrage approach to bond pricing was developed in a series of papers by Brennan and Schwartz [3], Dothan [10], Garman [14], Richard [28], and Vasicek [37]. Arguments similar to those employed in the proof of Theorem 2 of Cox, Ingersoll, and Ross [6] are used to show that if there are no arbitrage opportunities, Y must have the form

$$(34) \quad Y(r, t, T) = \psi(r, t) P_r(r, t, T),$$

where ψ is a function depending only on calendar time and not on the maturity date of the bond. This places definite restrictions on the form of the excess expected return; not all functions Y will satisfy both (33) and (34).

There are some potential problems, however, in going one step further and using the arbitrage approach to determine a complete and specific model of the term structure. The approach itself provides no way of guaranteeing that there is some underlying equilibrium for which assumptions (a) and (b) are consistent. Setting this problem aside, another difficulty arises from the fact that the arbitrage approach does not imply that every choice of ψ in (34) will lead to bond prices which do not admit arbitrage opportunities. Indeed, closing the model by assuming a specific functional form for ψ can lead to internal inconsistencies.

As an example of the potential problem, consider (33) with Y as shown in (34). This gives the valuation equation

$$(35) \quad \tfrac{1}{2}\sigma^2 r P_{rr} + \kappa(\theta - r)P_r + P_t - rP = \psi(r, t)P_r,$$

which is identical to (22) apart from a specification of the function ψ. We could now close the model by assuming that ψ is linear in the spot rate, $\psi(r, t) = \psi_0 + \lambda r$. The solution to (35) is then

$$(36) \quad P(r, t, T) = [A(t, T)]^{(\kappa\theta - \psi_0)/\kappa\theta} \exp[-rB(t, T)],$$

and the dynamic behavior of the bond price is given by

$$(37) \quad dP = [r - (\psi_0 + \lambda r)B(t, T)]P \, dt - B(t, T)\sigma\sqrt{r}P \, dz_1.$$

The linear form assumed for the risk premium seems quite reasonable and would appear to be a good choice for empirical work, but it in fact produces a model that is not viable. This is most easily seen when $r = 0$. In this case, the bond's return over the next instant is riskless; nevertheless, it is appreciating in price at the rate $-\psi_0 B(t, T)$, which is different from the prevailing zero rate of interest.[13] We thus have a model that guarantees arbitrage opportunities rather than precluding them. The difficulty, of course, is that there is no underlying equilibrium which would support the assumed premiums.

The equilibrium approach developed here thus has two important advantages over alternative methods of bond pricing in continuous time. First, it automatically insures that the model can be completely specified without losing internal consistency. Second, it provides a way to predict how changes in the underlying real economic variables will affect the term structure.

6. MULTIFACTOR TERM STRUCTURE MODELS AND THE USE OF PRICES AS INSTRUMENTAL VARIABLES

In Section 3, we specialized the general equilibrium framework of Cox, Ingersoll, and Ross [6] to develop a complete model of bond pricing. We purposely chose a simple specialization in order to illustrate the detailed information that such a model can produce. In the model, the prices of bonds of all maturities depended on a single random explanatory factor, the spot interest rate. Although the resulting term structure could assume several alternative shapes, it is inherent

---

[13] As stated earlier, the origin is accessible only if $\sigma^2 > 2\kappa\theta$. Somewhat more complex arguments can be used to demonstrate that the model is not viable even if the origin is inaccessible.

in a single factor model that price changes in bonds of all maturities are perfectly correlated. Such a model also implies that bond prices do not depend on the path followed by the spot rate in reaching its current level. For some applications, these properties may be too restrictive. However, more general specifications of technological opportunities will in turn imply more general bond pricing models. The resulting multifactor term structures will have more flexibility than the single factor model, but they will inevitably also be more cumbersome and more difficult to analyze.

To illustrate the possibilities, we consider two straightforward generalizations of our previous model. Suppose that in our description of technological change in (13) and (15), the central tendency parameter θ is itself allowed to vary randomly according to the equation

$$(38) \qquad d\theta = \nu(Y - \theta)\, dt,$$

where ν is a positive constant. That is, we let $\theta \equiv Y_2$ and $\mu_2 = \nu(Y_1 - Y_2)$. The value of θ at any time will thus be an exponentially weighted integral of past values of Y. It can then be verified that the interest rate r is again given by (14) and that the bond price P will have the form

$$(39) \qquad P(r, \theta, t, T) = \exp\lfloor -rf(t, T) - \theta g(t, T)\rfloor,$$

where f and g are explicitly determinable functions of time. In this case, both the yields-to-maturity of discount bonds and the expected values of future spot rates are linear functions of current and past spot rates.[14]

As a second generalization, suppose that the production coefficients α and GG' are proportional to the sum of two independent random variables, Y_1 and Y_2, each of which follows an equation of the form (13). Then it can be shown that the spot interest rate r will be proportional to the sum of Y_1 and Y_2 and that bond prices will again have the exponential form

$$(40) \qquad P(r, Y_2, t, T) = f(t, T)\exp[-rg(t, T) - Y_2 h(t, T)],$$

where f, g, and h are other explicitly determinable functions of time. In this model, price changes in bonds of all maturities are no longer perfectly correlated.

Each of these generalizations gives a two factor model of the term structure, and the resulting yield curves can assume a wide variety of shapes. Further multifactor generalizations can be constructed along the same lines.

In each of the models considered in this section, one of the explanatory variables is not directly observable. Multifactor generalizations will typically inherit this drawback to an even greater degree. Consequently, it may be very convenient for empirical applications to use some of the endogenously determined prices as instrumental variables to eliminate the variables that cannot be directly observed. In certain instances, it will be possible to do so. Let us choose the spot rate, r,

---

[14] Studies which have expressed expected future spot rates as linear combinations of current and past spot rates include Bierwag and Grove [2], Cagan [4], De Leeuw [8], Duesenberry [11], Malkiel [19], Meiselman [20], Modigliani and Shiller [24], Modigliani and Sutch [25], Van Horne [36], and Wood [38]. Cox, Ingersoll, and Ross [5] examine this issue in a diffusion setting.

and a vector of long interest rates, l, as instrumental variables. In general, each of these interest rates will be functions of W (unless the common utility function is isoelastic) and all the state variables. If it is possible to invert this system globally and express the latter as twice differentiable functions of r and l, then r and l can be used as instrumental variables in a manner consistent with the general equilibrium framework.

For the purposes of illustration, suppose that there are two state variables, Y_1 and Y_2, and that utility is isoelastic so that the level of wealth is immaterial. Then, for instrumental variables r and l, a scalar, direct but involved calculations show that the valuation equation (4) may be rewritten as:

$$(41) \quad \tfrac{1}{2}(\text{var } r)F_{rr} + (\text{cov } r, l)F_{rl} + \tfrac{1}{2}(\text{var } l)F_{ll} + [\mu_r - \lambda_r(r, l)]F_r$$
$$+ [\mu_l - \lambda_l(r, l)]F_l - rF + F_t + \delta = 0.$$

The functions λ_r and λ_l serve the role of the factor risk premiums in (5). They are related to the factor risk premiums, ϕ_Y, by:

$$\lambda_r(r, l) = \left[\psi_1 \frac{\partial g}{\partial l} - \psi_2 \frac{\partial f}{\partial l} \right] \Big/ \Delta,$$

$$\lambda_l(r, l) = \left[\psi_2 \frac{\partial f}{\partial r} - \psi_1 \frac{\partial g}{\partial r} \right] \Big/ \Delta,$$

where

$$(42) \quad Y_1 \equiv f(r, l, t), \qquad Y_2 \equiv g(r, l, t),$$
$$\phi_{Y_1}(Y_1, Y_2, t) \equiv \psi_1(r, l, t), \qquad \phi_{Y_2}(Y_1, Y_2, t) \equiv \psi_2(r, l, t),$$

and

$$\Delta \equiv \frac{\partial f}{\partial r} \frac{\partial g}{\partial l} - \frac{\partial f}{\partial l} \frac{\partial g}{\partial r}.$$

Thus far we have not used the fact that l is an interest rate, and the transformation of (4) to (41) can be performed for an arbitrary instrumental variable if the inversion is possible. The advantage of choosing an interest rate instrument is that the second risk factor premium λ_l and the drift μ_l can be eliminated from (41) as follows.

Let Q denote the value of the particular bond for which l is the continuously compounded yield-to-maturity. Denote the payment flow from the bond, including both coupons and return of principal, by $c(t)$. In general, this flow will be zero most of the time, with impulses representing an infinite flow rate when payments are made. Since by definition $Q \equiv \int_t^T c(s) \exp[-l(s - t)] \, ds$, we can write:

$$(43) \quad Q \equiv \Lambda_0(l), \quad Q_l = \Lambda_1(l),$$
$$Q_{ll} = \Lambda_2(l), \quad Q_t = -c(t) + l\Lambda_0(l) = -\delta + l\Lambda_0(l),$$
$$Q_r = Q_{rr} = Q_{rl} = 0,$$

where

$$\Lambda_n \equiv \int_t^T (t-s)^n c(s) \, e^{-l(s-t)} \, ds,$$

and the integral is to be interpreted in the Stieltjes sense. If (43) is substituted into (41), we then obtain:

(44) $\qquad \mu_l - \lambda_l(r, l) = \dfrac{(r-l)\Lambda_0(l) - \frac{1}{2}(\text{var } l)\Lambda_2(l)}{\Lambda_1(l)},$

and the unobservable factor risk premium may be replaced by the observable function in (44). If Q is a consol bond with coupons paid continuously at the rate c, then $\Lambda_0 = c/l$, $\Lambda_1 = -c/l^2$, $\Lambda_2 = 2c/l^3$, and (44) may be written as:[15]

(45) $\qquad \mu_l - \lambda_l(r, l) = \dfrac{(\text{var } l)}{l} + l(l-r).$

These representations may be a useful starting point for empirical work. However, it is important to remember that they cannot be fully justified without considering the characteristics of the underlying economy. In the next section, we examine some additional multiple state variable models, all of which could be reexpressed in this form.

7. UNCERTAIN INFLATION AND THE PRICING OF NOMINAL BONDS

The model presented here deals with a real economy in which money would serve no purpose. To provide a valid role for money, we would have to introduce additional features which would lead far afield of our original intent. However, for a world in which changes in the money supply have no real effects, we can introduce some aspects of money and inflation in an artificial way by imagining that one of the state variables represents a price level and that some contracts have payoffs whose real value depends on this price level. That is, they are specified in nominal terms. None of this requires any changes in the general theory.

Suppose that we let the price level, p, be the kth state variable. Since we assume that this variable has no effect on the underlying real equilibrium, the functions α, μ, G, S, and J will not depend on p. Of course, this would not preclude changes in p from being statistically correlated with changes in real wealth and the other state variables. Under these circumstances, the real value of a claim whose payoff is specified in nominal terms still satisfies equation (4). All that needs to be done is to express the nominal payoff in real terms for the boundary conditions. Alternatively, the valuation equation (4) will also still hold if p is a differentiable function of W, Y, and t.[16]

---

[15] See Brennan and Schwartz [3] for this representation.

[16] If one wished to make real money balances an argument in the direct utility function U, it would be straightforward to do so in our model. A utility-maximizing money supply policy would depend only on the state variables, real wealth, and time, so the induced price level would depend only on these variables as well.

We can illustrate some of these points in the context of the model of Section 3. Let us take a second state variable to be the price level, $p(\equiv Y_2)$, and consider how to value a contract which will at time T pay with certainty an amount $1/p(T)$. Call this a nominal unit discount bond, and denote its value at time t in real terms as $N(r, p, t, T)$. Suppose that the price level p moves according to

(46) $\qquad dp = \mu(p)\, dt + \sigma(p)\, dw_{n+2}(t)$

and that it is uncorrelated with W and Y_1. Assume also that the coefficients in (45) are such that $E[p^{-1}(s)]$ exists for all finite s.

We would then have the valuation equation for N

(47) $\qquad \frac{1}{2}\sigma^2 r N_{rr} + \frac{1}{2}\sigma^2(p) N_{pp} + [\kappa\theta - (\kappa + \lambda)r]N_r + \mu(p)N_p + N_t - rN = 0$

with terminal condition $N(r, p, T, T) = 1/p(T)$. It can be directly verified that the solution is

(48) $\qquad N(r, p, t, T) = P(r, t, T) \underset{p(t),t}{E}\, [1/p(T)]$

where P is the price of a real discount bond given in (23).

In this formulation, the expected inflation rate changes only with the price level. For the commonly assumed case of lognormally distributed prices, however, $\mu(p) = \mu_p p$, $\sigma(p) = \sigma_p p$, and

(49) $\qquad N(r, p, t, T) = e^{-(\mu_p - \sigma_p^2)(T-t)} P(r, t, T)/p(t),$

so in this case the price of a nominal bond in nominal terms, $\hat{N} \equiv p(t)N$, would be independent of the current price level. With lognormally distributed prices, the expected inflation rate is constant, although of course realized inflation will not be.

As a somewhat more general example, we can separate the expected inflation rate factor from the price level factor and identify it with a third state variable. Again no change in the general theory is necessary. Label the expected inflation rate as y. We propose two alternative models for the behavior of the inflation rate: (i) Model 1,

(50) $\qquad dy = \kappa_1 y(\theta_1 - y)\, dt + \sigma_1 y^{3/2}\, dz_3;$

(ii) Model 2,

(51) $\qquad dy = \kappa_2(\theta_2 - y)\, dt + \sigma_2 y^{1/2}\, dz_3$

with the stochastic differential equation governing the movement of the price level being in each case

(52) $\qquad dp = yp\, dt + \sigma_p p y^{1/2}\, dz_2$

with $(\text{cov } y, p) \equiv \rho\sigma_1\sigma_p y^2 p$ in Model 1, $(\text{cov } y, p) \equiv \rho\sigma_1\sigma_p yp$ in Model 2, and $\sigma_p < 1$. Here, as in (17), we have for convenience defined $z_2(t)$ and $z_3(t)$ as the appropriate linear combinations of $w_{n+2}(t)$ and $w_{n+3}(t)$.

Model 1 may well be the better choice empirically, since informal evidence suggests that the relative (percentage) variance of the expected inflation rate increases as its level increases. Model 1 has this property, while Model 2 does not. However, the solution to Model 2 is more tractable, so we will record both for possible empirical use. In both models the expected inflation rate is pulled toward a long-run equilibrium level. Both models also allow for correlation between changes in the inflation rate and changes in the price level, thus allowing for positive or negative extrapolative forces in the movement of the price level.

The valuation equation for the real value of a nominal bond, specialized for our example with Model 1, will then be

$$(53) \quad \tfrac{1}{2}\sigma^2 r N_{rr} + \tfrac{1}{2}\sigma_1^2 y^3 N_{yy} + \rho\sigma_1\sigma_p y^2 p N_{yp} + \tfrac{1}{2}\sigma_p^2 p^2 y N_{pp} + [\kappa\theta - (\kappa + \lambda)r]N_r$$
$$+ \kappa_1 y(\theta_1 - y)N_y + ypN_p + N_t - rN = 0$$

with $N(r, y, p, T, T) = 1/p(T)$. The solution to equation (53) is

$$N(r, y, p, t, T) = \frac{\Gamma(\nu - \delta)}{\Gamma(\nu)}\left[\frac{c(t)}{y}\right]^\delta M\left(\delta, \nu, \frac{c(t)}{y}\right)P(r, t, T)/p(t),$$

where

$$c(t) \equiv \frac{2\kappa_1\theta_1}{\sigma_1^2(e^{\kappa_1\theta_1(T-t)} - 1)},$$

$$(54) \quad \delta \equiv [[(\kappa_1 + \rho\sigma_1\sigma_p + \tfrac{1}{2}\sigma_1^2)^2 + 2(1 - \sigma_p^2)\sigma_1^2]^{1/2} - (\kappa_1 + \rho\sigma_1\sigma_p + \tfrac{1}{2}\sigma_1^2)]/\sigma_1^2,$$
$$\nu \equiv 2[(1 + \delta)\sigma_1^2 + \kappa_1 + \rho\sigma_1\sigma_p]/\sigma_1^2,$$

$M(\cdot, \cdot, \cdot)$ is the confluent hypergeometric function, and $\Gamma(\cdot)$ is the gamma function.[17]

Proceeding in the same way with Model 2, we obtain the valuation equation:

$$(55) \quad \tfrac{1}{2}\sigma^2 r N_{rr} + \tfrac{1}{2}\sigma_2^2 y N_{yy} + \rho\sigma_2\sigma_p yp N_{yp} + \tfrac{1}{2}\sigma_p^2 yp^2 N_{pp} + [\kappa\theta - (\kappa + \lambda)r]N_r$$
$$+ \kappa_2[\theta_2 - y]N_y + ypN_p + N_t - rN = 0$$

with $N(r, y, p, T, T) = 1/p(T)$. The corresponding valuation formula is:

$$(56) \quad N(r, y, p, t, T)$$
$$= \left(\frac{2\xi e^{[(\kappa_2 + \rho\sigma_2\sigma_p + \xi)(T-t)]/2}}{(\xi + \kappa_2 + \rho\sigma_2\sigma_p)(e^{\xi(T-t)} - 1) + 2\xi}\right)^{2\kappa_2\theta_2/\sigma_2^2}$$
$$\times \exp\left(\frac{-2(e^{\xi(T-t)} - 1)(1 - \sigma_p^2)y}{(\xi + \kappa_2 + \rho\sigma_2\sigma_p)(e^{\xi(T-t)} - 1) + 2\xi}\right)P(r, t, T)/p(t),$$

where

$$\xi \equiv [(\kappa_2 + \rho\sigma_2\sigma_p)^2 + 2\sigma_2^2(1 - \sigma_p^2)]^{1/2}.$$

[17] Slater [34] gives properties of the confluent hypergeometric function.

The term structure of interest rates implied by (54) and (56) can assume a wide variety of shapes, depending on the relative values of the variables and parameters. More complex models incorporating more detailed effects can be built along the same lines.

Throughout our paper, we have used specializations of the fundamental valuation equation (6). This equation determines the real value of a contingent claim as a function of real wealth and the state variables. For some empirical purposes, it may be convenient to have a corresponding valuation equation in which all values are expressed in nominal terms.

In our setting, this is given by the following proposition. In this proposition, we let nominal wealth be $X = pW$, the indirect utility function in terms of nominal wealth be $V(X, Y, t) \equiv J(X/p, Y, t) \equiv J(W, Y, t)$, and the nominal value of a claim in terms of nominal wealth be $H(X, Y, t) \equiv pF(X/p, Y, t) \equiv pF(W, Y, t)$. As before, we let p be the kth element of Y.

PROPOSITION: *The nominal value of a contingent claim in terms of nominal wealth, $H(X, Y, t)$, satisfies the partial differential equation*

$$(57) \quad \tfrac{1}{2}(\text{var } X)H_{XX} + \sum_{i=1}^{k} (\text{cov } X, Y_i)H_{XY_i} + \tfrac{1}{2}\sum_{i=1}^{k}\sum_{j=1}^{k} (\text{cov } Y_i, Y_j)H_{Y_iY_j}$$

$$+ (\iota X - pC^*)H_x + \sum_{i=1}^{k} \left[\mu_i - \left(\frac{-V_{XX}}{V_X}\right)(\text{cov } X, Y_i) \right.$$

$$\left. - \sum_{j=1}^{k} \left(\frac{-V_{XY_j}}{V_X}\right)(\text{cov } Y_i, Y_j) \right] H_{Y_i} + H_t + p\delta - \iota H = 0,$$

where the nominal interest rate, ι, is given by

$$(58) \quad \iota = \alpha_X - \left(\frac{-V_{XY}}{V_X}\right)\left(\frac{\text{var } X}{X}\right) - \sum_{i=1}^{k}\left(\frac{-V_{XY_i}}{V_X}\right)\left(\frac{\text{cov } X, Y_i}{X}\right)$$

and α_X is the expected rate of return on nominal wealth,

$$(59) \quad \alpha_X = a^{*\prime}\alpha + \left(\frac{\mu_p}{p}\right) + \left(\frac{\text{cov } p, X}{pX}\right) - \left(\frac{\text{var } p}{p^2}\right).$$

PROOF: Ito's multiplication rule implies that

$$(\text{var } W) = (1/p^2)(\text{var } X) - (2X/p^3)(\text{cov } X, p) + (X^2/p^4)(\text{var } p),$$

$$(\text{cov } W, p) = (1/p)(\text{cov } X, p) - (X/p^2)(\text{var } p),$$

$$(\text{cov } W, Y) = (1/p)(\text{cov } X, Y) - (X/p^2)(\text{cov } p, Y),$$

and

$$\alpha_X = a^{*\prime}\alpha + (\mu_p/p) + (1/pX)(\text{cov } X, p) - (1/p^2)(\text{var } p).$$

With

$$J(W, Y, t) \equiv J(X/p, Y, t) \equiv V(X, Y, t),$$

we have

$$(J_{WW}/J_W) = p(V_{XX}/V_X),$$

$$(J_{WY_i}/J_W) = (V_{XY_i}/V_X), \quad \text{and}$$

$$(V_{Xp}/V_X) = -(1/p) - (X/p)(V_{XX}/V_X).$$

Equation (57) follows by writing the derivatives of $F(W, Y, t)$ in terms of those of $H(X, Y, t)$ and substituting all of the above into (6). The nominal interest rate can then be identified as the nominal payout flow necessary to keep the nominal value of a security identically equal to one, which is ι as given in (58).

Q.E.D.

A comparison of (57) and (58) with (6) and (3) shows that the interest rate equation and the fundamental valuation equation have exactly the same form when all variables are expressed in nominal terms as when all variables are expressed in real terms. By using the arguments given in the proof of the proposition, the nominal interest rate can be expressed in terms of real wealth as

$$(60) \quad \iota = r + \left(\frac{1}{p}\right)\left[\mu_p - \left(\frac{-J_{WW}}{J_W}\right)(\text{cov } W, p)\right.$$

$$\left. - \sum_{i=1}^{k} \left(\frac{-J_{WY_i}}{J_W}\right)(\text{cov } Y_i, p) - \left(\frac{\text{var } p}{p}\right)\right],$$

where r, the real interest rate, is as given by equation (3). The term (μ_p/p) is the expected rate of inflation. The remaining terms may in general have either sign, so the nominal interest rate may be either greater or less than the sum of the real interest rate and the expected inflation rate.[18]

8. CONCLUDING COMMENTS

In this paper, we have applied a rational asset pricing model to study the term structure of interest rates. In this model, the current prices and stochastic properties of all contingent claims, including bonds, are derived endogenously. Anticipations, risk aversion, investment alternatives, and preferences about the timing of consumption all play a role in determining the term structure. The model thus includes the main factors traditionally mentioned in a way which is consistent with maximizing behavior and rational expectations.

By exploring specific examples, we have obtained simple closed form solutions for bond prices which depend on observable economic variables and can be tested. The combination of equilibrium intertemporal asset pricing principles and appropriate modelling of the underlying stochastic processes provides a powerful tool for deriving consistent and potentially refutable theories. This is the first

---

[18] For a related discussion, see Fischer [13].

such exercise along these lines, and the methods developed should have many applications beyond those which we considered here.

In a separate paper, Cox, Ingersoll, and Ross [5], we use our approach to examine some aspects of what may be called traditional theories of the term structure. There we show that some forms of the classical expectations hypothesis are consistent with our simple equilibrium model and more complex ones, while other forms in general are not. We also show the relationship between some continuous time equilibrium models and traditional theories which express expected future spot rates as linear combinations of past spot rates.

Massachusetts Institute of Technology
   and
Yale University

Manuscript received September, 1978; revision received October, 1984.

REFERENCES

[1] BEJA, A.: "State Preference and the Riskless Interest Rate: A Markov Model of Capital Markets," *Review of Economic Studies*, 46(1979), 435–446.

[2] BIERWAG, G. O., AND M. A. GROVE: "A Model of the Term Structure of Interest Rates," *Review of Economics and Statistics*, 49(1967), 50–62.

[3] BRENNAN, M. J., AND E. S. SCHWARTZ: "A Continuous Time Approach to the Pricing of Bonds," *Journal of Banking and Finance*, 3(1979), 133–155.

[4] CAGAN, P.: "The Monetary Dynamics of Hyperinflation," in *Studies in the Quantity Theory of Money*, ed. by M. Friedman. Chicago: University of Chicago Press, 1956.

[5] COX, J. C., J. E. INGERSOLL, JR., AND S. A. ROSS: "A Re-examination of Traditional Hypotheses about the Term Structure of Interest Rates, *Journal of Finance*, 36(1981), 769–799.

[6] ——: "An Intertemporal General Equilibrium Model of Asset Prices," *Econometrica*, 53 (1985), 363–384.

[7] CULBERTSON, J. M.: "The Term Structure of Interest Rates," *Quarterly Journal of Economics*, 71(1957), 485–517.

[8] DE LEEUW, F.: "A Model of Financial Behavior," in *The Brookings Quarterly Econometric Model of the United States*, ed. by J. S. Duesenberry et al. Chicago: Rand McNally, 1965.

[9] DIEFFENBACH, B. C.: "A Quantitative Theory of Risk Premiums on Securities with an Application to the Term Structure of Interest Rates," *Econometrica*, 43(1975), 431–454.

[10] DOTHAN, L. U.: "On the Term Structure of Interest Rates," *Journal of Financial Economics*, 6(1978), 59–69.

[11] DUESENBERRY, J. A.: *Business Cycles and Economic Growth*. New York: McGraw-Hill, 1958.

[12] FELLER, W.: "Two Singular Diffusion Problems," *Annals of Mathematics*, 54(1951), 173–182.

[13] FISCHER, S.: "The Demand for Index Bonds," *Journal of Political Economy*, 83(1975), 509–534.

[14] GERMAN, M. B.: "A General Theory of Asset Valuation Under Diffusion Processes," University of California, Berkeley, Institute of Business and Economic Research, Working Paper No. 50, 1977.

[15] HAKANSSON, N. H.: "Optimal Investment and Consumption Strategies under Risk for a Class of Utility Functions," *Econometrica*, 38(1970), 587–607.

[16] HICKS, J. R.: *Value and Capital*, 2nd edition. London: Oxford University Press, 1946.

[17] JOHNSON, N. L., AND S. KOTZ: *Distributions in Statistics: Continuous Univariate Distributions—2*. Boston: Houghton Mifflin Company, 1970.

[18] LONG, J. B.: "Stock Prices, Inflation, and the Term Structure of Interest Rates," *Journal of Financial Economics*, 1(1974), 131–170.

[19] MALKIEL, B. G.: *The Term Structure of Interest Rates: Excpectations and Behavior Patterns*. Princeton, New Jersey: Princeton University Press, 1966.

[20] MEISELMAN, D.: *The Term Structure of Interest Rates*. Englewood Cliffs, New Jersey: Prentice Hall, 1962.

[21] MERTON, R. C.: "A Dynamic General Equilibrium Model of the Asset Market and Its Application to the Pricing of the Capital Structure of the Firm," Massachusetts Institute of Technology, Sloan School of Management, Working Paper No. 497-70, 1970.

[22] ————: "Optimum Consumption and Portfolio Rules in a Continuous Time Model," *Journal of Economic Theory*, 3(1971), 373-413.

[23] ————: "Theory of Rational Option Pricing," *Bell Journal of Economics and Management Science*, 4(1973), 141-183.

[24] MODIGLIANI, F., AND R. J. SHILLER: "Inflation, Rational Expectations and the Term Structure of Interest Rates," *Economica*, 40 N.S. (1973), 12-43.

[25] MODIGLIANI, F., AND R. SUTCH: "Innovations in Interest Rate Policy," *American Economic Review*, 56(1966), 178-197.

[26] NELSON, C. R.: *The Term Structure of Interest Rates*. New York: Basic Books, Inc., 1972.

[27] OLIVER, F. W. J.: "Bessel Functions of Integer Order," *Handbook of Mathematical Functions*, ed. by M. A. Abramowitz and I. A. Stegun. New York: Dover, 1965.

[28] RICHARD, S. F.: "An Arbitrage Model of the Term Structure of Interest Rates," *Journal of Financial Economics*, 6(1978), 33-57.

[29] ROLL, R.: *The Behavior of Interest Rates*. New York: Basic Books, Inc., 1970.

[30] ————: "Investment Diversification and Bond Maturity," *Journal of Finance*, 26(1971), 51-66.

[31] RUBINSTEIN, M. E.: "The Valuation of Uncertain Income Streams and the Pricing of Options," *Bell Journal of Economics*, 7(1976), 407-425.

[32] SAMUELSON, P. A.: "Lifetime Portfolio Selection by Dynamic Stochastic Programming," *Review of Economics and Statistics*, 51(1969), 239-246.

[33] SARGENT, T. J.: "Rational Expectations and the Term Structure of Interest Rates," *Journal of Money, Credit, and Banking*, 4(1972), 74-97.

[34] SLATER, L. J.: "Confluent Hypergeometric Functions," in *Handbook of Mathematical Functions*, ed. by M. Abramowitz and I. A. Stegun. New York: Dover, 1965.

[35] STIGLITZ, J. E.: "A Consumption-Oriented Theory of Demand for Financial Assets and the Term Structure of Interest Rates," *Review of Economic Studies*, 37(1970), 321-351.

[36] VAN HORNE, J. C.: "Interest-Rate Risk and the Term Structure of Interest Rates," *Journal of Political Economy*, 73(1965), 344-351.

[37] VASICEK, O. A.: "An Equilibrium Characterization of the Term Structure," *Journal of Financial Economics*, 5(1977), 177-188.

[38] WOOD, J. H.: "The Expectations Hypothesis, the Yield Curve and Monetary Policy," *Quarterly Journal of Economics*, 78(1964), 457-470.

discussion | Modeling the Term Structure of Interest Rates in General Equilibrium

Kenneth J. Singleton

Graduate School of Industrial Administration
Carnegie-Mellon University

and

National Bureau of Economic Research

I. INTRODUCTION

Modeling the term structure has traditionally proceeded by studying the interrelations among short- and long-term bond returns and various types of "term premiums," without developing formally the relations between interest rates and the state of the economy. In a series of path-breaking papers, Cox, Ingersoll, and Ross (CIR) (1981, 1985a, b) have departed from this tradition and developed a general equilibrium model of the term structure of interest rates. The structure of interest rates in their economy is linked directly to the specifications of preferences, technologies, and the distributions of the underlying sources of uncertainty. Consequently, the relations among agents' expectations about the future values of the state variables in the economy, term premiums, and the shape of the yield curve are determined explicitly by these specifications. From their analyses it is now well understood that certain expectations-based theories of the term structure are mutually inconsistent, and many are incompatible with general equilibrium. Furthermore, the development of their models and subsequent extensions by others have led to more precise statements about how the degree of "risk" and "liquidity" in economic environments affects term premiums.

With the CIR studies in mind, we continue the exploration of the term structure in general equilibrium in two directions. First, in Section II, alternative approaches to the econometric analysis of the term structure are discussed. Particular attention is given to the inherent conflicts between model complexity or "richness" and the necessity of having econometrically identified and computationally tractable models. In the process of describing the trade-offs involved in model specification, we interpret the poor econometric

---

Comments from George Constantinides and financial support from the National Science Foundation are gratefully acknowledged.

fit of an important class of general equilibrium models and suggest some directions for future work.

The third section of this paper explores the properties of a simple monetary model of the term structure. By introducing money into general equilibrium models of the term structure, we can study the behavior of nominal interest rates and distinguish formally between the constructs or "risk" and "liquidity" premiums. Drawing upon the recent work of Lucas (1984) and Townsend (1984), we show that liquidity premiums can induce an upward bias to the slope of the yield curve. Moreover, the implied restrictions on the term structure of nominal interest rates are shown to be fundamentally different from the restrictions on the term structure of returns on discount bonds with goods-denominated payoffs.

II. ECONOMETRIC ANALYSIS OF GENERAL EQUILIBRIUM MODELS OF THE TERM STRUCTURE

We obtain the identification of econometric models of the term structure by restricting the structure of preferences, technologies, the distributions of disturbances, and the constraints facing economic agents. In practice, the choice of identifying restrictions is influenced by the goals of the analysis and the trade-offs between complexity and tractability. Estimation of the parameters of fairly general objective functions may be feasible without a complete characterization of the constraint set or the imposition of much structure on the distribution of shocks. On the other hand, calculating the implied equilibrium prices of bonds (either numerically or analytically) requires restrictions on all aspects of the economic environment. Given the complexity of these calculations, attention has typically been restricted to fairly simple specifications of objective functions and constraint sets. The choice of identifying restrictions may also influence the data requirements for empirical analyses. This section explores some of these trade-offs between model complexity, identification, and tractability in more detail.

Consider an economy with a finite number of homogeneous agents who choose consumption and investment plans in order to maximize expected utility from consumption. Let $m_{t,n}$ denote the marginal rate of substitution of consumption at date t for consumption at date $t + n$ of a numeraire good, and let $r_{t,n}$ denote a (real) n-period holding period return on a feasible investment strategy.[1] Then from the first-order conditions of an agent's intertemporal optimum problem, it follows that in equilibrium[2]

$$(1) \qquad E[m_{t,n}r_{t,n}|I_t] = 1,$$

where I_t is a common information set for all agents. An analogous expression holds for all feasible investment strategies over all holding periods. Equation (1), or its counterpart for monetary economies (see Section III), underlies most of the recent empirical studies of the term structure of interest rates. These studies are differentiated by the overidentifying restrictions imposed on the economy to deduce testable implications from (1).

A. Traditional Expectations Theories of the Term Structure

Perhaps the most widely studied models of the term structure of interest rates are the many variants of the expectations theory.[3] CIR (1981) have shown that all but one of the most common formulations of the expectations theory are incompatible with a continuous-time, rational expectations general equilibrium. The compatible version is the "local expectations theory," which assumes that agents have logarithmic preferences, the returns to physical capital are uncorrelated with changes in the state variables, and the state variables follow certain Markov processes. According to this theory, the expected holding period returns on long-term bonds over the next instant are equal to the instantaneous risk-free rate.

Besides the apparent intuitive appeal of this theory, it has the attractive feature of leading to restrictions on the joint stochastic process generating observable returns—data on nonasset market variables are not required for estimation and inference. This simplification is obtained by restricting substantially the underlying economic environment. It is natural to inquire then whether the local expectations theory can be deduced approximately from a general equilibrium model under weaker conditions. Shiller (1979) and Shiller, Campbell, and Schoenholtz (1983) have provided one affirmative answer to this question. By linearizing the present value formula for coupon-paying bonds with nonstochastic coupons, they deduce an approximate local expectations theory.

One can deduce a different, log-linear expectations formulation of interest rates in general equilibrium without approximations, using arguments similar to those in Hansen and Singleton (1983), Breeden (1985), and Dunn and Singleton (1986). Specifically, let r_t^f denote the one-period risk-free rate and suppose that $x_t \equiv (\log m_{t,1}, \log r_{t,1}, \log r_t^f)$ is a normal and stationary stochastic process. Under this distributional assumption,

(2) $$E[\log r_{t,1}|\psi_t] = \log r_t^f + \phi_1,$$

where

(3) $$\phi_1 = \tfrac{1}{2}\text{Var}[\log r_{t,1} + \log m_{t,1}|\psi_t] - \tfrac{1}{2}\text{Var}[\log m_{t,1}|\psi_t],$$

and ψ_t denotes the information set generated by $\{x_{t-s}:x \geqslant 0\}$. Since $\{x_t\}$ is a normally distributed stochastic process, the conditional expectations are linear functions. Furthermore, the conditional variances are constants, and, hence, ϕ_1 is a constant. Thus, equation (2) represents a logarithmic version of the local expectations theory (with constant intercept).

Relations (2) and (3) are satisfied for one-period holding period returns on pure discount bonds under the assumptions of common, constant relative risk-averse preferences across agents, homogeneous information, and an aggregate endowment process that follows a stationary lognormal process.[4] More generally, for given specifications of exchange or production economies, the distributional assumption underlying (2) can be interpreted as an implicit restriction on the joint distributions of the sources of uncertainty in the economy. That is, given specifications of preferences and technologies and the assumption that returns and $m_{t,n}$ are jointly lognormal, it may be possible to solve "backward" for the values of the disturbances to the economy that are consistent with the environment (see Sims 1985). The distribution of these disturbances will not, in general, have a simple parametric representation.

In practice, neither of these representations of the expectations theory appears to be supported by the data. Substantial evidence against the linearized model in Shiller, Campbell, and Schoenholtz (1983) is presented by Shiller (1979), Singleton (1980), Hansen and Sargent (1981), Shiller, Campbell, and Schoenholtz (1983), Fama (1984a, b), and Mankiw and Summers (1984), among others. The term structure relation (2) potentially accommodates these findings, since the difference between the holding period return and the one-period riskless rate, $r_{t,1} - r_t^f$, may vary stochastically over time in this model. However, since the logarithms of the total returns have historically been approximately equal to the real rates of return, previous tests of the traditional expectations hypothesis can be reinterpreted as tests of a close approximation to the general equilibrium model (2) with time-varying term premiums. These observations suggest that, in practice, the observed term structures are also not captured by (2); a less restrictive model is required to explain the data.[5]

B. Consumption Risk and the Historical Behavior of Interest Rates

More general term structure models can be studied empirically by working directly with (1). Specifically, suppose $m_{t,n}$ is observed up to a vector of unknown parameters. (Since specifying preferences parametrically is a prerequisite for solving equilibrium models, this assumption about $m_{t,n}$ is not unusually strong.) Let

$$(4) \qquad u_{t+n} = m_{t,n} r_{t,n} - 1.$$

Then (1) implies that the disturbance u_{t+n} is orthogonal to all variables in agents' information set: $E[u_{t+n} z_t] = 0, z_t \in I_t$. These orthogonality conditions can be used to construct estimates of the parameters governing preferences and to test the validity of the term structure model without specifying other features of the economic environment (Hansen and Singleton 1982). In this respect, the analysis of (1) can be interpreted as the first step in the process of building a complete model. Potential drawbacks of this approach are that observability precludes shocks to tastes, the use of aggregate consumption data requires certain homogeneity assumptions, and the consumption data may be measured with substantial error.[6]

Special cases of (1) have been examined by Hansen and Singleton (1982, 1983, 1984), Ferson (1983), Brown and Gibbons (1985), Dunn and Singleton (1986), Hall (1988), Litzenberger and Ronn (1986), and Singleton (1986). Based on conventional test criteria, these studies have found that representative agent models of asset prices are not consistent with the postwar United States data. To interpret the poor fit of these models, recall that if utility is a time-separable function of a single good and markets are complete, then asset prices are chosen in equilibrium to satisfy

(5)
$$E[u_{t+n}|I_t] \equiv E\left[\frac{\beta^n f(c_{t+n})}{f(c_t)r_{t,n}} - 1|I_t\right] = 0,$$

where $\beta \in (0, 1)$ is the subjective discount factor and $f(\cdot)$ is a monotonically decreasing function of aggregate consumption, c_t (see, e.g., Breeden and Litzenberger 1978, Constantinides 1982). From the condition $E[u_{t+n}|I_t] = 0$, it follows that $E[u_{t+n}] = 0$. Setting $n = 1$, linearizing $f(c_t)$ about c_{t-1} and assuming that the coefficient of relative risk aversion evaluated at aggregate consumption, $\alpha \equiv -c_{t-1}f(c_{t-1})/f(c_{t-1})$, is approximately constant lead to the approximate relation

(6)
$$(1 + \alpha)E[r_{t,1}] - \alpha E\left[\frac{c_{t+1}}{c_t}\right]E[r_{t,1}] = \beta^{-1} + \alpha\,\text{Cov}\left[\frac{c_{t+1}}{c_t}, r_{t,1}\right].$$

For plausible values of α and postwar United States data, $\text{Cov}[c_{t+1}/c_t, r_{t,1}]$ is negligible relative to the left side of (6). Since $E[c_{t+1}/c_t] > 1$, $E[r_{t,1}]$ must be greater than β^{-1} for (6) to be satisfied. And the implied difference between the average real returns on Treasury bills and β^{-1} is an increasing function of $E[c_{t+1}/c_t]$. Inspection of the data reveals that sample estimates of $E[r_{t+1}] - \beta^{-1}$ are too small (for plausible values of β and the sample estimate of $E[c_{t+1}/c_t]$) to be consistent with (6).

When agents are assumed to have constant relative risk-averse preferences $[f(c_t) = c_t^{-\alpha}]$, estimates of the parameters α and β are chosen to make the sample counterpart of $E[u_{t+n}]$ and other orthogonality conditions close to zero according to a certain metric (Hansen 1982, Hansen and Singleton 1982). Equation (6) suggests that in order for $\hat{\alpha}$ to be greater than zero (concave utility), $\hat{\beta}$ must be chosen to be larger than unity because $\hat{E}[c_{t+n}/c_t]$ is much larger than $\hat{E}[r_{t,n}]$ for real Treasury bill returns. Interestingly, this is exactly the pattern of results obtained by Hansen and Singleton (1982, 1984) and Dunn and Singleton (1986). Concave utility was associated with negative discount rates in models of bond returns. Essentially, the growth rate in consumption is too large relative to $\hat{E}[r_{t,n}]$ for this model to yield economically meaningful parameter estimates.[7] Indeed, when β is restricted to be less than unity, $\hat{\alpha}$ is substantially *smaller* than zero, and the probability values of the chi-square goodness-of-fit statistics are essentially zero (Singleton 1986).[8]

Admittedly this simple model omits decision variables that one may plausibly argue are not separable from consumption of nondurable goods. However, Deaton (1985) presents cogent arguments about why the introduction of leisure as a decision variable is unlikely to improve the fit of this model. Also, the same issues regarding average growth and returns and the value of β emerge in the models studied by Eichenbaum and Hansen (1985) and Dunn and Singleton (1986) in which consumers receive utility from the consumption of services of durable goods (Singleton 1986). Accounting for taxation of income by using after-tax returns leads to a further deterioration in the fit of these models, since the mean return is lowered. In sum, the evidence does not support these representative agent models of the term structure of real bond returns.

C. Econometric Analysis of Complete Models of the Term Structure

The analysis of Euler equations allows substantial flexibility in specifying objective functions, but only limited aspects of the temporal behavior of returns can be investigated using this approach. In particular, it may be difficult to assess the economic significance of large test statistics from the analysis of Euler equations alone. More information about the properties of bond prices can be obtained from the price series implied by a completely specified economic environment. This section discusses several approaches to solving general equilibrium models of interest rates as well as the relation between solution methods and the estimation problem.

Analytic solutions for bond prices can be obtained for a limited set of economic environments. Brock (1982) and Campbell (1986) present solutions for discrete-time economies, and Sundaresan (1984) and CIR (1985b) exhibit the solutions of several continuous-time economies. These models yield exact relations between bond prices and the state variables, which are convenient for analyzing the properties of bond returns. They also imply a stochastic singularity in the joint stochastic process for bond prices and other endogenous variables when the number of variables being examined exceeds the number of sources of uncertainty. This problem can be circumvented by introducing multiple goods and/or multiple shocks to endowments or technologies. However, except under fairly restrictive distributional assumptions, the resulting price equations will involve nonlinear functions of unobserved state variables.

To illustrate these econometric considerations, consider the continuous-time economies examined by CIR (1985b). Their single-state variable economy with logarithmic preferences yields the closed-form solution

$$(7) \qquad p(r, t, \tau) = A[\tau, \phi_0] \exp \{ - B[\tau, \phi_0] r \},$$

where r is the instantaneous rate, τ denotes the maturity of the bond, $A[\cdot]$ and $B[\cdot]$ are constants, and ϕ_0 denotes a vector of unknown parameters. Though (7) leads to a simple linear expression for $\log[p(r, t, \tau)]$ in terms of $\log r$, it also implies that price changes in bonds of all maturities are perfectly correlated. Therefore, models with multiple state variables may be more plausible empirically.[9]

In their econometric analysis of (7), Brown and Dybvig (1986) circumvented the problem of a stochastic singularity by introducing additive disturbances in (7). However, economic theory does not restrict the distributions of these disturbances, so ad hoc and possibly inconsistent assumptions about disturbances must be imposed. Gibbons and Ramaswamy (1987) circumvented these problems by introducing inflation as a state variable and then calculating method-of-moments estimators of the parameter vector ϕ_0. Their economic environment is not fully specified, however, so the equilibrium prices implied by their model cannot be calculated. Alternatively, one could introduce additional state variables, some of which are unobserved by the econometrician. This approach may lead not only to a potentially richer term structure but also to a consistent characterization of the disturbances across price equations for different maturities. The resulting expressions for prices are typically nonlinear functions of the unobserved state variables and, therefore, nontrivial identification and estimation problems may arise. Efficient estimation of multistate variable models in the presence of these econometric difficulties is an important topic for future research.

Another problem with expanding the dimension of the state vector is that the models may not yield analytic solutions. For continuous-time models, numerical solutions to the implied partial differential equation for bond prices are often feasible. Similarly, for discrete-time economies, the state space can be discretized and then numerical solutions can be obtained (e.g., Tauchen 1985).[10] The properties of alternative solution procedures, as well as the development of tractable estimation procedures that mix model solution with estimation, are also interesting topics for further research.

Finally, computational methods are also required for solving dynamic models that incorporate heterogeneity and incomplete markets. Either of these features of the economic environment could explain the failures of the representative agent models to fit the data. Private information, for instance, may explain the apparent limited opportunities to borrow against future income or why some agents are not always interior with regard to their labor supply decisions. Additionally, the frictions that induce agents to transact with money can lead to fundamentally different term structure relations than those described in this section.

III. INTRODUCING MONEY INTO A MODEL OF THE TERM STRUCTURE OF INTEREST RATES

The bonds being priced by all of the general equilibrium models discussed in Section II are goods-denominated bonds. Such bonds are not traded actively in the United States, so, strictly speaking, there do not exist empirical counterparts to the discount bond returns in CIR (1981, 1985a, b) or (2). In practice, ex post real returns on bonds with monetary payoffs have been used in empirical studies of equilibrium term structure relations like (2). This section investigates the validity of this practice in the context of the monetary model studied by Townsend (1984).

Hicks (1939) argued that the traditional expectations theory was incomplete and suggested in its stead what he called the liquidity preference hypothesis. He argued that due to risk aversion on the part of market participants, borrowers, in order to avoid interest rate risk, typically issue long-term securities, whereas lenders, to avoid fluctuation in portfolio value, prefer to hold short-term securities. These assumptions led him to conclude that lenders must be paid liquidity premiums over and above expected future short-term rates, and that these premiums increase monotonically with maturity. However, although risk aversion may lead to risk premiums of the type discussed in Section II, it seems that risk aversion per se cannot lead to a concern about "liquidity" in the presence of complete markets for contingent claims. In order for "liquidity" to be an important factor in asset pricing, some frictions must be introduced into the model that differentiate assets in terms of their exchangeability for consumption goods.

One way of creating a wedge between the liquidity of different types of assets is to introduce a friction that induces a transactions demand for money. Introducing money into a general equilibrium model of the term structure is of interest in its own right, because it also leads to a potentially important distinction between bonds with payoffs denominated in terms of goods and money.[11] For illustrative purposes, I shall follow Townsend (1984) and suppose that there are two types of goods. Good 2 must be purchased with money, and agents receive endowments of good 1 that may be either consumed or invested in a storage technology. Specifically, each agent maximizes

$$(8) \qquad E_0 \sum_{i=1}^{T} \beta^t U(c_t^1, c_t^2)$$

by choice of $c_t^1, c_t^2, I_{t+1}, M_{t+1}$, subject to

$$(9) \qquad p_t c_t^1 + p_t c_t^2 + M_{t+1} + p_t I_{t+1} \leqslant M_t + p_t w_t + p_t f[I_t, s_t] + z_t,$$

$$(10) \qquad p_t c_t^2 \leqslant M_t + z_t,$$

where p_t is the price of the goods in terms of money, I_t represents investment of good 1 in the storage technology $f[\cdot]$, which may depend on a vector of shocks s_t, M_t represents money holdings at the beginning of period t, w_t is the endowment of good 1, and z_t represents monetary injections at date t.[12]

Inequality (10) is a cash-in-advance constraint.[13] Households that exchange commodity 1 for money at date t in the market cannot use this money for the purchase of commodity 2 until date $t + 1$. Similarly, the proceeds from selling a security at date t for money cannot be used to purchase and consume good 2 until date $t + 1$. Thus, if bonds were traded in this economy, they would be perfectly illiquid relative to money over a single decision interval.[14] An interesting question is whether there are liquidity premiums associated with the term structure of nominal bond prices.

The first-order conditions for the optimum problem (8)–(10) are

$$(11) \qquad \beta^t U_{1,t} = \lambda_t p_t,$$

$$(12) \qquad \beta^t U_{2,t} = \lambda_t p_t + \phi_t p_t,$$

$$(13) \qquad \lambda_t = E_t(\phi_{t+1} + \lambda_{t+1}),$$

where $U_{s,t} = \partial U(c_t^1, c_t^2)/\partial c_t^s$ ($s = 1, 2$), λ_t and ϕ_t are the Lagrange multipliers associated with the constraints (9) and (10), respectively, and (13) is the intertemporal relation among multipliers. The expression $\lambda_t + \phi_t$ is the marginal utility of money at date t. The term λ_t represents an income effect, and

ϕ_t is the gain from relaxing the cash-in-advance constraint if it is binding in period t.

The price at the beginning of date t of a nominal pure discount bond that pays one dollar at the beginning of date $t+j$ is given by the ratio of the expected marginal utility of money at date $t+j$ to the marginal utility of money at date t:

$$(14) \qquad p_{t,j} = \frac{E_t[\lambda_{t+j} + \phi_{t+j}]}{\lambda_t + \phi_t}.$$

Repeated use of (13) and the law of iterated expectation leads to the equivalent expression

$$(15) \qquad p_{t,j} = p_{t,k} - \sum_{l=1}^{j-k} \frac{E_t[\phi_{t+j-l}]}{\lambda_t + \phi_t}$$

for $j > k$. Since $\phi_t \geq 0$ for all t, (15) implies that

$$(16) \qquad p_{t,k} \geq p_{t,j}.$$

It follows that the "price curve" of nominal pure discount bonds is unambiguously downward sloping in this model. Moreover, the difference between these prices is determined by the expected future values of the multipliers on the constraint (10).

Interestingly, the liquidity premiums show up in the prices and not in the returns in this model. That is, (16) is not equivalent to $r_{t,j} \geq r_{t,k}$, where $r_{t,j}$ is defined by the relation $p_{t,j} = (1 + r_{t,j})^{-j}$. Of course, the slope of the yield curve is influenced by the degree to which the cash-in-advance constraint is expected to be binding in the future or, equivalently, on how important holding liquid money will be for meeting desired consumption levels. If agents expect that the constraint will never be binding, then $r_{t,j} = 0$ for all time t and all maturities j.

Another interesting feature of Townsend's model is that the marginal rate of substitution pricing formula for nominal bonds is nearly identical to the Euler equation (1) for nonmonetary models when good 2 is chosen as the numeraire. This can be seen by dividing both sides of (11) by p_t and then substituting the resulting expression for $\lambda_t + \phi_t$ into (13), which after rearrangement gives

$$(17) \qquad E_t \left| \beta^j \frac{U_{2,t+j}}{U_{2,t}} (1 + r_{t,j})^j \frac{p_t}{p_{t+j}} \right| = 1.$$

Note that $[(1 + r_{t,j})^j p_t/p_{t+j}]$ is analogous to the ex post real return on a nominal bond that was used in empirical studies of nonmonetary models. It differs only in the dating convention—the holding period of the bond is from the beginning of date t to the beginning of date $t+j$, and the price deflators are typically measured at the end of the period.[15] Nevertheless, it turns out that tests of (17) give qualitatively similar results to tests of corresponding versions of (1) (Singleton 1985).

If, on the other hand, good 1 is taken to be the numeraire, then the appropriate marginal rate of substitution pricing formula is

(18)
$$E_t \left| \beta^j \frac{U_{1,t+j-1}}{U_{2,t}} (1 + r_{t,j})^j \frac{p_t}{p_{t+j-1}} \right| = 1.$$

Although the ex post real return is again similar to that used in studies of (1), the expression $[\beta^j (U_{1,t+j-1})/U_{2,t}]$ is very different from $[\beta^j U_{1,t+j}/U_{1,t}]$ which appears in (1).

In sum, this simple model has illustrated the often-neglected characteristic of general equilibrium models that the nominal yield curve may be fundamentally different than the yield curve associated with pure discount bonds that pay off in units of some good. In monetary models with more complicated transactions technologies or that introduce money in different ways, the liquidity premiums may not lead to a nonincreasing nominal price curve. And Lucas's (1984) model illustrates the fact that minor modifications of the timing of transactions and the nature of uncertainty may lead to pricing relations that are fundamentally different than (1) regardless of which good is the numeraire. These observations, together with the importance of monetary exchange in modern industrial economies, suggest that further analysis of asset prices in monetary economies may yield important insights about the term structure of interest rates.

NOTES

[1] Examples of investment strategies are buy and hold an n'-period security for n periods ($n' > n$) or roll over a sequence of short-term securities for n periods.

[2] Sufficient conditions for (1) to obtain in discrete time are given in Rubinstein (1976), Breeden and Litzenberger (1978), and Lucas (1978). Continuous-time versions of (1) were deduced by CIR (1985a), Richard and Sundaresan (1981), and Breeden (1985).

[3] The origins of this theory can be traced at least back to Fisher (1896). There are now many variants of this theory, several of which are summarized and critiqued in Nelson (1972) and CIR (1981).

[4] With common, constant relative risk-averse utility functions and complete markets, Rubinstein (1974) has shown that complete demand aggregation across consumers with possibly different endowment streams is possible. Eichenbaum, Hansen, and Richard (1985) discuss aggregation for more general classes of utility functions.

[5] To my knowledge, relation (2) has not been tested directly in the literature on the term structure. Hansen and Hodrick (1983) study an analogous relation to (2) for spot and forward exchange rates (i.e., no approximations were involved). They find substantial evidence against this relation for exchange rates.

[6] Some consequences of mismeasurement of consumption for empirical studies of intertemporal models have recently been explored by Breeden, Gibbons, and Litzenberger (1986). Miron (1986) and Singleton (1986) explore some of the consequences of seasonal adjustment for econometric studies of (1).

[7] Deaton (1985) reached a similar conclusion using certain monotonicity conditions implied by a perfect foresight version of this model.

[8] Another implications of (1) is that

$$Er_{t,n}^1 - Er_{t,n}^2 = -\frac{\text{Cov}[m_{t,n}, r_{t,m}^1 - r_{t,n}^2]}{E[m_{t,n}]},$$

where $r_{t,n}^1$ and $r_{t,n}^2$ are n-period returns on two different investment strategies. In fact, the sample covariances of returns and $m_{t,n}$ are much too small and of the wrong sign to explain the average differences in the returns on short-term investments in Treasury bills (Dunn and Singleton 1986). These findings are also symptomatic of the fact that consumption growth and real returns have not covaried in ways suggested by these utility-based models.

[9] Brennan and Schwartz (1979, 1980) use arbitrage arguments to deduce a two-state variable model of the term structure of interest rates, instead of working with a general equilibrium model. See CIR (1985b) for a discussion of several potential pitfalls in using arbitrage arguments to deduce econometric models of the term structure.

[10] Mehra and Prescott (1985) and Donaldson, Johnson, and Mehra (1985) assume a discrete state-space and then proceed to obtain numerical solutions to their model. Tauchen suggests a procedure for discretizing a continuous state-space as an initial step.

[11] LeRoy (1984) and Danthine and Donaldson (1986) examine asset prices in the context of monetary models with money introduced directly into agents' utility functions. LeRoy specifically examines the properties of "term premia" for nominal discount bonds. The signs of the term premia in his model depend on certain covariances of returns with aggregate endowments in a manner similar to the risk premia discussed in Section II.

[12] There is also a terminal condition on money holdings that will be ignored for the purposes of the discussion here; see Townsend (1984).

[13] Townsend (1984) provides a microeconomic justification for (10) based on the spatial separation of agents that precludes loan markets from coming into existence.

[14] Bonds are not traded in equilibrium in this model, because of the spatial separation of agents. Nevertheless, these securities can be priced.

[15] CIR (1985b) investigate nominal bond prices by introducing price levels and/or inflation as additional state variables. This approach presumes that changes in the money stock and inflation have no effect of real economic activity. However, the functions that typically underlie an economic role for money imply that money is nonneutral. Money is not superneutral in Townsend's cash-in-advance constraint economy, for instance (changes in growth rates affect real output).

REFERENCES

Breeden, D. T., and Litzenberger, R. H. 1978. "Prices of State-Contingent Claims Implicit in Option Prices." *Journal of Business* 51: 621–51.

——. 1985. "Consumption, Production, and Interest Rates: A Synthesis." *Journal of Financial Economics*.

Breeden, D.; Gibbons, M.; and Litzenberger, R. 1986. "Empirical Tests of the Consumption-Oriented CAPM." Stanford University, manuscript.

Brennan, M., and Schwartz, E. 1979. "A Continuous Time Approach to the Pricing of Bonds." *Journal of Banking and Finance* 3: 133–55.

——. 1980. "Conditional Predictions of Bond Prices and Returns." *Journal of Finance* 35: 405–17.

Brock, W. 1982. "Asset Prices in a Production Economy." In J. J. McCall, ed., *The Economics of Information and Uncertainty*. Chicago: University of Chicago Press.

Brown, D. P., and Gibbons, M. R. 1985. "A Simple Econometric Approach for Utility-Based Asset Pricing Models." *Journal of Finance* 40: 359–81.

Brown, S. J., and Dybvig, P. H. 1986. "The Empirical Implications of the Cox, Ingersoll, Ross Theory of the Term Structure of Interest Rates." *Journal of Finance* 41: 617–30.

Campbell, J. 1986. "Stock Returns and the Term Structure." Princeton University, manuscript.

Constantinides , G. 1982. "Intertemporal Asset Pricings with Heterogeneous Consumers and without Demand Aggregation." *Journal of Business* 55: 253–67.

Cox, J. C.; Ingersoll, J. E., Jr.; and Ross, S. A. 1981. "A Reexamination of the Traditional Hypotheses about the Term Structure of Interest Rates." *Journal of Finance* 36: 769–99.

―――. 1985a. "An Intertemporal General Equilibrium Model of Asset Prices." *Econometrica* 53: 363–84.

―――. 1985b. "A Theory of the Term Structure of Interest Rates." *Econometrica* 53: 385–407. Reprinted Chapter 5, this volume.

Danthine, J., and Donaldson, J. 1986. "Inflation and Asset Prices in an Exchange Economy." *Econometrica* 54: 585–606.

Deaton, A. 1985. "Life-Cycle Models of Consumption: Is the Evidence Consistent with the Theory?" Princeton University, manuscript.

Donaldson, J. B.; Johnsen, T.; and Mehra, R. 1985. "On the Term Structure of Interest Rates." Columbia University, manuscript.

Dunn, K. B., and Singleton, K. J. 1986. "Modeling the Term Structure of Interest Rates under Nonseparable Utility and Durability of Goods." *Journal of Financial Economics.* 17: 27–55.

Eichenbaum, M. S., and Hansen, L. P. 1985. "Estimating Consumption Models with Intertemporal Substitution Using Aggregate Time Series Data." Carnegie-Mellon University, manuscript.

Eichenbaum, M.; Hansen, L.; and Richard, S. 1985. "The Dynamic Equilibrium Pricing of Durable Consumption Goods." Carnegie-Mellon University, manuscript.

Fama, E. F. 1984a. "The Information in the Term Structure." *Journal of Financial Economics* 13: 509–28.

―――. 1984b. "Term Premiums in Bond Returns." *Journal of Financial Economics* 13: 529–46.

Ferson, W. E. 1983. "Expectations of Real Interest Rates and Aggregate Consumption: Empirical Tests." *Journal of Financial and Quantitative Analysis* 18: 477–97.

Fisher, I. 1896. "Appreciation and Interest." *Publications of the American Economic Association* 2: 23–29, 88–92.

Gibbons, M., and Ramaswamy, K. 1987. "The Term Structure of Interest Rates: Empirical Evidence." Stanford University, manuscript.

Hall, R. 1988. "Intertemporal Substitution in Consumption." *Journal of Political Economy* 96.

Hansen, L. P. 1982. "Large Sample Properties of Generalized Method of Moments Estimators." *Econometrica* 50: 1029–54.

Hansen, L. P., and Hodrick, R. J. 1980. "Forward Exchange Rates as Optimal Predictors of Future Spot Rates: An Econometric Analysis." *Journal of Political Economy* 88: 829–63.

―――. 1983. "Risk Averse Speculation in the Forward Foreign Exchange Market." In J. Frenkel, ed., *Exchange Rates and International Macroeconomics.* National Bureau of Economic Research, University of Chicago Press.

Hansen, L. P., and Sargent, T. J. 1981. "Exact Linear Rational Expectations Models: Specification and Estimation." Federal Reserve Bank of Minneapolis, manuscript.

Hansen, L. P., and Singleton, K. J. 1982. "Generalized Instrumental Variables Estimation of Nonlinear Rational Expectations Models." *Econometrica* 50: 1269–86.

————. 1983. "Stochastic Consumption, Risk Aversion, and the Temporal Behavior of Asset Returns." *Journal of Political Economy* 91: 249–65.

————. 1984. "Errata." *Econometrica* 52: 267–68.

Hicks, J. R. 1939. *Value and Capital*, 2nd ed. London: Clarendon Press.

LeRoy, S. 1984. "Nominal Prices and Interest Rates in General Equilibrium: Endowment Shocks." *Journal of Business* 57: 197–213.

Litzenberger, R., and Ronn, E. 1986. "A Utility Based Model of Common Stock Returns." *Journal of Finance* 41: 67–92.

Lucas, R. E., Jr. 1978. "Asset Prices in an Exchange Economy." *Econometrica* 46: 1429–46.

————. 1984. "Money in a Theory of Finance." *Carnegie-Rochester Conference Series on Public Policy* 21: 9–46.

Mankiw, G., and Summers, L. 1984. "Do Long-Term Interest Rates Overreact to Short-Term Interest Rates?" *Brookings Papers on Economic Activity* 1: 223–48.

Mehra, R., and Prescott, E. 1985. "The Equity Puzzle." *Journal of Monetary Economics* 15: 145–61.

Miron, J. 1986. "Seasonal Fluctuations and the Life Cycle-Permanent Income Model of Consumption." Working paper No. 1845, National Bureau of Economic Research.

Nelson, C. 1972. *The Term Structure of Interest Rates*. New York: Basic Books.

Richard, S. F., and Sundaresan, M. 1981. "A Continuous Time Equilibrium Model of Forward Prices and Future Prices in a Multigood Economy." *Journal of Financial Economics* 9: 347–71.

Rubinstein, M. E. 1974. "An Aggregation Theorem for Security Markets." *Journal of Financial Economics* 1: 225–44.

————. 1976. "The Valuation of Uncertain Income Streams and the Pricing of Options." *Bell Journal of Economics* 7: 407–25.

Shiller, R. J. 1979. "The Volatility of Long-Term Interest Rates and Expectations Models of the Term Structure." *Journal of Political Economy* 87: 1190–1219.

Shiller, R. J.; Campbell, J.; and Schoenholtz, K. 1983. "Forward Rates and Future Policy: Interpreting the Term Structure of Interest Rates." *Brookings Papers on Economic Activity*, no. 1.

Sims, C. 1985. "Solving Nonlinear Stochastic Equilibrium Models Backwards." University of Minnesota, manuscript.

Singleton, K. J. 1980. "Expectations Models of the Term Structure and Implied Variance Bounds." *Journal of Political Economy* 88: 1159–76.

————. 1985. "Testing Specifications of Economic Agents' Intertemporal Optimum Problems in the Presence of Alternative Models." *Journal of Econometrics* 30: 391–413.

————. 1986. "Specification and Estimation of Intertemporal Asset Pricing Models." In B. Friedman and F. Hahn, eds., *Handbook of Monetary Economics*. North-Holland.

Sundaresan, M. 1984. "Consumption and Equilibrium Interest Rates in Stochastic Production Economies." *Journal of Finance* 39: 77–92.

Tauchen, G. 1985. "Statistical Properties of Generalized Method of Moments Estimates of Utility Function Parameters Based on Financial Market Data." *Journal of Business and Economics Statistics.*

Townsend, R. 1984. "Asset Prices in a Monetary Economy." University of Chicago, manuscript.

Journal of Financial Economics 13 (1984) 299–335. North-Holland

OPTIMAL BOND TRADING WITH PERSONAL TAXES*

George M. CONSTANTINIDES

University of Chicago, Chicago, IL 60637, USA

Jonathan E. INGERSOLL, Jr.

Yale University, New Haven, CT 06520, USA

Received May 1982, final version received April 1984

Tax considerations governing bondholders' optimal trading include: capital loss realization; capital gain deferment; change of the long-term holding period status to short-term by sale of the bond and repurchase, to realize future losses short-term; raising the basis above par by sale of the bond and repurchase, to deduct the amortized premium from ordinary income. The optimal policy which incorporates transactions costs and conforms to the IRS code substantially differs from the buy-and-hold and continuous-realization policies. Failure to account for optimal trading may seriously bias econometric estimation of the yield curve and the tax bracket of the marginal bondholders.

1. Introduction

The yield curve implied by the prices of Treasury notes and bonds and corporate bonds is of interest to economists and practitioners alike: it reflects the investors' beliefs about the future course of the short-term interest rate. In calculating the yield curve, the tax bracket of the marginal bondholder is either taken to be some given number or is estimated simultaneously with the yield curve. The implied tax bracket of the marginal investor is of independent interest. It provides a direct (but incomplete) test of Miller's (1977) theory on the optimal capital structure of firms. It may also be useful for determining fair prices for other assets.

There are two major problems in estimating pure discount rates (the yield curve of zero coupon bonds) and the implied marginal tax rate. The first

*Earlier versions of the paper were presented at the annual AFA meeting in Washington, DC, and at workshops at the Universities of Chicago, Michigan, and Rochester, Massachusetts Institute of Technology, Yale University and New York University. We would like to thank Mark Wolfson, Steve Schaefer (the referee), Rene Stulz, and the participants at the above meeting and workshops for helpful comments. Part of this research was conducted during the academic year 1981–82 when the second author was a Batterymarch Fellow. Additional support was provided by the Sloan Foundation.

problem is that of differing clienteles, studied in detail by Schaefer (1981, 1982a). For a given investor some bonds of particular maturities and coupon rates may be dominated by combinations of other bonds. In this case tax clienteles naturally arise. If there is no one clientele for which every bond remains undominated, then the concept of the 'marginal taxable investor' who 'sets' all prices may well be meaningless.

The second problem is that of the assumed investment horizon. This is the focus of the present paper. By necessity we ignore the problem of tax clienteles. Extant estimation procedures assume either that the bond is held to maturity, without intermediate realization of capital gains and losses (the buy-and-hold policy), or that capital gains and losses are realized every period as they occur (the continuous realization policy). Both the buy-and-hold and the continuous realization policy lead to relatively simple bond pricing formulae. This facilitates the estimation of the yield curve and the implied tax bracket of the marginal investor.

The assumption that bondholders follow either a buy-and-hold or a continuous realization policy, rather than the optimal trading policy, is at variance with reality and, as we demonstrate, may seriously bias the estimation of the yield curve and the implied tax bracket of the marginal investor. Perusal of the *Wall Street Journal* provides convincing evidence that investment advisors – and presumably their clients – are aware of the optimal trading policies which frequently differ sharply from a buy-and-hold or continuous realization policy. By definition, the marginal bondholder is an economic agent (or group of agents) of sufficient stature to set bond prices at the margin. It is questionable then to assert that the marginal investor follows a suboptimal trading policy through ignorance.

The present paper unifies two recent strands of research, the pricing of bonds with stochastically varying interest rates and investment opportunity set and the pricing of stocks in the presence of personal taxes. Cox, Ingersoll and Ross (1981, 1983) present an equilibrium theory of bond pricing and the term structure of interest rates, in particular explaining the valuation of a deterministic stream of cash flows but with a stochastically varying interest rate and investment opportunity set. Constantinides (1983, 1984) and Constantinides and Scholes (1980) discuss the optimal trading of stocks and options in the presence of personal taxes and present an equilibrium theory of stock pricing, in particular explaining the effect of optimal realization of capital gains and losses on the pricing of stocks.

Tax considerations which govern a bondholder's optimal trading policy include the following: realization of capital losses, short-term if possible; deferment of the realization of capital gains, especially if they are short-term; changing the holding period status from long- to short-term by sale of the bond and repurchase, so that future capital losses may be realized short-term; and raising the basis through sale of the bond and repurchase in order to deduct from ordinary income the amortized premium. Because of the interaction of these factors, no simple characterization of the optimal trading policy is possible. We can say, however, that it differs substantially from the buy-and-hold irrespective of whether the bondholder is a bank, a bond dealer, or an individual. We obtain these strong results even when we allow for transactions costs and explicitly consider numerous IRS regulations designed to curtail tax avoidance.

The paper is organized as follows. In section 2 we outline the tax provisions in four representative tax scenarios which may apply to the elusive marginal bondholder. The formal model is presented in section 3. Closed-form solutions for the prices of consol bonds and the value of the timing option are presented in section 4 for a special case. In section 5 we derive the optimal trading policies under more general conditions, and in section 6 we illustrate the effect of taxes on the prices of bonds and on the value of the timing option. The estimation of the yield curve and the tax bracket of the marginal investor is grossly biased if the value of the timing option is ignored. This point is illustrated in section 7. In section 8 we discuss municipal bonds. Concluding remarks are offered in section 9.

2. The tax environment

To avoid a profusion of details in our discussion we abstract from many of the nuances of the regulations governing the taxation of income, as defined by the tax code and its interpretation by the Internal Revenue Service and the courts. We do emphasize, however, certain important aspects of the code, which, though largely ignored in finance, may materially affect bond prices and the estimation of the yield curve and the marginal tax rate. We also provide some historical perspective to familiarize the reader with major changes in the tax code which may be reflected in a time series of bond yields.

At least four broad classes of potential marginal investors warrant examination: individuals, banks and bond dealers, corporations, and tax-exempt institutions. Consider first the tax rules applicable to individual investors.

Coupon income (net of interest expense) is taxed at the individual's marginal tax rate on ordinary income, the maximum rate being currently 50%. Between 1970 and 1980, coupon income was classified as 'unearned income' and was taxed at a maximum rate of 72%. Prior to the seventies, the top marginal tax rate varied from a low of 7% in 1913 to a high of 95% in 1945. In our calculations we assume that the marginal tax rate on coupon income for an individual is $\tau_c = 0.5$.[1]

---

[1] Miller (1977) shows that, under simple tax rules, the marginal bondholder is in the corporate tax bracket, providing partial justification for our choice of the tax rate. In any case, our qualitative results are insensitive to the assumed rate.

The taxation of capital gains is complex. Unrealized gains and losses remain untaxed. Gains and losses are taxed in the year that they are realized. A realized gain or loss is the difference between the sales price (less cost of sale) and the basis. For most assets the basis is just the purchase price (plus cost of purchase), but for some bonds the purchase price is subject to adjustment.

We consider only original issue par bonds, defined as such by the IRS if the original issue discount does not exceed $\frac{1}{4}$ of 1 percent multiplied by the number of full years to maturity. For these bonds, if the purchase price in the secondary market is below par, no adjustment is made and the basis is just the purchase price. If the purchase price is above par, this difference is amortized linearly to the maturity date.[2] The amount amortized in a tax year is allowed as a deduction against ordinary income and the bond's basis is correspondingly reduced. There is no specific limitation on this deduction. In our calculations the amortized amount is (negatively) taxed at the rate $\tau_c = 0.5$.

Realized capital gains and losses are either short-term or long-term. The required holding period for long-term treatment is currently one year. This has varied many times since capital gains were first differentiated from ordinary income in 1922. In the years 1942–1977 the holding period was six months. Prior to that time there were three or more categories of long-term capital gains with required holding periods as long as ten years.

Net short-term capital gains are taxed as ordinary income. Net long-term capital gains are currently taxed at 40% of the investor's marginal tax rate on ordinary income. This treatment has also been changed. The tax rate on long-term gains has varied from 20% to 80% of the tax rate on ordinary income. In addition there have been periods in which alternate treatment could be elected (or, was required for large capital gains).

Net short-term capital losses and 50% of net long-term capital losses are deducted from ordinary income and may jointly reduce the taxable ordinary income by a maximum of $3,000 (until 1976, $1,000). Unused losses are carried forward indefinitely. Short-term losses and long-term gains, incurred in the same year, offset each other dollar for dollar, instead of being taxed at their respective rates.

We define τ_s to be the *marginal* tax rate on short-term capital gains and losses. This rate is not necessarily equal to the marginal tax rate on ordinary income: if the investor has net short-term losses and the deduction limit is binding, $\tau_s = 0$; if the investor has net short-term losses but larger long-term gains, τ_s is 40% of the marginal tax rate on ordinary income. Likewise, we define τ_L to be the *marginal* tax rate on long-term capital gains and losses.

---

[2]Amortization is optional for Treasury and corporate bonds. Since for practically all individuals the marginal tax rate on ordinary income is no less than the capital gains tax rate, amortization of the basis dominates foregoing this option. The amortization method need not be straight line, but may be that customarily used by the individual, if it is deemed to be reasonable. If the bond is callable, the basis is amortized to the call price at the call date or to par at maturity, whichever yields the smaller amortization. If there are alternate call dates the rule is complex.

If an asset is sold at a loss within thirty days before or after the acquisition of 'substantially identical' property, the IRS can disallow the loss deduction under the 'wash sale' rule. An investor has a high probability of circumventing this rule by purchasing instead another bond with a slightly different coupon or maturity. In any case, this rule is not applicable to dealers or individual taxpayers who are in the business of trading bonds. Consequently we ignore the wash sale rule throughout this paper.

We consider three representative tax scenarios for an individual bondholder and one scenario for banks or bond dealers, as defined by the marginal rates τ_c, τ_s, and τ_L.

(I) *The marginal investor is an individual. Coupon income is taxed at the rate* $\tau_c = 0.5$. *Realized short-term and long-term gains and losses are taxed at the rate* $\tau_s = \tau_L = 0.25$. *The deduction limit is not binding.*

This scenario is plausible if the individual is periodically forced to sell some of his portfolio assets by factors beyond his control (or, of more importance than the tax consequences) and, on average, realizes large long-term gains. Then the deduction limit is not binding. Since short-term losses must be used to offset the long-term gains, the marginal tax rate is the long-term gains rate.[3] We take the long-term gains rate to be half of the investor's marginal tax rate on ordinary income, as it was between 1942 and 1979. We also assume that the investor can always defer the realization of short-term gains until the holding period exceeds one year and then realize the gains long-term.

(II) *The marginal investor is an individual. Coupon income is taxed at the rate* $\tau_c = 0.5$. *Realized short-term gains and losses are taxed at the rate* $\tau_s = 0.5$. *Realized long-term gains and losses are taxed at the rate* $\tau_L = 0.25$. *The deduction limit is not binding.*

Scenario II is the least plausible one because it ignores both the deduction limit and the (unfavorable to the taxpayer) offsetting of long-term gains with short-term losses.[4] Since investors have a tax incentive to realize losses and defer gains (at least, short-term gains), the assumption that the deduction limit is not binding may be tenuous and is relaxed in the next scenario.

---

[3] Similarly the right to deduct half of the long-term losses from income, even under the current 40% rule for long-term capital gains, could not be used. Losses could only be deducted from other capital gains. Thus, the effective tax rate on both long-term gains and losses is the same.

[4] The individual may mitigate this offset provision of the tax law by realizing long-term gains and short- and long-term losses in alternate tax years; however, we do not explicitly model this. See Constantinides (1984). This procedure may also help to avoid the unfavorable long-term gain and loss offset.

(III)   *The marginal investor is an individual. Coupon income is taxed at the rate* $\tau_c = 0.5$. *Short- and long-term gains and losses remain untaxed, i.e.,* $\tau_s = \tau_L = 0$.

One justification for this scenario is to assume that the individual realizes losses and defers gains. At the margin losses can only be carried forward as the deduction limit is binding. The only tax 'game' permitted under this scenario is to realize a gain on a bond in order to raise its basis above par and start deducting the premium amortization against ordinary income. As we shall see, this policy is profitable.

Although corporations are taxed differently from individuals, the tax regulations on non-bank corporations that hold bonds for reasons not directly related to their business operations are sufficiently similar to those applying to individuals that the previous scenarios remain at least qualitatively correct. The primary distinction is that a net capital loss (short- and long-term combined) cannot be deducted in any amount from ordinary income, but may be carried back for three years and forward for five as a short-term loss to offset gains. Banks and (corporate or individual) bond dealers are taxed differently, however.

For banks and dealers, bond coupons and all realized capital gains and losses are treated as ordinary income or loss without explicit limitation. Net operating losses of banks are carried back for ten years and forward for five years. In the following scenario we effectively assume that the bank has positive net earnings in every ten-year period so that loss benefits are earned immediately. Corporate earnings and losses are taxed at the corporate rate of 50%. (The current corporate tax rate is 46% on earnings in excess of $100,000. In the past it has been as high as 54%.) The same scenario applies to a bond dealer with marginal personal or corporate tax rate on ordinary income equal to 50%.

(IV)   *The marginal holder is a bank or bond dealer. Coupon income and all capital gains and losses are taxed at the rate* $\tau_c = \tau_s = \tau_L = 0.5$. *There is no deduction limit.*

In each of the scenarios, I–IV, the tax rates τ_c, τ_s and τ_L are assumed to remain constant over time because we wish to focus on the long-run effect of taxes on bond prices. Certain trading policies not examined here would become optimal at the time that tax provisions were about to change. For example, when the effective maximum rate on long-term capital gains was changed from 28% to 20% by the 1978 Tax Revenue Act, individuals paying the 28% rate should have deferred realizing their capital gains, ceteris paribus. Similarly if an investor's income were to change sufficiently to place him in a different tax bracket, the optimal trading policy might be affected.

We also examine bond prices in each of the four tax scenarios under the assumption that the bondholder is (artificially) constrained to follow a buy-and-hold policy and compare the bond prices, tax timing option, and yields to the case when the investor follows optimal policies. The buy-and-hold economy is taken as our primary benchmark in which there are no price effects induced by tax trading.

We do not explicitly examine a scenario in which the marginal bondholder is exempt from all taxes. This might be considered a serious omission because tax-exempt intermediaries currently hold more than one-third of all the outstanding government and corporate bonds and account for an even greater proportion of the trading volume. Furthermore, liberalized tax-deferred retirement plans provide growing opportunities for taxable individuals to defer the tax on coupons, dividends and capital gains until retirement. If the marginal investor is tax-exempt, then there are obviously no tax-induced 'biases' in bond prices.[5] However, since the no-trading policy is not dominated by any other for a tax-exempt investor (in a perfect market), we may assume the buy-and-hold policy. Consequently bond prices should equal the benchmark values, and standard estimation techniques, such as McCulloch's (1975), should verify that the marginal tax bracket is zero.

3. The model

Our goal is to find the price of a default-free bond with par value one, continuous coupon rate c, and maturity date T. The bond is perfectly divisible and may be bought or sold with zero transactions costs.[6] The bond price is a function of the state vector Y (defined below) and time t, i.e., $P = P(Y, t; c, T)$.

We price the coupon bond relative to short-term (instantaneous) lending via a riskless, 'single-period' bond with maturity dt and before-tax yield $r(Y, t)$. The single-period bond is perfectly divisible and may be bought or sold with zero transactions costs. Effectively there is unlimited riskless lending over the time interval dt at the before-tax interest rate r. If an investor's tax rate on ordinary income is τ_c, his after-tax interest rate is $(1 - \tau_c)r$.

We assume that, throughout the term to this coupon bond's maturity, some investor with marginal tax rates τ_c, τ_s, and τ_L (on coupon income, short-term capital gains and losses, and long-term capital gains and losses, respectively) is indifferent between buying the coupon bond or investing in the single-period

---

[5]Even in this case, however, when taxes do not affect bond prices, taxed investors will still benefit from following trading policies different from the buy-and-hold. The value of trading optimally will of course depend upon what taxes they must pay. Thus, the timing option will have the same qualitative properties it does in one of the examined scenarios.

[6]Transactions costs on bonds are small and are of the order of magnitude of the bid–asked spread. In section 6 (table 6) we introduce transactions costs and show that the pricing implications and the value of the timing option remain largely unaffected.

bond. That there exists some tax bracket (τ_c, τ_s, τ_L) with the property that an investor in this tax bracket is indifferent between the two investments over a time interval dt, is a weak assumption. The strong part of our assumption is that *investors in the same tax bracket are at the margin throughout the bond's term to maturity.* In a richer model (beyond our present scope) one might allow for the possibility that the bond is passed from one tax clientele to another as it approaches maturity or as it becomes a premium or discount bond due to shifts in interest rates. Since we wish to focus on the already complex problem of the optimal realization of capital gains and losses, we abstract from issues related to changing tax clienteles.[7]

At each point of time and for each coupon bond there is a reservation purchase price defined to be such that a (marginal) investor in the given tax bracket (τ_c, τ_s, τ_L) is indifferent between purchasing the coupon bond now or investing in the single-period bond over the time interval dt. This equilibrium condition is formalized below as the after-tax version of the local expectations hypothesis. After purchasing the coupon bond, the investor follows the derived optimal trading policy as opposed to a continuous realization or a buy-and-hold policy.

Each bondholder also has a reservation sale price which depends on his cost basis and the length of time for which he has held the bond. In general the prevailing reservation purchase and sale prices differ. We assume that the government supplies all maturity and coupon bonds with infinite elasticity at the reservation purchase price of the (marginal) investor and that all trades take place at this price, denoted P.[8] When the reservation sale price exceeds the reservation purchase price, only the government supplies the bond. When the reservation purchase price exceeds the reservation sale price, the seller earns a 'producer's' surplus which we attribute to his tax timing option.

The value of the bond to an investor, $V(Y, t; c, T; \hat{P}, \hat{t})$, is defined as the present value of the stream of cash flows associated with the bond, assuming that the optimal policy in realizing capital gains and losses is followed. The symbols $\hat{P}$ and $\hat{t}$ denote the current cost basis and the time at which the bond

---

[7]Tax clienteles for bonds is an important issue extensively discussed by Schaefer (1981, 1982a, 1982b) under the assumption that bonds are held to maturity. As we demonstrate below, under tax laws similar to those in the U.S., a buy-and-hold policy is inferior to trading schemes which involve (among other things) early realization of capital losses. Under British regulations, which imposed no long-term capital gains tax on 'gilt' securities prior to 1962 or after 1969, such trading schemes have no direct benefits, so a buy-and-hold policy is not necessarily inferior. Neither need it be correct, however. Even in Schaefer's world, future changes in interest rates or the introduction of new bonds may cause an existing bond to become dominated for its current clientele. The anticipation of such events should be reflected in the bond's current price, and this may mask some clientele effects.

[8]Alternatively, we could assume that bonds are fixed in supply and some investors are occasionally forced to trade for reasons unrelated to optimal tax trading. 'Liquidity purchasers' will never pay above their reservation price because the discount bond is available. 'Liquidity sellers', however, may not be able to hold out for their reservation price.

was purchased. Because of amortization of the basis, $\hat{P}$ may differ from the price at which the bond was purchased.

At those 'stopping times' at which the investor either by choice or by force sells the bond and realizes a capital gain or loss, the value to the investor is simply the after-tax proceeds from its immediate sale. The bond's maturity date is an obvious stopping time for all investors. At maturity, the capital gain or loss is unavoidably realized, hence

$$V(Y, T; c, T; \hat{P}, \hat{t}) = 1 - \tau(t, \hat{t})(1 - \hat{P}), \tag{1}$$

where $\tau(t, \hat{t})$ is the short- or long-term tax rate depending on the bond's status.

A similar result is true at any stopping time prior to maturity when the investor sells his bonds. For the sequence of (possibly random) stopping times, $t = t_1, t_2, \ldots,$ at which the investor realizes a capital gain or loss,

$$V(Y, t; c, T, \hat{P}, \hat{t}) = P - \tau(t, \hat{t})(P - \hat{P}) \quad \text{at} \quad t = t_1, t_2, \ldots . \tag{2}$$

Stopping times may differ across investors. At the stopping times chosen by the investor the 'smooth-pasting' (or 'high contact') condition also must hold,[9]

$$\frac{\partial V}{\partial Y_n} = [1 - \tau(t, \hat{t})] \frac{\partial P}{\partial Y_n} \quad \text{for} \quad n = 1, 2, \ldots, N, \quad \text{at} \quad t_1^o, t_2^o, \ldots . \tag{3}$$

The smooth pasting condition is not imposed at those stopping times where a realization is forced. Forced realizations are assumed to be caused by events exogenous to the model, e.g., an unanticipated and unavoidable need for consumption or portfolio revision. Forced realizations are formally modelled as Poisson arrivals with constant force λ. The Poisson process is independent of the process which generates the movements of the state variables.

For a marginal investor the time of purchase is also an optimal stopping time since, by definition, he is indifferent to the purchase. Thus,

$$V(Y, t; c, T; P, t) = P, \tag{4a}$$

$$\frac{\partial V}{\partial Y_n} = (1 - \tau_s) \frac{\partial P}{\partial Y_n}, \quad n = 1, \ldots, N. \tag{4b}$$

This condition provides the link between the value of the bond and its market price. It may also be interpreted as an alternative description of the marginal investor. Eq. (4a) need not hold for non-marginal investors who either receive a

---

[9]Merton (1973) demonstrates that this condition is the result of optimizing behavior in the context of option pricing. It is formally derived in Grigelionis and Shiryaev (1966).

surplus by purchasing the bond at the prevailing price or find buying the bond to be dominated by lending at the short-term rate.

At all other times, the investor's value of the bond exceeds the after-tax proceeds from immediate sale, and the investor optimally defers the realization of a capital gain or loss. The set of states and times $\{Y, t\}$ at which this occurs is referred to as the continuation region, i.e., in the continuation region

$$V(Y, t; c, T; \hat{P}, \hat{\imath}) > P - \tau(t, \hat{\imath})(P - \hat{P}). \tag{5}$$

In the continuation region, the investor's after-tax rate of return on his bond is

$$\{dV + (1 - \tau_c)c\,dt + \max[0, (\hat{P} - 1)\tau_c dt/(T - t)]\}/V. \tag{6}$$

The term $(\hat{P} - 1)\tau_c dt/(T - t)$ is the tax benefit of the linearly amortized premium when the basis is above par.

We assume the after-tax version of the local expectations hypothesis:[10] The after-tax expected rate of return on the coupon bond (measured via the value function) equals the after-tax single-period rate of interest over the period $\{t, t + dt\}$, i.e.,

$$E\left[\{dV + (1 - \tau_c)c\,dt + \max[0, (\hat{P} - 1)\tau_c dt/(T - t)]\}/V\right]$$
$$= (1 - \tau_c)r\,dt, \tag{7}$$

for all Y, t, $\hat{P}$, and $\hat{\imath}$.

We assume that the state of the economy at time t is summarized by a vector $\{Y_n(t)\}_{N \times 1}$. This vector also summarizes the history of the economy, $Y(\tau)$, $\tau < t$, to the extent that it is of current economic relevance. The state variables are jointly Markov with movements determined by the system of stochastic differential equations

$$dY_n(t) = \mu_n(Y, t)\,dt + \sigma_n'(Y, t)\,dw(t), \qquad n = 1, 2, \ldots, N, \tag{8}$$

where μ_n is a scalar, σ_n is a K-dimensional vector, $K \le N$, and $dw(t)$ is the increment of the Wiener process $w(t)$ in R^K. The variance–covariance matrix $\{\sigma_n'\sigma_m\}$ is positive semidefinite and of rank K (positive definite, if $K = N$).

---

[10] See Cox, Ingersoll and Ross (1981) for a discussion of the different forms of the expectations hypothesis. In another paper (1983) they show how this assumption may be weakened by incorporating a risk premium into the drift terms for the state variables. As discussed there, the absence of arbitrage opportunities is insufficient to close the model as it is in option pricing. The difference here is that the state variables need not be prices.

If $\{Y, t\}$ lies in the continuation region, the expected value of dV due to the movement of the state variables Y, t, is given by Ito's Lemma, as the first three terms of eq. (9) below. The expected value of dV due to a stochastic forced realization is $[P - \tau(t, \hat{t})(P - \hat{P}) - V]\lambda dt$. The term in the brackets multiplying λ is the loss incurred when the investor is forced to deviate from his optimal policy. The term λdt is the probability of a forced realization over $[t, t + dt]$. Also, the expected value of dV due to the amortization of the premium is $-(\partial V / \partial \hat{P}) \max[0, (\hat{P} - 1) dt / (T - t)]$. Then eq. (7) becomes

$$\frac{1}{2} \sum_{n=1}^{N} \sum_{m=1}^{N} \frac{\partial^2 V}{\partial Y_n \partial Y_m} \sigma_n' \sigma_m + \sum_{n=1}^{N} \frac{\partial V}{\partial Y_n} \mu_n + \frac{\partial V}{\partial t}$$

$$+ [P - \tau(t, \hat{t})(P - \hat{P}) - V]\lambda + (1 - \tau_c)c$$

$$+ \left(\tau_c - \frac{\partial V}{\partial \hat{P}}\right) \max[0, (\hat{P} - 1)/(T - t)] - (1 - \tau_c)rV = 0. \qquad (9)$$

The solution to this differential equation, subject to the boundary conditions (1) through (5), provides the bond price, P, the value of a bond to the investor, V, and the optimal policy for the realization of capital gains and losses.[11]

For general functions $\sigma_n(Y, t)$ and $\mu_n(Y, t)$, a closed-form solution does not typically exist. In section 4 we illustrate the solution procedure in a simplified version of this problem and discuss the economic implications. In section 5 we provide numerical solutions to the general problem.

4. An example

In this section we begin to examine the value of the timing option regarding the realization of capital gains and losses on bonds and to analyze the effect of the capital gains tax on their pricing. To discuss these issues in the simplest possible setting and through closed-form solutions, we make a number of simplifying assumptions.

We assume that there is only one state variable, the short-term rate of interest, r, with movements determined by the stochastic differential equation

$$dr = \alpha r^2 dt + sr^{\frac{3}{2}} dw(t), \qquad (10)$$

---

[11] The now-familiar American put pricing problem provides a useful analogy. Let $G(S, K, T)$ denote the value of a put with striking price K and time to maturity T on a stock with price S. Eq. (2) is analogous to the condition at exercise, $G(S^*, K, T) = K - S^*$. The 'smooth-pasting' condition analogous to (3) is $G_S(S^*, K, T) = -1$. Together these relations are sufficient to derive both the pricing function G and the optimal exercise policy $S^*(T)$. Similarly here we derive both the value function and the optimal realization policy Y^* conditional on the bond price function. Eq. (4) then provides the closure finally giving all three.

where $dw(t)$ is the increment of the scalar Wiener process $w(t)$.[12] The price, $P(r; c)$, of an infinite maturity coupon bond is then a function of the short-term interest rate, r, but is independent of the current time, t, because the process generating interest rate movements is stationary.

We also assume that the tax rates on all capital gains and losses are equal, i.e., $\tau_s = \tau_L \equiv \tau$. Thus the length of time over which the bond has been held is irrelevant, and the consol's value to an investor, $V(r; c; \hat{P})$, is also independent of the current time, t. Finally, we assume away forced realizations, i.e., $\lambda = 0$.

It is easy to prove that any investor's optimal policy is to realize capital losses immediately and defer capital gains indefinitely.[13] Given the basis, $\hat{P}$, the continuation region is defined by the range of interest rates such that $P(r; c) > \hat{P}$. In the continuation region the differential equation (9) becomes

$$\frac{1}{2}s^2r^3\frac{\partial^2 V}{\partial r^2} + \alpha r^2\frac{\partial V}{\partial r} - (1 - \tau_c)rV + (1 - \tau_c)c = 0, \qquad P(r; c) > \hat{P}.$$

(11)

The boundary condition (4a) becomes

$$V(r; c; \hat{P}) = \hat{P} \quad \text{at} \quad P(r; c) = \hat{P},$$ (12)

and the 'smooth-pasting' conditions (3) and (4b) become

$$\frac{\partial V(r; c; \hat{P})}{\partial r} = (1 - \tau)\frac{\partial P(r, c)}{\partial r} \quad \text{at} \quad P(r; c) = \hat{P}.$$ (13)

The bond price $P(r; c)$ is a function of the interest rate, r, and of the parameters c, α, s, τ, and τ_c. Inspection of eq. (10) indicates that the parameters α and s are dimensionless as are the parameters τ and τ_c. The units of the coupon yield c are dollars per unit of time, and the unit of the interest rate is the inverse of the time unit. The bond price must be proportional to the coupon rate, and since it is invariant to changes in the unit of time, it must also

---

[12] We may alternatively consider (10) as the risk-adjusted interest rate dynamics with $\alpha = \mu + \pi$, where μ measures the expected change in the short rate and π captures the risk premium due on interest-rate-sensitive securities. Cox, Ingersoll and Ross (1980) discuss this interpretation for the stochastic process in (10).

[13] This statement is formally proved in Constantinides (1983). If the tax rates τ_s and τ_L are unequal the optimal policy is a great deal more complex. Under these circumstances, the optimal policy for trading stocks is discussed in Constantinides (1984) and the optimal policy for trading bonds is discussed in section 5 of this paper.

be inversely proportional to r. Hence

$$P(r; c) = Hc/r,$$

(14)

where H is a function of only the parameters α, s, τ, and τ_c.

Since we have determined the functional form of P, we can simplify (11) with the aid of eq. (14) to eliminate r and its derivatives, obtaining

$$\frac{s^2}{2}P^2V_{PP} + (s^2 - \alpha)PV_P - (1 - \tau_c)V + \frac{(1 - \tau_c)P}{H} = 0, \qquad P > \hat{P}.$$

(15)

The general solution to eq. (15) is given below:[14]

$$V = \frac{(1 - \tau_c)P}{(1 - \tau_c + \alpha - s^2)H} + A\hat{P}^{1-\eta}P^{\eta} + A'\hat{P}^{1-\eta'}P^{\eta'}, \qquad P > \hat{P},$$

(16)

where A, A' are arbitrary constants to be determined, and η, η' ($\eta < 0 < \eta'$) are the roots of the quadratic equation

$$\frac{s^2}{2}\eta(\eta - 1) + (s^2 - \alpha)\eta - (1 - \tau_c) = 0.$$

(17)

By homogeneity, the coefficients of P^{η} and $P^{\eta'}$ must be proportional to the parameters $\hat{P}^{1-\eta}$ and $\hat{P}^{1-\eta'}$, respectively. Thus, A and A' depend only on the parameters α, s, τ, and τ_c.

The following argument determines A'. Since the optimal trading policy involves no sales at any price above the basis, $\hat{P}$ must have a negligible effect on the value function whenever $P \gg \hat{P}$. Formally

$$\lim_{P/\hat{P} \to \infty} (\partial V/\partial \hat{P}) = 0.$$

(18)

This condition is satisfied only if $A' = 0$. The remaining two constants can be determined using (12) and (13). Substituting (16) into (12) and setting $A' = 0$, we obtain

$$\frac{(1 - \tau_c)P}{(1 - \tau_c + \alpha - s^2)H} + AP = P.$$

(19)

---

[14] For a meaningful solution the parameters of the interest rate process must satisfy $s^2 - \alpha < 1 - \tau_c$. From (22) and (23) the expected rate of price appreciation and the limit (as r goes to zero) of the expected rate of appreciation of the value function are both $(s^2 - \alpha)r$. Thus, if the stated condition is violated the expected rates of return including coupons must exceed the after-tax rate of interest $(1 - \tau_c)r$ and the expectations hypothesis cannot obtain as was assumed. Furthermore, given that the dynamics may be interpreted in a risk-adjusted sense, as discussed in footnote 12, no other equilibrium is possible either.

Similarly, substituting (16) into (13) and setting $A' = 0$, we obtain

$$\frac{1 - \tau_c}{(1 - \tau_c + \alpha - s^2)H} + A\eta = 1 - \tau. \tag{20}$$

We solve for H and A and obtain

$$P(r; c) = \frac{(1 - \tau_c)c}{(1 - \tau_c + \alpha - s^2)\{1 - \tau/(1 - \eta)\}r}, \tag{21}$$

and

$$V(r; c; \hat{P}) = (1 - \tau)P + \tau\hat{P}, \qquad\qquad P \leq \hat{P},$$

$$= \left(1 - \frac{\tau}{1 - \eta}\right)P + \left(\frac{\tau}{1 - \eta}\right)P^\eta\hat{P}^{1-\eta}, \qquad P > \hat{P}, \tag{22}$$

where

$$\eta \equiv -\left[s^2/2 - \alpha + \left\{(s^2/2 - \alpha)^2 + 2s^2(1 - \tau_c)\right\}^{\frac{1}{2}}\right]/s^2$$

is the negative root of (17).

Eq. (21) shows that the price of a consol bond is increasing in the capital gains tax rate of the marginal investor. A high capital gains rate does not hurt the investor because he is never forced to realize gains and his optimal policy is to defer indefinitely the realization of capital gains. In fact a high capital gains rate is a benefit because it enables him to obtain larger tax rebates by realizing a capital loss whenever such a loss occurs. Provided that forced realizations are not too frequent, the same conclusion also applies to a finite maturity par bond, as indeed is demonstrated in the numerical solutions of section 6. If the bond currently sells at par, the investor can be neutral to the capital gains tax by following the naive policy of deferring both gains and losses. The intelligent policy of deferring gains and realizing losses can only turn the taxation to his advantage, and he therefore benefits by a high capital gains tax rate.

Using Ito's Lemma and eqs. (10) and (11), we find the consol dynamics to be

$$dP/P = (s^2 - \alpha)r dt - s\sqrt{r}\, dw \equiv \gamma r dt - s\sqrt{r}\, dw. \tag{23}$$

The expected capital gains rate, γr, can be either positive or negative. We write the bond price in terms of γ and obtain

$$P(r; c) = \frac{c/r}{\{1 - \gamma/(1 - \tau_c)\}\{1 - \tau/(1 - \eta)\}}. \tag{21'}$$

We observe that the bond price is increasing (decreasing) in the ordinary income tax rate, if capital gains (losses) are expected. This indeterminancy is due to the light taxation of capital gains relative to interest and coupon income in this model. If capital gains are expected, the consol's current coupon yield is less than the interest rate, and an increase in τ_c represents a greater loss for potential holdings in the instantaneous bond than in the consol.

We use two benchmarks to measure the value of the tax timing option. The first is the price of the consol, P_H, in an economy where the marginal investor follows a buy-and-hold policy. This benchmark is also the consol's price in an economy with zero capital gains tax.[15] Hence, we write

$$P_H = \frac{(1 - \tau_c)c}{(1 - \tau_c - \gamma)r}. \tag{24}$$

The second benchmark is the consol price, P_C, in an economy where the marginal bondholder realizes all gains and losses continuously. Proceeding as before, we find that this consol price satisfies the equation

$$(1 - \tau)\left\{ \frac{\eta^2}{2}r^3 P_C'' + \alpha r^2 P_C' \right\} - (1 - \tau_c)rP_C + (1 - \tau_c)c = 0, \tag{25}$$

with solution

$$P_C = \frac{(1 - \tau_c)c}{\{1 - \tau_c - \gamma(1 - \tau)\}r}. \tag{26}$$

Note that $P_C \gtrless P_H$ as $\gamma \lessgtr 0$: A continuous realization policy dominates the buy-and-hold policy whenever capital losses are expected.

The tax effect on the consol's price is expressed relative to the two benchmarks as follows:

$$\frac{P - P_H}{P} = \frac{\tau}{1 - \eta}, \tag{27a}$$

$$\frac{P - P_C}{P} = \frac{\tau}{1 - \eta}\left[1 + \frac{\gamma(1 - \eta - \tau)}{1 - \tau_c - \gamma(1 - \tau)} \right]. \tag{27b}$$

When the buy-and-hold benchmark is used, the timing option's value derives from the right to realize capital losses early. When the continuous-realization

---

[15] The buy-and-hold price is unaffected by the capital gains tax rate of the marginal investor for the simple reason that no capital gains tax is ever paid. This result differs from that reported in Constantinides (1983) for stocks. Although the tax liability is also postponed indefinitely for equities, the expected rate of growth in price, adjusted for risk, equals the discount rate so the present value of the tax liability is not negligible. In our problem, the expected rate of growth in price, γr, must be smaller than the discount rate $(1 - \tau_c)r$. See footnote 14.

Table 1

The value of the timing option as a percentage of the consol price.[a]

	s = 0.604			s = 0.172		
	$\alpha = 0$	$\alpha = s^2$	$\alpha = 0.44$	$\alpha = 0$	$\alpha = s^2$	$\alpha = 0.44$
Buy-and-hold benchmark	7.7	11.2	11.9	3.4	3.9	11.7
Continuous realization benchmark	44.9	11.2	9.0	4.9	3.9	0.5

[a] Computed for infinitely lived investors. Interest rate follows the risk-adjusted stochastic process $dr = \alpha r^2 dt + sr^{\frac{3}{2}} dw$. Marginal bondholder's tax rates are $\tau_c = 0.5$ on coupon income and $\tau = 0.25$ on all capital gains.

benchmark is used, the timing option measures the value of deferring capital gains.

To measure the magnitude of the timing option we require estimates of the parameters α and s and the marginal tax bracket. Using the Ibbotson and Sinquefield (1982) data the annualized standard deviation of changes in the short rate over the period 1926–1981 is 2.2%. Using eq. (10) and $r = 0.11$ we set $s = (0.022)(0.11)^{-\frac{3}{2}} = 0.604$. In the same study the reported standard deviation of annualized returns on long-term U.S. Treasury bonds is 5.7%. If we take this number as an estimate of the standard deviation of returns on a consol, then using (23) and $r = 0.11$ we obtain $s = (0.057)/\sqrt{0.11} = 0.172$.[16]

Ibbotson and Sinquefield do not report the average change in the interest rate, so somewhat arbitrarily we examine the two cases $\alpha = 0$ and $\alpha = s^2$ which correspond to zero expected change in the interest rate and in the consol price, respectively. If we choose to interpret α as a risk premium measure, then under the assumption of no drift in the interest rate, the expected rate of return on a consol is $r(1 + \alpha)$. Ibbotson and Sinquefield estimate that investors expected on average a premium of 131 basis points on twenty-year bonds. This gives an estimate for α of 0.44 based on the average interest rate.

Table 1 displays the value of the timing option as a percentage of price [eqs. (27a) and (27b)]. For the higher variance process the timing option contributes a significant portion of the bond's value as measured against either benchmark. For the lower variance process the timing option remains important except in the case when large capital losses are expected and the continuous realization

[16] The Ibbotson and Sinquefield estimate based on a portfolio of long-term bonds may be a downwardly biased estimate of the standard deviation of a consol's rate of return for two reasons:

(a) They considered a portfolio of bonds with an average maturity of 20 years (not infinite).

(b) The variability of a portfolio of bonds generally underestimates the return variability of each bond. For example, a shock in the economy which raises the price of ten-year bonds and lowers the price of thirty-year bonds may leave the portfolio's price essentially unchanged and contribute little to the variability of the portfolio's return. The same shock, however, may have a significant impact on the consol's return.

Both of our estimates of s, particularly the first, may also be negatively biased because the interest rate was substantially less than 11% for most of this period.

benchmark is employed. We conclude that the potential effect of tax trading on bond prices cannot be safely ignored in practice.

5. Optimal bond trading: The general case

We examine a discrete-time version of the model outlined in section 3, focusing on the distinction between short- and long-term gains and losses, the effect of the amortization deduction and transactions costs. Since our primary concern is on how optimal trading affects the bond prices, we confine our attention to the marginal bondholder.

We assume that the trading interval is one year.[17] If an asset is sold one year after purchase, we assume that the holding period is short-term or long-term at the investor's discretion. Since the cutoff point is one year after purchase, the investor can make the holding period long- or short-term, by delaying or advancing the bond sale by only one day. By a simple dominance argument, all capital gains are realized long-term. Similarly, whenever the investor realizes a capital loss one year after purchasing the bond, he does so short-term.

We maintain our assumption that there are no forced realizations. On each trading date the investor either holds his bond, deferring the realization of a capital gain or loss, or sells his bond and immediately repurchases its, thereby realizing a capital gain or loss and re-establishing a short-term status. The following set of factors determines whether the investor holds his bond or executes a wash sale:

(a) If the bond price is below the basis, the investor would like to sell the bond and receive the tax deduction immediately. The reason becomes more compelling if the bond was purchased one year earlier, so that this is the only chance to realize the capital loss short-term.

(b) If the bond price is above the basis, the investor would like to defer the realization of the capital gain and thereby defer the tax liability. As stated previously, he never realizes a short-term gain because he can wait one more day. Nevertheless, he may wish to realize a long-term gain as explained in (c) and (d).

(c) A short-term holding status is beneficial to the investor. This status helps when he realizes a capital loss, because he realizes it short-term, and it never hurts, even when the investor realizes a capital gain, because he can always wait one more day and convert to the long-term status. The short-term status turns out to be a very important factor governing the optimal liquidation policy. Under certain realistic conditions, an investor may realize a capital gain solely to convert to the beneficial short-term status.

---

[17] The choice of one year is primarily a matter of convenience, coinciding with both the minimum holding period for long-term gains and the length of the tax year. If the holding period were shorter, as it was until recently, and the offset provision were to be considered, then an additional complication would arise. The value of short-term losses in the first part of the year could not be determined until it was known if there were later offsetting long-term capital gains.

(d) The peculiar amortization rules on bonds introduce another twist to this already complex problem. If the bond's basis is above par, this difference is linearly amortized over its remaining term to maturity with the 'loss' applied against the investor's ordinary income. The present value of this tax deduction is high for short maturity bonds, but decreases with longer maturity, because of the linearity of the amortization rule. For short maturity bonds the benefit in establishing a basis above par may be sufficiently large to make it optimal to realize a capital gain.

We assume that the short-term rate of interest, r, is the only state variable and that it follows a driftless binomial random walk with two reflecting barriers. We consider two specifications for the interest rate process. In the low-variance process, the interest rate takes on the twenty-one values, $0.04, 0.05, 0.06, \ldots, 0.24$. At each point in time the interest rate either increases or decreases by 0.01, each with probability one half, unless it is currently at one of the reflecting barriers, 0.04 or 0.24. If the interest rate is equal to one of the reflecting barriers, then at the next date it remains unchanged or takes on the value 0.05 or 0.23, respectively, with probability one half. The reader may verify that the unconditional distribution of r is uniform over the twenty-one points. The standard deviation of changes in the interest rate is $\sigma_r \equiv \text{std}(r(t + 1)|r(t)) = 0.01$ per year, independent of the state (except in the end-point states).

In the high-variance process, the interest rate takes one of the eleven values, $0.04, 0.06, \ldots, 0.24$. The probabilities of increase or decrease by 0.02 are as in the low-variance process with the same reflecting barriers at 0.04 and 0.24. The standard deviation of the changes in the interest rate in the high-variance process is $\sigma_r = 0.02$ per year. From the Ibbotson and Sinquefield (1982) study, the annualized standard deviation of the short-term rate is 0.022. The low-variance process then underestimates the interest rate variability, while the high-variance process reflects the average variability in the period 1926–1981.

As we shall see, the low-variance process implies, on average, that the standard deviation of the annual rate of return of twenty-year Treasury bonds is 5.66%, if priced under the buy-and-hold policy, and 5.82% if priced under the optimal policy with $\tau_s = \tau_L = 0.25$ (scenario I). For the high-variance process, the corresponding numbers are 9.47% and 8.73%. From the Ibbotson and Sinquefield (1982) study this standard deviation is 5.7% for long-term Treasury bonds over the 1926–1981 period. Therefore the low-variance process reflects the actual *initial* variability of long-term bonds over that period.[18] The high-variance process, however, may be more representative of recent history.

In discrete time, the differential equation (9) becomes a difference equation which we may solve numerically subject to the boundary conditions. Equiva-

---

[18]See, however, the second caveat in footnote 16. In addition, when the low-variance process is used, the simulated volatility of a twenty-year bond over its life will be lower than the historic average because the low-variance process understates the variance of the short-term rate and hence the variance of short-term bonds.

lently and more directly we obtain the bond price and the value of a bond to the marginal investor by dynamic programming, at dates $T, T-1, T-2, \ldots$, etc.

Eqs. (28) and (29) establish the bond price and value of a bond to the investor at maturity, i.e., at $t = T$. At maturity the ex-coupon bond is priced at par which we take to be unity,

$$P(r, T; c, T) = 1. \tag{28}$$

The value of the bond to an investor is the after-tax sale proceeds. By the maturity date, the bond basis cannot exceed one, because the excess will have been completely amortized by then. Thus only a gain can be realized at maturity, and the appropriate capital gains tax rate is the long-term rate. Thus,

$$V(r, T; c, T; \hat{P}, \hat{\iota}) = 1 - \tau_L + \tau_L \hat{P}. \tag{29}$$

With the terminal values established, the bond's price and its value to a given investor at points in time prior to maturity can now be obtained through dynamic programming. We distinguish between the cases in which amortization is and is not utilized.

The bond price is what a marginal investor is willing to pay for it. His alternative is investing in the short-term asset over the next year in which case his investment increases at the prevailing after-tax interest rate. He is indifferent to buying the bond, therefore, only if the after-tax coupon and amortization benefit plus the expectation of the value function next period is greater than the current bond price by exactly the after-tax foregone interest. If the bond is selling today for less than par, then its price is the appropriate basis in the value function. If the bond is priced above par, then $(P - 1)/(T - t)$ will be amortized in the next year, and the basis in the value function next year is less than the prevailing price by this amount. Thus at time t,

$$P = \left[1 + (1 - \tau_c)r\right]^{-1}\{(1 - \tau_c)c$$
$$+ E_t[V(\tilde{r}(t+1), t+1; c, T; P, t]\} \quad \text{if} \quad P \le 1, \tag{30}$$

and

$$P = \left[1 + (1 - \tau_c)r\right]^{-1}\{(1 - \tau_c)c + (P - 1)\tau_c/(T - t)$$
$$+ E_t[V(\tilde{r}(t+1), t+1; c, T; P - (P - 1)/(T - t), t]\} \quad \text{if} \quad P > 1. \tag{31}$$

The bond price, P, is the solution to (30) and (31).[19]

---

[19] The right-hand side of (30) is positive at $P = 0$ since the first term is, and the right-hand side of (31) is less than P for large values [since the maximum benefit of future tax losses is $\tau_c(P - 1)$]. These expressions are continuous at $P = 1$. Therefore a solution to (30) and (31) exists. For the dynamics assumed, the solution is also unique.

The value of a long position in the bond is the greater of the after-tax proceeds from immediate sale and the discounted value of the benefits if the bond is retained. The after-tax proceeds from immediate sale are

$$P - \tau(t, \hat{\imath})(P - \hat{P}). \tag{32}$$

If the bond is retained, the discounted benefits are

$$\left[1 + (1 - \tau_c)r\right]^{-1}\{(1 - \tau_c)c$$
$$+ E_t[V(\tilde{r}(t+1), t+1; c, T; \hat{P}, t)]\} \quad \text{if} \quad \hat{P} \le 1, \tag{33}$$

and

$$\left[1 + (1 - \tau_c)r\right]^{-1}\{(1 - \tau_c)c + (\hat{P} - 1)\tau_c/(T - t)$$
$$+ E_t[V(\tilde{r}(t+1), t+1; c, T; \hat{P} - (\hat{P} - 1)/(T - t), \hat{\imath})]\} \quad \text{if} \quad \hat{P} > 1. \tag{34}$$

In comparing eqs. (30) and (33) we note that $P = V(r, t; c, T; P, t)$ so the relation in (4a) is satisfied.

We illustrate the optimal trading policies for a bond with a 14 percent stated coupon payable annually, in the four tax scenarios.

(I)   *Treasury bond held by a high-tax-bracket individual, with* $\tau_c = 0.5$, $\tau_s = \tau_L = 0.25$.

Table 2 reports the bond prices and values, V, for the high variance interest rate process, for a range of interest rates and bases, and for maturities 1, 5 and 20 years.[20] If both the basis and the bond price are less than one, the amortization feature is not in effect and the simple trading rule is to realize a loss and defer a gain as indicated by daggers. If either the basis or the bond price exceeds one, the amortization feature becomes relevant and complicates the rule. Asterisks and daggers mark the states in which a wash sale is optimal. In these states the value function is equal to the after-tax proceeds from an immediate sale as stated in (32). Asterisks indicate the realization of capital gains establishing a new or higher amortizable basis. Daggers denote the realization of a capital loss. In unmarked states the value of holding exceeds

---

[20] Some of the entries in this table as well as those in table 3 give the value function for states which could never arise along the optimal path. For example, since losses are always realized when the basis is below par, the basis can never be substantially in excess of the current price in this situation. These entries, therefore, give the value of changing to the optimal policy from a suboptimal position.

Table 2

Treasury bond prices and values of a long position under tax scenario I.[a]

Interest rate	Bond price	Basis						
		0.7	0.8	0.9	1.0	1.1	1.2	1.3
		Maturity = 1 year						
0.06	1.0755	*0.98	*1.01	*1.03	*1.06	1.09	1.14	1.18
0.10	1.0364	*0.95	*0.98	*1.00	*1.03	1.07	1.11	1.16
0.14	1.0000	0.93	0.95	0.98	*1.00	1.05	1.09	1.14
0.18	0.9762	0.91	0.94	0.96	†0.98	1.03	1.07	1.12
0.22	0.9535	0.90	0.92	0.94	†0.97	1.01	1.05	1.10
		Maturity = 5 years						
0.06	1.3363	*1.18	*1.20	*1.23	*1.25	*1.28	*1.30	*1.33
0.10	1.1771	*1.06	*1.08	*1.11	*1.13	*1.16	1.18	1.22
0.14	1.0197	0.95	0.97	0.99	*1.01	1.05	1.08	1.12
0.18	0.9110	0.88	0.89	0.91	†0.93	0.96	1.00	1.04
0.22	0.8354	0.81	0.83	†0.85	†0.88	†0.90	0.93	0.97
		Maturity = 20 years						
0.06	1.7358	1.48	†1.50	*1.53	*1.55	*1.58	*1.60	*1.63
0.10	1.4187	1.26	1.27	1.29	1.31	1.34	1.36	*1.39
0.14	1.1044	1.03	1.04	1.06	1.08	1.10	†1.13	†1.15
0.18	0.8793	0.85	0.86	†0.88	†0.91	†0.93	†0.96	†0.98
0.22	0.7429	0.74	†0.76	†0.78	†0.81	†0.83	†0.86	†0.88

[a] Tax scenario I is characterized by a tax rate on coupon income of $\tau_c = 0.5$ and a tax rate on short- and long-term capital gains of $\tau_s = \tau_L = 0.25$ corresponding to a situation in which the offset rule is binding but the deduction limit is not. Coupon rate on bond is 0.14 paid annually. Interest rate follows high-variance process with standard deviation of 0.02 per year. The solid line divides the states with capital gains, realized or not, from those with capital losses. Asterisks and daggers mark the states in which the optimal policy is to perform a wash sale. Asterisks indicate the realization of a long term capital gain establishing a new or higher amortizable basis. Daggers denote the realization of a long-term capital loss.

the after-tax proceeds from a sale and no sale is executed. For example, when the interest rate is 14% a five-year bond sells for 1.0197. With a basis of 1.3 a tax rebate of 0.07 could be earned by realizing a capital loss; however, the total value of the wash sale, 1.02 + 0.07 = 1.09, is less than that of holding the bond, 1.12, and continuing to amortize the higher basis.

For one-year bonds, if the bond sells at a premium, $P > 1$, and the basis is below the bond price, $\hat{P} < P$, the investor realizes a capital gain in order to establish a higher basis and benefit from the amortization of the basis, Conversely, if the bond price drops below the basis, $P < \hat{P}$, the investor defers realization of the loss to continue amortizing the original premium. For five-year bonds the amortization benefit is reduced and large capital gains may be deferred, or capital losses may be realized even at the expense of foregoing future amortization benefits. For example, if the bond price rises to 1.1097 from a basis of 1.0, the investor realizes a capital gain; but if $\hat{P} < 1.0$, the investor defers the capital gain. The amortization benefit becomes negligible for twenty-year bonds. For example, if $P = 1.42$ and $\hat{P} \leq 1.3$, the investor optimally defers the realization of a capital gain and thereby foregoes the amortization benefit of increasing the basis to 1.42. In fact, if $P = 0.88$ and $\hat{P} = 1.1, 1.2$, or 1.3, the investor foregoes the amortization benefit and realizes the capital loss.

(II) *Treasury bond held by a high-tax-bracket individual with* $\tau_c = 0.5$, $\tau_s = 0.5$, $\tau_L = 0.25$.

Table 3 reports the bond price and values, V, for the high variance interest rate process, for a range of interest rates and bases, and for maturities 1, 5, and 20 years. Asterisks, daggers and double daggers mark the states where the optimal policy is to perform a wash sale. Panel A reports results when the bond has been held for longer than one year, $t - \hat{t} > 1$, while panel B reports results when the bond has been held for just one year, $t - \hat{t} = 1$. Note that the value function in the two panels can differ only when a wash sale is executed and a capital loss is realized. When a gain is realized, it is presumed to be long-term so the taxes paid are the same. When no wash sale occurs, the ensuing status must be long-term regardless of the current status.

These tables indicate that the investor performs a wash sale of long-term bonds practically every year in order to revert to the short-term status. This is emphasized by the double daggers which mark states in which a wash sale is executed to this end alone. The desirability of the short-term status seems to dominate all other considerations.

(III) *Treasury bond held by a high-tax-bracket individual with* $\tau_c = 0.5$, $\tau_s = \tau_L = 0$.

The optimal trading policy is quite simple and need not be illustrated in a table. Whenever the bond price is above par and the basis, the investor makes a wash sale to establish a higher basis and deduct from future ordinary income the premium amortization. The investor has no tax incentives to perform any other trades.

(IV) *Treasury bond held by a bank or bond dealer with* $\tau_c = \tau_s = \tau_L = 0.5$.

Again the optimal policy can be described without a table. The investor optimally realizes all capital losses and defers the realization of capital gains. He never realizes a capital gain in order to establish a higher basis with the benefit of the amortization deduction. The tax rate on ordinary income is the same as that on capital gains so amortization 'losses' at best exactly offset the capital gain and occur later. Neither does he defer the realization of a capital loss in order to maintain the benefit of the amortization deduction.

Table 3

Treasury bond prices and values of a long position under tax scenario II.[a]

Interest rate	Bond price	Basis						
		0.7	0.8	0.9	1.0	1.1	1.2	1.3

		Panel A: Long-Term Status						
		Maturity = 1 year						
0.06	1.0755	*0.98	*1.01	*1.03	*1.06	1.09	1.14	1.18
0.10	1.0364	*0.95	*0.98	*1.00	*1.03	1.07	1.11	1.16
0.14	1.0000	0.93	0.95	0.98	‡1.00	1.05	1.09	1.14
0.18	0.9762	0.91	0.94	0.96	†0.98	1.03	1.07	1.12
0.22	0.9535	0.90	0.92	0.94	†0.97	1.01	1.05	1.10
		Maturity = 5 years						
0.06	1.3476	*1.19	*1.21	*1.24	*1.26	*1.29	*1.31	*1.34
0.10	1.1919	*1.07	*1.09	*1.12	*1.14	*1.17	†1.19	1.22
0.14	1.0368	0.95	*0.98	*1.00	*1.03	†1.05	1.08	1.12
0.18	0.9177	0.88	0.89	‡0.91	†0.94	†0.96	1.00	1.04
0.22	0.8357	0.81	0.83	†0.85	†0.88	†0.90	0.93	0.97
		Maturity = 20 years						
0.06	1.9200	*1.62	*1.64	*1.67	*1.69	*1.72	*1.74	*1.77
0.10	1.6138	*1.39	*1.41	*1.44	*1.46	*1.49	*1.51	*1.54
0.14	1.2672	*1.13	*1.15	*1.18	*1.20	*1.23	*1.25	†1.28
0.18	0.9791	‡0.91	‡0.93	‡0.96	†0.98	†1.01	†1.03	†1.06
0.22	0.7856	‡0.76	*0.79	†0.81	†0.84	†0.86	†0.89	†0.91
		Panel B: Short-Term Status						
		Maturity = 1 year						
0.06	1.0755	*0.98	*1.01	*1.03	*1.06	†1.09	†1.14	†1.19
0.10	1.0364	*0.95	*0.98	*1.00	*1.03	†1.07	†1.12	†1.17
0.14	1.0000	0.93	0.95	0.98	‡1.00	†1.05	†1.10	†1.15
0.18	0.9762	0.91	0.94	0.96	†0.99	†1.04	†1.09	†1.14
0.22	0.9535	0.90	0.92	0.94	†0.98	†1.03	†1.08	†1.13
		Maturity = 5 years						
0.06	1.3476	*1.19	*1.21	*1.24	*1.26	*1.29	*1.31	*1.34
0.10	1.1919	*1.07	*1.09	*1.12	*1.14	*1.17	†1.20	†1.25
0.14	1.0368	0.95	*0.98	*1.00	*1.03	†1.07	†1.12	†1.17
0.18	0.9177	0.88	0.89	†0.91	†0.96	†1.01	†1.06	†1.11
0.22	0.8375	0.81	0.83	†0.87	†0.92	†0.97	†1.02	†1.07
		Maturity = 20 years						
0.06	1.9200	*1.62	*1.64	*1.67	*1.69	*1.72	*1.74	*1.77
0.10	1.6138	*1.39	*1.41	*1.44	*1.46	*1.49	*1.51	*1.54
0.14	1.2672	*1.13	*1.15	*1.18	*1.20	*1.23	*1.25	†1.28
0.18	0.9791	‡0.91	‡0.93	‡0.96	†0.99	†1.04	†1.09	†1.14
0.22	0.7856	‡0.76	†0.79	†0.84	†0.89	†0.94	†0.99	†1.04

[a] Tax scenario II is characterized by a tax rate on coupon income and short-term capital gains of $\tau_c = \tau_s = 0.5$ and a tax rate on long-term capital gains of $\tau_L = 0.25$ corresponding to a situation in which neither the offset rule nor the deduction limit is binding. Coupon rate on bond is $c = 0.14$, paid annually. Interest rate follows the high-variance process with standard deviation of 0.02 per year. The solid line divides the states with capital gains, realized or not, from those with capital losses. Asterisks, daggers, and double daggers mark the states in which the optimal policy is to perform a wash sale. In each case, one of the benefits is re-establishing a short-term holding status. Asterisks and double daggers indicate the realization of a long-term capital gain. The former also denote the establishing of a new or higher amortizable basis. Double daggers also indicate the realization of a long-term capital gain; however, in these cases the only benefit is the re-establishing of a short-term holding period. Daggers indicate the realization of a long- or short-term capital loss in panels A and B, respectively.

6. Bond prices and the tax timing option

Table 4 displays simulated Treasury bond prices that would be established by the marginal investor following the optimal trading policy under each of the four tax scenarios. We assume that the current value of the short-term interest rate is 14%. For comparison, the 14% coupon bond would be priced just above par if the marginal investor followed a buy-and-hold policy. The exact buy-

Table 4

Treasury bond prices established by optimal trading policies; tax scenarios I–IV.[a,b]

Maturity	High-variance process $\sigma_r = 0.02$ per year				Low-variance process $\sigma_r = 0.01$ per year			
	I	II	III	IV	I	II	III	IV
	Coupon rate c = 0.06							
5	0.802	0.803	0.837	0.748	0.801	0.801	0.836	0.746
10	0.690	0.706	0.728	0.642	0.681	0.683	0.721	0.628
15	0.624	0.664	0.655	0.592	0.607	0.613	0.641	0.568
20	0.584	0.644	0.605	0.566	0.561	0.578	0.586	0.535
25	0.558	0.633	0.570	0.551	0.531	0.560	0.548	0.516
30	0.540	0.627	0.545	0.542	0.512	0.553	0.523	0.505
	Coupon rate c = 0.10							
5	0.904	0.912	0.923	0.878	0.901	0.901	0.918	0.874
10	0.861	0.903	0.889	0.840	0.844	0.855	0.864	0.821
15	0.841	0.923	0.874	0.833	0.812	0.842	0.831	0.800
20	0.832	0.947	0.865	0.836	0.796	0.846	0.812	0.792
25	0.828	0.969	0.859	0.841	0.787	0.857	0.801	0.791
30	0.825	0.986	0.853	0.847	0.783	0.869	0.796	0.792
	Coupon rate c = 0.14							
5	1.020	1.037	1.039	1.010	1.009	1.017	1.018	1.004
10	1.054	1.118	1.103	1.043	1.023	1.054	1.048	1.019
15	1.082	1.199	1.153	1.080	1.035	1.096	1.075	1.037
20	1.104	1.267	1.188	1.113	1.047	1.137	1.097	1.055
25	1.120	1.320	1.209	1.139	1.057	1.172	1.114	1.071
30	1.132	1.359	1.221	1.159	1.067	1.201	1.127	1.085
	Coupon rate c = 0.18							
5	1.161	1.176	1.184	1.147	1.150	1.157	1.163	1.142
10	1.276	1.344	1.342	1.255	1.244	1.275	1.282	1.231
15	1.350	1.484	1.453	1.339	1.301	1.367	1.365	1.292
20	1.401	1.593	1.527	1.402	1.337	1.440	1.422	1.337
25	1.436	1.676	1.574	1.450	1.363	1.496	1.460	1.370
30	1.460	1.746	1.601	1.485	1.382	1.536	1.484	1.396

[a]Computed at the midpoint of the interest rate range, $r = 0.14$. For each process σ_r is the annual standard deviation of changes in the short-term rate of interest.

[b]Tax scenarios are described by their capital gains tax rates, τ_s short-term and τ_L long-term. If the investor is an individual, these depend on whether the short-term loss/long-term gain offset rule and the $3,000 deduction limit are binding. For banks and dealers these rules are not applicable. In each case the ordinary tax rate is $\tau_c = 0.5$.

(I)   Offset rule binding, deduction limit not binding, $\tau_s = \tau_L = 0.25$.
(II)   Neither rule binding, $\tau_s = 0.5$, $\tau_L = 0.25$.
(III) Deduction limit binding, offset rule irrelevant, $\tau_s = \tau_L = 0$.
(IV) Bank or dealer at margin, $\tau_s = \tau_L = 0.5$

and-hold prices range from 1.002 to 1.071 for the high-variance process and from 1.001 to 1.030 for the low-variance process.[21]

The prices which prevail under tax scenario II are uniformly higher than those under scenario I since investors are not subject to the restrictive offset provision of the tax code but can exploit in full their short-term losses. Furthermore, except for the bonds of five-year maturity, tax scenario II typically results in the highest price. We would expect the second scenario to yield high prices because short-term losses provide valuable rebates and a short-term holding period is relatively cheap to establish. This advantage is least valuable for short maturity bonds because they are the least volatile. Consequently all of the five-year bonds and a few of the other short maturity bonds are priced highest under tax scenario III. There are two distinct reasons.

First, for discount bonds the buy-and-hold price is highest under tax scenario III since the guaranteed capital gain escapes all taxation. Second, with a zero capital gains tax rate, it is costless to establish an above-par amortizable basis. For sufficiently short maturities these two effects dominate.

A comparison of the pricing under scenarios I, III, and IV is also of interest. While their interpretation is radically different, they actually differ in only one respect. The capital gain tax rates, both long- and short-term, are 0.25, 0, and 0.5, respectively. All other taxes are the same. Scenario III with the lowest tax rate has prices which are uniformly highest; nevertheless, the high tax rate in scenario IV does not always induce the lowest price. Again there is a tradeoff between the value of capital losses and the cost of capital gains. The former is more important for the volatile longer maturity bonds. The latter is more important for the shorter maturity bonds, particularly those selling below par.

Litzenberger and Rolfo (1984b) note that, under the buy-and-hold policy, the price of a discount bond is linearly increasing in the coupon rate: in comparing three discount bonds with the same maturity, prices P_1, P_2, P_3, and coupon rates c_1, c_2, c_3, where $c_1 < c_2 < c_3$, the after-tax cash flows of the bond P_2 are replicated by a portfolio of bonds P_1 and P_3 with weights α and $1 - \alpha$, where $c_2 = \alpha c_1 + (1 - \alpha)c_3$. A similar argument also applied to premium bonds, but the rate at which the bond price increases in the coupon rate is higher for premium than for discount bonds, reflecting the tax-advantageous amortization of the premium. Considering discount and premium bonds together, under the buy-and-hold policy the bond price is piece-wise linear, increasing, and convex in the coupon rate.

Examination of table 4 reveals that the price–coupon relation is also convex for the bond prices under the various optimal policies. However, now the

---

[21] Buy-and-hold prices are computed with the formula (35) below. Even though the interest rate is not expected to increase or decrease from 14%, the yield curve is slightly downward sloping due to Jensen's inequality, and prices are above par. For these and other premium bonds the buy-and-hold policy assumes that the excess above par is amortized and deducted year by year. Thus no capital losses (or gains) are earned on premium bonds under the buy-and-hold policy. Therefore this benchmark price is the same for all scenarios.

Table 5

Value of the timing option on Treasury bonds measured as the percentage difference between the prices under the optimal and buy-and-hold policies; tax scenarios I–IV.[a,b]

Maturity	High-variance process $\sigma_r = 0.02$ per year				Low-variance process $\sigma_r = 0.01$ per year			
	I	II	III	IV	I	II	III	IV
Coupon rate c = 0.06								
5	0.0%	0.1	0.0	0.1	0.0	0.0	0.0	0.0
10	0.5	2.8	0.2	1.6	0.1	0.3	0.0	0.4
15	1.3	7.2	0.4	3.4	0.4	1.4	0.0	1.3
20	2.0	11.1	0.5	5.1	0.9	3.7	0.1	2.4
25	2.6	14.2	0.4	6.3	1.3	6.5	0.2	3.4
30	3.0	16.4	0.4	7.1	1.8	8.9	0.3	4.2
Coupon rate c = 0.10								
5	0.2	1.1	0.4	0.4	0.0	0.1	0.0	0.1
10	1.5	6.1	2.5	2.2	0.3	1.6	0.2	0.9
15	2.6	11.2	4.3	4.2	0.8	4.4	0.9	2.0
20	3.4	15.1	5.5	5.8	1.4	7.4	1.6	3.1
25	3.9	17.9	6.9	6.9	2.0	10.0	2.4	4.0
30	4.1	19.7	6.2	7.7	2.4	12.1	3.0	4.7
Coupon rate c = 0.14								
5	1.7	3.3	3.5	0.8	0.8	1.6	1.7	0.4
10	3.9	9.4	8.1	2.8	1.9	4.8	4.2	1.5
15	5.0	14.2	10.8	4.7	2.6	8.0	6.1	2.7
20	5.4	17.6	12.0	6.1	3.0	10.7	7.4	3.7
25	5.5	19.8	12.4	7.0	3.3	12.7	8.2	4.5
30	5.4	21.2	12.2	7.6	3.4	14.3	8.6	5.0
Coupon rate c = 0.18								
5	1.7	2.9	3.6	0.5	0.9	1.5	2.0	0.2
10	3.5	8.4	8.3	2.0	1.9	4.3	4.8	0.8
15	4.2	12.8	11.0	3.4	2.3	7.0	6.9	1.6
20	4.4	15.9	12.3	4.5	2.3	9.3	8.2	2.3
25	4.4	18.1	12.8	5.3	2.4	11.1	8.9	2.9
30	4.3	20.0	12.7	5.9	2.5	12.2	9.2	3.4

[a]Computed at the midpoint of the interest rate range, $r = 0.14$. For each process σ_r is the annual standard deviation of changes in the short-term rate of interest.

[b]Tax scenarios are described by their capital gains tax rates τ_s short-term and τ_L long-term. If the investor is an individual, these depend on whether the short-term loss/long-term gain offset rule and the $3000 deduction limit are binding. For banks and dealers these rules are not applicable. In each case the ordinary tax rate is $\tau_c = 0.5$.

(I)   Offset rule binding, deduction limit not binding, $\tau_s = \tau_L = 0.25$.
(II) Neither rule binding, $\tau_s = 0.5$, $\tau_L = 0.25$.
(III) Deduction limit binding, offset rule irrelevant, $\tau_s = \tau_L = 0$.
(IV) Bank or dealer at margin, $\tau_s = \tau_L = 0.5$.

relation is strictly convex throughout for both premium and discount bonds.[22] The different buy-and-hold linear relations contribute to this, but the strict convexity is due to the tax timing effect. The basic intuition for this convexity comes from Merton's (1973) study of stock purchase options. The right to realize capital gains and losses optimally and the right to amortize (even under

[22] The strict convexity cannot be illustrated in table 4 because at least three premium and three discount bonds would be required.

a buy-and-hold policy) convey a valuable option to the bondholder. If we compare a single bond to a portfolio of bonds with the same total coupons and face value, the latter must be at least as valuable since its 'options' can be exercised singly. The convexity is empirically tested in Litzenberger and Rolfo (1984b).

With different tax clientelles each following a buy-and-hold policy, the linear price–coupon relation may become convex or concave. Thus, the tax timing effect discussed in this paper and the buy-and-hold clientele effect may reinforce or cancel one another and it is difficult to distinguish them empirically. Previous evidence in support of clientele effects could be due, at least in part, to tax trading within a single tax bracket.

It is frequently asserted that discount bond prices are higher than what is justified by the term structure of interest rates, reflecting the fact that a portion of the return is realized as a lightly taxed capital gain. Our discussion of table 4 demonstrates that this is just one of several tax effects on bond prices. The direction and magnitude of the tax effect depends critically on the tax scenario applicable to the marginal investor and on whether the marginal investor follows a passive or optimal trading policy.

We now turn our attention to the tax timing option, defined as the difference between the bond prices under the optimal and buy-and-hold policies.[23,24] Table 5 reports the value of the timing option as a percentage of the bond price under the optimal policy. In each case the buy-and-hold price is calculated using the corresponding long-term capital gains tax rate $(0.25, 0.25, 0, 0.5)$. If this price is above par, the amortization is deducted every year. Thus no capital losses (or gains) are earned under the buy-and-hold policy for premium bonds, and the benchmark price is the same for all scenarios. For discount bonds the buy-and-hold prices vary across the scenarios and are inversely related to the long-term capital gains tax rate. The timing option varies widely for different coupon rates, maturities, and tax scenarios, but in most cases it represents a substantial fraction of the bond price just as the example in section 4 illustrates.

The one exception is deep discount bonds under tax scenario III. Here the timing option is worth little since there is only a small probability of ever amortizing a premium and no other tax trading benefit is possible. For bonds selling near or above par, however, the timing option is more important under tax scenario III than under scenarios I or IV. The binding deduction limit under scenario III is a mixed blessing. On the one hand the individual may not

[23]An alternative definition of the timing option is the difference between the bond prices under the optimal and continuous realization policies. The assumption of a buy-and-hold policy is by far the more common in previous research. The two definitions are compared in the example of section 4.

[24]Since the interest rate dynamics employed here are without drift, the results are most similar to the case $\alpha = 0$ in the continuous time model. The buy-and-hold benchmark resulted in smaller timing options in that case so our choice is conservative.

obtain tax rebates from the government by realizing capital losses. On the other hand he can costlessly realize capital gains in order to raise the basis and take advantage of the amortization deduction.

For tax scenario III the timing option's relative value is increasing in the coupon rate. The only tax trading benefit comes from the establishment of an amortizable basis. For deep discount bonds the probability of ever doing so is low and the timing option has little value. For bonds with higher coupon rates, and therefore higher prices, the timing option is increasingly valuable. For premium bonds, however, the rate of increase of the timing option slackens since the expected capital gains component of the bond's return is negative and there is a decreasing chance of future price rises to create the opportunity for further amortization deductions.

For the other three tax scenarios the option–coupon relation has an inverted U-shape. Low coupon, deep discount bonds have large expected capital gains and therefore little chance of future deductible losses. Near par bonds can benefit from either a deductible decrease in price or an increase in price which is later amortizable. As under scenario III premium bonds have reduced changes for future increases in amortization. While they do have the largest expected decreases in price, these are deductible only to the extent that they exceed the amortization and only if future amortization is foregone.

The reported values show that the tax timing option is typically increasing in maturity. This is due to both the increased value of standard options when their maturities are lengthened and the greater volatility of the longer maturity bonds underlying these options. This feature explains why the 25- and 30-year 10% coupon bonds are more expensive than those with 10- to 20-year maturities even though the interest rate is above the coupon rate at 14% and the yield curve is essentially flat.

Although longer maturity bonds generally have more valuable timing options, it does not follow that a larger tax subsidy flow is available on long bonds. For example, holding two 15-year bonds in succession may provide greater total tax benefit than a single 30-year bond provides. One way to compare the benefits of different maturity bonds is to express the timing option on an annualized basis. The maturity of bonds with the largest annualized benefits would then represent the natural 'habitat' of investors particularly concerned with tax benefits. The annualized tax subsidy on a T-year bond is approximately $r(1 - \tau_c)/[1 - \exp(-r(1 - \tau_c)T)]$ per dollar value of the timing option. Using this approximation we establish that the lowest annual subsidy is on short maturity bonds. On bonds with ten or more years to maturity the benefits are fairly constant, regardless of the tax scenario.

Annualizing the timing option also permits us to normalize the tax benefits relative to the rate of return earned on the bond. For example, under the four scenarios tax benefits provide on average 7, 32, 18 and 10%, respectively, of the total return expected on the 25-year, 14% coupon bond.

The tax timing effect on bond prices also provides a possible explanation of why discounts are so prevalent in the seasoned bond market. Since Treasury bonds are issued at par and are not callable (except occasionally during their last five years before maturity), we should, in the absence of tax timing effects, expect an equal probability of observing seasoned bonds at a premium or discount under a random walk assumption and in the absence of any risk or term premiums. If long-term bonds are riskier and command higher expected returns, then bonds issued at par should later sell at premium prices, at least on average, when these high-term premiums are no longer justified by their reduced risk. Only if interest rates rise dramatically should discounts be observed.

The value added to a long-term bond by its tax timing option lets it be issued at par with a coupon rate below what would otherwise be required. For example (see table 4) under scenario II and no term premiums, a thirty-year bond could be issued at par with a coupon rate just above 10%, even though the interest rate was 14% and rates were not expected to change. The other prices in this section of table 4 show the expected path of this bond's price over its life. With no change in the interest rate, the expected outcome is that the bond would fall in price about ten points over a period of twenty years before recovering in value.

We have so far ignored transactions costs. A bid–ask spread or other costs of trading will reduce the value of the timing option since the optimal policies involve substantially more trading than the buy-and-hold policy. Constantinides has examined the optimal tax trading policy on stocks in the presense of proportional transactions costs.[25] In a simple continuous-time lognormal model he found that investors should not realize losses immediately, but should wait until the price falls to a specific fraction of the basis. A similar rule applies to our model in section 4. The modifications to the optimal trading policies of the models here are more complicated, but the basic idea remains the same: Trades are deferred until capital gains and losses are larger than in the absence of transactions costs.

Table 6 displays the value of the timing option when trading is costly. The round-trip transaction cost is represented by a bid–ask spread of 0.2, 0.5 or 1.0 percent of par.[26] The timing option retains a large fraction of its value even with sizeable transactions costs. Bonds of ten or more years to maturity retain at least half of the original timing option even with one percent transactions costs. The reduction may not be as large as we might have expected because transactions costs are not entirely a dead weight loss. The cost of purchase is

---

[25] In an earlier version of Constantinides (1983).

[26] U.S. Treasury bonds are typically quoted with spreads of one-quarter to one-half of a point in the *Wall Street Journal*. A few have spreads of one-eighth of one point. Treasury note spreads are usually one-eighth to one-quarter of a point.

Table 6

Effects of transactions costs on the timing option; tax scenarios I–IV.[a,b]

Maturity	Value of timing option (%) for $k =$				Value of timing option (%) for $k =$			
	0.0	0.2	0.5	1.0	0.0	0.2	0.5	1.0
	Tax scenario I				*Tax scenario II*			
5	1.7%	1.4	1.0	0.5	3.3	2.8	2.0	1.2
10	3.9	3.3	2.7	2.0	9.4	8.4	7.0	5.0
15	5.0	4.4	3.8	3.0	14.2	13.1	11.4	8.7
20	5.4	4.8	4.2	3.5	17.6	16.3	14.4	11.4
25	5.5	4.9	4.3	3.7	19.8	18.4	16.5	13.2
30	5.4	4.8	4.2	3.6	21.2	19.9	17.8	14.4
	Tax scenario III				*Tax scenario IV*			
5	3.5	3.2	2.7	1.9	0.8	0.6	0.4	0.2
10	8.1	7.6	6.9	5.9	2.8	2.6	2.3	1.9
15	10.8	10.1	9.3	8.2	4.7	4.5	4.2	3.7
20	12.0	11.3	10.4	9.2	6.1	5.8	5.5	5.0
25	12.4	11.6	10.7	9.4	7.0	6.7	6.4	5.9
30	12.2	11.4	10.5	9.2	7.6	7.4	7.0	6.6

[a] Computed at midpoint of interest rate range, $r = 0.14$. Interest rate follows high-variance process with standard deviation of 0.02 per year. Coupon rate on bond is $c = 0.14$. k measures the transactions costs (bid–ask spread) as a percent of par.

[b] Tax scenarios are described by their capital gains tax rates τ_s short-term and τ_L long-term. If the investor is an individual, these depend on whether the short-term loss/long term gain offset rule and the $3,000 deduction limit are binding. For banks and dealers these rules are not applicable. In each case the ordinary tax rate is $\tau_c = 0.5$.

(I)   Offset rule binding, $\tau_s = \tau_L = 0.25$.
(II)   Neither rule binding, $\tau_s = 0.5$, $\tau_L = 0.25$.
(III) Deduction limit binding, offset rule irrelevant, $\tau_s = \tau_L = 0$.
(IV) Bank or dealer at margin, $\tau_s = \tau_L = 0.5$.

added to the basis while the cost of sale is deducted from the sales proceeds. Effectively, the taxing authority subsidizes the costs of trading.

Transactions costs decrease the value of the timing option on short maturity bonds more than they do on long maturity bonds. With one point bid-ask spread, the five-year bond losses 71, 64, 46 or 75 percent of its timing option under the four tax scenarios while bonds of at least fifteen years to maturity never give up more than 40 percent. At thirty-year maturities the examined bonds always retain at least two-thirds of the value of their timing option.

7. The tax-adjusted yield curve and implied tax rates

We have demonstrated that bond prices set by the marginal investor following the optimal trading policy are markedly different from those set under a buy-and-hold or continuous-realization policy. In this section we explore the implications of these differences when interest rate and tax bracket estimates are inferred from market prices.

Previous authors typically have assumed that a particular marginal investor holds the bond to maturity. Under this assumption the price at time zero of a bond with maturity date T, coupon rate c, and par value one is the solution to

$$P = (1 - \tau_c)c \sum_{t=1}^{T} \pi_t + (1 - \tau_L + \tau_L P)\pi_T, \qquad P \le 1, \qquad (35a)$$

or

$$P = [(1 - \tau_c)c + \tau_c(P - 1)/T] \sum_{t=1}^{T} \pi_t + \pi_T, \qquad P > 1, \qquad (35b)$$

where π_t is the price at time zero of one dollar after tax at time t. Given a set of bond prices, the resulting set of eqs. (35) can be inverted to solve for the discount factors and the tax rates.[27]

Robichek and Niebuhr (1970) do this by imposing the additional assumptions, $\tau_L = 0.5\tau_c$, and a flat term structure, $\pi_t = (1 + y)^{-t}$. They then solve for the remaining unknowns, τ_c and y, using just two bonds. Their estimates of the marginal tax bracket for the year 1968 range from 37.5% to 50%, depending on the pair of bonds used (and disregarding the cheapest flower bond).

McCulloch (1975) also assumes $\tau_L = 0.5\tau_c$. He does not require a flat term structure but estimates the tax bracket and a cubic spline for the discount function to minimize a weighted sum of the squared deviations between actual and modeled prices. Using data from 1963–1966 he concludes that 'the effective tax rate that best explains the prices of U.S. Treasury securities lies somewhere in the range 0.22 to 0.33'. For later data from 1973 the best estimate of the tax rate is only 0.19.

Litzenberger and Rolfo (1984a) estimate tax brackets under a variety of assumptions about the capital gains tax rate. When they set $\tau_L = 0.5\tau_c$ ($\tau_L = 0.4\tau_c$ after October 1978), they confirm McCulloch's estimates. For the period 1973 to 1980 their yearly U.S. tax bracket estimates range from 12% in 1979 to 45% in 1976. The average is 28%.

Pye (1969) estimates the tax bracket of the marginal bondholder using various combinations of discount and par, taxable and exempt bonds. The analysis closest to ours compares par and moderately discounted taxable bonds. Pye concludes that the effective tax rate at the margin varies between 10% and 36% over the period 1967–1968.

Our analysis provides a possible explanation of these findings which is nevertheless consistent with the true marginal tax bracket being substantially higher as suggested by Miller (1977). If bond prices are set by investors who

---

[27]McCulloch (1975) and Litzenberger and Rolfo (1984a) explicitly and Caks (1977) implicitly use equations identical to (35a). Only McCulloch and Litzenberger and Rolfo recognize the premium amortization embodied in (35b). See also Pye (1969), Robichek and Niebuhr (1970), and Schaefer (1981).

follow an optimal trading policy, estimates of the yield curve and the marginal tax bracket obtained under the assumption of a naive buy-and-hold policy may be biased. To test for bias, we generate a sample of simulated bond prices under the assumption of optimal trading policies with known tax rates and yield curves. We then estimate the yield curve and tax rate from this sample by a procedure which is in the spirit of the methods discussed.

Since our 'data' is simulated and, therefore, not subject to measurement error, there is no statistical advantage in using many prices. Thus, like Robichek and Niebuhr, we use an exact 'estimation' requiring only a few bonds. We eliminate the need of assuming a flat term structure, however, by using four rather than two bonds. In fact with four bonds no smoothness requirement for the yield curve even of the weak type assumed by McCulloch is required.

For each estimation we use two different coupon bonds from each of two adjacent maturities. Under an assumed buy-and-hold policy, the two longer bonds with maturity $T + 1$ are priced according to

$$P' = (1 - \tau_c)c \sum_{t=1}^{T} \pi_t + \left[1 - \tau_L + \tau_L P' + (1 - \tau_c)c\right]\pi_{T+1}, \qquad P' \leq 1,$$

(36a)

or

$$P' = \left[(1 - \tau_c)c + \tau_c(P' - 1)/(T + 1)\right] \sum_{t=1}^{T} \pi_t$$

$$+ \left[(1 - \tau_c)c + \tau_c(P' - 1)/(T + 1) + 1\right]\pi_{T+1}, \qquad P' > 1, \quad (36b)$$

while the shorter maturity bonds are priced by (35).

Substituting the four bond prices into (35) and (36) gives four equations in the five unknowns, $\Sigma\pi_t$, π_T, π_{T+1}, τ_c, and τ_L. If we assume $\tau_L = \tau_c/2$, the system of equations is now fully specified. We eliminate π_T, π_{T+1}, τ_c, and τ_L to obtain a quadratic equation in the variable $\Sigma\pi_t$. Solving for this unknown and then the others yields two solution sets. Only one of these satisfies the constraints $0 \leq \pi_{T+1} \leq \pi_T \leq 1$ and $\tau_c \leq 100\%$, and this is the one chosen.[28]

Tables 7 and 8 report the errors in the estimated forward rates and the estimated tax brackets on coupon income (correct tax bracket $\tau_c = 50\%$ in each case) for different maturities, tax scenarios, coupon rates and interest rate variances.[29] The errors are usually opposite in sign since an increase in the tax

[28] In some cases the estimated tax rates are negative.

[29] The error in the estimated forward rate is the deviation between the estimate and the true forward rate calculated from the binomial model. The true forward rate is not equal to the future expected spot rate, 14% in this case, due to Jensen's inequality.

Table 7

Errors (basis points) in estimated forward rates under the buy-and-hold assumption with $\tau_L = 0.5\tau_c$; tax scenarios I–IV.[a,b]

Forecast period	Std. dev.[c]	High-variance process $\sigma_r = 0.02$ per year				Std. dev.[c]	Low-variance process $\sigma_r = 0.01$ per year			
		I	II	III	IV		I	II	III	IV
					Coupon rates c = 0.08, 0.10					
5	400	39	203	-136	466	200	5	27	-201	470
10	549	85	266	22	357	300	17	201	-134	350
15	595	98	255	126	287	403	33	243	-64	284
20	620	105	283	243	238	426	42	271	10	246
25	625	98	296	391	198	468	50	292	87	212
30	631	82	338	657	179	497	57	318	175	192
					Coupon rates c = 0.04, 0.06					
5	400	5	30	-200	467	200	0	0	-201	420
10	549	7	129	-146	328	300	13	45	-167	338
15	595	6	112	-125	260	403	6	65	-138	262
20	620	4	97	-105	211	426	7	141	-114	222
25	625	0	67	-97	151	468	7	149	-94	188
30	631	-23	47	-83	94	497	0	127	-79	138

[a] Computed at midpoint of interest rate range $r = 0.14$. Errors reported in basis points. For each process σ_r is the annual standard deviation of changes in the short-term rate of interest.

[b] Tax scenarios are described by their capital gains tax rates τ_s short-term and τ_L long-term. If the investor is an individual, these depend on whether the short-term loss/long-term gain offset rule and the $3,000 deduction limit are binding. For banks and dealers these rules are not applicable. In each case the ordinary tax rate is $\tau_c = 0.5$.

(I)   Offset rule binding, deduction limit not binding, $\tau_s = \tau_L = 0.25$.
(II)   Neither rule binding, $\tau_s = 0.5$, $\tau_L = 0.25$.
(III) Deduction limit binding, offset rule irrelevant, $\tau_s = \tau_L = 0$.
(IV)   Bank or dealer at margin, $\tau_s = \tau_L = 0.5$.

[c] Standard deviation of single-period interest rate being forecasted.

rate decreases the effective discount rate and errors of opposite signs have partially offsetting effects. In most cases the interest rate is overestimated while the tax bracket is underestimated. In the extreme, the tax rate is estimated to be negative.

The errors are usually smaller for the low-variance process, as we would expect, since the timing option then has less value and buy-and-hold prices are more accurate. For the same reason, errors are smaller when the deep discount bonds are used in the estimation.

The estimates are generally most accurate under tax scenario I. Again this corresponds to the case when the timing option has the least value. Tax scenario II yields very poor results as does scenario III when near par bonds are used. Tax scenario IV is interesting because the implied tax bracket is about the same for all maturities. It ranges between 20% to 30%, disturbingly reminiscent of the tax rate estimated by McCulloch. (By construction, the actual tax rates in this case are all 50%.)

While the errors in the forward rates are often large, the computed numbers are almost invariably within one standard deviation of both the true forward

Table 8

Estimated tax brackets under the buy-and-hold assumption with $\tau_L = 0.5\tau_c$; tax scenarios I–IV.[a,b]

Maturity	High-variance process $\sigma_r = 0.02$ per year				Low-variance process $\sigma_r = 0.01$ per year			
	I	II	III	IV	I	II	III	IV
	Coupon rates c = 0.08, 0.10							
5	44%	17	52	20	49	45	63	18
10	36	17	28	23	47	11	53	27
15	35	0	14	25	44	7	42	31
20	35	−17	−6	26	42	−2	30	31
25	38	−26	−36	29	40	−15	16	31
30	44	−48	−108	27	38	−33	−4	30
	Coupon rates c = 0.04, 0.06							
5	49	44	63	18	50	50	63	26
10	48	20	55	27	47	39	59	28
15	47	20	56	29	48	30	56	32
20	47	18	54	30	47	8	54	32
25	48	24	56	39	47	5	52	33
30	55	27	55	50	49	11	51	43

[a] Computed at the midpoint of interest rate range, $r = 0.14$. For each process σ_r is the annual standard deviation of changes in the short-term rate of interest.

[b] Tax scenarios are described by their capital gains tax rates τ_s, short-term and τ_L long-term. If the investor is an individual, these depend on whether the short-term loss/long-term gain offset rule and the \$3,000 deduction limit are binding. For banks and dealers these rules are not applicable. In each case the ordinary tax rate is $\tau_c = 0.5$.

(I) Offset rule binding, deduction limit not binding, $\tau_s = \tau_L = 0.25$.
(II) Neither rule binding, $\tau_s = 0.5$, $\tau_L = 0.25$.
(III) Deduction limit binding, offset rule irrelevant, $\tau_s = \tau_L = 0$.
(IV) Bank or dealer at margin, $\tau_s = \tau_L = 0.5$.

rate and the single-period rate expected to prevail at the forecast time. Consequently, verifying the induced tax trading bias in the forward rates would require a large sample of data. Furthermore, even with large amounts of data available, the errors probably could not be distinguished from liquidity or other term premia. It is interesting to note that the positive errors are at least qualitatively consistent with the usually claimed upward bias in the yield curve.

We also tried estimation under the buy-and-hold assumption with $\tau_L = 0$ and $\tau_L = \tau_c$. These rates are correct for tax scenarios III and IV, respectively, but the estimates are not noticeably improved, probably because the buy-and-hold policy is 'too far' from optimal.

8. Municipal bonds

The tax treatment of municipal bonds differs from the tax treatment of Treasury and corporate bonds in two important respects. First, coupon income on municipal bonds is exempt from Federal tax. Second, if the purchase price

Table 9

Value of the timing option on municipal bonds measured as the percentage difference between the prices under the optimal and buy-and-hold policies; tax scenarios I, II and IV.[a,b]

Maturity	High-variance process $\sigma_r = 0.02$ per year			Low-variance process $\sigma_r = 0.01$ per year		
	I	II	IV	I	II	IV
	Coupon rate c = 0.03					
5	0.0%	0.1	0.1	0.0	0.0	0.0
10	0.5	2.6	1.6	0.1	0.3	0.4
15	1.2	6.6	3.4	0.4	1.0	1.3
20	1.9	10.5	5.1	0.7	1.9	2.4
25	2.5	13.6	6.3	1.0	3.0	3.4
30	3.0	15.9	7.1	1.2	4.1	4.2
	Coupon rate c = 0.05					
5	0.1	0.8	0.4	0.0	0.1	0.1
10	0.7	3.8	2.2	0.2	1.2	0.9
15	1.5	7.2	4.2	0.6	2.9	2.0
20	2.2	10.0	5.8	1.0	4.5	3.1
25	2.8	12.2	6.1	1.3	5.8	4.0
30	3.2	13.8	7.7	1.5	6.8	4.7
	Coupon rate c = 0.07					
5	0.2	1.0	0.8	0.1	0.5	0.4
10	0.9	3.3	2.8	0.5	1.7	1.5
15	1.8	5.7	4.7	0.9	2.9	2.7
20	2.4	7.9	6.1	1.2	3.9	3.7
25	3.0	9.6	7.0	1.5	4.8	4.5
30	3.4	11.1	7.6	1.7	5.4	5.0
	Coupon rate c = 0.09					
5	0.6	1.2	0.5	0.3	0.6	0.2
10	1.4	3.1	2.0	0.7	1.5	0.8
15	2.1	4.9	3.4	1.0	2.2	1.6
20	2.6	6.6	4.5	1.3	2.7	2.3
25	2.9	8.1	5.3	1.4	3.2	2.9
30	3.2	9.4	5.9	1.5	3.7	3.4

[a] Computed at the midpoint of the interest rate range $r = 0.14$. For each process σ_r is the annual standard deviation of changes in the short-term rate of interest.

[b] Tax scenarios are described by their capital gains tax rates. If the investor is an individual, these depend on whether the short-term loss/long-term gain offset rule and the $3,000 deduction limit are binding. For banks and dealers these rules are not applicable. In each case the ordinary tax rate is $\tau_c = 0.5$.
(I)　Offset rule binding, deduction limit not binding, $\tau_s = \tau_L = 0.25$.
(II)　Neither rule binding, $\tau_s = 0.5$, $\tau_L = 0.25$.
(IV)　Bank or dealer at margin, $\tau_s = \tau_L = 0.5$.
Timing option is always zero under tax scenario III.

in the secondary market is above par the difference must be amortized but the amortized amount is not allowed as a deduction, even though the bond's tax basis is correspondingly reduced. In effect the taxation of bond coupons and of premium amortization are symmetric: for Treasury bonds, the coupons and premium amortization are taxed at the individual's marginal tax rate on ordinary income; for municipal bonds the coupons and premium amortization remain untaxed.

Coupon income on municipal bonds may be subject to state tax, but in our calculations we ignore state taxes. We consider this a good first approximation for two reasons. Many states exempt from state tax the coupons on bonds issued by municipalities within the state so the marginal holders of such bonds may well be exempt from taxes. Also, while state tax rates vary widely across states, they are generally very low relative to the Federal tax rates of investors who would consider holding municipal bonds.[30]

The main difference between the optimal trading policies for municipal and taxable bonds is that no trades are ever made at a price above par since there is no advantage in establishing an amortizeable basis. Since this is the only trading advantage of taxable bonds under tax scenario III, the value of the timing option on municipal bonds is zero in this scenario. At the opposite extreme is tax scenario IV. In this case it is never optimal to establish an above par basis on a taxable bond, so the right to amortize such a basis contributes nothing to the value of the timing option. Thus under scenario IV, the value of the timing option on a municipal bond is equal to that on a taxable bond with the same after-tax coupons. Under tax scenarios I and II the timing option on municipal bonds is less valuable than the option on coupon-equivalent taxable bonds.

Table 9 presents the value of the timing option on municipal bonds. When municipals are deep discount, the timing option under scenarios I and II is nearly as valuable as on coupon-equivalent taxable bonds. The same is true on short-maturity municipals even if the discount is small. These, of course, are the cases when the right to amortize the basis in the future has negligible value. On premium municipal bonds the timing option is substantially smaller than on coupon equivalent taxables, especially if the comparison is made between short-maturity bonds. For example, under tax scenario II the timing option on short-maturity municipals is one-third as large as the timing option on short-term taxables; the timing option on long-term municipals is one-half as large as the timing option on long-term taxables.

9. Concluding remarks

This paper extended the work of Cox, Ingersoll and Ross (1981, 1983) on valuing bonds and combined it with the work of Constantinides (1983, 1984) and Constantinides and Scholes (1980) on optimal trading policies. We determined that the tax timing option is an important fraction of the bond price.

We also discussed how the price distortion affects standard estimation techniques for extracting interest rates and marginal tax brackets from observed bond prices. We found the implied errors to be substantial.

---

[30]As of 1980 seven states had no individual income tax on interest. More than half the states had maximum marginal tax rates at or below 7%. In only three states was the maximum tax rate above 11%. The highest rate was Minnesota's 16%.

Our paper only examined the case when the tax bracket of the marginal bondholder remains unchanged. That is, an investor may buy and sell the bond in the course of the optimal trading policy, but the bond remains in the hands of investors in the same tax bracket throughout its term to maturity. The next step should be to recognize the existence of tax clienteles as in Schaefer (1981); but unlike Schaefer, to explore the implications of the bondholders' following optimal trading policies and of the bond being passed from one tax bracket investor to another as its maturity shortens or as it changes from a discount to a premium bond.

References

Caks, J., 1977, The coupon effect on yield to maturity, Journal of Finance 32, 103–115.

Constantinides, G.M., 1984, Optimal stock trading with personal taxes: Implications for prices and the abnormal January returns, Journal of Financial Economics 13, 65–89.

Constantinides, G.M., 1983, Capital market equilibrium with personal tax, Econometrica 51, 611–636.

Constantinides, G.M. and M.S. Scholes, 1980, Optimal liquidation of assets in the presence of personal taxes: Implications for asset pricing, Journal of Finance 35, 439–449.

Cox, J.C., J.E. Ingersoll, Jr. and S.A. Ross, 1980, An analysis of variable rate loan contracts, Journal of Finance 35, 389–403.

Cox, J.C., J.E. Ingersoll, Jr. and S. A. Ross, 1981, A re-examination of traditional hypotheses about the term structure of interest rates, Journal of Finance 36, 769–799.

Cox, J.C., J.E. Ingersoll, Jr. and S.A. Ross, 1983, A theory of the term structure of interest rates, Econometrica, forthcoming.

Grigelionis, B.I. and A.N. Shiryaev, 1966, On Stefan's problem and optimal stopping rules for Markov processes, Theory of Probability and Its Applications 11, 541–558.

Ibbotson, R.G. and R.A. Sinquefield, 1982, Stocks, bonds, bills and inflation: The past and the future (Financial Analysts Research Foundation, University of Virginia, Charlottesville, VA).

Litzenberger, R.H. and J. Rolfo, 1984a, An international study of tax effects on government bonds, Journal of Finance 39, 1–22.

Litzenberger, R.H. and J. Rolfo, 1984b, Arbitrage pricing, transaction costs and taxation of capital gains: A study of government bonds with the same maturity date, Journal of Financial Economics, this issue.

McCulloch, J.H., 1975, The tax-adjusted yield curve, Journal of Finance 30, 811–830.

Merton, R.C., 1973, Theory of rational option pricing, Bell Journal of Economics and Management Science 4, 141–183.

Miller, M.H., 1977, Debt and Taxes, Journal of Finance 32, 261–275.

Miller, M.H. and M.S. Scholes, 1978, Dividends and taxes, Journal of Financial Economics 6, 333–364.

Pye, G., 1969, On the tax structure of interest rates, Quarterly Journal of Economics 83, 562–579.

Robichek, A. A. and W. D. Niebuhr, 1970, Tax-induced bias in reported treasury yields, Journal of Finance 25, 1081–1090.

Schaefer, S.M., 1981, Measuring a tax-specific term structure of interest rates in the market for British government securities, Economic Journal 91, 415–438.

Schaefer, S.M., 1982a, Tax induced clientele effects in the market for British government securities: Placing bounds on security values in an incomplete market, Journal of Financial Economics 10, 121–159.

Schaefer, S.M., 1982b, Taxes and security market equilibrium, in: W.F. Sharpe and C.M. Cootner, eds., Financial economics: Essays in honor of Paul H. Cootner (Prentice-Hall, Englewood Cliffs, NJ), 159–178.

discussion | **Tax Effects on the Pricing of Government Securities**

Robert H. Litzenberger

University of Pennsylvania

The purpose of this discussion is to provide a brief summary of static models of the impact of taxes on government security prices and to relate these studies to the path-breaking study of Constantinides and Ingersoll (1984) on a dynamic model of the impact of taxes on government security prices.

The influence of taxes on the relative pricing of government securities has been studied in the context of a static equilibrium in which the prices of bonds reflect the tax status of marginal purchasers who hold the bonds to maturity. The capital gain from holding to maturity a coupon bond that is selling at a discount in the secondary market is taxed at a preferential rate for most classes of taxable investors. A pioneering article by Robichek and Niebuhr (1970) demonstrated that the preferential tax treatment accorded capital gains has a major impact on the prices of deeply discounted coupon bonds. Early attempts to measure the tax rates implicit in the relative pricing of government securities compared yields of bonds with the same or similar maturities but different coupons (McCallum 1973 and Pye 1969).

An innovative article by McCulloch (1975) viewed coupon bonds as packages of tax-free pure discount bonds. Consider a simplified example of a 10-year bond that pays interest annually, has a 6 percent coupon yield, and a current market price of 80. If the tax rates on ordinary income and on capital gains for the marginal investor are T_p and $0.5T_p$, respectively, then the coupon bond is characterized as a package consisting of $6(1 - T_p)$ tax-exempt pure-discount bonds for each maturity year 1 through 9 and for year 10, $6(1 - T_p) + 80 + (100 - 80)(1 - 0.5T_p)$ tax-exempt pure discount bonds. Since the number of coupon bonds is considerably less than the number of coupon dates, the tax-exempt pure discount bond prices and the ordinary income tax rate of the marginal investor cannot be identified without placing some restrictions on the relative prices of tax-exempt pure discount bonds of different maturities. A minimal economic restriction is that the pure discount bond price is 1 for a zero maturity and is monotonically decreasing with respect to maturity. This restriction follows from the existence of money, which places a lower bound of zero on future interest rates. Other economically plausible restrictions are the existence of a continuous forward rate, which implies a continuous first derivative with respect to maturity, and the smoothness of the forward yield curve, which implies a continuous second derivative. McCulloch (1975) developed an estimation procedure that incorporates these economic restrictions using a cubic spline, which is a piecewise cubic function constrained to be continuous and to have continuous first and second derivatives at the points where the respective cubic functions are connected together. Constraining the capital gains rate to be equal to one half the ordinary income tax rate and using the cubic spline, McCulloch estimated the tax rate implicit in the relative pricing of government securities. His estimates of the implicit tax rate from 1963 to 1966 are between 22 and 33 percent. He interprets these rates as a weighted average tax rate of investors in government securities. The theoretical basis for McCulloch's model was the existence of an equilibrium in a market where a complete set of tax-exempt and taxable pure discount bonds are spanned by existing securities.

Schaefer (1981, 1982a, b) questions the existence of an equilibrium when there are no restrictions on short selling and individuals have constant but divergent tax rates because of the possibility of tax arbitrage. He uses his existence argument to motivate short-selling restrictions on government securities, which are the cornerstone of his model of a bond market where investors in government securities are segmented into tax-related clienteles. Using a linear programming model, Schaefer (1982a) demonstrates that for most of his sample period there were tax brackets for which some British government bonds were dominated by a portfolio consisting of long positions in other bonds, and that for many periods there did not exist a single tax rate for which all bonds were undominated. Consistent with Schaefer's evidence of tax clienteles for British government securities, Van Horne (1983) shows that his estimates of implied tax rates for a limited number of United States government securities vary inversely with yield levels. These theoretical and empirical studies question the prior work of McCulloch (1975) and others, which indicated that an average tax rate is consistent with the relative prices of United States government securities.

Litzenberger and Rolfo (1984a) discuss equilibrium in a bond market where there is a complete set of dated nominal claims on tax-exempt wealth, ordinary income, and capital gains income. They note that, under progressive taxation, unrestricted short selling would result in the existence of tax arbitrage until an allocation of the three classes of dated nominal claims is reached where all investors are in the same marginal tax bracket. They explain that an equilibrium is feasible under divergent marginal tax rates when there are nonnegativity restrictions on net holdings of taxable and tax-exempt dated nominal claims, which are effectively embodied in the tax laws. Thus, short-selling restrictions on coupon bonds is not a necessary condition for equilibrium in a complete bond market. However, the primary contribution of their study is a discussion of equilibrium in a semicomplete bond market where the available securities consist of two or more coupon bonds for every date. The prices of bonds of a given maturity are a linear function of their coupons. Hence, the vectors of payoffs of the three classes of time-dated claims from holding a given coupon bond can be replicated by a portfolio of two other bonds of the same maturity. The three classes of dated nominal claims are not spanned by coupon bonds, because for each maturity date there are a maximum of two linearly independent coupon bonds. Under these conditions, an equilibrium with investors in diverse tax brackets holding positive amounts of all bonds is feasible, and there is a locus of ordinary income and capital gains tax rates that is consistent with the relative prices of coupon bonds. It is shown that in Germany, Japan, the United Kingdom, and the United States this locus includes the interest income and capital gains tax rates of major taxable holders of government securities. For example, in the United States where commercial banks hold 31.5 percent of privately held government securities, the estimated interest income tax rate conditional on their capital gains tax rate was not significantly different from the statutory rates of 46 and 48 percent over their sample period.

Commercial banks are also major holders of municipal debt. Skelton (1983) has argued that high-grade corporate taxable debt and municipal bonds, aside from tax considerations, are close substitutes, and that tax arbitrage by commercial banks would ensure that the tax rate implicit in relative prices of corporate and municipal debt would be equal to the corporate statutory rate. Empirical studies by Skelton (1983) and Trzcinka (1982) obtain estimates of this implicit tax rate that are equal to the corporate statutory rate. The Litzenberger and Rolfo (1984a) empirical results reconcile the tax rate estimated by McCulloch, based on the constraint that the capital gains rate is one half the ordinary income tax rate (which is applicable to individuals but not to commercial banks), with the higher tax rates (equal to the corporate statutory rate) estimated by Skelton (1983) and Trzcinka (1982).

The previously discussed studies of the effect of taxes on the relative pricing of government securities was based on static models where investors held bonds to maturity. Although turnover rates in many bond issues are quite low, a buy-and-hold policy is not generally optimal for taxable investors. The path-breaking contribution of Constantinides and Ingersoll (1984) notes that a dynamic strategy gives an investor the option of realizing losses and gains prior to maturity and of setting coupon bonds to permit the amortization of a premium. A taxable investor would find it optimal to exercise these tax options for some but not all bonds of a given maturity. This implies that a portfolio of two bonds that would offer the same cash-flow stream as a third bond if held to maturity would have a higher value for a taxable investor than would the single bond. Thus, both the Schaefer (1982a, b) tax clientele model of a segmented bond market and the tax option model of Constantinides and Ingersoll (1984) predict that the prices of coupon bonds would be convex in their coupon. This implies that the two bond portfolios offering the identical pre-tax return stream if held to maturity would not sell for the same price. In absence of restrictions on short sales and in absence of transaction costs, this would imply the existence of an arbitrage opportunity for tax-exempt investors. In the Schaefer model, restrictions on short selling are used to prevent arbitrage by tax-exempt investors. Constantinides and Ingersoll (1984) formally consider only a single class of investors and the problem of the consistency of their tax option effect with a no-arbitrage condition does not arise. However, the extension of their analysis to divergent tax rates would require future assumptions in the structure of the market. Transaction costs in the form of a bid/ask spread and/or impediments to shorting bonds, such as an absence of an active term repro, are sufficient to inhibit arbitrage by tax-exempt investors. A study of the pricing of coupon bonds with the maturity dates by Litzenberger and Rolfo (1984b) is consistent with the convex relation implied by both the Schaefer (1982b) and Constantinides and Ingersoll (1984) models. However, the convexity is within the bounds implied by tax-exempt arbitrage when the bid/ask spread and error in estimated prices are taken into account.

Constantinides and Ingersoll (1984) determine bond prices based on simulations of a number of simple tax strategies and tax rates. For example, they consider commercial banks, which are taxed at a 50 percent rate on both interest income and capital gains and optimally realize all capital losses and defer all capital gains. They then attempt to determine the bias inherent in estimates of tax rates based on static equilibrium models. For simulated data from the aforementioned scenario they find tax rate estimates of between 20 and 30 percent based on a static model with a constraint that the capital gains rate is one half the ordinary income tax rate. Since this range of estimates is similar to that obtained by McCulloch, even though the tax rate that generated the data using their dynamic equilibrium model was 50 percent, they conclude that the static models resulted in downward-biased tax rate estimates. However, this comparison is misleading because a static equilibrium implies that an entire locus of interest income and capital gains rates is consistent with the relative prices of coupon bonds. The correct comparison with the price data that was generated by a dynamic model with an equal capital gains and interest tax rates is based on a static estimate of the tax rate that constrains the capital gains rate to equal the ordinary income tax rate. Although they do not reproduce these results, they note that the implied estimates based on the static model were correct when this constraint was used. Thus, although the Constantinides and Ingersoll article provides important and empirically verifiable predictions concerning the impact of dynamic tax strategies on bond prices, the interpretation of their simulation results concerning a possible bias inherent in estimates of tax rates based on static models is problematic.

REFERENCES

Constantinides, G , and Ingersoll, J. 1984. "Optimal Bond Trading with Personal Taxes." *Journal of Financial Economics* 13: 299–336. Reprinted Chapter 6, this volume.

Litzenberger, R. H., and Rolfo, J. 1984a. "An International Study of Tax Effects on Government Bonds." *Journal of Finance* 39: 1–22.

———. 1984b. "Arbitrage Pricing, Transaction Costs and Taxation of Capital Gains: A Study of Government Bonds with the Same Maturity Date." *Journal of Financial Economics* 13: 337–51.

McCallum, J. S. 1973. "The Impact of Capital Gains Tax on Bond Yields." *National Tax Journal* 26: 575–83.

McCulloch, J. H. 1975. "The Tax-Adjusted Yield Curve." *Journal of Finance* 30: 811–30.

Pye, G. 1969. "On the Tax Structure of Interest Rates." *Quarterly Journal of Economics* 83: 562–79.

Robichek, A. A., and Niebuhr, W. D. 1970. "Tax-Induced Bias in Reported Treasury Yields." *Journal of Finance* 25: 1081–90.

Schaefer, S. M. 1981. "Measuring a Tax-Specific Term Structure of Interest Rates in the Market for British Government Securities." *Economic Journal* 91: 415–38.

———. 1982a. "Tax Induced Clientele Effects in the Market for British Government Securities: Placing Bounds on Security Values in an Incomplete Market." *Journal of Financial Economics* 10: 121–59.

———. 1982b. "Taxes and Security Market Equilibrium." In W. F. Sharpe and C. M. Cootner (eds.), *Financial Economics: Essays in Honor of Paul H. Cootner*. Englewood Cliffs, N.J.: Prentice-Hall.

Skelton, J. L. 1983. "Banks, Firms and the Relative Pricing of Tax-Exempt and Taxable Bonds." *Journal of Financial Economics* 12: 343–57.

Trzcinka, C. 1982. "The Pricing of Tax-Exempt Bonds and the Miller Hypothesis." *Journal of Finance* 37: 907–23.

Van Horne, J. 1983. "Implied Tax Rates and the Valuation of Discount Bonds." Research paper, Graduate School of Business, Stanford University.

Capital Market Equilibrium with Transaction Costs

George M. Constantinides

University of Chicago and Harvard University

A two-asset, intertemporal portfolio selection model is formulated incorporating proportional transaction costs. The demand for assets is shown to be sensitive to these costs. However, transaction costs have only a second-order effect on the liquidity premia implied by equilibrium asset returns: the derived utility is insensitive to deviations from the optimal portfolio proportions, and investors accommodate large transaction costs by drastically reducing the frequency and volume of trade. A single-period model with an appropriately chosen length of period does not imply the same liquidity premium as the intertemporal model because the appropriate length of the time period is asset specific.

I. Introduction

Transaction costs are an essential feature of some economic theories, such as the transactions demand for money. They are, however, an inessential nuisance in the real asset pricing theory of Sharpe (1964) and Lintner (1965) and its intertemporal extensions. Although inessential, transaction costs may be safely ignored in the real asset pricing theory only if it can be shown that they induce merely second-order effects on the theory's empirically testable implications.

In a two-asset intertemporal model without transaction costs and with isoelastic utility of consumption, the optimal investment policy is characterized by one number, the ratio of the two asset values in the

I thank Darrell Duffie and the referee for helpful comments. I also thank Duane Seppi for helpful comments and computational assistance. I remain responsible for errors.

[*Journal of Political Economy*, 1986, vol. 94, no. 4]

portfolio. When proportional transaction costs are introduced, a simple investment policy is characterized by a region of no transactions, which is an interval on the real line: an investor refrains from transacting as long as the ratio of asset values lies in this interval. One finds that the region of no transactions is wide, and, therefore, an investor's demand for the assets is sensitive to the current composition of the portfolio. Furthermore, the average (over time) demand for one of the two assets, which is subject to transaction costs, is substantially reduced. Therefore, transaction costs have a first-order effect on the assets' demand. This is the bad news.

The good news and the primary result of this paper is that transaction costs have only a second-order effect on equilibrium asset returns: investors accommodate large transaction costs by drastically reducing the frequency and volume of trade. It turns out that an investor's expected utility of the future consumption stream is insensitive to deviations of the asset proportions from those proportions that are optimal in the absence of transaction costs. Therefore, a small liquidity premium is sufficient to compensate an investor for deviating significantly from the target portfolio proportions.

In this paper trades are generated by the endogenously determined adjustments of the portfolio assets in a way that maximizes the investor's expected utility of the infinite lifetime's consumption stream. This contrasts with models in which investors randomly arrive in the market to trade and with single-period models in which investors must liquidate their assets and consume the entire proceeds at the end of the period.

To illustrate the significance of endogenous trading, consider two risky assets with perfectly correlated rates of return and the same variance of their rate of return. The first is traded without transaction costs. The second is subject to proportional transaction costs, where k is the one-way transaction cost rate. The liquidity premium is defined as the difference in these two assets' annual expected rates of return such that an investor is indifferent between holding the one or the other. Suppose that the investor is endowed with the optimal portfolio proportions. In a single-period model in which the period length is 1 year, the liquidity premium is k per year. By contrast, in the infinite-horizon model with proportional transaction costs the investor trades infrequently. For a stock with the standard deviation of the annual rate of return .20, the liquidity premium is only about .15k per year; that is, it is smaller by one order of magnitude (see table 1).

Transaction costs may play a significant role in dissipating arbitrage profits, that is, preventing an investor from purchasing an underpriced asset with the intention of selling it a few months later and realizing a profit net of transaction costs. I find, however, that transaction costs do not explain systematic and significant deviations of assets' expected returns adjusted for risk premia.

The starting point of the analysis is Merton's (1973) intertemporal consumption and investment model, outlined in Section II. I keep the discussion tractable by allowing for only two assets in the economy, one riskless and one risky.

In Section III, I introduce proportional transaction costs and define the set of simple investment and consumption policies. I argue that the optimal investment policy is simple if one assumes that it exists and that the derived utility function is differentiable. The optimal consumption policy is not in the set of simple consumption policies, but it is argued in Section III and in the Appendix that this is not a major issue. I solve for the optimal simple consumption and investment policy. I correct a technical error in Magill and Constantinides (1976), pointed out by Duffie (1983), but, more to the point, I provide numerical solutions that quantify the effect of transaction costs on the optimal simple investment and consumption policy (see tables 1, 2, and 3 and fig. 1).

Two measures of the liquidity premium are defined in Section IV and are estimated for a wide range of parameter values (see tables 1, 2, and 3). These estimates are obtained under the constraint that the optimal policy is simple and, therefore, represent an upper bound to the true liquidity premium. These upper bounds substantiate the main claim of this paper, that even large transaction costs give rise to a modest liquidity premium.

I find that the liquidity premium is strongly positively related to the variance of the asset's rate of return. By contrast, a single-period model with proportional transaction costs states that the liquidity premium is independent of the variance.

Finally, in Section V, I outline extensions and provide concluding remarks.

II. The Model

I consider an exchange economy with a single consumption good as the numeraire. There exist two securities only, with prices $P_0(t)$ and $P_1(t)$ at time t. The investor takes the prices as given and may trade continuously at these prices. The shares of the securities are infinitely divisible. Short sales are permitted with full use of the proceeds. Taxes on capital gains are zero. The securities pay no dividend, and the capital gains are as follows:

$$dP_0(t) = P_0(t)rdt \qquad (1a)$$

and

$$dP_1(t) = P_1(t)[\mu dt + \sigma dw(t)], \tag{1b}$$

where r, μ, and σ are constants and $dw(t)$ is the increment of a Wiener process in R^1.

The investor has wealth $W(t)$ at time t, denominated in units of the consumption good. The investor consumes $c(t)dt$ over $[t, t + dt]$ and invests fraction $\alpha(t)$ of the wealth in the risky asset and the remaining fraction $1 - \alpha(t)$ in the riskless asset. When zero transaction costs and zero labor income are assumed, the wealth dynamics is

$$dW(t) = \{[(\mu - r)\alpha(t) + r]W(t) - c(t)\}dt + \sigma\alpha(t)W(t)dw(t). \tag{2}$$

The investor makes sequential consumption, $c(t)$, and investment, $\alpha(t)$, decisions with the objective to maximize expected utility subject to the wealth dynamics (2) and given initial endowment $W(0) = W_0$. The expected utility is

$$E_0 \int_0^\infty e^{-\rho t} \gamma^{-1} c^\gamma(t) dt \quad (\equiv J[W_0]), \tag{3}$$

where E_0 is the expectation at time zero over the Wiener process $w(t)$. The impatience factor ρ is a constant. The relative risk aversion coefficient, $1 - \gamma$, is assumed to be positive.[1] A solution exists provided that

$$0 < \left(\frac{1}{1 - \gamma}\right)\left[\rho - \gamma r - \frac{(\mu - r)^2 \gamma}{2(1 - \gamma)\sigma^2}\right] \quad (\equiv h) \tag{4}$$

and is given in Merton (1973):

$$\frac{c^*(t)}{W(t)} = h, \tag{5a}$$

$$\alpha^*(t) = \frac{\mu - r}{(1 - \gamma)\sigma^2}, \tag{5b}$$

and

$$J(W_0) = \frac{h^{\gamma-1} W_0^\gamma}{\gamma}. \tag{5c}$$

---

[1] Given the assumption that one of the assets is riskless, it is straightforward to generalize the utility function c^γ/γ to $[c - \hat{c}(t)]^\gamma/\gamma$: the investor invests $\int_0^\infty e^{-rt}\hat{c}(t)dt$ in the riskless asset and allocates the remaining wealth between the risky and riskless assets by maximizing the expected utility as given by eq. (3). The same transformation applies to the problem with proportional transaction costs defined in the following section. In the remainder of the paper I set $\hat{c}(t) = 0$ without loss of generality.

In the next section I reexamine this problem in the presence of proportional transaction costs.

III. Proportional Transaction Costs

Prior to a transaction at time t, the investor's holdings in the riskless and risky securities are $x(t)$ and $y(t)$, respectively, denominated in units of the consumption good. If the investor increases (or decreases) the holding of the risky asset to $y(t) + v(t)$, the holding of the riskless asset decreases (or increases) to $x(t) - v(t) - |v(t)|k$. The proportional transaction cost rate, k, is a given constant. I employ the convention that transaction costs and consumption deplete the riskless, but not the risky, asset.[2]

An investment policy is defined as *simple* if it is characterized by two reflecting barriers, $\underline{\lambda}$, $\bar{\lambda}$, $\underline{\lambda} \leq \bar{\lambda}$, such that the investor refrains from transacting as long as the ratio $y(t)/x(t)$ lies in the interval $[\underline{\lambda}, \bar{\lambda}]$ and transacts to the closest boundary, $\underline{\lambda}$ or $\bar{\lambda}$, of the region of no transactions, $[\underline{\lambda}, \bar{\lambda}]$, whenever the ratio $y(t)/x(t)$ lies outside this interval. In a discrete-time version of the proportional transaction costs model above, Constantinides (1979) proves that the optimal investment policy is simple. In the continuous-time framework characterized by equations (1a) and (1b), Taksar, Klass, and Assaf (1983) assume that the investor does not consume but maximizes the expected rate of growth of wealth. They prove that the optimal investment policy is simple.

For the problem at hand, with asset price dynamics given by (1a) and (1b), the objective given by (3), and proportional transaction costs, results on the existence and form of the optimal consumption and investment policy have not been derived.[3] I therefore confine my attention to the set of simple investment policies, as defined above, and to the set of simple consumption policies, defined by the property that the consumption rate is a constant fraction of the holding in the riskless asset; that is, $\beta \equiv c(t)/x(t)$ is independent of $x(t)$, $y(t)$, and t.[4]

---

[2] The assumption that the transaction costs are charged to the riskless asset instead of to the risky asset can be changed. Also the assumption that the transaction cost rate for increasing the holding of the risky asset equals the rate for decreasing it is innocuous and can be relaxed. Finally, the assumption that consumption depletes the riskless rather than the risky asset can also be relaxed.

[3] The difficult task is proving the existence of an optimal policy. If the existence of an optimal policy and differentiability of J are assumed, one can prove that an optimal investment policy is simple. However, the optimal consumption policy is not, in general, simple, and this issue is taken up below and in the App.

[4] An alternative approach is to replace the continuous-time problem at hand by a discrete-time problem, in which the decision interval is h. Equation (1a) is replaced by $P_0(t + h) = e^{rh}P_0(t)$. Equation (1b) is replaced by a binomial process $P_1(t + h) = aP_1(t)$

An optimal simple policy is defined as a simple policy that maximizes expected utility among all simple policies.

The primary goal of this paper is to show that transaction costs have only a second-order effect on the liquidity premium of an asset's rate of return. In Section IV the liquidity premium is defined and is shown to be a decreasing function of the maximized expected utility of consumption in the presence of transaction costs. By limiting the investor's consumption and investment policy to the set of simple policies, I underestimate the maximized expected utility of consumption and, therefore, overestimate the liquidity premium. The finding that the overestimated liquidity premium is small strengthens the claim that the actual liquidity premium is small. The sensitivity of my results to the assumed simple consumption policy is further discussed in the Appendix.

A given simple investment policy is characterized by the two parameters $\underline{\lambda}$, $\bar{\lambda}$, and a given simple consumption policy is characterized by the parameter β, $\beta \equiv c(t)/x(t)$. The expected derived utility function of $x(t)$ and $y(t)$ is defined as

$$J[x(t), y(t); \beta, \underline{\lambda}, \bar{\lambda}] \equiv E_t \int_t^\infty e^{-\rho(\tau - t)} \gamma^{-1} c^\gamma(\tau) d\tau, \qquad (6)$$

where E_t is the expectation at time t over the Wiener process $w(\tau)$. In the region of no transactions the dynamics of $x(t)$ and $y(t)$ are given by

$$dx(t) = rx(t)dt - c(t)dt \qquad (7a)$$

and

$$dy(t) = \mu y(t)dt + \sigma y(t)dw(t). \qquad (7b)$$

The derived utility satisfies the Bellman equation

$$\frac{c^\gamma}{\gamma} + (rx - c)J_x + \mu y J_y + \frac{\sigma^2}{2} y^2 J_{yy} - \rho J = 0, \quad \underline{\lambda} \le \frac{y}{x} \le \bar{\lambda}. \qquad (8)$$

Subscripts on J denote derivatives, and the arguments of x, y, c, and J are suppressed.

---

with probability p and $P_1(t + h) = a^{-1}P_1(t)$ with probability $1 - p$. Equation (2) is replaced by its obvious discrete-time counterpart, and the objective function (3) is replaced by $E_0 \Sigma_{n=0}^\infty e^{-\rho nh} \gamma^{-1} c^\gamma(nh)$. For this problem the optimal investment policy is known to be simple, as argued above. One can proceed by deriving a difference equation analogous to the differential equation (8) and obtain a general solution that is of the same general form as eq. (11). The whole discussion may be couched in this framework. With the appropriate choice of the parameters $a = a(h)$ and $p = p(h)$, the stochastic process of $P_1(t)$ tends to either the diffusion process (1b) or a Poisson process. For an illustration of this approach in option pricing, see Cox, Ross, and Rubinstein (1979).

For $y/x \leq \underline{\lambda}$, the assumed investment policy is to sell $(1 + k)v$ units of the riskless asset and purchase v units of the risky asset so that the investment proportions equal $\underline{\lambda}$; that is, $(y + v)/[x - (1 + k)v] = \underline{\lambda}$. Solving for v, we obtain $v = (\underline{\lambda}x - y)/[1 + (1 + k)\underline{\lambda}]$. Hence $J(x, y) = J[x - (1 + k)v, y + v] = J\{x - (1 + k)(\underline{\lambda}x - y)/[1 + (1 + k)\underline{\lambda}], y + (\underline{\lambda}x - y)/[1 + (1 + k)\underline{\lambda}]\}$. It is easily shown that J is homogeneous of degree one in its arguments. Invoking homogeneity, we can simplify the expression above into $J(x, y) = [x + (1 + k)y]J\{1/[1 + (1 + k)\underline{\lambda}], \underline{\lambda}/[1 + (1 + k)\underline{\lambda}]\}$, which satisfies the boundary condition

$$(1 + k)J_x = J_y, \quad \frac{y}{x} \leq \underline{\lambda}. \tag{9a}$$

Essentially, the marginal rate of substitution of the riskless asset for the risky asset equals $1 + k$ because in the range $y/x \leq \underline{\lambda}$ the optimal simple policy is to sell $(1 + k)v$ units of the riskless asset and use the proceeds to purchase v units of the risky asset.

On the other side of the region of no transactions the boundary condition is

$$(1 - k)J_x = J_y, \quad \frac{y}{x} \geq \bar{\lambda}, \tag{9b}$$

stating that the marginal rate of substitution of the riskless asset for the risky asset equals $1 - k$.

I invoke continuity of the first derivatives of the J function and impose the conditions that the solution to equation (8) satisfies equation (9a) at $y/x = \underline{\lambda}$ and equation (9b) at $y/x = \bar{\lambda}$.[5]

We can substitute $c = \beta x$ in equation (8) and obtain

$$\frac{(\beta x)^\gamma}{\gamma} + (r - \beta)xJ_x + \mu y J_y + \frac{\sigma^2}{2} y^2 J_{yy} - \rho J = 0, \quad \underline{\lambda} \leq \frac{y}{x} \leq \bar{\lambda}. \tag{10}$$

We can easily show that J is homogeneous of degree γ in x and y. If x and y are both positive, the general solution to equation (10) is[6]

---

[5] The problem defined by eqq. (8) and (9) and without the restriction that the consumption policy be simple is a two-security version of the multisecurity problem formulated in Magill and Constantinides (1976). Unable to solve the partial differential equation, they solve a closely related "ϵ problem" and obtain the control parameters $\underline{\lambda}$, $\bar{\lambda}$, by taking the limit as $\epsilon \to 0^+$. In a private communication, Duffie (1983) points out that the claimed solution to the ϵ problem does not satisfy the partial differential equation in the continuation region because certain χ_{vi} functions are mistakenly treated as constants. The quantitative results in Magill and Constantinides (1976) are invalid and are corrected in the present paper in the special case of two securities and a simple consumption policy.

[6] If x is positive but y is negative, the general solution to eq. (10) is given by eq. (11), where y is replaced by $-y$. If y is positive but x is negative, the general solution is still given by eq. (11), where x and β^γ are replaced by $-x$ and $(-\beta)^\gamma$, respectively. In either case, the parameters s_1 and s_2 are the roots of the quadratic equation (12).

$$J(x, y; \beta, \underline{\lambda}, \bar{\lambda}) = \frac{\beta^\gamma}{\rho - \gamma(r - \beta)} \left(\frac{x^\gamma}{\gamma} + A_1 x^{\gamma - s_1} y^{s_1} + A_2 x^{\gamma - s_2} y^{s_2} \right), \quad (11)$$

where A_1 and A_2 are free parameters and s_1 and s_2 are the roots of the quadratic equation

$$\frac{\sigma^2}{2} s^2 + \left(\mu - \frac{\sigma^2}{2} - r + \beta \right) s - [\rho - \gamma(r - \beta)] = 0. \quad (12)$$

If we substitute the solution (11) in the boundary conditions (9) and divide by x^γ, we obtain the following pair of linear equations in A_1 and A_2:

$$(1 + k)[1 + A_1(\gamma - s_1)\underline{\lambda}^{s_1} + A_2(\gamma - s_2)\underline{\lambda}^{s_2}]$$
$$= A_1 s_1 \underline{\lambda}^{s_1 - 1} + A_2 s_2 \underline{\lambda}^{s_2 - 1} \quad (13)$$

and

$$(1 - k)[1 + A_1(\gamma - s_1)\bar{\lambda}^{s_1} + A_2(\gamma - s_2)\bar{\lambda}^{s_2}]$$
$$= A_1 s_1 \bar{\lambda}^{s_1 - 1} + A_2 s_2 \bar{\lambda}^{s_2 - 1}. \quad (14)$$

Assuming that the corresponding matrix of coefficients is nonsingular, we see that these equations uniquely determine $A_1 = A_1(\beta, \underline{\lambda}, \bar{\lambda})$ and $A_2 = A_2(\beta, \underline{\lambda}, \bar{\lambda})$ in terms of the controls β, $\underline{\lambda}$, and $\bar{\lambda}$.

Before we assert that

$$J^*(x, y) \equiv \max_{\beta, \underline{\lambda}, \bar{\lambda}} J(x, y; \beta, \underline{\lambda}, \bar{\lambda}), \quad \underline{\lambda} \le \frac{y}{x} \le \bar{\lambda}, \quad (15)$$

determine the optimal controls, we need to demonstrate that the maximizing triplet $(\beta, \underline{\lambda}, \bar{\lambda})$ is independent of x and y. Since (13) is not an explicit function of $\bar{\lambda}$, differentiating this equation with respect to $\bar{\lambda}$, we obtain the result that $\partial A_1 / \partial \bar{\lambda} = 0$ implies $\partial A_2 / \partial \bar{\lambda} = 0$, and vice versa. Likewise, from equation (14) we see that $\partial A_1 / \partial \underline{\lambda} = 0$ implies $\partial A_2 / \partial \underline{\lambda} = 0$. We conclude that the same pair $(\underline{\lambda}, \bar{\lambda})$ that satisfies the necessary conditions of optimality of A_1 also satisfies the necessary conditions of optimality of A_2 and, more to the point, of $J(x, y; \beta, \underline{\lambda}, \bar{\lambda})$ irrespective of x, y.

We cannot prove that the control β maximizing $J(x, y; \beta, \underline{\lambda}, \bar{\lambda})$ is independent of x, y. This is to be expected because of the constraint imposed on $c(t)/x(t)$ to be independent of $x(t)$ and $y(t)$.

In the numerical solution we can proceed as follows. For a given triplet $(\beta, \underline{\lambda}, \bar{\lambda})$ we obtain $A_1(\beta, \underline{\lambda}, \bar{\lambda})$ from equations (13) and (14). We maximize $A_1(\beta, \underline{\lambda}, \bar{\lambda})/[\rho - \gamma(r - \beta)]$ with respect to $(\underline{\lambda}, \bar{\lambda})$. By the earlier argument, this pair also maximizes $J(x, y; \beta, \underline{\lambda}, \bar{\lambda})$. Defining

$$J(x, y, \beta) \equiv \max_{(\underline{\lambda}, \bar{\lambda})} J(x, y; \beta, \underline{\lambda}, \bar{\lambda}), \quad (16)$$

we then maximize $J(x, y, \beta)$ with respect to β at the value of y/x corresponding to the optimal portfolio proportions in the absence of transaction costs. From equation (5b), this value of y/x is

$$\lambda^* = \left[\frac{\mu - r}{(1 - \gamma)\sigma^2} \right] \left[1 - \frac{\mu - r}{(1 - \gamma)\sigma^2} \right]^{-1}. \tag{17}$$

In tables 1, 2, and 3 I report the maximizing triplet $(\beta, \underline{\lambda}, \bar{\lambda})$ for various values of the model parameters. The properties of the region of no transactions and the optimal consumption rate are summarized below.

A. Transaction costs broaden the region of no transactions. In table 1 and figure 1 I report the lower ($\underline{\lambda}$) and upper ($\bar{\lambda}$) bounds of the risky to the riskless asset ratio in the region of no transactions for different transaction cost rates and for parameter values $\gamma = -1$, $\rho = .10$/year, $r = .10$/year, $\mu = .15$/year, and $\sigma^2 = .04$/year. The bounds of the region of no transactions are sensitive to a change in transaction costs, especially for low levels of the transaction cost rate.

B. Transaction costs shift the region of no transactions toward the riskless asset. Table 1 and figure 1 illustrate that the lower bound $\underline{\lambda}$ is decreasing in k faster than the upper bound is increasing in k. As expected, the average demand for the risky asset is decreasing in the transaction cost rate.

The same conclusion obtains if the control limits are expressed in terms of the ratio of the risky asset to total wealth, $y/(x + y)$, instead of the ratio y/x. With the same parameter values as in table 1, the optimal ratio $y/(x + y)$ in the absence of transaction costs is .625 and the control limits with $k = .20$ are .670 and .394, respectively, illustrating that the lower bound is decreasing in k faster than the rate at which the upper bound is increasing in k.

C. The width of the region of no transactions is insensitive to risk aversion. Table 2 presents the bounds of the region of no transactions for different levels of risk aversion for $k = .01$ or $.10$, $\rho = .10$/year, $r = .10$/year, $\mu = .15$/year, and $\sigma^2 = .04$/year. Whereas the region of no transactions narrows as measured by $\bar{\lambda} - \underline{\lambda}$, the terms $\underline{\lambda}/\lambda^*$ and $\bar{\lambda}/\lambda^*$ are insensitive to the level of risk aversion. Also the width of the region of no transactions, as measured by the difference in the ratio $y/(x + y)$ at the boundaries, is insensitive to risk aversion. For $k = .01$ and $\gamma = -1$ this width is $.64 - .58 = .06$, and for $k = .01$ and $\gamma = -5$ it is $.22 - .17 = .05$.

D. An increase in risk aversion shifts the region of no transactions toward the riskless asset. This is illustrated in table 2. Also the average demand for the risky asset is decreasing in risk aversion.

E. The width of the region of no transactions is insensitive to the variance of the asset's rate of return. Table 3 presents the bounds of

TABLE 1

OPTIMAL POLICY PARAMETERS AND LIQUIDITY PREMIA FOR DIFFERENT VALUES OF THE TRANSACTION COST RATE

	0	.005	.01	.02	.03	.04	.05	.10	.15	.20
$\underline{\lambda}$	1.667	1.450	1.377	1.277	1.202	1.140	1.087	.891	.754	.650
$\bar{\lambda}$	1.667	1.767	1.784	1.803	1.818	1.832	1.844	1.905	1.965	2.026
β	.2875	.2869	.2869	.2864	.2859	.2852	.2845	.2803	.2754	.2700
$\delta(k)$/year	0	.0008	.0014	.0025	.0037	.0049	.0061	.0130	.0216	.0347
$\delta(k)/k$	...	.16	.14	.13	.12	.12	.12	.13	.14	.17
$\hat{\delta}(k)$/year	0	.0013	.0024	.0046	.0068	.0091	.0114	.0250	>.0500	>.0500
$\hat{\delta}(k)/k$	...	.26	.24	.23	.23	.23	.23	.25	N.A.	N.A.

NOTE.—The table displays the lower ($\underline{\lambda}$) and upper ($\bar{\lambda}$) bounds of the risky to the riskless asset ratio in the region of no transactions, the optimal consumption rate (β), and the liquidity premia (δ, $\hat{\delta}$) on the risky asset, for different values of the transaction cost rate (k). The assumed parameter values are $\gamma = -1$, $\rho = .10$/year, $r = .10$/year, $\mu = .15$/year, and $\sigma^2 = .04$/year.

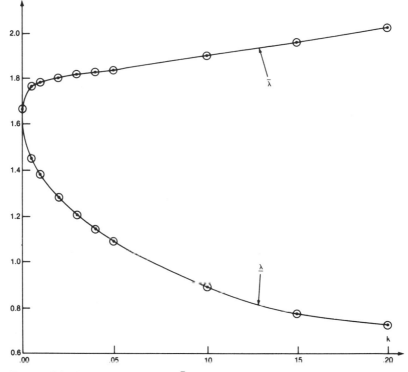

Fɪɢ. 1.—The lower ($\underline{\lambda}$) and upper ($\bar{\lambda}$) bounds of the risky to the riskless asset ratio in the region of no transactions for different values of the transaction cost rate (k). The assumed parameter values are $\gamma = -1$, $\rho = .10$/year, $r = .10$/year, $\mu = .15$/year, and $\sigma^2 = .04$/year.

the region of no transactions for different levels of variance for $k = .01$ or $.10$, $\gamma = -1$, $\rho = .10$/year, $r = .10$/year, and $\mu = .15$/year. Whereas the region of no transactions widens as measured by $\bar{\lambda} - \underline{\lambda}$, the width of the region of no transactions, as measured by the difference in the ratio $y/(x + y)$ at the boundaries, is insensitive to risk aversion. For $k = .01$ and $\sigma^2 = .2^2$/year, the width is $.64 - .58 = .06$, and for $k = .01$ and $\sigma^2 = .5^2$/year the width is $.13 - .06 = .07$.

F. An increase in the variance of the risky asset's rate of return shifts the region of no transactions toward the riskless asset.

G. Transaction costs decrease the consumption rate, but the effect is weak. The consumption rate (β) as a function of the transaction cost rate is reported in table 1. Transaction costs affect the consumption rate in two ways. First, through an income effect, transaction costs decrease the consumption rate. Second, through a substitution effect, they make current consumption less costly (in terms of transaction costs) than future consumption and shift consumption to the earlier

TABLE 2

OPTIMAL POLICY PARAMETERS AND LIQUIDITY PREMIA FOR DIFFERENT VALUES
OF THE RISK AVERSION PARAMETER

	γ				
	-1	-2	-3	-4	-5
			$k = .01$		
$\underline{\lambda}$	1.377	.576	.364	.266	.209
$\underline{\lambda}/\lambda*$	.83	.81	.80	.80	.80
$\lambda*$	1.667	.714	.455	.333	.263
$\bar{\lambda}$	1.784	.767	.489	.360	.284
$\bar{\lambda}/\lambda*$	1.07	1.07	1.08	1.08	1.08
$\beta\ (k = 0)$	.2875	.1833	.1540	.1400	.1318
$\beta\ (k = .01)$	.2868	.1814	.1524	.1387	.1307
δ/year	.0014	.0016	.0017	.0018	.0019
$\hat{\delta}$/year	.0024	.0026	.0027	.0028	.0028
			$k = .10$		
$\underline{\lambda}$	.892	.374	.236	.172	.135
$\underline{\lambda}/\lambda*$	.54	.52	.52	.52	.51
$\lambda*$	1.667	.714	.455	.333	.263
$\bar{\lambda}$	1.905	.825	.528	.388	.306
$\bar{\lambda}/\lambda*$	1.14	1.16	1.16	1.16	1.16
$\beta\ (k = .1)$	.2803	.1783	.1501	.1368	.1291
δ/year	.0130	.0133	.0134	.0136	.0136
$\hat{\delta}$/year	.0250	.0236	.0230	.0226	.0224

NOTE.—The table displays the lower ($\underline{\lambda}$) and upper ($\bar{\lambda}$) bounds of the risky to the riskless asset ratio in the region of no transactions, the target portfolio ratio ($\lambda*$), the optimal consumption rate (β), and the liquidity premia (δ, $\hat{\delta}$) on the risky asset for different values of the risk aversion parameter (γ) and the transaction cost rate (k). The assumed parameter values are $\rho = .10$/year, $r = .10$/year, $\mu = .15$/year, and $\sigma^2 = .04$/year.

periods. Whereas it is not a priori obvious which effect should dominate, table 1 illustrates that the consumption rate is decreasing in the transaction cost rate. This point is discussed further in the Appendix.

Finally, tables 2 and 3 illustrate that an increase in risk aversion or in the risky asset's variance of return increases the consumption rate. These properties are the same as in the absence of transaction costs.

IV. The Liquidity Premium

Consider two assets with perfectly correlated rates of return and equal variance of their rates of return. Trading in the first asset is subject to proportional transaction costs k. Trading in the second asset is exempt from transaction costs. I refer to the second asset as the liquid counterpart of the first one. If both assets are held in equilib-

TABLE 3

OPTIMAL POLICY PARAMETERS AND LIQUIDITY PREMIA FOR DIFFERENT VALUES
OF THE VARIANCE OF THE RISKY ASSET'S RATE OF RETURN

	$.2^2$	$.25^2$	$.3^2$	$.35^2$	$.4^2$	$.45^2$	$.5^2$
				σ^2/YEAR			
				$k = .01$			
$\underline{\lambda}$	1.377	.506	.274	.172	.118	.086	.064
$\underline{\lambda}/\lambda^*$	.83	.76	.71	.67	.64	.61	.58
λ^*	1.667	.667	.385	.256	.185	.141	.111
$\bar{\lambda}$	1.784	.739	.442	.305	·228	.178	.144
$\bar{\lambda}/\lambda^*$	1.07	1.11	1.15	1.19	1.23	1.26	1.30
$\beta\ (k = 0)$	.2875	.1750	.1433	.1289	.1208	.1159	.1125
$\beta\ (k = .01)$	.2869	.1727	.1412	.1270	.1192	.1144	.1112
$\underline{\delta}$/year	.0014	.0018	.0023	.0028	.0033	.0038	.0043
$\bar{\delta}$/year	.0024	.0028	.0032	.0036	.0041	.0046	.0051
				$k = .10$			
$\underline{\lambda}$	.891	.294	.140	.078	.047	.030	.020
$\underline{\lambda}/\lambda^*$	.53	.44	.36	.30	.25	.21	.18
λ^*	1.667	.667	.385	.256	.185	.141	.111
$\bar{\lambda}$	1.905	.805	.488	.341	.259	.205	.168
$\bar{\lambda}/\lambda^*$	1.14	1.21	1.27	1.33	1.40	1.45	1.51
$\beta\ (k = .1)$	.2803	.1692	.1379	.1239	.1163	.1116	.1086
$\underline{\delta}$/year	.0130	.0137	.0150	.0166	.0185	.0205	.0227
$\bar{\delta}$/year	.0250	.0225	.0217	.0219	.0225	.0235	.0247

NOTE.—The lower ($\underline{\lambda}$) and upper ($\bar{\lambda}$) bounds of the risky to the riskless asset ratio in the region of no transactions, the target portfolio ratio (λ^*), the optimal consumption rate (β), and the liquidity premia ($\underline{\delta}$, $\bar{\delta}$) for different values of the variance of the risky asset's rate of return (σ^2) and the transaction cost rate (k). The assumed parameter values are $\gamma = -1$, $\rho = .10$/year, $r = .10$/year, and $\mu = .15$/year.

rium, the expected rate of return on the first asset must exceed that of its liquid counterpart by some liquidity premium $\delta(k)$.

I assume that the investor follows an optimal simple consumption and investment policy. I define the liquidity premium, $\delta(k)$, on the risky asset in the presence of proportional transaction costs (k) as the decrease in the risky asset's mean return (μ), which, combined with the elimination of transaction costs, leaves unchanged the investor's expected utility at $y/x = \lambda^*$.

From equation (11) the maximized expected utility in the presence of transaction costs is the left-hand side of the following equation:

$$
\frac{\beta^\gamma}{\rho - \gamma(r - \beta)} \left(\frac{x^\gamma}{\gamma} + A_1 x^{\gamma - s_1} y^{s_1} + A_2 s^{\gamma - s_2} y^{s_2} \right)
$$
$$
= \left(\left(\frac{1}{1 - \gamma} \right) \left\{ \rho - \gamma r - \frac{[\mu - \delta(k) - r]^2 \gamma}{2(1 - \gamma)\sigma^2} \right\} \right)^{\gamma - 1} \frac{(x + y)^\gamma}{\gamma}. \tag{18}
$$

The right-hand side is the maximized expected utility in the absence of transaction costs and with the expected rate of return on the risky asset replaced by $\mu - \delta(k)$. If we divide both sides of equation (18) by x^γ and substitute λ^* for y/x, we obtain

$$\frac{\beta^\gamma}{(1 + \lambda^*)^\gamma[\rho - \gamma(r - \beta)]} [\gamma^{-1} + A_1(\lambda^*)^{s_1} + A_2(\lambda^*)^{s_2}]$$

$$= \left(\left(\frac{1}{1 - \gamma}\right)\left\{\rho - \gamma r - \frac{[\mu - \delta(k) - r]^2\gamma}{2(1 - \gamma)\sigma^2}\right\}\right)^{\gamma - 1} \Big/ \gamma. \tag{19}$$

This definition of the liquidity premium does not reflect the transaction costs of initially adjusting the portfolio proportions to the ratio λ^*. An alternative definition that accounts for the initial transaction costs is provided shortly.

The liquidity premium is a decreasing function of the left-hand side of equation (19). This left-hand side is the maximized expected utility under the constraint that the policy is simple and, therefore, underestimates the unconstrained maximized expected utility. Thus the liquidity premium, as defined by equation (19), is an upper bound to the liquidity premium when the investor is not constrained to follow a simple policy.

Table 1 presents the liquidity premium $\delta(k)$ and the ratio $\delta(k)/k$ for parameter values $\gamma = -1$, $\rho = .10/\text{year}$, $r = .10/\text{year}$, $\mu = .15/\text{year}$, and $\sigma^2 = .04/\text{year}$. The liquidity premium is one order of magnitude smaller than the one-way proportional transaction cost rate; that is, $\delta(k)/k \cong .15$ for $k = .005$ to $.20$. As the investor becomes more risk averse, the liquidity premium rises but only slightly. Table 2 shows that, for $k = .01$, the liquidity premium rises from $\delta = .0014$ to $.0019$ as γ decreases from -1 to -5; and for $k = .10$, the liquidity premium rises only from $\delta = .0130$ to $.0136$ as γ decreases from -1 to -5.

An increase in the risky asset's variance of return increases the frequency of transactions, increases the transaction costs, and raises the liquidity premium. Table 3 shows that, for $k = .01$, the liquidity premium triples as the variance increases from $\sigma^2 = .04/\text{year}$ to $.25/\text{year}$: for $k = .10$, the liquidity premium doubles as the variance increases from $\sigma^2 = .04/\text{year}$ to $.25/\text{year}$.

Banz (1981) documents a negative association between average returns to stocks and the market value of the stocks after controlling for risk. Classifying all New York Stock Exchange–listed stocks into 10 groups by the market value of the stock, he finds that the difference in the annual mean rate of return between the smallest and largest deciles is about .15. I readily dismiss transaction costs as an explanation for this anomaly. If small firms are traded with .10 one-way proportional transaction costs and if $\sigma^2 = .25/\text{year}$, table 3 indicates that the liquidity premium is .023/year. The liquidity premium is one order of magnitude smaller than the observed anomaly even with the assumed large transaction costs and variance of return.

The second definition of a liquidity premium, $\hat{\delta}(k)$, incorporates the transaction costs both in setting up the portfolio and in maintaining the portfolio proportions within the region of no transactions. The investor's endowment is x_1, y_1, where $y_1 = 0$; that is, the endowment is in the riskless asset alone. The investor optimally purchases $y_2 = \underline{\lambda}x_1/[1 + (1 + k)\underline{\lambda}]$ units of the risky asset. Net of transaction costs, the investment in the riskless asset becomes

$$x_2 = x_1 - \frac{(1 + k)\underline{\lambda}x_1}{1 + (1 + k)\underline{\lambda}} = \frac{x_1}{1 + (1 + k)\underline{\lambda}}. \tag{20}$$

The ratio y_2/x_2 is $\underline{\lambda}$; that is, the investor optimally transacts to the lower boundary of the region of no transactions.

The definition of the liquidity premium $\hat{\delta}(k)$ is given by

$$\frac{\beta^\gamma}{\rho - \gamma(r - \beta)} \left(\frac{x_2^\gamma}{\gamma} + A_1 x_2^{\gamma - s_1} y_2^{s_1} + A_2 x_2^{\gamma - s_2} y_2^{s_2} \right)$$

$$= \left(\left(\frac{1}{1 - \gamma} \right) \left\{ \rho - \gamma r - \frac{[\mu - \hat{\delta}(k) - r]^2 \gamma}{2(1 - \gamma)\sigma^2} \right\} \right)^{\gamma - 1} \Big/ \gamma. \tag{21}$$

Dividing both sides by x_2^γ, we obtain

$$\frac{\beta^\gamma}{[1 + (1 + k)\underline{\lambda}]^\gamma [\rho - \gamma(r - \beta)]} (\gamma^{-1} + A_1 \underline{\lambda}^{s_1} + A_2 \underline{\lambda}^{s_2})$$

$$= \left(\left(\frac{1}{1 - \gamma} \right) \left\{ \rho - \gamma r - \frac{[\mu - \hat{\delta}(k) - r]^2 \gamma}{2(1 - \gamma)\sigma^2} \right\} \right)^{\gamma - 1} \Big/ \gamma. \tag{22}$$

Tables 1, 2, and 3 report the liquidity premium $\hat{\delta}(k)$ and illustrate that it is almost double the liquidity premium $\delta(k)$. Recall that $\delta(k)$ is the liquidity premium that compensates for the transaction costs in maintaining the portfolio proportions within the region of no transactions. I interpret the difference $\hat{\delta}(k) - \delta(k)$ as the liquidity premium in setting up the portfolio if the endowment is in the form of the riskless asset. The difference $\hat{\delta}(k) - \delta(k)$ is small compared with the transaction cost rate because the transaction costs of setting up the portfolio are amortized over the investor's infinite lifetime.

A major difficulty in incorporating transaction costs in the intertemporal consumption and investment problem is that the (stopping) times at which the investor optimally trades are endogenously determined. In the particular problem examined here, trades occur when the ratio of the risky to the riskless asset falls outside the region of no transactions.

By contrast, in single-period models trades may occur only at the two exogenously determined times, the beginning and the end of the period. The problem is reduced to the determination of the optimal size of a trade at the beginning of the period. The simplification associated with single-period models comes at a cost. Since the assumed length of the time period is arbitrary, the length of time over which the transaction costs are amortized is also arbitrary. The liquidity premium (to be defined) implied by a single-period model is a function of the arbitrary length of the time period. The problem may not be resolved by simply choosing the "correct" length of the time period. The following example illustrates that the correct length of the time period is asset specific.

An investor is endowed with W_0 units of the consumption good. The investor buys y_0 units of the risky asset and $W_0 - y_0$ units of the riskless asset without incurring transaction costs. No trading is allowed between now and date T. The asset dynamics are given by equation (1). At date T the risky asset becomes $y(T) = y_0 \exp \int_0^T [\mu dt + \sigma dw(t)]$, gross of transaction costs; it is converted into $(1 - k)y_0 \exp \int_0^T [\mu dt + \sigma dw(t)]$ units of the riskless asset and is consumed along with the $(W_0 - y_0)\exp(rT)$ units of the riskless asset. The corresponding definition of the liquidity premium, $\delta(k)$, is

$$
(1 - k)y_0 \exp \int_0^T [\mu dt + \sigma dw(t)]
$$
$$
= y_0 \exp \int_0^T \{[\mu - \delta(k)]dt + \sigma dw(t)\}, \tag{23}
$$

which implies

$$
\delta(k) = -\frac{1}{T} \ln(1 - k). \tag{24}
$$

The single-period model states that the liquidity premium is independent of the variance of the asset's rate of return unlike the optimal trading model, which states that the liquidity premium is strongly positively related to the variance of the asset's rate of return. Thus the single-period model either underestimates the liquidity premium of high-variance stocks or overestimates the liquidity premium of low-variance stocks.[7] The single-period model also states that the liquidity premium is independent of the risk aversion of the investor unlike

---

[7] Single-period models of capital market equilibrium with fixed transaction costs have been presented in Levy (1978) and Mayshar (1979, 1981). The argument may be extended to the case of fixed transaction costs to show that single-period models imply a substantially different liquidity premium than the optimal trading model. See the discussion in Constantinides (1985).

the optimal trading model, which states that the liquidity premium is weakly positively related to the risk aversion of the investor.

With parameter values $\gamma = -1$, $\rho = .10$/year, $r = .10$/year, $\mu = .15$/year, $\sigma^2 = .04$/year, and $k = .01$, the optimal trading model states that the liquidity premium is $\delta(.01) = .0014$ (see table 3). If the single-period model is to give the same liquidity premium in equation (24), the length of the period must be 7.2 years. If, instead, the variance is $\sigma^2 = .25$/year, the optimal trading model gives a liquidity premium $\delta(.01) = .0043$, and the length of the period in the single-period model must shrink to 2.3 years.

Despite their shortcomings, single-period models capture the realistic possibility that the investor may be forced to liquidate the portfolio at some future time. The infinite-horizon model ignores the possibility of forced liquidation. A simple modification of the basic model accommodates forced liquidations.

We can model forced liquidations as Poisson arrivals uncorrelated with the stock return realization. We can add one term to the right-hand side of equation (8), which is the product of the force of the Poisson process and the utility of consumption, net of transaction costs, in the event of a forced liquidation. The problem can be solved by the numerical methods discussed earlier. If the expected time of arrival of the forced liquidation is short, the model resembles the single-period model, while if it is long, it resembles the infinite-horizon model.

V. Extensions and Concluding Remarks

There are several directions in which the model presented in this paper can be extended. First, we can allow for more than one risky asset. In principle this extension is straightforward. The computational requirements, however, are enormous. I conjecture that, as the number of risky assets is increased, each with the same variance of their rate of return and correlation less than one, the liquidity premium drops. Indirect supporting evidence is provided in Mayshar (1979) and Kovenock and Rothschild (1985).

Second, we can introduce fixed transaction costs. Single-period models with fixed transaction costs are discussed in Leland (1974), Mukherjee and Zabel (1974), Brennan (1975), Goldsmith (1976), Levy (1978), and Mayshar (1979, 1981). In multiperiod extensions of these models the optimal investment policy is complex because the derived utility function, $J(x, y)$, is no longer homogeneous of some degree in x and y. Kandel and Ross (1983) introduce quasi-fixed transaction costs in a multiperiod model. They capture some aspects of fixed transaction costs yet maintain the homogeneity of the derived utility function in its arguments. Constantinides (1985) computes the liquidity premium with quasi-fixed transaction costs and confirms the earlier conclusion that transaction costs have only a second-order effect on equilibrium asset returns.

Third, we can model the process by which firms supply their shares, endogenize share prices, and study the serial correlation of stock returns. Fourth, we can model the way in which the release of information by firms affects prices and trading volume around the event date. Finally, we can study the process by which market makers facilitate trade and endogenize prices and transaction costs.

In this paper I abstract from many realistic features of the market in order to highlight the implications of the endogenously chosen times to trade in the presence of transaction costs. My first conclusion is that investors accommodate transaction costs by drastically reducing the frequency and volume of trade. Second, an investor's expected utility is insensitive to deviations from the optimal portfolio proportions. Hence the liquidity premium due to transaction costs is small. Third, the higher the variance of an asset's return, the more frequent the trade in this particular asset and the higher the liquidity premium. Fourth, even large transaction costs may not explain the empirical anomaly that small firms have mean returns that are substantially larger than the mean returns of large firms. Finally, the implications of the model with endogenous tradings are fundamentally different from those of a single-period model.

Appendix

A Generalized Consumption Policy

In the text I confine my attention to simple consumption policies, defined by the property that the consumption rate is a constant fraction of the holding in the riskless asset; that is, $c(t)/x(t)$ is a constant β in the region $\underline{\lambda} \leq y(t)/x(t) \leq \bar{\lambda}$. As a first step in exploring the sensitivity of the calculated liquidity premium to the assumed simple policy, I derive the liquidity premium under the assumption that the consumption policy is of the following generalized form: The ratio $c(t)/x(t)$ is a constant $\underline{\beta}$ in the region $\underline{\lambda} \leq y(t)/x(t) \leq \lambda^*$ and is a possibly different constant $\bar{\beta}$ in the region $\lambda^* \leq y(t)/x(t) \leq \bar{\lambda}$. The constant λ^* is defined by equation (17), and $\underline{\lambda}$, $\bar{\lambda}$ are the parameters of the simple investment policy in the presence of proportional transaction costs.

I proceed as in Section III to find the optimal parameter values $\underline{\beta}, \bar{\beta}, \underline{\lambda}$, and $\bar{\lambda}$ in the presence of proportional transaction costs. I define $J(x, y; \underline{\beta}, \bar{\beta}, \underline{\lambda}, \bar{\lambda})$ to be the expected utility of consumption given x and y and given policy parameters $\underline{\beta}, \bar{\beta}, \underline{\lambda}$, and $\bar{\lambda}$. The function J satisfies equation (8) and the boundary conditions (9).

In the region $\underline{\lambda} \leq y(t)/x(t) \leq \lambda^*$, I set $c = \underline{\beta}x$ and obtain equation (10) with solution given by (11), where β is replaced by $\underline{\beta}$ and the free parameters A_1 and A_2 are replaced by $\underline{A}_1$ and $\underline{A}_2$. The boundary condition (9a) imposes a

TABLE A1

COMPARISONS OF THE OPTIMAL POLICY PARAMETERS AND LIQUIDITY PREMIA UNDER
DIFFERENT CONSTRAINTS ON THE CONSUMPTION POLICY

	PANEL 1*		PANEL 2†		PANEL 3‡		PANEL 4§	
	$\underline{\beta} = \bar{\beta}$	$\beta \lessgtr \bar{\beta}$	$\underline{\beta} = \bar{\beta}$	$\beta \lessgtr \bar{\beta}$	$\underline{\beta} = \bar{\beta}$	$\beta \lessgtr \bar{\beta}$	$\underline{\beta} = \bar{\beta}$	$\beta \lessgtr \bar{\beta}$
$\underline{\lambda}$	.891	.776	1.377	1.297	.172	.152	.047	.042
$\bar{\lambda}$	1.905	1.892	1.784	1.826	.388	.406	.259	.288
$\underline{\beta}$	.2803	.2589	.2869	.2753	.1368	.1327	.1163	.1129
$\bar{\beta}$	.2803	.2832	.2869	.2959	.1368	.1403	.1163	.1232
δ	.0130	.0127	.0014	.0012	.0136	.0128	.0185	.0169

NOTE.—The lower ($\underline{\lambda}$) and the upper ($\bar{\lambda}$) bounds of the risky to the riskless asset ratio in the region of no transactions, the optimal consumption rates ($\underline{\beta}$, $\bar{\beta}$) in the regions ($\underline{\lambda}$, λ^*) and (λ^*, $\bar{\lambda}$), and the liquidity premium (δ) for different values of the risk aversion parameter (γ), variance of the risky asset's rate of return (σ^2), and transaction cost rate (k). The assumed parameter values are $\rho = .10$/year, $r = .10$/year, and $\mu = .15$/year.
* $\gamma = -1$, $\sigma^2 = .04$/year, $k = .1$.
† $\gamma = -1$, $\sigma^2 = .04$/year, $k = .01$.
‡ $\gamma = -4$, $\sigma^2 = .04$/year, $k = .1$.
§ $\gamma = -1$, $\sigma^2 = .16$/year, $k = .1$.

restriction equivalent to equation (13):

$$(1 + k)[1 + \underline{A}_1(\gamma - s_1)\underline{\lambda}^{s_1} + \underline{A}_2(\gamma - s_2)\underline{\lambda}^{s_2}]$$
$$= \underline{A}_1 s_1 \underline{\lambda}^{s_1 - 1} + \underline{A}_2 s_2 \underline{\lambda}^{s_2 - 1}. \quad (A1)$$

In the region $\lambda^* \leq y(t)/x(t) \leq \bar{\lambda}$, I set c and $\bar{\beta}x$ and proceed as above. The boundary condition (9b) imposes a restriction equivalent to (14):

$$(1 - k)[1 + \bar{A}_1(\gamma - s_1)\bar{\lambda}^{s_1} + \bar{A}_2(\gamma - s_2)\bar{\lambda}^{s_2}]$$
$$= \bar{A}_1 s_1 \bar{\lambda}^{s_1 - 1} + \bar{A}_2 s_2 \bar{\lambda}^{s_2 - 1}. \quad (A2)$$

Continuity of $\partial J/\partial x$ at $y/x = \lambda^*$ imposes the restriction

$$\frac{\underline{\beta}^\gamma}{\rho - \gamma(r - \underline{\beta})} [1 + \underline{A}_1(\gamma - s_1)(\lambda^*)^{s_1} + \underline{A}_2(\gamma - s_2)(\lambda^*)^{s_2}]$$
$$= \frac{\bar{\beta}^\gamma}{\rho - \gamma(r - \bar{\beta})} [1 + \bar{A}_1(\gamma - s_1)(\lambda^*)^{s_1} + \bar{A}_2(\gamma - s_2)(\lambda^*)^{s_2}]. \quad (A3)$$

Continuity of $\partial J/\partial y$ at $y/x = \lambda^*$ imposes the restriction

$$\frac{\underline{\beta}^\gamma}{\rho - \gamma(r - \underline{\beta})} [\underline{A}_1 s_1 (\lambda^*)^{s_1 - 1} + \underline{A}_2 s_2 (\lambda^*)^{s_2 - 1}]$$
$$= \frac{\bar{\beta}^\gamma}{\rho - \gamma(r - \bar{\beta})} [\bar{A}_1 s_1 (\lambda^*)^{s_1 - 1} + \bar{A}_2 s_2 (\lambda^*)^{s_2 - 1}]. \quad (A4)$$

The four equations (A1)–(A4) are linear in $\underline{A}_1$, $\underline{A}_2$, $\bar{A}_1$, and $\bar{A}_2$ and uniquely determine these parameters in terms of the policy parameters $\underline{\beta}$, $\bar{\beta}$, $\underline{\lambda}$, and $\bar{\lambda}$, provided the corresponding matrix of coefficients is nonsingular. Finally I maximize $J(x, y; \underline{\beta}, \bar{\beta}, \underline{\lambda}, \bar{\lambda})$ at $y/x = \lambda^*$ with respect to the policy parameters.

In table A1 I compare the optimal simple investment policy and liquidity premium in the case that the optimal consumption policy is constrained to be simple and in the case that it is generalized as above. Throughout the table I set $\rho = .10$/year, $r = .10$/year, and $\mu = .15$/year. In panel 1 I set $\gamma = -1$, $\sigma^2 = .04$/year, and $k = .1$. If the optimal consumption policy is constrained to be simple, the liquidity premium is $\delta = .0130$/year. If the optimal consumption policy is of the generalized form, the investor has greater flexibility in accommodating the adverse effects of transaction costs and the liquidity premium is reduced to .0127/year. The striking conclusion from panel 1 as well as from panels 2, 3, and 4 is that the liquidity premium with the generalized consumption policy is only slightly lower than the liquidity premium with the simple policy. I also conclude that the optimal simple investment policy and consumption rate are robust to the assumption that the consumption policy is simple.

In principle I can further generalize the set of consumption policies by dividing the region of no transactions into N subregions with the ratio c/x in the nth region given by the parameter β_n. I can then proceed as above to find the optimal parameter values β_n, $n = 1, 2, \ldots, N$. However, table A1 provides convincing evidence that the primary results of the paper remain essentially unchanged as the set of consumption policies is generalized.

References

Banz, Rolf W. "The Relationship between Return and Market Value of Common Stocks." *J. Financial Econ.* 9 (March 1981): 3–18.

Brennan, Michael J. "The Optimal Number of Securities in a Risky Asset Portfolio When There Are Fixed Costs of Transacting: Theory and Some Empirical Results." *J. Financial and Quantitative Analysis* 10 (September 1975): 483–96.

Constantinides, George M. "Multiperiod Consumption and Investment Behavior with Convex Transactions Costs." *Management Sci.* 25 (November 1979): 1127–37.

———. "Capital Market Equilibrium with Transaction Costs." Working Paper no. 130. Chicago: Univ. Chicago, Grad. School Bus., Center Res. Security Prices, April 1985.

Cox, John C.; Ross, Stephen A.; and Rubinstein, Mark. "Option Pricing: A Simplified Approach." *J. Financial Econ.* 7 (September 1979): 229–63.

Duffie, J. Darrell. "An Error in Portfolio Selection with Transactions Costs." Mimeographed. Stanford, Calif.: Stanford Univ., Engineering–Econ. Systems Dept., 1983.

Goldsmith, David. "Transactions Costs and the Theory of Portfolio Selection." *J. Finance* 31 (September 1976): 1127–39.

Kandel, Shmuel, and Ross, Stephen A. "Some Intertemporal Models of Portfolio Selection with Transaction Costs." Working Paper no. 107. Chicago: Univ. Chicago, Grad. School Bus., Center Res. Security Prices, 1983.

Kovenock, Daniel J., and Rothschild, Michael. "Notes on the Effect of Capital Gains Taxation on Non-Austrian Assets." Working Paper no. 1568. Cambridge, Mass.: N.B.E.R., 1985.

Leland, Hayne E. "On Consumption and Portfolio Choices with Transaction Costs." In *Essays on Economic Behavior under Uncertainty*, edited by Michael Balch, Daniel McFadden, and Shih-yen Wu. Amsterdam: North-Holland, 1974.

Levy, Haim. "Equilibrium in an Imperfect Market: A Constraint on the Number of Securities in the Portfolio." *A.E.R.* 68 (September 1978): 643–58.

Lintner, John. "The Valuation of Risk Assets and the Selection of Risky Investments in Stock Portfolios and Capital Budgets." *Rev. Econ. and Statis.* 47 (February 1965): 13–37.

Magill, Michael J. P., and Constantinides, George M. "Portfolio Selection with Transactions Costs." *J. Econ. Theory* 13 (October 1976): 245–63.

Mayshar, Joram. "Transaction Costs in a Model of Capital Market Equilibrium." *J.P.E.* 87 (August 1979): 673–700.

———. "Transaction Costs and the Pricing of Assets." *J. Finance* 36 (June 1981): 583–97.

Merton, Robert C. "An Intertemporal Capital Asset Pricing Model." *Econometrica* 41 (September 1973): 867–87.

Mukherjee, Robin, and Zabel, Edward. "Consumption and Portfolio Choices with Transaction Costs." In *Essays on Economic Behavior under Uncertainty,* edited by Michael Balch, Daniel McFadden, and Shih-yen Wu. Amsterdam: North-Holland, 1974.

Sharpe, William F. "Capital Asset Prices: A Theory of Market Equilibrium under Conditions of Risk." *J. Finance* 19 (September 1964): 425–42.

Taksar, M.; Klass, Michael; and Assaf, D. "Diffusion Model for Optimal Portfolio Selection in Presence of Brokerage Fees." Technical Report no. 4. Stanford, Calif.: Stanford Univ., Dept. Operations Res., 1983.

Theory of rational option pricing

Robert C. Merton

■ The theory of warrant and option pricing has been studied extensively in both the academic and trade literature.[1] The approaches taken range from sophisticated general equilibrium models to ad hoc statistical fits. Because options are specialized and relatively unimportant financial securities, the amount of time and space devoted to the development of a pricing theory might be questioned. One justification is that, since the option is a particularly simple type of contingent-claim asset, a theory of option pricing may lead to a general theory of contingent-claims pricing. Some have argued that all such securities can be expressed as combinations of basic option contracts, and, as such, a theory of option pricing constitutes a

1. Introduction

Robert C. Merton received the B.S. in engineering mathematics from Columbia University's School of Engineering and Applied Science (1966), the M.S. in applied mathematics from the California Institute of Technology (1967), and the Ph.D. from the Massachusetts Institute of Technology (1970). Currently he is Assistant Professor of Finance at M.I.T., where he is conducting research in capital theory under uncertainty.

The paper is a substantial revision of sections of Merton [34] and [29]. I am particularly grateful to Myron Scholes for reading an earlier draft and for his comments. I have benefited from discussion with P. A. Samuelson and F. Black. I thank Robert K. Merton for editorial assistance. Any errors remaining are mine. Aid from the National Science Foundation is gratefully acknowledged.

[1] See the bibliography for a substantial, but partial, listing of papers.

theory of contingent-claims pricing.[2] Hence, the development of an option pricing theory is, at least, an intermediate step toward a unified theory to answer questions about the pricing of a firm's liabilities, the term and risk structure of interest rates, and the theory of speculative'markets. Further, there exist large quantities of data for testing the option pricing theory.

The first part of the paper concentrates on laying the foundations for a rational theory of option pricing. It is an attempt to derive theorems about the properties of option prices based on assumptions sufficiently weak to gain universal support. To the extent it is successful, the resulting theorems become necessary conditions to be satisfied by any rational option pricing theory.

As one might expect, assumptions weak enough to be accepted by all are not sufficient to determine uniquely a rational theory of option pricing. To do so, more structure must be added to the problem through additional assumptions at the expense of losing some agreement. The Black and Scholes (henceforth, referred to as B-S) formulation[3] is a significant "break-through" in attacking the option problem. The second part of the paper examines their model in detail. An alternative derivation of their formula shows that it is valid under weaker assumptions than they postulate. Several extensions to their theory are derived.

2. Restrictions on rational option pricing[4]

■ An "American"-type warrant is a security, issued by a company, giving its owner the right to purchase a share of stock at a given ("exercise") price on or before a given date. An "American"-type call option has the same terms as the warrant except that it is issued by an individual instead of a company. An "American"-type put option gives its owner the right to sell a share of stock at a given exercise price on or before a given date. A "European"-type option has the same terms as its "American" counterpart except that it cannot be surrendered ("exercised") before the last date of the contract. Samuelson[5] has demonstrated that the two types of contracts may not have the same value. All the contracts may differ with respect to other provisions such as antidilution clauses, exercise price changes, etc. Other option contracts such as strips, straps, and straddles, are combinations of put and call options.

The principal difference between valuing the call option and the warrant is that the aggregate supply of call options is zero, while the aggregate supply of warrants is generally positive. The "bucket shop" or "incipient" assumption of zero aggregate supply[6] is useful

---

[2] See Black and Scholes [4] and Merton [29].

[3] In [4].

[4] This section is based on Merton [34] cited in Samuelson and Merton [43], p. 43, footnote 6.

[5] In [42].

[6] See Samuelson and Merton [43], p. 26 for a discussion of "incipient" analysis. Essentially, the incipient price is such that a slightly higher price would induce a positive supply. In this context, the term "bucket shop" was coined in oral conversation by Paul Samuelson and is based on the (now illegal) 1920's practice of side-bets on the stock market.

Myron Scholes has pointed out that if a company sells a warrant against stock already *outstanding* (not just authorized), then the incipient analysis is valid as well. (E.g., Amerada Hess selling warrants against shares of Louisiana Land

because the probability distribution of the stock price return is unaffected by the creation of these options, which is not in general the case when they are issued by firms in positive amounts.[7] The "bucketshop" assumption is made throughout the paper although many of the results derived hold independently of this assumption.

The notation used throughout is: $F(S, \tau; E)$ — the value of an American warrant with exercise price E and τ years before expiration, when the price per share of the common stock is S; $f(S, \tau; E)$ — the value of its European counterpart; $G(S, \tau; E)$ — the value of an American put option; and $g(S, \tau; E)$ — the value of its European counterpart.

From the definition of a warrant and limited liability, we have that

$$F(S, \tau; E) \geqq 0; \quad f(S, \tau; E) \geqq 0 \tag{1}$$

and when $\tau = 0$, at expiration, both contracts must satisfy

$$F(S, 0; E) = f(S, 0; E) = \text{Max}[0, S - E]. \tag{2}$$

Further, it follows from conditions of arbitrage that

$$F(S, \tau; E) \geqq \text{Max}[0, S - E]. \tag{3}$$

In general, a relation like (3) need not hold for a European warrant.

Definition: Security (portfolio) A is *dominant* over security (portfolio) B, if on some known date in the future, the return on A will exceed the return on B for some possible states of the world, and will be at least as large as on B, in all possible states of the world.

Note that in perfect markets with no transactions costs and the ability to borrow and short-sell without restriction, the existence of a dominated security would be equivalent to the existence of an arbitrage situation. However, it is possible to have dominated securities exist without arbitrage in imperfect markets. If one assumes something like "symmetric market rationality" and assumes further that investors prefer more wealth to less,[8] then any investor willing to purchase security B would prefer to purchase A.

Assumption 1: A necessary condition for a rational option pricing theory is that the option be priced such that it is neither a dominant nor a dominated security.

Given two American warrants on the same stock and with the same exercise price, it follows from Assumption 1, that

$$F(S, \tau_1; E) \geqq F(S, \tau_2; E) \quad \text{if} \quad \tau_1 > \tau_2, \tag{4}$$

and that

$$F(S, \tau; E) \geqq f(S, \tau; E). \tag{5}$$

Further, two warrants, identical in every way except that one has a larger exercise price than the other, must satisfy

$$F(S, \tau; E_1) \leqq F(S, \tau; E_2)$$
$$f(S, \tau; E_1) \leqq f(S, \tau; E_2) \quad \text{if} \quad E_1 > E_2. \tag{6}$$

and Exploration stock it owns and City Investing selling warrants against shares of General Development Corporation stock it owns.)

[7] See Merton [29], Section 2.

[8] See Modigliani and Miller [35], p. 427, for a definition of "symmetric market rationality."

Because the common stock is equivalent to a perpetual ($\tau = \infty$) American warrant with a zero exercise price ($E = 0$), it follows from (4) and (6) that

$$S \geq F(S, \tau; E), \qquad (7)$$

and from (1) and (7), the warrant must be worthless if the stock is, i.e.,

$$F(0, \tau; E) = f(0, \tau; E) = 0. \qquad (8)$$

Let $P(\tau)$ be the price of a riskless (in terms of default), discounted loan (or "bond") which pays one dollar, τ years from now. If it is assumed that current and future interest rates are positive, then

$$1 = P(0) > P(\tau_1) > P(\tau_2) > \cdots > P(\tau_n)$$
$$\text{for} \quad 0 < \tau_1 < \tau_2 < \cdots < \tau_n, \quad (9)$$

at a given point in calendar time.

Theorem 1. If the exercise price of a European warrant is E and if no payouts (e.g. dividends) are made to the common stock over the life of the warrant (or alternatively, if the warrant is protected against such payments), then $f(S, \tau; E) \geq \text{Max}[0, S - EP(\tau)]$.

Proof: Consider the following two investments:

A: Purchase the warrant for $f(S, \tau; E)$;
Purchase E bonds at price $P(\tau)$ per bond.
Total investment: $f(S, \tau; E) + EP(\tau)$.
B: Purchase the common stock for S.
Total investment: S.

Suppose at the end of τ years, the common stock has value S^*. Then, the value of B will be S^*. If $S^* \leq E$, then the warrant is worthless and the value of A will be $0 + E = E$. If $S^* > E$, then the value of A will be $(S^* - E) + E = S^*$. Therefore, unless the current value of A is at least as large as B, A will dominate B. Hence, by Assumption 1, $f(S, \tau; E) + EP(\tau) \geq S$, which together with (1), implies that $f(S, \tau; E) \geq \text{Max}[0, S - EP(\tau)]$. Q.E.D.

From (5), it follows directly that Theorem 1 holds for American warrants with a fixed exercise price over the life of the contract. The right to exercise an option prior to the expiration date always has nonnegative value. It is important to know when this right has zero value, since in that case, the values of an European and American option are the same. In practice, almost all options are of the American type while it is always easier to solve analytically for the value of an European option. Theorem 1 significantly tightens the bounds for rational warrant prices over (3). In addition, it leads to the following two theorems.

Theorem 2. If the hypothesized conditions for Theorem 1 hold, an American warrant will never be exercised prior to expiration, and hence, it has the same value as a European warrant.

Proof: If the warrant is exercised, its value will be $\text{Max}[0, S - E]$. But from Theorem 1, $F(S, \tau; E) \geq \text{Max}[0, S - EP(\tau)]$, which is larger than $\text{Max}[0, S - E]$ for $\tau > 0$ because, from (9), $P(\tau) < 1$. Hence, the warrant is always worth more "alive" than "dead." Q.E.D.

Theorem 2 suggests that if there is a difference between the American and European warrant prices which implies a positive probability of a premature exercise, it must be due to unfavorable changes in the exercise price or to lack of protection against payouts to the common stocks. This result is consistent with the findings of Samuelson and Merton.[9]

It is a common practice to refer to $\text{Max}[0, S - E]$ as the *intrinsic value* of the warrant and to state that the warrant must always sell for at least its intrinsic value [condition (3)]. In light of Theorems 1 and 2, it makes more sense to define $\text{Max}[0, S - EP(\tau)]$ as the intrinsic value. The latter definition reflects the fact that the amount of the exercise price need not be paid until the expiration date, and $EP(\tau)$ is just the present value of that payment. The difference between the two values can be large, particularly for long-lived warrants, as the following theorem demonstrates.

Theorem 3. If the hypothesized conditions for Theorem 1 hold, the value of a perpetual ($\tau = \infty$) warrant must equal the value of the common stock.

Proof: From Theorem 1, $F(S, \infty ; E) \geq \text{Max}[0, S - EP(\infty)]$. But, $P(\infty) = 0$, since, for positive interest rates, the value of a discounted loan payable at infinity is zero. Therefore, $F(S, \infty ; E) \geq S$. But from (7), $S \geq F(S, \infty ; E)$. Hence, $F(S, \infty ; E) = S$. Q.E.D.

Samuelson, Samuelson and Merton, and Black and Scholes[10] have shown that the price of a perpetual warrant equals the price of the common stock for their particular models. Theorem 3 demonstrates that it holds independent of any stock price distribution or risk-averse behavioral assumptions.[11]

The inequality of Theorem 1 demonstrates that a finite-lived, rationally-determined warrant price must be a function of $P(\tau)$. For if it were not, then, for some sufficiently small $P(\tau)$ (i.e., large interest rate), the inequality of Theorem 1 would be violated. From the form of the inequality and previous discussion, this direct dependence on the interest rate seems to be "induced" by using as a variable, the exercise price instead of the present value of the exercise price (i.e., I conjecture that the pricing function, $F[S, \tau; E, P(\tau)]$, can be written as $W(S, \tau; e)$, where $e = EP(\tau)$.[12] If this is so, then the qualitative effect of a change in P on the warrant price would be similar to a change in the exercise price, which, from (6), is negative. Therefore, the warrant price should be an increasing function of the interest rate. This finding is consistent with the theoretical models of Samuel-

---

[9] In [43], p. 29 and Appendix 2.

[10] In [42], [43], and [4], respectively.

[11] It is a bit of a paradox that a perpetual warrant with a positive exercise price should sell for the same price as the common stock (a "perpetual warrant" with a zero exercise price), and, in fact, the few such outstanding warrants do not sell for this price. However, it must be remembered that one assumption for the theorem to obtain is that no payouts to the common stock will be made over the life of the contract which is almost never true in practice. See Samuelson and Merton [43], pp. 30–31, for further discussion of the paradox.

[12] The only case where the warrant price does not depend on the exercise price is the perpetuity, and the only case where the warrant price does not depend on $P(\tau)$ is when the exercise price is zero. Note that in both cases, $e = 0$, (the former because $P(\infty) = 0$, and the latter because $E = 0$), which is consistent with our conjecture.

son and Merton and Black and Scholes and with the empirical study by Van Horne.[13]

Another argument for the reasonableness of this result comes from recognizing that a European warrant is equivalent to a long position in the common stock levered by a limited-liability, discount loan, where the borrower promises to pay E dollars at the end of τ periods, but in the event of default, is only liable to the extent of the value of the common stock at that time.[14] If the present value of such a loan is a decreasing function of the interest rate, then, for a given stock price, the warrant price will be an increasing function of the interest rate.

We now establish two theorems about the effect of a change in exercise price on the price of the warrant.

Theorem 4. If $F(S, \tau; E)$ is a rationally determined warrant price, then F is a convex function of its exercise price, E.

Proof: To prove convexity, we must show that if

$$E_3 \equiv \lambda E_1 + (1 - \lambda)E_2,$$

then for every $\lambda, 0 \leq \lambda \leq 1$,

$$F(S, \tau; E_3) \leq \lambda F(S, \tau; E_1) + (1 - \lambda)F(S, \tau; E_2).$$

We do so by a dominance argument similar to the proof of Theorem 1. Let portfolio A contain λ warrants with exercise price E_1 and $(1 - \lambda)$ warrants with exercise price E_2 where by convention, $E_2 > E_1$. Let portfolio B contain one warrant with exercise price E_3. If S^* is the stock price on the date of expiration, then by the convexity of $\text{Max}[0, S^* - E]$, the value of portfolio A,

$$\lambda \text{ Max}[0, S^* - E_1] + (1 - \lambda) \text{ Max}[0, S^* - E_2],$$

will be greater than or equal to the value of portfolio B,

$$\text{Max}[0, S^* - \lambda E_1 - (1 - \lambda)E_2].$$

Hence, to avoid dominance, the current value of portfolio B must be less than or equal to the current value of portfolio A. Thus, the theorem is proved for a European warrant. Since nowhere in the argument is any factor involving τ use¦, the same results would obtain if the warrants in the two portfolios were exercised prematurely. Hence, the theorem holds for American warrants. Q.E.D.

Theorem 5. If $f(S, \tau; E)$ is a rationally determined European warrant price, then for $E_1 < E_2$, $-P(\tau)(E_2 - E_1) \leq f(S, \tau; E_2) - f(S, \tau; E_1) \leq 0$. Further, if f is a differentiable function of its exercise price, $-P(\tau) \leq \partial f(S, \tau; E)/\partial E \leq 0$.

Proof: The right-hand inequality follows directly from (6). The left-hand inequality follows from a dominance argument. Let portfolio A contain a warrant to purchase the stock at E_2 and $(E_2 - E_1)$ bonds at price $P(\tau)$ per bond. Let portfolio B contain a warrant to purchase the stock at E_1. If S^* is the stock price on the

---

[13] In [43], [4], and [54], respectively.
[14] Stiglitz [51], p. 788, introduces this same type loan as a sufficient condition for the Modigliani-Miller Theorem to obtain when there is a positive probability of bankruptcy.

date of expiration, then the terminal value of portfolio A,

$$\text{Max}[0, S^* - E_2] + (E_2 - E_1),$$

will be greater than the terminal value of portfolio B, $\text{Max}[0, S^* - E_1]$, when $S^* < E_2$, and equal to it when $S^* \geq E_2$. So, to avoid dominance, $f(S, \tau; E_1) \leq f(S, \tau; E_2) + P(\tau)(E_2 - E_1)$. The inequality on the derivative follows by dividing the discrete-change inequalities by $(E_2 - E_1)$ and taking the limit as E_2 tends to E_1. Q.E.D.

If the hypothesized conditions for Theorem 1 hold, then the inequalities of Theorem 5 hold for American warrants. Otherwise, we only have the weaker inequalities, $-(E_2 - E_1) \leq F(S, \tau; E_2) - F(S, \tau; E_1) \leq 0$ and $-1 \leq \partial F(S, \tau; E)/\partial E \leq 0$.

Let $Q(t)$ be the price per share on a common stock at time t and $F_Q(Q, \tau; E_Q)$ be the price of a warrant to purchase one share of stock at price E_Q on or before a given date τ years in the future, when the current price of the common stock is Q.

Theorem 6. If k is a positive constant; $Q(t) = kS(t)$; $E_Q = kE$, then $F_Q(Q, \tau; E_Q) \equiv kF(S, \tau; E)$ for all S, τ, E and each k.

Proof: Let S^* be the value of the common stock with initial value S when both warrants either are exercised or expire. Then, by the hypothesized conditions of the theorem, $Q = Q^* = kS^*$ and $E_Q = kE$. The value of the warrant on Q will be $\text{Max}[0, Q^* - E_Q]$ $= k\,\text{Max}[0, S^* - E]$ which is k times the value of the warrant on S. Hence, to avoid dominance of one over the other, the value of the warrant on Q must sell for exactly k times the value of the warrant on S. Q.E.D.

The implications of Theorem 6 for restrictions on rational warrant pricing depend on what assumptions are required to produce the hypothesized conditions of the theorem. In its weakest form, it is a dimensional theorem where k is the proportionality factor between two units of account (e.g., $k = 100$ cents/dollar). If the stock and warrant markets are purely competitive, then it can be interpreted as a scale theorem. Namely, if there are no economies of scale with respect to transactions costs and no problems with indivisibilities, then k shares of stock will always sell for exactly k times the value of one share of stock. Under these conditions, the theorem states that a warrant to buy k shares of stock for a total of (kE) dollars when the stock price per share is S dollars, is equal in value to k times the price of a warrant to buy one share of the stock for E dollars, all other terms the same. Thus, the rational warrant pricing function is homogeneous of degree one in S and E with respect to scale, which reflects the usual constant returns to scale results of competition.

Hence, one can always work in standardized units of $E = 1$ where the stock price and warrant price are quoted in units of exercise price by choosing $k = 1/E$. Not only does this change of units eliminate a variable from the problem, but it is also a useful operation to perform prior to making empirical comparisons across different warrants where the dollar amounts may be of considerably different magnitudes.

Let $F_i(S_i, \tau_i; E_i)$ be the value of a warrant on the common stock of firm i with current price per share S_i when τ_i is the time to expiration and E_i is the exercise price.

Assumption 2. If $S_i = S_j = S$; $\tau_i = \tau_j = \tau$; $E_i = E_j = E$, and the returns per dollar on the stocks i and j are identically distributed, then $F_i(S, \tau; E) = F_j(S, \tau; E)$.

Assumption 2 implies that, from the point of view of the warrant holder, the only identifying feature of the common stock is its (*ex ante*) distribution of returns.

Define $z(t)$ to be the one-period random variable return per dollar invested in the common stock in period t. Let $Z(\tau) \equiv \prod_{t=1}^{\tau} z(t)$ be the τ-period return per dollar.

Theorem 7. If $S_i = S_j = S$, $i, j = 1, 2, \ldots, n$;

$$Z_{n+1}(\tau) \equiv \sum_1^n \lambda_i Z_i(\tau)$$

for $\lambda_i \epsilon [0, 1]$ and $\sum_1^n \lambda_i = 1$, then

$$F_{n+1}(S, \tau; E) \leq \sum_1^n \lambda_i F_i(S, \tau; E).$$

Proof: By construction, one share of the $(n + 1)$st security contains λ_i shares of the common stock of firm i, and by hypothesis, the price per share, $S_{n+1} = \sum_1^n \lambda_i S_i = S \sum_1^n \lambda_i = S$. The proof follows from a dominance argument. Let portfolio A contain λ_i warrants on the common stock of firm i, $i = 1, 2, \ldots, n$. Let portfolio B contain one warrant on the $(n + 1)$st security. Let S_i^* denote the price per share on the common stock of the ith firm, on the date of expiration, $i = 1, 2, \ldots, n$. By definition, $S_{n+1}^* = \sum_1^n \lambda_i S_i^*$. On the expiration date, the value of portfolio A, $\sum_1^n \lambda_i \text{Max}[0, S_i^* - E]$, is greater than or equal to the value of portfolio B, $\text{Max}[0, \sum_1^n \lambda_i S_i^* - E]$, by the convexity of $\text{Max}[0, S - E]$. Hence, to avoid dominance,

$$F_{n+1}(S, \tau; E) \leq \sum_1^n \lambda_i F_i(S, \tau; E). \quad \text{Q.E.D.}$$

Loosely, Theorem 7 states that a warrant on a portfolio is less valuable than a portfolio of warrants. Thus, from the point of view of warrant value, diversification "hurts," as the following special case of Theorem 7 demonstrates:

Corollary. If the hypothesized conditions of Theorem 7 hold and if, in addition, the $z_i(t)$ are identically distributed, then

$$F_{n+1}(S, \tau; E) \leq F_i(S, \tau; E)$$

for $i = 1, 2, \ldots, n$.

Proof: From Theorem 7, $F_{n+1}(S, \tau; E) \leq \sum_1^n \lambda_i F_i(S, \tau; E)$. By hypothesis, the $z_i(t)$ are identically distributed, and hence, so are the $Z_i(\tau)$. Therefore, by Assumption 2, $F_i(S, \tau; E) = F_j(S, \tau; E)$ for i, $j = 1, 2, \ldots n$. Since $\sum_1^n \lambda_i = 1$, it then follows that $F_{n+1}(S, \tau; E) \leq F_i(S, \tau; E)$, $i = 1, 2, \ldots n$. Q.E.D.

Theorem 7 and its Corollary suggest the more general proposition that the more risky the common stock, the more valuable the warrant. In order to prove the proposition, one must establish a careful definition of "riskiness" or "volatility."

Definition: Security one is *more risky* than security two if $Z_1(\tau) = Z_2(\tau) + \epsilon$ where ϵ is a random variable with the property

$$E[\epsilon \mid Z_2(\tau)] = 0.$$

This definition of more risky is essentially one of the three (equivalent) definitions used by Rothschild and Stiglitz.[15]

Theorem 8. The rationally determined warrant price is a nondecreasing function of the riskiness of its associated common stock.

Proof: Let $Z(\tau)$ be the τ-period return on a common stock with warrant price, $F_Z(S, \tau; E)$. Let $Z_i(\tau) = Z(\tau) + \epsilon_i$, $i = 1, \ldots, n$, where the ϵ_i are independently and identically distributed random variables satisfying $E[\epsilon_i | Z(\tau)] = 0$. By definition, security i is more risky than security Z, for $i = 1, \ldots, n$. Define the random variable

return $Z_{n+1}(\tau) \equiv \frac{1}{n} \sum_1^n Z_i(\tau) = Z(\tau) + \frac{1}{n} \sum_1^n \epsilon_i$. Note that, by con-

struction, the $Z_i(\tau)$ are identically distributed. Hence, by the Corollary to Theorem 7 with $\lambda_i = 1/n$, $F_{n+1}(S, \tau; E) \leq F_i(S, \tau; E)$ for $i = 1, 2, \ldots, n$. By the law of large numbers, $Z_{n+1}(\tau)$ converges in probability to $Z(\tau)$ as $n \to \infty$, and hence, by Assumption 2, $\lim_{n \to \infty} F_{n+1}(S, \tau; E) = F_Z(S, \tau; E)$. Therefore, $F_Z(S, \tau; E) \leq F_i(S, \tau; E)$ for $i = 1, 2, \ldots, n$. Q.E.D.

Thus, the more uncertain one is about the outcomes on the common stock, the more valuable is the warrant. This finding is consistent with the empirical study by Van Horne.[16]

To this point in the paper, no assumptions have been made about the properties of the distribution of returns on the common stock. If it is assumed that the $\{z(t)\}$ are independently distributed,[17] then the distribution of the returns per dollar invested in the stock is independent of the initial level of the stock price, and we have the following theorem:

Theorem 9. If the distribution of the returns per dollar invested in the common stock is independent of the level of the stock price, then $F(S, \tau; E)$ is homogeneous of degree one in the stock price per share and exercise price.

Proof: Let $z_i(t)$ be the return per dollar if the initial stock price is S_i, $i = 1, 2$. Define $k = (S_2/S_1)$ and $E_2 = kE_1$. Then, by Theorem 6, $F_2(S_2, \tau; E_2) = kF_2(S_1, \tau; E_1)$. By hypothesis, $z_1(t)$ and $z_2(t)$ are identically distributed. Hence, by Assumption 2, $F_2(S_1, \tau; E_1) = F_1(S_1, \tau; E_1)$. Therefore, $F_2(kS_1, \tau; kE_1) \equiv kF_1(S_1, \tau; E_1)$ and the theorem is proved. Q.E.D.

Although similar in a formal sense, Theorem 9 is considerably stronger than Theorem 6, in terms of restrictions on the warrant pricing function. Namely, given the hypothesized conditions of Theorem 9, one would expect to find in a table of rational warrant values for a given maturity, that the value of a warrant with exercise price E when the common stock is at S will be exactly k times as

---

[15] The two other equivalent definitions are: (1) every risk averter prefers X to Y (i.e., $EU(X) \geq EU(Y)$, for all concave U); (2) Y has more weight in the tails than X. In addition, they show that if Y has greater variance than X, then it need not be more risky in the sense of the other three definitions. It should also be noted that it is the *total* risk, and not the *systematic* or portfolio risk, of the common stock which is important to warrant pricing. In [39], p. 225.

[16] In [54].

[17] Cf. Samuelson [42].

valuable as a warrant on the same stock with exercise price E/k when the common stock is selling for S/k. In general, this result will not obtain if the distribution of returns depends on the level of the stock price as is shown by a counter example in Appendix 1.

Theorem 10. If the distribution of the returns per dollar invested in the common stock is independent of the level of the stock price, then $F(S, \tau; E)$ is a convex function of the stock price.

Proof: To prove convexity, we must show that if

$$S_3 \equiv \lambda S_1 + (1 - \lambda)S_2,$$

then, for every λ, $0 \leq \lambda \leq 1$,

$$F(S_3, \tau; E) \leq \lambda F(S_1, \tau; E) + (1 - \lambda)F(S_2, \tau; E).$$

From Theorem 4,

$$F(1, \tau; E_3) \leq \gamma F(1, \tau; E_1) + (1 - \gamma)F(1, \tau; E_2),$$

for $0 \leq \gamma \leq 1$ and $E_3 = \gamma E_1 + (1 - \gamma)E_2$. Take $\gamma \equiv \lambda S_1/S_3$, $E_1 \equiv E/S_1$, and $E_2 \equiv E/S_2$. Multiplying both sides of the inequality by S_3, we have that

$$S \cdot F(1, \tau; E_3) \leq \lambda S_1 F(1, \tau; E_1) + (1 - \lambda)S_2 F(1, \tau; E_2).$$

From Theorem 9, F is homogeneous of degree one in S and E. Hence,

$$F(S_3, \tau; S_3 E_3) \leq \lambda F(S_1, \tau; S_1 E_1) + (1 - \lambda)F(S_2, \tau; S_2 E_2).$$

By the definition of E_1, E_2, and E_3, this inequality can be rewritten as $F(S_3, \tau; E) \leq \lambda F(S_1, \tau; E) + (1 - \lambda)F(S_2, \tau; E)$. Q.E.D.

Although convexity is usually assumed to be a property which always holds for warrants, and while the hypothesized conditions of Theorem 10 are by no means necessary, Appendix 1 provides an example where the distribution of future returns on the common stock is sufficiently dependent on the level of the stock price, to cause perverse local concavity.

Based on the analysis so far, Figure 1 illustrates the general shape that the rational warrant price should satisfy as a function of the stock price and time.

FIGURE 1

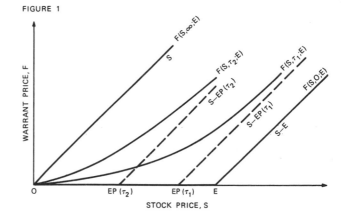

■ A number of the theorems of the previous section depend upon the assumption that either no payouts are made to the common stock over the life of the contract or that the contract is protected against such payments. In this section, the adjustments required in the contracts to protect them against payouts are derived, and the effects of payouts on the valuation of unprotected contracts are investigated. The two most common types of payouts are stock dividends (splits) and cash dividends.

In general, the value of an option will be affected by unanticipated changes in the firm's investment policy, capital structure (e.g., debt-equity ratio), and payout policy. For example, if the firm should change its investment policy so as to lower the riskiness of its cash flow (and hence, the riskiness of outcomes on the common stock), then, by Theorem 8, the value of the warrant would decline for a given level of the stock price. Similarly, if the firm changed its capital structure by raising the debt-equity ratio, then the riskiness of the common stock would increase, and the warrant would become more valuable. If that part of the total return received by shareholders in the form of dividends is increased by a change in payout policy, then the value of an unprotected warrant would decline since the warrant-holder has no claim on the dividends.[18]

While it is difficult to provide a set of adjustments to the warrant contract to protect it against changes in investment or capital structure policies without severely restricting the management of the firm, there do exist a set of adjustments to protect the warrant holders against payouts.

Definition: An option is said to be *payout protected* if, for a fixed investment policy and fixed capital structure, the value of the option is invariant to the choice of payout policy.

Theorem 11. If the total return per dollar invested in the common stock is invariant to the fraction of the return represented by payouts and if, on each expayout date during the life of a warrant, the contract is adjusted so that the number of shares which can be purchased for a total of E dollars is increased by (d/S^z) percent where d is the dollar amount of the payout and S^z is the expayout price per share of the stock, then the warrant will be payout protected.

Proof: Consider two firms with identically distributed total returns per dollar invested in the common stock, $z_i(t)$, $i = 1, 2$, and whose initial prices per share are the same ($S_1 = S_2 = S$). For firm i, let $\lambda_i(t)(t \geq 1)$ be the return per dollar in period t from payouts and $x_i(t)$ be the return per dollar in period t from capital gains, such that $z_i(t) \equiv \lambda_i(t)x_i(t)$. Let $N_i(t)$ be the number of shares of firm i which the warrant of firm i has claim on for a total price of E, at time t where $N_1(0) = N_2(0) = 1$. By definition, $\lambda_i(t) \equiv 1 + d_i(t)/S_i^z(t)$, where $S_i^z(t) = \prod_{k=1}^{t} x_i(k)S$ is the expayout price per share at time t. Therefore, by the hypothesized conditions of the theorem, $N_i(t) = \lambda_i(t)N_i(t - 1)$. On the date when the warrants are either exercised

---

[18] This is an important point to remember when valuing unprotected warrants of companies such as A. T. & T. where a substantial fraction of the total return to shareholders comes in the form of dividends.

or expire, the value of the warrant on firm i will be

$$\text{Max}[0,\ N_i(t)S_i{}^z(t) - E].$$

But, $N_i(t)S_i{}^z(t) = [\prod_{k=1}^{t} \lambda_i(t)][\prod_{k=1}^{t} x_i(t)S] = \prod_{k=1}^{t} z_i(t)S$. Since, by hypothesis, the $z_i(t)$ are identically distributed, the distribution of outcomes on the warrants of the two firms will be identical. Therefore, by Assumption 2, $F_1(S,\ \tau;\ E) = F_2(S,\ \tau;\ E)$, independent of the particular pattern chosen for the $\lambda_i(t)$. Q.E.D.

Note that if the hypothesized conditions of Theorem 11 hold, then the value of a protected warrant will be equal to the value of a warrant which restricts management from making any payouts to the common stock over the life of the warrant (i.e., $\lambda_i(t) \equiv 1$). Hence, a protected warrant will satisfy all the theorems of Section 2 which depend on the assumption of no payouts over the life of the warrant.

Corollary. If the total return per dollar invested in the common stock is invariant to the fraction of the return represented by payouts; if there are no economies of scale; and if, on each expayout date during the life of a warrant, each warrant to purchase one share of stock for exercise price E, is exchanged for $\lambda(\equiv 1 + d/S^z)$ warrants to purchase one share of stock for exercise price E/λ, then the warrant will be payout protected.

Proof: By Theorem 11, on the first expayout date, a protected warrant will have claim on λ shares of stock at a total exercise price of E. By hypothesis, there are no economies of scale. Hence, the scale interpretation of Theorem 6 is valid which implies that the value of a warrant on λ shares at a total price of E must be identically (in λ) equal to the value of λ warrants to purchase one share at an exercise price of E/λ. Proceeding inductively, we can show that this equality holds on each payout date. Hence, a warrant with the adjustment provision of the Corollary will be payout protected. Q.E.D.

If there are no economies of scale, it is generally agreed that a stock split or dividend will not affect the distribution of future per dollar returns on the common stock. Hence, the hypothesized adjustments will protect the warrant holder against stock splits where λ is the number of postsplit shares per presplit share.[19]

The case for cash dividend protection is more subtle. In the absence of taxes and transactions costs, Miller and Modigliani[20] have shown that for a fixed investment policy and capital structure, dividend policy does not affect the value of the firm. Under their hypothesized conditions, it is a necessary result of their analysis that the total return per dollar invested in the common stock will be invariant to payout policy. Therefore, warrants adjusted according to either Theorem 11 or its Corollary, will be payout protected in the same

---

[19] For any particular function, $F(S,\ \tau;\ E)$, there are many other adjustments which could leave value the same. However, the adjustment suggestions of Theorem 11 and its Corollary are the only ones which do so for every such function. In practice, both adjustments are used to protect warrants against stock splits. See Braniff Airways 1986 warrants for an example of the former and Leasco 1987 warrants for the latter. λ could be less than one in the case of a reverse split.

[20] In [35].

sense that Miller and Modigliani mean when they say that dividend policy "doesn't matter."

The principal cause for confusion is different definitions of payout protected. Black and Scholes[21] give an example to illustrate "that there may not be any adjustment in the terms of the option that will give adequate protection against a large dividend." Suppose that the firm liquidates all its assets and pays them out in the form of a cash dividend. Clearly, $S^z = 0$, and hence, the value of the warrant must be zero no matter what adjustment is made to the number of shares it has claim on or to its exercise price.

While their argument is correct, it also suggests a much stronger definition of payout protection. Namely, since their example involves changes in investment policy and if there is a positive supply of warrants (the nonincipient case), a change in the capital structure, in addition to a payout, their definition would seem to require protection against all three.

To illustrate, consider the firm in their example, but where management is prohibited against making any payouts to the shareholders prior to expiration of the warrant. It seems that such a warrant would be called payout protected by any reasonable definition. It is further assumed that the firm has only equity outstanding (i.e., the incipient case for the warrant) to rule out any capital structure effects.[22]

Suppose the firm sells all its assets for a fair price (so that the share price remains unchanged) and uses the proceeds to buy riskless, τ-period bonds. As a result of this investment policy change, the stock becomes a riskless asset and the warrant price will fall to $\mathrm{Max}[0, S - EP]$. Note that if $S < EP$, the warrant will be worthless even though it is payout protected. Now lift the restriction against payouts and replace it with the adjustments of the Corollary to Theorem 11. Given that the shift in investment policy has taken place, suppose the firm makes a payment of γ percent of the value of the firm to the shareholders. Then, $S^z = (1 - \gamma)S$ and

$$\lambda = 1 + \gamma/(1 - \gamma) = 1/(1 - \gamma).$$

The value of the warrant after the payout will be

$$\lambda \, \mathrm{Max}[0, S^z - EP/\lambda] = \mathrm{Max}[0, S - EP],$$

which is the same as the value of the warrant when the company was restricted from making payouts. In the B-S example, $\gamma = 1$ and so, $\lambda = \infty$ and $E/\lambda = 0$. Hence, there is the indeterminancy of multiplying zero by infinity. However, for every $\gamma < 1$, the analysis is correct, and therefore, it is reasonable to suspect that it holds in the limit.

A similar analysis in the nonincipient case would show that both investment policy and the capital structure were changed. For in this case, the firm would have to purchase γ percent of the warrants outstanding to keep the capital structure unchanged without issuing new stock. In the B-S example where $\gamma = 1$, this would require purchasing

---

[21] In [4].
[22] The incipient case is a particularly important example since in practice, the only contracts that are adjusted for cash payouts are options. The incipient assumption also rules out "capital structure induced" changes in investment policy by malevolent management. For an example, see Stiglitz [50].

the entire issue, after which the analysis reduces to the incipient case. The B-S emphasis on protection against a "large" dividend is further evidence that they really have in mind protection against investment policy and capital structure shifts as well, since large payouts are more likely to be associated with nontrivial changes in either or both.

It should be noted that calls and puts that satisfy the incipient assumption have in practice been the only options issued with cash dividend protection clauses, and the typical adjustment has been to reduce the exercise price by the amount of the cash dividend which has been demonstrated to be incorrect.[23]

To this point it has been assumed that the exercise price remains constant over the life of the contract (except for the before-mentioned adjustments for payouts). A variable exercise price is meaningless for an European warrant since the contract is not exercisable prior to expiration. However, a number of American warrants do have variable exercise prices as a function of the length of time until expiration. Typically, the exercise price increases as time approaches the expiration date.

Consider the case where there are n changes of the exercise price during the life of an American warrant, represented by the following schedule:

Exercise Price	Time until Expiration (τ)
E_0	$0 \leqq \tau \leqq \tau_1$
E_1	$\tau_1 \leqq \tau \leqq \tau_2$
$\vdots$	$\vdots$
E_n	$\tau_n \leqq \tau,$

where it is assumed that $E_{j+i} < E_j$ for $j = 0, 1, \ldots, n - 1$. If, otherwise the conditions for Theorems 1–11 hold, it is easy to show that, if premature exercising takes place, it will occur only at points in time just prior to an exercise price change, i.e., at $\tau = \tau_j^+$, $j = 1, 2, \ldots, n$. Hence, the American warrant is equivalent to a *modified European warrant* which allows its owner to exercise the warrant at discrete times, just prior to an exercise price change. Given a technique for finding the price of an European warrant, there is a systematic method for valuing a modified European warrant. Namely, solve the standard problem for $F_0(S, \tau; E_0)$ subject to the boundary conditions $F_0(S, 0: E_0) = \text{Max}[0, S - E_0]$ and $\tau \leqq \tau_1$. Then, by the same technique, solve for $F_1(S, \tau; E_1)$ subject to the boundary conditions $F_1(S, \tau_1; E_1) = \text{Max}[0, S - E_1, F_0(S, \tau_1; E_0)]$ and $\tau_1 \leqq \tau \leqq \tau_2$. Proceed inductively by this dynamic-programming-like technique, until the current value of the modified European warrant is determined. Typically, the number of exercise price changes is small, so the technique is computationally feasible.

Often the contract conditions are such that the warrant will never be prematurely exercised, in which case, the correct valuation will be the standard European warrant treatment using the exercise

---

[23] By Taylor series approximation, we can compute the loss to the warrant holder of the standard adjustment for dividends: namely, $F(S - d, \tau; E - d) - F(S, \tau; E) = -dF_S(S, \tau; E) - dF_E(S, \tau; E) + o(d) = -[F(S, \tau; E) - (S - E)F_S(S, \tau; E)](d/E) + o(d)$, by the first-degree homogeneity of F in (S, E). Hence, to a first approximation, for $S = E$, the warrant will lose (d/S) percent of its value by this adjustment. Clearly, for $S > E$, the percentage loss will be smaller and for $S < E$, it will be larger.

price at expiration, E_0. If it can be demonstrated that

$$F_j(S, \tau_{j+1}; E_j) \geqq S - E_{j+1}$$
$$\text{for all } S \geqq 0 \text{ and } j = 0, 1, \ldots, N - 1, \quad (10)$$

then the warrant will always be worth more "alive" than "dead," and the no-premature exercising result will obtain. From Theorem 1, $F_j(S, \tau_{j+1}; E_j) \geqq \text{Max}[0, S - P(\tau_{j+1} - \tau_j)E_j]$. Hence, from (10), a sufficient condition for no early exercising is that

$$E_{j+1}/E_j > P(\tau_{j+1} - \tau_j). \quad (11)$$

The economic reasoning behind (11) is identical to that used to derive Theorem 1. If by continuing to hold the warrant and investing the dollars which would have been paid for the stock if the warrant were exercised, the investor can with certainty earn enough to overcome the increased cost of exercising the warrant later, then the warrant should not be exercised.

Condition (11) is not as simple as it may first appear, because in valuing the warrant today, one must know for certain that (11) will be satisfied at some future date, which in general will not be possible if interest rates are stochastic. Often, as a practical matter, the size of the exercise price change versus the length of time between changes is such that for almost any reasonable rate of interest, (11) will be satisfied. For example, if the increase in exercise price is 10 percent and the length of time before the next exercise price change is five years, the yield to maturity on riskless securities would have to be less than 2 percent before (11) would not hold.

As a footnote to the analysis, we have the following Corollary.

Corollary. If there is a finite number of changes in the exercise price of a payout-protected, perpetual warrant, then it will not be exercised and its price will equal the common stock price.

Proof: applying the previous analysis, consider the value of the warrant if it survives past the last exercise price change, $F_0(S, \infty; E_0)$. By Theorem 3, $F_0(S, \infty; E_0) = S$. Now consider the value just prior to the last change in exercise price, $F_1(S, \infty; E_1)$. It must satisfy the boundary condition,

$$F_1(S, \infty; E_1) = \text{Max}[0, S - E_1, F_0(S, \infty; E_0)]$$
$$= \text{Max}[0, S - E_1, S] = S.$$

Proceeding inductively, the warrant will never be exercised, and by Theorem 3, its value is equal to the common stock. Q.E.D.

The analysis of the effect on unprotected warrants when future dividends or dividend policy is known,[24] follows exactly the analysis of a changing exercise price. The arguments that no one will prematurely exercise his warrant except possibly at the discrete points in time just prior to a dividend payment, go through, and hence, the modified European warrant approach works where now the boundary conditions are $F_j(S, \tau_j; E) = \text{Max}[0, S - E, F_{j-1}(S - d_j, \tau_j; E)]$

---

[24] The distinction is made between knowing future dividends and dividend policy. With the former, one knows, currently, the actual amounts of future payments while, with the latter, one knows the conditional future payments, conditional on (currently unknown) future values, such as the stock price.

where d_j equals the dividend per share paid at τ_j years prior to expiration, for $j = 1, 2, \ldots, n$.

In the special case, where future dividends and rates of interest are known with certainty, a sufficient condition for no premature exercising is that[25]

$$E > \sum_{t=0}^{\tau} d(t)P(\tau - t)/[1 - P(\tau)]. \qquad (12)$$

I.e., the net present value of future dividends is less than the present value of earnings from investing E dollars for τ periods. If dividends are paid continuously at the constant rate of d dollars per unit time and if the interest rate, r, is the same over time, then (12) can be rewritten in its continuous form as

$$E > \frac{d}{r}. \qquad (13)$$

Samuelson suggests the use of discrete recursive relationships, similar to our modified European warrant analysis, as an approximation to the mathematically difficult continuous-time model when there is some chance for premature exercising.[26] We have shown that the only reasons for premature exercising are lack of protection against dividends or sufficiently unfavorable exercise price changes. Further, such exercising will never take place except at boundary points. Since dividends are paid quarterly and exercise price changes are less frequent, the Samuelson recursive formulation with the discrete-time spacing matching the intervals between dividends or exercise price changes is actually the correct one, and the continuous solution is the approximation, even if warrant and stock prices change continuously!

Based on the relatively weak Assumption 1, we have shown that dividends and unfavorable exercise price changes are the only rational reasons for premature exercising, and hence, the only reasons for an American warrant to sell for a premium over its European counterpart. In those cases where early exercising is possible, a computationally feasible, general algorithm for modifying a European warrant valuation scheme has been derived. A number of theorems were proved putting restrictions on the structure of rational European warrant pricing theory.

4. Restrictions on rational put option pricing

■ The put option, defined at the beginning of Section 2, has received relatively little analysis in the literature because it is a less popular option than the call and because it is commonly believed[27] that, given the price of a call option and the common stock, the value of a put is uniquely determined. This belief is false for American put

---

[25] The interpretation of (12) is similar to the explanation given for (11). Namely, if the losses from dividends which are smaller than the gains which can be earned risklessly, from investing the extra funds required to exercise the warrant and hold the stock, then the warrant is worth more "alive" than "dead."

[26] See [42], pp. 25–26, especially equation (42). Samuelson had in mind small, discrete-time intervals, while in the context of the current application, the intervals would be large. Chen [8] also used this recursive relationship in his empirical testing of the Samuelson model.

[27] See, for example, Black and Scholes [4] and Stoll [52].

options, and the mathematics of put options pricing is more difficult than that of the corresponding call option.

Using the notation defined in Section 2, we have that, at expiration,

$$G(S, 0; E) = g(S, 0; E) = \text{Max } [0, E - S]. \qquad (14)$$

To determine the rational European put option price, two portfolio positions are examined. Consider taking a long position in the common stock at S dollars, a long position in a τ-year European put at $g(S, \tau; E)$ dollars, and borrowing $[EP'(\tau)]$ dollars where $P'(\tau)$ is the current value of a dollar payable τ-years from now at the borrowing rate[28] (i.e., $P'(\tau)$ may not equal $P(\tau)$ if the borrowing and lending rates differ). The value of the portfolio τ years from now with the stock price at S^* will be: $S^* + (E - S^*) - E = 0$, if $S^* \leq E$, and $S^* + 0 - E = S^* - E$, if $S^* > E$. The pay-off structure is identical in every state to a European call option with the same exercise price and duration. Hence, to avoid the call option from being a dominated security,[29] the put and call must be priced so that

$$g(S, \tau; E) + S - EP'(\tau) \geq f(S, \tau; E). \qquad (15)$$

As was the case in the similar analysis leading to Theorem 1, the values of the portfolio prior to expiration were not computed because the call option is European and cannot be prematurely exercised.

Consider taking a long position in a τ-year European call, a short position in the common stock at price S, and lending $EP(\tau)$ dollars. The value of the portfolio τ years from now with the stock price at S^* will be: $0 - S^* + E = E - S^*$, if $S^* \leq E$, and $(S^* - E) - S^* + E = 0$, if $S^* > E$. The pay-off structure is identical in every state to a European put option with the same exercise price and duration. If the put is not to be a dominated security,[30] then

$$f(S, \tau; E) - S + EP(\tau) \geq g(S, \tau; E) \qquad (16)$$

must hold.

Theorem 12. If Assumption 1 holds and if the borrowing and lending rates are equal [i.e., $P(\tau) = P'(\tau)$], then

$$g(S, \tau; E) = f(S, \tau; E) - S + EP(\tau).$$

Proof: the proof follows directly from the simultaneous application of (15) and (16) when $P'(\tau) = P(\tau)$. Q.E.D.

Thus, the value of a rationally priced European put option is determined once one has a rational theory of the call option value. The formula derived in Theorem 12 is identical to B-S's equation (26), when the riskless rate, r, is constant (i.e., $P(\tau) = e^{-r\tau}$). Note

---

[28] The borrowing rate is the rate on a τ-year, noncallable, discounted loan. To avoid arbitrage, $P'(\tau) \leq P(\tau)$.

[29] Due to the existent market structure, (15) must hold for the stronger reason of arbitrage. The portfolio did not require short-sales and it is institutionally possible for an investor to issue (sell) call options and reinvest the proceeds from the sale. If (15) did not hold, an investor, acting unilaterally, could make immediate, positive profits with no investment and no risk.

[30] In this case, we do not have the stronger condition of arbitrage discussed in footnote (29) because the portfolio requires a short sale of shares and, under current regulations, the proceeds cannot be reinvested. Again, intermediate values of the portfolio are not examined because the put option is European.

that no distributional assumptions about the stock price or future interest rates were required to prove Theorem 12.

Two corollaries to Theorem 12 follow directly from the above analysis.

Corollary 1. $EP(\tau) \geqq g(S, \tau; E)$.

Proof: from (5) and (7), $f(S, \tau; E) - S \leqq 0$ and from (16), $EP(\tau) \geqq g(S, \tau; E)$. Q.E.D.

The intuition of this result is immediate. Because of limited liability on the common stock, the maximum value of the put option is E, and because the option is European, the proceeds cannot be collected for τ years. The option cannot be worth more than the present value of a sure payment of its maximum value.

Corollary 2. The value of a perpetual ($\tau = \infty$) European put option is zero.

Proof: the put is a limited liability security $[g(S, \tau; E) \geqq 0]$. From Corollary 1 and the condition that $P(\infty) = 0$, $0 \geqq g(S, \infty; E)$. Q.E.D.

Using the relationship $g(S, \tau; E) = f(S, \tau; E) - S + EP(\tau)$, it is straightforward to derive theorems for rational European put pricing which are analogous to the theorems for warrants in Section 2. In particular, whenever f is homogeneous of degree one or convex in S and E, so g will be also. The correct adjustment for stock and cash dividends is the same as prescribed for warrants in Theorem 11 and its Corollary.[31]

Since the American put option can be exercised at any time, its price must satisfy the arbitrage condition

$$G(S, \tau; E) \geqq \text{Max}[0, E - S]. \tag{17}$$

By the same argument used to derive (5), it can be shown that

$$G(S, \tau; E) \geqq g(S, \tau; E), \tag{18}$$

where the strict inequality holds only if there is a positive probability of premature exercising.

As shown in Section 2, the European and American warrant have the same value if the exercise price is constant and they are protected against payouts to the common stock. Even under these assumptions, there is almost always a positive probability of premature exercising of an American put, and hence, the American put will sell for more than its European counterpart. A hint that this must be so comes from Corollary 2 and arbitrage condition (17). Unlike European options, the value of an American option is always a nondecreasing function of its expiration date. If there is no possibility of premature exercising, the value of an American option will equal the value of its European counterpart. By the Corollary to Theorem 11, the value of a perpetual American put would be zero, and by the monotonicity argument on length of time to maturity, all American puts would have zero value.

---

[31] While such adjustments for stock or cash payouts add to the value of a warrant or call option, the put option owner would prefer not to have them since lowering the exercise price on a put decreases its value. For simplicity, the effects of payouts are not considered, and it is assumed that no dividends are paid on the stock, and there are no exercise price changes.

This absurd result clearly violates the arbitrage condition (17) for $S < E$.

To clarify this point, reconsider the two portfolios examined in the European put analysis, but with American puts instead. The first portfolio contained a long position in the common stock at price S, a long position in an American put at price $G(S, \tau; E)$, and borrowings of $[EP'(\tau)]$. As was previously shown, if held until maturity, the outcome of the portfolio will be identical to those of an American (European) warrant held until maturity. Because we are now using American options with the right to exercise prior to expiration, the interim values of the portfolio must be examined as well. If, for all times prior to expiration, the portfolio has value greater than the exercise value of the American warrant, $S - E$, then to avoid dominance of the warrant, the current value of the portfolio must exceed or equal the current value of the warrant.

The interim value of the portfolio at T years until expiration when the stock price is S^*, is

$$S^* + G(S^*, T; E) - EP'(T)$$
$$= G(S^*, T; E) + (S^* - E) + E[1 - P'(T)] > (S^* - E).$$

Hence, condition (15) holds for its American counterparts to avoid dominance of the warrant, i.e.,

$$G(S, \tau; E) + S - EP'(\tau) \geqq F(S, \tau; E). \tag{19}$$

The second portfolio has a long position in an American call at price $F(S, \tau; E)$, a short position in the common stock at price S, and a loan of $[EP(\tau)]$ dollars. If held until maturity, this portfolio replicates the outcome of a European put, and hence, must be at least as valuable at any interim point in time. The interim value of the portfolio, at T years to go and with the stock price at S^*, is

$$F(S^*, T; E) - S^* + EP(T)$$
$$= (E - S^*) + F(S^*, T; E) - E[1 - P(T)] < E - S^*,$$

if $F(S^*, T; E) < E[1 - P(T)]$, which is possible for small enough S^*. From (17), $G(S^*, T; E) \geqq E - S^*$. So, the interim value of the portfolio will be less than the value of an American put for sufficiently small S^*. Hence, if an American put was sold against this portfolio, and if the put owner decided to exercise his put prematurely, the value of the portfolio could be less than the value of the exercised put. This result would certainly obtain if $S^* < E[1 - P(T)]$. So, the portfolio will not dominate the put if inequality (16) does not hold, and an analog theorem to Theorem 12, which uniquely determines the value of an American put in terms of a call, does not exist. Analysis of the second portfolio does lead to the weaker inequality that

$$G(S, \tau; E) \leqq E - S + F(S, \tau; E). \tag{20}$$

Theorem 13. If, for some $T < \tau$, there is a positive probability that $f(S, T; E) < E[1 - P(T)]$, then there is a positive probability that a τ-year, American put option will be exercised prematurely and the value of the American put will strictly exceed the value of its European counterpart.

Proof: the only reason that an American put will sell for a premium over its European counterpart is that there is a positive probability of exercising prior to expiration. Hence, it is sufficient to prove that $g(S, \tau; E) < G(S, \tau; E)$. From Assumption 1, if for some $T \leqq \tau$, $g(S^*, T; E) < G(S^*, T; E)$ for some possible value(s) of S^*, then $g(S, \tau; E) < G(S, \tau; E)$. From Theorem 12, $g(S^*, T; E) = f(S^*, T; E) - S^* + EP(T)$. From (17), $G(S^*, T; E) \geqq \text{Max} [0, E - S^*]$. But $g(S^*, T; E) < G(S^*, T; E)$ is implied if $E - S^* > f(S^*, T; E) - S^* + EP(T)$, which holds if $f(S^*, T; E) < E[1 - P(T)]$. By hypothesis of the theorem, such an S^* is a possible value. Q.E.D.

Since almost always there will be a chance of premature exercising, the formula of Theorem 12 or B-S equation (26) will not lead to a correct valuation of an American put and, as mentioned in Section 3, the valuation of such options is a more difficult analytical task than valuing their European counterparts.

5. Rational option pricing along Black-Scholes lines

■ A number of option pricing theories satisfy the general restrictions on a rational theory as derived in the previous sections. One such theory developed by B-S[32] is particularly attractive because it is a complete general equilibrium formulation of the problem and because the final formula is a function of "observable" variables, making the model subject to direct empirical tests.

B-S assume that: (1) the standard form of the Sharpe-Lintner-Mossin capital asset pricing model holds for intertemporal trading, and that trading takes place continuously in time; (2) the market rate of interest, r, is known and fixed over time; and (3) there are no dividends or exercise price changes over the life of the contract.

To derive the formula, they assume that the option price is a function of the stock price and time to expiration, and note that, over "short" time intervals, the stochastic part of the change in the option price will be perfectly correlated with changes in the stock price. A hedged portfolio containing the common stock, the option, and a short-term, riskless security, is constructed where the portfolio weights are chosen to eliminate all "market risk." By the assumption of the capital asset pricing model, any portfolio with a zero ("beta") market risk must have an expected return equal to the risk-free rate. Hence, an equilibrium condition is established between the expected return on the option, the expected return on the stock, and the riskless rate.

Because of the distributional assumptions and because the option price is a function of the common stock price, B-S in effect make use of the Samuelson[33] application to warrant pricing of the Bachelier-Einstein-Dynkin derivation of the Fokker-Planck equation, to express the expected return on the option in terms of the option price function and its partial derivatives. From the equilibrium condition on the option yield, such a partial differential equation for the option price is derived. The solution to this equation for a European call option is

$$f(S, \tau; E) = S\Phi(d_1) - Ee^{-r\tau}\Phi(d_2), \qquad (21)$$

where Φ is the cumulative normal distribution function, σ^2 is the

---

[32] In [4].
[33] In [42].

instantaneous variance of the return on the common stock,

$$d_1 \equiv [\log (S/E) + (r + \tfrac{1}{2}\sigma^2)\tau]/\sigma\sqrt{\tau},$$

and $d_2 \equiv d_1 - \sigma\sqrt{\tau}$.

An exact formula for an asset price, based on observable variables only, is a rare finding from a general equilibrium model, and care should be taken to analyze the assumptions with Occam's razor to determine which ones are necessary to derive the formula. Some hints are to be found by inspection of their final formula (21) and a comparison with an alternative general equilibrium development.

The manifest characteristic of (21) is the number of variables that it does *not* depend on. The option price does not depend on the expected return on the common stock,[34] risk preferences of investors, or on the aggregate supplies of assets. It does depend on the rate of interest (an "observable") and the *total* variance of the return on the common stock which is often a stable number and hence, accurate estimates are possible from time series data.

The Samuelson and Merton[35] model is a complete, although very simple (three assets and one investor) general equilibrium formulation. Their formula[36] is

$$f(S, \tau; E) = e^{-r\tau} \int_{E/S}^{\infty} (ZS - E)dQ(Z; \tau), \tag{22}$$

where dQ is a probability density function with the expected value of Z over the dQ distribution equal to $e^{r\tau}$. Equations (22) and (21) will be the same only in the special case when dQ is a log-normal density with the variance of $\log (Z)$ equal to $\sigma^2\tau$.[37] However, dQ is a risk-adjusted ("util-prob") distribution, dependent on both risk-preferences and aggregate supplies, while the distribution in (21) is the objective distribution of returns on the common stock. B-S claim that one reason that Samuelson and Merton did not arrive at formula (21) was because they did not consider other assets. If a result does not obtain for a simple, three asset case, it is unlikely that it would in a more general example. More to the point, it is only necessary to consider three assets to derive the B-S formula. In connection with this point, although B-S claim that their central assumption is the capital asset pricing model (emphasizing this over their hedging argument), their final formula, (21), depends only on the interest rate (which is exogenous to the capital asset pricing model) and on the *total* variance of the return on the common stock. It does not depend on the betas (covariances with the market) or other assets' characteristics. Hence, this assumption may be a "red herring."

Although their derivation of (21) is intuitively appealing, such an

---

[34] This is an important result because the expected return is not directly observable and estimates from past data are poor because of nonstationarity. It also implies that attempts to use the option price to estimate expected returns on the stock or risk-preferences of investors are doomed to failure (e.g., see Sprenkle [49]).

[35] In [43].

[36] *Ibid.*, p. 29, equation 30.

[37] This will occur only if: (1) the objective returns on the stock are log-normally distributed; (2) the investor's utility function is iso-elastic (i.e., homothetic indifference curves); and (3) the supplies of *both* options and bonds are at the incipient level.

important result deserves a rigorous derivation. In this case, the rigorous derivation is not only for the satisfaction of the "purist," but also to give insight into the necessary conditions for the formula to obtain. The reader should be alerted that because B-S consider only terminal boundary conditions, their analysis is strictly applicable to European options, although as shown in Sections 2 through 4, the European valuation is often equal to the American one.

Finally, although their model is based on a different economic structure, the formal analytical content is identical to Samuelson's "linear, $\alpha = \beta$" model when the returns on the common stock are log-normal.[38] Hence, with different interpretation of the parameters, theorems proved in Samuelson and in the difficult McKean appendix[39] are directly applicable to the B-S model, and vice versa.

6. An alternative derivation of the Black-Scholes model[40]

■ Initially, we consider the case of a European option where no payouts are made to the common stock over the life of the contract. We make the following further assumptions.

(1) *"Frictionless"* markets: there are no transactions costs or differential taxes. Trading takes place continuously and borrowing and short-selling are allowed without restriction.[41] The borrowing rate equals the lending rate.

(2) *Stock price dynamics:* the instantaneous return on the common stock is described by the stochastic differential equation[42]

$$\frac{dS}{S} = \alpha dt + \sigma dz, \qquad (23)$$

where α is the instantaneous expected return on the common stock, σ^2 is the instantaneous variance of the return, and dz is a standard Gauss-Wiener process. α may be a stochastic variable of quite general type including being dependent on the level of the stock price or other assets' returns. Therefore, no presumption is made that dS/S is an independent increments process or stationary, although dz clearly is. However,

---

[38] In [42]. See Merton [28] for a brief description of the relationship between the Samuelson and B-S models.

[39] In [26].

[40] Although the derivation presented here is based on assumptions and techniques different from the original B-S model, it is in the spirit of their formulation, and yields the same formula when their assumptions are applied.

[41] The assumptions of unrestricted borrowing and short-selling can be weakened and still have the results obtained by splitting the created portfolio of the text into two portfolios: one containing the common stock and the other containing the warrant plus a long position in bonds. Then, as was done in Section 2, if we accept Assumption 1, the formulas of the current section follow immediately.

[42] For a general description of the theory of stochastic differential equations of the Itô type, see McKean [27] and Kushner [24]. For a description of their application to the consumption-portfolio problem, see Merton [32], [33], and [31]. Briefly, Itô processes follow immediately from the assumption of a continuous-time stochastic process which results in continuous price changes (with finite moments) and some level of independent increments. If the process for price changes were functions of stable Paretian distributions with infinite moments, it is conjectured that the only equilibrium value for a warrant would be the stock price itself, independent of the length of time to maturity. This implication is grossly inconsistent with all empirical observations.

σ is restricted to be nonstochastic and, at most, a known function of time.

(3) *Bond price dynamics:* $P(\tau)$ is as defined in previous sections and the dynamics of its returns are described by

$$\frac{dP}{P} = \mu(\tau)dt + \delta(\tau)dq(t; \tau), \tag{24}$$

where μ is the instantaneous expected return, δ^2 is the instantaneous variance, and $dq(t; \tau)$ is a standard Gauss-Wiener process for maturity τ. Allowing for the possibility of habitat and other term structure effects, it is not assumed that dq for one maturity is perfectly correlated with dq for another, i.e.,

$$dq(t; \tau)dq(t; T) = \rho_{\tau T}dt, \tag{24a}$$

where $\rho_{\tau T}$ may be less than one for $\tau \neq T$. However, it is assumed that there is no serial correlation[43] among the (unanticipated) returns on any of the assets, i.e.,

$$dq(s; \tau)dq(t; T) = 0 \quad \text{for} \quad s \neq t$$
$$dq(s; \tau)dz(t) = 0 \quad \text{for} \quad s \neq t, \tag{24b}$$

which is consistent with the general efficient market hypothesis of Fama and Samuelson.[44] $\mu(\tau)$ may be stochastic through dependence on the level of bond prices, etc., and different for different maturities. Because $P(\tau)$ is the price of a discounted loan with no risk of default, $P(0) = 1$ with certainty and $\delta(\tau)$ will definitely depend on τ with $\delta(0) = 0$. However, δ is otherwise assumed to be nonstochastic and independent of the level of P. In the special case when the interest rate is nonstochastic and constant over time, $\delta \equiv 0$, $\mu = r$, and $P(\tau) = e^{-r\tau}$.

(4) *Investor preferences and expectations:* no assumptions are necessary about investor preferences other than that they

---

[43] The reader should be careful to note that it is assumed only that the *unanticipated* returns on the bonds are not serially correlated. Cootner [11] and others have pointed out that since the bond price will equal its redemption price at maturity, the total returns over time cannot be uncorrelated. In no way does this negate the specification of (24), although it does imply that the variance of the unanticipated returns must be a function of time to maturity. An example to illustrate that the two are not inconsistent can be found in Merton [29]. Suppose that bond prices for all maturities are only a function of the current (and future) short-term interest rates. Further, assume that the short-rate, r, follows a Gauss-Wiener process with (possibly) some drift, i.e., $dr = adt + gdz$, where a and g are constants. Although this process is not realistic because it implies a positive probability of negative interest rates, it will still illustrate the point. Suppose that all bonds are priced so as to yield an expected rate of return over the next period equal to r (i.e., a form of the expectations hypothesis):

$$P(\tau; r) = \exp\left[-r\tau - \frac{a}{2}\tau^2 + \frac{g^2\tau^3}{6}\right]$$

and

$$\frac{dP}{P} = rdt - g\tau dz.$$

By construction, dz is not serially correlated and in the notation of (24), $\delta(\tau) = -g\tau$.

[44] In [13] and [41], respectively.

satisfy Assumption 1 of Section 2. All investors agree on the values of σ and δ, and on the distributional characteristics of dz and dq. It is *not* assumed that they agree on either α or μ.[45]

From the analysis in Section 2, it is reasonable to assume that the option price is a function of the stock price, the riskless bond price, and the length of time to expiration. If $H(S, P, \tau; E)$ is the option price function, then, given the distributional assumptions on S and P, we have, by Itô's Lemma,[46] that the change in the option price over time satisfies the stochastic differential equation,

$$dH = H_1 dS + H_2 dP + H_3 d\tau$$
$$+ \tfrac{1}{2}[H_{11}(dS)^2 + 2H_{12}(dSdP) + H_{22}(dP)^2], \quad (25)$$

where subscripts denote partial derivatives, and $(dS)^2 \equiv \sigma^2 S^2 dt$, $(dP)^2 \equiv \delta^2 P^2 dt$, $d\tau = -dt$, and $(dSdP) \equiv \rho\sigma\delta SPdt$ with ρ, the instantaneous correlation coefficient between the (unanticipated) returns on the stock and on the bond. Substituting from (23) and (24) and rearranging terms, we can rewrite (25) as

$$dH = \beta H dt + \gamma H dz + \eta H dq, \quad (26)$$

where the instantaneous expected return on the warrant, β, equals $[\tfrac{1}{2}\sigma^2 S^2 H_{11} + \rho\sigma\delta SPH_{12} + \tfrac{1}{2}\delta^2 P^2 H_{22} + \alpha SH_1 + \mu PH_2 - H_3]/H$, $\gamma \equiv \sigma SH_1/H$, and $\eta \equiv \delta PH_2/H$.

In the spirit of the Black-Scholes formulation and the analysis in Sections 2 thru 4, consider forming a portfolio containing the common stock, the option, and riskless bonds with time to maturity, τ, equal to the expiration date of the option, such that the aggregate investment in the portfolio is zero. This is achieved by using the proceeds of short-sales and borrowing to finance long positions. Let W_1 be the (instantaneous) number of dollars of the portfolio invested in the common stock, W_2 be the number of dollars invested in the option, and W_3 be the number of dollars invested in bonds. Then, the condition of zero aggregate investment can be written as $W_1 + W_2 + W_3 = 0$. If dY is the instantaneous dollar return to the portfolio, it can be shown[47] that

$$dY = W_1 \frac{dS}{S} + W_2 \frac{dH}{H} + W_3 \frac{dP}{P}$$

$$= [W_1(\alpha - \mu) + W_2(\beta - \mu)]dt + [W_1\sigma + W_2\gamma]dz$$
$$+ [W_2\eta - (W_1 + W_2)\delta]dq, \quad (27)$$

where $W_3 \equiv -(W_1 + W_2)$ has been substituted out.

---

[45] This assumption is much more acceptable than the usual homogeneous expectations. It is quite reasonable to expect that investors may have quite different estimates for current (and future) expected returns due to different levels of information, techniques of analysis, etc. However, most analysts calculate estimates of variances and covariances in the same way: namely, by using previous price data. Since all have access to the same price history, it is also reasonable to assume that their variance-covariance estimates may be the same.

[46] Itô's Lemma is the stochastic-analog to the fundamental theorem of the calculus because it states how to differentiate functions of Wiener processes. For a complete description and proof, see McKean [27]. A brief discussion can be found in Merton [33].

[47] See Merton [32] or [33].

Suppose a strategy, $W_j = W_j^*$, can be chosen such that the coefficients of dz and dq in (27) are always zero. Then, the dollar return on that portfolio, dY^*, would be nonstochastic. Since the portfolio requires zero investment, it must be that to avoid "arbitrage"[48] profits, the expected (and realized) return on the portfolio with this strategy is zero. The two portfolio and one equilibrium conditions can be written as a 3×2 linear system,

$$(\alpha - \mu)W_1^* + (\beta - \mu)W_2^* = 0$$
$$\sigma W_1^* + \gamma W_2^* = 0 \tag{28}$$
$$- \delta W_1^* + (\eta - \delta)W_2^* = 0.$$

A nontrivial solution $(W_1^* \neq 0;\ W_2^* \neq 0)$ to (28) exists if and only if

$$\frac{\beta - \mu}{\alpha - \mu} = \frac{\gamma}{\sigma} = \frac{\delta - \eta}{\delta}. \tag{29}$$

Because we make the "bucket shop" assumption, μ, α, δ, and σ are legitimate exogeneous variables (relative to the option price), and β, γ, and η are to be determined so as to avoid dominance of any of the three securities. If (29) holds, then $\gamma/\sigma = 1 - \eta/\delta$, which implies from the definition of γ and in (26), that

$$\frac{SH_1}{H} = 1 - \frac{PH_2}{H} \tag{30}$$

or

$$H = SH_1 + PH_2. \tag{31}$$

Although it is not a sufficient condition, by Euler's theorem, (31) is a necessary condition for H to be first degree homogeneous in (S, P) as was conjectured in Section 2.

The second condition from (29) is that $\beta - \mu = \gamma(\alpha - \mu)/\sigma$, which implies from the definition of β and γ in (26) that

$$\tfrac{1}{2}\sigma^2 S^2 H_{11} + \rho\sigma\delta SPH_{12} + \tfrac{1}{2}\delta^2 P^2 H_{22}$$
$$+ \alpha SH_1 + \mu PH_2 - H_3 - \mu H = SH_1(\alpha - \mu), \tag{32}$$

or, by combining terms, that

$$\tfrac{1}{2}\sigma^2 S^2 H_{11} + \rho\sigma\delta SPH_{12} + \tfrac{1}{2}\delta^2 P^2 H_{22} + \mu SH_1$$
$$+ \mu PH_2 - H_3 - \mu H = 0. \tag{33}$$

Substituting for H from (31) and combining terms, (33) can be rewritten as

$$\tfrac{1}{2}[\sigma^2 S^2 H_{11} + 2\rho\sigma\delta SPH_{12} + \delta^2 P^2 H_{22}] - H_3 = 0, \tag{34}$$

which is a second-order, linear partial differential equation of the parabolic type.

---

[48] "Arbitrage" is used in the qualified sense that the distributional and other assumptions are known to hold with certainty. A weaker form would say that if the return on the portfolio is nonzero, either the option or the common stock would be a dominated security. See Samuelson [44] or [45] for a discussion of this distinction.

If H is the price of a European warrant, then H must satisfy (34) subject to the boundary conditions:

$$H(0, P, \tau; E) = 0 \qquad (34a)$$

$$H(S, 1, 0; E) = \text{Max}[0, S - E], \qquad (34b)$$

since by construction, $P(0) = 1$.

Define the variable $x \equiv S/EP(\tau)$, which is the price per share of stock in units of exercise price-dollars payable at a *fixed date* in the future (the expiration date of the warrant). The variable x is a well-defined price for $\tau \geq 0$, and from (23), (24), and Itô's Lemma, the dynamics of x are described by the stochastic differential equation,

$$\frac{dx}{x} = [\alpha - \mu + \delta^2 - \rho\sigma\delta]dt + \sigma dz - \delta dq. \qquad (35)$$

From (35), the expected return on x will be a function of S, P, etc., through α and μ, but the instantaneous variance of the return on x, $V^2(\tau)$, is equal to $\sigma^2 + \delta^2 - 2\rho\sigma\delta$, and will depend only on τ.

Motivated by the possible homogeneity properties of H, we try the change in variables, $h(x, \tau; E) \equiv H(S, P, \tau; E)/EP$ where h is assumed to be independent of P and is the warrant price evaluated in the same units as x. Substituting (h, x) for (H, S) in (34), (34a) and (34b), leads to the partial differential equation for h,

$$\tfrac{1}{2}V^2x^2h_{11} - h_2 = 0, \qquad (36)$$

subject to the boundary conditions, $h(0, \tau; E) = 0$, and $h(x, 0; E) = \text{Max}[0, x - 1]$. From inspection of (36) and its boundary conditions, h is only a function of x and τ, since V^2 is only a function of τ. Hence, the assumed homogeneity property of H is verified. Further, h does not depend on E, and so, H is actually homogeneous of degree one in $[S, EP(\tau)]$.

Consider a new time variable, $T \equiv \int_0^\tau V^2(s)ds$. Then, if we define $y(x, T) \equiv h(x, \tau)$ and substitute into (36), y must satisfy

$$\tfrac{1}{2}x^2y_{11} - y_2 = 0, \qquad (37)$$

subject to the boundary conditions, $y(0, T) = 0$ and $y(x, 0) = \text{Max}[0, x - 1]$. Suppose we wrote the warrant price in its "full functional form," $H(S, P, \tau; E, \sigma^2, \delta^2, \rho)$. Then,

$$y = H(x, 1, T; 1, 1, 0, 0),$$

and is the price of a warrant with T years to expiration and exercise price of one dollar, on a stock with unit instantaneous variance of return, when the market rate of interest is zero over the life of the contract.

Once we solve (37) for the price of this "standard" warrant, we have, by a change of variables, the price for any European warrant. Namely,

$$H(S, P, \tau; E) = EP(\tau)y\left[S/EP(\tau), \int_0^\tau V^2(s)ds\right]. \qquad (38)$$

Hence, for empirical testing or applications, one need only compute tables for the "standard" warrant price as a function of two variables, stock price and time to expiration, to be able to compute warrant prices in general.

To solve (37), we first put it in standard form by the change in variables $Z \equiv \log(x) + T/2$ and $\phi(Z, T) \equiv y(x, T)/x$, and then substitute in (37) to arrive at

$$0 = \tfrac{1}{2}\phi_{11} - \phi_2, \qquad (39)$$

subject to the boundary conditions: $|\phi(Z, T)| \leq 1$ and $\phi(Z, 0) = \text{Max}[0, 1 - e^{-Z}]$. Equation (39) is a standard free-boundary problem to be solved by separation of variables or Fourier transforms.[49] Its solution is

$$y(x, T) = x\phi(Z, T) = [x\, erfc(h_1) - erfc(h_2)]/2, \qquad (40)$$

where $erfc$ is the error complement function which is tabulated, $h_1 \equiv -[\log x + \tfrac{1}{2}T]/\sqrt{2T}$, and $h_2 \equiv -[\log x - \tfrac{1}{2}T]/\sqrt{2T}$. Equation (40) is identical to (21) with $r = 0$, $\sigma^2 = 1$, and $E = 1$. Hence, (38) will be identical to (21) the B-S formula, in the special case of a non-stochastic and constant interest rate (i.e., $\delta = 0$, $\mu = r$, $P = e^{-r\tau}$, and $T \equiv \sigma^2\tau$).

Equation (37) corresponds exactly to Samuelson's equation[50] for the warrant price in his "linear" model when the stock price is log-normally distributed, with his parameters $\alpha = \beta = 0$, and $\sigma^0 = 1$. Hence, tables generated from (40) could be used with (38) for valuations of the Samuelson formula where $e^{-\alpha\tau}$ is substituted for $P(\tau)$ in (38).[51] Since α in his theory is the expected rate of return on a risky security, one would expect that $e^{-\alpha\tau} < P(\tau)$. As a consequence of the following theorem, $e^{-\alpha\tau} < P(\tau)$ would imply that Samuelson's forecasted values for the warrants would be higher than those forecasted by B-S or the model presented here.

Theorem 14. For a given stock price, the warrant price is a nonincreasing function of $P(\tau)$, and hence, a nondecreasing function of the τ-year interest rate.

Proof: it follows immediately, since an increase in P is equivalent to an increase in E which never increases the value of the warrant. Formally, H is a convex function of S and passes through the origin. Hence, $H - SH_1 \leq 0$. But from (31), $H - SH_1 - PH_2$, and since $P \geq 0$, $H_2 \leq 0$. By definition, $P(\tau)$ is a decreasing function of the τ-year interest rate. Q.E.D.

Because we applied only the terminal boundary condition to (34), the price function derived is for an European warrant. The correct boundary conditions for an American warrant would also include the arbitrage-boundary inequality

$$H(S, P, \tau; E) \geq \text{Max}[0, S - E]. \qquad (34c)$$

Since it was assumed that no dividend payments or exercise price changes occur over the life of the contract, we know from Theorem 1, that if the formulation of this section is a "rational" theory, then

---

[49] For a separation of variables solution, see Churchill [9], pp. 154–156, and for the transform technique, see Dettman [12], p. 390. Also see McKean [26].

[50] In [42], p. 27.

[51] The tables could also be used to evaluate warrants priced by the Sprenkle [49] formula. Warning: while the Samuelson interpretation of the "$\beta = \alpha$" case implies that expected returns are equated on the warrant and the stock, the B-S interpretation does not. Namely, from [29], the expected return on the warrant satisfies $\beta = r + H_1 S(\alpha - r)/H$, where H_1 can be computed from (21) by differentiation.

it will satisfy the stronger inequality $H \geq$ Max$[0, S - EP(\tau)]$ [which is homogeneous in S and $EP(\tau)$], and the American warrant will have the same value as its European counterpart. Samuelson argued that solutions to equations like (21) and (38) will always have values at least as large, as Max$[0, S - E]$, and Samuelson and Merton[52] proved it under more general conditions. Hence, there is no need for formal verification here. Further, it can be shown that (38) satisfies all the theorems of Section 2.

As a direct result of the equal values of the European and American warrants, we have:

Theorem 15. The warrant price is a nondecreasing function of the variance of the stock price return.

Proof: from (38), the change in H with respect to a change in variance will be proportional to y_2. But, y is the price of a legitimate American warrant and hence, must be a nondecreasing function of time to expiration, i.e., $y_2 \geq 0$. Q.E.D.

Actually, Theorem 15 is a special case of the general proposition (Theorem 8) proved in Section 2, that the more risky is the stock, the more valuable is the warrant. Although Rothschild and Stiglitz[53] have shown that, in general, increasing variance may not imply increasing risk, it is shown in Appendix 2 that variance is a valid measure of risk for this model.

We have derived the B-S warrant pricing formula rigorously under assumptions weaker than they postulate, and have extended the analysis to include the possibility of stochastic interest rates. Because the original B-S derivation assumed constant interest rates in forming their hedge positions, it did not matter whether they borrowed or lent long or short maturities. The derivation here clearly demonstrates that the correct maturity to use in the hedge is the one which matches the maturity date of the option. "Correct" is used in the sense that if the price $P(\tau)$ remains fixed while the price of other maturities changes, the price of a τ-year option will remain unchanged.

The capital asset pricing model is a sufficient assumption to derive the formula. While the assumptions of this section are necessary for the intertemporal use of the capital asset pricing model,[54] they are not sufficient, e.g., we do not assume that interest rates are nonstochastic, that price dynamics are stationary, nor that investors have homogeneous expectations. All are required for the capital asset pricing model. Further, since we consider only the properties of three securities, we do not assume that the capital market is in full general equilibrium. Since the final formula is independent of α or μ, it will hold even if the observed stock or bond prices are transient, nonequilibrium prices.

The key to the derivation is that any one of the securities' returns over time can be perfectly replicated by continuous portfolio combinations of the other two. A complete analysis would require that

---

[52] In [42] and [43], respectively.

[53] In [39].

[54] See Merton [31] for a discussion of necessary and sufficient conditions for a Sharpe-Lintner-Mossin type model to obtain in an intertemporal context. The sufficient conditions are rather restrictive.

all three securities' prices be solved for simultaneously which, in general, would require the examination of all other assets, knowledge of preferences, etc. However, because of "perfect substitutability" of the securities and the "bucket shop" assumption, supply effects can be neglected, and we can apply "partial equilibrium" analysis resulting in a "causal-type" formula for the option price as a function of the stock and bond prices.

This "perfect substitutability" of the common stock and borrowing for the warrant or the warrant and lending for the common stock explains why the formula is independent of the expected return on the common stock or preferences. The expected return on the stock and the investor's preferences will determine how much capital to invest (long or short) in a given company. The decision as to whether to take the position by buying warrants or by leveraging the stock depends only on their relative prices and the cost of borrowing. As B-S point out, the argument is similar to an intertemporal Modigliani-Miller theorem. The reason that the B-S assumption of the capital asset pricing model leads to the correct formula is that because it is an equilibrium model, it must necessarily rule out "sure-thing" profits among perfectly correlated securities, which is exactly condition (29). Careful study of both their derivations shows that (29) is the only part of the capital asset pricing model ever used.

The assumptions of this section are necessary for (38) and (40) to hold.[55] The continuous-trading assumption is necessary to establish perfect correlation among nonlinear functions which is required to form the "perfect hedge" portfolio mix. The Samuelson and Merton model[56] is an immediate counter-example to the validity of the formula for discrete-trading intervals.

The assumption of Itô processes for the assets' returns dynamics was necessary to apply Itô's Lemma. The further restriction that σ and δ be nonstochastic and independent of the price levels is required so that the option price change is due only to changes in the stock or bond prices, which was necessary to establish a perfect hedge and to establish the homogeneity property (31).[57] Clearly if investors did not agree on the value of $V^2(\tau)$, they would arrive at different values for the same warrant.

The B-S claim that (21) or (38) is the only formula consistent with capital market equilibrium is a bit too strong. It is not true that if the market prices options differently, then arbitrage profits are ensured. It is a "rational" option pricing theory relative to the assumptions of this section. If these assumptions held with certainty, then the B-S formula is the only one which all investors could agree on, and no deviant member could prove them wrong.[58]

---

[55] If most of the "frictionless" market assumptions are dropped, it may be possible to show that, by substituting current institutional conditions, (38) and (40) will give lower bounds for the warrant's value.

[56] In [43].

[57] In the special case when interest rates are nonstochastic, the variance of the stock price return can be a function of the price level and the derivation still goes through. However, the resulting partial differential equation will not have a simple closed-form solution.

[58] This point is emphasized in a critique of Thorp and Kassouf's [53] "sure-thing" arbitrage techniques by Samuelson [45] and again, in Samuelson [44], footnote 6.

7. Extension of the model to include dividend payments and exercise price changes

■ To analyze the effect of dividends on unprotected warrants, it is helpful to assume a constant and known interest rate r. Under this assumption, $\delta = 0$, $\mu = r$, and $P(\tau) = e^{-r\tau}$. Condition (29) simplifies to

$$\beta - r = \gamma(\alpha - r)/\sigma. \qquad (41)$$

Let $D(S, \tau)$ be the dividend per share unit time when the stock price is S and the warrant has τ years to expiration. If α is the instantaneous, *total* expected return as defined in (23), then the instantaneous expected return from price appreciation is $[\alpha - D(S, \tau)/S]$. Because $P(\tau)$ is no longer stochastic, we suppress it and write the warrant price function as $W(S, \tau; E)$. As was done in (25) and (26), we apply Itô's Lemma to derive the stochastic differential equation for the warrant price to be

$$dW = W_1(dS - D(S, \tau)dt) + W_2 d\tau + \tfrac{1}{2}W_{11}(dS)^2$$
$$= [\tfrac{1}{2}\sigma^2 S^2 W_{11} + (\alpha S - D)W_1 - W_2]dt + \sigma S W_1 dz. \qquad (42)$$

Note: since the warrant owner is not entitled to any part of the dividend return, he only considers that part of the expected dollar return to the common stock due to price appreciation. From (42) and the definition of β and γ, we have that

$$\beta W = \tfrac{1}{2}\sigma^2 S^2 W_{11} + (\alpha S - D)W_1 - W_2$$
$$\gamma W = \sigma S W_1. \qquad (43)$$

Applying (41) to (43), we arrive at the partial differential equation for the warrant price,

$$\tfrac{1}{2}\sigma^2 S^2 W_{11} + (rS - D)W_1 - W_2 - rW = 0, \qquad (44)$$

subject to the boundary conditions, $W(0, \tau; E) = 0$, $W(S, 0; E) = \text{Max}[0, S - E]$ for a European warrant, and to the additional arbitrage boundary condition, $W(S, \tau; E) \geq \text{Max}[0, S - E]$ for an American warrant.

Equation (44) will not have a simple solution, even for the European warrant and relatively simple functional forms for D. In evaluating the American warrant in the "no-dividend" case ($D = 0$), the arbitrage boundary inequalities were not considered explicitly in arriving at a solution, because it was shown that the European warrant price never violated the inequality, and the American and European warrant prices were equal. For many dividend policies, the solution for the European warrant price will violate the inequality, and for those policies, there will be a positive probability of premature exercising of the American warrant. Hence, to obtain a correct value for the American warrant from (44), we must explicitly consider the boundary inequality, and transform it into a suitable form for solution.

If there exists a positive probability of premature exercising, then, for every τ, there exists a level of stock price, $C[\tau]$, such that for all $S > C[\tau]$, the warrant would be worth more exercised than if held. Since the value of an exercised warrant is always $(S - E)$, we have the appended boundary condition for (44),

$$W(C[\tau], \tau; E) = C[\tau] - E, \qquad (44a)$$

where W satisfies (44) for $0 \leq S \leq C[\tau]$.

If $C[\tau]$ were a known function, then, after the appropriate change of variables, (44) with the European boundary conditions and (44a) appended, would be a semiinfinite boundary value problem with a time-dependent boundary. However, $C[\tau]$ is not known, and must be determined as part of the solution. Therefore, an additional boundary condition is required for the problem to be well-posed.

Fortunately, the economics of the problem are sufficiently rich to provide this extra condition. Because the warrant holder is not contractually obliged to exercise his warrant prematurely, he chooses to do so only in his own best interest (i.e., when the warrant is worth more "dead" than "alive"). Hence, the only rational choice for $C[\tau]$ is that time-pattern which maximizes the value of the warrant. Let $f(S, \tau; E, C[\tau])$ be a solution to (44)–(44a) for a given $C[\tau]$ function. Then, the value of a τ-year American warrant will be

$$W(S, \tau; E) = \underset{\{c\}}{\text{Max}} f(S, \tau; E, C). \qquad (45)$$

Further, the structure of the problem makes it clear that the optimal $C[\tau]$ will be independent of the current level of the stock price. In attacking this difficult problem, Samuelson[59] postulated that the extra condition was "high-contact" at the boundary, i.e.,

$$W_1(C[\tau], \tau; E) = 1. \qquad (44b)$$

It can be shown[60] that (44b) is implied by the maximizing behavior described by (45). So the correct specification for the American warrant price is (44) with the European boundary conditions plus (44a) and (44b).

Samuelson and Samuelson and Merton[61] have shown that for a proportional dividend policy where $D(S, \tau) = \rho S, \rho > 0$, there is always a positive probability of premature exercising, and hence, the arbitrage boundary condition will be binding for sufficiently large stock prices.[62] With $D = \rho S$, (44) is mathematically identical to Samuelson's[63] "nonlinear" ("$\beta > \alpha$") case where his $\beta = r$ and his $\alpha = r - \rho$. Samuelson and McKean[64] analyze this problem in great detail. Although there are no simple closed-form solutions for finite-lived warrants, they did derive solutions for perpetual warrants which are power functions, tangent to the "$S - E$" line at finite values of S.[65]

---

[59] In [42].

[60] Let $f(x, c)$ be a differentiable function, concave in its second argument, for $0 \leq x \leq c$. Require that $f(c, c) = h(c)$, a differentiable function of c. Let $c = c^*$ be the c which maximizes f, i.e.,

$$f_2(x, c^*) = 0,$$

where subscripts denote partial derivatives. Consider the total derivative of f with respect to c along the boundary $x = c$. Then,

$$df/dc = dh/dc = f_1(c, c) + f_2(c, c).$$

For $c = c^*, f_2 = 0$. Hence, $f_1(c^*, c^*) = dh/dc$. In the case of the text, $h = c - E$, and the "high-contact" solution, $f_1(c^*, c^*) = 1$, is proved.

[61] In [42] and [43], respectively.

[62] For $D = \rho S$, the solution to (44) for the European warrant is

$$W = [e^{-\rho\tau}S\Phi(d_1) - Ee^{-r\tau}\Phi(d_2)]$$

where Φ, d_1, and d_2 are as defined in (21). For large S,

$$W \sim [e^{-\rho\tau}S - Ee^{-r\tau}]$$

which will be less than $(S - E)$ for large S and $\rho > 0$. Hence, the American warrant can be worth more "dead" than "alive."

[63] In [42].

[64] *Ibid.* In the appendix.

[65] *Ibid.*, p. 28.

A second example of a simple dividend policy is the constant one where $D = d$, a constant. Unlike the previous proportional policy, premature exercising may or may not occur, depending upon the values for d, r, E, and τ. In particular, a sufficient condition for no premature exercising was derived in Section 3. Namely,

$$E > \frac{d}{r}. \tag{13}$$

If (13) obtains, then the solution for the European warrant price will be the solution for the American warrant. Although a closed-form solution has not yet been found for finite τ, a solution for the perpetual warrant when $E > d/r$, is[66]

$$W(S, \infty; E)$$

$$= S - \frac{d}{r} \left[1 - \frac{\left(\dfrac{2d}{\sigma^2 S} \right)^{2r/\sigma^2}}{\Gamma \left(2 + \dfrac{2r}{\sigma^2} \right)} M \left(\frac{2r}{\sigma^2}, 2 + \frac{2r}{\sigma^2}, \frac{-2d}{\sigma^2 S} \right) \right] \tag{46}$$

where M is the confluent hypergeometric function, and W is plotted in Figure 2.

FIGURE 2

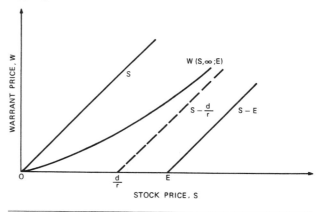

WARRANT PRICE, W

STOCK PRICE, S

[66] Make the change in variables: $Z \equiv \delta/S$ and

$$h(Z) \equiv \exp[Z]Z^{-\gamma}W$$

where

$$\delta \equiv 2d/\sigma^2$$

and

$$\gamma \equiv 2r/\sigma^2.$$

Then, substituting in (44), we have the differential equation for h:

$$Zh'' + (\gamma + 2 - Z)h' - 2h = 0,$$

whose general solution is $h = c_1 M(2, 2 + \gamma, Z) + c_2 Z^{-(\gamma+1)} M(1 - \gamma, -\gamma, Z)$ which becomes (46) when the boundary conditions are applied. Analysis of (46) shows that W passes through the origin, is convex, and is asymptotic to the line $(S - d/r)$ for large S, i.e., it approaches the common stock value less the present discounted value of all future dividends forgone by holding the warrant.

Consider the case of a continuously changing exercise price, $E(\tau)$, where E is assumed to be differentiable and a decreasing function of the length of time to maturity, i.e., $dE/d\tau = -dE/dt = -\dot{E} < 0$. The warrant price will satisfy (44) with $D = 0$, but subject to the boundary conditions,

$$W[S, 0; E(0)] = \text{Max}[0, S - E(0)]$$

and

$$W[S, \tau; E(\tau)] \geqq \text{Max}[0, S - E(\tau)].$$

Make the change in variables $X \equiv S/E(\tau)$ and

$$F(X, \tau) \equiv W[S, \tau; E(\tau)]/E(\tau).$$

Then, F satisfies

$$\tfrac{1}{2}\sigma^2 X^2 F_{11} + \eta(\tau) X F_1 - \eta(\tau) F - F_2 = 0, \qquad (47)$$

subject to $F(X, 0) = \text{Max}[0, X - 1]$ and $F(X, \tau) \geqq \text{Max}[0, X - 1]$ where $\eta(\tau) \equiv r - \dot{E}/E$. Notice that the structure of (47) is identical to the pricing of a warrant with a fixed exercise price and a variable, but nonstochastic, "interest rate" $\eta(\tau)$. (I.e., substitute in the analysis of the previous section for $P(\tau)$, $\exp[-\int_0^\tau \eta(s)ds]$, except $\eta(\cdot)$ can be negative for sufficiently large changes in exercise price.) We have already shown that for $\int_0^\tau \eta(s)ds \geqq 0$, there will be no premature exercising of the warrant, and only the terminal exercise price should matter. Noting that $\int_0^\tau \eta(s)ds = \int_0^\tau [r + dE/d\tau]ds = r\tau + \log[E(\tau)/E(0)]$, formal substitution for $P(\tau)$ in (38) verifies that the value of the warrant is the same as for a warrant with a fixed exercise price, $E(0)$, and interest rate r. We also have agreement of the current model with (11) of Section 3, because $\int_0^\tau \eta(s)ds \geqq 0$ implies $E(\tau) \geqq E(0) \exp[-r\tau]$, which is a general sufficient condition for no premature exercising.

■ As the first example of an application of the model to other types of options, we now consider the rational pricing of the put option, relative to the assumptions in Section 7. In Section 4, it was demonstrated that the value of an European put option was completely determined once the value of the call option is known (Theorem 12). B-S give the solution for their model in equation (26). It was also demonstrated in Section 4 that the European valuation is not valid for the American put option because of the positive probability of premature exercising. If $G(S, \tau; E)$ is the rational put price, then, by the same technique used to derive (44) with $D = 0$, G satisfies

$$\tfrac{1}{2}\sigma^2 S^2 G_{11} + rSG_1 - rG - G_2 = 0, \qquad (48)$$

subject to $G(\infty, \tau; E) = 0$, $G(S, 0; E) = \text{Max}[0, E - S]$, and $G(S, \tau; E) \geqq \text{Max}[0, E - S]$.

From the analysis by Samuelson and McKean[67] on warrants, there is no closed-form solution to (48) for finite τ. However, using their techniques, it is possible to obtain a solution for the perpetual put option (i.e., $\tau = \infty$). For a sufficiently low stock price, it will be advantageous to exercise the put. Define C to be the largest value of the stock such that the put holder is better off exercising than continuing to hold it. For the perpetual put, (48) reduces to the ordinary

8. Valuing an American put option

[67] In [42].

differential equation,

$$\tfrac{1}{2}\sigma^2 S^2 G_{11} + rSG_1 - rG = 0, \qquad (49)$$

which is valid for the range of stock prices $C \leqq S \leqq \infty$. The boundary conditions for (49) are:

$$G(\infty, \infty; E) = 0, \qquad (49a)$$

$$G(C, \infty; E) = E - C, \text{ and} \qquad (49b)$$

choose C so as to maximize the value of the option, which follows from the maximizing behavior arguments of the previous section. $\qquad (49c)$

From the theory of linear ordinary differential equations, solutions to (49) involve two constants, a_1 and a_2. Boundary conditions (49a), (49b), and (49c) will determine these constants along with the unknown lower-bound, stock price, C. The general solution to (49) is

$$G(S, \infty; E) = a_1 S + a_2 S^{-\gamma}, \qquad (50)$$

where $\gamma \equiv 2r/\sigma^2 > 0$. Equation (49a) requires that $a_1 = 0$, and (49b) requires that $a_2 = (E - C)C^\gamma$. Hence, as a function of C,

$$G(S, \infty; E) = (E - C)(S/C)^{-\gamma}. \qquad (51)$$

To determine C, we apply (49c) and choose that value of C which maximizes (51), i.e., choose $C = C^*$ such that $\partial G/\partial C = 0$. Solving this condition, we have that $C^* = \gamma E/(1 + \gamma)$, and the put option price is,

$$G(S, \infty; E) = \frac{E}{(1 + \gamma)} [(1 + \gamma)S/\gamma E]^{-\gamma}. \qquad (52)$$

The Samuelson "high-contact" boundary condition

$$G_1(C^*, \infty; E) = -1,$$

as an alternative specification of boundary condition (49c), can be verified by differentiating (52) with respect to S and evaluating at $S = C^*$. Figure 3 illustrates the American put price as a function of the stock price and time to expiration.

FIGURE 3

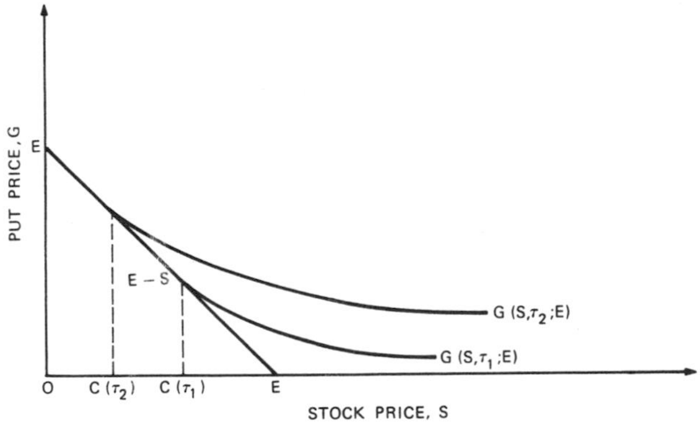

■ As a second example of the application of the model to other types of options, we consider the rational pricing of a new type of call option called the "down-and-outer."[68] This option has the same terms with respect to exercise price, antidilution clauses, etc., as the standard call option, but with the additional feature that if the stock price falls below a stated level, the option contract is nullified, i.e., the option becomes worthless.[69] Typically, the "knock-out" price is a function of the time to expiration, increasing as the expiration date nears.

Let $f(S, \tau; E)$ be the value of an European "down-and-out" call option, and $B[\tau] = bE \exp[-\eta\tau]$ be the "knock-out" price as a function of time to expiration where it is assumed that $\eta \geq 0$ and $0 \leq b \leq 1$. Then f will satisfy the fundamental partial differential equation,

$$\tfrac{1}{2}\sigma^2 S^2 f_{11} + rSf_1 - rf - f_2 = 0, \qquad (53)$$

subject to the boundary conditions,

$$f(B[\tau], \tau; E) = 0$$
$$f(S, 0; E) = \text{Max}[0, S - E].$$

Note: if $B(\tau) = 0$, then (53) would be the equation for a standard European call option.

Make the change in variables, $x \equiv \log[S/B(\tau)]$; $T \equiv \sigma^2 r$;

$$H(x, T) \equiv \exp[ax + \gamma\tau]f(S, \tau; E)/E,$$

and $a \equiv [r - \eta - \sigma^2/2]/\sigma^2$ and $\gamma = r + a^2\sigma^2/2$. Then, by substituting into (53), we arrive at the equation for H,

$$\tfrac{1}{2}H_{11} - H_2 = 0 \qquad (54)$$

subject to

$$H(0, T) = 0$$
$$H(x, 0) = e^{ax}\,\text{Max}[0, be^x - 1],$$

which is a standard, semiinfinite boundary value problem to be solved by separation of variables or Fourier transforms.[70]

Solving (54) and substituting back, we arrive at the solution for the "down-and-out" option,

$$f(S, \tau; E) = [S\,erfc(h_1) - Ee^{-rr}\,erfc(h_2)]/2$$
$$- (S/B[\tau])^{-\delta}[B[\tau]\,erfc(h_3) - (S/B[\tau])\,Ee^{-rr}\,erfc(h_4)]/2, \quad (55)$$

---

[68] See Snyder [48] for a complete description. A number of Wall Street houses are beginning to deal in this option. See *Fortune*, November, 1971, p. 213.

[69] In some versions of the "down-and-outer," the option owner receives a positive rebate, $R(\tau)$, if the stock price hits the "knock-out" price. Typically, $R(\tau)$ is an increasing function of the time until expiration [i.e., $R'(\tau) > 0$] with $R(0) = 0$. Let $g(S, \tau)$ satisfy (53) for $B(\tau) \leq S < \infty$, subject to the boundary conditions (a) $g(B[\tau], \tau) = R(\tau)$ and (b) $g(S, 0) = 0$. Then, $F(S, \tau; E) \equiv g(S, \tau) + f(S, \tau; E)$ will satisfy (53) subject to the boundary conditions (a) $F(B[\tau], \tau; E) = R(\tau)$ and (b) $F(S, 0; E) = \text{Max}[0, S - E]$. Hence, F is the value of a "down-and-out" call option with rebate payments $R(\tau)$, and $g(S, \tau)$ is the additional value for the rebate feature. See Dettman [12], p. 391, for a transform solution for $g(S, \tau)$.

[70] See Churchill [9], p. 152, for a separation of variables solution and Dettman [12], p. 391, for a transform solution.

where

$$h_1 \equiv - \left[\log (S/E) + (r + \sigma^2/2)\tau \right] / \sqrt{2\sigma^2\tau},$$
$$h_2 \equiv - \left[\log (S/E) + (r - \sigma^2/2)\tau \right] / \sqrt{2\sigma^2\tau},$$
$$h_3 \equiv - \left[2 \log (B[\tau]/E) - \log (S/E) + (r + \sigma^2/2)\tau \right] / \sqrt{2\sigma^2\tau},$$
$$h_4 \equiv - \left[2 \log (B[\tau]/E) - \log (S/E) + (r - \sigma^2/2)\tau \right] / \sqrt{2\sigma^2\tau},$$

and $\delta \equiv 2(r - \eta)/\sigma^2$. Inspection of (55) and (21) reveals that the first bracketed set of terms in (55) is the value of a standard call option, and hence, the second bracket is the "discount" due to the "down-and-out" feature.

To gain a better perspective on the qualitative differences between the standard call option and the "down-and-outer," it is useful to go to the limit of a perpetual option where the "knock-out" price is constant (i.e., $\eta = 0$). In this case, (53) reduces to the ordinary differential equation

$$\tfrac{1}{2}\sigma^2 S^2 f'' + rSf' - rf = 0 \tag{56}$$

subject to

$$f(bE) = 0 \tag{56a}$$

$$f(S) \leqq S, \tag{56b}$$

where primes denote derivatives and $f(S)$ is short for $f(S, \infty; E)$. By standard methods, we solve (56) to obtain

$$f(S) = S - bE(S/bE)^{-\gamma}, \tag{57}$$

where $\gamma \equiv 2r/\sigma^2$. Remembering that the value of a standard perpetual call option equals the value of the stock, we may interpret $bE(S/bE)^{-\gamma}$ as the "discount" for the "down-and-out" feature. Both (55) and (57) are homogeneous of degree one in (S, E) as are the standard options. Further, it is easy to show that $f(S) \geqq \text{Max } [0, S - E]$, and although a tedious exercise, it also can be shown that $f(S, \tau; E) \geqq \text{Max } [0, S - E]$. Hence, the option is worth more "alive" than "dead," and therefore, (55) and (57) are the correct valuation functions for the American "down-and-outer."

From (57), the elasticity of the option price with respect to the stock price $[Sf'(S)/f(S)]$ is greater than one, and so it is a "levered" security. However, unlike the standard call option, it is a concave function of the stock price, as illustrated in Figure 4.

FIGURE 4

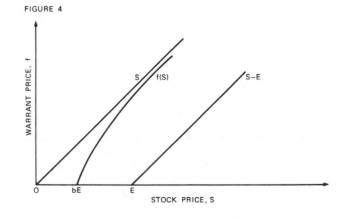

■ As our third and last example of an application of the model to other types of options, we consider the rational pricing of a callable American warrant. Although warrants are rarely issued as callable, this is an important example because the analysis is readily carried over to the valuation of other types of securities such as convertible bonds which are almost always issued as callable.

We assume the standard conditions for an American warrant except that the issuing company has the right to ("call") buy back the warrant at any time for a fixed price. Because the warrant is of the American type, in the event of a call, the warrant holder has the option of exercising his warrant rather than selling it back to the company at the call price. If this occurs, it is called "forced conversion," because the warrant holder is "forced" to exercise, if the value of the warrant exercised exceeds the call price.

The value of a callable warrant will be equal to the value of an equivalent noncallable warrant less some "discount." This discount will be the value of the call provision to the company. One can think of the callable warrant as the resultant of two transactions: the company sells a noncallable warrant to an investor and simultaneously, purchases from the investor an option to either "force" earlier conversion or to retire the issue at a fixed price.

Let $F(S, \tau; E)$ be the value of a callable American warrant; $H(S, \tau; E)$ the value of an equivalent noncallable warrant as obtained from equation (21), $C(S, \tau; E)$ the value of the call provision. Then $H = F + C$. F will satisfy the fundamental partial differential equation,

$$\tfrac{1}{2}\sigma^2 S^2 F_{11} + rSF_1 - rF - F_2 = 0 \qquad (58)$$

for $0 \leq S \leq \overline{S}$ and subject to

$$F(0, \tau; E) = 0,$$
$$F(S, 0; E) = \text{Max}[0, S - E]$$
$$F(\overline{S}, \tau; E) = \text{Max}[K, \overline{S} - E],$$

where K is the call price and $\overline{S}$ is the (yet to be determined) level of the stock price where the company will call the warrant. Unlike the case of "voluntary" conversion of the warrant because of unfavorable dividend protection analyzed in Section 7, $\overline{S}$ is not the choice of the warrant owner, but of the company, and hence will not be selected to maximize the value of the warrant.

Because $C = H - F$ and H and F satisfy (58), C will satisfy (58) subject to the boundary conditions,

$$C(0, \tau; E) = 0$$
$$C(S, 0; E) = 0$$
$$C(\overline{S}, \tau; E) = H(\overline{S}, \tau; E) - \text{Max}[K, \overline{S} - E].$$

Because $\overline{S}$ is the company's choice, we append the maximizing condition that $\overline{S}$ be chosen so as to maximize $C(S, \tau; E)$ making (58) a well-posed problem. Since $C = H - F$ and H is not a function of $\overline{S}$, the maximizing condition on C can be rewritten as a minimizing condition on F.

In general, it will not be possible to obtain a closed-form solution to (58). However, a solution can be found for the perpetual warrant. In this case, we known that $H(S, \tau; E) = S$, and (58) reduces to the ordinary differential equation

$$\tfrac{1}{2}\sigma^2 S^2 C'' + rSC' - rC = 0 \tag{59}$$

for $0 \leq S \leq \bar{S}$ and subject to

$$C(0) = 0$$
$$C(\bar{S}) = \bar{S} - \text{Max}\,(K, \bar{S} - E)$$
$$\text{Choose } \bar{S} \text{ so as to maximize } C,$$

where $C(S)$ is short for $C(S, \infty; E)$ and primes denote derivatives. Solving (59) and applying the first two conditions, we have

$$C(S) = (1 - \text{Max}[K/\bar{S}, 1 - E/\bar{S}])S. \tag{60}$$

Although we cannot apply the simple calculus technique for finding the maximizing $\bar{S}$, it is obviously $\bar{S} = K + E$, since for $\bar{S} < K + E$, C is an increasing function of $\bar{S}$ and for $\bar{S} > K + E$, it is a decreasing function. Hence, the value of the call provision is

$$C(S) = \left(\frac{E}{K+E}\right)S, \tag{61}$$

and because $F = H - C$, the value of the callable perpetual warrant is

$$F(S) = \left(\frac{K}{K+E}\right)S. \tag{62}$$

11. Conclusion

■ It has been shown that a B-S type model can be derived from weaker assumptions than in their original formulation. The main attractions of the model are: (1) the derivation is based on the relatively weak condition of avoiding dominance; (2) the final formula is a function of "observable" variables; and (3) the model can be extended in a straightforward fashion to determine the rational price of any type option.

The model has been applied with some success to empirical investigations of the option market by Black and Scholes and to warrants by Leonard.[71]

As suggested by Black and Scholes and Merton,[72] the model can be used to price the various elements of the firm's capital structure. Essentially, under conditions when the Modigliani-Miller theorem obtains, we can use the total value of the firm as a "basic" security (replacing the common stock in the formulation of this paper) and the individual securities within the capital structure (e.g., debt, convertible bonds, common stock, etc.) can be viewed as "options" or "contingent claims" on the firm and priced accordingly, So, for example, one can derive in a systematic fashion a risk-structure of interest rates as a function of the debt-equity ratio, the risk-class of the firm, and the riskless (in terms of default) debt rates.

Using the techniques developed here, it should be possible to develop a theory of the term structure of interest rates along the

---

[71] In [5] and [25], respectively.
[72] In [4] and [29], respectively.

lines of Cootner and Merton.[73] The approach would also have application in the theory of speculative markets.

Appendix 1[74]

■ Theorems 9 and 10 state that warrants whose common stock per dollar returns possess *distributions* that are independent of *stock price* levels (henceforth, referred to as D.I.S.P.) are: (1) homogeneous of degree one in stock price S and exercise price E—Theorem 9 and (2) convex in S—Theorem 10. This appendix exhibits via counterexample the insufficiency of the posited assumptions *sans* D.I.S.P. for the proof of Theorems 9 and 10.

First, we posit a very simple, noncontroversial, one-period European warrant pricing function, W:

$$W(S, \lambda) = K \int_{E/S}^{\infty} (S\hat{Z} - E)dP(\hat{Z}; S, \lambda), \qquad (A1)$$

wherein: $1 > K > 0$ is a discounting factor which is deemed (somewhat erroneously) to be constant at this point in time (i.e., independent of S),

$\lambda \epsilon [0,1]$ is a parameter of the distribution, dP,

$$\hat{Z} \equiv Z + \lambda g(S)\epsilon \equiv Z + U(S, \lambda) \equiv \text{Common stock per} \atop \text{dollar return,} \qquad (A2)$$

Z and ϵ are independent random variables such that $E(\epsilon|Z) = 0$.

The function $g(S)$ has the following properties for our example: $g(S)\epsilon(0, 1)$, $\dfrac{dg(S)}{ds} < 0$, $dP(\hat{Z}; S, \lambda)$ is the Stieltjes integral representation of the probability density which is equivalent to the convolution of the probability densities of Z and U.

In constructing the counterexample, we choose the following uniform distributions for Z and U:

$$f(\epsilon) = (1/2) \quad \text{for} \quad -1 \leq \epsilon \leq 1 \qquad (A3)$$
$$= 0 \quad \text{elsewhere}$$

$$\rightarrow f(U) = \frac{1}{2\lambda g(S)} \quad \text{for} \quad -\lambda g(S) \leq U \leq \lambda g(S)$$
$$= 0 \quad \text{elsewhere}$$

$$h(Z) = (1/2) \quad \text{for} \quad 1 \leq Z \leq 3$$
$$= 0 \quad \text{elsewhere.} \qquad (A4)$$

The convoluted density would then be:

$$\frac{dP}{d\hat{Z}}(\hat{Z}; S, \lambda) = \frac{\hat{Z} - 1 + \lambda g(S)}{4\lambda g(S)}$$
$$\text{for} \quad 1 - \lambda g(S) \leq \hat{Z} \leq 1 + \lambda g(S) \quad (A5)$$

---

[73] In [11] and [29], respectively.

[74] I thank B. Goldman of M.I.T. for constructing this example and writing the appendix.

$$= (1/2) \quad \text{for} \quad 1 + \lambda g(S) \le \hat{Z} \le 3 - \lambda g(S)$$

$$= \frac{3 + \lambda g(S) - \hat{Z}}{4\lambda g(S)}$$

$$\text{for} \quad 3 - \lambda g(S) \le \hat{Z} \le 3 + \lambda g(S)$$

$$= 0 \quad \text{elsewhere.}$$

As a further convenience, we choose the exercise price, E, to be in the neighborhood of twice the stock price, S, and evaluate (A1):

$$W(S, \lambda) = K[E^2/4S - 3E/2 + 9S/4 + \lambda^2 g(S)^2 S/12]. \quad (A6)$$

By inspection of (A6), we notice that W is not homogeneous of degree one in S and E. Moreover, the convexity of W can be violated (locally) $\left(\text{i.e., } \dfrac{d^2W}{dS^2} \text{ can become negative} \right)$ by choosing a sufficiently negative $\dfrac{d^2g(S)}{dS^2}$:

$$\frac{d^2W}{dS^2} = \qquad\qquad\qquad\qquad\qquad\qquad\qquad (A7)$$
$$K\left(E^2/2S^3 + \lambda^2/6 \left[2g(S)dg/ds + \frac{S(dg)^2}{(dS)} + Sg(S)\frac{d^2g(S)}{dS^2} \right] \right) \gtreqless 0.$$

Thus, our example has shown Theorems 9 and 10 to be not generally consistent with a non-D.I.S.P. environment; however, we can verify Theorems 9 and 10 for the D.I.S.P. subcase of our example, since by construction setting $\lambda = 0$ reinstates the D.I.S.P. character of the probability distribution. By inspection, we observe that when $\lambda = 0$, the right-hand side of (A6) is homogeneous of degree one in S and E, while the right-hand side of (A7) is $KE^2/2S^3 > 0$, verifying the convexity theorem.

Appendix 2

■ It was stated in the text that Theorem 15 is really a special case of Theorem 8, i.e., variance is a consistent measure of risk in the B-S model. To prove consistency, we use the equivalent, alternative definition (Rothschild and Stiglitz')[75] of more risky that X is more risky than Y if $E[X] = E[Y]$ and $EU(X) \le EU(Y)$ for every concave function U.

Since the B-S formula for warrant price, (21), is independent of the expected return on the stock and since the stock returns are assumed to be log normally distributed, different securities are distinguished by the single parameter, σ^2. Therefore, without loss of generality, we can assume that $\alpha = 0$, and prove the result by showing that for every concave U, $EU(Z)$ is a decreasing function of σ, where Z is a log-normal variate with $E[Z] = 1$ and the variance of

[75] In [39].

log (Z) equal to σ^2:

$$EU(Z) = \frac{1}{\sqrt{2\pi\sigma^2}} \int_0^\infty U(Z)\exp\{ -[\log Z + (1/2)\sigma^2]^2/2\sigma^2\}dZ/Z$$

$$= \frac{1}{\sqrt{2\pi}} \int_{-\infty}^\infty U(e^{\sigma x - (1/2)\sigma^2})e^{(-1/2)x^2}dx,$$

$$\text{for} \quad x \equiv [\log Z + (1/2)\sigma^2]/\sigma;$$

$$\partial EU(Z)/\partial\sigma = \frac{1}{\sqrt{2\pi}} \int_{-\infty}^\infty U'(\quad)\exp[-(1/2)(x-\sigma)^2](x-\sigma)dx$$

$$= \frac{1}{\sqrt{2\pi}} \int_{-\infty}^\infty U'(e^{\sigma y + (1/2)\sigma^2})ye^{-1/2y^2}dy, \quad \text{for} \quad y \equiv x - \sigma$$

$$\equiv \text{Covariance } [U'(e^{\sigma y + (1/2)\sigma^2}), y].$$

But, $U'(\quad)$ is a decreasing function of y by the concavity of U. Hence, by Theorem 236, Hardy et al.,[76] Cov$[U', y] < 0$. Therefore, $\partial EU/\partial\sigma < 0$ for all concave U

---

[76] In [16], p. 168

References

1. AYRES, R. F. "Risk Aversion in the Warrant Markets." *Industrial Management Review*, Vol. 50, No. 1 (Fall 1963), pp. 45–53; reprinted in Cootner [10], pp. 497–505.
2. BACHELIER, L. *Theory of Speculation* (translation of 1900 French edition), in Cootner [10], pp. 17–78.
3. BAUMOL, W. J., MALKIEL, B. G., AND QUANDT, R. E. "The Valuation of Convertible Securities." *Quarterly Journal of Economics*, Vol. 80, No. 1 (February 1966), pp. 48–59.
4. BLACK, F. AND SCHOLES, M. "The Pricing of Options and Corporate Liabilities," forthcoming in *Journal of Political Economy*.
5. ———. "The Valuation of Option Contracts and a Test of Market Efficiency." *Journal of Finance*, Vol. 27, No. 2 (May 1972).
6. ———. "Some Evidence on the Profitability of Trading in Put and Call Options," in Cootner [10], pp. 475–496.
7. BONESS, A. J. "Elements of a Theory of Stock-Option Value," *Journal of Political Economy*, Vol. 72, No. 2 (April 1964), pp. 163–175.
8. CHEN, A. H. Y. "A Model of Warrant Pricing in a Dynamic Market," *Journal of Finance*, Vol. 25, No. 5 (December 1970).
9. CHURCHILL, R. V. *Fourier Series and Boundary Value Problems*. 2nd ed. New York: McGraw-Hill, 1963.
10. COOTNER, P. H., ed. *The Random Character of Stock Market Prices*. Cambridge: M.I.T. Press, 1964.
11. ———. "The Stochastic Theory of Bond Prices." Mimeographed. Massachusetts Institute of Technology, December 1966.
12. DETTMAN, J. W. *Mathematical Methods in Physics and Engineering*. 2nd ed. New York: McGraw-Hill, 1969.
13. FAMA, E. F. "Efficient Capital Markets: A Review of Theory and Empirical Work." *Journal of Finance*, Vol. 25, No. 2 (May 1970).
14. GIGUERE, G. "Warrants: A Mathematical Method of Evaluation." *Analysts Journal*, Vol. 14, No. 5 (November 1958), pp. 17–25.
15. HALLINGBY, P., JR. "Speculative Opportunities in Stock Purchase Warrants." *Analysts Journal*, Vol. 3, No. 3 (1947).
16. HARDY, G. H., LITTLEWOOD, J. E. AND PÓLYA, G. *Inequalities*. Cambridge: The University Press, 1959.

17. HAUSMAN, W. H. AND WHITE, W. L. "Theory of Option Strategy under Risk Aversion." *Journal of Financial and Quantitative Analysis*, Vol. 3, No. 3 (September 1968).
18. KASSOUF, S. T. *Evaluation of Convertible Securities*. Maspeth, N. Y.: Analytic Investors Inc., 1962.
19. ———. "Stock Price Random Walks: Some Supporting Evidence." *Review of Economics and Statistics*, Vol. 50, No. 2 (May 1968), pp. 275–278.
20. ———. *A Theory and an Econometric Model for Common Stock Purchase Warrants*. Ph.D. dissertation, Columbia University. New York: Analytical Publishers Co., 1965.
21. KRUIZENGA, R. J. "Introduction to the Option Contract," in Cootner [10], pp. 277–391.
22. ———. "Profit Returns from Purchasing Puts and Calls," in Cootner [10], pp. 392–411.
23. ———. *Put and Call Options: A Theoretical and Market Analysis*. Unpublished Ph.D. dissertation. M.I.T., 1956.
24. KUSHNER, H. J. *Stochastic Stability and Control*. New York: Academic Press, 1967.
25. LEONARD, R. J. "An Empirical Examination of a New General Equilibrium Model for Warrant Pricing." Unpublished M.S. thesis, M.I.T., September 1971.
26. McKEAN, H. P., JR. "Appendix: A Free Boundary Problem for the Heat Equation Arising from a Problem in Mathematical Economics." *Industrial Management Review*, Vol. 6, No. 2 (Spring 1965), pp. 32–39; reprinted in [40], Chapter 199.
27. MERTON, R. C. *Stochastic Integrals*. New York: Academic Press, 1969.
28. ———. "Appendix: Continuous-Time Speculative Processes." (Appendix to Samuelson [45]), in *Mathematical Topics in Economic Theory and Computation*, SIAM, Philadelphia, 1972.
29. ———. "A Dynamic General Equilibrium Model of the Asset Market and its Application to the Pricing of the Capital Structure of the Firm." Sloan School of Management Working Paper # 497-70, M.I.T., (December 1970).
30. ———. "An Empirical Investigation of the Samuelson Rational Warrant Pricing Theory," Chapter V in *Analytical Optimal Control Theory as Applied to Stochastic and Non-Stochastic Economics*, unpublished Ph.D. dissertation, M.I.T., 1970.
31. ———. "An Intertemporal Capital Asset Pricing Model," forthcoming in *Econometrica*.
32. ———. "Lifetime Portfolio Selection under Uncertainty: The Continuous-Time Case," *Review of Economics and Statistics*, Vol. 51, No. 3 (August 1969).
33. ———. "Optimum Consumption and Portfolio Rules in a Continuous-Time Model." *Journal of Economic Theory*, Vol. 3, No. 4 (December 1971).
34. ———. "Restrictions on Rational Option Pricing: A Set of Arbitrage Conditions." Mimeographed. Massachusetts Institute of Technology, August 1968.
35. MILLER, M. AND MODIGLIANI, F. "Dividend Policy, Growth, and the Valuation of Shares." *Journal of Business*, Vol. 34, No. 4 (October 1961).
36. MORRISON, R. J. "The Warrants or the Stock?" *Analysts Journal*, Vol. 13, No. 5 (November 1957).
37. PEASE, F. "The Warrant—Its Powers and Its Hazards." *Financial Analysts Journal*, Vol. 19, No. 1 (January-February 1963).
38. PLUM, V. L. AND MARTIN, T. J. "The Significance of Conversion Parity in Valuing Common Stock Warrants." *The Financial Review* (February 1966).
39. ROTHSCHILD, M. AND STIGLITZ, J. E. "Increasing Risk: I. A Definition." *Journal of Economic Theory*, Vol. 2, No. 3 (September 1970).
40. SAMUELSON, P. A. *The Collected Scientific Papers of Paul A. Samuelson*. Vol. 3. R. C. Merton, ed. Cambridge: M.I.T. Press, 1972.
41. ———. "Proof That Properly Anticipated Prices Fluctuate Randomly." *Industrial Management Review*, Vol. 6, No. 2 (Spring 1965), pp. 41–50; reprinted in [40], Chapter 198.
42. ———. "Rational Theory of Warrant Pricing." *Industrial Management Review*, Vol. 6, No. 2 (Spring 1965), pp. 13–31; reprinted in [40], Chapter 199.
43. ——— AND MERTON, R. C. "A Complete Model of Warrant Pricing That Maximizes Utility." *Industrial Management Review*, Vol. 10, No. 2 (Winter 1969), pp. 17–46; reprinted in [40], Chapter 200.

44. ———. "Mathematics of Speculative Price," in *Mathematical Topics in Economic Theory and Computation*, SIAM, Philadelphia, 1972.

45. ———. Review of [53]. *Journal of American Statistical Association*, Vol. 63, No. 323 (September 1968), pp. 1049–1051.

46. SHELTON, J. P. "The Relation of the Pricing of a Warrant to the Price of Its Associated Stock." *Financial Analysts Journal*, Vol. 23, Nos. 3–4 (Part I: May-June 1967) and (Part II: July-August 1967).

47. SLATER, L. J. "Confluent Hypergeometric Functions," Chapter 13 in *Handbook of Mathematical Functions*. National Bureau of Standards, Applied Mathematics Series, 55, August, 1966.

48. SNYDER, G. L., "Alternative Forms of Options." *Financial Analysts Journal*, Vol. 25, No. 1 (September–October 1969), pp. 93–99.

49. SPRENKLE, C. M. "Warrant Prices as Indicators of Expectations and Preferences." *Yale Economic Essays* I, pp. 172–231; reprinted in Cootner [10], pp. 412–474.

50. STIGLITZ, J. E. "On Some Aspects of the Pure Theory of Corporate Finance: Bankruptcies and Take-Overs." *The Bell Journal of Economics and Management Science*, Vol. 3, No. 2 (Autumn 1972), pp. 458–482.

51. ———. "A Re-Examination of the Modigliani-Miller Theorem." *The American Economic Review*, Vol. 59, No. 5 (December 1969).

52. STOLL, H. R. "The Relationship between Put and Call Option Prices." *Journal of Finance*, Vol. 24, No. 4 (December 1969), pp. 802–824.

53. THORP, E. O. AND KASSOUF, S. T. *Beat the Market*. New York. Random House, 1967.

54. VAN HORNE, J. C. "Warrant Valuation in Relation to Volatility and Opportunity Costs." *Industrial Management Review*, Vol. 10, No. 3 (Spring 1969), pp. 17–32.

| # Option Pricing Theory and Its Applications

John C. Cox and Chi-fu Huang

Sloan School of Management
Massachusetts Institute of Technology

I. INTRODUCTION

Option pricing theory has a long and illustrious history. The first scientific study of options was done by Louis Bachelier in 1900 in a remarkable work that also contained several pioneering results in the theory of stochastic processes. Unfortunately, Bachelier's work fell into obscurity and remained undiscovered by economists for over 50 years. Little research was done on options during that time, but subsequently the field became more active. Key contributions were made in the 1960s by Samuelson (1965) and Samuelson and Merton (1969). It was not until the 1970s, however, that a completely satisfactory theory of option pricing was developed. This new theory, which revolutionized the field, was initiated by Black and Scholes (1973) and extended in important ways by Merton (1973). Their path-breaking articles have formed the basis for nearly all subsequent work in the area.

Recent work on option pricing has tended to fall into two broad categories. The first category is foundational work whose objective is to refine, extend, and elucidate the basic ideas underlying the Black-Scholes theory. In Section II we present this line of research by rederiving the basic Black-Scholes results from the perspective of subsequent work. In the second category are articles that have developed applications of this basic theory. It is the tremendous variety and power of these applications that has given the field much of its vitality. As one illustration of this, we show in Section III how option pricing theory can be fruitfully applied to a classical issue in financial economics, the intertemporal portfolio problem. In Section IV we briefly survey a number of other applications of the theory.

II. THE MARTINGALE APPROACH TO OPTION PRICING

In this section we develop option pricing theory from a somewhat different perspective than the way in which it was originally presented in Black and Scholes (1973) and Merton (1973). We exploit the martingale connection of an arbitrage-free price system as first observed by Cox and Ross (1976) and formalized by Harrison and Kreps (1979). This approach leads naturally to a discussion in Section III on some fundamental issues in portfolio theory.

To simplify notation, we will take the Black-Scholes model of securities prices as a starting point and later discuss directions for generalization. Throughout we will consider an economy with a long horizon. However, we focus our attention only on the time interval $[0, 1]$.

A. The Setup

Let there be two securities, one risky and another riskless. The risky security does not pay dividends on $[0, 1]$ and has a price process

$$(1) \qquad S(t) = \exp\{(\mu - \tfrac{1}{2}\sigma^2)t + \sigma W(t)\},$$

where μ and σ are two strictly positive constants and $\{W(t)\}$ is a standard Brownian motion under a probability $P.$[1] The interpretation of μ and σ will be clear if we take the differential of (1):

$$dS(t) = \mu S(t)\, dt + \sigma S(t)\, dW(t).$$

The σ is the *instantaneous* standard deviation, and μ is the *instantaneous* expected value of the rate of return of the risky asset. The riskless asset does not pay dividends on $[0, 1]$ and has a price process

$$(2) \qquad B(t) = \exp\{rt\}, \quad t \in [0, 1].$$

The vector price processes (B, S) will be termed a *price system*.

An investor in the economy is interested in trading in the two securities to achieve an optimal random wealth at time 1. We shall assume that the random time 1 wealths in which he is interested have finite second moments[2] and that he has no sources of income other than his endowed wealth at time 0.

One immediate question that comes to mind is how do we know the price system written down is a *reasonable* price system? In the least, the price system should not allow us to create something out of nothing or create *free lunches*. In order to formulate what we mean by *creating*, we have to talk about what types of investment strategies, or *trading strategies*, are allowed and what kind of information can be used by investors. For a rich model of securities trading, we would certainly like to include as many trading strategies as possible, as long as there is no free lunch that can arise.

The information an investor has at any time t is the past realization of the price system. Since the riskless asset has a purely deterministic price process, at time 0, an investor knows its future price behavior completely. Thus, the information that an investor has learned between any time t and time 0 is just the realizations of the risky asset price process there. We shall use $\mathcal{F}_t$ to denote the information that an investor possesses at time $t.$[3] Compactly denoted, the information structure of an investor is $\mathbf{F} = \{\mathcal{F}_t; t \in [0, 1]\}$, or a *filtration generated by S*. Note that from (1) we can write

$$W(t) = \left\{\frac{\ln S(t) - (\mu - (\sigma^2/2))}{\sigma}\right\}, \quad t \in [0, 1].$$

Thus knowing the realizations of S is equivalent to knowing those of the Brownian motion W. Thus the filtration (information) generated by S is equivalent to the filtration (information) generated by W.

A process is said to be consistent with the information structure if its values at time t can only depend on the information at that time. Alternatively, a consistent process is also said to be *adapted*. A process is said to be *predictable* if its values at time t depend only on the information strictly before time t. A predictable process is certainly adapted.

A trading strategy is a pair of predictable processes $\{\alpha(t), \theta(t)\}$. For every $t \in (0, 1]$, interpret $\alpha(t)$ and $\theta(t)$ to be the number of shares of the riskless and risky security, respectively, held at time t before time t trading. That is, $\alpha(t)$ is the number of shares of the riskless security carried by an investor from an instant before time t into t; likewise for $\theta(t)$. Then naturally, the informational constraint is that the values of $(\alpha(t), \theta(t))$ be dependent only on the information strictly before time t. As for $(\alpha(0), \theta(0))$, they represent the initial holdings of the two securities and are therefore nonstochastic.

A trading strategy is said to be *simple* if it is bounded and if it only changes its values or trades at finitely many points of time. The number of those time points, although finite in number, can be arbitrarily large.

Since a simple strategy can easily be implemented in real life, it seems that we should at least allow all the simple strategies that satisfy an appropriate budget constraint. Formally, a simple strategy (α, θ), with trading dates $0 = t_0 < t_1 < \cdots < t_n = 1$, is *admissible* if

(3) $\quad \alpha(t_i)B(t_i) + \theta(t_i)S(t_i) = \alpha(t_{i+1})B(t_i) + \theta(t_{i+1})S(t_i) \quad \forall i = 0, 1, \ldots, n-1.$

The left side of (3) is the value of the strategy at time t_i before the trading, and the right side is the value after the trading at t_i. That they are equal is a natural budget constraint, since an investor does not have income other than his endowed time 0 wealth. The value of the strategy at time 0 will be equal to an investor's time 0 wealth. Here we note that any simple strategy generates a time 1 wealth with a finite second moment. It can be easily verified that (3) implies that

$$\alpha(t)B(t) + \theta(t)S(t) = \alpha(0)B(0) + \theta(0)S(0) + \int_0^t \alpha(s)\,dB(s)$$

(4)

$$+ \int_0^t \theta(s)\,dS(s); \quad t \in [0, 1].$$

That is, the value of a strategy at time t is equal to its initial value plus accumulated capital gains or losses. Any trading strategy, not necessarily simple, that satisfies (4) will henceforth be termed a *self-financing* strategy for obvious reasons. (Implicit in this statement is the requirement that all the integrals are well defined.)

Let H denote the space of admissible strategies. We will specify H carefully later; for the time being, we only say that it includes all the admissible simple strategies and any element of it must be self-financing. Here we are obliged to explain why we are not content with simple strategies, since it seems that those are the ones that are likely to be carried out in real life. Besides certain technical reasons, here we can only point out that some financial assets, like options, cannot be *manufactured* by simple strategies. Thus, for the *richness* of the model, we would like also to consider strategies that are not simple. For technically inclined readers, we note that the space of simple strategies lacks the closure property that is convenient for many purposes.

Now we shall formalize what we mean by a free lunch. In words first, a *free lunch* is a sequence of admissible trading strategies whose initial costs go to a nonpositive real number and whose time 1 value goes to a nonzero positive random variable. Formally, a free-lunch is a sequence of admissible trading strategies $(\alpha^n, \theta^n) \in H, n = 1, 2, \ldots,$ such that $\lim_n \alpha^n(0)B(0) + \theta^n(0)S(0) \leqslant 0$ and that $\lim_n \alpha^n(1)B(1) + \theta^n(1)S(1) \geqslant k,$ where k is some nonzero positive random variable.[4]

Now we are ready to discuss an important consequence of the no-free-lunch condition. We shall first fix some notation. Let $S^*(t) = S(t)/B(t)$ and $B^*(t) = 1.$ Then (B^*, S^*) is a *normalized* or *discounted* price system where the riskless asset is the numeraire.

The following theorem, an application of Harrison and Kreps (1979) and Kreps (1981), gives the connection between the normalized price system and martingales.

THEOREM 1. *Suppose that* (B, S) *admits no free lunches. Then there exists a probability* Q *under which* S^* *is a martingale. The probabilities* Q *and* P *are equivalent in the sense that an event is of probability zero under* P *if and only if it is of probability zero under* Q. *Moreover, the derivative of* Q *with respect to* P, *denoted by* dQ/dP, *has a finite variance. Conversely, if there exists such a probability* Q, *then there are no free lunches for simple admissible strategies.*

Remark 1. In a finite state model with finitely many discrete periods, Theorem 1 follows from the absence of simple free lunches, as an application of the Farkas lemma (see, e.g., Holmes 1975, p. 92). A *simple free lunch* is an admissible strategy whose initial cost is nonpositive and whose time 1 value is a nonzero positive random variable. Moreover, when there is an agent whose preferences have a von Neumann–Morgenstern expected utility representation, dQ/dP can be viewed as his marginal utility per unit of probability P. When there are an infinite number of states, the absence of simple free lunches is no longer sufficient for the theorem for some technical reasons. We refer interested readers to Kreps (1981) for a host of related issues.

Normally we would not expect price processes to be martingales. A set of sufficient conditions for that to be true is this: investors are risk neutral, and the interest rate is zero. In the theorem the normalization takes out the positive interest rate, and the change of probability subsumes risk aversion. We shall call the probability Q a *martingale measure*. We will see shortly that a martingale measure is just a Cox and Ross (1976) risk-neutral probability.

The task now is to verify that there exists a martingale measure for the price system (B, S). Our approach will be through construction. We will define a probability and show that it is a martingale measure.

Put

(5)
$$\xi = \exp\left\{ -\left(\frac{\mu - r}{\sigma}\right) W(1) - \frac{1}{2}\left(\frac{\mu - r}{\sigma}\right)^2 \right\}.$$

Since $W(1)$ is a normally distributed random variable with mean 0 and variance 1, ξ is a lognormal random variable. A lognormal random variable has finite arbitrary moments and is strictly positive. Define a probability Q by

$$Q(A) = E[1_A \xi] \quad \forall A \in \mathscr{F}_1,$$

where A is any distinguishable event at time 1 and 1_A is an indicator function of the event A taking the value 1 if the true state of nature lies in A and taking the value 0 otherwise. The density of Q with respect to P is just ξ. The two probabilities P and Q are equivalent since ξ is strictly positive.

Now we claim that Q is a martingale measure. To prove this, we need a mathematical result, the Girsanov theorem, which states that the Brownian motion $\{W(t)\}$ under P becomes a Brownian motion plus a drift term under Q (see, e.g., Liptser and Shiryayev 1977).

THEOREM 2. (*Girsanov*) *Let*

$$z^*(t) = W(t) + \left(\frac{\mu - r}{\sigma}\right) t.$$

Then $\{z^*(t)\}$ *is a standard Brownian motion under* Q.

The drift term in the theorem comes from equation (5). The Girsanov theorem holds more generally than stated here. When the parameters μ, σ, and r are not constant but are stochastic processes themselves, we simply replace $((\mu - r)/\sigma)t$ by the integral of $(\mu - r)/\sigma$ from 0 to t. When there is more than one risky security and μ and σ are a vector and a matrix, respectively, we replace $(\mu - r)/\sigma$ by $\sigma^{-1}(\mu - r)$. (In the general case there are some additional regularity conditions.)

Given the Girsanov theorem, we can write, for all $0 \leqslant s \leqslant t \leqslant 1$,

(6)
$$\begin{aligned} S^*(t) &= \exp\{(\mu - \tfrac{1}{2}\sigma^2 - r)t + \sigma W(t)\} \\ &= S^*(s) \exp\{-\tfrac{1}{2}\sigma^2(t - s) + \sigma(z^*(t) - z^*(s))\}. \end{aligned}$$

Given $S^*(s)$, $S^*(t)$ is equal to $S^*(s)$ times a lognormal random variable with unit mean under Q. Letting $E^*[\cdot|\mathscr{F}_t]$ be the conditional expectation under Q given the information at time t, we immediately have

$$E^*[S^*(t)|\mathscr{F}_S] = S^*(s),$$

which simply says that $\{S^*(t)\}$ is a martingale under Q. Thus according to Theorem 1, (B, S) admits no free lunches for admissible simple strategies.

The question that remains is whether the existence of a martingale measure implies no free lunch for a strategy space containing nonsimple strategies. For example, consider all the self-financing strategies. The answer is no by an example due to Harrison and Kreps (1979). They conceive of a self-financing strategy termed the *doubling strategy*. This strategy is like borrowing to double your bet in roulette each time you lose. As long as you can borrow an unbounded amount and can bet infinitely often, you are sure to win in the end. By way of doing this, you will essentially create something out of nothing. This kind of scheme is certainly self-financing. It is feasible in our economy since there are infinitely many trading opportunities in [0, 1] and there are no bounds on the numbers of shares of securities that an investor can hold, and hence no limit on the amount of borrowing that can be done.

There are two approaches that one can take to make (B, S) a viable model of securities prices while allowing nonsimple strategies. The first is suggested by Harrison and Kreps. To implement a doubling strategy, one has to allow the possibility that one's wealth can go negative and be unbounded from below before one actually wins. Hence, prohibiting an investor from having negative wealth will certainly rule out the doubling strategies. Harrison and Kreps conjectured that the nonnegative wealth constraint may also rule out all the free lunches. Dybvig (1980) confirmed their conjecture; see also Latham (1984).

The second approach is to put a condition on the number of shares of securities that an investor can hold. The idea is that a doubling strategy will involve shorting more and more of the riskless security and going long in the risky one in some state of nature. If we put a bound on the position in the risky security that one can take over time, then the doubling strategy will not be implementable. It turns out, however, that even unbounded strategies can be admitted without allowing doubling strategies. The admissible strategies only need to satisfy the square-integrability condition

$$(7) \qquad E^*\left[\int_0^1 (\theta(t)S^*(t))^2 dt \right] < \infty,$$

where $E^*[\cdot]$ is the expectation at time 0 under Q. This approach has been adopted by Harrison and Pliska (1981) and Duffie and Huang (1985). It turns out that any self-financing strategy satisfying (7) is the limit of a sequence of admissible simple strategies.[5] In words, a nonsimple self-financing strategy satisfying (7) can be approximated arbitrarily closely by an admissible simple strategy that trades very frequently. It can be easily shown that any simple strategy satisfies (7).

The two approaches turn out to be functionally equivalent when investors prefer more to less. The nonnegative wealth constraint rules out free lunches but still allows suicidal strategies—strategies that are mirror images of free lunches and throw money away. Condition (7), however, rules out both free lunches and suicidal strategies. For nonsatiated investors, suicidal strategies will never be employed. Thus the two approaches are equivalent for a nonsatiated investor in that they yield the same solution set for the investor. Interested readers should consult Dybvig and Huang (1987) for details. Here we take the second route by defining H to be the collection of self-financing strategies (α, θ) satisfying (7) such that $\alpha(1)B(1) + \theta(1)S(1) \in L^2(P)$, where we have used $L^2(P)$ to denote the space of random variables consistent with $\mathscr{F}_1$ and having finite variances under P. Thus defined, H is a linear space and that makes our discussion to follow on dynamic spanning easier. (If we took the first approach, the space of admissible trading strategies would not be a linear space.)

Now we summarize in the following theorem:

THEOREM 3. (B, S) *admits no free lunches with respect to* H.

Before we leave this section, we note two things. First, if we substitute for P the martingale measure Q, we will only change the drift term of the price process of the risky security. The instantaneous standard deviation term will not be affected. To see this, we apply Itô's lemma to (6) and get

$$(8) \qquad dS^*(t) = \sigma S^*(t) dz^*(t).$$

Under Q, S^* is a martingale and does not have a drift term. The instantaneous standard deviation under Q of the rate of return on S^* is still σ. This property is not particular to the normalized price process. For S we have

$$(9) \qquad dS(t) = rS(t) dt + \sigma S(t) dz^*(t).$$

Under the martingale measure, the instantaneous expected rate of return of S is equal to the riskless rate and the σ is unaffected. So, as we mentioned previously, the martingale measure is just the risk-neutral probability of Cox and Ross (1976).

Second, Itô's lemma implies that $(\alpha, \theta) \in H$ if and only if

$$(10) \qquad \alpha(t) + \theta(t)S^*(t) = \alpha(0) + \theta(0)S^*(0) + \int_0^t \theta(s)\sigma S^*(s)dz^*(s).$$

Now note a result in the theory of stochastic integration: Let θ satisfy (7). Then

$$\int_0^t \theta(s)\sigma S^*(s) dz^*(s), \quad t \in [0, 1],$$

is a martingale having finite second moment under Q. It follows that the left side of (10), the value of the strategy $(\alpha, \theta) \in H$ in units of the riskless security, is a martingale with a finite second moment under Q:

$$(11) \qquad \alpha(t) + \theta(t)S^*(t) = E^*[\alpha(1) + \theta(1)S^*(1)|\mathscr{F}_t], \quad t \in [0, 1].$$

A consequence of this is that if we know the final value of a strategy $(\alpha, \theta) \in H$ and θ, then we know α by rearranging (11):

$$(12) \qquad \alpha(t) = E^*[\alpha(1) + \theta(1)S^*(1)|\mathscr{F}_t] - \theta(t)S^*(t).$$

That is, the final wealth generated by an admissible trading strategy is *completely* determined by the number of shares of the risky security that is held over time. The number of shares of the riskless security held over time will then be determined through the budget constraint as manifested by (12).

B. Dynamic Spanning and the Martingale Representation Theorem

Recall that an investor's task is to find an optimal time 1 wealth through trading dynamically in the two securities. We learned in the previous section that there do not exist free lunches for admissible strategies. In this section we first examine the kinds of time 1 random wealth that can be achieved by trading in the two long-lived securities. We will show that although there are only two long-lived securities, *any* time 1 wealth that has a finite second moment under both P and Q is achievable through some strategy in H. Through the sequential trading opportunity, one can turn the two long-lived securities into an achievable final wealth space infinite in dimension.

In particular, a European call option written on the risky asset expiring at time 1 with any exercise price $K > 0$ is achievable and thus has a well-defined price. We will compute its price and demonstrate the strategy that manufactures it.

To fix notations, let $L^2(Q)$ be the collection of random variables that are consistent with the information at time 1 and have finite second moments under Q. We will first show that any element of $L^2(P) \cap L^2(Q)$ is achievable through some strategy in H. This is a direct consequence of the *martingale representation theorem*, due originally to Kunita and Watanabe (1967). Before recording this theorem, we note that since $z^*(t) = W(t) + ((\mu - r)/\sigma)t$, the information structure $\mathbf{F}$ is also generated by z^*.

THEOREM 4. (*Kunita and Watanabe*) *Suppose that the information structure $\mathbf{F}$ is generated by z^*, a Brownian motion under Q. Then any finite second-moment martingale $\{m(t)\}$ under Q consistent with $\mathbf{F}$ can be represented as a stochastic integral with respect to $\{z^*(t)\}$:*

$$m(t) = m(0) + \int_0^t \eta(s) \, dz^*(s), \quad t \in [0, 1],$$

where $\{\eta(t)\}$ is predictable and satisfies

(13)
$$E^* \left[\int_0^1 |\eta(t)|^2 \, dt \right] < \infty.$$

(Note that although here $\{z^*(t)\}$ is a one-dimensional Brownian motion under Q, the theorem applies also to the case where the Brownian motion is multidimensional.)

Now let $x \in L^2(P) \cap L^2(Q)$. We want to show that there exists $(\alpha, \theta) \in H$ that manufactures x. Since x has a finite second moment under Q, xe^{-r} does too. Hence, $\{E^*[xe^{-r} | \mathscr{F}_t]\}$ is a finite second-moment martingale under Q. By the martingale representation theorem, we know there exists $\{\eta(t)\}$ satisfying (13) such that

$$xe^{-r} = E^*[xe^{-r}] + \int_0^1 \eta(t) \, dz^*(t)$$

(14)
$$= E^*[xe^{-r}] + \int_0^1 \frac{\eta(t)}{S^*(t)\sigma} S^*(t)\sigma \, dz^*(t).$$

Putting $\theta(t) \equiv \eta(t)/S^*(t)\sigma$ and defining $\alpha(t)$ by (12), we can easily verify that $(\alpha, \theta) \in H$ and it manufactures x.[6] Hence *any* element x of $L^2(P) \cap L^2(Q)$ is achievable through some strategy (α, θ) in H. From the previous section, we also know how to compute the price for x: the price for x at time t is $E^*[xe^{-(1-t)r}|\mathscr{F}_t]$.

Consider now a European call option written on the risky security with an exercise price of $K > 0$ and an expiration date of time 1. The payoff of this option at time 1 is $y \equiv \max[S(1) - K(0)]$. Note that $S(1)$ is a lognormal random variable under P and Q, so $y \in L^2(P) \cap L^2(Q)$. That is, this call option can be manufactured by some $(\alpha, \theta) \in H$. Its price at time t, denoted by $C(t)$, is

$$(15) \qquad C(t) = E^*[ye^{-(1-t)r}|\mathscr{F}_t].$$

Carrying out the computation, we get the Black-Scholes formula.

From the Black-Scholes formula, we know that the price of a European call option at any time t depends on $S(t)$, σ, r, K, and t. Since σ, r, and K are constants, we can write $C(t) = C(S(t), t)$. It is easily verified that $C(S(t), t)$ is twice continuously differentiable with respect to $S(t)$ and once continuously differentiable with respect to t. Itô's lemma implies

$$
\begin{aligned}
(16) \qquad C(S(t), t)e^{-rt} = C(0) &+ \int_0^t C_S(S(s), s)S^*(s)\sigma \, dz^*(s) \\
&+ \int_0^t e^{-rs}(\tfrac{1}{2}\sigma^2 S^2(s)C_{SS}(S(s), s) + rS(s)C_S(S(s), s) \\
&+ C_s(S(s), s) - rC(S(s), s))ds.
\end{aligned}
$$

One can verify that

$$E^*\left[\int_0^1 (C_S(S(t), t)S^*(t))^2 \, dt\right] < \infty.$$

Thus the second term on the right side of (16) is a martingale under Q. Recall that the normalized price for any achievable time 1 wealth is a martingale under Q. Hence, the third term on the right side of (16) is also a martingale. A martingale does not have any drift term. It then follows that the third term on the right side of (16) must be zero; therefore

$$(17) \quad \tfrac{1}{2}\sigma^2 S^2(t)C_{SS}(S(t), t) + rS(t)C_S(S(t), t) + C_t(S(t), t) - rC(S(t), t) = 0.$$

Since $S(t)$ is lognormally distributed and therefore has a support equal to the positive real line excluding zero, the option price must be a solution to the partial differential equation

$$(18) \quad \tfrac{1}{2}\sigma^2 x^2 C_{xx}(x, t) + rxC_x(x, t) + C_t(x, t) - rC(x, t) = 0 \quad \forall x \in (0, \infty), t \in [0, 1].$$

This is the *fundamental partial differential equation for valuation* in the option pricing literature. Here we derived this partial differential equation as a byproduct of the option pricing formula.

Given (16), it is then clear what is the strategy that manufactures the call option: $\theta(t) = C_S(S(t), t)$, and $\alpha(t)$ is defined by (12). The number of shares of the risky security held at time t is just the partial derivative of the option price with respect to $S(t)$. The number of shares of the riskless security held is then determined through the budget constraint. One can also verify easily that Itô's lemma can be applied to C_S. Thus C_S is itself an Itô process that fluctuates very fast and is not a simple strategy on S.

We note that in the above demonstration of the strategy for a call option, the only property that we made use of $C(S(t), t)$ is that it has certain continuous partial derivatives for Itô's lemma to work. Thus we have demonstrated a general method for constructing a strategy for an achievable time 1 wealth whose value at any time t is a function of $S(t)$ and t to which Itô's lemma can be applied. We will see this point again in the next section.

Using the martingale approach in option pricing theory has several advantages. First, the interplay between the existence of free lunches and admissible trading strategies is clearly revealed. Second, it brings forth the observation that a *reasonable* price system should, in the least, be a martingale after a normalization and a change of probability. Third, the space of reachable final wealths can be explicitly characterized. Not only options, but also everything else that lies in $L^2(P) \cap L^2(Q)$ is reachable. Hence, we have the amazing fact that the number of traded securities is finite, but the space of reachable time 1 wealths has infinite dimension. This is not a mystery, however, since we have an uncountably infinite number of trading opportunities.

C. Some Generalizations

We have mentioned that the martingale approach can be applied to very general stochastic environments. The following is such a scenario: There are a finite number of securities indexed by $j = 0, 1, 2, \ldots, J$, which, for simplicity, do not pay dividends. Except for the zeroth security, all the others are risky. Denote by $\{B(t), S(t) = (S_1(t), \ldots, S_J(t))^T\}$ the price processes for the riskless and the risky securities, where ^{T} denotes the *transpose*. We assume that $B(t) = \exp\{\int_0^t r(s)\, ds\}$ and that S is a J-dimensional Itô process:

$$S(t) = S(0) + \int_0^t \mu(s)\, ds + \int_0^t \sigma(s)\, dW(s) \quad \forall t \in [0, 1],$$

where W is a J-dimensional standard Brownian motion. Itô's lemma implies that $S^*(t) \equiv S(t)/B(t)$ can be written as

$$S^*(t) = S^*(0) + \int_0^t \frac{1}{B(s)}(\mu(s) - r(s)S(s))\, ds + \int_0^t \frac{\sigma(s)}{B(s)}\, dW(s)$$

$$\equiv S^*(0) + \int_0^t \mu^*(s)\, ds + \int_0^t \sigma^*(s)\, dW(s).$$

Now under some regularity conditions, and especially with the nonsingularity of the $J \times J$ matrix process $\{\sigma(t)\}$, there exists a unique martingale measure. Therefore, as an application of Theorem 1, there are no free lunches for self-financing simple strategies. When we consider the space of self-financing trading strategies $\{\alpha(t), \theta(t) = (\theta_1(t), \ldots, \theta_J(t))^T\}$ that satisfy the square-integrability condition

$$E^* \left[\int_0^1 \theta(t) \sigma^*(t) \sigma^*(t)^T \theta(t)^T \, dt \right] < \infty,$$

no free lunches exist, where, as usual, $E^*[\cdot]$ denotes the expectation under the martingale measure Q. Under some regularity conditions and a generalization of theorem 4, any final wealth in $L^2(P) \cap L^2(Q)$ is reachable by a self-financing strategy satisfying the above integrability condition. The value at time t of any reachable final wealth, in units of the zeroth asset, is just the conditional expectation at that time of the final wealth under the martingale measure. Readers are referred to Cox and Huang (1986a) and Harrison and Kreps (1979) for complete details.

We have also noted earlier that, using the martingale approach to price a call option in the Black-Scholes context, the price of an option can be computed by evaluating the conditional expectation of (15). As a consequence, the fundamental partial differential equation for valuation (18) becomes an implication of the Black-Scholes option pricing formula; it is no longer the vehicle through which the call option price is solved, as it was in the original treatments of Black and Scholes (1973) and Merton (1973). The two approaches are indeed equivalent in the simple setup of the Black-Scholes economy.

In many situations, however, it is impossible to evaluate the relevant conditional expectation explicitly. For example, consider valuing an American put option expiring at time 1 in the setup of Section II.A. It is well known that it may be optimal for the holder of such an option to exercise it before the expiration date (see Merton 1973). Then the value of the put option depends on the optimal exercise policy and will be given by the supremum of the conditional expectation over all exercise strategies. In this case, no analytic expression has yet been found for the value of the option. However, we do know that the fundamental partial differential equation for valuation will be satisfied by the put option price before exercise and that the exercise strategy will be chosen to maximize the value of the option. Hence, one can use numerical techniques for solving partial differential equations to find the approximate optimal exercise policy and the approximate value of the put option. Readers may consult Brennan and Schwartz (1977a) and Parkinson (1977) for details.

Even without the optimal exercise problem, conditional expectations will usually be impossible to evaluate explicitly in situations with general stochastic environments such as the one depicted in the beginning of this section. Hence it will again be necessary to solve the fundamental partial differential equation numerically in order to obtain specific results.

Note that all of the results we have described express the value of an option in terms of the value of some other security or set of securities. It is the derivation of relative pricing results using only a few properties of the underlying equilibrium that characterizes option pricing as a separate field of study. In any situation in which the relative pricing methodology cannot be applied, option valuation must be considered in the context of a complete general equilibrium model (see, e.g., Rubinstein 1976). In those cases, option pricing theory becomes indistinguishable from the more general theory of asset valuation.

III. EXISTENCE AND PROPERTIES OF OPTIMAL STRATEGIES

Let us come back to an investor's maximization problem. We learned from the previous section that there are no free lunches. Hence, it is sensible now to ask whether there exists a solution to an investor's dynamic optimization program. For ease of exposition we assume that the investor seeks to maximize his expected utility of time 1 wealth and that his utility function is of the constant relative risk-aversion type: $u(w) - (b - 1)^{-1}w^{1-b}$, with $h \neq 1$. Formally stated, the problem the investor tries to solve is

$$(19) \qquad \max_{(\alpha,\theta)\in H} \frac{1}{1-b} E[w^{1-h}] \quad \text{s.t.} \quad \alpha(0)B(0) + \theta(0)S(0) = K_0,$$

$$\alpha(1)B(1) + \theta(1)S(1) = w \in L_+^2(P),$$

where K_0 is the investor's initial wealth at time 0 and $L_+^2(P)$ is the collection of all the nonnegative elements of $L^2(P)$.

Merton (1971) has solved this problem by stochastic dynamic programming. There are two approaches to show that there exists a solution to a problem like (19) using dynamic programming. The first is through some existence theorems in the theory of stochastic control. Those existence theorems often require an admissible control to take its values in a compact set, but here that is not satisfactory. If we are modeling frictionless markets, any compactness assumption on the values of controls or strategies is arbitrary. Moreover, most of the treatments of stochastic control theory are extremely complicated (e.g., Krylov 1980). More comprehensible treatments, such as Fleming and Rishel (1975), do not consider cases where the controls affect the diffusion term of the controlled processes. This, unfortunately, rules out the portfolio problem under consideration. (The *control* referred to above is a strategy in our context.)

This second approach is through construction: construct a control or a strategy and show that it satisfies Bellman's equation. Merton's solution to (19) uses the second approach. In general, however, it is difficult to construct a solution.

Using the insights from the martingale approach to the contingent-claims pricing theory, we will demonstrate a technique that proves the existence of a solution to (19) when the space of admissible controls is a linear space. This technique is easier to understand than the theory of stochastic control, and the properties of a solution can be easily characterized. Kreps (1979) was the first to recognize the possibility of this new technique.

We know from the previous sections that any element x of $L^2(P) \cap L^2(Q)$ is achievable and has a price $E^*[xe^{-r}]$. Thus the investor can be viewed as facing the static problem of choosing an element of $L^2_+(P) \cap L^2(Q)$ subject to his budget constraint. We shall consider a slightly different problem that is easier to solve.

Consider the static maximization problem

$$(20) \qquad \max_{w \in L^2_+(P)} \frac{1}{1-b} E[w^{1-b}] \quad \text{s.t.} \quad E^*[we^{-r}] = K_0.$$

Noting that $E^*[we^{-r}] = E[we^{-r}\xi]$, we can use the Lagrangian method to get the unique solution to (20):

$$\hat{w} = K_0 \exp\left\{ r - \frac{1}{2}\left(\frac{\mu - r}{\sigma}\right)^2 \frac{1}{b^2} + \frac{1}{b}\left(\frac{\mu - r}{\sigma}\right) z^*(1) \right\},$$

a lognormally distributed random variable under Q. Thus $\hat{w}$ has a finite second moment under Q. That is, $\hat{w} \in L^2_+(P) \cap L^2(Q)$ and, by the martingale representative theorem, is achievable through some strategy $(\hat{a}, \hat{\theta}) \in H$.

We claim that $(\hat{a}, \hat{\theta})$ is a solution to (19). If this is not the case, there must exist a $(\alpha, \theta) \in H$ that satisfies the constraints of (19) such that

$$\frac{1}{1-b} E[w^{1-b}] > \frac{1}{1-b} E[\hat{w}^{1-b}],$$

where $w = \alpha(1)B(1) + \theta(1)S(1)$. We know $w \in L^2(P)$ and $E^*[we^{-r}] = K_0$ and is thus feasible in (20). This contradicts the fact that $\hat{w}$ is a solution to (20). In fact, given that H is a linear space and that the utility function is strictly concave, $(\hat{a}, \hat{\theta})$ is the unique solution to (19).

Using a static maximization method together with the martingale representation theorem, we have demonstrated the existence of a solution to (19). The space of admissible controls H is a linear space embodying the notion of frictionless markets. Here we used a specific utility function, but the idea can be applied to a large class of utility functions and a very general stochastic environment (see Cox and Huang 1986a and Pliska 1986).

As in option pricing theory, we can readily compute the optimal strategy. Let $f(t)$ be the value of $\hat{w}$ at time t. We know

$$f(t)e^{-rt} = E^*[\hat{w}e^{-r}|\mathcal{F}_t]$$

$$= K_0 \exp\left\{ -\frac{1}{2}\left(\frac{\mu - r}{\sigma}\right)^2 \frac{1}{b^2} + \frac{1}{b}\left(\frac{\mu - r}{\sigma}\right) z^*(t) \right\}$$

$$= K_0 \left\{ -\frac{1}{2}\left(\frac{\mu - r}{\sigma}\right)^2 \frac{1}{b^2} + \frac{1}{b}\frac{(\mu - r)}{\sigma^2} \ln S^*(t) + \frac{1}{2b}(\mu + \frac{1}{2b}(\mu - r)t \right\}.$$

Thus we can write $f(t) = f(S(t), t)$. It is easily checked that we can apply Itô's lemma to f. Since $f(t)e^{-rt}$ is a martingale having a finite second moment under Q, Itô's lemma implies that

$$f(S(t), t)e^{-rt} = f(0) + \int_0^t \frac{f(S(s), s)e^{-rs}}{S^*(s)} \frac{1}{b}\frac{\mu - r}{\sigma^2} dS^*(s).$$

The same arguments as in the option pricing part show that

$$\hat{\theta}(t) = \frac{f(S(t),t)e^{-rt}}{S^*(t)} \frac{1}{b} \frac{\mu - r}{\sigma^2} = \frac{f(S(t),t)}{S(t)} \frac{1}{b} \frac{\mu - r}{\sigma^2}.$$

The proportion of the investor's wealth invested in the risky asset is a constant:

$$\frac{\hat{\theta}(t)S(t)}{f(S(t),t)} = \frac{1}{b} \frac{\mu - r}{\sigma^2}.$$

By applying Itô's lemma to $f(S(t), t)$, we find that $\hat{\theta}(t)$ is equal to $f_S(S(t), t)$. Then $\hat{\alpha}(t)$ is determined through (12). This technique for characterizing optimal portfolio policies can be applied more generally. It is especially effective in situations in which utility is derived from intermediate consumption as well as terminal wealth. The natural nonnegativity constraint on consumption and terminal wealth can be handled with no added difficulty. For example, in the maximization of the terminal wealth case, the solution for the constrained problem can be decomposed into two parts. The first part is an unconstrained solution for a fraction of the initial wealth, and the second part is a put option written on the first part with a zero exercise price. The fraction of the initial wealth in the first part is determined such that the value of the put option in the second part exhausts the remaining initial wealth. Readers are referred to Cox and Huang (1986b) for details.

IV. APPLICATIONS TO CONTINGENT-CLAIM PRICING

As is evident from the previous sections, option pricing theory can potentially be applied to any security whose future payoffs are contractually related to the value of some other security or group of securities. Option pricing theory thus leads directly to a general theory of contingent-claim pricing relevant for a wide variety of financial instruments. This theory has been especially useful for practitioners because it not only provides a standard of value but also provides a production technology for duplicating the payoffs of any contingent claim by using an appropriate dynamic strategy. Consequently, it provides a constructive technique for exploiting mispricing opportunities and for hedging the risk associated with holding positions in contingent claims.

A particularly important application of contingent-claim pricing theory has been in the relative valuation of corporate securities. Here the theory links the value of a single corporate security to the total value of all of the firm's outstanding securities. For example, consider a firm that has outstanding common stock and a single issue of zero coupon bonds with a promised payment B and a maturity date T. If the value of the firm on the maturity date is greater than B, the bondholders will be paid in full; otherwise, the firm will be in default, and the ownership of the firm will pass to the bondholders. Thus, in a perfect and frictionless market, the value of the bonds at date T will be the maximum of B and the value of the firm. This is exactly the same as the value at date T of a portfolio containing a long position in a default-free zero coupon bond with promised payment B and maturity date T and a short position in one European put option on the value of the firm with exercise price B and expiration date T. Since the bonds and the portfolio have the same future value in all circumstances, they must have the same current value. Consequently, the proper discount to the corporate bonds for the possibility of default is exactly equal to the value of the put option. Among the early work in this area are articles by Merton (1974) and Black and Cox (1976) on ordinary bonds and Ingersoll (1977) and Brennan and Schwartz (1977b) on convertible bonds.

Some especially interesting recent work concerns the game-theoretic issues associated with corporate securities whose owners have certain discretionary conversion rights, such as warrants. Warrants differ from ordinary options in several important ways. When an option is exercised, the number of shares outstanding of the underlying stock remains unchanged and the exercise price is transferred to the individual who sold the option. As a consequence, setting aside informational issues, the exercise of any one option has no effect on the value of any other outstanding option. Therefore, all options with identical terms will optimally be exercised at the same time. By analogy, warrant issues have traditionally been valued under the assumption that all of the warrants would be exercised simultaneously. However, when a warrant is exercised, new shares are issued and the exercise price becomes part of the assets of the firm. By employing option pricing methodology, Emanuel (1983) showed that the differences between options and warrants imply that simultaneous exercise may no longer be optimal for a warrant issue owned by a single agent. The exercise of any one warrant influences the value of the remaining ones, and a monopolist can use this situation to his advantage by, in effect, sacrificing some warrants for the good of the others. Competing owners of individual warrants would not have this opportunity, so the distribution of ownership may affect both the value of the warrants and the optimal pattern of their exercise. In subsequent work, Constantinides (1984) found that the total value of a warrant issue held by competing individuals is in some situations the same as that derived under the assumption of simultaneous exercise. Surprisingly, this is true even though the competing individuals may not exercise their warrants simultaneously. Constantinides and Rosenthal (1984) explicitly modeled the exercise of a warrant issue held by competing individuals as a noncooperative game and provided some existence results. Spatt and Sterbenz (1986) examined the interaction between optimal warrant exercise strategies and the firm's capital structure, dividend, and reinvestment policies. Among other things, they showed that the firm can follow policies that will eliminate any advantage to sequential exercise strategies. These papers are part of a growing body of literature on strategic issues in the valuation of corporate securities, and this will undoubtedly be an active area of research in the future.

NOTES

[1] A standard Brownian motion is a Brownian motion that starts at zero at time zero.

[2] Any random variable that has a finite second moment must have a finite mean and a finite variance.

[3] Mathematicians call $\mathscr{F}_t$ the sigma field generated by $\{S(s); 0 \leqslant s \leqslant t\}$.

[4] The convergence of the time 0 investment is in real numbers. The convergence of the time 1 value is in the sense of the expectation of the square of the difference.

[5] That is, if θ satisfies (7), then there is a sequence of simple θ_n, $n = 1, 2, \ldots$, such that $E^*[\int_0^1 ((\theta(t) - \theta^n(t))S^*(t))^2 \, dt] \to 0$ as $n \to \infty$.

[6] A technical argument can show that (α, θ) is predictable.

REFERENCES

Bachelier, L. 1900. *Théorie de la Speculation*. Paris: Gauthier-Villars.

Black, F., and Cox, J. 1976. "Valuing Corporate Securities: Some Effects of Bond Indenture Provisions." *Journal of Finance* 31: 351–68.

Black, F., and Scholes, M. 1973. "The Pricing of Options and Corporate Liabilities." *Journal of Political Economy* 81: 637–54.

Brennan, M., and Schwartz, E. 1977. "The Valuation of American Put Options." *Journal of Finance* 32: 449–62.

———. 1977. "Convertible Bonds: Valuation and Optimal Strategies for Call and Conversion." *Journal of Finance* 32: 1699–1716.

Constantinides, G. 1984. "Warrant Exercise and Bond Conversion in Competitive Markets." *Journal of Financial Economics* 13: 371–97.

Constantinides, G., and Rosenthal, R. 1984. "Strategic Analysis of the Competitive Exercise of Certain Financial Options." *Journal of Economic Theory* 32: 128–38.

Cox, J., and Huang, C. 1986a. "A Variational Problem Arising in Financial Economics with an Application to a Portfolio Turnpike Theorem." Working paper No. 1751–86, Sloan School of Management, M.I.T.

———. 1986b. "Optimal Consumption and Portfolio Policies When Asset Prices Follow a Diffusion Process." M.I.T. (mimeo).

Cox, J., and Ross, S. 1976. "The Valuation of Options for Alternative Stochastic Processes." *Journal of Financial Economics* 3: 145–66.

Duffie, D., and Huang, C. 1985. "Implementing Arrow-Debreu Equilibria by Continuous Trading of Few Long-Lived Securities." *Econometrica* 53: 1337–56. Reprinted Chapter 4, this volume.

Dybvig, P. 1980. "A Positive Wealth Constraint Precludes Arbitrage in the Black-Scholes Model." Yale University, unpublished manuscript.

Dybvig, P., and Huang, C. 1987. "Nonnegative Wealth, Absence of Arbitrage, and Feasible Consumption Streams." Sloan School of Management, M.I.T. (mimeo).

Emanuel, D. 1983. "Warrant Valuation and Exercise Strategy." *Journal of Financial Economics* 12: 211–35.

Fleming, W., and Rishel, R. 1975. *Deterministic and Stochastic Optimal Control*. New York: Springer-Verlag.

Harrison, M. 1982. "Lecture Notes on Stochastic Calculus." Graduate School of Business, Stanford University.

Harrison, M., and Kreps, D. 1979. "Martingales and Multiperiod Securities Markets." *Journal of Economic Theory* 20: 381–408.

Harrison, M., and Pliska, S. 1981. "Martingales and Stochastic Integrals in the Theory of Continuous Trading." *Stochastic Processes and Their Applications* 11: 215–60.

Holmes, R. 1975. *Geometric Functional Analysis and Its Applications*. New York: Springer-Verlag.

Ingersoll, J. 1977. "A Contingent-Claims Valuation of Convertible Securities." *Journal of Financial Economics* 4: 289–322.

Kreps, D. 1979. "Three Essays on Capital Markets." Technical report 298, Institute for Mathematical Studies in the Social Sciences, Stanford University.

———. 1981. "Arbitrage and Equilibrium in Economies with Infinitely Many Commodities." *Journal of Mathematical Economics* 8: 15–35.

———. 1982. "Multiperiod Securities and the Efficient Allocation of Risk: A Comment on the Black-Scholes Option Pricing Model." In J. McCall, ed., *The Economics of Uncertainty and Information.* Chicago: University of Chicago Press.

Krylov, N. 1980. *Controlled Diffusion Processes.* New York: Springer-Verlag.

Kunita, H., and Watanabe, S. 1967. "On Square-Integrable Martingales." *Nagoya Mathematics Journal* 30: 209–45.

Latham, M. 1984. "Doubling Strategies and the Nonnegative Wealth Constraint." University of California at Berkeley (mimeo).

Liptser, R., and Shiryayev, A. 1977. *Statistics of Random Processes I: General Theory.* New York: Springer-Verlag.

Merton, R. 1971. "Optimum Consumption and Portfolio Rules in a Continuous Time Model." *Journal of Economic Theory* 3: 373–413.

———. 1973. "Theory of Rational Option Pricing." *Bell Journal of Economics and Management Science* 4: 141–83. Reprinted Chapter 8, this volume.

———. 1974. "On the Pricing of Corporate Debt: The Risk Structure of Interest Rates." *Journal of Finance* 29: 449–70.

Parkinson, M. 1977. "Option Pricing: The American Put." *Journal of Business* 50: 21–36.

Pliska, S. 1986. "A Stochastic Calculus Model of Continuous Trading: Optimal Portfolios." *Mathematics of Operations Research* 11: 371–82.

Rubinstein, M. 1976. "The Valuation of Uncertain Income Streams and the Pricing of Options." *Bell Journal of Economics* 7: 407–25.

Samuelson, P. 1965. "Rational Theory of Warrant Pricing." *Industrial Management Review* 6: 13–32.

Samuelson, P., and Merton, R. 1969. "A Complete Model of Warrant Pricing That Maximizes Utility." *Industrial Management Review* 10: 17–46.

Spatt, C., and Sterbenz, F. 1986. "Warrant Exercise, Dividends and Reinvestment Policy." GSIA Working Paper No. 33-84-85, Carnegie-Mellon University.

Reprinted from JOURNAL OF ECONOMIC THEORY
All Rights Reserved by Academic Press, New York and London

Vol. 28, No. 1, October 1982
Printed in Belgium

A Simple Approach to Arbitrage Pricing Theory

Gur Huberman*

*Graduate School of Business, University of Chicago,
Chicago, Illinois 60637*

Received August 18, 1980; revised March 16, 1981

1. Introduction

The arbitrage theory of capital asset pricing was developed by Ross [9, 10, 11] as an alternative to the mean-variance capital asset pricing model (CAPM), whose main conclusion is that the market portfolio is mean-variance efficient. Its formal statement entails the following notation. A given asset i has mean return E_i and the market portfolio has mean return E_m and variance σ_m^2. The covariance between the return on asset i and the return on the market portfolio is σ_{im}, and the riskless interest rate is r. The CAPM asserts that

$$E_i = r + \lambda b_i, \tag{1.1}$$

where

$$\lambda = E_m - r,$$

and

$$b_i = \sigma_{im}/\sigma_m^2 \tag{1.2}$$

is the "beta coefficient" of asset i.

Normality of the returns of the capital assets or quadratic preferences of their holders are the assumptions which lead to (1.1)–(1.2). Theoretically and empirically it is difficult to justify the assumptions of the CAPM. Moreover, the CAPM has been under strong criticism because of its dubious empirical content (cf. [7]). The market portfolio is practically not obser-

* This is a modified version of the third chapter in my Ph.D. dissertation which was written at Yale University. I am grateful to Gregory Connor, who inspired some of the ideas in the paper. Comments from my advisor, Steve Ross, as well as from Jon Ingersoll, Uriel Rothblum and Michael Rothschild were helpful in my attempts to bring this work to a lucid form. This research was supported by NSF Grants ENG-78-25182 and SOC-77-22301.

0022-0531/82/050183–09$02.00/0

vable, and a statement on the market portfolio (such as the CAPM) is difficult to test empirically. Yet the linear relation (1.1) is appealing in its simplicity and in its ready interpretations. The arbitrage pricing theory [10, 11] is an alternative theory to mean-variance theories, an alternative which implies an approximately linear relation like (1.1). In [10] Ross elaborated on the economic interpretation of the arbitrage pricing theory and its relation to other models, whereas in [11] he provided a rigorous treatment of the theory. Recent interest in the APT is evident from papers elaborating on the theory (e.g., Chamberlin and Rothschild [1], Connor [4] and Kwon [5, 6]) as well as on its empirical aspects (e.g., Chen [2, 3] and Roll and Ross [8]).

The main advantage of Ross' arbitrage pricing theory is that its empirical testability does not hinge upon knowledge of the market's portfolio. Unfortunately, Ross' analysis is difficult to follow. He does not provide an explicit definition of arbitrage and his proof—unlike the intuitively appealing introductory remarks in [11]—involves assumptions on agents' preferences as well as "no arbitrage" assumptions.

Here arbitrage is defined and the intuition is formalized to obtain a simple proof that no arbitrage implies Ross' linear-like relation among mean returns and covariances. The main lines of the proof are illustrated in the following paragraphs.

Consider an economy with n risky assets whose returns are denoted by $\tilde{x}_i$ ($i = 1,..., n$) and they are generated by a factor model

$$\tilde{x}_i = E_i + \beta_i \tilde{\delta} + \tilde{\varepsilon}_i \qquad (i = 1,..., n), \tag{1.3}$$

where the expectations $E\tilde{\delta} = E\tilde{\varepsilon}_i = 0$ ($i = 1,..., n$), the $\tilde{\varepsilon}_i$ are uncorrelated and their variances are bounded. Relying on results from linear algebra, express the vector E (whose ith component is E_i) as a linear combination of the vector e (whose ith component is 1), the vector β (whose ith component is β_i) and a third vector c which is *orthogonal* both to e and to β.[1] In other words, one can always find a vector c such that

$$E = \rho e + \gamma \beta + c, \tag{1.4}$$

where ρ and γ are scalars,

$$ec \equiv \sum_{i=1}^{n} c_i = 0, \tag{1.5}$$

and

$$\beta c \equiv \sum_{i=1}^{n} \beta_i c_i = 0. \tag{1.6}$$

[1] Gregory Connor used this idea in an earlier work of his [4].

Next, consider a portfolio which is proportional to c, namely ac (a is a scalar). Note that it costs nothing to acquire such a portfolio because its components (the dollar amount put into each asset) sum to zero by (1.5). We shall call such a portfolio an arbitrage portfolio. Also, by (1.6) this is a zero-beta portfolio. The return on this portfolio is

$$a\tilde{x}c = a \sum_{i=1}^{n} \tilde{x}_i c_i = a \sum_{i=1}^{n} c_i^2 + a \sum_{i=1}^{n} c_i \tilde{\varepsilon}_i, \tag{1.7}$$

by virtue of the decomposition (1.4) and the orthogonality relations (1.5) and (1.6). It is important to notice that the expected return on the portfolio ac is proportional to a (and $\sum_{i=1}^{n} c_i^2$), whereas an upper bound on the variance of its return is proportional to a^2 (and $\sum_{i=1}^{n} c_i^2$).

Suppose now that the number of assets n increases to infinity. Think of arbitrage in this environment as the opportunity to create a sequence of arbitrage portfolios whose expected returns increase to infinity while the variances of their returns decrease to zero. If the sum $\sum_{i=1}^{n} c_i^2$ increased to infinity as n did, then one could find such arbitrage opportunities as follows. Set $a = 1/(\sum_{i=1}^{n} c_i^2)^{3/4}$ and use the portfolio ac. The reason why such a choice of a will create the arbitrage is that the expected return on the portfolio is proportional to a (and with $a = 1/(\sum_{i=1}^{n} c_i^2)^{3/4}$ it equals $a \sum_{i=1}^{n} c_i^2 = (\sum_{i=1}^{n} c_i^2)^{1/4}$), while its variance is proportional to a^2 (and with $a = 1/(\sum_{i=1}^{n} c_i^2)^{3/4}$ it equals $a^2 \sum_{i=1}^{n} c_i^2 = 1/(\sum_{i=1}^{n} c_i^2)^{1/2}$).

Therefore, if there are no arbitrage opportunities (as described above) the sum $\sum_{i=1}^{n} c_i^2$ cannot increase to infinity as n does. In particular, when the number of assets n is large, most of the c_i's are small and approximately zero. Going back to the original decomposition (1.4) we conclude that $E_i \approx \rho + \gamma \beta_i$ for most of the assets.

When motivating his proof, Ross [11, p. 342] emphasized the role of "well-diversified" arbitrage portolios. He indicated that the law of large numbers was the driving force behind the diminishing contribution of the idiosyncratic risks $\tilde{\varepsilon}_i$ to the overall risks of the arbitrage portfolios. The portfolios presented above, ac, need not be well diversified, but they satisfy the orthogonality conditions (1.5) and (1.6). It is the judicious choice of the scalar a that enables us to apply an idea, which is in the spirit of the proof of the law of large numbers.

Section 2 of this paper pesents the formal model, a precise statement of the result and a rigorous proof. In the closing section an attempt is made to interpret the linear-like pricing relation and to justify the no-arbitrage assumption in an equilibrated economy of von Neumann–Morgenstern expected utility maximizers.

2. Arbitrage Pricing

The arbitrage pricing theory considers a sequence of economies with increasing sets of risky assets. In the nth economy there are n risky assets whose returns are generated by a k-factor model (k is a fixed number). Loosely speaking, arbitrage is the possibility to have arbitrarily large returns as the number of available assets grows. We will show that in the absence of arbitrage a relation like (1.1) holds, namely (2.9).

Formally, in the nth economy, we consider an array of returns on risky assets $\{\tilde{x}_i^n : i = 1,..., n\}$. These returns are generated by a k-factor linear model of the form

$$\tilde{x}_i^n = E_i^n + \beta_{i1}^n \, \tilde{\delta}_1^n + \beta_{i2}^n \, \tilde{\delta}_2^n + \cdots + \beta_{ik}^n \, \tilde{\delta}_k^n + \tilde{\varepsilon}_i^n \qquad (i = 1, 2,..., n), \quad (2.1)$$

where

$$E \tilde{\delta}_j^n = 0 \qquad (j = 1,..., k), \qquad E \tilde{\varepsilon}_i^n = 0 \qquad (i = 1,..., n), \qquad (2.2)$$

$$E \tilde{\varepsilon}_i^n \tilde{\varepsilon}_j^n = 0 \qquad \text{if} \quad i \neq j, \qquad (2.3)$$

$$\text{and } \operatorname{Var} \tilde{\varepsilon}_i^n \leqslant \bar{\sigma}^2 \qquad (i = 1,..., n), \qquad (2.4)$$

where $\bar{\sigma}^2$ is a fixed (positive) number. Using standard matrix notation we can rewrite (2.1) as

$$\tilde{x}^n = E^n + \beta^n \, \tilde{\delta}^n + \tilde{\varepsilon}^n, \qquad (2.5)$$

where β^n is the $n \times k$ matrix whose elements are β_{ij}^n ($i = 1,..., n; j = 1,..., k$).

A portfolio $c^n \in R^n$ in the nth economy is an *arbitrage portfolio* if $c^n e^n = 0$, where $e^n = (1, 1,..., 1) \in R^n$. The return on a portfolio c is

$$\tilde{z}(c) = c\tilde{x}^n = cE^n + c\beta^n \, \tilde{\delta}^n + c\tilde{\varepsilon}^n. \qquad (2.6)$$

Arbitrage is the existence of a subsequence n' of arbitrage portfolios whose returns $\tilde{z}(c^{n'})$ satisfy

$$\lim_{n' \to \infty} E\tilde{z}(c^{n'}) = +\infty, \qquad (2.7)$$

and

$$\lim_{n' \to \infty} \operatorname{Var} \tilde{z}(c^{n'}) = 0. \qquad (2.8)$$

In Section 3 we relate (2.7)–(2.8) to standard probabilistic convergence concepts, and discuss how von Neumann–Morgenstern expected utility maximizers view (2.7)–(2.8).

In Theorem 1 we show that the absence of arbitrage implies an approximation to a linear relation like (1.1).

THEOREM 1. *Suppose the returns on the risky investments satisfy (2.1)–(2.4) and there is no arbitrage. Then for $n = 1, 2,...$, there exists $\rho^n, \gamma_1^n,..., \gamma_k^n$, and an A such that*

$$\sum_{i=1}^{n} \left(E_i^n - \rho^n - \sum_{j=1}^{k} \beta_{ij}^n \gamma_j^n \right)^2 \leqslant A, \quad for \quad n = 1, 2,... \tag{2.9}$$

Proof. Using the orthogonal projection of E^n into the linear subspace spanned by e^n and the columns of β^n, one obtains the representation

$$E^n = \rho^n e + \beta^n \gamma^n + c^n, \tag{2.10}$$

where

$$\gamma^n \in R^k,$$
$$e^n c^n = 0, \tag{2.11}$$

and

$$\beta^n c^n = 0. \tag{2.12}$$

Note that $\|c^n\|^2 \equiv \sum_{i=1}^{n} (c_i^n)^2 = \sum_{i=1}^{n} (E_i^n - \rho^n - \sum_{j=1}^{k} \gamma_j^n \beta_{ij}^n)^2$, and assume that the result is false. Consequently, there is an increasing subsequence (n') with

$$\lim_{n' \to \infty} \|c^{n'}\| = +\infty \tag{2.13}$$

Let p be fixed between -1 and $-1/2$, and consider the portfolio $d^{n'} = \alpha_{n'} c^{n'}$, where

$$\alpha_{n'} = \|c^{n'}\|^{2p}. \tag{2.14}$$

By (2.11), $d^{n'}$ is an arbitrage portfolio for each n'. Use (2.10)–(2.12) to see that its return

$$\tilde{z}(d^{n'}) = \alpha_{n'} \|c^{n'}\|^2 + \alpha_{n'} c^{n'} \tilde{\varepsilon}^{n'}. \tag{2.15}$$

Note that

$$E\tilde{z}(d^{n'}) = \alpha_{n'} \|c^{n'}\|^2 = \|c^{n'}\|^{2+2p}, \tag{2.16}$$

so (by (2.13)–(2.14)),

$$\lim_{n' \to \infty} E\tilde{z}(d^{n'}) = +\infty. \tag{2.17}$$

On the other hand (using (2.3), (2.4))

$$\text{Var } \tilde{z}(d^{n'}) \leqslant \bar{\sigma}^2 \alpha_{n'}^2 \| c^{n'} \|^2 = \bar{\sigma}^2 \| c^{n'} \|^{2+4p}, \tag{2.18}$$

so (by (2.13)),

$$\lim_{n' \to \infty} \text{Var } \tilde{z}(d^{n'}) = 0,$$

thus completing the proof. ∎

Next, consider a stationary model, in which $E_i^n = E_i$ and $\beta_{ij}^n = \beta_{ij}$ for all i, j and n. In other words, (2.5) is replaced by

$$\tilde{x}^n = E + \beta \tilde{\delta}^n + \tilde{\varepsilon}^n. \tag{2.5'}$$

The stationary model is the one considered originally by Ross [11]. The nonstationary model is more general than the stationary model but its result (2.9) is not as elegantly presentable as the result in the stationary case (2.9').

THEOREM 2. *Suppose the returns on the risky investments satisfy* (2.5'), *(2.2)–(2.4), and there is no arbitrage. Then there exist* $\rho, \gamma_1, ..., \gamma_k$ *such that*

$$\sum_{i=1}^{\infty} \left(E_i - \rho - \sum_{j=1}^{k} \beta_{ij} \gamma_j \right)^2 < \infty. \tag{2.9'}$$

Proof. Consider the $n \times (k+1)$ matrix B^n whose (i,j) entry is 1 if $j = 1$ and β_{ij-1} if $1 < j \leqslant k+1$. Let $r(n)$ be the rank of B^n. Since $1 \leqslant r(n) \leqslant r(n+1) \leqslant k+1$ for all n, and $r(n)$ is an integer, there is an $\bar{n}$ such that $r(n) = r(\bar{n})$ for all $n \geqslant \bar{n}$. Let $n \geqslant \bar{n}$ be fixed. By permuting the columns of B^n we may assume that its first $r(\bar{n})$ columns can be expressed as linear combinations of the first $r(\bar{n})$ columns. Define the set H^n by

$$H^n = \left\{ (\rho, \gamma_1, ..., \gamma_k) : \sum_{i=1}^{n} \left(E_i - \rho - \sum_{j=1}^{k} \beta_{ij} \gamma_j \right)^2 \leqslant A, \gamma_j = 0, \right.$$

$$\left. \text{for} \quad r(\bar{n}) < j \leqslant k \right\},$$

where A is the A whose existence was asserted in Theorem 1. Note that H^n is nonempty (by Theorem 1), compact for $n \geqslant \bar{n}$ and $H^n \subset H^{n+1}$. Therefore, $\bigcap_{n=1}^{\infty} H^n$ is nonempty. Since every $k+1$ tuple $(\rho, \gamma_1, ..., \gamma_k) \in \bigcap_{n=1}^{\infty} H^n$ satisfies (2.9'), the proof is complete. ∎

Finally, we turn attention to the case where a risk free asset exists, i.e., where there is an additional asset in the nth economy, whose return, say, x_0^n, satisfies

$$x_0^n = r_0^n. \tag{2.19}$$

Now look at excess returns of the risky assets (excess relative to the riskless rate), i.e., at

$$\tilde{y}_i^n \equiv \tilde{x}_i^n - r_0^n, \qquad i = 1, 2, ..., n.$$

Note that any arbitrage portfolio $(c_0, c_1, ..., c_n) \in R^{n+1}$ of $x_0^n, \tilde{x}_1^n, ..., \tilde{x}_n^n$ (which of course satisfies $\sum_{i=0}^{n} c_i = 0$) is equivalent to a vector $(c_1, ..., c_n) \in R^n$ indicating a wealth allocation among the risky assets. Using this idea one can go through the same analysis as in Theorem 1 with the excess returns vector $\tilde{y}^n$, the decomposition (2.10) replaced by

$$E^n - r_0^n e = \beta^n \gamma^n + c^n, \tag{2.10'}$$

and (2.11) deleted.

Consequently, one has

COROLLARY. *Suppose the returns on the risky investments satisfy* (2.1)–(2.4), *there is a risk free asset satisfying* (2.19) *and there is no arbitrage. Then there exist* $\gamma_1^n, \gamma_2^n, ..., \gamma_k^n$ *such that*

$$\sum_{i=1}^{n} \left(E_i^n - r_0^n - \sum_{j=1}^{k} \beta_{ij}^n \gamma_j^n \right)^2 \leqslant A \qquad \text{for} \quad n = 1, 2, ... \tag{2.20}$$

Remark. Analogously, a similar result holds for the stationary model.

3. DISCUSSION

The interpretation of (2.9) or (2.9′) is straightforward: for most of the assets in a large economy, the mean return on an asset is approximately linearly related to the covariances of the asset's returns with economy-wide common factors. As the number of assets becomes large, the linear approximation improves and most of the assets' mean returns are almost exact linear functions of the appropriate covariances.

Next, consider the probabilistic implications of arbitrage returns satisfying (2.7)–(2.8). Given a sequence of random returns $\tilde{z}(c^{n'})$ which satisfy (2.7)–(2.8), we can apply Chebychev's inequality to see that along this sequence $\lim_{n' \to \infty} \tilde{z}(c^{n'}) = +\infty$ in probability (i.e., for all $M > 0$, $\lim_{n \to \infty} \Pr\{\tilde{z}(c^{n'}) \geqslant M\} = 1$). Furthermore, along a subsequence $\hat{n}$, a stronger convergence holds: $\lim_{\hat{n} \to \infty} \tilde{z}(c^{\hat{n}}) = +\infty$ almost surely (i.e., for all $M > 0$, $\Pr\{\lim \inf_{\hat{n} \to \infty} \tilde{z}(c^{\hat{n}}) \geqslant M\} = 1$).

Are arbitrage portfolio which satisfy (2.7)–(2.8) desirable for an expected utility maximizer? In other words, do (2.7)–(2.8) suffice to assert that $\lim_{n \to \infty} EU(\tilde{z}(c^n)) = U(+\infty)$ for any monotone concave utility function U? The negative answer is illustrated by the following examples.

The first example considers a utility function which is $-\infty$ for nonpositive wealth levels, whereas the second example is for an exponential utility which takes finite values for finite wealth levels.

1.   The returns $\tilde{z}(c^n)$ are 0, n and $2n$ with probabilities $1/n^3$, $1 - 2/n^3$, and $1/n^3$, respectively. The utility function $U(x) = -1/x$ for $x > 0$ and $U(x) = -\infty$ for $x \leqslant 0$. Then $EU(\tilde{z}(c^n)) = -\infty$ although $\tilde{z}(c^n)$ satisfies (2.7)–(2.8).

2.   The returns $\tilde{z}(c^n)$ are $-n$, n, and $3n$ with probabilities $1/n^3$, $1 - 2/n^3$, and $1/n^3$, respectively. The utility function is $U(x) = -\exp(-x)$. Then $EU(\tilde{z}(c^n)) \leqslant -n^3 \exp(n)$, so $\lim_{n \to \infty} EU(\tilde{z}(c^n)) = -\infty$, although (2.7)–(2.8) are met.

General conditions which assert that (2.7)–(2.8) imply $\lim_{n' \to \infty} EU(\tilde{z}(c^{n'})) = U(+\infty)$ are not known. As shown in [11, Appendix 2], utility functions which are bounded below or uniformiy integrable utility functions will possess this property.

We conclude that one needs to make assumptions on agents' preferences in order to relate existence of equilibria to absence of arbitrage. This task is beyond the scope of this paper. However, it is straightforward to see that if the economies satisfy the assumptions made by Ross (see [11], especially the first paragraph on p. 349 and Appendix 2), then no arbitrage can exist. In fact, a result of the type "no arbitrage implies a certain behavior of returns," should involve no consideration of the preference structure of the agents involved. Our analysis is in this spirit, because it involves no assumptions on utilities. Other than the simple proof, this may be another contribution of this work.

REFERENCES

1. G. CHAMBERLAIN AND M. ROTHCHILD, Arbitrage and mean-variance analysis of large asset markets, mimeo, University of Wisconsin–Madison, 1980.
2. NAI-FU CHEN, Empirical evidence of the arbitrage pricing theory, mimeo, UCLA, 1980.
3. NAI-FU CHEN, The arbitrage pricing theory: Estimation and applications, mimeo, UCLA, 1980.
4. G. CONNOR, "Asset Prices in a Well-Diversified Economy," Technical Report No. 47, Yale School of Organization and Management, July 1980.
5. Y. KWON, Counterexaples to Ross' arbitrage asset pricing model, mimeo, University of Kansas, 1980.
6. Y. KWON, "On the negligibility of diversifiable risk components at the capital market equilibrium," mimeo, University of Kansas, 1980.
7. R. ROLL, A critique of the asset pricing theory's tests: Part I: On past and potential testability of the theory, Financial Econ. 4 (1977), 129–179.
8. R. ROLL AND S. ROSS, An empirical investigation of the arbitrage pricing theory, J. Finance 35 (1980), 1073–1103.

9. S. Ross, "The General Validity of the Mean-Variance Approach in Large Markets," Discussion Paper No. 12–72, Rodney L. White Center for Financial Research, University of Pennsylvania.

10. S. Ross, Return, risk and arbitrage, *in* "Risk and Return in Finance" (I. Friend and J. Bicksler, Eds.), Ballinger, Cambridge, Mass., 1977.

11. S. Ross, The arbitrage theory of capital asset pricing, *J. Econ. Theory* **13**, No. 3 (1976), 341–360

Printed by the St. Catherine Press Ltd., Tempelhof 41, Bruges, Belgium

discussion | Notes on the Arbitrage Pricing Theory

Gregory Connor

University of California, Berkeley

The arbitrage pricing theory (APT) constitutes one of the most important models of security market pricing. The chief aim of Huberman's justly famous paper, reprinted in this volume, is to clarify and simplify Ross's model. He does an admirable job of this. His presentation is so clear that a detailed critical review would be superfluous. I will attempt, instead, a general overview of the APT. A novice to the field might use this broad discussion as a way to solidify his or her understanding of the original papers. An economist familiar with the APT may benefit from seeing another economist's conceptual framework laid out simply.

Section I describes a few results from "pure" arbitrage pricing theory. "Pure" arbitrage pricing theory is only distantly related to *the* arbitrage pricing theory. Part of the intent of Section I is to clarify this relationship. The results of this section also have independent interest; Key Result 2 in Section I must be one of the most elegant theorems in financial economics.

Section II develops the APT using Ross's original "approximate arbitrage" argument. Ross conjectured that several assumptions of his model could be weakened, and acknowledged that some of its features could be refined. Section III describes one of the most important refinements: the generalization of the factor model assumption that Ross uses. Section IV develops the competitive equilibrium version of the APT. Section V summarizes the paper and suggests some fruitful directions for future research. Each section (except V) ends with a selective list of references to guide further reading.

I. PURE ARBITRAGE PRICING THEORY

An arbitrage opportunity is the existence of a collection of assets that can be combined into a costless portfolio with some chance of a positive payoff and no chance of a negative payoff. There are two strong arguments for assuming that arbitrage opportunities will not appear in security market price relationships. First, *any* investor who observes such an opportunity can make limitless profits (unless prices adjust). Second, *all* investors can improve on their current portfolios by reshuffling their holdings to take advantage of the arbitrage opportunity. Chaos follows unless prices adjust.

The absence of arbitrage opportunities is a minimal condition for well-functioning capital markets. The standard tool for price analysis in free markets is the concept of competitive equilibrium. The absence of arbitrage is a more general condition than the presence of competitive equilibrium, as codified below.

KEY RESULT 1. *If the economy is in competitive equilibrium (and there exists at least one ·nonsatiated investor) then there do not exist any arbitrage opportunities.*

See Harrison and Kreps (1979, p. 385) for a proof. Arbitrage (more correctly "nonarbitrage" or "the absence of arbitrage") places linear restrictions on the relationships among asset prices. (In security market analysis we usually describe price in terms of expected return, which is essentially the reciprocal of price.) A complete characterization of these restrictions is provided in Key Result 2.

For simplicity, assume that the economy lasts one period and there is a finite set of l possible outcomes, or states of the world, denoted by $\theta_1, \theta_2, \ldots, \theta_l$. Assume that there are N assets in the economy; asset i is represented by an l-vector R_i giving the gross return of the asset for each possible state. The set of possible returns for all assets can be represented by an $N \times l$ matrix R. The assumption of no arbitrage creates linear restrictions on R. Let 1^N denote an N-vector of 1's.

KEY RESULT 2. R *allows no arbitrage opportunities if and only if there exists an l-vector p_θ that consists entirely of positive numbers such that $1^N = Rp_\theta$.*

See Ross (1978, p. 474) for the proof of this simple version and Kreps (1981, Theorem 3) for a more complex version allowing for continuous time and a continuum of states. The elements of p_θ can be viewed as the "fundamental prices" of the l states of nature; a security that pays one dollar only in state θ_j costs P_{θ_j}. The theorem can be interpreted to say that there must exist some set of positive state prices. Note, however, that these state prices need not be uniquely defined. In the continuous-time, continuous-state-space version, the vector p_θ is replaced by an infinite-dimensional linear operator; the theorem guarantees the existence of a positive linear operator that relates the price of a security to its payoff density over states.

Key result 1 shows that competitive equilibrium implies the nonexistence of arbitrage opportunities. The next theorem proves, in a restricted sense, that a converse relationship also holds. For any returns that do not permit arbitrage, there exists some economic model (specified by investor preferences and endowments) in which the returns are consistent with competitive equilibrium. Without loss of generality, one can restrict the analysis to representative investor economies—economies in which all investors are identical. One must also assume that the representative investor is nonsatiated in all states.

KEY RESULT 3. *R does not permit arbitrage if and only if there exists a representative investor economy in which R is consistent with competitive equilibrium.*

See Harrison and Kreps (1979, Theorem 1) for a proof. This theorem describes in what sense a competitive equilibrium pricing theory can be reduced to a nonarbitrage pricing theory. Any competitive equilibrium model that does not depend on preferences or endowments can be derived by a nonarbitrage argument. The Black-Scholes option pricing model, originally proven with a competitive equilibrium argument, is an example of such a model. Most other security market pricing models rely on preferences or endowments in some fashion and so cannot be reduced to nonarbitrage models.

Arbitrage theory has produced powerful results using fairly weak assumptions. Research has branched in three directions. First, arbitrage theory has played a key role in developing the mathematical foundations of asset pricing theory. See Kreps (1981), Duffie (1985), and Duffie and Huang (1985) for a taste of this field of research. Second, arbitrage theory has been applied to the pricing of derivative assets. A derivative asset is an asset whose payoff is a function of one or more other observable assets (the primary assets). If all assets are traded continuously and price changes are "smooth," then the relationship between the price of the derivative asset and that of the primary assets is determined by arbitrage. Applications range from the pricing of put and call options (Black and Scholes 1973, Merton 1973) to the valuation of oil drilling rights (Paddock, Siegel, and Smith 1985) to choice of investment in higher education (Dothan and Williams 1981). See Smith (1976) for a general review of this area.

The third direction for research is to place more structure on the relationship among primary asset payoffs so that arbitrage restricts their price relationship. This is the intent of Ross's APT and the topic of the rest of this chapter.

II. APPROXIMATE ARBITRAGE AND THE APT

Many successful theories begin with a simple model that captures some empirical regularity. Ross's APT is based on a readily observable feature of securities markets: asset returns have strong patterns of positive covariation. First, Ross captures this observation with a very simple model called a *noiseless factor model*. All asset returns are assumed to be exact linear combinations of a constant term and a set of K random variates called factors:

$$(1) \qquad r = \bar{r} + Bf, \quad r_0 = \bar{r}_0,$$

where r_0 is the riskless return, B is an $N \times k$ matrix of factor betas, $\bar{r}$ is an N-vector of expected returns, and f is a K-vector of mean-zero random variables called factors. Since the returns are linearly related, nonarbitrage guarantees that the expected returns also have a linear relationship.

KEY RESULT 4. *If returns obey (1), then in the absence of arbitrage there exists a K-vector* γ *such that* $\bar{r} = 1^N r_0 + B\gamma$.

The proof is in Ross (1977, p. 197); briefly, it goes as follows. Any portfolio with zero risk and zero cost must have zero expected return to prevent arbitrage. Letting α denote an arbitrary portfolio, we can state this non-arbitrage condition as follows:

(2) $\qquad\qquad$ If $\alpha'B = 0$ and $\alpha'1^N = 0$, then $\alpha'\bar{r} = 0$.

The duality theorem of linear algebra can now be applied.[1] Statement (2) says that the dual space of B and 1^N belongs to the dual space of $\bar{r}$. This implies (by the duality theorem) that $\bar{r}$ is a linear combination of B and 1^N,

$$\bar{r} = 1^N \gamma_0 + B\gamma,$$

for some γ_0 and γ. It is easy to show (by nonarbitrage) that $\gamma_0 = r_0$.

Next, Ross generalizes the model to the case of a standard factor model (sometimes called a *strict factor model* to differentiate it from the *approximate factor model* discussed in Section III). He assumes the assets have uncorrelated, mean-zero random terms added to the noiseless factor model of (1):

$$r = \bar{r} + Bf + \varepsilon.$$

He also assumes that there are many assets (N is large). The weak law of large numbers guarantees that if we take a large convex combination of uncorrelated random variates and each of the linear coefficients is small, then the randomness approximately disappears from the sum. Note that the random return in a portfolio is a convex combination of the random returns to assets. Since there are many assets and the terms in ε are uncorrelated, these terms obey the weak law of large numbers. By choosing each individual element of α to be small, an investor can approximately eliminate the ε variates from his or her portfolio return.

Because of the ε terms, pure arbitrage pricing theory does not give an exact pricing restriction. A portfolio with $\alpha'1^N = 0, \alpha'B = 0$, and $\alpha'\bar{r} > 0$ is no longer an arbitrage portfolio because the investor must incur idiosyncratic risk. However, by relying on the diversification of ε in portfolios, we can get an approximate form of (2) that holds if N is large. If $\alpha_i \approx 0$ for every i, then $\alpha'\varepsilon \approx 0$, where the "$\approx$" will be used loosely to mean "approximately equal." This gives an approximate version of (2):

(3) $\qquad\qquad$ If $\alpha'1^N = 0, \alpha'B = 0$, and $\alpha'\varepsilon \approx 0$, then $\alpha'\bar{r} \approx 0$.

Invoking the duality theorem together with (3) gives

(4) $\qquad\qquad\qquad\qquad \bar{r} \approx 1^N \gamma_0 + B\gamma.$

Equation (4) is the central conclusion of the APT. Unfortunately, the informal intuition given above cannot be formalized directly—the duality theorem is an exact theorem and does not allow for the approximate equality $\alpha'\varepsilon \approx 0$ in (3). Ross uses a quadratic programming problem to mimic (3). This provides an approximate form of the duality theorem. Most recent theoretical papers abandon duality theory entirely and rely on projection theory instead. A clear and simple proof using projection theory appears in Huberman's paper in this volume.

There are two distinct uses of the symbol " $\approx$ " in the intuitive description of the APT given above. I will follow Huberman in defining each of these precisely. A sequence of approximate arbitrage opportunities (for shorthand, an approximate arbitrage opportunity) is a sequence of portfolios with expected payoff going to infinity and the probability of negative payoff going to zero. This clarifies the meaning of " $\approx$ " in (3).

The symbol " $\approx$ " in (4) will be defined as follows. Let d^N denote the N-vector of pricing errors in the equality version of (4): $\bar{r} = 1^N \gamma_0 + B\gamma + d^N$. The sequence obeys the *Ross pricing bound* if the sum of squared pricing errors, $d^{N'} d^N$, does not go to infinity with N. That is, there exists some finite number C such that $d^{N'} d^N < C$ for all N.

KEY RESULT 5. *If there do not exist any appropriate arbitrage opportunities, then the Ross pricing bound holds.*

See Ross (1976, Theorem 1) or Huberman (1982, Theorem 1) for a proof. Next, we describe in what sense this gives approximate pricing for large N. The proof is straightforward and is left to the reader.

KEY RESULT 6. *Given the Ross pricing bound, the mean square pricing error is less than C/N; for any $\delta > 0$ the proportion of assets with squared pricing errors less than δ is greater than $1 - C/\delta N$; and the squared pricing error of any individual asset is less than C.*

This is not a standard approximation: even for large N it only guarantees accurate pricing on average or for most assets. The error bound for an individual asset $(C < \infty)$ does not change with N. For now, let us view this as a useful, although unconventional, form of approximation and return for a second look when we discuss competitive equilibrium.

III. APPROXIMATE FACTOR MODELS

Ross's original derivation assumes that the idiosyncratic risks have zero correlation. This is one of the features of a standard factor model. This obviously allows a diversification of idiosyncratic risk, but, as Ross notes, a weaker condition could also suffice. Chamberlain and Rothschild (1983) and Ingersoll (1984) (working independently) developed a very appealing alternative, called an approximate factor model.

First, recall that in a strict factor model random returns can be written in the form $r - \bar{r} = Bf + \varepsilon$, where ε_i is uncorrelated with ε_j and f_k for every i, j, k, $i \neq j$. Without loss of generality we can set $E[ff'] = I$ (the $K \times K$ identity matrix). The assumption of an exact factor model is identical to assuming the following form for the return covariance matrix:

$$E[(r - \bar{r})(r - \bar{r})'] = \Sigma = BB' + D,$$

where $D = E[\varepsilon\varepsilon']$ is diagonal.

We wish to relax some of the restrictiveness of the strict factor model. We maintain the assumption that f_k, ε_i are uncorrelated, but we drop the assumption that $\varepsilon_i, \varepsilon_j$ are uncorrelated. This gives the more general form

(5) $$\Sigma = BB' + V,$$

where $V = E[\varepsilon\varepsilon']$ need not be diagonal.

We need to place sufficient structure on (5) to derive the APT. Recall that the APT is an asymptotic theory dealing with approximate relationships for large N. Let $V^N = E[\varepsilon^N \varepsilon^{N'}]$ be the idiosyncratic covariance matrix indexed by the number of assets. A basic concept of the APT is that the randomness captured by ε_i, $i = 1, 2, \ldots, N$, should disappear from portfolios with holdings spread evenly over a large collection of assets. Define a *sequence of diversified portfolios* as a sequence of N-vectors α^N such that $\alpha^{N'} 1^N = 1$ for all N and $\text{limit}_{N \to \infty} \alpha^{N'} \alpha^N = 0$. Call a sequence of random variables ε^N *diversifiable* if $\text{limit}_{N \to \infty} E[(\alpha^{N'} \varepsilon^N)^2] = 0$ for all sequences of diversified portfolios α^N.

KEY RESULT 7. *The sequence of random variates ε^N is diversifiable if there exists a $C < \infty$ such that the maximum eigenvalue of V^N is less than C for all N.*

See Chamberlain (1983, Lemma 2) for a proof. There is a useful restriction on $B^N B^{N'}$ that is symmetrical to the restriction on V^N. The factors in Ross's model are intended to represent economywide shocks to asset returns. As such, each factor should have a broad-based influence affecting many assets in the economy. This means that each of the columns of B^N should have many nonzero components. Through a technical argument (see Connor 1982, appendix) this gives rise to a restriction called the *pervasiveness condition*. The pervasiveness condition requires that the minimum eigenvalue of $B^N B^{N'}$ approaches infinity as N goes to infinity.

Asset returns follow an *approximate factor model* if the sequence of covariance matrices can be written in the form (5) and the minimum eigenvalue of $B^N B^{N'}$ approaches infinity with N while the maximum eigenvalue of V^N is bounded for all N.

KEY RESULT 8. *If returns obey an approximate factor model, then the nonexistence of approximate arbitrage implies Ross's pricing bound.*

See Chamberlain and Rothschild (1983, Theorem 3) or Ingersoll (1984, Corollary) for a proof. Besides generalizing Ross's assumptions, the approximate factor model has implications for the econometrics of the APT. Let H^N denote the $N \times K$ matrix consisting of the K eigenvectors of Σ^N associated with the K largest eigenvalues. Chamberlain and Rothschild (1983, Corollary 3) show that, in an important sense, H^N is approximately equal to B^N for large N. Hence, the econometrician can estimate B^N by estimating the first K eigenvectors of Σ^N.

IV. THE COMPETITIVE EQUILIBRIUM VERSION OF THE APT

In the simple case of a noiseless factor model, the APT only requires the nonexistence of arbitrage in its derivation. For strict or approximate factor models, many theorists now believe that assuming competitive equilibrium improves the model. A competitive equilibrium approach avoids two weaknesses of the approximate arbitrage proof. First, approximate arbitrage can only give a pricing bound rather than a pricing approximation in the conventional sense. Second, the Ross-Huberman model of approximate arbitrage, although clever, is very different from the classic economic model of competitive market pricing. This separates the approximate arbitrage version of the APT from a wide range of applications and extensions that rely on classic price theory.

The extra assumptions needed for a competitive equilibrium proof of the APT are very natural to Ross's framework. Rather than weakening the APT by restricting its applicability, these extra assumptions actually strengthen the theory by clarifying the economic principles behind it.

First, for the competitive equilibrium proof, the market portfolio must be well diversified. This merely requires that no single asset in the economy accounts for a significant proportion of market wealth. If aggregate wealth is spread evenly across assets, then, by definition, so are the market portfolio weights.

Second, the market factors must be pervasive. As discussed in Section III, this restriction is justified by the economic rationale behind Ross's model. In the competitive equilibrium model this assumption guarantees that investors can efficiently trade factor risk and idiosyncratic risk by exchanging available securities. It allows investors to diversify away idiosyncratic risk without restricting their choice of factor risk exposure.

The competitive equilibrium proof relies on the most basic notions of economics. The first tool we need is the "invisible hand" of Adam Smith (1776), which guarantees that all mutually beneficial trades will be consummated in a competitive market. Given that investors are risk-averse, idiosyncratic risk is undesirable to them. With the market portfolio diversification and pervasiveness assumptions, it is possible to eliminate this risk from all portfolios via market trading. Rational investors will take advantage of these trading opportunities, and, in competitive equilibrium, all investors' portfolios will be free of idiosyncratic risk.

Another basic principle of economics is the notion that prices accurately reflect the marginal preferences of agents (see, for example, Marshall 1890). The randomness of security returns has two parts in an approximate factor model: a linear combination of factor variates and an additive component of idiosyncratic risk. We deduced above that each investor will be protected from idiosyncratic risk; hence, this risk will not affect his marginal preferences and will not be reflected in expected returns. The remaining risk (factor risk) is in linear combinations across assets. It follows, by the same logic that Ross uses for the noiseless factor model case, that the risk premia for each type of factor risk will be proportional to the linear coefficients.

KEY RESULT 9. *Given the pervasiveness and market portfolio diversification assumptions, then in competitive equilibrium the APT holds with a conventional approximation. In particular, it holds approximately for every asset for large N and exactly for every asset for infinite N.*

See Connor (1982, 1984) for proofs of the large-N and infinite-N cases, respectively, along the lines outlined above. Dybvig (1983) and Grinblatt and Titman (1983) develop alternative versions of the large-N model that simplify the proof and provide explicit bounds on the rate of convergence of the approximation.

The advantages of the competitive equilibrium proof of the APT are obvious: it provides a stronger conceptual basis for the theory by embedding it in a competitive market setting, and it leads to a more conventional approximation of asset prices. One disadvantage is that the model depends on an economywide pricing equilibrium. The approximate arbitrage model only depends on the hedging behavior of any single investor trading any large collection of assets. That some assets (for example, real estate, human capital, corporate bonds) might not be included in the model does not affect the pricing restriction. The equilibrium model analyzes economywide market equilibrium and *all* the trading interactions between investors. It does require that all assets are included in the model; in particular, the model assumes that the market portfolio (the value-weighted portfolio of *all* assets traded in the economy) is well diversified. In this respect, the equilibrium version is similar to the CAPM (capital asset pricing model), which also requires a joint hypothesis on the market portfolio. (For the CAPM the return on the market index used for empirical analysis must be a good proxy for the true market portfolio return.) One must trade off the necessity for a joint hypothesis about economywide aggregates against the fact that the equilibrium version gives a conventional approximation rather than a pricing bound.

Some of the papers in this area are Connor (1982, 1984), Dybvig (1983), Dybvig and Ross (1985), Grinblatt and Titman (1983), Shanken (1982, 1985), and Sharpe (1977).

V. CONCLUSION

Stripping the APT model to its barest essentials, it has two central ideas. The first is contained in Key Result 3—the absence of arbitrage implies linear pricing under (noiseless) factor linearity of returns. This takes the pure APT, which provides an intuitively appealing but empirically sterile result, and gives it usable empirical content.

A noiseless factor model involves an overly restrictive assumption on asset returns. The second central idea of the APT is that asset-specific risks will be diversified out of large portfolios. The weak law of large numbers states that all randomness disappears from a many-term, convex combination of random variables, given that the linear weights are spread "evenly" across terms and there are appropriate limits on the interdependencies between the random variables. A portfolio return is a convex combination of asset returns. If a portfolio consists of weights that are spread "evenly" across many assets, and asset-specific risks have limited independence, then these risks will disappear from the portfolio return. Risks that disappear from portfolio returns ought not affect the market prices of assets. This is the logical tool that allows the analyst to generalize the arbitrage-based pricing result of the noiseless factor model to a strict or approximate factor model.

One feature that is *not* essential to the APT is the approximate arbitrage approach, which Ross and Huberman use to prove the theory. Arbitrage (including approximate arbitrage) deals with the portfolio strategies of individual investors. It cannot be used to analyze the influence of investor interaction on prices. To more fully understand the diversification pheno-menon, the analyst must examine marketwide equilibrium. Diversification is then viewed as a consequence of the invisible hand acting on investors. Investors eliminate asset-specific risks from their portfolios because it is mutually beneficial for them to do so. In this form the APT has its basis in the most fundamental principles of economics.

The greatest weakness of the APT is the large amount of ambiguity in its empirical predictions, particularly when compared to the CAPM. The CAPM is explicitly a one-beta model. The APT only guarantees a K-beta form, with K determined (one hopes) empirically. The CAPM specifies the market portfolio return as its "factor." We do not have a perfect proxy for the market portfolio return, but at least we know what we are searching for. The APT gives very little guidance on the identity of the factors beyond the restriction that they should obey the pervasiveness condition. Even with a perfect statistical procedure for extracting factors, a level of ambiguity would remain: any rotation of the factors provides an equally valid set of factors.

The APT assumes a factor model of returns a priori. A stronger model would generate the returns process endogenously, as a consequence of the economic forces in the economy acting on asset prices. In such a model the factors would be "labeled" as money shocks, production shocks, fiscal shocks, and so on, and so identified theoretically rather than empirically. This would greatly diminish the empirical ambiguity in the APT. The paper of Chen, Roll, and Ross (1986), although it does not provide a formal model, constitutes an important first step in this direction.

The APT is winning increasing favor as the best available model of stock market prices. Yet there is a dearth of applications of the model to related areas, such as capital structure, tax effects, dividend policy, and capital budgeting. For these tangential areas the CAPM remains the dominant paradigm. This situation may change with time.

This chapter has been devoted entirely to the theoretical side of the model. One of the most exciting directions for future research is toward tying together the theoretical and empirical approaches to the APT. This tendency is evident, for example, in Chamberlain and Rothschild (1983), Ingersoll (1984), and Stambaugh (1983), where theoretical models lead directly to new econometric insights.

The APT, despite its weaknesses, has made a permanent contribution to our understanding of security market pricing. The model will continue to change and grow due to new theoretical developments and empirical findings. The key insights, however, are here to stay.

NOTE

[1] Let A be an $N \times M$ matrix and b an N-vector. The duality theorem says that if $c'b = 0$ for all N-vectors c such $c'A = 0$, then there exists an M-vector γ such that $b = A\gamma$.

REFERENCES

Black, Fischer, and Scholes, Myron. 1973. "The Pricing of Options and Corporate Liabilities." *Journal of Political Economy* 81: 637–54.

Chamberlain, Gary. 1983. "Funds, Factors and Diversification in the Arbitrage Pricing Theory." *Econometrica* 51: 1303–24.

Chamberlain, Gary, and Rothschild, Michael. 1983. "Arbitrage and Mean Variance Analysis on Large Asset Markets." *Econometrica* 51: 1281–1304.

Chen, Nai-fu, and Ingersoll, Jonathan, Jr. 1983. "Exact Pricing in Linear Factor Models with Finitely Many Assets: A Note." *Journal of Finance* 38: 985–88.

Chen, N.; Roll, Richard; and Ross, Stephen A. 1986. "Economic Forces and the Stock Market." *Journal of Business* 59: 383–403.

Connor, Gregory. 1982. "A Factor Pricing Theory for Capital Assets." Working paper, Kellogg Graduate School of Management, Northwestern University.

———. 1984. "A Unified Beta Pricing Theory." *Journal of Economic Theory* 34: 13–31.

Dothan, Uri, and Williams, Joseph T. 1981. "Education as an Option." *Journal of Business* 54: 117–39.

Duffie, Darrell. 1985. "Price Operators: Extensions, Potentials, and the Markov Valuation of Securities." Research paper No. 813, Graduate School of Business, Stanford University.

Duffie, Darrell, and Huang, Chi-fu. 1985. "Implementing Arrow-Debreu Equilibria by Continuous Trading of Few Long-Lived Securities." *Econometrica* 53: 1337–56. Reprinted Chapter 4, this volume.

Dybvig, Philip, H. 1985. "An Explicit Bound on Individual Assets' Deviations from APT Pricing in a Finite Economy." *Journal of Financial Economics* 12: 483–96.

Dybvig, Philip, H., and Ross, Stephen A. 1985. "Yes, the APT Is Testable." *Journal of Finance* 40: 1173–88.

Grinblatt, Mark, and Titman, Sheridan. 1983. "Factor Pricing in a Finite Economy." *Journal of Financial Economics* 12: 497–507.

Harrison, J., and Kreps, D. 1979. "Martingales and Arbitrage in Multiperiod Securities Markets." *Journal of Economic Theory* 20: 381–408.

Huberman, G. 1982. "A Simple Approach to Arbitrage Pricing Theory." *Journal of Economic Theory* 28: 183–91.

Ingersoll, J., Jr. 1984. "Some Results in the Theory of Arbitrage Pricing." *Journal of Finance* 39: 1021–39.

Kreps, David, M. 1981. "Arbitrage and Equilibrium in Economies with Infinitely Many Commodities." *Journal of Mathematical Economics* 8: 15–35.

Marshall, Alfred. 1920. *Principles of Economics*, 8th ed. Reprinted 1946, London: Macmillan & Co.

Merton, Robert, C. 1973. "Theory of Rational Option Pricing." *Bell Journal of Economics and Management Science* 4: 141–83. Reprinted Chapter 8, this volume.

Paddock, James; Siegel, Daniel; and Smith, James. 1985. "Options Valuation of Claims on Real Assets: The Case of Offshore Petroleum Leases." Northwestern University, manuscript.

Ross, S. A. 1976. "The Arbitrage Theory of Capital Asset Pricing." *Journal of Economic Theory* 13: 341–60.

———. 1977. "Return, Risk, and Arbitrage." In Irwin Friend and James L. Bicksler, eds., *Risk and Return in Finance, I*. Cambridge, Mass.: Ballinger.

———. 1978. "A Simple Approach to the Valuation of Risky Streams." *Journal of Business* 51: 453–75.

Shanken, J. 1982. "The Arbitrage Pricing Theory: Is It Testable." *Journal of Finance* 37: 1129–40.

———. 1985. "Multi-Beta CAPM or Equilibrium APT? A Reply to Dybvig and Ross." *Journal of Finance* 40: 1189–96.

Sharpe, W. 1977. "The Capital Asset Pricing Model: A 'Multi-Beta' Interpretation." In H. Levy and M. Sarnat, eds., *Financial Decision Making under Uncertainty*. New York: Academic Press.

Smith, Adam. 1776. *The Wealth of Nations*. Reprinted 1936. New York: Random House, 10–19.

Smith, Clifford. 1976. "Options Pricing: A Review." *Journal of Financial Economics* 3: 3–51.

Stambaugh, Robert F. 1983. "Arbitrage Pricing with Information." *Journal of Financial Economics* 12: 357–70.

Reprinted from JOURNAL OF ECONOMIC THEORY
All Rights Reserved by Academic Press, New York and London

Vol. 17, No. 2, April 1978
Printed in Belgium

Mutual Fund Separation in Financial Theory—The Separating Distributions

STEPHEN A. ROSS

*School of Organization and Management and Department of Economics, Yale University,
New Haven, Connecticut 06520*

Received May 17, 1976; revised December 22, 1976

This paper finds necessary and sufficient conditions on the stochastic structure of
asset returns for portfolio choice to be equivalent to choice among a limited
number of mutual funds of assets, independent of investors' preferences. This
type of separation result is central to modern financial theory and the distributions which satisfy these conditions, the separating distributions, form the underlying basis for much of this theory.

INTRODUCTION

Modern financial theory derives its analytic power from a few strong
assumptions it imposes on the models it develops. Without such assumptions
the special problems of the financial theorist, e.g., the comparative statics
of portfolio positions, the pricing of financial instruments and, quite generally,
the behavior of speculative markets would be as intractible and empirically
empty in finance as they are in general equilibrium theory. Perhaps the most
successful of the theoretical assumptions employed has been that of separability. Roughly speaking, separation occurs in a portfolio problem of allo-
cating wealth across many risky assets when the problem can be simplified
to that of choosing amongst combinations of a few funds formed from these
assets.

The first rigorous separation results in portfolio theory were due to
Markowitz [22] and Tobin [37], but the intuition if not the rigor of separation
had long played an important role in the neoclassical literature. Earlier work
by Knight [18] and Hicks [17] had made it clear that the relevant parameters
in asset choice problems were those of return and risk, and it was well
understood that the problem of valuing risky assets in equilibrium was
essentially the problem of determining the risk premium, i.e., the differential
anticipated return of the risky asset over that of a sure asset. In their development of the mean variance analysis in portfolio theory, Markowitz and Tobin
were the first to put the tradeoff between return and risk on a solid analytic
footing.

0022-0531/78/0172-0254$02.00/0

In a mean variance analysis the investor is concerned with only two parameters of the probability distribution of total returns on investment, the mean return and the variance of the return. For a risk averse investor the latter is a "bad" to be traded off against higher mean returns; risk in such an analysis is equivalent to variance. Aside from simply putting earlier notions into mathematical notation within this framework, Markowitz and Tobin obtained a number of important results. Most notably, the analysis stressed the role played by covariance, or, more generally, co-relations among assets, in determining the optimal portfolio proportions. In addition, the authors obtained the first separation theorem. In a world with a riskless asset they showed that an investor's portfolio decision could be separated into two stages. In the first stage an efficient portfolio or fund, m, of risky assets could be chosen, and in the second the investor's attitudes towards risk could be introduced to determine the optimal allocation of wealth between the riskless asset and the efficient portfolio of risky assets. The important simplification is that all efficient portfolios are simply combinations of the same fund, m, of risky assets and the riskless asset.

The extension of the mean variance theory to an equilibrium theory completed the neoclassical analysis and was first accomplished by Sharpe [35] and Lintner [20]. Since the separation principle holds in a mean variance world, all investors with the same ex ante beliefs, regardless of their attitudes towards risk, must hold the same fund of risky assets. Sharpe and Lintner recognized that this must imply that the efficient fund of risky assets, m, is the same as the market portfolio of risky assets and from the conditions which guarantee the efficiency of the market portfolio they derived the mean variance capital asset pricing model that forms the core of much of modern finance. In an important contribution, Black [3] generalized their results to a mean variance world without a riskless asset by showing that separation would still occur, using two efficient funds of risky assets.

The simplicity and intuitive appeal of the mean variance portfolio and equilibrium results attracted a great deal of attention and much effort has been directed toward determining their generality. Both Markowitz and Tobin noted that if investors were von-Neumann Morgenstern expected utility maximizers, then a mean variance analysis could be justified either by assuming that utility functions were quadratic or by assuming that asset returns were distributed by a multivariate normal distribution. Tobin further remarked that "any 'two parameter' family of random variables" would be sufficient to justify a two parameter risk-return theory.

The use of quadratic utility functions (even in their monotone range) to justify the mean variance approach has become somewhat unfashionable. This is due largely to Arrow's [2] observation that the quadratic utility function exhibits increasing absolute risk aversion which implies that risky assets are inferior assets in a portfolio problem. Efforts to find acceptable, tractable classes of utility functions for financial work have proved most successful in intertemporal work. Here separation theorems of a somewhat different kind have been obtained by Leland [19], Mossin [24], Hakansson [16], and Ross [26], who were concerned with questions of the intertemporal stationarity of optimal portfolio policies and found that the constant relative risk aversion utility functions played a pivotal role; under certain circumstances they implied the separation result that portfolio composition was wealth independent. In a definitive paper, Cass and Stiglitz [6] thoroughly examined the utility function approach to separation. They were able to completely characterize the classes of utility functions that would permit separation in any stochastic environment, in the sense that for all wealth levels an investor with a utility function in one of their classes would divide his wealth between a limited number of specific funds of the assets; the composition of the funds being independent of wealth.

The dual side to this research, i.e., the delineation of the classes of stochastic processes that permit separation for all utility functions, has also been the object of research-perhaps spurred to some extent by Tobin's rather cryptic remark. In fact, it soon became clear that just "any 'two parameter' family of random variables" would not do and that further restrictions had to be imposed. Feldstein [9], for example, showed that lognormal random variables, while defined by two parameters, would not admit of separation. Merton [23] and Ross [27], however, demonstrated that the use of continuous time log normal diffusion processes would allow separation. The additional criterion that seemed to be required was that of closure of the random law under addition. The well known Pareto-Levy class of stable distributions not only served as limiting laws in central limit theorems, but also were defined in terms of a type of closure under addition. Mandelbrot [21] introduced this class of distributions into financial work and Fama [7] examined the portfolio implications of stability and proved a separation theorem for these distributions. This work led Cass and Stiglitz to conjecture that the stable distributions were both necessary and sufficient for separation.

In fact, however, there exist a number of counterexamples to this conjecture. Agnew [1] displayed an example of a multivariate distribution which was not stable (and, a fortiori, not normal) for which all risk averse individuals would choose mean variance efficient portfolios and, hence, obey the earlier Markowitz and Tobin separation rules. Somewhat less idiosyncratically, a body of what might be called symmetry results has been collected. For example, Samuelson [34] pointed out that if the multivariate distribution function of the random assets is unchanged by permuting the assets, then all risk averse investors will allocate their wealth equally across the assets.

The intent of this paper is to resolve the question of what distributions permit separation and, in so doing, to tie together a number of the results cited above. Section 1 introduces the formal definition of separation and describes the class of distributions with the property that all investors choose the same optimal portfolio. Section 2 proves a two fund separability result which will provide the desired generalization of the mean variance and two parameter theories. Section 3 analyzes the analogous k fund case, and Section 4 discusses some further extensions. Section 5 summarizes and concludes the paper. Portions of the proofs of a technical and supportive nature are contained in the Appendix.

1. One Fund Separability

This section introduces the concept of separability and provides necessary and sufficient conditions for the simplest example, one fund separability. Some previous results in the literature are then examined with the help of these equivalent conditions. A word on notation is in order.

Throughout, $\tilde{x}$ will denote the n-vector, $(\tilde{x}_1, ..., \tilde{x}_n)$, of individual random returns. Tildes over variables indicate that they are random, and if one of the assets (or a portfolio) is explicitly assumed to be riskless, it will be taken to be the 0th asset. Lower case Greek letters will denote portfolios, n vectors which sum to unity, i.e., α is a portfolio if and only if

$$\sum_i \alpha_i \equiv \alpha e = 1,$$

where

$$e \equiv (1, ..., 1).$$

(We will permit free short sales, $\alpha_i < 0$.) The only exception to this rule will be the vector η which will denote an arbitrage portfolio which uses no wealth,

$$\eta e = 0.$$

Separability, as looked at from the distributional side, is a somewhat ambiguous concept and a variety of possible definitions suggest themselves. We will deal explicitly with only the two that seem most natural, but several other formulations can be shown to be equivalent. A particularly strong form of separation can be defined in terms of the principle of stochastic dominance. Let U denote the set of all monotone increasing, concave (i.e., utility) functions on R. A random return $\tilde{y}$ is said to stochastically dominate an alternative, $\tilde{w}$, written $\tilde{y} \gtrsim \tilde{w}$, iff ($\forall u \in U$).

$$E\{u[\tilde{y}]\} \geqslant E\{u[\tilde{w}]\}, \tag{1}$$

where $E\{\cdot\}$ denotes the expectation operator. In other words, by (1), no risk averse investor prefers $\tilde{w}$ to $\tilde{y}$.[1]

In the mathematics literature, Strassen [36], and in economics, Ross [25], have independently demonstrated that the statement $\tilde{y} \gtrsim \tilde{w}$ is equivalent to asserting the existence of two random variables $\tilde{z}$ and $\tilde{\epsilon}$ with

$$\tilde{w} \sim \tilde{y} + \tilde{z} + \tilde{\epsilon}, \tag{2}$$

where "$\sim$" is read "is distributed as," $\tilde{z} \leqslant 0$, is a nonpositive random return and $\tilde{\epsilon}$ is a noise term, i.e.,

$$E\{\tilde{\epsilon} \mid \tilde{y} + \tilde{z}\} = 0.$$

It is important to recognize that (2) does not say that $\tilde{w}$ and $\tilde{y} + \tilde{z} + \tilde{\epsilon}$ are equal, only that they are identically distributed. For example, the number of atoms of radium that decay in a second might have the same distribution as the number of telephone calls made to a central exchange, but the two variables are not necessarily equal. The sufficiency of (2) for (1) should be clear since (2) simply asserts that $\tilde{w}$ can be constructed from $\tilde{y}$ by shifting some probability mass downward and adding noise, changes that make $\tilde{w}$ of less value for all $u \in U$.

A special case of (2) that is of some economic interest occurs when $\tilde{z} = 0$, and $\tilde{w}$ is distributed as $\tilde{y}$ plus a noise term. This representation is still sufficient for $\tilde{y}$ to dominate $\tilde{w}$ for $u \in U$ but there is a more interesting result. Dropping the monotonicity requirement, and letting C denote the class of concave functions, a necessary and sufficient condition for (1) to hold for all $u \subset C$ is that (2) holds with $\tilde{z} = 0$. In either case, dominance for U or for C, what is somewhat surprising is the necessity part of these propositions, i.e., the two conditions (1) and (2) are actually equivalent. Similarly if $\tilde{\epsilon} = 0$, then (2) becomes a necessary and sufficient condition for dominance, i.e., for (1) to hold for the class of monotone increasing functions, M. Notice that wealth has been suppressed in the utility functions in (1) since we are regarding the same utility function at different wealth levels as different members of U, C or M.

The following definition of separability uses the concept of stochastic dominance.

---

[1] This definition only makes sense if the expectation is well defined. See Ross [29], for a glimpse at some of the paradoxes that can arise when the expectation doesn't exist. Rothschild and Stiglitz [32, 33] were the first economists to study stochastic dominance and they verified (2) with $\tilde{z} = 0$, i.e., concave dominance, for random variables with compact support.

DEFINITION 1.   A set of returns, $\tilde{x}$, is said to exhibit strong k-fund separability, s$k$fs, iff there exist k mutual funds of the n assets, $\alpha^1,..., \alpha^k$, such that for any portfolio β, there exists a portfolio α,

$$\alpha = a_1\alpha^1 + \cdots + a_k\alpha^k,$$

with

$$\alpha\tilde{X} \gtrsim \beta\tilde{X},$$

where a_i is the weight given fund α^i and $\sum_{i=1}^{k} a_i = 1$.

The definition of s$k$fs requires that for any portfolio, β, there is a portfolio of the k mutual funds that stochastically dominates β. Trivially, the property has force only when $k < n$, and it is really only useful when k is substantially less than n. In addition, throughout the paper we will limit ourselves to the class of distributions for which there exists some strictly monotone and strictly concave $u \in U$ for which $E\{u(\alpha\tilde{x})\}$ exists and attains its maximum at some α^*. This only insures that there is some utility function for which the portfolio problem has a solution. For example, if there were two riskless assets with different returns, this requirement would be violated, and it would be artificial to permit separation in such a case. (Of course, with short sales restrictions such problems would not arise.)

The central concept of separability for financial economics is somewhat weaker than Definition 1. Formally, we can define weak separability as follows.

DEFINITION 2.   A set of returns, $\tilde{x}$, is said to exhibit weak k-fund separability, w$k$fs, iff there exist k mutual funds of the n assets, $\alpha^1,..., \alpha^k$, such that for any portfolio β and any $u \in U$, there exists a portfolio α,

$$\alpha = a_1\alpha^1 + \cdots + a_k\alpha^k,$$

with

$$E\{u(\alpha\tilde{x})\} \geq E\{u(\beta\tilde{x})\}$$

(if the expectations exist).

For w$k$fs we do not require $\alpha\tilde{x}$ to stochastically dominate $\beta\tilde{x}$, rather we permit the choice of α to depend on u, the particular utility function under consideration. From the definitions, s$k$fs implies w$k$fs, that is, if $\tilde{x}$ is strongly k-fund separable then it is weakly k-fund separable. We shall, in fact, show below that these two definitions are equivalent (for $k \leq 2$). Notice also, that while both definitions of separation were made with respect to the class of utility functions, U, similar definitions can be used with respect to any class of functions. We will refer to separation with respect to the broader classes, M and C, as monotone separation and concave separation, respectively.

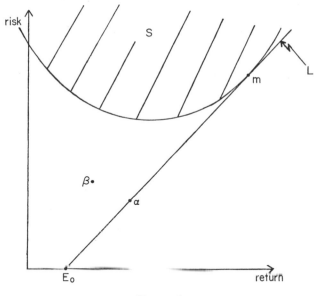

FIGURE 1

It might be useful, at this stage, to examine these definitions in the traditional mean variance or general two-parameter case. Figure 1 illustrates the familiar geometry in the presence of a riskless asset with return E_0. The set S is the set of (return, risk) pairs that can be obtained by forming portfolios of the risky assets alone, and we will assume that S is strictly convex. The efficient frontier is the set of pairs with maximum return for a given level of risk. If we permit free borrowing and lending in the riskless asset, the efficient frontier will be the line L formed by investment at E_0 and investment in m, a unique and efficient fund of risky assets. This is an illustration of a two fund separation theorem, since all risk averse investors will choose positions along L, i.e., portfolios made up of investment in a fund consisting of only the riskless asset and the fund (m) of risky assets.[2]

Furthermore, this type of separation is s2fs, since for any choice of β there is a point, α, on L that dominates β for all choices of $u \in U$; such a point will have the same risk level and at least as high a return. If w2fs, but not s2fs had been satisfied there would exist a portfolio β such that different points on L bested it for different utility functions, but no single point, α, was best for all utility functions. The geometry of Fig. 1 makes it clear that such a situation cannot occur in the two parameter case.

---

[2] The efficient frontier for the concave class, C, is the set of pairs that minimize risk for a given return. For the risky assets alone it is the whole lower boundary of S, and with a riskless asset it is the line L and a line from E_0 asymptotic to S on the left side.

The two concepts come to the same thing, of course, if $k = 1$. Since in both cases we are requiring that there is a single dominant portfolio for all $u \in U$, w1fs and s1fs are equivalent. This is a statement of stochastic dominance and in Theorem 1, below, we will use the stochastic dominance results cited above to establish necessary and sufficient conditions on $\tilde{x}$ for 1fs. Some of the technical aspects of the proof have been put in the Appendix.

THEOREM 1. *A vector of asset returns, $\tilde{x}$, exhibits 1fs if and only if the following conditions are satisfied*:

$$(\exists \tilde{y}, \tilde{\epsilon}, \alpha)$$

(i) $\tilde{x}_i = \tilde{y} + \tilde{\epsilon}_i$,

(ii) $E\{\tilde{\epsilon}_i \mid \tilde{y}\} = 0$,   a.e.,   (C1)

and

(iii) $\alpha\tilde{\epsilon} \equiv 0$, $\alpha e = 1$.

Proof. We can verify the sufficiency of (C1) by showing that the portfolio α stochastically dominates any alternative portfolio β. Define η by

$$\beta = \alpha + \eta, \eta e = 0.$$

From (C1) (i) and (iii)

$$\alpha\tilde{x} = \alpha(\tilde{y} + \tilde{\epsilon}) = \tilde{y}.$$

and by (C1) (ii)

$$\begin{aligned} E\{\beta\tilde{x} \mid \alpha\tilde{x}\} &= E\{(\alpha + \eta)(\tilde{y} + \tilde{\epsilon}) \mid \tilde{y}\} \\ &= E\{\tilde{y} + \eta\tilde{\epsilon} \mid \tilde{y}\} \\ &= \tilde{y}. \end{aligned}$$

It follows from (2) that $\alpha\tilde{x}$ stochastically dominates $\beta\tilde{x}$.

The difficult part of the proof is necessity. Suppose that $\tilde{x}$ exhibits 1fs. Let α be the dominant portfolio and define

$$\tilde{y} \equiv \alpha\tilde{x}.$$

Since α is the dominant portfolio, for all η with $\eta e = 0$ we must have

$$\alpha\tilde{x} + \eta\tilde{x} \sim \alpha\tilde{x} + \tilde{\epsilon}_\eta \tag{3}$$

or

$$\tilde{y} + \eta\tilde{x} \sim \tilde{y} + \tilde{\epsilon}_\eta,$$

where $\tilde{\epsilon}_n$ is a noise term that depends on η, i.e.,

$$E\{\tilde{\epsilon}_n \mid \alpha\tilde{x}\} = 0. \tag{4}$$

(Notice, that, since U contains only monotone increasing u, we could have $E\{\tilde{\epsilon}_n \mid \alpha\tilde{x}\} < 0$ (on a set of positive measure) and still satisfy stochastic dominance, but then $E\{\eta\tilde{x}\} < 0$ and $E\{\epsilon_{-\eta} \mid \alpha\tilde{x}\} > 0$, which would be a violation.) Since (4) must hold for arbitrary choices of η ($\eta e = 0$) we can apply Theorem A2 in the Appendix to show that

$$E\{\eta\tilde{x} \mid \tilde{y}\} = 0. \tag{5}$$

Notice, too, that this result is not immediate from (3) and (4) and it is here that the distinction between equality and distributional equivalence, "$\sim$," becomes important. Consider the following example. Let

and

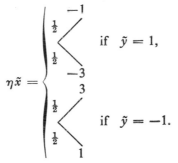

If we take

then

$$\tilde{y} + \eta\tilde{x} = \tilde{y} + \tilde{\epsilon}_n =$$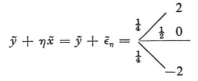

and

$$E\{\tilde{\epsilon}_n \mid \tilde{y}\} = 0,$$

but

$$E\{\eta\tilde{x} \mid \tilde{y}\} = \pm 2 \neq 0.$$

Demonstrating that (5) holds when (4) holds for all η is the technical portion of the proof which is done in the appendix. Given (5), though, the remainder of the argument is straightforward. Letting

$$\eta^i \equiv e_i - \alpha,$$

where e_i is the ith unit vector we can define

$$\tilde{\epsilon}_i \equiv \eta^i \tilde{x} = \tilde{x}_i - \tilde{y},$$

so that

$$\alpha\tilde{\epsilon} = \alpha\tilde{x} - \alpha\tilde{y} = \tilde{y} - \tilde{y} = 0.$$

Rearranging terms yields,

$$\tilde{x}_i = \tilde{y} + (\tilde{x}_i - \tilde{y})$$
$$= \tilde{y} + \tilde{\epsilon}_i,$$

and from (5)

$$E\{\tilde{\epsilon}_i \mid \tilde{y}\} = 0. \qquad\qquad \text{Q.E.D.}$$

The conditions (C1) provide a *constructive* characterization that permits one to generate multivariate distributions satisfying 1fs. By picking an arbitrary $\tilde{y}$ random return and $n - 1$ arbitrarily chosen (conditionally mean zero random variables) and by defining the nth, $\tilde{\epsilon}_n$, so as to satisfy (C1)(iii) for some α, the resulting $\tilde{x}$ will exhibit 1fs. Of course, it follows from (C1) that a necessary condition for 1fs is that all n assets have the same expected return, $E\{\tilde{y}\}$.

In addition, if the $\tilde{x}_i$ have finite variances, then α will simply be the minimum variance portfolio. (This is true even if the $\tilde{x}_i$ do not have compact support, and, consequently, no monotone quadratic utility function can be defined on their range.) To see this, note that the variance of any alternative portfolio, $\beta = \alpha + \eta$, is given by

$$\text{Var}\{(\alpha + \eta)\,\tilde{x}\} = \text{Var}\{\tilde{y}\} + \eta V \eta$$
$$\geqslant \text{Var}\{\tilde{y}\},$$

where V is the covariance matrix of $\tilde{\epsilon}$.

Condition (C1) and the sufficiency portion of Theorem 1 also contain a number of previous results as special cases. Rothschild and Stiglitz [32] observed that if the $\tilde{x}_i$ were identically independently distributed, then the unique optimal portfolio would be the equal weight portfolio, $(1/n,..., 1/n)$. Samuelson [34] had earlier generalized this result to the case where the distribution function, $F(x_1,..., x_n)$, is unaltered under permutations of the variables. Suppose that Samuelson's condition is satisfied. Define

$$\tilde{\epsilon}_i \equiv \tilde{x}_i - \frac{1}{n} \sum_i \tilde{x}_i \, ,$$

and

$$\tilde{y} \equiv \frac{1}{n} \sum_i \tilde{x}_i \, .$$

Clearly,

$$E\{\tilde{\epsilon}_i \mid \tilde{z}\} = E\left\{\tilde{x}_i - \frac{1}{n} \sum_i \tilde{x}_i \,\middle|\, \frac{1}{n} \sum_i x_i\right\}$$

$$= E\left\{\tilde{x}_i \,\middle|\, \frac{1}{n} \sum_i \tilde{x}_i\right\} - \frac{1}{n} \sum_i \tilde{x}_i$$

$$- \frac{1}{n} \sum_i \tilde{x}_i - \frac{1}{n} \sum_i \tilde{x}_i$$

$$= 0,$$

where we have used the symmetry of the distribution function to conclude that the conditional expectation of any $\tilde{x}_i$, given the average of the $\tilde{x}_i$'s must be the average.[3]

These cases are too specialized to be terribly important in their own right, but they are useful preliminary results and they serve to illustrate that 1fs can occur with a variety of different distributions. In particular, there is no

[3] We should also note, at this stage, the work of Hadar and Russell [13, 14], and Fishburn [10–12]. Fishburn has derived a number of conditions which are equivalent to one portfolio dominating another in a stochastic sense. For example, in our notation, he derived the result that a portfolio, α, would dominate a portfolio β (in U) if and only if for every choice of $u \in U$ there is one investment in the α portfolio which is preferred to one in the β portfolio. This result can then be applied to the question of whether diversification as opposed to "plunging" is optimal. This latter question has occupied Hadar and Russell in their work. Our concern is somewhat different; we are interested in restrictions on the underlying distributions which guarantee separability in the k-fund sense defined above. That is, we are asking under what conditions the class of optimal portfolios may be simply characterized.

necessity that the $\tilde{x}_i$ follow a multivariate stable distribution.[4] Finding necessary conditions on distribution functions equivalent to (C1), though, is awkward and since it also does not seem to be a natural way to pose the problem of separation we will not consider the question of equivalent conditions on distribution functions further. As we shall see, what matters for separation is not the marginal distributions of the returns, but, rather, their co-relations which are properties of the joint distribution.

In the next section we will develop the notion of 2fs and it is with this concept that we will be able to generalize the traditional two parameter portfolio theory.[5]

2. Two Fund Separability

Two fund separability is, of course, the central theme of modern portfolio and capital asset pricing theory. Before proceeding to prove the main theorem, however, it might be instructive to examine the question of separation in a state-space context.

If the admissible preference structure is augmented beyond U to include state dependent utility functions, then 1fs requires all assets to be identical, which implies that there can be no noise terms in (C1). This is easy to see since if two assets, x_i and x_j, had different patterns of returns across states of nature, then two state dependent utility functions can be constructed one of which is optimized by holding x_i and the other of which is optimized by holding x_j. By restricting choice, as we have done, to be represented by von-Neumann Morgenstern utility functions, the class of admissible distributions enlarges in an interesting fashion to include the noise terms of (C1). This is illustrated in a two-state example displayed in Fig. 2. The states θ_1 and θ_2 are equally probable and x_1 and x_2 are pure contingent returns. A state dependent utility function that only assigned weight to state θ_1 would pick x_1 and one that only had weight on θ_2 would pick x_2 and by varying the weights

---

[4] On the other hand, while it is possible to use Theorem 1 to *directly* verify the sufficiency for 1fs of a multivariate stable distribution with identical means, to do so requires the development of some multivariate distribution theory for these laws that does not appear to be readily available in the literature. In the normal case, for example, it is well known that if $\eta' V\alpha = 0$, then $E\{\eta\tilde{x} \mid \alpha\tilde{x}\} = 0$, where V is the covariance matrix of $\tilde{x}$. What is required for other stable variances is a similar notion of conditional independence given zero cospread.

[5] Before concluding, it might be useful to briefly consider monotone and concave separation. Since monotone separation implies U separation, a fortiori (C1) remains a necessary condition. For sufficiency, though, we require Prob$\{\tilde{\varepsilon}_\eta > 0 \mid \alpha\tilde{x}\} = 0$ (a.e.) and this implies that $\tilde{\varepsilon}_\eta = 0$, a.e.. In other words, a necessary and sufficient condition for M separation (with no short sales restrictions) is that $\tilde{x}_i = \tilde{y}$, all i. Concave separation, i.e., separation for all $u \in C$, requires the same conditions (C1) as separation for all $u \in U$.

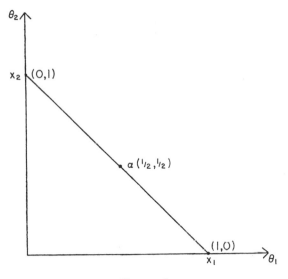

FIGURE 2

any point on L can be chosen. All convace von-Neuman Morgenstern functions, though, would pick the portfolio $\alpha = (\frac{1}{2}, \frac{1}{2})$ with returns $\tilde{y} = \frac{1}{2}$ for sure. Notice that this example satisfies the conditions for 1fs in (C1), with each x_i equal to a common $\tilde{y}$ plus noise terms giving $-\frac{1}{2}$ or $\frac{1}{2}$ with equal probability. Thus, with state dependent utility functions (x_1, x_2) cannot exhibit 1fs, but for von-Neumann Moregenstern utilities separation does obtain.

This suggests a similar approach to 2fs. Figure 3 illustrates a three-state example of the requirement that for 2fs with state dependent utility functions all assets must lie on a line, L, in the state space. (This result is not confined to finite dimensional state spaces and is quite robust with respect to the structure of the state space. Similarly, $k$fs would require that all assets lie in a $(k-1)$ dimensional subspace of the state space.) All random returns are linearly dependent in the sense that any asset is a portfolio of two funds, α and β.

The equation of the line, L, can be written in the form

$$x_i(\theta) = y(\theta) + b_i z(\theta).$$

If state dependent utility functions are permitted, 2fs requires that this linear relation hold.

With von-Neumann Morgenstern utility functions, though, a number of multivariate distributions (e.g., the normal) which are not linearly dependent are known to be sufficient for 2fs. The following theorem fully characterizes 2fs.

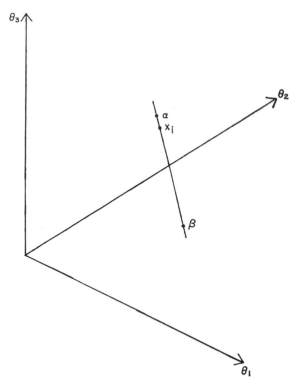

FIGURE 3

THEOREM 2. *A vector of asset returns, $\tilde{x}$, exhibits w2fs if and only if the following conditions are satisfied:*

$$(\exists \tilde{y}, \tilde{z}, \epsilon b, \alpha, \beta)$$

(i) $\tilde{x}_i = \tilde{y} + b_i \tilde{z} + \tilde{\epsilon}_i \,,$

$$E_i \equiv E\{\tilde{x}_i\} = E_y + b_i E_z \qquad\qquad \text{(C2)}$$

(ii) $(\forall \xi \in A) \, E\{\tilde{\epsilon}_i \mid \tilde{y} + \xi \tilde{z}\} = 0, \qquad a.e.,$

(iii) $\alpha \tilde{\epsilon} = \beta \tilde{\epsilon} \equiv 0, \qquad \alpha e = \beta e = 1,$

and

(iv) *if b is not a constant vector, then*

$$\alpha b > \beta b.$$

Defining

$$\gamma(u) \equiv \arg\max E\{u(\gamma\tilde{x})\},$$

the set

$$A = (\inf_{u \in U} \gamma(u) \, b, \, \sup_{u \in U} \gamma(u) \, b),$$

and

$$A = (\inf_{u \in U} \gamma(u) \, b, \, \infty),$$

if $E_z b$ is not a constant vector.

Proof. The proof of sufficiency is still straightforward, as in the case of 1fs. Let γ be a portfolio that is optimal for u and suppose that γ is not a linear combination of α and β. By (C2) (iv) we can define λ such that

$$\gamma b = \lambda \alpha b + (1 - \lambda) \beta b,$$

and define η by

$$\gamma = \lambda \alpha + (1 - \lambda) \beta + \eta.$$

Since $\eta b = 0$, we have

$$\begin{aligned}
E\{\eta\tilde{x} \mid \lambda\alpha\tilde{x} + (1 - \lambda) \beta\tilde{x}\} &= E\{\eta b\tilde{z} + \eta\tilde{\epsilon} \mid \lambda(\tilde{y} + (\alpha b) \tilde{z}) \\
&\quad + (1 - \lambda)(\tilde{y} + (\beta b) \tilde{z}) \\
&= E\{\eta\tilde{\epsilon} \mid \tilde{y} + (\gamma b) \tilde{z}\} = 0,
\end{aligned}$$

by (C2)(ii) and (iii). This verifies that $(\lambda\alpha + (1 - \lambda) \beta) \tilde{x}$ stochastically dominates $\gamma\tilde{x}$. (If γb is on the boundary of A, the result follows by a simple closure argument from the continuity of expected utility.)

The proof of necessity, again, is more difficult. Suppose that $\tilde{x}$ exhibits w2fs. By definition, $(\forall u \in U, \gamma)(\exists\lambda)$

$$E\{u[\lambda\alpha\tilde{x} + (1 - \lambda) \beta\tilde{x}]\} \geqslant E\{u[\gamma\tilde{x}]\}.$$

To put the point somewhat differently, for every $u \in U$, the optimum is attained at a portfolio that is a linear combination (simplicial) of two portfolios α and β. If $u(\cdot)$ is chosen to be everywhere differentiable and if it has an internal optimum, then $\lambda\alpha + (1 - \lambda) \beta$ must satisfy the first order conditions for an optimum at some value of λ,

$$E\{u'[\lambda\alpha\tilde{x} + (1 - \lambda) \beta\tilde{x}](\tilde{x}_i - x_j)\} = 0; \qquad \text{all } i, j.[6] \tag{6}$$

---

[6] By assumption a $u \in U$ exists with a determinate optimum portfolio and, without loss of generality, we can take u to be differentiable.

On the other hand, we can also find the optimal value of λ by the first order condition

$$E\{u'[\lambda\alpha\tilde{x} + (1 - \lambda)\,\beta\tilde{x}](\alpha\tilde{x} - \beta\tilde{x})\} = 0. \tag{7}$$

This condition, (7), then, must imply that (6) is satisfied. Furthermore, given λ, this implication must hold for all positive, monotone declining functions. Picking a particular λ value and defining

$$\tilde{q} \equiv \lambda\alpha\tilde{x} + (1 - \lambda)\,\beta\tilde{x},$$
$$v(\tilde{q}) \equiv E\{\alpha\tilde{x} - \beta\tilde{x} \mid \tilde{q}\},$$

and

$$S_i(\tilde{q}) \equiv E\{\tilde{x}_i \mid \tilde{q}\},$$

it must be the case that for all positive, monotone declining functions $h(\cdot)$,

$$E\{h(\tilde{q})\,v(\tilde{q})\} = 0,$$

implies that

$$E\{h(\tilde{q})|\,S_i(\tilde{q}) - S_j(\tilde{q})]\} = 0; \text{ all } i, j.$$

From Theorem A1 in the Appendix this implies that $(\forall i)(\exists b_i)$

$$S_i(\tilde{q}) - S_1(\tilde{q}) = b_i v(\tilde{q}), \text{ a.e.} . \tag{8}$$

Taking expectations over the conditioning variable, $\tilde{q}$, in (8) we have that

$$E_i - E_1 = b_i(\alpha E - \beta E), \quad \text{for all } i, \tag{9}$$

and if $v(\tilde{q}) \neq 0$, a.e., (8) also implies that

$$\alpha b - \beta b = 1. \tag{10}$$

Now define $\tilde{y}$ and $\tilde{z}$ by the two equation system

$$\alpha\tilde{x} = \tilde{y} + (\alpha b)\,\tilde{z} \tag{11}$$

and

$$\beta\tilde{x} = \tilde{y} + (\beta b)\,\tilde{z}, \tag{11}$$

and let

$$\tilde{\varepsilon}_i \equiv \tilde{x}_i - [\tilde{y} + b_i\tilde{z}]. \tag{12}$$

From (8), (9), and (10) we have that for $\xi = \lambda \alpha b + (1 - \lambda) \beta b$

$$E\{\tilde{\epsilon}_i - \tilde{\epsilon}_1 \mid \tilde{y} + \xi \tilde{z}\}$$
$$= E\{\tilde{x}_i - \tilde{x}_1 - (b_i - b_1) \tilde{z} \mid \tilde{y} + \xi \tilde{z}\}$$
$$= E\{\tilde{x}_i - \tilde{x}_1 - b_i(\alpha \tilde{x} - \beta \tilde{x}) \mid \tilde{y} + \xi \tilde{z}\}$$
$$= 0, \quad \text{a.e.,}$$

and, from (11), $\alpha \tilde{\epsilon} \equiv 0$, which implies that

$$E\{\tilde{\epsilon}_i \mid \tilde{y} + \xi \tilde{z}\} = 0, \quad \text{a.e.,}$$

Let

$$A \equiv \{\xi \mid \xi = \gamma(u) b, \, u \in U\}.$$

From Lemmas A1, A2 and A3, A is an interval and is unbounded from the right if E and, therefore, $E_n b$ is not a constant vector. Lemma A4 implies that (C2)(ii) is satisfied for all $\xi \in A$. Combining (9) and (12) we have

$$\tilde{x}_i = \tilde{y} + b_i \tilde{z} + \tilde{\epsilon}_i,$$

and $\hspace{10cm}$ (C2)(i)

$$E_i = E_y + b_i E_z.$$

If $v(\tilde{q}) = 0$, a.e., from (8) the conditions reduce to those of one fund separability. $\hspace{8cm}$ Q.E.D.

COROLLARY 1. *A vector of asset returns, X, exhibits concave w2fs (i.e., separation for all $u \in C$) if and only if (C2) is satisfied with $A = (-\infty, \infty)$ if all expectations are not identical and A an interval if they are.*[7]

Proof. The proof follows directly from that of Theorem 2 with the application of Lemma A3. $\hspace{6cm}$ Q.E.D.

The role of the set A in (C2) should now be clear. In the mean variance case, for example, concave separation is equivalent to picking points on the lower boundary of the mean variance feasible set. In other words, the points of minimum variance for a given return-including those to the left of the minimum variance point in Fig. 1—are permissible and A is unbounded. When we add to concavity the additional requirement of monotonicity, A is restricted so that only returns at or above the minimum variance point are permitted. This accounts for the lower bound on A in (C2), i.e., only port-

[7] Monotone 2fs requires all $\tilde{\epsilon}_i$ to be zero, as in the one fund case.

[8] I am grateful to Oliver Hart for having impressed me with the need to specify A in detail.

folios which maximize return for a given variance are efficient for monotone, concave utility functions.[8]

While the form of (C2), particularly (C2)(i), might seem both specialized and somewhat odd, in relation to the traditional sufficiency conditions—multivariate normality—it is quite general. In the first place, conditions (C2), as with (C1), offer a *constructive* approach to the separation problem. We are free to pick $\tilde{y}$ and $\tilde{z}$ arbitrarily and any $n - 2$ random variables $\tilde{\epsilon}_i$ which satisfy (C2)(ii), and then we can define $\tilde{\epsilon}_{n-1}$ and $\tilde{\epsilon}_n$ to satisfy (C2)(iii) for some choice of α and β. Conversely, Theorem 2 can also be used to directly check for separation. By simply selecting any two utility functions with (unique different) optimal portfolios, α and β, we can verify whether the residuals satisfy (C2)(ii). Moreover, the thrust of the theorem is that (C2) represents the *most* general set of conditions that can be found which permit the usual development of portfolio theory. To see this more clearly we can use Theorem 2 to examine a number of alternative theoretical developments of portfolio separation. To facilitate the exposition, we will implicitly be considering cases where E, the expected return vector, is not a constant vector.

Two Parameter Models

The two parameter models introduced by Tobin require that the expected utility of a portfolio be a function of only two parameters, the mean return, m, and a risk variable, σ. For a given risk level, σ, then, the objective is to maximize the return, m. If this procedure implies a 2 fund separation result for all choices of a utility function, then by Theorem 2 the random distribution must be of the form of (C2).[9] We can, however, say a bit more than this.

Consider any portfolio, γ, with an expected return, $\gamma E = m$. If we choose λ so that

$$\lambda \alpha E + (1 - \lambda) \beta E = m,$$

then

$$\gamma \tilde{x} = (\lambda \alpha + (1 - \lambda) \beta) \, \tilde{x} + \eta \tilde{x}, \tag{13}$$

where $\eta e = \eta E = 0$ and, consequently,

$$E\{\eta \tilde{x} \,|(\lambda \alpha + (1 - \lambda) \beta) \, \tilde{x}\} = 0.$$

[9] Notice that, a priori, the problem of maximizing αE subject to a constraint on $\sigma(\alpha)$ does not generally yield a separation result without some restrictions on the spread function, σ.

In other words, whatever spread parameter, σ, is used the portfolio $\lambda\alpha + (1 - \lambda)\beta$ has minimum spread for the given expected return. This permits us to compute the two funds, α and β, when separation occurs, and facilitates testing for 2fs.

Furthermore, suppose that the random variables $\tilde{x}_i$ possess variances. It is clear from (13) that $\lambda\alpha + (1 - \lambda)\beta$ must be the minimum variance portfolio with the given return $\lambda\alpha E + (1 - \lambda)\beta E$. The portfolios α and β then will be two portfolios which span the mean variance efficient frontier. In fact any two such portfolios can be chosen for separation, and this illustrates an important general point about separation theorems.

In (C2) we did not require that α and β be unique. Rather, all we can say is that α and β span a space in which any two linearly independent members can serve as separating funds. For example, choosing $\lambda_1 \neq \lambda_2$ we can define

$$\gamma^1 = \lambda^1\alpha + (1 - \lambda^1)\beta,$$

and

$$\gamma^2 = \lambda^2\alpha + (1 - \lambda^2)\beta,$$

and the portfolios γ^1 and γ^2 will be separating funds. In addition, if we pick γ^2 (say to be the market portfolio in a pricing model) then γ^1 can be chosen to be uncorrelated with γ^2 (e.g., as a "zero beta" portfolio in a mean variance pricing model.[10])

In the two parameter case, then, the spread parameter can be taken to be the variance (if it exists). It should be stressed, though, that this two parameter evaluation is valid if and only if the random returns are of the form of (C2). In summary, if a two parameter return-risk tradeoff can be taken and yields separation, then (C2) must be satisfied. Conversely, if (C2) holds, i.e., given w2fs, then the relevant separating portfolios will be minimum spread portfolios and this will permit a two parameter interpretation.

Normally Distributed Returns

What of the normal distribution then, or the continuous time version, the lognormal price diffusion process? Since we know that these distributions exhibit two fund separation, it must follow that all multivariate normal random variables take the form of (C2). It is instructive, though, to demonstrate this directly since (C2) is, at least at first appearances, a somewhat restrictive form.

---

[10] If there is a riskless asset with return E_0 it can be chosen as one of the separating funds. This follows from the requirement that a riskless asset must also satisfy (C2). Hence, $\tilde{\varepsilon}_0 \equiv 0$ which implies that $\tilde{y} + b_0\tilde{z} \equiv E_0$, and scaling $\tilde{z}$ yields $\tilde{x}_i = E_i + (E_i - E_0)\tilde{z} + \tilde{\varepsilon}_i$. Since $\alpha\tilde{x}$ and $\beta\tilde{x}$ are now dependent only on $\tilde{z}$, they span the riskless asset, and it can be chosen as one of the separating funds.

If the covariance matrix, V, is singular, then a riskless portfolio can be formed and for simplicity of exposition alone we will assume that V refers to the $(n-1)$ risky assets and is nonsingular, and explicitly assume a riskless asset with return E_0. If (C2) is to be satisfied, the riskless asset must also take the form of (C2)(i) and, as a consequence, $\bar{\epsilon}_0 \equiv 0$ and

$$\tilde{y} + b_0\tilde{z} \equiv 0.$$

In other words, scaling $\tilde{z}$ so that $E_z = 1$ we must be able to write the risky assets in the form

$$\tilde{x}_i - E_0 = (E_i - E_0)\tilde{z} + \tilde{\epsilon}_i,$$

where

$$E\{\tilde{\epsilon}_i \mid \tilde{z}\} = 0. \tag{14}$$

To do this we choose $\tilde{z}$ to be the excess random return on the separating combination, α, defined by

$$\alpha = kV^{-1}(E - E_0),$$

where E_0 now denotes a constant vector with E_0 in all entries, and k is a constant chosen to normalize α to have unit excess return, $\alpha'(E - E_0) = 1$. Thus,

$$\begin{aligned} \tilde{z} &\equiv \alpha'\tilde{x} - \alpha'E_0 \\ &= k(E - E_0)'\,V^{-1}(\tilde{x} - E_0). \end{aligned}$$

It is well known that a sufficient condition for conditional independence, (14), of normal random variables is that they be uncorrelated. Since, for any γ,

$$\begin{aligned} \text{covariance } (\gamma'\tilde{\epsilon}, \tilde{z}) \\ = \text{covariance } (\gamma'[\tilde{x} - E_0 - (E - E_0)\tilde{z}], \tilde{z}) \\ = \gamma'[I - k(E - E_0) \cdot (E - E_0)'\,V^{-1}]\,V \cdot kV^{-1}(E - E_0) \\ = k\gamma'(E - E_0) - k\gamma'(E - E_0)[k(E - E_0)'\,V^{-1}(E - E_0)] \\ = k\gamma'(E - E_0) - k\gamma'(E - E_0) \\ = 0, \end{aligned}$$

it follows that all multivariate normal random variables satisfy the conditions of (C2).

The same is true of the stable distributions, but since the use of stable distributions in portfolio theory is generally closely linked with the use of market factor models (see, e.g., Fama [7, 8]), it is more instructive to treat them as special cases of the factor model approach.

Market Factor Models

The one factor generating model is written in the form

$$\tilde{x}_i = E_i + b_i \tilde{z} + \tilde{\epsilon}_i \,, \tag{15}$$

or with a common risk as

$$\tilde{x}_i = E_i + \tilde{y} + b_i \tilde{z} + \tilde{\epsilon}_i \,, \tag{16}$$

where

$$E_y = E_z = E\{\tilde{\epsilon}_i \mid \tilde{y} + b_i \tilde{z}\} = 0.$$

Generally, $\tilde{z}$ is interpreted as a systematic or market risk and $\tilde{\epsilon}$ as the unsystematic risk of the asset.

Until something more is said about the random factors and $\tilde{\epsilon}$ terms, though, these models are without content, i.c., all random variables can be put into these forms. Furthermore, even when it is required that there exist α such that

$$\alpha b = 1$$

and

$$\alpha \tilde{\epsilon} \equiv 0,$$

it should be emphasized that this, too, imposes no constraints on the random variables. A meaningful restriction is obtained when we require the $\tilde{\epsilon}_i$ to have a degree of independence (e.g., mutually uncorrelated).

Without any restrictions there can be no separation results, but unfortunately, the requirement that the $\tilde{\epsilon}_i$ be linearly independent while a strong and interesting assumption, is not sufficient for two fund separation. We will say more about these models in Section IV, and for the present show only that either model (15) or (16) with $\tilde{\epsilon} \equiv 0$ is sufficient for two fund separation. In this case the generating mechanism restricts the rank of the state space tableau of returns (see Ross [28, 30]). Since the only discretionary source of risk in the two models is the amount of market risk, $\tilde{z}$, borne in the portfolio, this implies that a two parameter model is applicable. Directly, though, with

$\tilde{\epsilon} \equiv 0$, if arbitrage is not possible then both (15) and (16) must actually be written in the form of (C2).[11]

Suppose, now, that $\tilde{\epsilon}$ is not identically zero, and suppose that there exist two portfolios α and β for which

$$\alpha b \neq \beta b, \tag{17}$$

and

$$\alpha \tilde{\epsilon} \equiv \beta \tilde{\epsilon} \equiv 0.$$

Given any portfolio, γ, it is possible to combine α and β so that the resulting portfolio has the same systematic $\tilde{z}$ risk as the γ portfolio and no $\tilde{\epsilon}$ risk, but there is no assurance that such a portfolio combination will have as high an expected return as that of the γ portfolio. In other words, unless (C2)(i) holds and E_i is a linear function of b_i, we cannot have 2fs in the market model. We will return to the problem of separation with market models in Sections III and IV below.

Capital Asset Pricing Theory

The traditional results of the two parameter capital asset pricing models follow in a straightforward fashion from w2fs. This can be shown in any of a number of ways, but it is most instructive to derive the theory directly from the separating conditions (C2). For expositional purposes, suppose that there is a riskless asset. From (C2) w2fs implies that (setting $b_0 = 0$)

$$x_i = E_0 + b_i \tilde{z} + \tilde{\epsilon}_i ,$$

and

$$E_i - E_0 = E_z b_i . \tag{18}$$

Since all efficient portfolios have no $\tilde{\epsilon}$ risk, the market portfolio which is a convex combination of such portfolios must also have no $\tilde{\epsilon}$ risk and takes the form

$$x_m = E_0 + b_m \tilde{z}, \tag{19}$$

and scaling $\tilde{z}$ so that $b_m = 1$ we have the familiar Sharpe-Lintner pricing result

$$E_i - E_0 = (E_m - E_0) b_i . \tag{20}$$

---

[11] Consider (15), for example, with $\tilde{\epsilon} = 0$. If b is constant, then all portfolios have the same risk, $b\tilde{z}$, and unless E is also constant it will be possible to have arbitrarily high returns at no cost or risk with an arbitrage portfolio η. If b is not constant, to prevent the same sort of arbitrage, all portfolios with $\eta e = \eta b = 0$, must also have $\eta E = 0$, hence there must exist constants a_0 and a_1 such that $E_i = a_0 + a_1 b_i$.

This derivation is deceptively simple and it is worth recapitulating. Once we know that the distribution permits w2fs, then from (C2)(i) it is clear that the market portfolio is efficient and can be taken to be one of the separating funds. The basic pricing result (20) is an immediate consequence.

Stochastic Dominance Theory

There has long been a hope that the principles of stochastic dominance could be applied in portfolio problems to eliminate the need for strong distributional assumptions. To date, the results have been somewhat weak and Theorem 2 offers an explanation. Conditions (C2) are required of any portfolio theory that obtains separation results and this makes any attempt to search for weaker or more distribution free results unrewarding. This is not to say that work on stochastic dominance is futile, but, rather, that results will be forthcoming only in special cases.[12]

Before generalizing Theorem 2 to the case of kfs, we will end this section with a simple corollary that establishes the promised equivalence between w2fs and s2fs.

COROLLARY 2. w2fs *and* s2fs *are equivalent.*

Proof. As we observed before, s2fs implies w2fs. To prove that w2fs implies strong 2fs, let γ be a given portfolio. If $\gamma b \epsilon A$, then, the sufficiency proof of Theorem 2 applies. If $\gamma b \notin A$, suppose that $\gamma b \leqslant \inf_{u \in U} \alpha(u) b$. For any $u \in U$, there exists a linear combination of α and β, $\lambda \alpha + (1 - \lambda) \beta$, with $\lambda \alpha b + (1 - \lambda) \beta b \in \bar{A}$ and such that

$$E\{u((\lambda \alpha + (1 - \lambda) \beta) \tilde{x})\} \geqslant E\{u(\gamma \tilde{x})\}.$$

It follows by the concavity of u that a portfolio, ξ, of $\lambda \alpha + (1 - \lambda) \beta$ and γ with $\xi b = \inf_{u \in U} \alpha(u) b$ will have

$$E\{u(\xi \tilde{x})\} \geqslant E\{u(\gamma \tilde{x})\}.$$

From the sufficiency proof of Theorem 2, though, all such portfolios ξ are stochastically dominated by the portfolio of α and β, $t\alpha + (1 - t)\beta$ with $(t\alpha + (1 - t)\beta) b = \inf_{u \in U} \alpha(u) b$. The proof for $\alpha b \geqslant \sup \alpha(u) b$ is identical. Q.E.D.

---

[12] For example, it is possible to use the results of stochastic dominance, together with Theorem 2, to derive some interesting theorems about multivariate distribution theory. Theorem 2 permits a characterization of those distributions beyond the normal with the property that under specified linear restrictions, lack of co-relation is equivalent to conditional independence. (See Ross [31].)

In what follows we will drop the distinction between strong and weak two fund separability.

3. k-Fund Separability

The following theorem generalizes Theorem 2 to the case of w$k$fs. As is to be anticipated, the k funds are not unique and the funds given in the theorem, as with the 2fs result, should be interpreted as defining a $(k-1)$ dimensional space within which all optimal portfolios lie. Any basis for this space will be a set of k separating funds. Distributions which satisfy the conditions of the theorem, (CK), for some $k < n$ will be termed separating distributions.

THEOREM 3. *A vector of asset returns, X, exhibits* w$k$fs *if and only if the following conditions are satisfied*

$$(\exists \tilde{y}, \tilde{z}^1,..., \tilde{z}^{k-1}, \tilde{\epsilon}, B, \alpha^1,..., \alpha^k)$$

(i) $\tilde{X}_i = \tilde{y} + \sum_{j=1}^{k-1} b_{ij}\tilde{z}^j + \tilde{\epsilon}_i$,

$$E_i = E_y + \sum_{j=1}^{k-2} E_{z^j}b_{ij} ,$$

(ii) $(\forall \xi \epsilon A)\ E\left\{\tilde{\epsilon}_i \mid \tilde{y} + \sum_{j=1}^{k-1} \xi_j\tilde{z}^j\right\} = 0,$ (CK)

where

$$A \equiv \{\xi \mid \xi = \gamma(u)\ B,\ u \in U\},\ B = [b_{ij}],$$

(iii) $\alpha^1\tilde{\epsilon} = \cdots = \alpha^k\tilde{\epsilon} \equiv 0,$

and

the two matrices

$$\left[e \;\vdots\; B\right] \quad \text{and} \quad \left[e \;\vdots\; [\alpha^i B^j]\right]$$

have identical rank on all submatrices formed from corresponding columns.

Proof. The proof is a straightforward generalization of that for Theorem 2.[13]   Q.E.D.

[13] The exact structure of A is not known, but by Lemma A1 it is pathwise connected, and Theorems A3 and A4 are trivially extended to imply that optimal portfolios generated by D are dense in S and that, as in the case of $k = 2$, A is bounded in some directions.

The generalization to w$k$fs is of some interest beyond that of the two fund separation result. In particular, CK permits the presence of systematic factors, $\tilde{z}^j$ with arbitrary coefficients, b_{ij}. The rank conditions of (CK)(iii) do not interfere with this; they only insure that separation obtains in situations where the factors cannot be combined into a smaller set of basic factors. (This is necessary since while $k$fs is sufficient for k'fs when $k' > k$ the latter implication is, of course, not true.) In general, we need to span all feasible factor weights and the rank conditions are necessary and sufficient for this purpose. The analogous situation arises with (C2)(iii) in the case of 2fs. If E is not a constant vector then $[e \vdots E]$ is of full rank 2, and we require that $\alpha E \neq \beta E$ for the two separating funds, α and β, to span all returns.

The conditions (CK) also indicate the pivotal importance of general linear factor models for separation. For k-fund separation it is both necessary and sufficient that returns be generated by a k factor generating mechanism of the form of (CK)(i). Furthermore, the expected returns, E_i, cannot be arbitrary, but must be linearly dependent on the factor beta weights. Once these factors are identified as observable portfolios, the separability conditions become testable capital market equilibrium conditions.

4. Some Extensions

One of the consequences of the above representations of separability is that separation occurs only under certain restrictive conditions. If exact separation does not occur, though, there remains the possibility of approximate separation. Suppose, for example, that returns are generated by the simple one factor model (Eq. (15))

$$\tilde{x}_i - E_i + b_i \tilde{z} + \tilde{\epsilon}_i,$$

where the $\tilde{\epsilon}_i$ are linearly independent. As we have seen, this model generally fails to satisfy the separation conditions.

Suppose, though, that by the law of large numbers, portfolios, α, can be formed that diversify away the nonsystematic $\tilde{\epsilon}$ risk.

$$\alpha \tilde{\epsilon} \approx 0.$$

For such portfolios the generating model is essentially of the form

$$\alpha \tilde{x} \cong (\alpha E) + (\alpha b) \tilde{z},$$

and we have already shown that (if arbitrage possibilities are eliminated) this model exhibits 2fs. These concepts are developed into the basis of a capital asset pricing theory in Ross [28, 30].

5. SUMMARY AND CONCLUSION

This paper has described the conditions on the stochastic distributions of asset returns that are both necessary and sufficient for separation for all risk averse utility functions. In this sense it is the dual to the papers by Cass and Stiglitz [6], Hakansson [15, 16], Leland [19], Mossin [24] and others who have developed the theory of utility functions which permit separation for all stochastic environments. The results may be somewhat surprising in that certain common distributions, in particular, the Paretian stable distributions, do not emerge as central to the analysis. Rather, what we are concerned with in portfolio theory is not so much the marginal distributions of asset returns as the interrelationships amongst random assets. For the problems of separation and, therefore, for portfolio theory in general, the linear factor models occupy a central canonical role in describing these co-relations.

APPENDIX

The purpose of this appendix is to establish some results used in the proofs in the text.

Define M^+ to be the class of all nonnegative monotone declining functions with a derivative bounded away from zero on compact intervals, and let L_a^b denote the class of functions that are continuous and piecewise linear on $[a, b]$ and vanish elsewhere.

THEOREM A1. *Let integrals be taken with respect to a distribution function* Q. *If for all* $h \in M^+$

$$\int hv = 0 \Rightarrow \int hs = 0, \tag{1}$$

and if $(\exists \hat{h} \in M^+)$ *such that*

$$\int \hat{h}v = 0,$$

then there exists a constant, k, such that

$$s = kv, \text{ a.e.}, \tag{2}$$

Proof. First we show that the implication (1) holds for all $h \in L_a^b$. If $h \in L_a^b$, then there exists a $\delta \neq 0$ and sufficiently small so that $h + \delta h \in M^+$. Hence, if

$$\int hv = 0,$$

then

$$\int (\hat{h} + \delta h) \, v = 0,$$

which implies by (1) that

$$\int (\hat{h} + \delta h) \, s = 0,$$

and, therefore,

$$\int hS = 0.$$

Now, pick $g, h \in L_a^b$ and choose c such that

$$\int hv = c \int gv.$$

Since $h - cg \in L_a^b$,

$$\int (h - cg) \, v = 0$$

implies that

$$\int (h - cg) \, s = 0,$$

or

$$\int hs = c \int gs.$$

It follows, then, that $(\exists k)(\forall h \in L_a^b)$

$$\int hs = k \int hv, \tag{3}$$

where k is independent of the choice of interval $[a, b]$. The members of L_a^b are known to constitute a separating family of functions in the sense that (3) implies (2) (see, e.g., Breiman [5, Proposition 8.17]). Q.E.D.

In applying Theorem A1 in the proof of Theorem 2, we take $s = [S_i(\tilde{q}) - S_j(\tilde{q})]$, and Q as the distribution function of $\tilde{q}$.

The next theorem, Theorem A2, is used in the proof of Theorem 1 in the text. Just as Theorem 1 is only a special case of Theorem 2, the proof of Theorem A2 is really just a specialization of the proof of Theorem 2 in the text. It has been separated out, though, both for expositional purposes and because it might be of some independent interest.

THEOREM A2. *If* $(\forall \lambda)$

$$\tilde{y} + \lambda \tilde{p} \sim \tilde{y} + \tilde{\epsilon}(\lambda),$$

where

$$E\{\tilde{\epsilon}(\lambda)|\ \tilde{y}\} = 0,$$

then

$$E\{\tilde{p}\ |\ \tilde{y}\} = 0.$$

Proof. For all $u \in U$, Jensen's inequality implies that

$$E\{u[\tilde{y} + \lambda \tilde{p}]\} = E\{u[\tilde{y} + \tilde{\epsilon}]\} \leqslant E\{u[\tilde{y}]\}. \tag{4}$$

Concavity also implies that

$$u[\tilde{y}] = u[\tilde{y} + \lambda \tilde{p} - \lambda \tilde{p}]$$
$$\leqslant u[\tilde{y} + \lambda \tilde{p}] + (-\lambda \tilde{p})\ u'[\tilde{y} + \lambda \tilde{p}],$$

and taking expectations yields

$$E\{u[\tilde{y}]\} \leqslant E\{u[\tilde{y} + \lambda \tilde{p}]\} - E\{\lambda \tilde{p} u'[\tilde{y} + \lambda \tilde{p}]\}. \tag{5}$$

The inequalities (4) and (5) imply that $(\forall \lambda)$

$$E\{\lambda \tilde{p} u'[\tilde{y} + \lambda \tilde{p}]\} \leqslant E\{u[\tilde{y} + \lambda \tilde{p}]\} - E\{u[\tilde{y}]\} \tag{6}$$
$$\leqslant 0.$$

From (6) it follows that $(\forall \lambda > 0)$

$$E\{\tilde{p} u'[\tilde{y} + \lambda \tilde{p}]\} \leqslant 0,$$

which implies that

$$E\{\tilde{p} u'[\tilde{y}]\} \leqslant 0,$$

and $(\forall \lambda) < 0$

$$E\{\tilde{p} u'[\tilde{y} + \lambda \tilde{p}]\} \geqslant 0,$$

which implies that

$$E\{\tilde{p} u'[\tilde{y}]\} \geqslant 0,$$

hence

$$E\{\tilde{p} u'[\tilde{y}]\} = 0.$$

Since $u \in U$, we can take u' to be an arbitrary element of M^+, and by Theorem A1,

$$E\{\hat{p} \mid \tilde{y}\} = 0, \text{ a.e. .} \qquad\qquad \text{Q.E.D.}$$

The following results determine the sets of portfolio returns for which separation holds. They are used to define the set A introduced in Theorems 2 and 3 in the text to describe the relevant domain over which the noise terms in (C2) and (CK) must have zero conditional means. We will adopt the following notation

$$u(\alpha) \equiv E\{u(\alpha\tilde{X})\},$$

and

$$\alpha(u) \equiv \text{arg max } u(\alpha),$$

and throughout the analysis $\tilde{x}$ will be fixed and expected returns are not equal. Defining

$$m(u) \equiv \sup_{\alpha(u)} \alpha(u) \, E,$$

the sets we are interested in are of the form

$$A_Q \equiv \{m \mid (\exists u \in Q) \, m = m(u)\},$$

where Q is a given class of functions. The classes we consider are U, the monotone, concave functions, C, the concave functions, and D the monotone concave functions with a second derivative bounded from zero on compact sets. Notice that $D \subset U \subset C$. Lastly, we will assume that there is a strictly concave $u \in U$ for which $m(u)$ exists.

The next lemmas are used to prove the basic results on the sets A_Q.

LEMMA A1. *Define*

$$\alpha(a) \equiv \text{arg max } u(\alpha, a),$$

where u is strictly concave in α and uniformly continuous in a. It follows that where $\alpha(a)$ exists it is continuous on an open neighborhood of a.

Proof. Let B be any open ball centered at $\alpha(a^0)$. By strict concavity

$$2\epsilon \equiv u(\alpha(a^0), a^0) - \sup_{\alpha \in B^C} u(\alpha, a^0) > 0,$$

where B^C denotes the complement of B. By concavity, the supremum of u on

B^C is attained on the boundary of B, ∂B. By continuity, if $a^\nu \to a^0$ then $(\exists n)(\forall \nu > n)$

$$\left| \sup_{\alpha \in B} u(\alpha, a^\nu) - u(\alpha(a^0), a^0) \right| < \epsilon,$$

and

$$\left| \sup_{\alpha \in \partial B} u(\alpha, a^\nu) - \sup_{\alpha \in B^C} u(\alpha, a^0) \right| < \epsilon.$$

Hence,

$$\sup_{\alpha \in B} u(\alpha, a^\nu) - \sup_{\alpha \in \partial B} u(\alpha, a^\nu) > 0,$$

which with the strict concavity of u implies that $\alpha(a^\nu) \in B$.   Q.E.D.

The following lemma is used to show that A is composed of a union of intervals.

LEMMA A2. *Let* $a \geqslant 0$,

$$g(\alpha, a) \equiv (1 - a) U(\alpha) + a(\alpha E),$$

and let

$$m(a) \equiv \alpha(a) E,$$

where u is strictly concave, and $\alpha(u)$ exists. It follows that m(a) is continuous, monotone increasing and assumes all values in

$$[m(u), \infty).$$

Proof. Monotonicity follows directly from optimality and continuity from Lemma A1. Since $u(\cdot)$ is strictly concave, for some a, $m(0)$ exists and if for some a, $m(a)$ exists, then it exists on an open neighborhood of a. If, for some a^*, $m(a)$ exists for $a < a^*$, but not for $a \geqslant a^*$, then $(\exists \alpha^\nu)(\forall \alpha)(\exists n)$ $(\forall \nu > n)$

$$g(\alpha^\nu, a^*) > g)\alpha, a^*). \tag{7}$$

Now, suppose that

$$m^* \equiv \lim_{a \uparrow a^*} m(a) < \infty,$$

then

$$\alpha^* \equiv \arg \max g(\alpha, a^*)$$

subject to

$$\alpha E \leqslant m^*.$$

The existence of α^* is assured by the strict concavity of u. As $a \uparrow a^*$

$$g(\alpha(a), a) \uparrow g(\alpha^*, a^*),$$

but from (7) ($\exists \nu$) such that

$$g(\alpha^\nu, a^*) > g(\alpha^*, a^*).$$

By continuity, though for a sufficiently close to a^*

$$g(\alpha^\nu, a) > g(\alpha(a), a),$$

violating the optimality of $\alpha(a)$. It follows that m^* is unbounded. Since $m(a)$ is continuous it must assume all values in $[m(u), \infty)$. Q.E.D.

Now we can combine these two lemmas to prove our basic theorems on the range of the mean.

LEMMA A3. *The set A_U is an interval unbounded on the right, and A_C is the line.*

Proof. From Lemma A2 we know that $[m(u), \infty) \subset A_U$. If $v \in U$, then from Lemma A1, $[m(u), m(v) \subset A_U$, hence A_U is an interval unbounded on the right.

Since $C \supset U, A_C \supset A_U$. In addition, $u(\alpha) \in U$ implies that $u(-\alpha) \in C$, hence $-A_U \subset A_C$. Lastly, by forming linear combinations of $u(\alpha)$ and $u(-\alpha)$ and applying Lemma A1 it follows that $[-m(u), m(u)] \subset A_C$, and, therefore, $A_C = (-\infty, \infty)$. Q.E.D.

LEMMA A4:

$$\bar{A}_D = \bar{A}_U$$

Proof. By the same argument as above A_D is an interval unbounded on the right, and clearly $A_D \subset A_U$. Since D is dense in U, the lemma follows by a straightforward closure argument. Q.E.D.

Whether A_U is open or closed depends on the distribution of $\tilde{x}$. If $\tilde{x}$ has compact support, then A_U is closed, but if not then A_U may be open. For example, if $\tilde{x}$ is a nonsingular multivariate normal, then the minimum variance point defines the left boundary and is not attainable.

ACKNOWLEDGMENTS

The author is grateful to the Rodney L. White Center, the Guggenheim Foundation, and the National Science Foundation (Grant No. SOC-20292) for their financial support.

An unknown referee, David Cass, Sandy Grossman, Philip Dybvig, and especially Richard Roll and Oliver Hart are to be thanked for helpful comments. All errors are the responsibility of the author.

REFERENCES

1. R. A. AGNEW, Counter-examples to an assertion concerning the normal distributions and a new stochastic price fluctuation model, *Rev. Econ. Statist.* **38** (1971), 381–383.
2. K. J. ARROW, "Essays on the Theory of Risk-Bearing," Markham, Chicago, 1971.
3. F. BLACK, Capital market equilibrium with restricted borrowing, *J. Business* **45** (1972), 444–454.
4. K. BORCH, A note on uncertainty and indifference curves, *Rev. Econ. Statist.* **36** (1969), 1–4.
5. L. BREIMAN, "Probability," Addison–Wesley, Reading, Mass., 1968.
6. D. CASS AND J. STIGLITZ, The structure of investor preferences and asset returns, and separability in portfolio selection: A contribution to the pure theory of mutual funds, *J. Econ. Theory* **2** (1970), 122–160.
7. E. FAMA, Portfolio analysis in a stable Paretian market, *Management Sci.* **11** (January 1965), 404–419.
8. E. FAMA, Risk, return and equilibrium: Some clarifying comments, *J. Finance* **23** (1968), 29–40.
9. M. S. FELDSTEIN, Mean-variance analysis in the theory of liquidity preference and portfolio selection, *Rev. Econ. Studies* **36** (1969), 5–12.
10. P. C. FISHBURN, Convex stochastic dominance with continuous distribution functions, *J. Econ. Theory* **7** (1974), 143–158.
11. P. C. FISHBURN, Majority voting on risky investments, *J. Econ. Theory* **8** (1974), 85–99.
12. P. C. FISHBURN, Separation theorems and expected utilities, *J. Econ. Theory* **11** (1975), 16–34.
13. J. HADAR AND W. R. RUSSELL, Stochastic dominance and diversification, *J. Econ. Theory* **3** (1971), 288–305.
14. J. HADAR AND W. R. RUSSELL, Diversification of interdependent prospects, *J. Econ. Theory* **7** (1974), 231–241.
15. N. HAKANSSON, On optimal myopic portfolio policies, with and without serial correlation of yields, *J. Business* **44** (1971), 324–334.
16. N. HAKANSSON, Convergence in multiperiod portfolio choice, *J. Financial Econ.* **1** (1974), 201–224.
17. J. R. HICKS, "Value and Capital," Oxford Univ. Press, Fair Lawn, N. J., 1939.
18. F. H. KNIGHT, "Risk, Uncertainty and Profit," *Reprints of Economic Classics*, New York, 1964.
19. H. LELAND, On turnpike portfolios, *in* "Mathematical Methods in Investment and Finance" (G. P. Szego and K. Shell, Eds.), pp. 24–33, North–Holland, Amsterdam, 1972.
20. J. LINTNER, The valuation of risky assets and the selection of risky investments in stock porfolios and capital budgets, *Rev. Econ. Statist.* **47** (1965), 13–37.
21. B. MANDELBROT, The variation of certain speculative prices, *J. Business* **36** (1963), 394–411.
22. H. M. MARKOWITZ, "Portfolio Selection; Efficient Diversification of Investments," Wiley, New York, 1959.
23. R. C. MERTON, Optimum consumption and portfolio rules in a continuous-time model, *J. Econ. Theory* **3** (1971), 373–413.

24. J. Mossin, Optimal multiperiod portfolio policies, *J. Business* **41** (1969), 215–229.

25. S. A. Ross, "Risk and Efficiency," University of Pennsylvania Discussion Paper No. 196, February 1971.

26. S. A. Ross, Portfolio turnpike theorems for constant policies, *J. Financial Econ.* **1** (1974), 171–198.

27. S. A. Ross, Uncertainty and the heterogeneous capital good model, *Rev. Econ. Studies* **42** (1975), 133–146.

28. S. A. Ross, The arbitrage theory of capital asset pricing, *J. Econ. Theory* **13** (1976), 341–360.

29. S. A. Ross, A note on a paradox in portfolio theory, Mimeograph, 1976.

30. S. A. Ross, Return, risk and arbitrage, *in* "Risk and Return in Finance" (I. Friend and J. Bicksler, Eds.), Ballinger, Cambridge, Mass., 1976.

31. S. A. Ross, Stability and separability: The role of the stable distributions in portfolio theory, *Econometrica*, to appear.

32. M. Rothschild and J. Stiglitz, Increasing Risk. I. A definition, *J. Econ. Theory* **2** (1970), 225–243.

33. M. Rothschild and J. Stiglitz, Increasing Risk. II. Its economic consequences, *J. Econ. Theory* **3** (1971), 66–84.

34. P. Samuelson, General proof that diversification pays, *J. Financial Quantitative Anal.* **2** (1967), 1–13.

35. W. Sharpe, Capital asset prices: A theory of market equilibrium under conditions of risk, *J. Finance* **19** (1964), 425–442.

36. V. Strassen, The existence of probability measures with given marginals, *Ann. Math. Statist.* **36** (1965), 423–439.

37. J. Tobin, Liquidity preference as behavior toward risk, *Rev. Econ. Studies* **25** (1958), 65–85.

38. J. Tobin, Comment on Borch and Feldstein, *Rev. Econ. Studies* **36** (1969), 13–14

Printed by the St Catherine Press Ltd., Tempelhof 37, Bruges, Belgium.

discussion | Mutual Funds, Capital Structure, and Economic Efficiency

Joseph E. Stiglitz

Princeton University

James Tobin, in his justly celebrated paper "Liquidity Preference as Behavior Towards Risk," established a remarkable result: all individuals, regardless of their attitudes towards risk, purchased all risky securities in the same proportions. This theorem became known as the *portfolio separation theorem*: one could decompose the portfolio allocation problem into two stages: first, one decided on the proportions in which different risky assets should be held; and then one decided on the proportion of one's total wealth to invest in the safe asset, the remainder being invested in the risky portfolio.

In the late 1960s Dave Cass and I turned our attention to the question of investigating the generality of this result.[1] There were several reasons for our interest. First, the portfolio separation theorem is an example of a general class of theorems encountered in the theory of consumer behavior, identifying circumstances in which individuals could separate their budget decisions (e.g., first determining what fraction to spend on cheese, and then, of that amount, what fraction to spend on blue cheese). Individuals often seem to act as if they allocate their expenditures in this way; in any case, these theorems provide a structure to the individual's budgeting process; they enable the economist to say more than just, "Everything depends on everything else." But the conditions under which these theorems had been shown to hold were very restrictive: depending on the nature of the result being established, they required separability of the utility function and/or linearity of Engel curves.

Though the expected utility theorem imposed a kind of additive separability structure to the utility function, the utility function was not separable in terms of quantities of different assets purchased. Thus, the portfolio separation theorem could not be viewed simply as a special case of the more common forms of budget-separation theorems.

The earlier results from the general theory of consumer behavior *suggested* that the Tobin portfolio separation theorem would have an equally restricted domain of validity. The assumptions employed by Tobin were very restrictive: the individual had a quadratic utility function (or there was some other specification of utility functions cum probability distribution of returns that allowed for an evaluation of portfolios in terms of two parameters alone), there was a perfectly safe asset, there were no restrictions on short sales or borrowing, and individuals had no other (stochastic) sources of income.

Moreover, for all individuals to purchase the same risky portfolio, all individuals had to have the same beliefs concerning the probability distribution of returns. These assumptions were sufficiently restrictive that they cast doubt on the generality of any conclusions derived making use of them; it thus seemed important to see whether, and to what extent, the result held under less restrictive conditions.

The portfolio separation theorem has four important implications: it implies that the firm's choice of a debt-equity ratio has no consequences; it has strong implications for the structure of prices of risky assets; it has strong implications for firm decision making; and it has strong welfare implications. Thus, a second objective of our research program was to ascertain to what extent these implications were robust; that is, were they valid only under the restrictive condition under which the mutual funds theorems were valid? After discussing the general structure of the portfolio separation theorem, I turn to a discussion of each of these implications.

I. THE MUTUAL FUND THEOREMS

It quickly became apparent to us that Tobin's assertion that an individual need evaluate portfolios only in terms of two parameters was not quite correct. Even if the returns to a security could be described by two parameters (for example, a lognormal distribution), a portfolio consisting of lognormal securities would not be described by two parameters (that is, a linear combination of lognormals is not lognormal). We decomposed the problem into two parts: (a) assuming we imposed no restrictions on the distributions, for what utility functions could a portfolio separation theorem be established? (b) assuming we imposed no restrictions on the utility functions, for what distributions could a portfolio separation theorem be established?

Rather than investigating the portfolio separation theorem itself, we decided to explore a more general class of questions, of which the portfolio separation theorem was a special case. (The reasons for this will become apparent later.) We asked, for what class of utility functions could we find a set of mutual funds (linear combination of existing assets) such that, for all individuals within the class, portfolio allocations could be described as simply different combinations of these mutual funds? Thus the portfolio separation theorem was a special case, where one mutual fund consisted of all risky assets, the other mutual fund consisted simply of the safe asset.

Since we wished to establish these results regardless of the assets' distributions of returns, we postulated a particularly simple structure of asset returns—the Arrow-Debreu state contingent class; and since we wished the result to hold for all individuals within a class, we postulated that the individuals had the same utility function and differed only in their wealth. We then were able to show that the class of utility functions for which a *generalized mutual fund theorem* held was indeed very restrictive, though more general than the quadratic utility function: it included all the utility functions with linear risk tolerance functions (i.e., for which U'/U'' was a linear function of wealth, special cases of which include the quadratic, constant absolute, and constant relative risk-aversion utility functions). We had thus established a *necessary condition* for the mutual fund theorem to be true: for we had, at this juncture, only considered a limited class of distributions and a limited class of variations in utility functions (individuals differed only in wealth). We then showed that in the absence of a safe asset, the constant absolute risk-aversion utility function might not work; and if individuals had different parameters in their utility function (for instance, different degrees of constant or absolute risk aversion), then they would buy different mutual funds. If they all had quadratic utility functions, then they would buy the same mutual funds regardless of the parameters of the utility function. Thus, it seemed Tobin had stumbled on the only class of utility functions for which any mutual fund theorem of interest could be established.

Indeed, we were able to establish for the quadratic utility function (or for the other "two-parameter" case, constant absolute risk aversion with normal distributions) that a more general two-fund theorem was valid, even in the absence of a safe asset. Of the different ways to characterize the two funds, we found particularly attractive one that represented a direct generalization of the Tobin result, in which one fund was the minimum-variance portfolio (corresponding to the safe asset in Tobin's model), and the other of which was the market portfolio.

On the other hand, our analysis also made clear that if there were nonmarketed risks (stochastic wages), then individuals would hold different risky portfolios; the portfolio separation theorem would not hold.

Though the proofs in our original paper were rather complicated, there are simple proofs for a slightly more restricted class of questions (Stiglitz 1972c). From the earlier literature on the theory of consumer behavior, one might have suspected that the only utility functions for which mutual funds could be derived would be utility functions that generated linear Engel curves. One could ask, what utility functions generate linear Engel curves, regardless of the distribution of underlying assets? The answer leads directly to the class of linear risk tolerance utility functions. Note that this provides directly testable empirical implications; casual empiricism suggests that the remarkably different pattern of portfolio allocations at different wealth levels is inconsistent with the hypothesis of linear Engel curves.[2]

This, as I have noted, is only one of the two possible approaches to mutual fund theorems. The other is to ask for what restrictions on the distribution functions can a mutual fund theorem be established regardless of the utility functions that individuals have. We did not pursue this for three reasons. First, it seemed clear to us that the natural restrictions to be imposed were not on the returns to the financial assets, which were endogenous, but on the underlying assets. Thus, by issuing different securities, firms could alter the set of financial assets available. Even if the underlying assets had normal distributions, the return on a risky bond would not be normal nor would the return on a preferred share be normal. In a competitive market with many different firms having the same pattern of returns of the underlying assets, one could generate what is effectively a complete set of securities by having different firms with different debt-equity ratios (see Grossman and Stiglitz 1980). But for these securities we already knew the answer: there was no set of distributions of underlying assets such that, for all utility functions, a mutual fund could be established; a mutual fund theorem could be established only for very restricted classes of utility functions.

Second, even if we restricted ourselves to a fixed set of financial assets and asked what restrictions on the pattern of the returns of these assets would generate a mutual fund theorem, prospects for proving a general result of interest seemed bleak: for the individual is concerned about the probability distribution of returns, and the class of distributions such that all linear combinations of these assets belong to that class is very limited—with finite variances the class is just the normal distribution. This does not settle the matter, for the question of when a mutual fund theorem is valid is not quite the same as the question of when will the portfolio distribution belong to the same class as the distribution of returns for the individual asset (see Chamberlain 1983).[3] But our pessimism was confirmed by the article by Ross reprinted in Chapter 10, which provides the definitive solution to this problem.

II. ON THE USES AND ABUSES OF ECONOMIC THEORY: SOME METHODOLOGICAL REMARKS

If, as our analysis suggested, the mutual fund theorems (and, in particular, the special case of the portfolio separation theorem) are valid only under extremely restrictive conditions, of what use are they?

Three answers suggest themselves:

1. We live in but one of the many possible worlds. It may be that in our particular world, these conditions are satisfied. The fact that there are other worlds in which they are not is noteworthy but of little practical importance.

2. It may be that though the conditions are not satisfied precisely, they are satisfied well enough that some of the central lessons to be learned from the mutual funds theorems are (at least approximately) valid.

3. It may be that the conditions are not even approximately satisfied. The analysis serves a vital cautionary role: to the extent that the analyst employs the parameterizations for which the mutual funds theorems are valid, the results of the analysis are suspect.

There is a peculiar perversion of the positivist doctrine that was popularized by Milton Friedman, which held that the validity of a theory depended not on the reasonableness of the assumptions but on the verification of the implications of the theory. This view has been extended by some to suggest that a theory is a good theory if any of its implications are verified. This is sheer nonsense. For a theory to be verified requires that none of its implications be falsified.[4] Among the implications of a theory are the direct implications— including the assumptions themselves—as well as the more subtle implications derived in the analysis. It is true that the fact that an assumption is not verified or directly verifiable should not lead us to reject the theory; but in those cases where an assumption is falsifiable, the direct falsification of an assumption should lead to the theory's rejection.[5]

Attempts to verify the mutual funds models have focused on testing one of the more subtle implications of the theory—those for the structure of asset prices. The statistical tests typically are unable to reject the model. Yet there are more straightforward tests of the theory and of its underlying assumptions. These overwhelmingly cast doubt on the relevance of the model.

Consider first those assumptions that are directly testable:

(a) Individuals can borrow and lend at the same (safe) rate of interest; individuals can easily sell short risky securities.

Not only is this assumption patently false, but if it were true it would lead to some well-known paradoxes. For instance, under these "perfect capital market" assumptions, I have shown elsewhere (Stiglitz 1983, 1985) that, given our tax code, there are a multitude of ways by which individuals could eliminate all their tax obligations or at least their taxes on capital income. It does not require detailed empirical work to reject this hypothesis.

(b) All individuals' wage (nonportfolio) income is nonrisky. For if it were risky, even if all individuals had the same pattern of risky income, they would wish their total portfolio—including the risky human capital—to have the same proportions, and it would be fortuitous if the ratio of risky portfolio income to the total desired risk, including human capital, happened to be the same for all individuals; a fortiori if individuals have different risky wage incomes, they will wish to have different securities portfolios.[6]

(c) All individuals have the same expectations concerning the returns to each security. The presence of significant differences in beliefs should be obvious to anyone who has engaged in conversations concerning the prospects of different securities, and these differences are readily confirmed by attitude surveys. Yet the more positivist among the economists may argue that actions speak louder than words, that though they talk as if they have different beliefs, they act in a manner consistent with the theory. On the contrary, it seems to me that their behavior—which as we shall see later seems so at odds in many details with the theory—is indeed perfectly consistent with the simple hypothesis that individuals believe what they say, and that there are important and fundamental differences in beliefs.

(d) The tax rate imposed on all forms of income must be the same (or, more precisely, if risky and safe assets are taxed at different rates, the ratio of the tax rates must be the same for all individuals). If some individuals are tax exempt (below the tax threshold), then if these individuals were to purchase the same risky portfolio as a taxed individual, the taxed individual must face the same tax rate on safe and risky investments.[7] Again, this is an assumption that can be tested (and rejected).

Clearly, the assumptions concerning the utility functions are not themselves directly testable; but the theory has strong implications for individual portfolio behavior, and these may be subjected to testing. Some of these implications are clearly false.

(a) The first implication (valid for a wider range of models) is that everyone holds a widely diversified portfolio. On the contrary, there appears to be considerable evidence that, at least within their stock market portfolio, individuals are far less diversified than the theory would suggest.[8] This behavior is consistent either with the hypothesis that individuals are not risk averse or that there are strong differences in beliefs.[9]

(b) The portfolio separation theorem has the stronger implication that all individuals purchase all risky assets in the same proportions. This hypothesis can easily be rejected. The extensions, for example, to two mutual funds, can also be rejected.

Two of the corollary implications (which also may be rejected) are that (i) all trading in, say, agricultural futures markets consists of farmers (and similar individuals) attempting to offset their risky income with those without this source of risky income (hence all nonfarmers take the same position in the market); and (ii) all trading in the stock market is life-cycle trading (as individuals get older they sell off their assets) or trading intended to offset changes in the riskiness of wage income.

(c) The parameterizations of utility functions/probability distributions of returns for which the mutual funds theorems are valid have strong implications for asset demand functions: the linearity hypothesis can be tested and, I suspect, rejected.

Since we have shown that the assumptions under which the mutual funds theorems are valid are indeed special and that there are direct implications of these conditions that can be tested and rejected, why proceed further? Why would anyone bother testing the subtler implications of the model, such as those for the structure of prices? Even were those implications verified, it would only imply that there must exist an alternative theory giving rise to similar pricing structures.

But, alas, economic science does not always proceed in an orderly way; and several of the implications of the model are of interest in their own right. In the following sections we discuss four of these implications. The central question with which we are concerned is, are these conclusions sufficiently "robust" that, even if the special mutual funds model is rejected, these conclusions can be viewed as being "approximately" correct?

III. IMPLICATIONS FOR DEBT-EQUITY RATIOS

One of the interesting implications of the portfolio separation theorem was that the firm's financial structure was of no relevance: since individuals purchased all risky assets in the same proportion, a mutual fund consisting of all corporate bonds and equity is all that is required. But since the mutual fund purchases all of the firm's bonds and equities, clearly the mutual fund must be indifferent to the debt-equity ratio: the mutual fund just receives the total profits of the firm.

This is a rather different argument for the irrelevance of corporate financial policy than that originally presented by Modigliani and Miller (1958), though the intuition behind the result is similar; their analysis required arbitrage between two assets with the same pattern of returns. When the one-mutual-fund theorem held, one did not need two assets with the same pattern of returns.

This implication, however, is of rather limited interest for several reasons. First, a far more general theorem, showing the irrelevance of corporate financial policies (not only debt-equity ratios, but dividend policies, maturity structure of debts, etc.) within a general equilibrium model, not requiring the restrictive conditions of either the mutual funds theorems or the restrictive assumptions that there are many firms within the same risk class, has been established (Stiglitz 1969, 1974b). The one restrictive assumption required was that there is no probability of default. The one advantage that the portfolio separation approach has is that bankruptcy is irrelevant whereas the Stiglitz and Modigliani-Miller approaches assume no bankruptcy. On the other hand, the portfolio separation approach yields the irrelevance of corporate financial policy only under the stringent conditions under which there is a single mutual fund embracing all risky assets. It is not true, in general, if there are two mutual funds embracing risky assets, for then an increase in the debt-equity ratio beyond the point where there is no chance of bankruptcy changes the opportunity set of the economy.

Second, for reasons given above, both the assumptions and the other implications of the models yielding the strong portfolio separation theorems are sufficiently implausible that this particular implication of the model, were it derived solely from it, could not be taken seriously.

Third, I have now come to believe that even apart from the consequences to the opportunity set that follow from firms increasing the debt-equity ratio in the presence of bankruptcy risk, the debt-equity ratio is relevant because of (i) the effects it has on the firms' behavior (Stiglitz and Weiss 1981, 1983; Grossman and Hart 1980, 1982), and (ii) the information that it may give about the firms' returns (Stiglitz 1974a, Ross 1977, Leland and Pyle 1977, Gale and Stiglitz 1982a).

Moreover, as Modigliani and Miller themselves recognized, tax considerations imply that the debt-equity ratio matters, though a full analysis is rather complicated, necessitating an integrated examination of the corporate and individual tax structures and taking into account the specific rules relating to the treating of capital gains as well as the deductibility of interest (Stiglitz 1973, 1976).

Finally, we should note that firms seem to act as if they are concerned about their debt-equity ratio. This is consistent with a number of the hypotheses we have put forward, but not with the mutual funds model.

This presents a dilemma. How are we to reconcile firms' claims with our theory? At first blush, the allegation that firms talk as if the debt-equity ratio matters looks much like similar allegations concerning firms' pricing behavior, allegations that economists are used to dealing with. Firms claim, for instance, that they determine prices by a simple markup over costs. We economists know better: we know that they must, in equilibrium, set prices equal to marginal cost. But there is a difference here (a difference I shall note again in the next section): it is reasonable to hypothesize that firms look for rules of thumb to simplify their life, and that these rules of thumb adjust, in subtle ways, to reflect true economic forces. But here, we find that the businessman is complicating his life unnecessarily. The economist tells him, Dismiss your corporate treasurer who worries about debt-equity ratio. Any financial policy will do.

Accordingly, here we have a real dilemma: for as long as resources are spent on thinking about (and implementing) a corporate financial strategy, we cannot simultaneously hold to the view that firms are rational profit maximizing (shareholders are rational investors) and that debt-equity ratios (and financial policies more generally) are irrelevant.

IV. PRICING STRUCTURE OF ASSETS

The most widely tested of the implications of the portfolio separation theory is that for the structure of prices of risky assets: it predicts that stock market values should be a linear function of mean returns and the covariance with the market.

The theory has quite correctly emphasized one important aspect of risk analysis—the covariance with the market. Securities that are negatively correlated with the market, and thus provide insurance, should sell at a premium. And stocks that are more highly correlated with the business cycle, which are, in this sense, more cyclical, should sell at a discount. This qualitative proposition would hold in a wide variety of models. Thus, the verification of the relationship, although an important empirical finding, does not by itself constitute a verification of the model.[10]

I do not wish to engage here in an evaluation of the more detailed econometric work attempting to assess the validity of the linear relationship[11] except to note that, in many cases, were the so-called attempts to verify the theory[12] successful they would have constituted almost a refutation of the theory, for what is relevant is not just the market for stock market securities but the entire market (including risky wage income, returns from land, etc.) and what is relevant in after-tax returns.

V. FIRM DECISION MAKING

The mutual funds theory has two strong implications for firm decision making.

First, it suggests that when managers use the term "risk," they refer to "covariance with the market," not own-risk. This is at odds with how managers use the term: they do seem to be concerned with the risk of the project itself (which is not to say they ignore the counter or procyclical aspects of the returns). Again, we could claim that words are cheap: when it comes to actions, firms are concerned about covariance with the market as a whole. But here again we face a dilemma similar to that noted earlier: firms gather information about own-risk. There is at least anecdotal evidence that they pay attention to this information; but at the very least, if they do not, they cannot be profit maximizing.[13]

Second, there will be unanimity among all shareholders on the action that maximizes the stock market value. One of the important properties of the Arrow-Debreu model is that there is *unanimity* among all shareholders, both about what the firm's objectives should be—all shareholders wish the firm to maximize its stock market value—and about how this is to be attained. Differences in subjective probabilities concerning different states are irrelevant. In my Tokyo lecture, I asked if these properties extend to economies with a more limited set of securities markets and, in particular, to economies in which the mean-variance model held. There, I assumed that there were no differences about judgments concerning the probability distribution of returns. I showed that there still would not be unanimity, except in what seemed to me then—and seem to me now—to be certain irrelevant cases. I drew attention to two such cases: (a) clearly, if all current shareholders plan to sell all of their shares, they will wish the firm to maximize its stock market value, whereas (b) if all current shareholders plan neither to buy nor to sell shares, there will be unanimity about the objective of the firm, but they will not wish the firm to maximize market value. In the former case the action taken will not be Pareto efficient, but in the latter case it will be (see Section VI below). An extensive literature has developed extending the second case, showing that as long as a "spanning" condition is satisfied unanimity obtains.

The case where individuals are planning neither to buy nor to sell shares has a certain superficial resemblance to conventional exchange equilibrium (where individuals hold the commodities that they wish to consume). But the resemblance is little more than superficial, and it has always seemed to be peculiar that so much attention was paid to this case: it makes little sense to attempt to model a stock market in which no trade occurs. There are innumerable reasons for trade in a dynamic economy (life cycle, changes in circumstances, etc.). In subsequent work, Grossman and I (1977, 1980) have shown how under these more general circumstances unanimity will not arise.

(Besides, as I emphasized in Section I, even if one believed that the underlying probability distributions of returns were jointly normal, the returns to individual securities will not, in general, be normal. Accordingly, there is no reason to believe that the relevant spanning condition will, in general, be satisfied. Grossman and I showed, in particular, that if among the firm's decisions was a decision on financial structure the spanning condition would only be satisfied under conditions that were little weaker than the condition that there existed a complete set of Arrow-Debreu securities.)[14]

But more fundamentally, our interest in whether there would be unanimity was an analytical interest: when the condition was satisfied, at least we as analysts could describe what we thought the firm would do. But the fact that the unanimity property was satisfied hardly served to make the model more plausible; on the contrary, there seem to be many disagreements about objectives and consequences. There is a vast literature about the conflicts of insiders (management, controlling stockholders) and outsiders; there are disagreements about whether the firms should pursue a policy of short-run profit maximization or long-run profit maximization. And when there are disagreements about the consequences of a given policy, they are concerned both with the likelihood of various events and with how the market will react to alternative courses of actions. Many firms spend large amounts of money to find out the likelihood of various possibilities.

Two of the important manifestations of these disagreements are takeovers and proxy battles. These battles are often symptomatic of more widespread disagreements about objectives or evaluations of policies; the takeover or proxy battles occur when a group of individuals feels that the consequences of the mistaken policy of the firm are sufficiently large (the benefits to be gained from pursuing alternative policies are sufficiently great) that it pays to undertake the usually large expenses associated with these battles. In the world of the mutual funds theorems, these battles would never occur. (See, e.g., Stiglitz 1972b, Grossman and Hart 1980, Hart 1977.)

Another manifestation of the importance of the possibility of disagreement is that the market puts a value on control. In some instances there are two kinds of shares that are identical in their claims on the profits of the firm, but one of which is nonvoting (or has fewer voting rights). These shares often sell at a large differential.[15]

VI. WELFARE PROPERTIES

One of the most important properties of the Arrow-Debreu model was that it extended to situations where there was uncertainty in the basic welfare theorems asserting the Pareto efficiency of the economy. The question naturally arose: how robust was this result? In particular, would it be true if there were a more limited set of risk markets?

P. Diamond (1967) and I (1972a and b) investigated two alternative parameterizations to answer this question. Diamond considered an economy in which there was a single commodity, the pattern of returns for each firm was fixed, and the only decision variable of the firm was the scale; moreover, he assumed that there were enough firms with any particular pattern of returns that there was, in effect, a competitive market for that particular security, for what might be thought of as a particular composite commodity. He showed that given that the only available securities were safe securities and claims on the risky assets, the economy was Pareto efficient.

I considered the mean-variance model. In this world, exchange efficiency is trivial to establish: since in the world in which the mutual funds theorems are valid, all individuals purchase all risky securities in the same proportion, all that is required is that there be a single mutual fund; additional securities are simply redundant. The subtler question was production efficiency. Here, it seemed to me that if the capital asset model had any relevance, it provided guidance to firms about the consequences of their actions; that is, it provided a simple formula describing for them what their market value would be as a function of their mean return and the covariance with the market as a whole. Each small firm should take the risk discount factor as a parameter, just as it took the time discount factor (the rate of interest) as a parameter, unaffected by its actions. When firms did this and maximized their stock market value, then the market equilibrium was not Pareto efficient.

There have been several attempts to reconcile this result with religious beliefs concerning the efficiency of the market. Some have suggested that as the small firm changes its investment level or choice of technique, the risk discount factor changes, and firms take this into account. In a general equilibrium model everything does indeed depend on everything else; but the spirit of competitive analysis is that small firms ignore their effect on prices. It seems inconsistent with the spirit of competitive analysis to assume that any small firm takes into account how its actions are going to affect how the market evaluates risk in general.

A second approach has been to observe that as long as the risk discount factor is positive, it pays to create new firms, as long as their returns are not perfectly correlated with existing firms. Hence, entry will occur until the risk discount factor is driven to zero; and in a risk-neutral world, the market is (not surprisingly) Pareto efficient. This analysis errs both in its assumptions and in its conclusions. Fixed costs are associated with creating firms, which means that market equilibrium (and Pareto efficiency) entails a finite number of firms and a finite risk discount factor. But there is no presumption that the number of firms in the market will be Pareto optimal (Stiglitz 1975). Moreover, evidence against a zero risk discount factor seems sufficiently overwhelming to dismiss this approach out of hand.

It is now apparent that these debates of the early 1970s are irrelevant: the more general results of Greenwald and Stiglitz (1986) make it clear that when there are a limited set of risk markets, the economy will essentially always be Pareto inefficient. Even under the stringent assumptions assumed by P. Diamond, the market is only Pareto efficient if there is a single good being produced. If there are two goods, the market is not Pareto efficient (Stiglitz 1982b).[16]

The intuition behind why the market is (constrained) Pareto efficient with one good and not with many goods is easy to see. With one good and multiplicative uncertainty[17] it is as if the firm produced a single composite commodity; if there are many firms in each risk class (i.e., producing each composite commodity), we obtain a standard competitive model, with the "goods" being produced being the composite commodities—that is, particular patterns of returns across the states of nature. Now, when there are two or more commodities, the profits of the firm depend not only on the outputs but also on the prices; and the relative prices across states of nature will, in general, change as the levels of investment in different industries change. In making their investment decisions, small firms ignore the effects of their investment on prices; but in analyzing the Pareto-efficient allocations, one takes into account how the allocation of investment affects the patterns of prices. In other words, the set of "composite commodities" (patterns of profits across the states of nature) available depends on the pattern of *aggregate* investment decisions; individual firms do not take into account how their investment decisions affect this set.

VII. CONCLUSIONS

In conclude, then, that the major use of the mutual funds theorems has been a cautionary one. The parameterizations that give rise to these results are extremely convenient, particularly for obtaining closed-form results. Their widespread use within finance is, accordingly, hardly surprising. The problem is, what credence can we give to the generality of the results derived?[18]

NOTES

[1] See D. Cass and J. E. Stiglitz (1970, 1972), Stiglitz (1972).

[2] Part of the reason for this may lie in the different marginal tax rates faced by individuals at different wealth levels.

[3] He shows, in particular, that the class of functions for which expected utility is a function only of the portfolio's mean and variance (when there exists a riskless asset) consists of distributions satisfying spherical symmetry ("a random vector is spherically distributed about the origin if its distribution is invariant under orthogonal linear transformations that leave the origin fixed," p. 186). If the components of x are independent, then (with a riskless asset) the only distribution (with finite variance) that works is the normal; but without independence, there is a larger class of distributions (see Agnew 1971).

[4] I am not here commenting on whether I agree with the logical positivist doctrine that the acceptability of a theory depends on its verifiability or falsifiability. The criticisms of this philosophical position were well known even at the time that the doctrine became fashionable in economics.

[5] Again, without entering into a discussion of the sociology of knowledge, it should be apparent that in the social sciences the falsification of an important implication of a theory has not necessarily led to its rejection.

[6] If we redefine the individual's portfolio to include all human and physical capital, then a mutual funds theorem (of little practical relevance) could be established, provided there existed a traded security (or a linear combination of securities) that was perfectly correlated with each individual's wage income.

[7] And, if wage income is risky, on wage and investment income.

[8] That individuals own only two or three or four stocks does not mean that they are undiversified, for their stock market portfolio represents only a fraction of their total wealth, including pension funds, social security, housing, etc.

[9] Even with strong differences in beliefs, individuals should have (in positive or negative amounts) virtually all securities. That so many individuals are at corners only reinforces the previous observation concerning the importance of transactions costs, the difficulties of selling short and borrowing.

Differences in information (between the original owners-founders of firms and outsiders) can also give rise to concentrated portfolios. See Stiglitz (1982a).

[10] Note, in particular, that in a complete market, the generalized (expected utility maximizing for some utility function) efficient set of portfolios is convex (Peleg and Yaari 1975, Dybvig and Ross 1982). Hence, the *market portfolio* is (generalized) efficient, and thus efficient in a mean-variance sense among the subset of assets (including the market) ordered by mean-variance criteria. So the CAPM pricing structure holds for this subset. (See also Dybvig and Ingersoll 1982.)

[11] For a survey see, for instance, Fama (1970) or Jensen (1972). For an excellent critique, see Roll (1977).

[12] This occurred when the "market" was limited to the market for traded securities, and where tax considerations were ignored or not modeled correctly. More recent work has attempted at least to take account of some tax considerations, but the problems of modeling capital gains taxation correctly make this an extremely difficult task.

[13] In Stiglitz (1982a) I explain why asymmetric information may give rise to concentrated ownership patterns; given this, the risk-averse behavior of firms, reflecting their dominant shareholders, is not surprising.

Moreover, imperfect information concerning managerial performance may lead to the use of managerial compensation schemes that induce risk-averse behavior on their part.

[14] Unanimity may also arise when firms are sufficiently close substitutes that investors obtain, in the limit, no surplus out of owning shares in any one firm; that is, at the margin they are indifferent to further diversification. This is *not* true, for instance, if firms have independently normally distributed returns. In that model it would imply, in effect, that the risk discount factor should be zero. The observed patterns of portfolio composition suggest that this is not a good model for analyzing the stock market.

[15] A related phenomenon is that in the world of the mutual funds theorems, mergers are irrelevant.

[16] In addition, I showed in my 1972a paper that there may be multiple Nash equilibria, some of which Pareto dominated others. Similar conclusions were reached by Hart (1975).

[17] That is, where the ratios of outputs in each state are fixed, independent of the level of investment.

[18] Another example of a misleading result derived within these parameterizations is that establishing the informational efficiency of futures markets. Grossman and I (1976) showed, for instance, that when farmers have information about their own crop, the futures prices efficiently aggregate that information to provide a forecast of the future spot price under the standard normality-constant absolute risk-aversion assumptions. But this parametrization and the quadratic utility function are essentially the only parametrizations for which this is true (Gale and Stiglitz 1985).

REFERENCES

Agnew, R. A. 1971. "Counter-examples to an Assertion Concerning the Normal Distribution and a New Stochastic Price Fluctuation Model." *Review of Economic Studies* 38: 381–83.

Cass, D., and Stiglitz, J. E. 1970. "The Structure of Investor Preferences and Asset Returns, and Separability in Portfolio Allocation: A Contribution to the Pure Theory of Mutual Funds." *Journal of Economic Theory* 2: 122–60.

———. 1972. "Risk Aversion and Wealth Effects on Portfolios with Many Assets." *Review of Economic Studies* 39: 331–54.

Chamberlain, G. 1983. "A Characterization of the Distributions That Imply Mean Variance Utility Functions." *Journal of Economic Theory* 29: 185–201.

Diamond, P. 1967. "The Role of a Stock Market in a General Equilibrium Model with Technological Uncertainty." *American Economic Review* 57: 759–76.

Dybvig, P., and Ingersoll, J. 1982. "Mean-Variance Theory in Complete Markets." *Journal of Business* 55: 233–51.

Dybvig, P., and Ross, S. A. 1982. "Portfolio Efficient Sets." *Econometrica* 50: 1525–46.

Fama, E. 1970. "Efficient Capital Markets: A Review of Theory and Empirical Work." *Journal of Finance* 25: 383–417.

Gale, I., and Stiglitz, J. E. 1985. "Futures Markets Are Almost Always Informationally Inefficient." Memorandum No. 57, Princeton University Financial Research Center, February.

———. 1986. "Multiple Stock Offerings and the Financing of New Firms." Financial Research Center Memorandum No. 75, Princeton University.

Greenwald, B., and Stiglitz, J. E. 1986. "Externalities in Economies with Imperfect Information and Incomplete Markets." *Quarterly Journal of Economics* 100: 229–64.

Grossman, S., and Stiglitz, J. E. 1976. "Information and Competitive Price Systems." *American Economic Review* 66: 246–53.

———. 1977. "On Value Maximization and Alternative Objectives of the Firm." *Journal of Finance* 32: 389–402.

———. 1980. "Stockholder Unanimity in the Making of Production and Financial Decisions." *Quarterly Journal of Economics* 94: 543–66.

Hart, O. 1975. "On the Optimality of Equilibrium When the Market Structure Is Incomplete." *Journal of Economic Theory* 11: 418–43.

———. 1977. "Takeover Bids and Stock Market Equilibrium." *Journal of Economic Theory* 16: 53–83. Reprinted Chapter 3, volume 2.

Jensen, M. C. 1972. "Capital Markets: Theory and Evidence." *Bell Journal of Economics and Management Science* 3: 357–98.

Leland, H., and Pyle, D. 1977. "Informational Asymmetrics, Financial Structure, and Financial Intermediation." *Journal of Finance* 32: 371–87. Reprinted Chapter 8, volume 2.

Miller, M. H. 1977. "Debt and Taxes." *Journal of Finance* 32: 261–75.

Modigliani, F., and Miller, M. H. 1958. "The Cost of Capital, Corporation Finance, and the Theory of Investment." *American Economic Review* 48: 261–97.

Peleg, B., and Yaari, M. E. 1975. "A Price Characterization of Efficient Random Variables." *Econometrica* 43: 283–92.

Radner, R. 1974. "A Note on Unanimity of Stockholders' Preferences among Alternative Production Plans: A Reformulation of the Ekern-Wilson Model." *Bell Journal of Economics and Management Science* 5: 181–86.

Roll, R. 1977. "A Critique of the Asset Pricing Theory's Tests. Part I: On Past and Potential Testability of the Theory." *Journal of Financial Economics* 4: 129–76.

Ross, S. 1977. "The Determination of Financial Structure: The Incentive-Signalling Approach." *Bell Journal of Economics* 8: 23–40.

Stiglitz, J. E. 1969. "A Re-examination of the Modigliani-Miller Theorem." *American Economic Review* 59: 784–93.

———. 1970. "On the Optimality of the Stock Market Allocation of Investment." Invited lecture, Far Eastern Meetings of the Econometric Society, Tokyo, June. Printed in 1972 in *Quarterly Journal of Economics* 86: 25–60.

———. 1972a. "Four Lectures on Portfolio Allocation with Many Risky Assets." In G. Szego and K. Shell, eds., *Mathematical Methods in Investment and Finance*. Amsterdam, Netherlands: North-Holland, pp.766–826.

———. 1972b. "Some Aspects of the Pure Theory of Corporate Finance: Bankruptcies and Takeover." *Bell Journal of Economics and Management Science* 3: 458–82.

———. 1973. "Taxation, Corporate Financial Policy and the Cost of Capital." *Journal of Public Economics* 2: 1–34.

————. 1974a. "Incentives and Risk Sharing in Sharecropping." *Review of Economic Studies* 41: 219–55.

————. 1974b. "On the Irrelevance of Corporate Financial Policy."*American Economic Review* 64: 851–66.

————. 1974c. "Information and Capital Markets." Oxford University (mimeo). Revised as 1982a.

————. 1975. "Monopolistic Competition and the Capital Market." IMSSS Technical Report 161, Stanford, February. Forthcoming in G. Feiwel (ed.), *Essays in Memory of Joan Robinson.*

————. 1976. "The Corporation Tax." *Journal of Public Economics* 5: 303–11.

————. 1982a. "Information and Capital Markets." In W. F. Sharpe and Cathryn Cootner, eds., *Financial Economics: Essays in Honor of Paul Cootner.* Englewood Cliffs, N.J.: Prentice-Hall, pp. 118–58.

————. 1982b. "The Inefficiency of the Stock Market Equilibrium." *Review of Economic Studies* 49: 241–61.

————. 1983. "Some Aspects of the Taxation of Capital Gains." *Journal of Public Economics* 21: 257–94.

————. 1985. "The General Theory of Tax Avoidance." *National Tax Journal* 38: 325–38.

Stiglitz, J. E., and Weiss, A. 1981. "Credit Rationing in Markets with Imperfect Information." *American Economic Review* 71: 393–410.

————. 1983. "Incentive Effects of Termination: Applications to the Credit and Labor Markets." *American Economic Review* 73: 912–27.

Tobin, J. 1958. "Liquidity Preference as Behavior Towards Risk." *Review of Economic Studies* 25: 65–86.